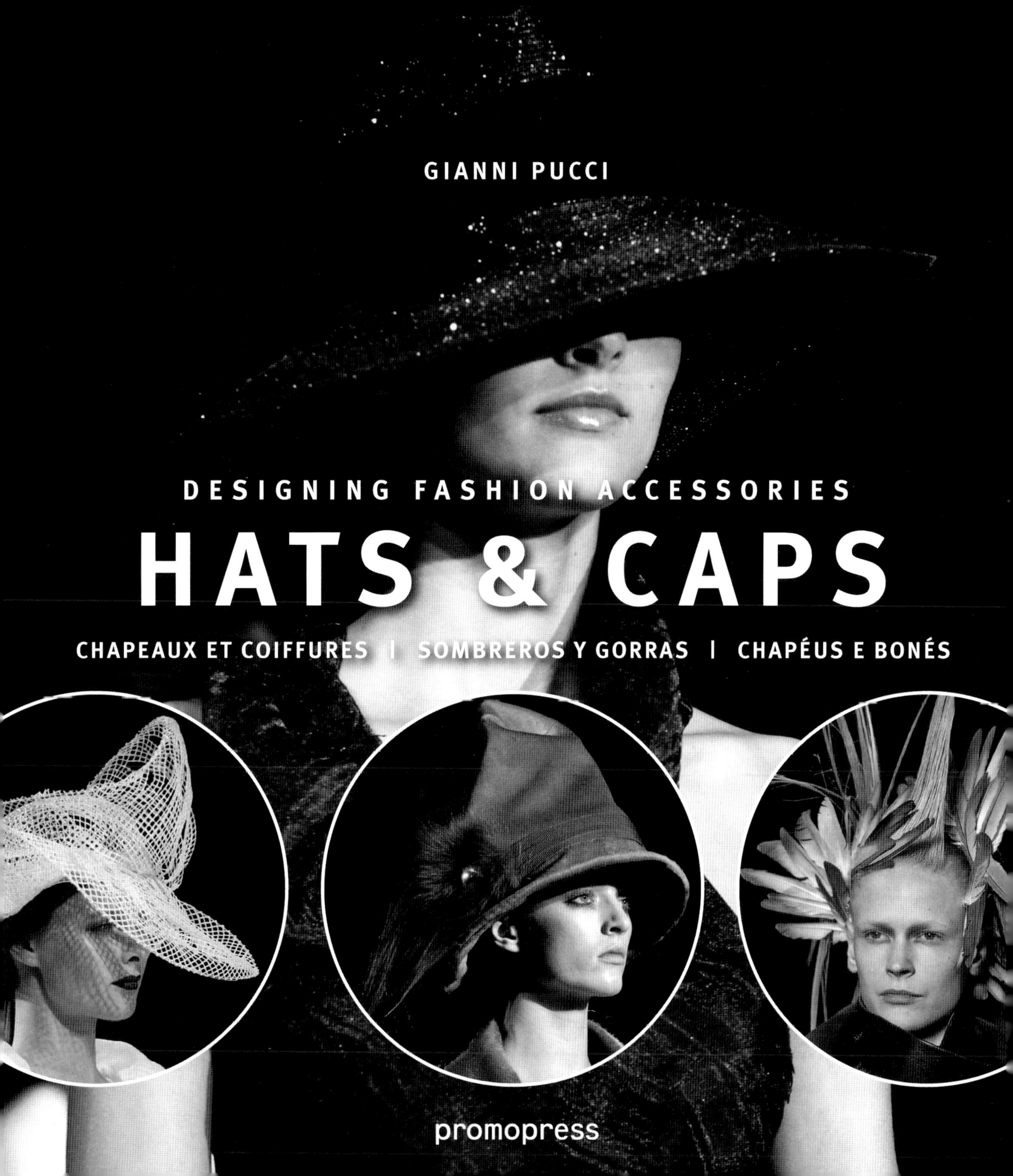

GIANNI PUCCI

DESIGNING FASHION ACCESSORIES

# HATS & CAPS

CHAPEAUX ET COIFFURES | SOMBREROS Y GORRAS | CHAPÉUS E BONÉS

promopress

THE AUTHOR
Gianni Pucci has made his stylistic mark the harmony between light and subject, an instinctive talent for "seeing" the photograph and capturing it in the same instant. His resumè is filled with fashion and even more runway shoots; he was a 2.0 photographer before the term was even invented and was one of the first to use digital. He has been published by the biggest fashion and design sites, from Style.com to Vogue.it.

L'AUTEUR
Gianni Pucci sait combiner harmonieusement lumière et sujet. Il a un talent inné pour «voir» la scène à immortaliser et la capturer dans l'instant. Il s'est spécialisé dans la photographie de mode, et en particulier les défilés. Gianni Pucci a été un des premiers à utiliser la technologie numérique : il était déjà un photographe de la deuxième génération alors que le terme n'existait pas encore. Ses œuvres ont été publiées sur les plus importants sites de mode et de design, de Style.com Vogue.it.

THANKS
Our thanks go to the entire team that made this work possible, and in particular, Monica Feudi, Carola Guaineri, Maddalena Mazzola, Tiziana Universi, Paolo Pucci, Massimo Ferrario, Luca Cannonieri, and Pier Pietro Brunelli.

REMERCIEMENTS
Je remercie toute l'équipe qui m'a aidé à réaliser cet ouvrage, et en particulier Monica Feudi, Carola Guaineri, Maddalena Mazzola, Tiziana Universi, Paolo Pucci, Massimo Ferrario, Luca Cannonieri et Pier Pietro Brunelli.

*EL AUTOR*
*La armonía entre iluminación y modelo es la marca personal del estilo de Gianni Pucci, una capacidad instintiva de ver la fotografía y realizarla al mismo tiempo. Su currículum está lleno de moda y más aún de pasarelas; fotógrafo 2.0 avant la lettre, fue pionero en el uso del medio digital y ha publicado en las páginas web de moda y diseño más importantes, desde Style.com hasta Vogue.it.*

*O AUTOR*
*Gianni Pucci fez a harmonia entre a luz e o objeto com um talento instintivo para "ver" a foto e capturá-la instantaneamente em suas características estilísticas. Seu currículo é repleto de fotos de moda, especialmente da passarela. Ele era um fotógrafo 2.0 antes mesmo de ter sido inventado esse termo e foi um dos primeiros a usar o digital. Seu trabalho foi publicado nos maiores sites de moda e design, desde o Style.com até o Vogue.it.*

*AGRADECIMIENTOS*
*Gracias a todo el equipo que ha hecho posible este trabajo, y en particular a Monica Feudi, Carola Guaineri, Maddalena Mazzola, Tiziana Universi, Paolo Pucci, Massimo Ferrario, Luca Cannonieri y Pier Pietro Brunelli.*

*AGRADECIMENTOS*
*Nossos agradecimentos a toda a equipe que tornou possível este trabalho e, em especial, a Monica Feudi, Carola Guaineri, Maddalena Mazzola, Tiziana Universi, Paolo Pucci, Massimo Ferrario, Luca Cannonieri, e Pier Pietro Brunelli.*



Original title:
CAPPELLI & CAPELLI - Accessori nel Fashion design


Design and layout: Pause Design
Drafting: Beata Sperczynska
Selection of the images: Maristella Olivotto, B. Sperczynska

Printed in Italy
by T.E.P. - Milano



PROMOPRESS is a commercial brand of: Promotora de Prensa Internacional S.A. C/ Ausias March, 124 - 08013 Barcelona, Spain
Phone: +34 93 245 14 64 Fax: +34 93 265 48 83
info@promopress.es
www.promopress.es - www.promopresseditions.com

*HATS & CAPS - CHAPEAUX ET COIFFURES*
*SOMBREROS Y GORRAS - CHAPÉUS E BONÉS*
English preface revised by: Tom Corkett
Translators of the preface: French / Spanish / Brazilian Portuguese translator: Marie-Pierre Teuler / Jesús de Cos Pinto / Élcio Carillo
Cover adaptation: Stan van Steendam

ISBN: 978-84-92810-90-1

## THE HAT: A SYMBOL OF STATUS AND PERSONALITY

The hat enhances and protects the head of the persona, like a cathedral dome crowning and protecting its place of worship. In fact, the hat is a status symbol that both metaphorically and literally goes over the top in its enhancement of the personality, something that is demonstrated by its significations, which have deep and ancient roots in magic and religion. A brief glimpse at the history and legends of the hat reveals extraordinary cultures, figures, and personalities. Since the earliest times, the hat—decorated with amulets, symbols, feathers, or precious stones and made from felt, fabrics, animal skins, or plant materials—propitiated benign spirits and drove away the evil ones, while of course also protecting from inclement weather and various natural incidents and accidents. The coronation of the powerful with headdresses and precious crowns was a sacred rite that conferred on common mortals practically immortal religious and political powers. Headdresses and hats have also characterized the images and feats of the lower classes, and therefore the customs, rites, and folklore of every place and time.

It was between the thirteenth century and the Renaissance that the hat became popular not only as a functional accessory, but also as a symbolic and aesthetic one. From then on fashion reinvented the "divine hat" according to infinite stylistic and expressive variations that became more and more refined as millenary craft and later industry became more sophisticated. Fashion has therefore strongly contributed to playing up the hat's ability to enhance the value of personality. It has become the mark of many qualities and characteristics of identity, sometimes even contrasting ones. It has been able to express humility and moderation rather than boldness and courage, and vanity rather than shyness and polite conformism, though always through that driving force of fashion: beauty. The hat became adopted by society and culture as an aesthetic sign of respect and merit, civilizing and ceremonial. After that, the hat was seen as a carrier of altruistic sentiments and solidarity, denoting affiliation with a group, a team, or a class, so that, on a more playful and personal level, it served as a salute from afar when waved in the air, as if to demonstrate good feelings and thoughts in one's heart and in one's mind about the departing person.

While women traditionally covered their heads in church, men uncovered theirs as a sign of reverence, and it was the same when one was before one's superiors, or with the custom of

## LE CHAPEAU SYMBOLE DE STATUT SOCIAL ET D'IDENTITÉ

Le chapeau met en valeur et protège la tête, comme le dôme d'une cathédrale couronne et abrite le lieu de culte. Le couvre-chef est un symbole de statut social qui annonce la personnalité de celui qui le porte et confirme son identité. Son rôle a des racines anciennes et profondes qui remontent aux origines de la magie et de la religion. Un bref aperçu de l'histoire du chapeau et des légendes qui l'entourent évoque des cultures extraordinaires et des personnalités hors du commun. Depuis l'aube des temps, le chapeau — orné d'amulettes, de symboles, de plumes ou de pierres précieuses et fabriqué en feutre, en tissu, en peau ou en fourrure d'animal ou en matière végétale — attirait les esprits bénéfiques et chassait le mal. Il protégeait en même temps des intempéries, de certains désagréments naturels et des accidents. La consécration des puissants que l'on coiffait de tiares ou de couronnes de précieux matériaux était un rite sacré qui conférait à un mortel des pouvoirs religieux et politiques quasi immortels. Coiffures et chapeaux ont aussi caractérisé les représentations et les exploits des classes populaires et nous ont transmis les coutumes, les rites et le folklore des diverses régions du monde et époques de l'humanité.

C'est entre le XIIIe siècle et la Renaissance que le chapeau devient répandu, non seulement comme accessoire fonctionnel, mais aussi comme objet symbolique et esthétique. À partir de cette époque, la mode réinvente le chapeau au gré des innombrables styles et expressions qui se succèdent, et devient de plus en plus raffiné à mesure que l'artisanat, puis l'industrie se développe. C'est ainsi que la mode a largement contribué au renforcement du rôle du chapeau en tant que marqueur de personnalité. Le couvre-chef est devenu l'emblème de certaines qualités et signes d'identité parfois opposés. Par exemple, il peut exprimer l'humilité et la modération, ou l'audace et le courage, ou la vanité et le conformisme poli. Emporté par la force vive de la mode, la seule constante est la beauté. Le chapeau a été adopté par les diverses sociétés et les cultures comme une marque esthétique de respect et de mérite, et a joué un rôle social et cérémonial Par la suite, il a représenté l'affiliation et la solidarité par rapport à un groupe, une équipe ou une classe sociale. À un niveau plus personnel et plus informel, le chapeau que l'on agite permet de saluer de loin. Il transmet les sentiments et les pensées de son propriétaire à la personne qui arrive ou qui s'en va.

Autrefois, les femmes se couvraient la tête lorsqu'elles allaient

tipping one's hat to convey class, prestige, and respect. Aside from these customs, an adorned and covered female head implies a ritual enchantment, as the protection of a propitiative gift, erotic and divine, that is offered like a flower blooming on the woman's body, rendering thanks to both mortal and spiritual life. After all, women—at least in the Western world—have, following many long ages of sad misogyny, finally managed to free themselves of the bigoted morality of the covered head, letting down their hair and styling it as they wish. However, in doing so they also freed the "hat culture" of sacro-magical, militaristic, and paternalistic rules, and by extension from rigidly formalizing and predominantly functional aesthetics. Sometimes this occurred through the appropriation of men's hats, even borrowing ideas from military uniforms, as Charlotte Rampling does, for example, with a tormented and neo-romantic S&M look in the film *Night Porter*, directed by Liliana Cavani. More so than those of men, women's hat fashions have, since the end of the 1800s, unleashed a creativity that was expressed then as now using every possible kind of material and shape, ornament, and surprise.

Whatever protects and adorns the human head—whether a man's or a woman's—can thus contribute a special something to it, and the more unique, particular, or chic that headwear, the more special that something is. The hat elevates the person to personage, and by the same token lends personality to the personage. So, for example, it makes a person physically and symbolically taller, loftier, or even haughtier. This happens every time the head is adorned by anything, whether real or imaginary, and whether the halos of saints or the horns of devils, the laurel crowns of the philosophers and the poets, the starry blue cones of fairies and wizards, or the raggedy old hats of Halloween witches. Then there are fashion hats that imitate institutional hats and hats of caste that elevate the person to a "superior" role of high stature and pedigree, either of a spiritual or earthly nature, such as those inspired by the calottes worn by priests, or the headwear of Eastern mystics, or even that worn by magistrates or other *notables* and so-called bigwigs. There are also hats that "uplift" the lower classes, such as workers and peasants, who thus seem to participate more fully in a progressive iconography of the social classes that settles on the working class head a "hat" that is practical and meant to standardize, but which also possesses a noble sense of equity and solidarity that at times manages to become fashionable, as a more or less ideological and idealistic "popular trend". Think of in this regard certain revolutionary berets or the countless versions of hoods that are often embraced by the protester or the ultra.

Then there are hats that confer a kooky amiability to the broadest range of personalities, and we could also mention various eccentric artists in connection with a defiant and anti-conven-

à l'église alors que les hommes se découvraient en signe de révérence. Un homme ôtait aussi son chapeau devant un supérieur et dans toutes les circonstances où il devait incarner élégance, prestige et respect. Au-delà des traditions laïques ou religieuses, une femme qui portait un chapeau se conformait à un rituel incantatoire de protection. En rendant grâce à son corps et à son esprit, cette coiffe lui conférait un pouvoir à la fois érotique et divin. Après des siècles de misogynie, la femme — au moins en Occident — a réussi à se libérer des pressions sectaires et moralisatrices qui l'obligeaient à se couvrir la tête. Elle a pu enfin sortir «en cheveux» et se coiffer comme bon lui semble. Cette révolution a également libéré la «culture du chapeau» de son carcan sacré-magique, militaire et paternaliste, et par extension, de son esthétique codifiée principalement fonctionnelle. La femme a parfois adopté des chapeaux masculins, voire emprunté des détails aux uniformes militaires, comme Charlotte Rampling dans le film *Portier de nuit*, de Liliana Cavani, aux accents sadomasochistes tourmentés et néoromantiques. Depuis la fin du XIXe siècle, la mode féminine, plus que la masculine, laisse libre cours à la créativité et élabore des chapeaux à partir de tous les matériaux, formes, ornements et détails insolites possibles.

Tout ce qui protège et orne la tête d'une personne, homme ou femme, lui assigne un caractère propre, voire un certain chic qui la distingue de la masse. Le chapeau transforme la personne en personnage en lui conférant une personnalité. Par exemple, quelqu'un qui porte un chapeau a l'air physiquement et symboliquement plus grand, plus noble, presque plus hautain. L'effet produit est le même, que le couvre-chef soit réel ou imaginaire, qu'il s'agisse du halo des saints ou des cornes des démons, des couronnes de lauriers des philosophes et des poètes, des chapeaux pointus des fées et des mages ou des coiffes toutes cabossées des sorcières d'Halloween. Sans oublier les chapeaux à la mode s'inspirant de couvre-chefs emblématiques qui élèvent la personne qui les porte au rang de leur modèle, qu'il soit spirituel ou matériel, comme ceux évoquant les calottes de prélats, les turbans de mystiques orientaux, les toques de magistrats ou d'autres notables, etc. Il y a aussi les couvre-chefs qui «anoblissent» la classe ouvrière et paysanne et font partie de l'iconographie de la masse laborieuse. Ils sont pratiques et servent de marqueurs d'appartenance, mais ils représentent aussi des sentiments nobles comme l'égalité et la solidarité. Ils deviennent parfois à la mode et expriment une tendance idéologique et idéaliste populaire, comme c'est le cas de certains bérets révolutionnaires et des multiples variantes de capuches et cagoules portées par les contestataires et les opposants de tous bords.

N'oublions pas non plus les chapeaux qui donnent l'air un peu «décalé» à ceux qui les portent, ni les excentriques qui dé-

tional use of the hat (from Dalí to Picasso and Magritte, for example). Just as every personality has its opposite, hats likewise denote opposite roles and personalities. Just think of the Maigret-style investigator's Borsalino or the hats worn by gangsters and criminals (for example, the infamous coppola, or flat cap, of the Sicilian Mafia). Then there are returns to traditional wear such as the cowboy hat, depicted in the incredible *Indiana Jones* movies and TV series set in Texas. And could we imagine Napoleon, Garibaldi, Che Guevara, Dante, or Robin Hood without their hats? Likewise, think of certain movie stars who unfailingly wore a hat, cap, or beret: Greta Garbo, Audrey Hepburn, Charlie Chaplin, Humphrey Bogart, and so many others, right on up to our own years of youthful exuberance—the fifties and sixties—with Marlon Brando in *On the Waterfront* or James Dean in *Rebel Without a Cause* (or young people who, in spite of losing their heads, have the rebel's cap of experience!).

From this kaleidoscopic survey, which perhaps might fit in well with the mad hatter's dreams and imagination in *Alice in Wonderland*, hat styles can take their inspiration, nurtured in a context of creative freedom that is at times extravagant, at other times conformist, and made of *coups de théâtre* and revisitations ranging from vintage and passé aesthetics to future and futuristic ones. This is how, in hat and headwear styles and trends in particular, we often find cross-pollination from and revivals of primitive cultures, from both the East and the West, where exotic hats are taken up and remodeled, from the fez to the turban, dreadlocks to the neo-Japanese, the sombrero to the South American chullo, and the icy-weather colback to the Italian straw boater. The expressly transcultural—or not—hat-trend, far from generating creativity for itself alone, has often inspired entire looks from head to toe, leading the way to new fashions. Here we have stirred up a confusion of myths, periods, costumes, and historical and legendary figures, all to highlight, hat in hand—as someone presenting himself rather than collecting, as a street artist would—how the hat puts the stress on personality, just like an accent over someone's head, placed to highlight his status, charm, and personality in his sentiments and thoughts. The hat sits *caput mundi*, or rather at the top of the physical body—the head—and is therefore the expressive symbol of the personality, which is to say of the absolute value of every person in his thoughts and sentiments alike. Everything we have said, and everything that this precious book will tell you again through a gallery of images—some famous, some unusual, but in all cases vital for a visual understanding of the charm and elegance of the hat—invites the observer to reflect on why and how it came to be such a beloved and celebrated accessory.

**Pier Pietro Brunelli** (an expert in the psychology of fashion)

tournent le couvre-chef de sa fonction, de Dali à Picasso en passant par Magritte, par exemple. Pour chaque trait de caractère il existe son contraire. Il en va de même des couvre-chefs. Le chapeau mou du commissaire Maigret s'oppose à la casquette coppola de la mafia sicilienne. Notons également le retour en force du chapeau, comme celui des cow-boys et qu'arbore fièrement Indiana Jones et les héros des téléfilms de type Dallas. Pourrait-on imaginer Napoléon, Garibaldi, Che Guevara, Dante ou Robin des Bois sans leur couvre-chef ? De même, pensez à tous les acteurs et actrices qui ont systématiquement porté un chapeau, une casquette ou un béret dans leurs films, comme Greta Garbo, Audrey Hepburn, Charlie Chaplin, Humphrey Bogart et tant d'autres. Sans oublier dans les années cinquante et soixante, les jeunes premiers comme Marlon Brando dans *Sur les quais* et James Dean dans *La Fureur de vivre*.

Cette collection d'images qui semble sortie tout droit d'un kaléidoscope ou de l'imagination du chapelier toqué d'*Alice aux pays des merveilles* montre que les styles de chapeaux naissent dans un contexte où la liberté de création favorise tantôt l'extravagance tantôt le conformisme, où les coups de théâtre changent d'un seul coup la norme et où les modes du passé resurgissent avec vigueur pour créer des tendances allant du vintage à la réinterprétation d'anciens standards, en passant par leur intégration à des esthétiques futuristes. C'est ainsi que dans les styles et les modes de chapeaux on retrouve souvent des influences d'origines diverses, comme la reprise de traditions anciennes d'Orient et d'Occident. Du fez au turban, des dreadlocks au sombrero, du bonnet péruvien au colback ou au canotier, les couvre-chefs de peuples venus d'ailleurs sont récupérés et adaptés. L'inspiration transculturelle (ou non) du chapeau ne se limite pas au seul couvre-chef mais s'étend à l'ensemble de la tenue (de la tête aux pieds) pour créer de nouvelles tendances.

Nous évoquons dans cet ouvrage des personnages historiques et légendaires — auxquels nous tirons notre chapeau pour leur rendre hommage —, dignes représentants de différents mythes, périodes et styles de costumes, pour illustrer l'importance du couvre-chef comme marqueur de personnalité et symbole de statut social, charme et trait de caractère. «Autant de têtes, autant d'avis» dit Jean de La Fontaine et «Qui a une bonne tête ne manque pas de chapeaux», précise le proverbe. Les illustrations du présent ouvrage, certaines étant très connus et d'autres un peu moins, nous permettent de mieux comprendre le rôle d'ambassadeur de charme et de prince de l'élégance joué par cet accessoire prisé et célébré depuis toujours.

**Pier Pietro Brunelli** (expert en psychologie de la mode)

# EL SOMBRERO, SÍMBOLO DE ESTATUS Y PERSONALIDAD

El sombrero destaca y protege la cabeza de la persona igual que la cúpula de una catedral corona y protege el lugar de culto. De hecho, el sombrero, en su refuerzo de la personalidad, es un símbolo de estatus que se ubica literal y metafóricamente por encima de la cumbre, algo que queda demostrado por sus significados, que tienen profundas y antiguas raíces en la magia y la religión. Un vistazo a la historia y las leyendas del sombrero revela culturas, figuras y personalidades extraordinarias. Desde épocas primitivas, el sombrero –decorado con amuletos, símbolos, plumas o piedras preciosas y hecho de fieltro, tela, pieles de animales o materiales vegetales– acercaba a los espíritus benignos y alejaba a los malignos, además, por supuesto, de proteger de las inclemencias del tiempo y de diversos incidentes y accidentes naturales. La coronación de los poderosos con tocados y coronas preciosas era un rito sagrado por el cual se confería a los mortales poderes religiosos y políticos prácticamente inmortales. Los tocados y los sombreros también caracterizaban las imágenes y las hazañas de las clases inferiores y, por lo tanto, las costumbres, ritos y folclore de todos los lugares y en todas las épocas.

Fue entre el siglo XIII y el Renacimiento cuando el sombrero se popularizó no sólo como accesorio funcional sino también como complemente simbólico y estético. Desde entonces, la moda reinventó el «divino sombrero» de acuerdo con infinitas variaciones estilísticas y expresivas que se refinaron cada vez más a medida que la artesanía milenaria, y después la industria, se hacían más sofisticadas. La moda, por ello, ha contribuido en gran medida a desplegar la capacidad del sombrero de reforzar el valor de la personalidad. Se ha convertido en el sello de muchas cualidades y características de la identidad, en ocasiones incluso contradictorias. Ha servido para expresar humildad y moderación en lugar de osadía y coraje, o vanidad en lugar de timidez y educado conformismo, pero siempre a través de esa fuerza divina de la moda: la belleza. El sombrero fue adoptado por la sociedad y la cultura como símbolo estético de respeto y mérito, civilización y ceremonial. Después, el sombrero fue visto como portador de sentimientos altruistas y solidaridad, denotó la afiliación a un grupo, un equipo o una clase social y sirvió también, en un contexto más informal y personal, como saludo a distancia cuando era agitado en el aire para mostrar buenos deseos del corazón y pensamientos de la mente hacia la persona que se marchaba.

Tradicionalmente, las mujeres se cubrían la cabeza en la iglesia, mientras que los hombres se quitaban el sombrero como señal de reverencia. Lo mismo se hacía en presencia de superiores, y la acción de descubrirse también indicaba clase, prestigio y respeto. Aparte de estas costumbres, la cabeza adornada y cubierta de la mujer implica un

# O CHAPÉU: UM SÍMBOLO DE STATUS E PERSONALIDADE

O chapéu valoriza e protege a cabeça do personagem, tal como a cúpula de uma catedral coroa e protege o seu lugar de culto. Na verdade, o chapéu é um símbolo de status que metafórica e literalmente fica por cima em sua valorização da personalidade, algo que é demonstrado por seus significados, que têm profundas e antigas raízes na magia e na religião. Um breve olhar para a história e lendas do chapéu revela extraordinárias culturas, figuras e personalidades. Desde os tempos mais remotos, o chapéu – decorado com amuletos, símbolos, penas, ou pedras preciosas e feitos de feltro, tecidos, peles de animais, materiais vegetais – propiciou espíritos benignos e afastou os maus, ao mesmo tempo que, claro, também protegeu do mau tempo e de vários incidentes e acidentes naturais. A coroação dos poderosos com cocares e coroas preciosas era um rito sagrado que conferia aos mortais comuns poderes políticos e religiosos praticamente imortais. Cocares e chapéus também têm caracterizado as imagens e feitos das classes mais baixas e, portanto, os costumes, ritos e folclore de cada tempo e lugar.

Entre o século XIII e o Renascimento, o chapéu tornou-se popular não só como um acessório funcional, mas também simbólico e estético. A partir de então, a moda reinventou o «chapéu divino» de acordo com infinitas variações estilísticas e expressivas que se tornaram mais e mais refinadas como artesanato milenar, convertendo-se depois numa indústria mais sofisticada. Portanto, a moda contribuiu intensamente para aumentar a capacidade do chapéu de valorizar a personalidade. Tornou-se o símbolo de muitas qualidades e características de identidade, por vezes até mesmo contrastantes. Ele tem sido capaz de expressar humildade e moderação em vez de ousadia e coragem, e vaidade em vez de timidez e conformismo polido, ainda que sempre através da força motriz da moda: a beleza. O chapéu foi adotado pela sociedade e pela cultura como sinal estético de respeito e mérito, civilizador e cerimonial. Depois disso, o chapéu foi visto como portador de sentimentos altruístas e solidários, denotando afiliação a um grupo, a uma equipe ou a uma classe, de modo que, num nível mais lúdico e pessoal, serviu como saudação à distância quando acenado no ar, e também para demonstrar bons sentimentos e pensamentos, no coração e na mente, em relação à pessoa que parte.

Enquanto as mulheres, tradicionalmente, cobriam a cabeças na igreja, os homens descobriam-na como sinal de reverência, e o mesmo acontecia quando alguém estava diante de um superior seu, ou com o costume de fazer uma inflexão do chapéu como manifestação de classe, prestígio e respeito. Afora esses costumes, uma cabeça feminina adornada e coberta envolve um encantamento ritual, como a proteção de um dom propício, erótico e divino, que é oferecido como uma

encantamiento ritual, semejante a la protección que brinda un regalo propiciatorio, erótico y divino, ofrecido como una flor que florece en el cuerpo femenino en acción de gracias por la vida mortal y espiritual. Al final, las mujeres –al menos en el mundo occidental– han conseguido, después de siglos de lamentable misoginia, liberarse de la moral intolerante de la cabeza cubierta, dejar suelto su cabello y peinarlo según sus deseos. Además, al hacerlo así, también han liberado la «cultura del sombrero» de normas mágico-religiosas, militares y paternalistas, y por extensión la han desvinculado de rígidas estéticas formalizadoras y predominantemente funcionales.

En ocasiones, esto ocurrió mediante la apropiación de los sombreros de los hombres, incluso tomando ideas de los uniformes militares, como, por ejemplo, hace Charlotte Rampling con el estilo sadomasoquista atormentado y neorromántico que luce en el filme *Portero de noche*, dirigido por Liliana Cavani. Desde finales del siglo XVIII, la moda del sombrero femenino, más que la del masculino, ha desencadenado una creatividad que se expresa, entonces como ahora, empleando todos los materiales, formas, adornos y sorpresas posibles.

Cualquier cosa que proteja y adorne la cabeza humana, sea de hombre o de mujer, puede añadirle un factor especial; y cuanto más singular, particular o chic sea el tocado más especial será ese factor. El sombrero eleva a la persona a personaje y, por la misma fórmula, aporta personalidad al personaje. Así, por ejemplo, el sombrero hace a la persona física y simbólicamente más alta, más elevada o incluso más altiva. Esto ocurre cada vez que se adorna la cabeza con algo, real o imaginario, ya sea el halo de los santos o los cuernos de los demonios, las coronas de laurel de filósofos y poetas, los cucuruchos azules adornados con estrellas de hadas y magos o los sombreros harapientos de las brujas de Halloween. Tenemos también sombreros de moda que imitan los sombreros institucionales, y sombreros de clase social que elevan a la persona a un papel *superior*, de estatura y casta elevadas, ya sean de naturaleza espiritual o terrenal, como los inspirados en los bonetes de los sacerdotes o en el tocado de los místicos orientales, o incluso en los sombreros de los magistrados y otros notables y potentados. También hay sombreros que *elevan* a las clases bajas, obreros y campesinos, que de este modo parecen tomar parte en una iconografía progresista de las clases sociales que pone en la cabeza de la clase obrera un tipo de tocado que es práctico y unificador pero que también denota un noble sentimiento de igualdad y solidaridad, y que en ocasiones se pone de moda como tendencia popular más o menos ideológica e idealista. En ese sentido, pensemos en ciertas boinas revolucionarias, o en las incontables versiones de las capuchas que a menudo adoptan los inconformistas o los ultras.

Por otra parte, hay sombreros que confieren un aire raro y simpático a un amplio espectro de personalidades, y también podríamos mencionar a diversos artistas excéntricos en relación con el uso provocador y anticonvencional del sombrero, de Dalí a Picasso pasando por Magritte, por ejemplo. Del mismo modo que hay persona-

flor que brota no corpo da mulher, rendendo graças à vida, tanto mortal como espiritual. Afinal, as mulheres – pelo menos no mundo ocidental – após muitos e longos séculos de misoginia triste, finalmente conseguiram libertar-se da moralidade intolerante da cabeça coberta, soltando seu cabelo e modelando-o como desejam. Contudo, ao fazer isso, elas também libertaram a «cultura do chapéu» das regras sacro-mágicas, militaristas e paternalistas e, por extensão, da estética rígida e predominantemente funcional. Algumas vezes, isso ocorreu através da apropriação de chapéus dos homens, mesmo por empréstimo de ideias de uniformes militares, como faz Charlotte Rampling, por exemplo, com um atormentado e neo-romântico visual S & M no filme *Night Porter,* dirigido por Liliana Cavani. Mais do que os dos homens, a moda do chapéu feminino, desde o final de 1800, desencadeou uma criatividade que se expressa, tanto naquela época como agora, com a utilização de todo tipo imaginável de material e forma, ornamentação, e surpresa.

Tudo o que protege e adorna a cabeça humana – seja de um homem ou de uma mulher – pode então contribuir com algo especial, e quanto as mais originais, particulares, ou chiques forem os chapéus, mais especial será esse algo. O chapéu eleva a pessoa à categoria de personagem e, por isso mesmo, confere personalidade à personagem. Assim, por exemplo, torna uma pessoa física e simbolicamente mais alta, mais elevada, ou até mesmo mais altiva. Isto acontece cada vez que a cabeça é adornada por qualquer coisa, seja ela real ou imaginária como as auréolas dos santos ou os chifres dos diabos, as coroas de louros dos filósofos e dos poetas, os cones azuis estrelados das fadas e magos, ou os velhos e esfarrapados chapéus das bruxas do Dia das Bruxas. Deste modo, há chapéus de moda que imitam chapéus institucionais e chapéus de casta que elevam a pessoa a um papel «superior» de estatura elevada e pedigree, ou de natureza espiritual ou terrena, tais como os inspirados nos solidéus usados pelos sacerdotes ou pelos místicos orientais, ou mesmo aqueles usados por magistrados ou outros notáveis e assim chamados figurões. Há também chapéus que «elevam» as classes mais baixas, como operários e camponeses, que assim parecem participar mais plenamente uma iconografia progressiva das classes sociais que se instala na cabeça classe trabalhadora um «chapéu» que é prático e destinado a padronizar, mas que também possui um sentido nobre de equidade e de solidariedade que, por vezes, torna-se moda, mais ou menos como uma «tendência popular» ideológica e idealista. Neste sentido, pense em certas boinas revolucionárias ou nas inúmeras versões de capuzes frequentemente adotados por manifestantes de protestos ou ultra radicais.

Depois, há chapéus que conferem uma amabilidade excêntrica para uma ampla gama de personalidades, e também poderíamos mencionar vários artistas excêntricos ligados ao uso desafiador e anticonvencional do chapéu (de Dalí a Picasso e a Magritte, por exemplo). Assim como toda personalidade tem o seu oposto, chapéus igualmente denotam papéis e personalidades opostos. Bas-

lidades opuestas, los sombreros pueden denotar roles y personalidades contrarios. Pensemos en el Borsalino de investigador estilo Maigret o en los sombreros que llevan gángsteres y criminales (por ejemplo, el infame *coppola*, o sombrero plano, de la mafia siciliana). También tenemos retornos a la tradición, como el sombrero de cow boy que aparece en las increíbles películas de Indiana Jones y en las series de televisión ambientadas en Texas. ¿Y podríamos imaginarnos a Napoleon, Garibaldi, Che Guevara, Dante o Robin Hood sin sus sombreros? Del mismo modo, ciertas estrellas del cine siempre llevaban sombrero, gorra o boina: Greta Garbo, Audrey Hepburn, Charlie Chaplin, Humphrey Bogart y tantos otros, y hasta en los años de nuestra juventud –los cincuenta y los sesenta– con Marlon Brando en *La ley del silencio* o James Dean en *Rebelde sin causa* (y otros jóvenes que, a pesar de perder la cabeza, llevan en ella el sombrero de la rebeldía).

De este caleidoscópico recorrido, que quizá encajaría en los sueños y fantasías del Sombrerero Loco de *Alicia en el país de las maravillas*, pueden extraer su inspiración los estilos de sombreros, una inspiración que se alimenta en un contexto de libertad creativa a veces extravagante, conformista en otras ocasiones, y que está hecha de golpes de efecto y revisiones que van desde las estéticas vintage y antiguas hasta las futuras y futuristas. De este modo, en los estilos y tendencias, en especial los de sombreros y tocados, a menudo encontramos cruces con culturas primitivas de Oriente y Occidente, cuyos sombreros exóticos se toman y se remodelan, del fez al turbante, de las rastas al neojaponés, del sombrero mexicano al chullo de Sudamérica y del sombrero de húsar para el frío al canotier italiano. Las tendencias del sombrero –expresamente transculturales o no– lejos de ceñirse a su propio ámbito creativo, han inspirado a menudo estilos completos de la cabeza a los pies, señalando el camino para nuevas modas.

Hemos hurgado en una confusión de mitos, periodos, atuendos y figuras históricas y legendarias para señalar, sombrero en mano –como alguien que se presenta a sí mismo, no como un artista callejero que pasa el sombrero– cómo el sombrero pone el acento en la personalidad, como si fuera una tilde sobre la cabeza, para resaltar su estatus, su encanto y la naturaleza de sus sentimientos y pensamientos. El sombrero se asienta *caput mundi* o, más bien, en lo alto del cuerpo físico –la cabeza– y es por ello el símbolo expresivo de la personalidad, es decir, del valor absoluto de cada persona en sus pensamientos y en sus sentimientos. Todo lo dicho, y todo lo que ese precioso libro le dirá a través de su galería de imágenes –algunas famosas, otras inusuales, pero en todos los casos vitales para la comprensión visual del encanto y elegancia del sombrero– invita al observador a reflexionar sobre cómo y por qué ha llegado a ser un accesorio tan querido y celebrado.

**Pier Pietro Brunelli,** experto en psicología de la moda.

ta pensar no estilo-investigador-Maigret, de Borsalino ou nos chapéus usados pelos gangsters e criminosos (por exemplo, no famoso coppola, ou nos bonés da máfia siciliana). E no retorno ao tradicional, como o chapéu de cowboy, retratado nos incríveis filmes de Indiana Jones e nas séries de TV no Texas. E será que poderíamos imaginar Napoleão, Garibaldi, Che Guevara, Dante, ou Robin Hood sem os seus chapéus? Assim como, pensar em certas estrelas de cinema que, infalivelmente, usavam um chapéu, boné ou boina: Greta Garbo, Audrey Hepburn, Charlie Chaplin, Humphrey Bogart, e tantas outras dos nossos anos de exuberante juventude – dos anos cinquenta e sessenta – com Marlon Brando em On the Waterfront ou James Dean em Rebel Without a Cause (ou jovens que, apesar de perder a cabeça, têm o quepe dos rebeldes da experiência!).

A partir deste exame caleidoscópico, que talvez possa se encaixar bem com os sonhos e imaginações do chapeleiro maluco de Alice no País das Maravilhas, os estilos de chapéus podem inspirar-se, alimentando-se num contexto de liberdade criativa que é algumas vezes extravagante e outras conformista, feito de reviravoltas e revisitações que vão desde a estética de épocas passadas até as futuras e futuristas. É por isso que na moda e nos estilos de chapéus, e em suas tendências em particular, encontramos frequentemente a polinização cruzada de revivals das culturas primitivas, tanto no Oriente como no Ocidente, onde chapéus exóticos são tomados e remodelados, desde o fez até o turbante, dos rastafáris aos neo-Japoneses, do sombrero ao chullo sul americano, e do colback para climas gelados ao chapéu de palha italiano. As tendências – transculturais ou não – do chapéu, longe de gerar criatividade por si mesmas, frequentemente se inspiraram em olhares integrais, dos pés à cabeça, abrindo caminho para novas modas.

Despertamos aqui uma confusão de mitos, períodos, costumes e figuras históricas e lendárias, tudo para destacar, de chapéu na mão – como alguém que se apresenta e não como quem coleta doações, como faria um artista de rua – de que modo o chapéu coloca o ênfase sobre a personalidade, assim como um acento gramatical sobre a cabeça de alguém, colocado para destacar seu status, charme e personalidade em também dos seus sentimentos e pensamentos. O chapéu fica caput mundi, ou melhor, no topo do corpo físico – a cabeça – e é, portanto, o símbolo expressivo da personalidade, ou seja, do valor absoluto de cada pessoa em seus pensamentos e sentimentos. Tudo o que dissemos e tudo o que este precioso livro vai lhe dizer mais uma vez através de uma galeria de imagens – algumas famosas, outras incomuns, mas em todos os casos vitais para uma compreensão visual do charme e elegância do chapéu – convida o observador a refletir sobre o porquê e o como ele se tornou um acessório amado e celebrado.

**Pier Pietro Brunelli** (um especialista em psicologia da moda)

# index

10
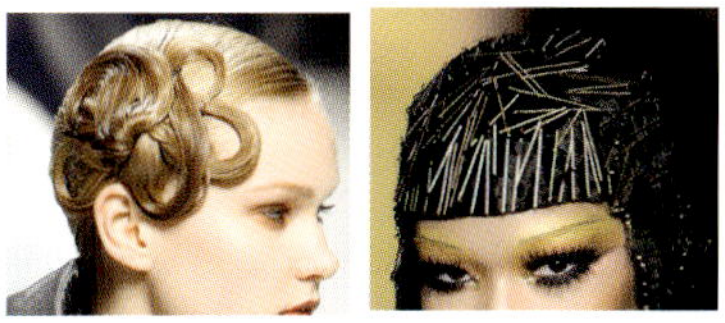
32
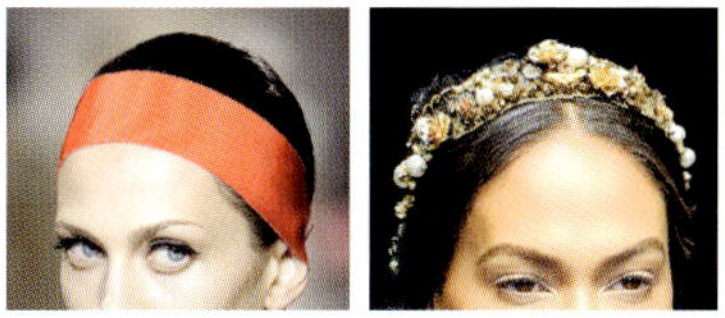
46
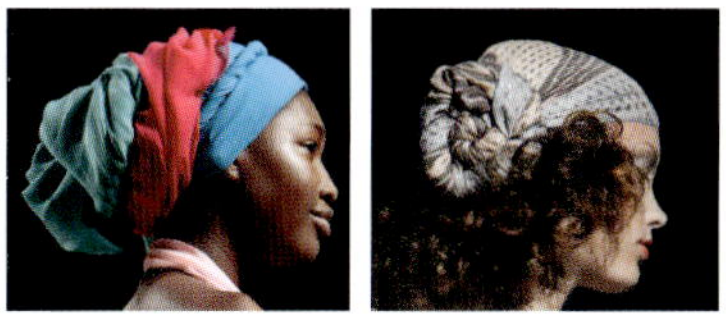
58
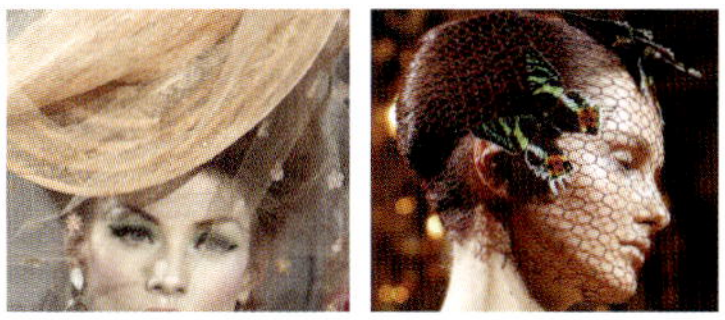
70
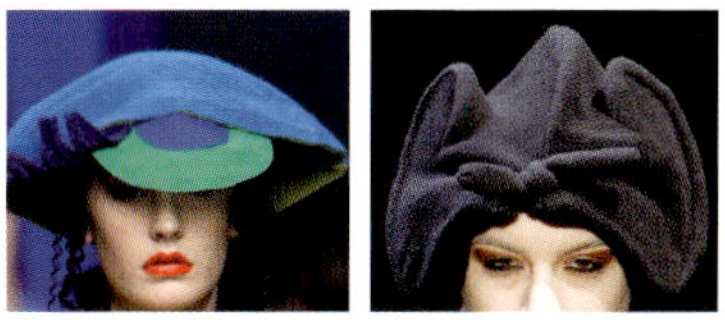
84
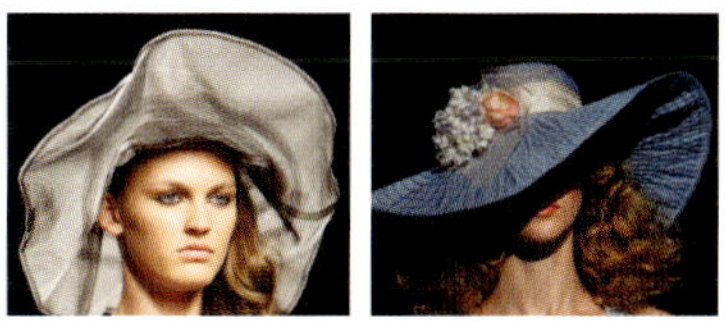
98
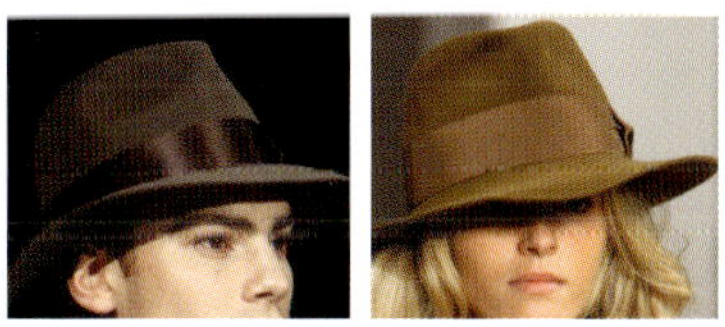
104
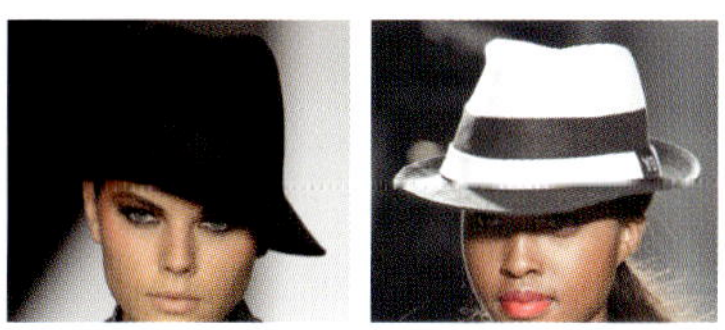
108
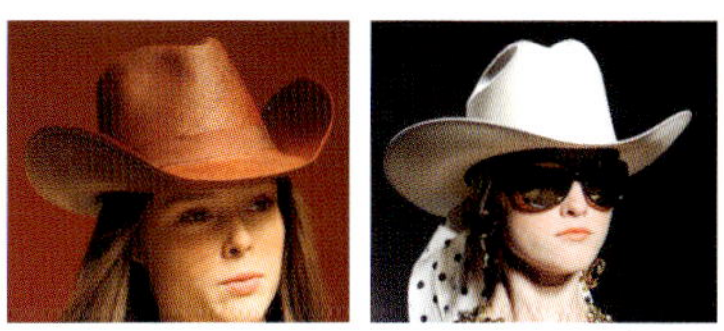
112
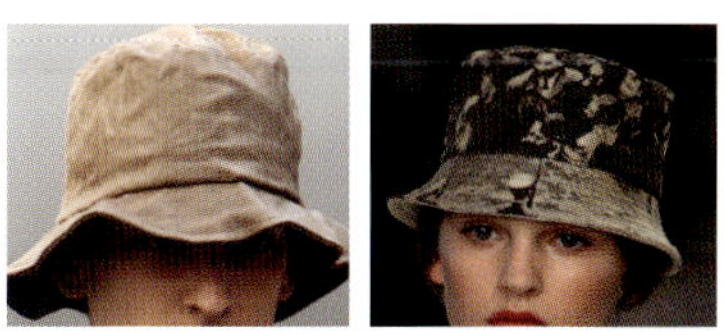
116
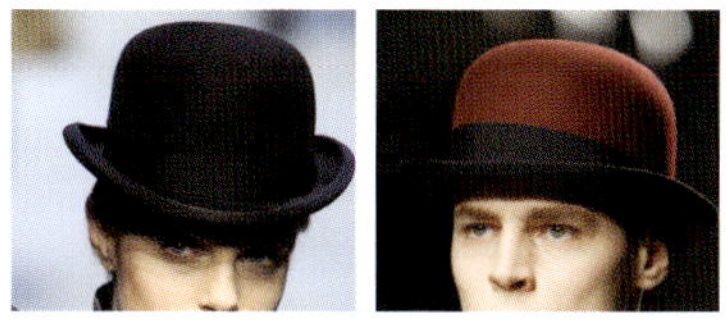
124
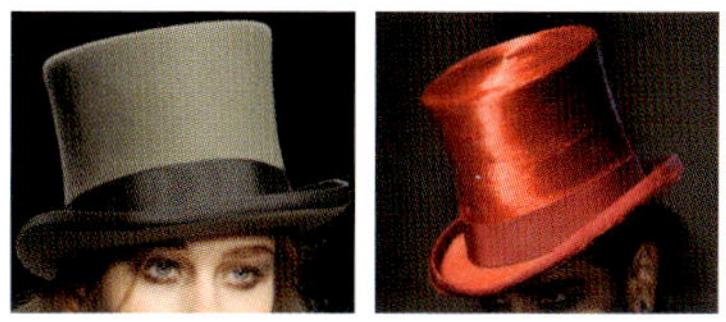
128
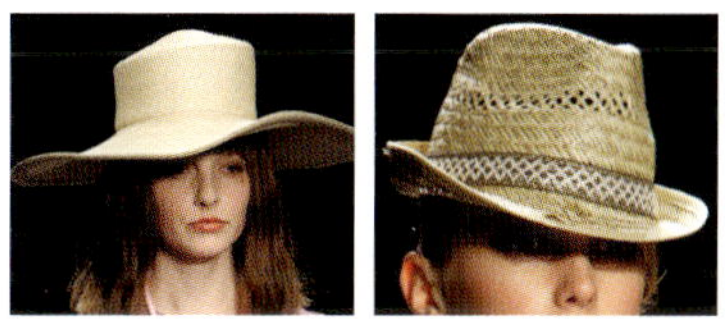
142
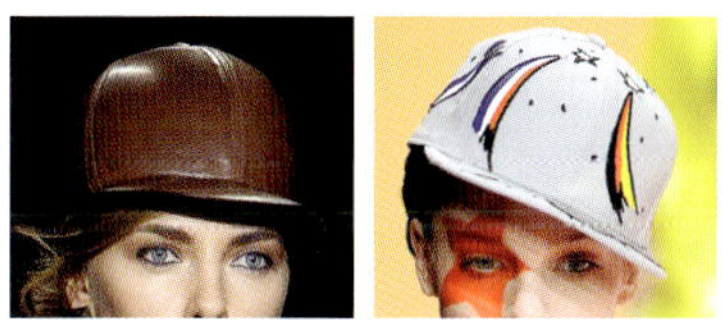
146
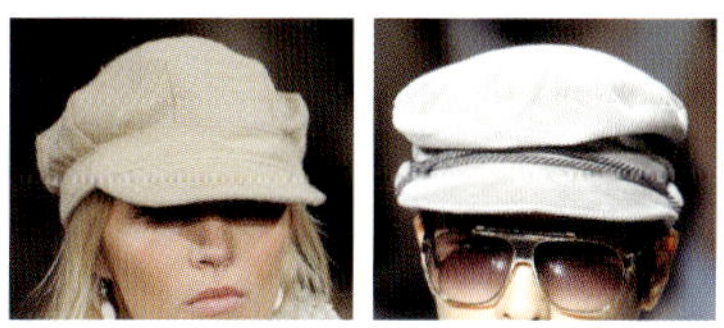
150
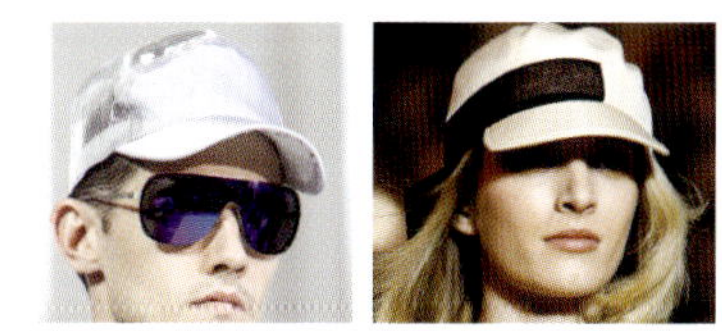
156
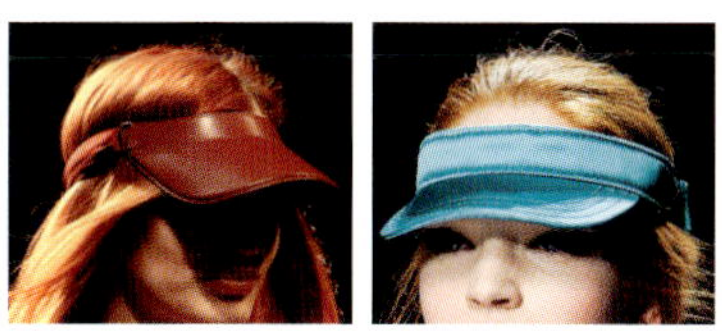
158
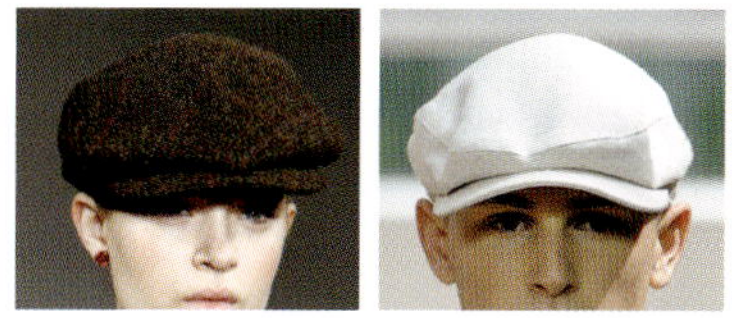
164
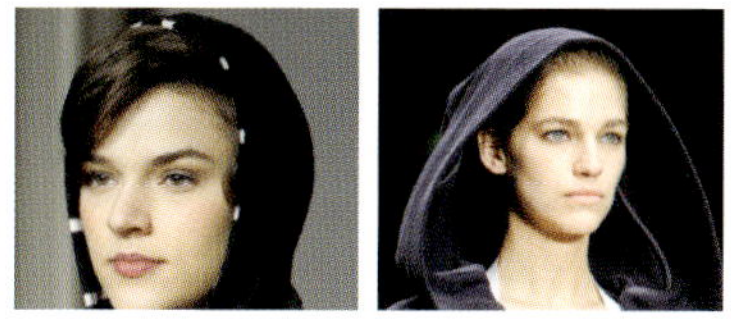
174
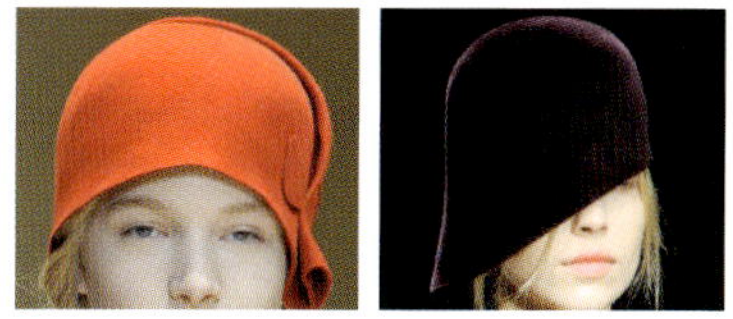
176
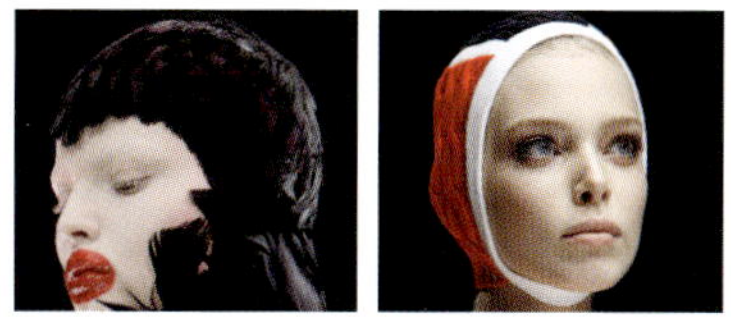
184
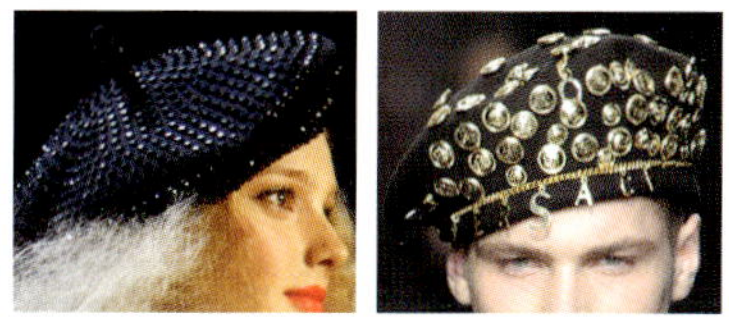
190
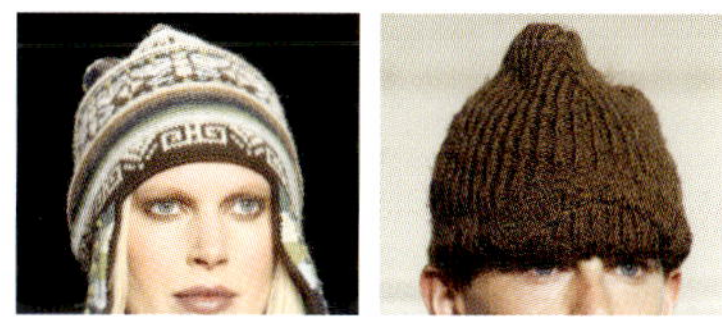
198
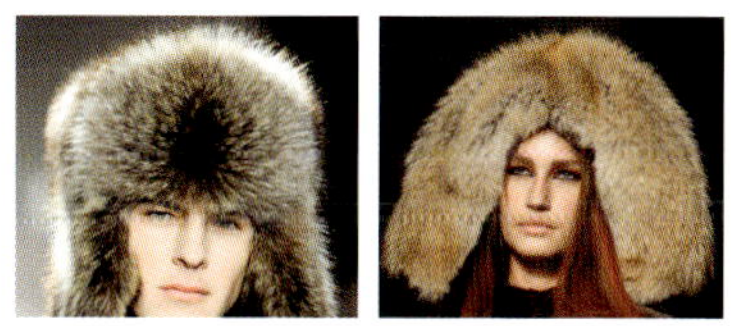
202
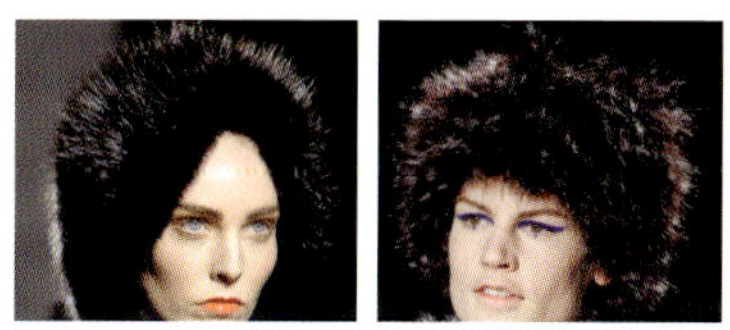
214
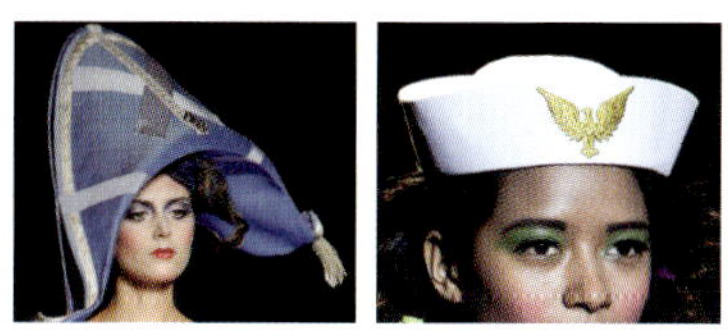
220
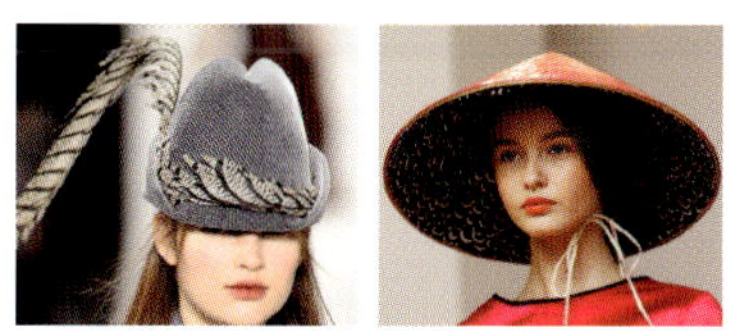

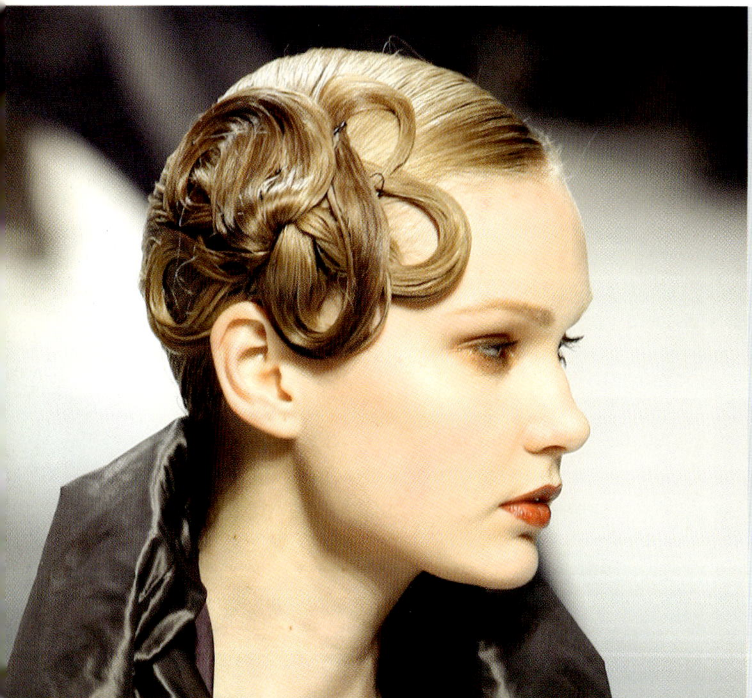
Issey Miyake

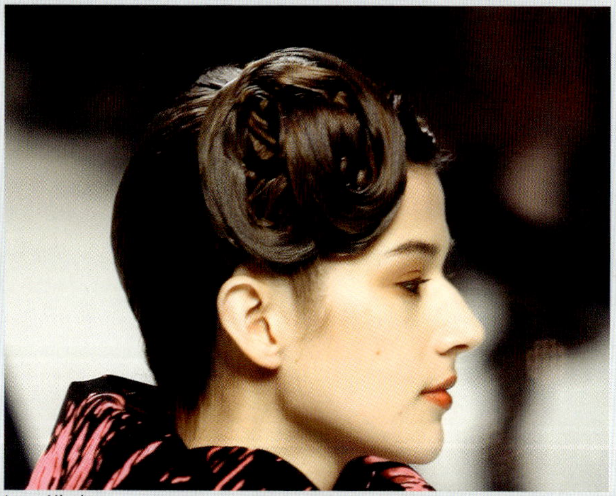
Issey Miyake

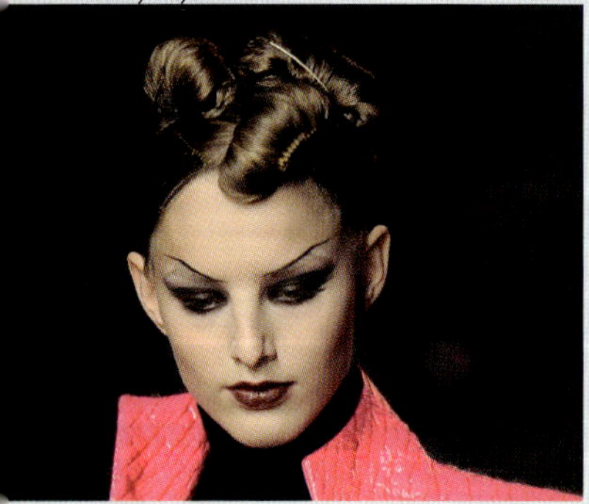
Christian Lacroix

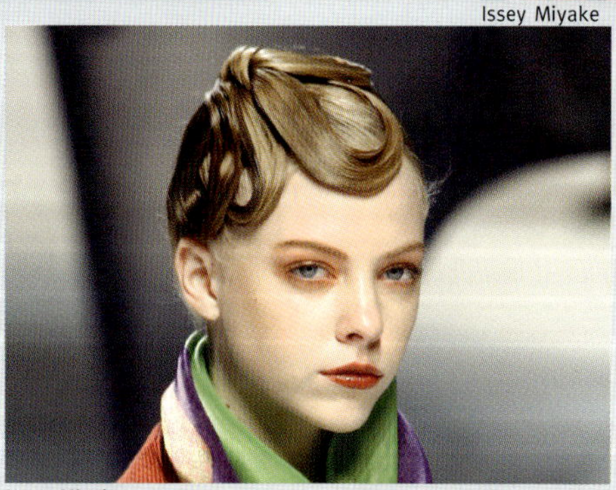
Issey Miyake

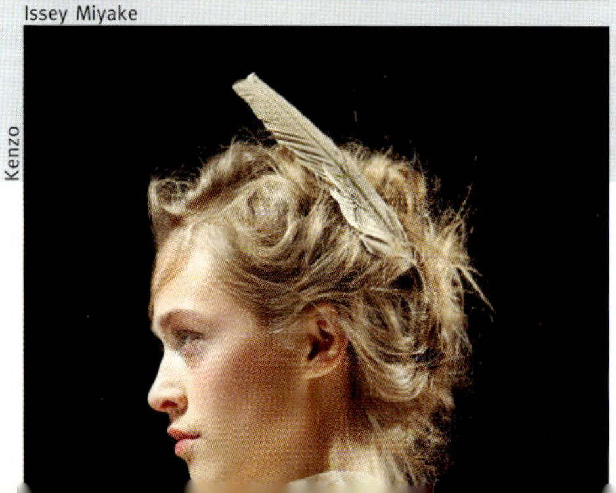
Kenzo

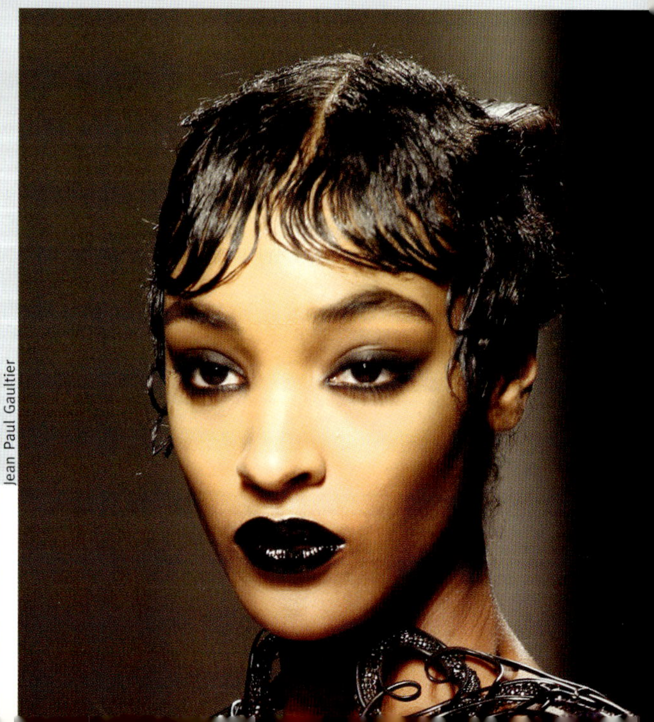
Jean Paul Gaultier

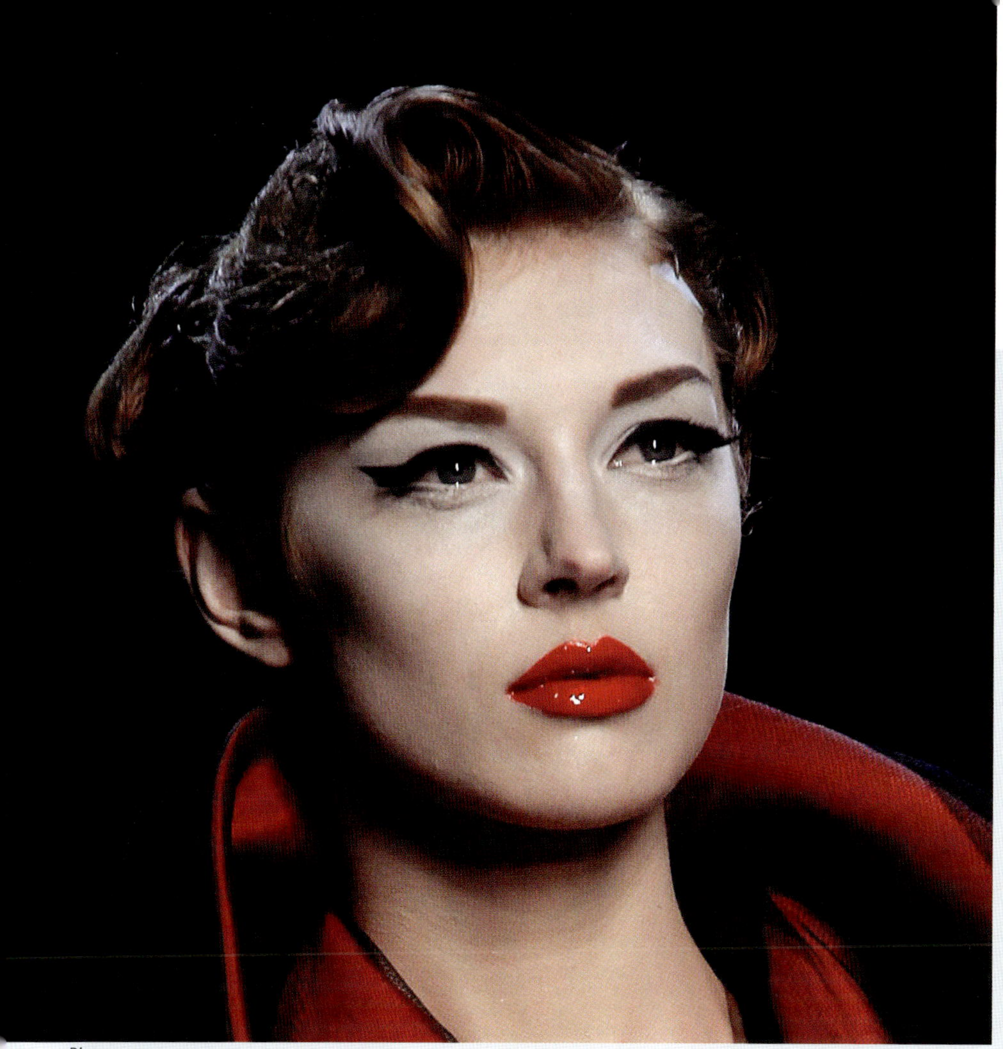

Dior

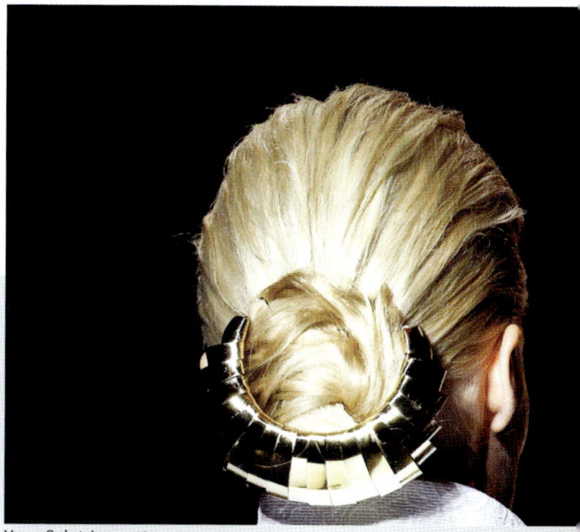

Yves Saint Laurent

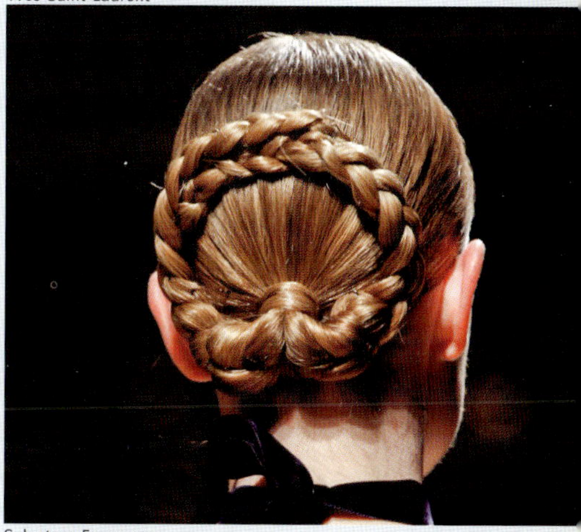

Salvatore Ferragamo

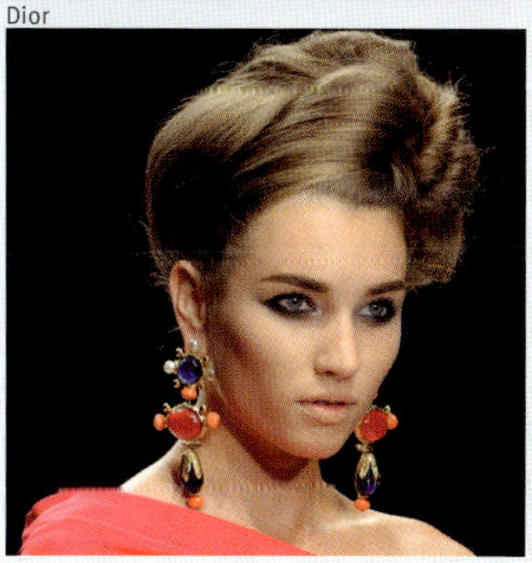

Issa

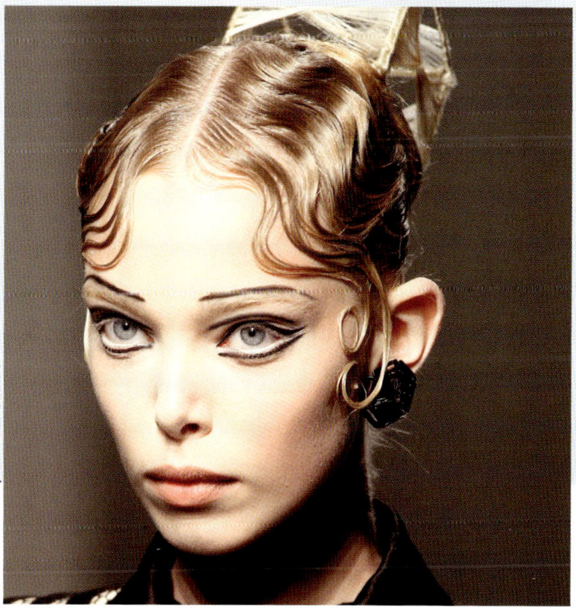

Jean Paul Gaultier

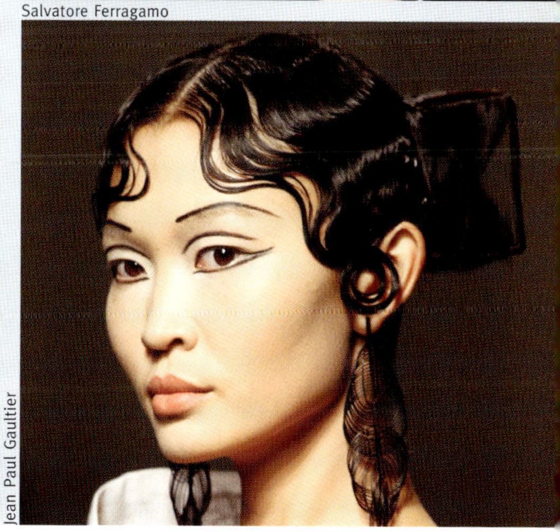

Jean Paul Gaultier

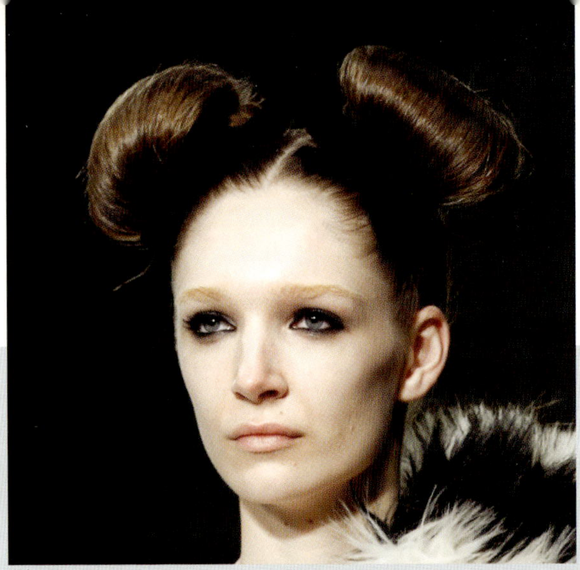

Unique

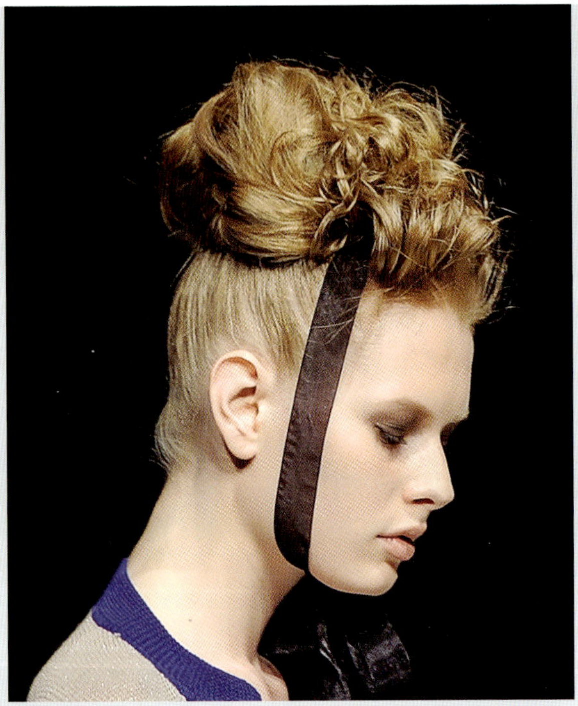

Lala Berlin

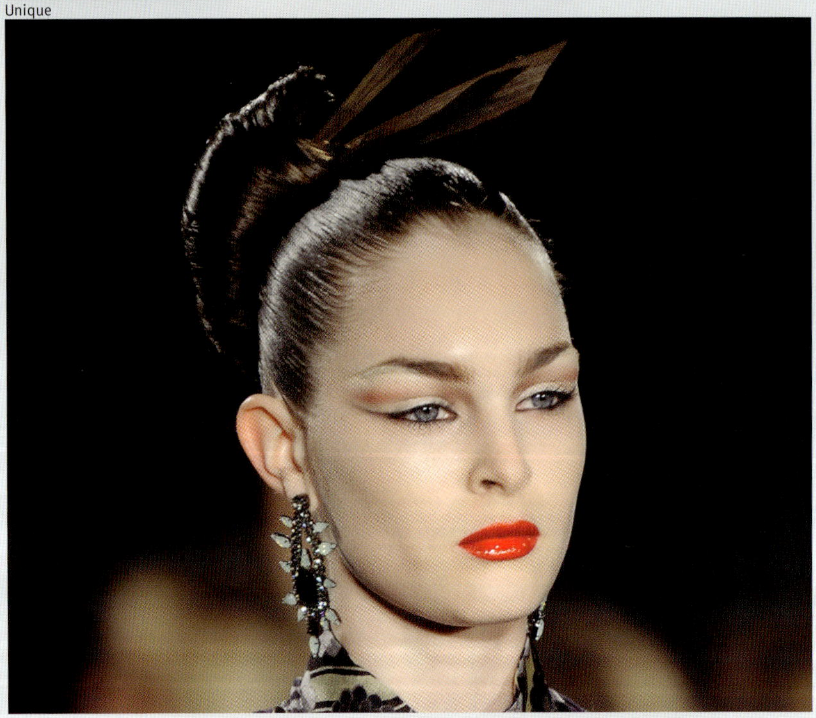

Zac Posen

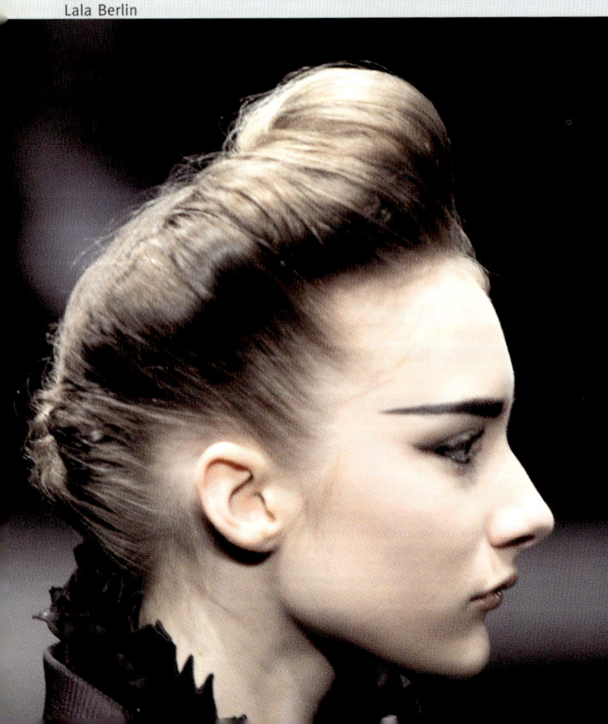

Gianfranco Ferré

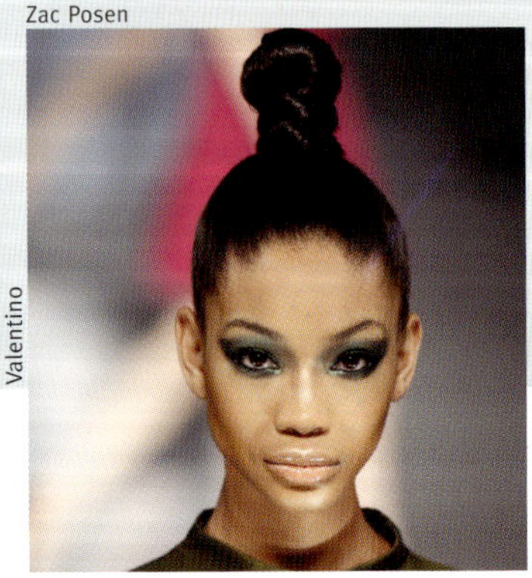

Valentino

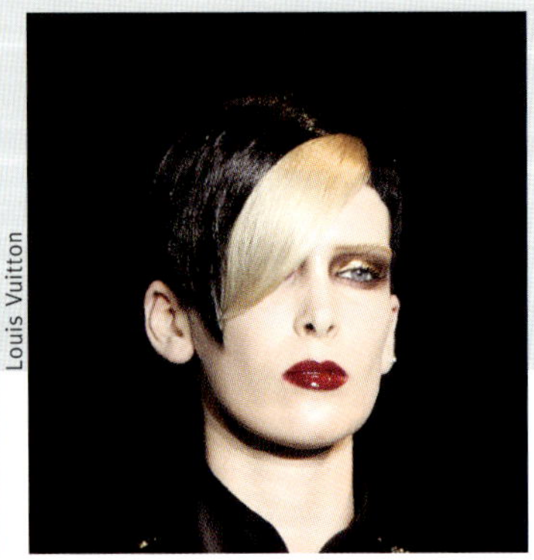

Louis Vuitton

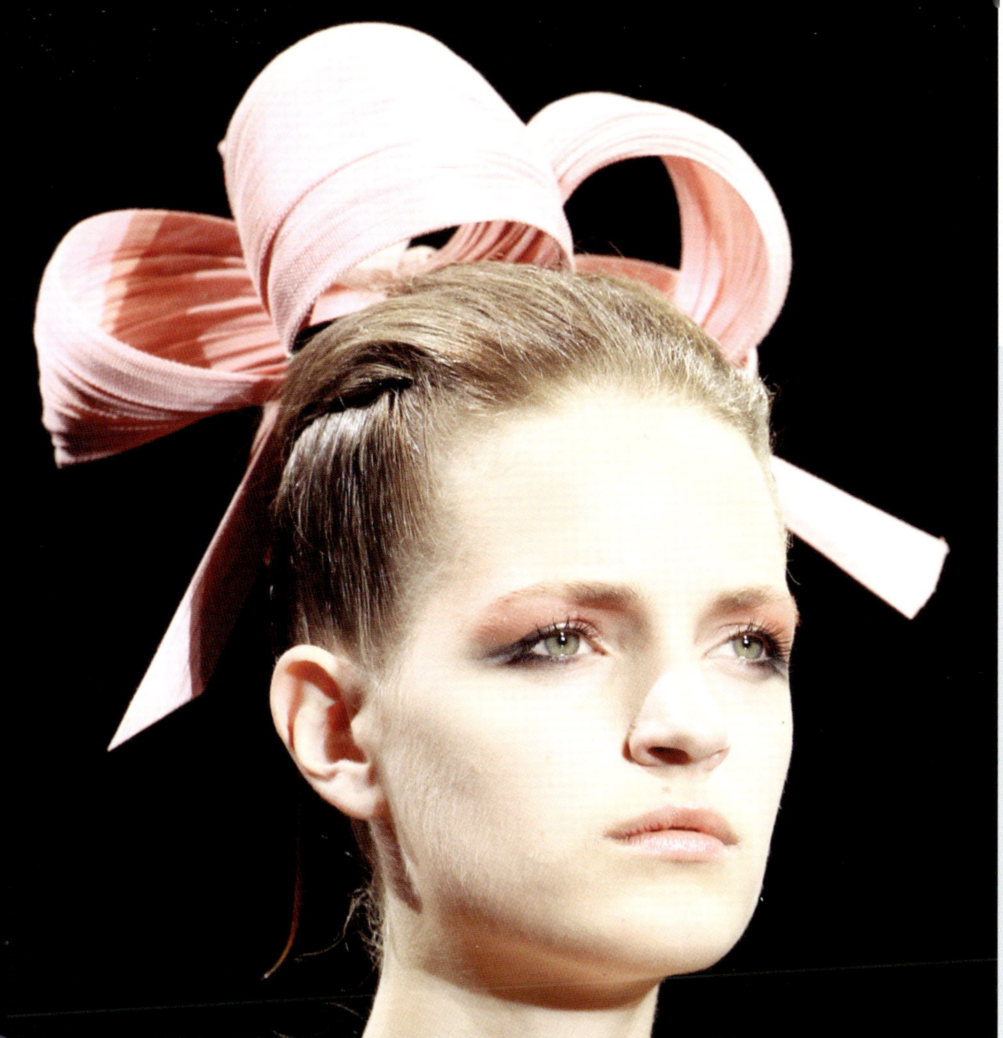

Armani Privè

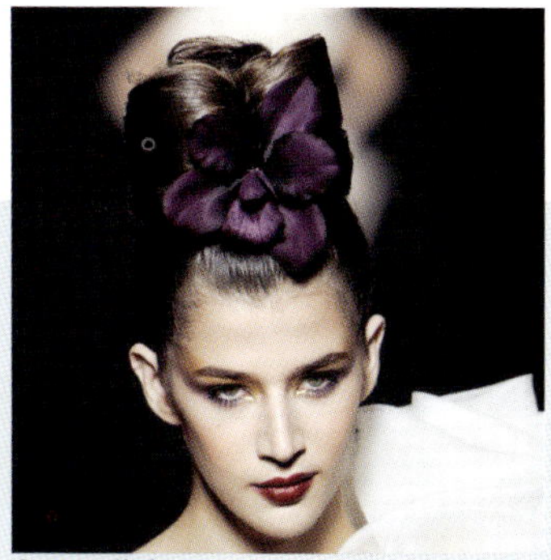

Georges Chakra

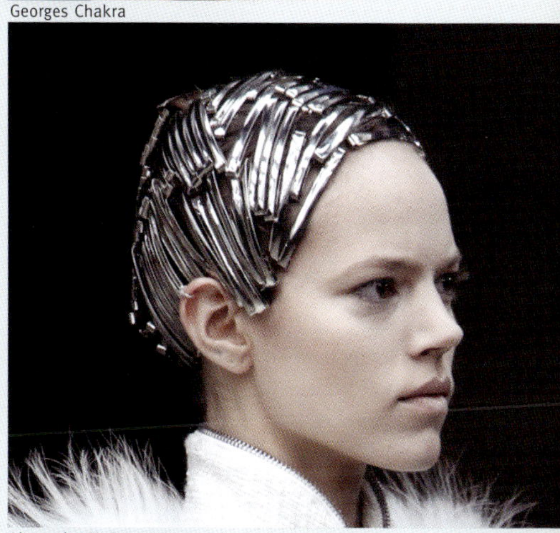

Alexander McQueen

Yves Saint Laurent

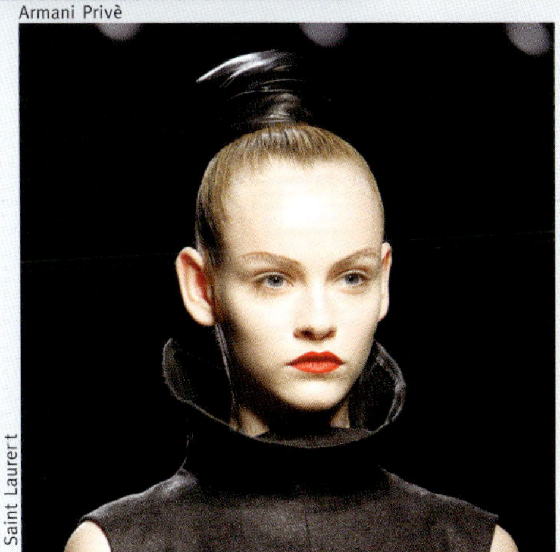

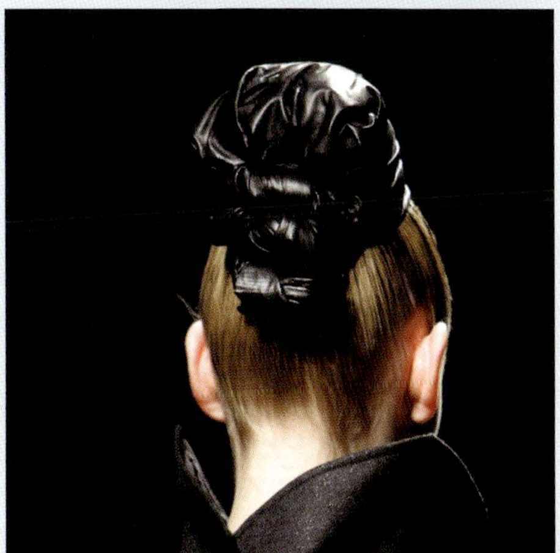

Jean Paul Gaultier

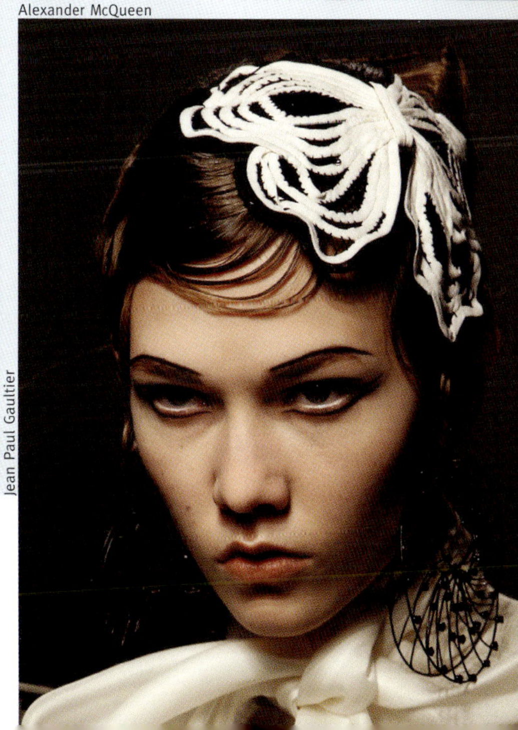

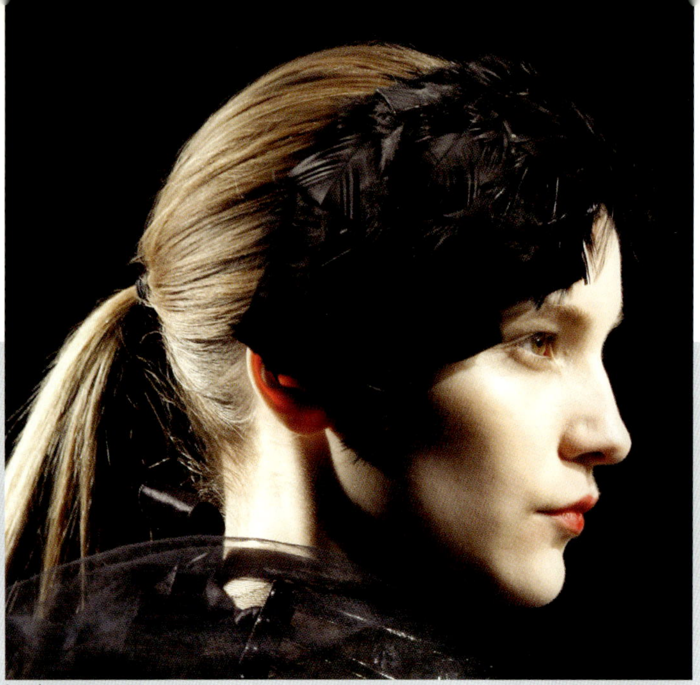

Lanvin

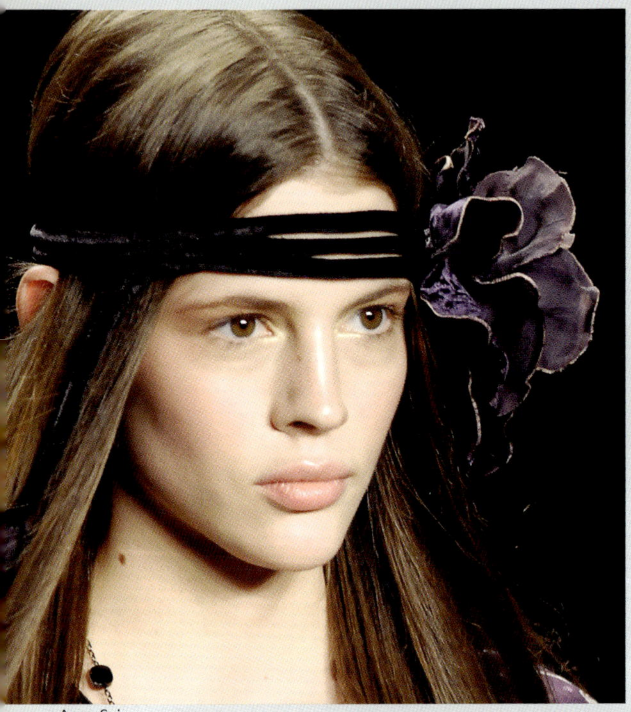

Anna Sui

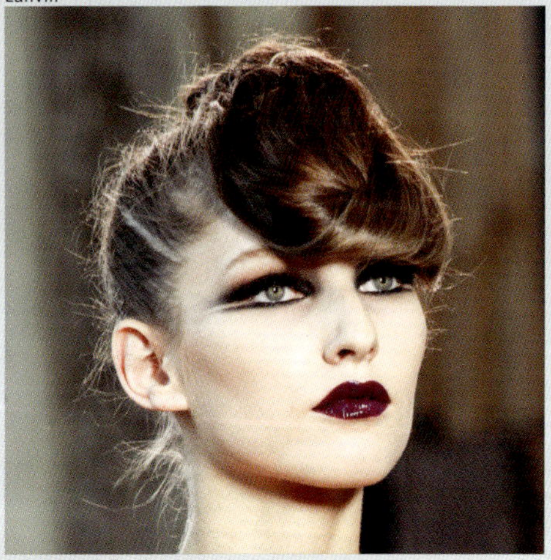

Stéphane Rolland

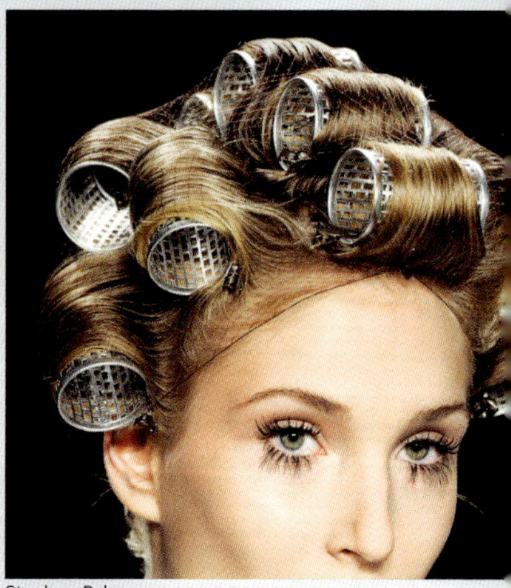

Stephan Pelger

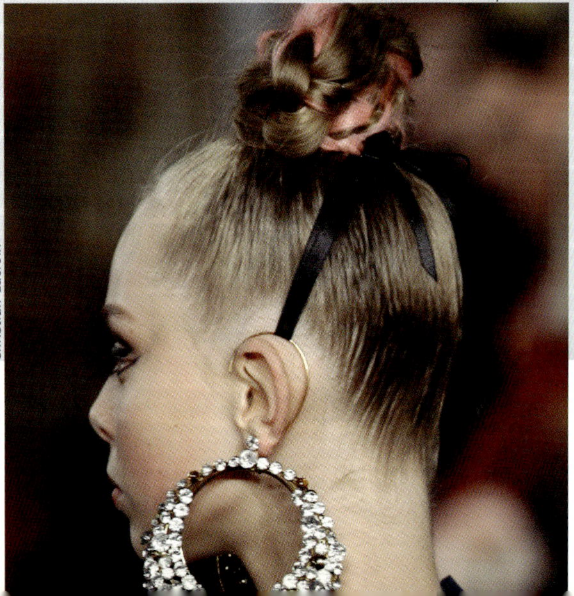

Christian Lacroix

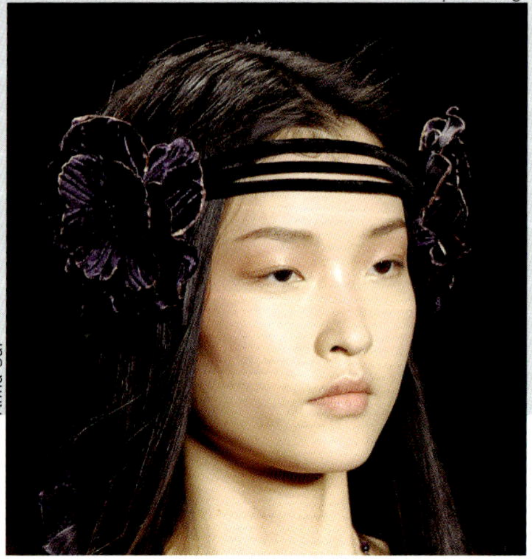

Anna Sui

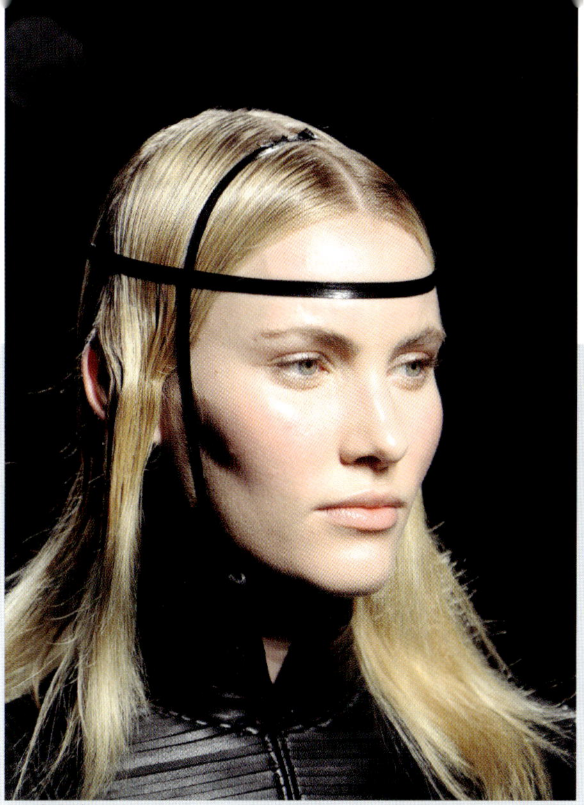
Gareth Pugh

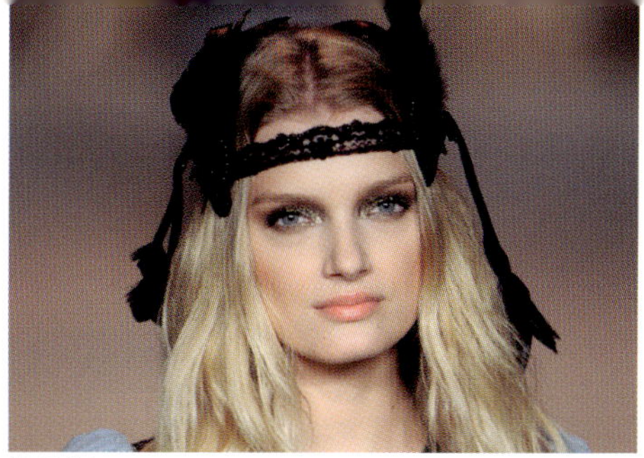
Anna Sui

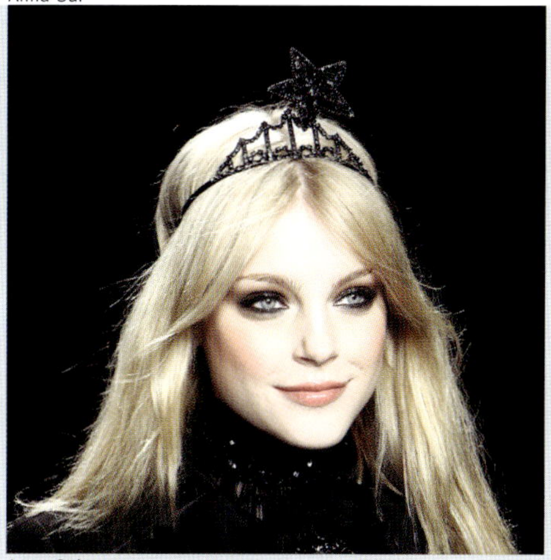
Anna Sui

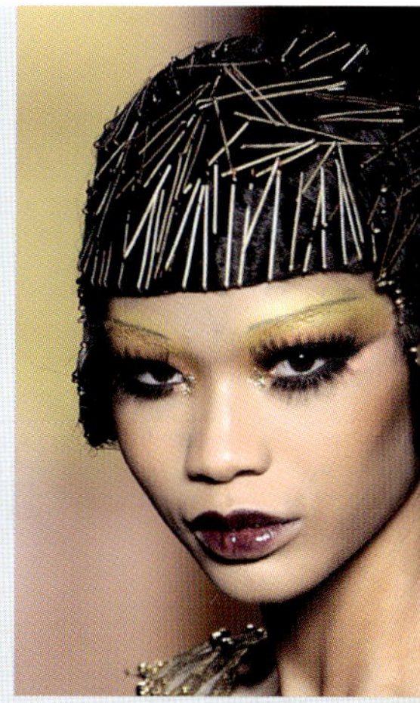
Dior

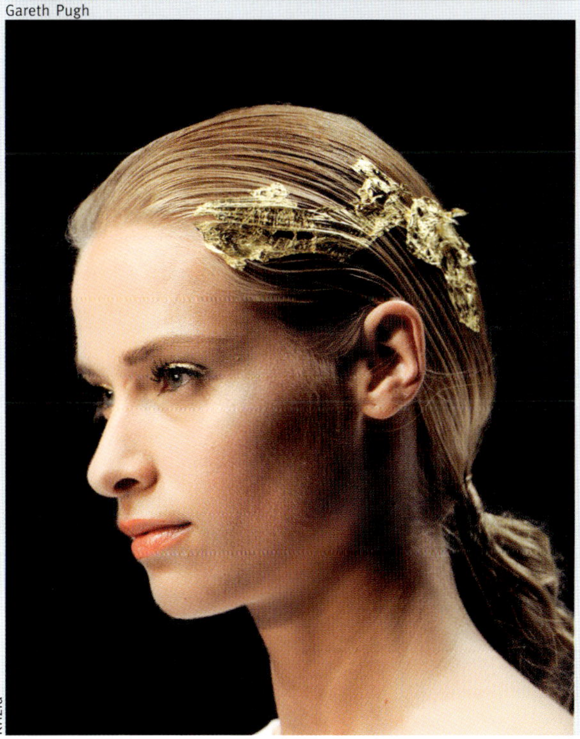
Krizia

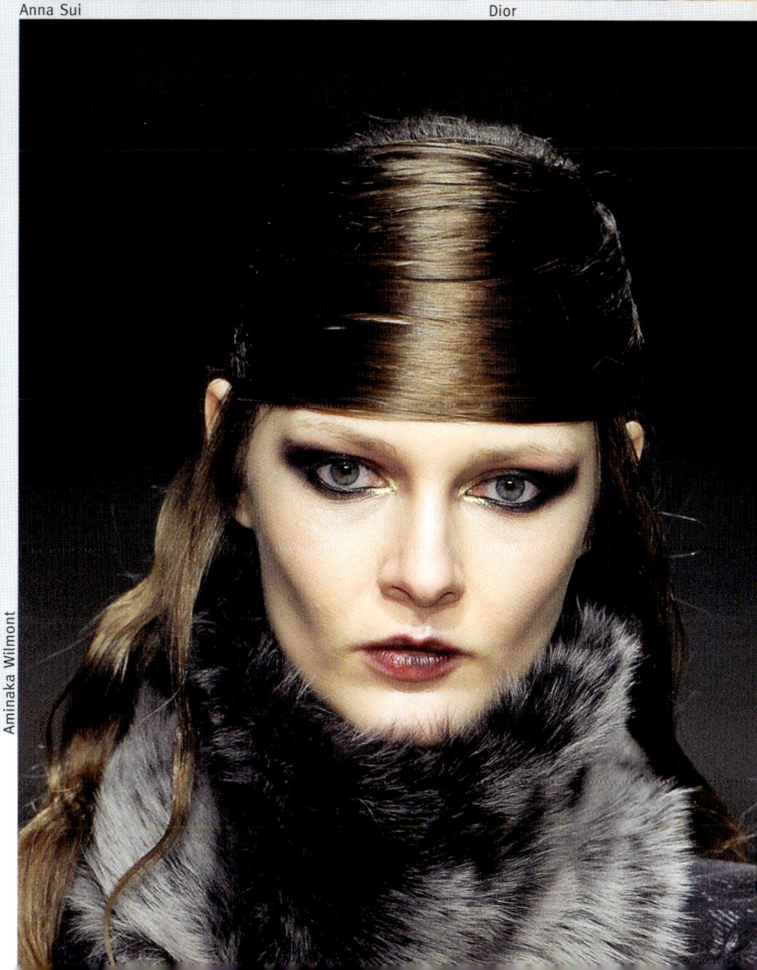
Aminaka Wilmont

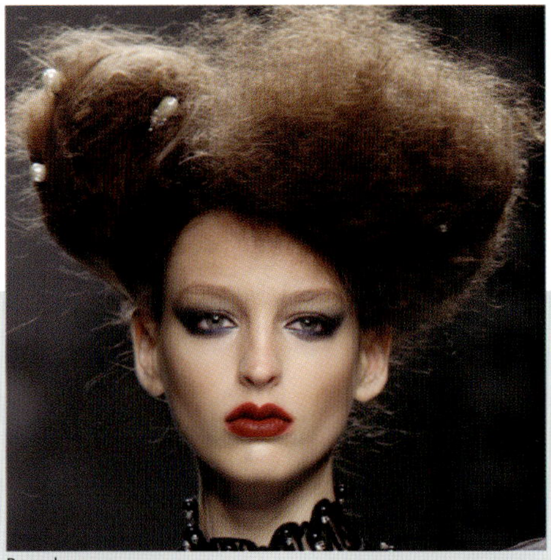
Roccobarocco

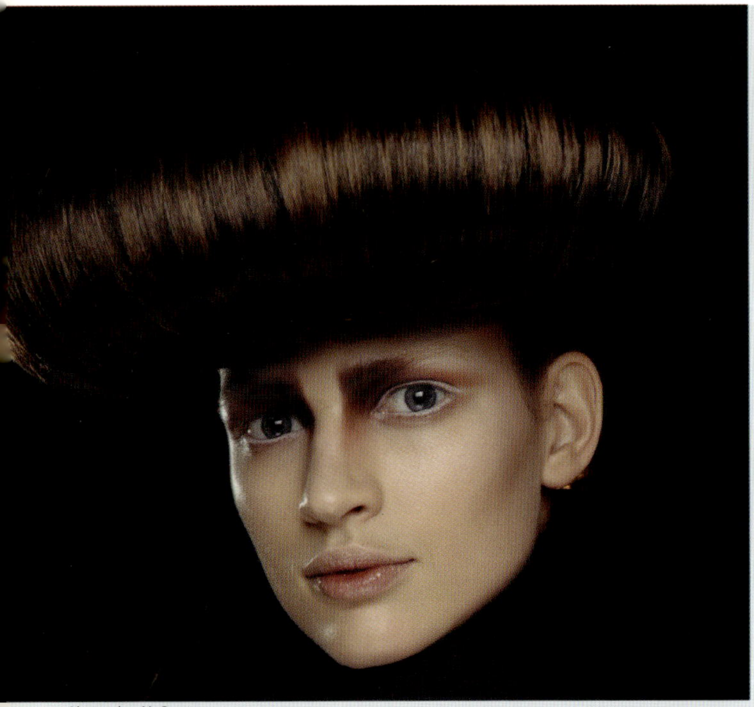
Alexander McQueen

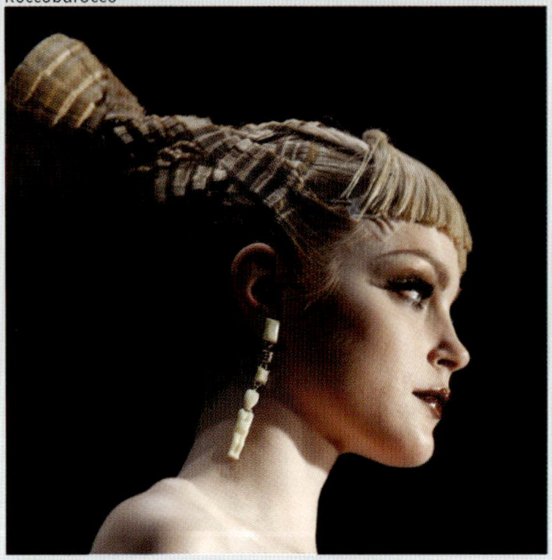
Dior

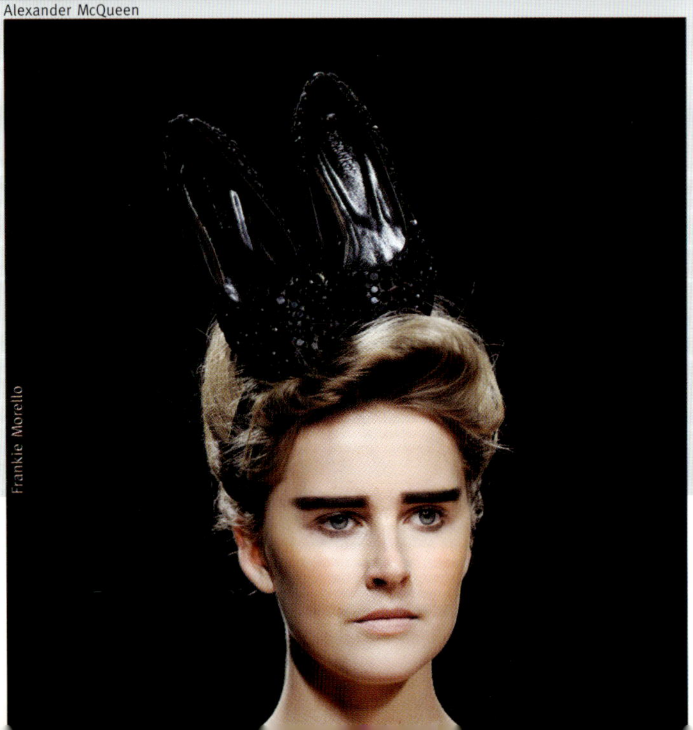
Frankie Morello

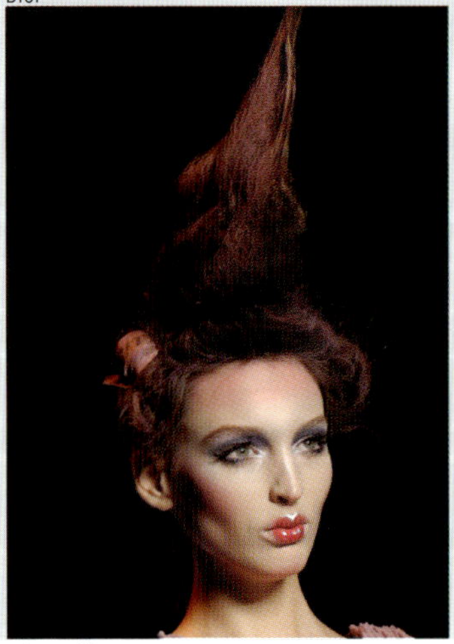
John Galliano

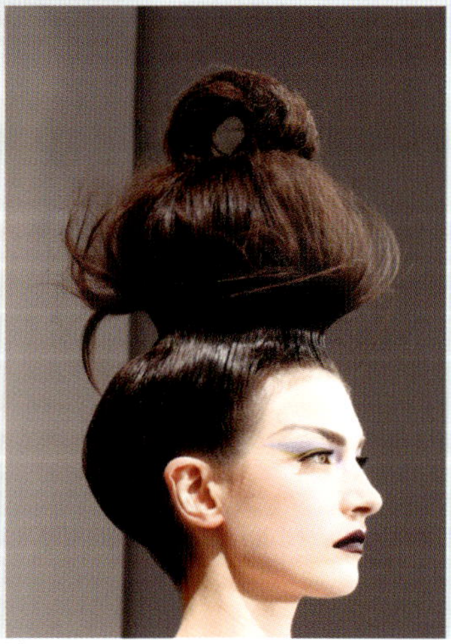
Dior

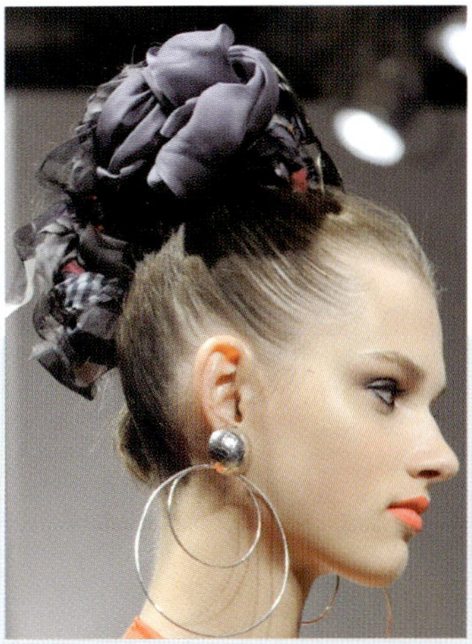
Danielle Scutt

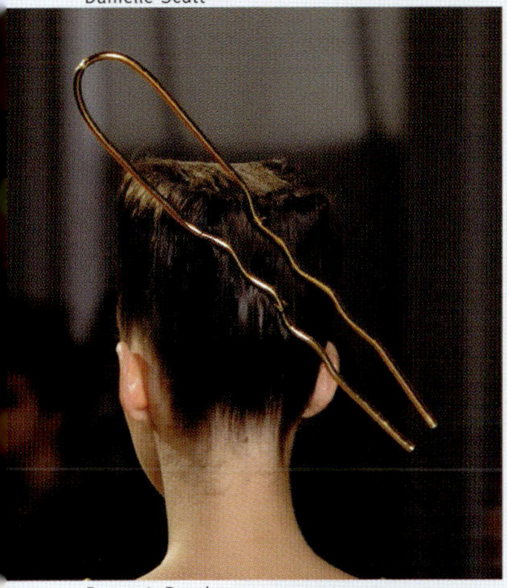
Basso & Brooke

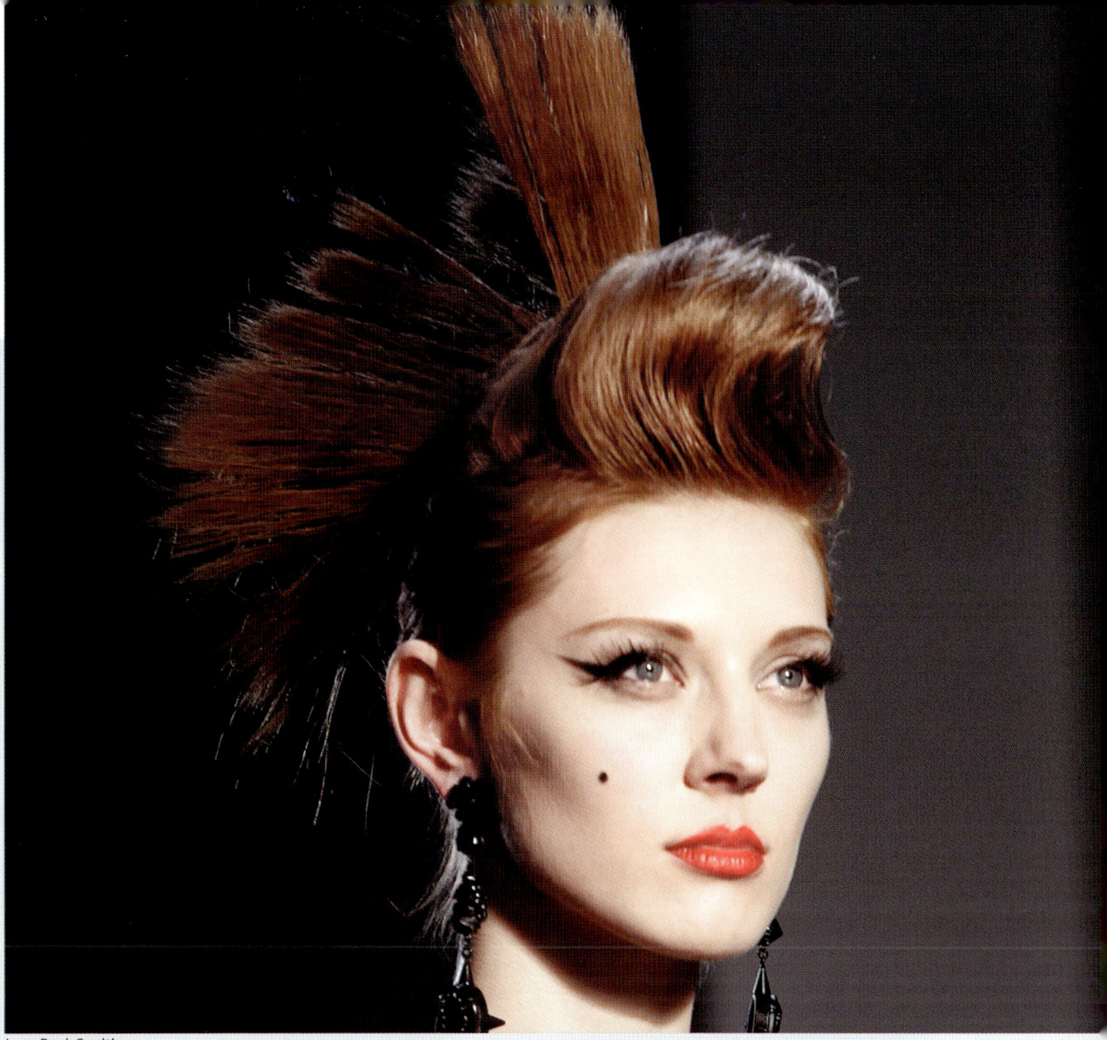
Jean Paul Gaultier

Junko Shimada
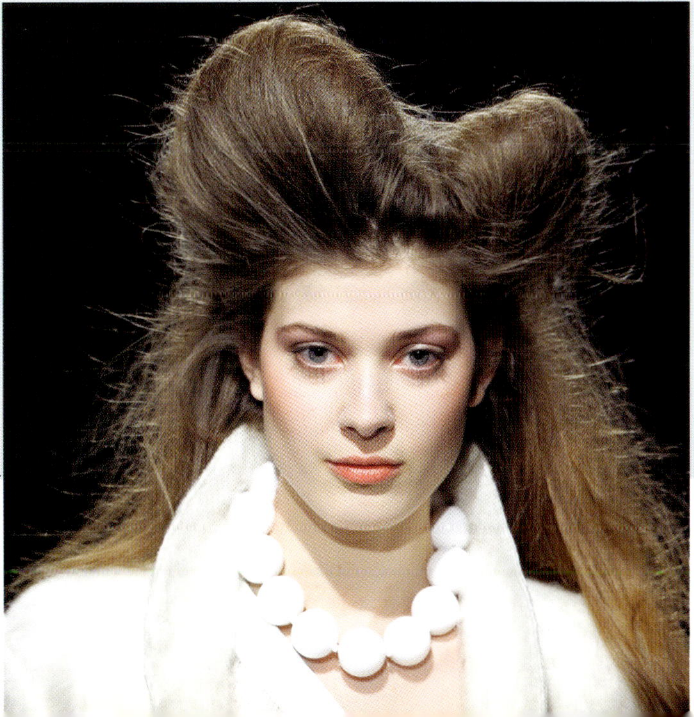

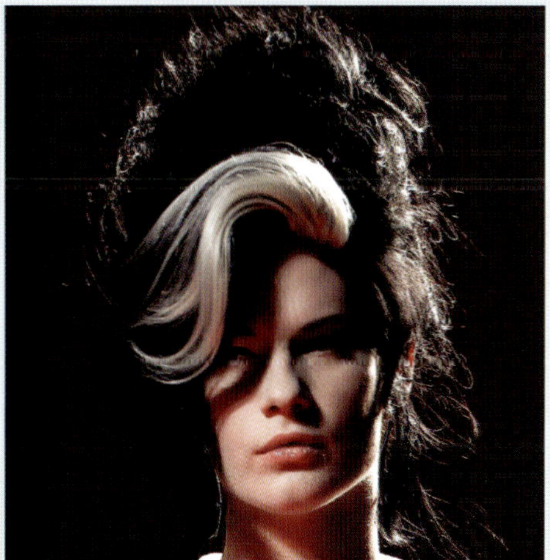
Jean Paul Gaultier

18

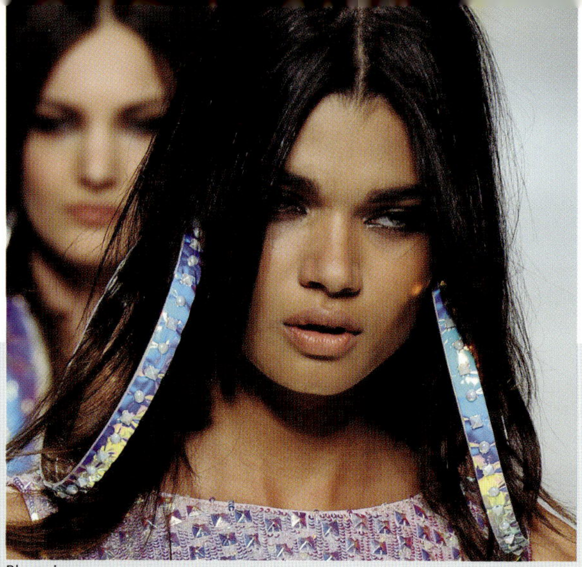

Blumarine

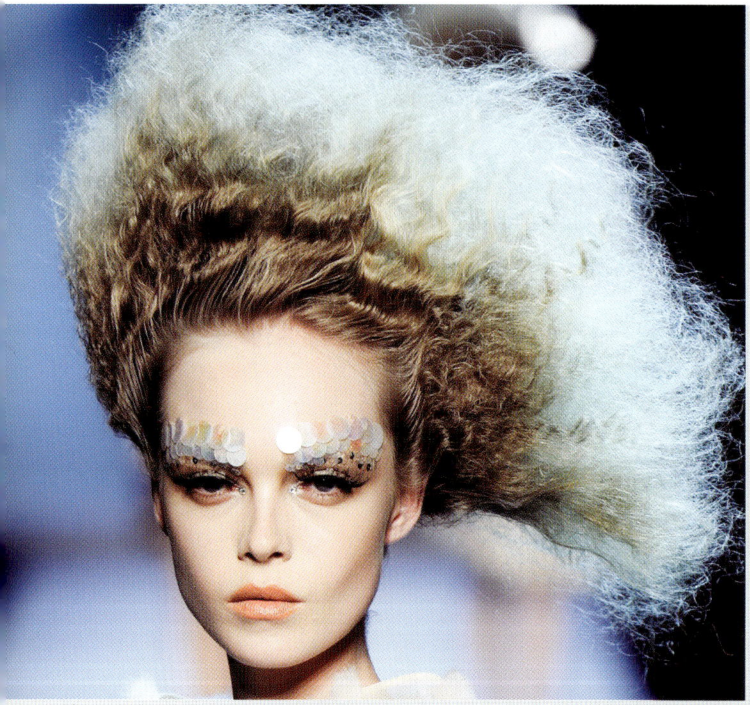

Dior

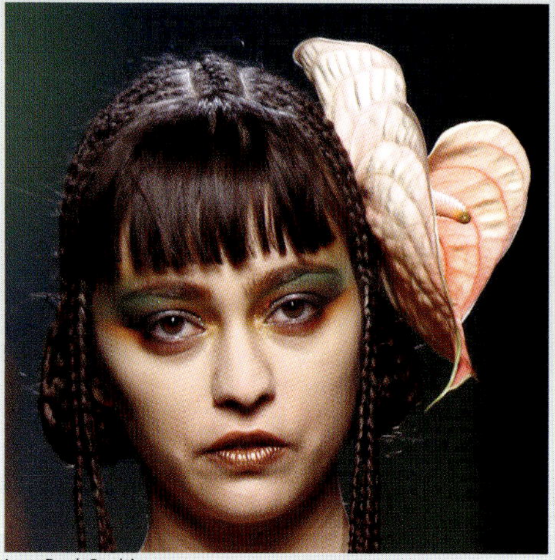

Jean Paul Gaultier

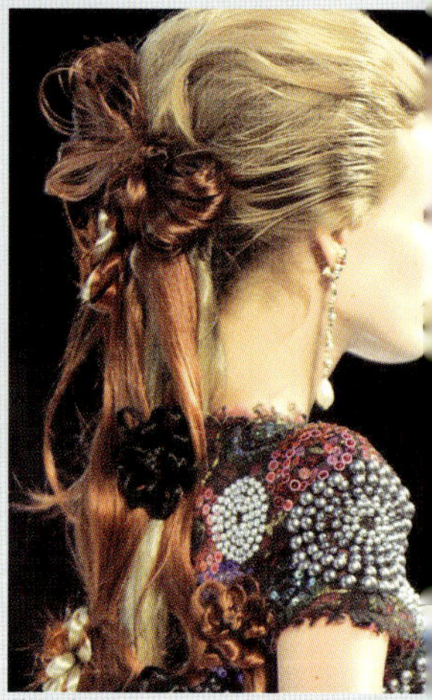

Chanel

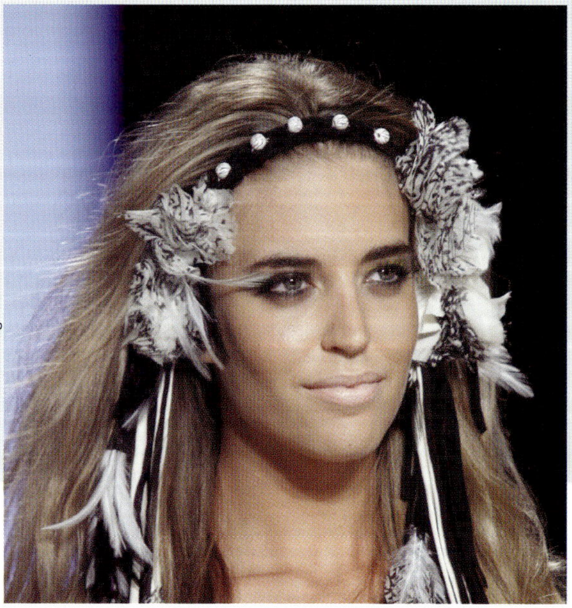

Diane Von Furstenberg

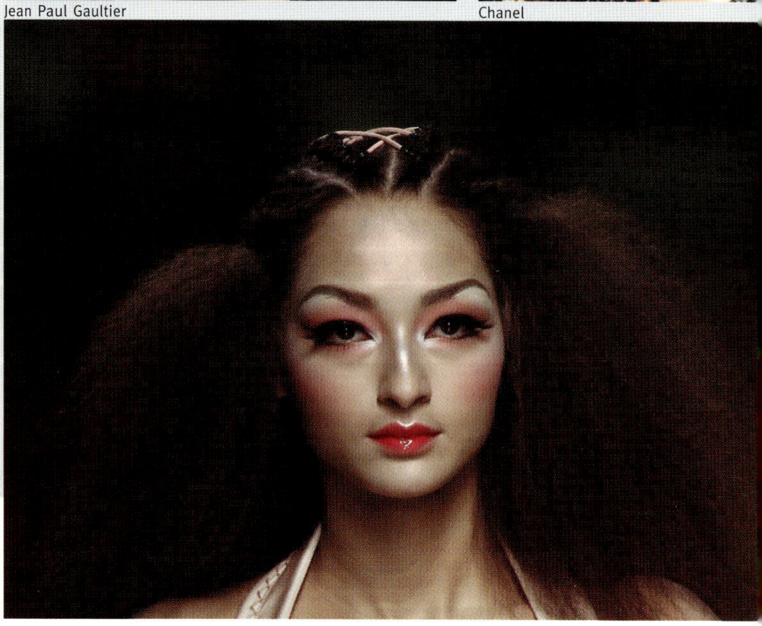

Dior

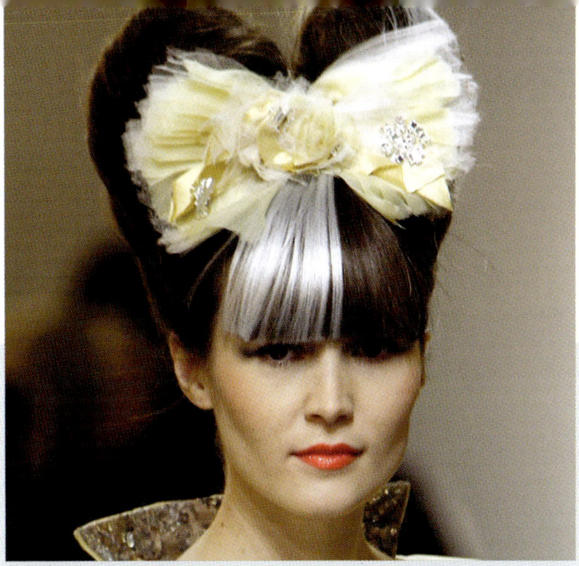
Chanel

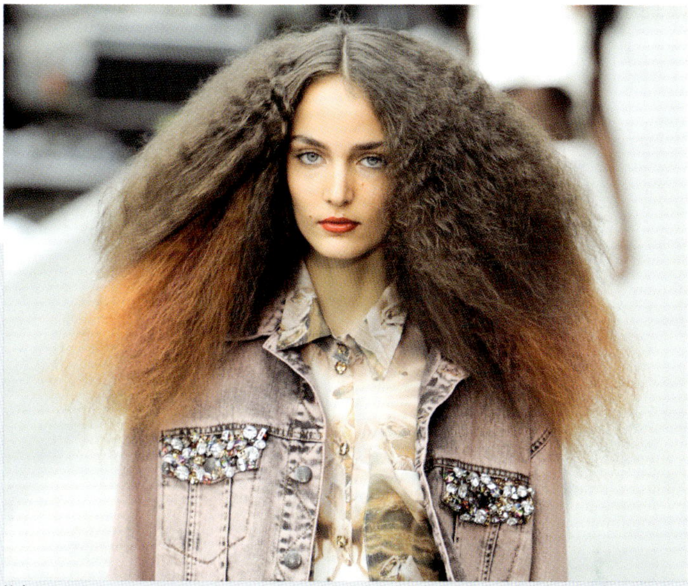
Unique

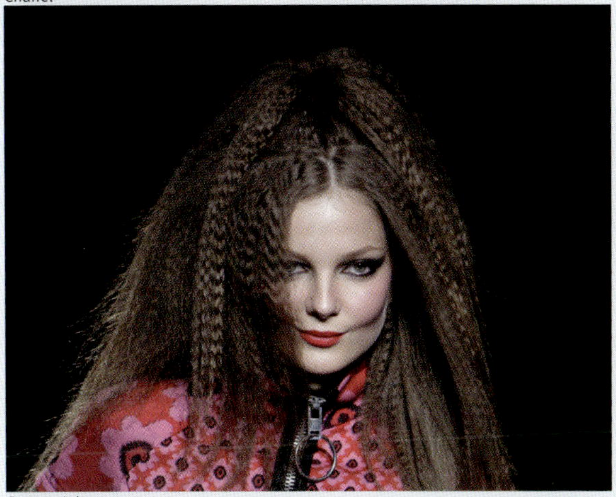
Betsey Johnson

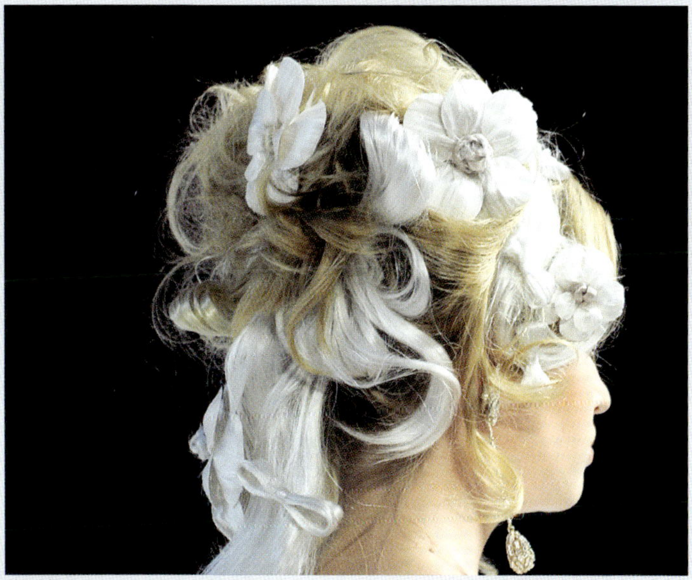
Chanel

Vivienne Westwood
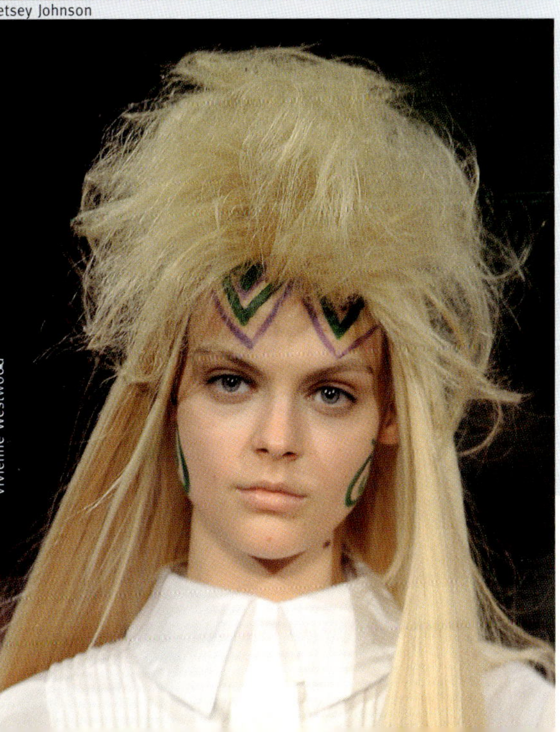

Vivienne Westwood Red Label
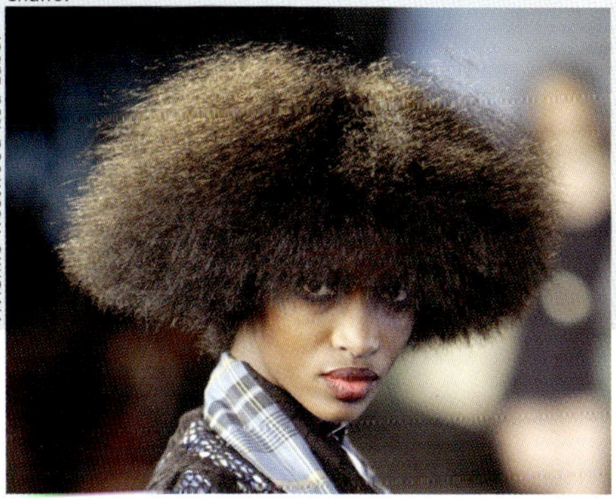

Dior
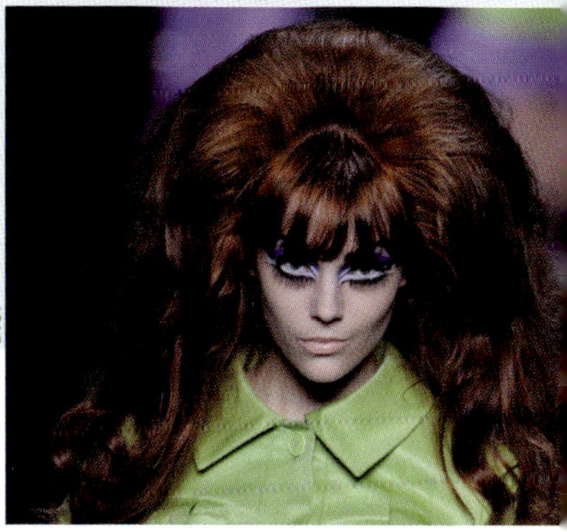

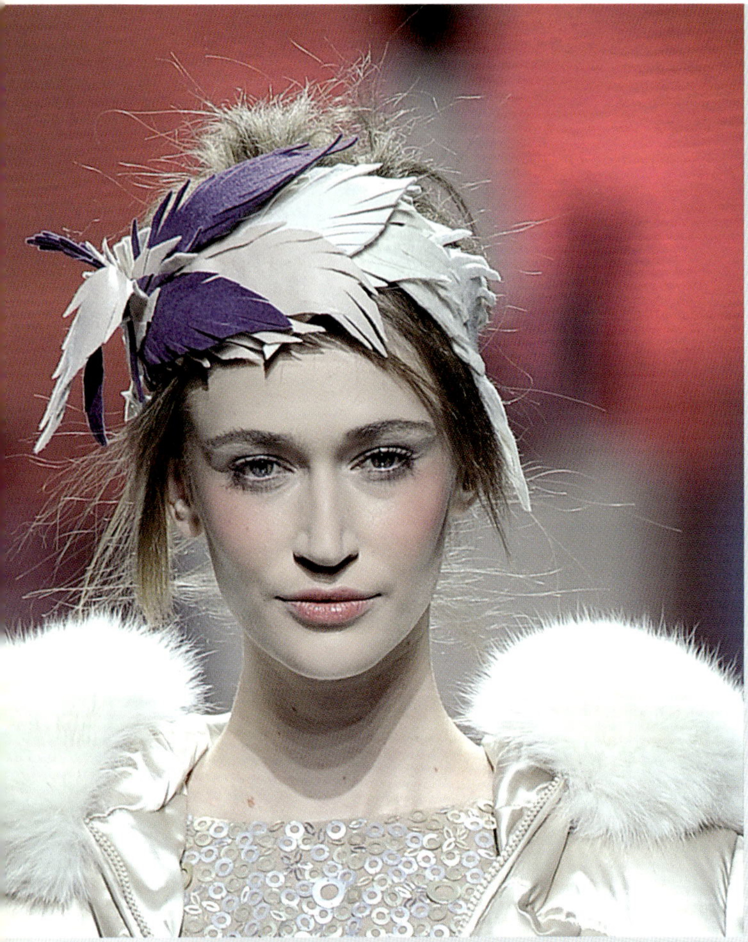

Blugirl

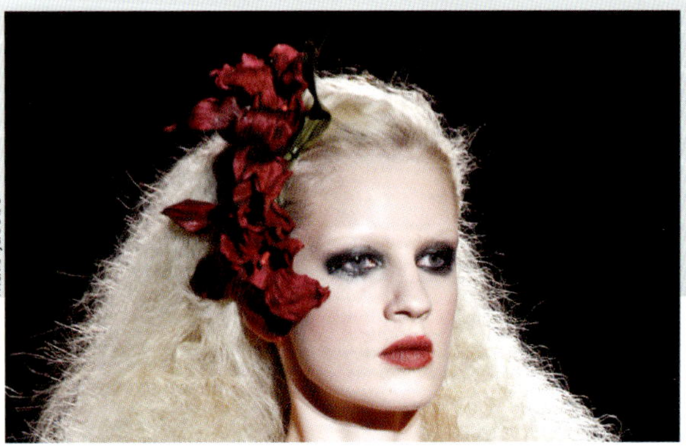

Marc Jacobs

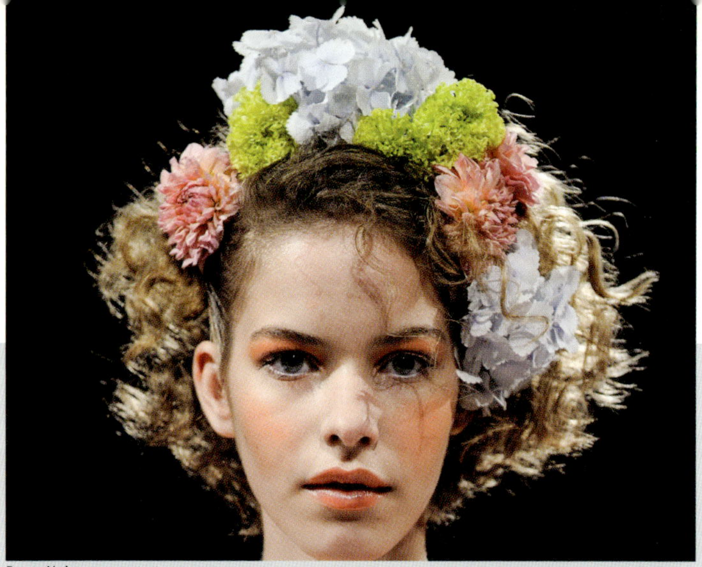

Barre Noire

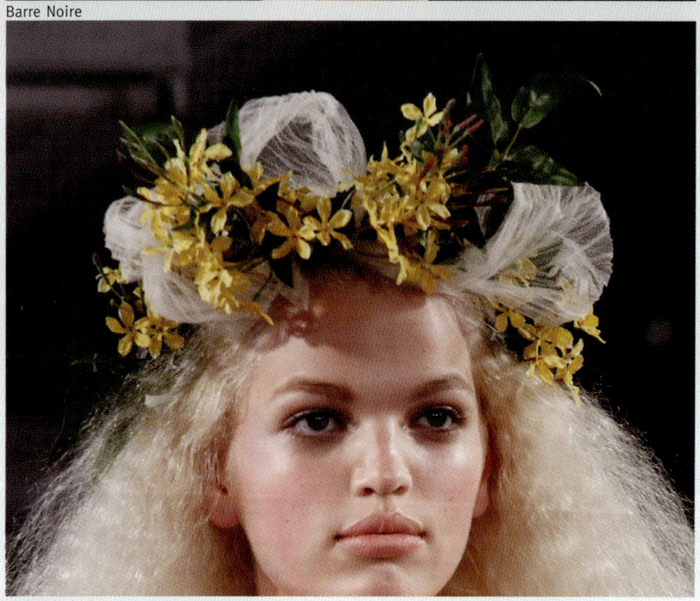

Oscar de la Renta

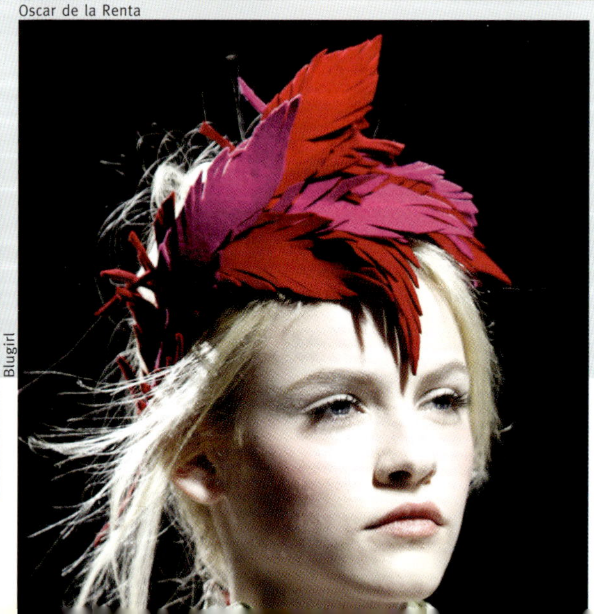

Blugirl

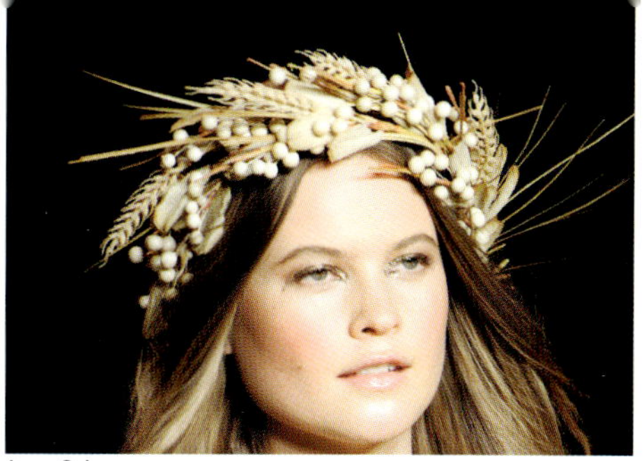

Anna Sui

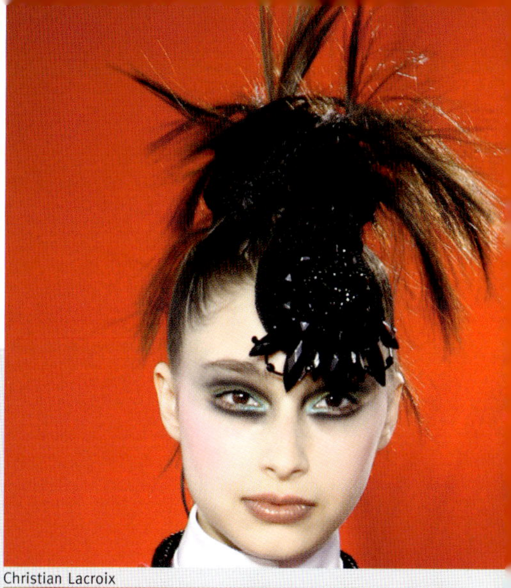

Christian Lacroix

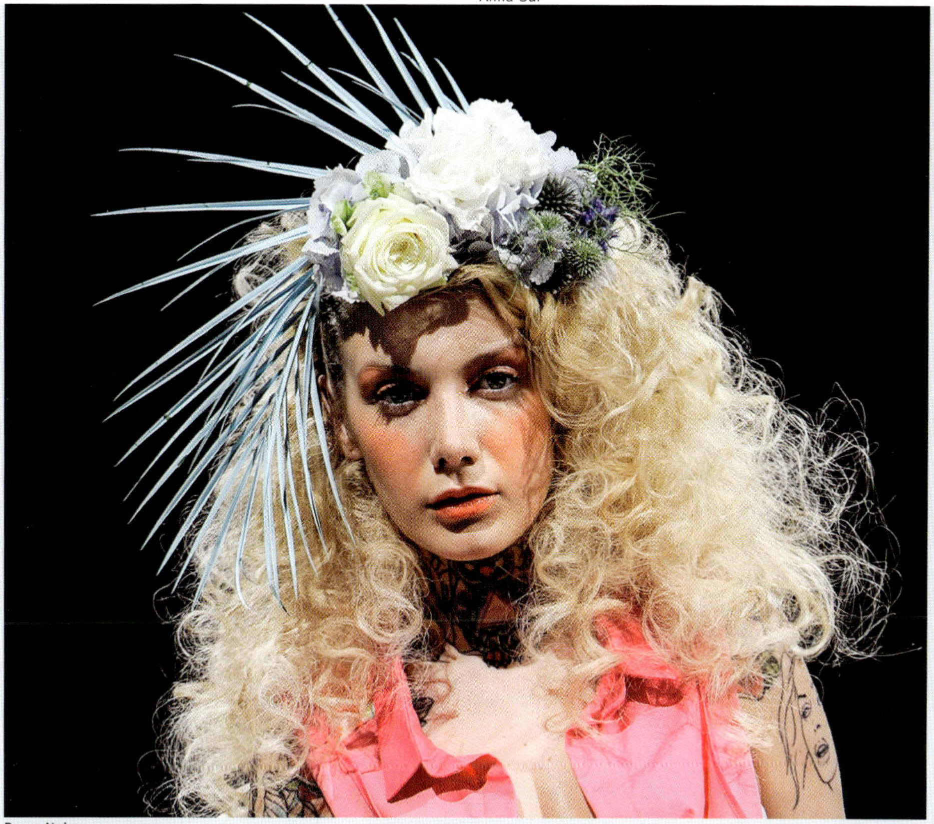

Barre Noire

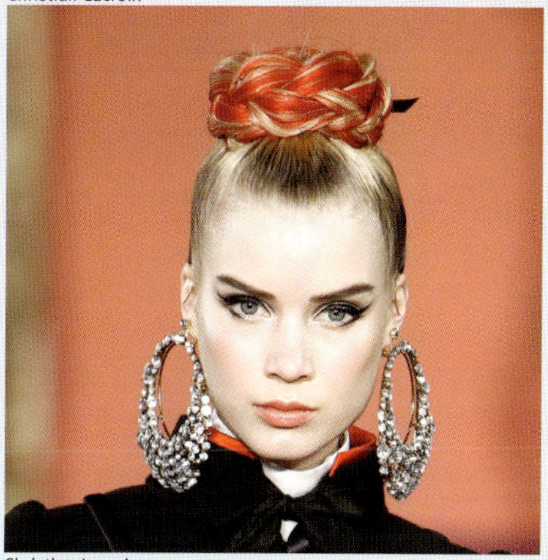

Christian Lacroix

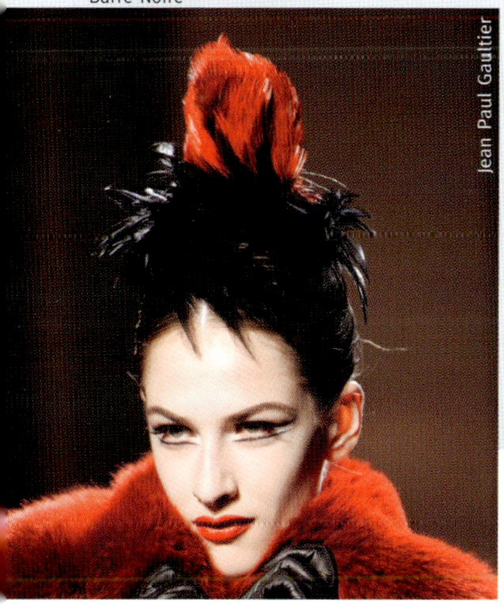

Jean Paul Gaultier

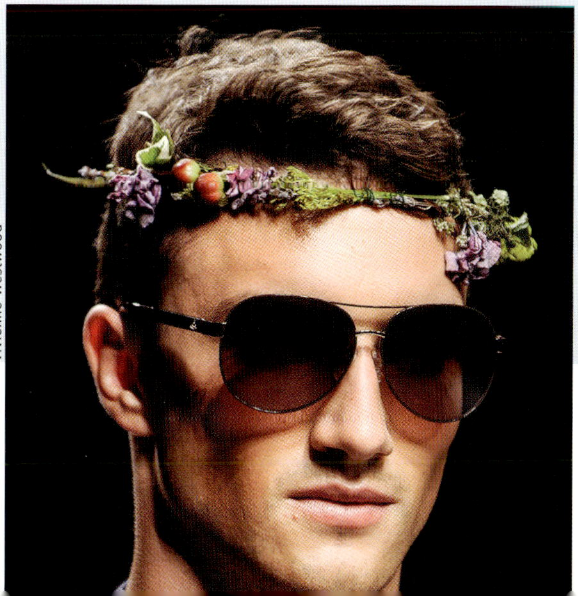

Vivienne Westwood

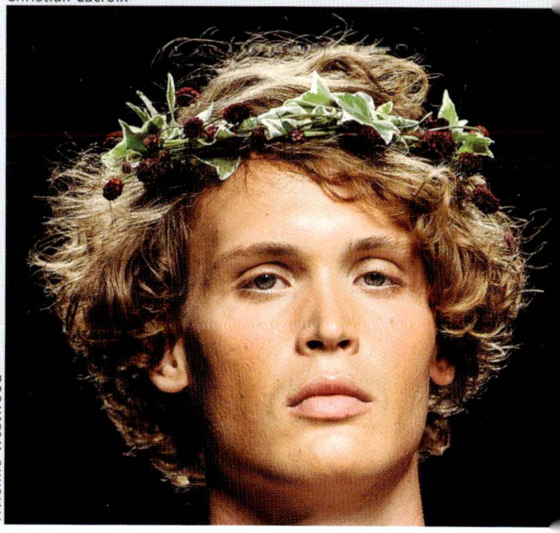

Vivienne Westwood

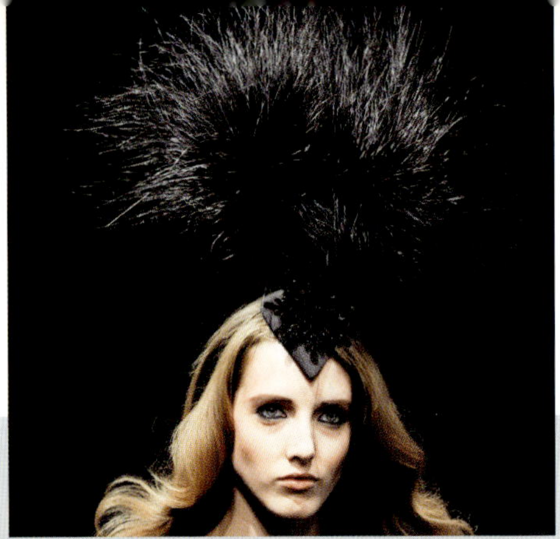
Francesco Scognamiglio

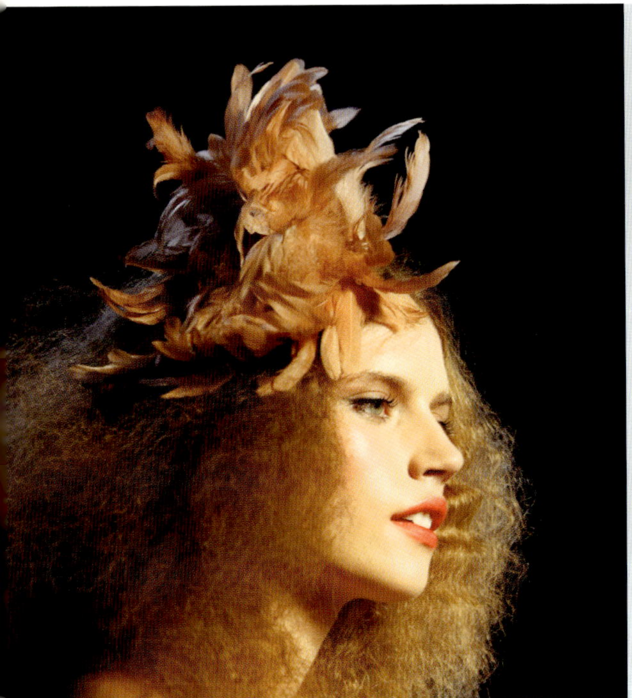
Sonia Rykiel

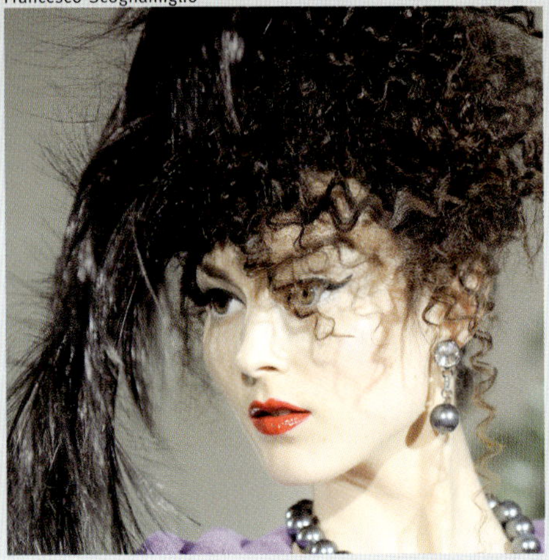
Dior

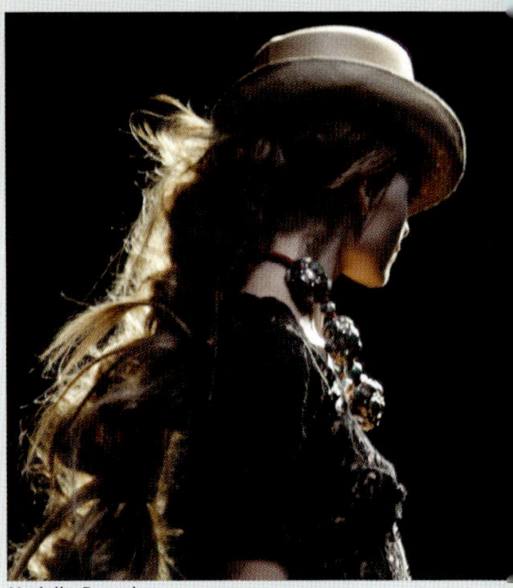
Mariella Burani

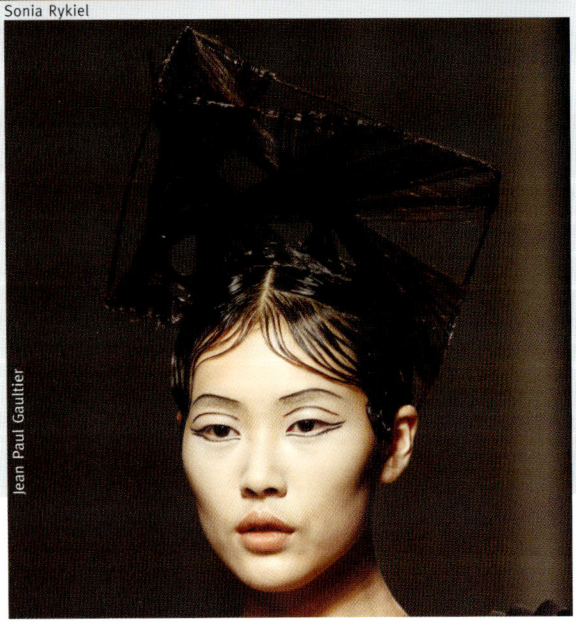
Jean Paul Gaultier

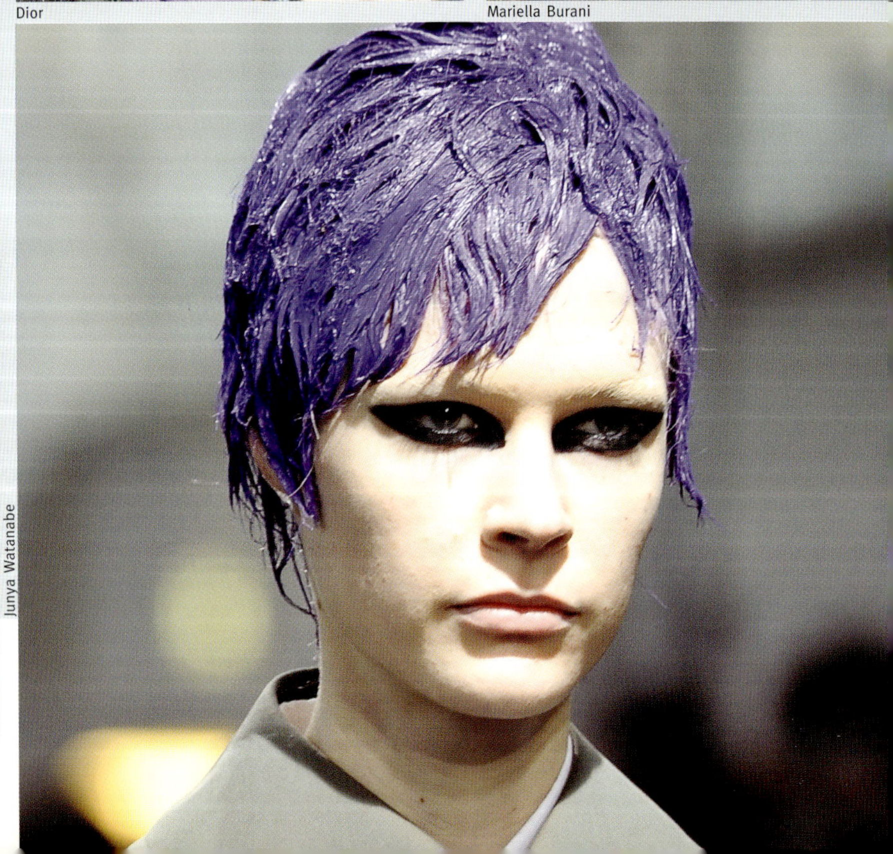
Junya Watanabe

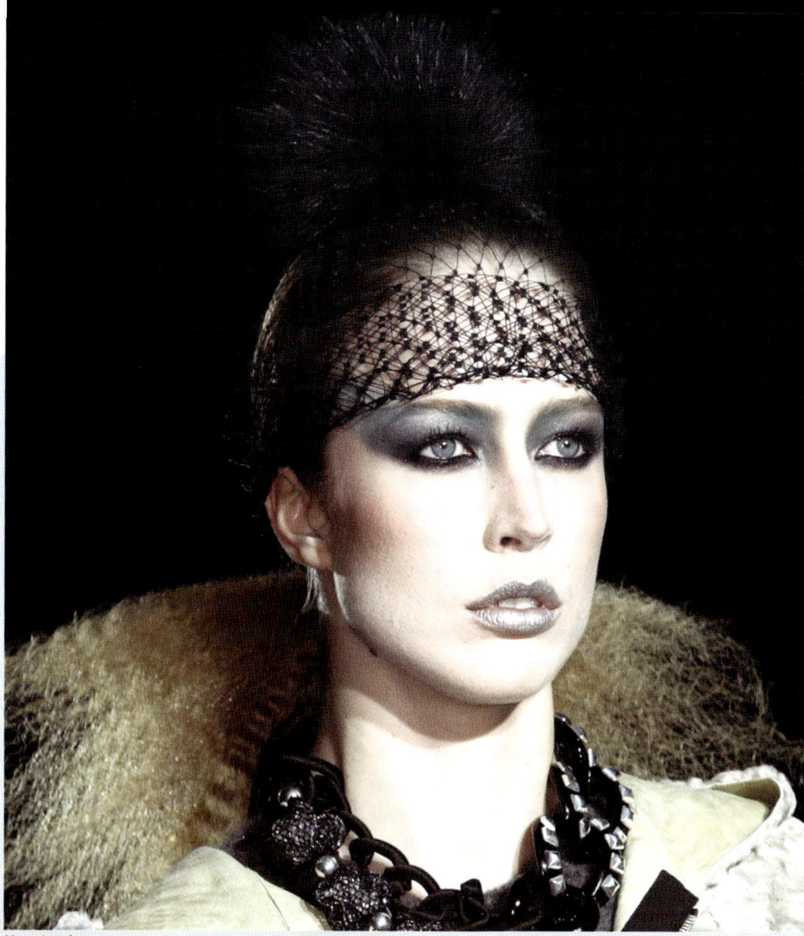

Marc Jacobs

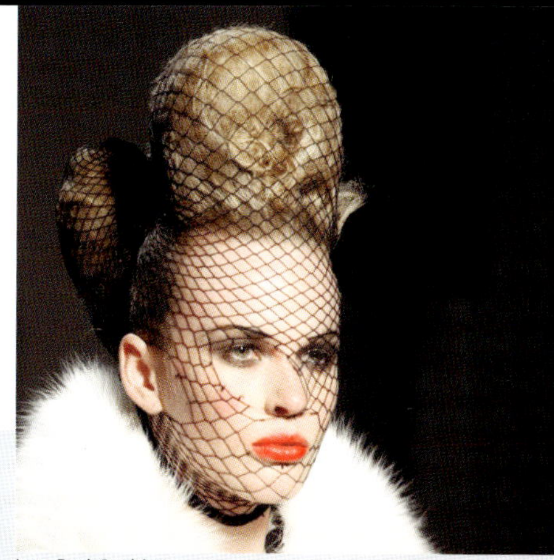

Jean Paul Gaultier

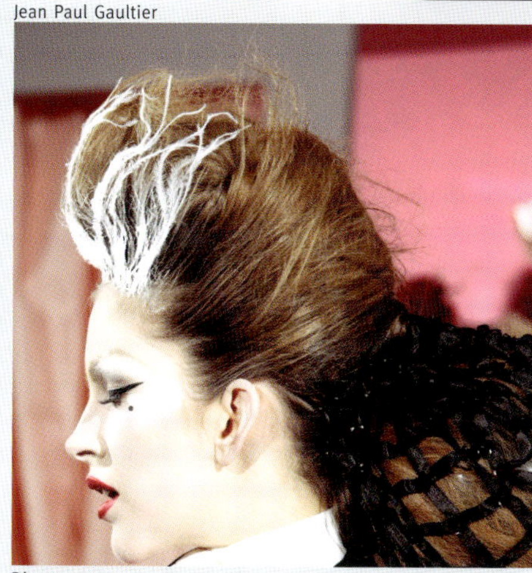

Dior

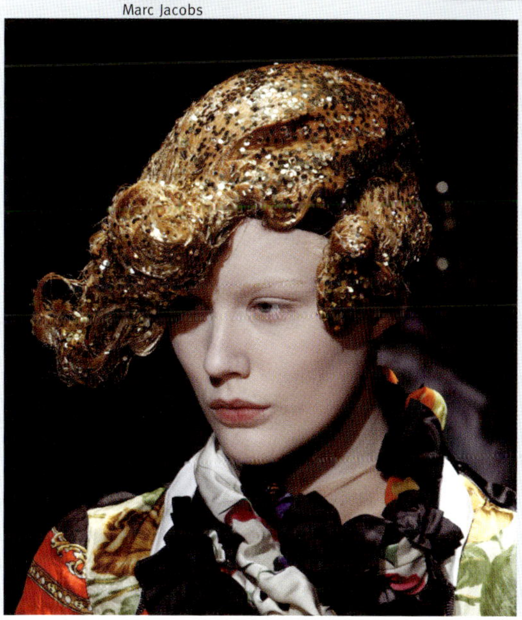

Comme des Garçons

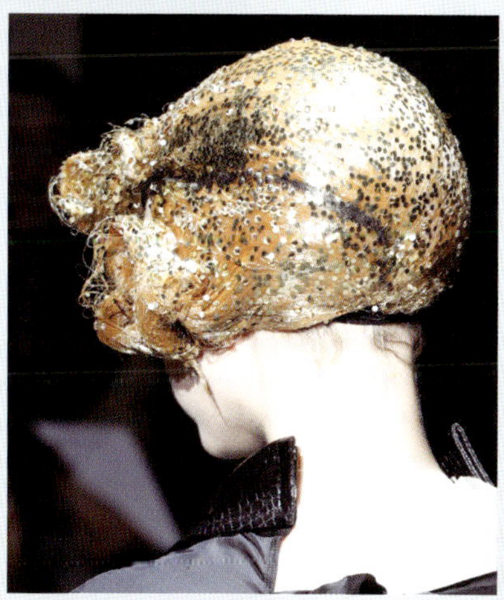

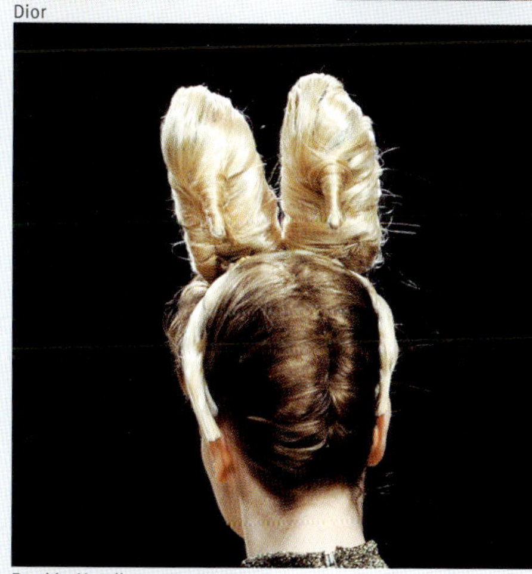

Frankie Morello

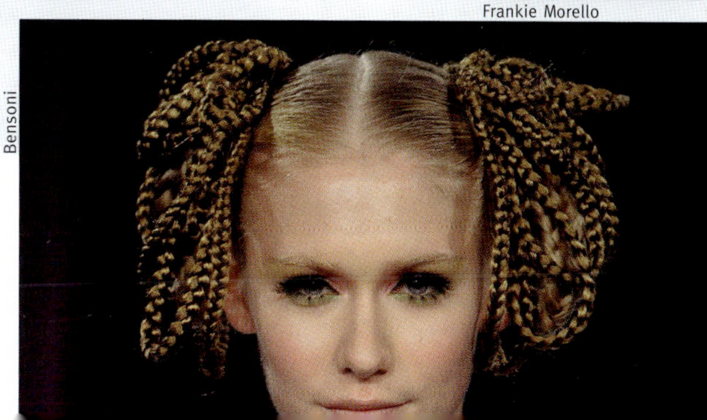

Bensoni

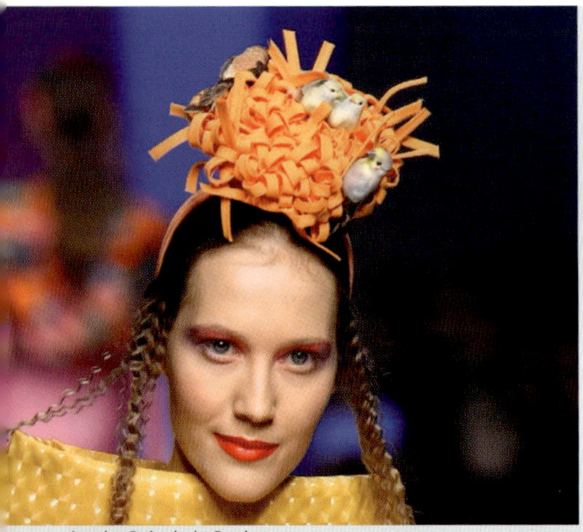
Agatha Ruiz de la Prada

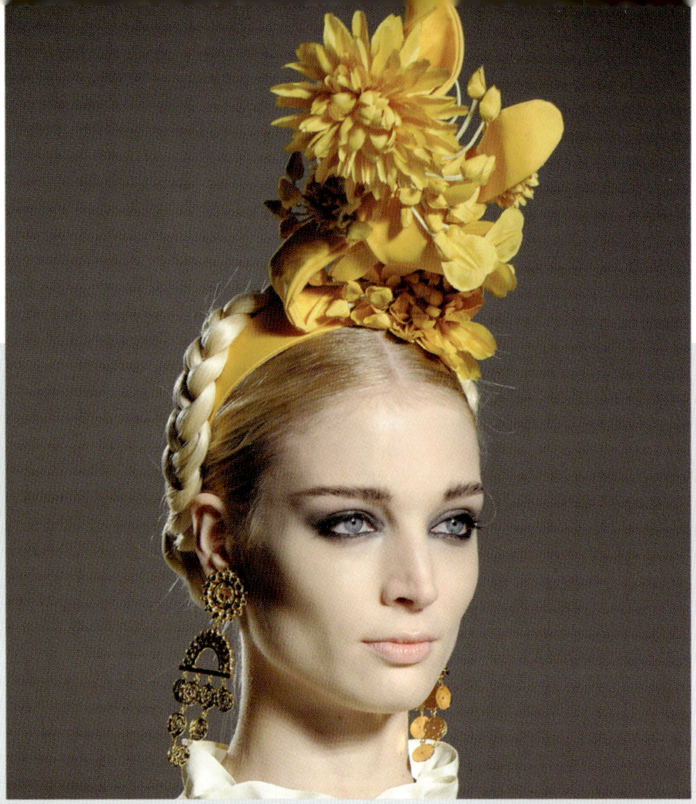
Moschino

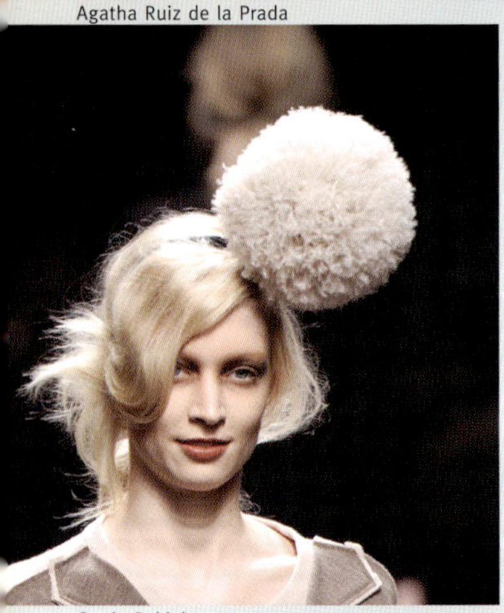
Sonia Rykiel

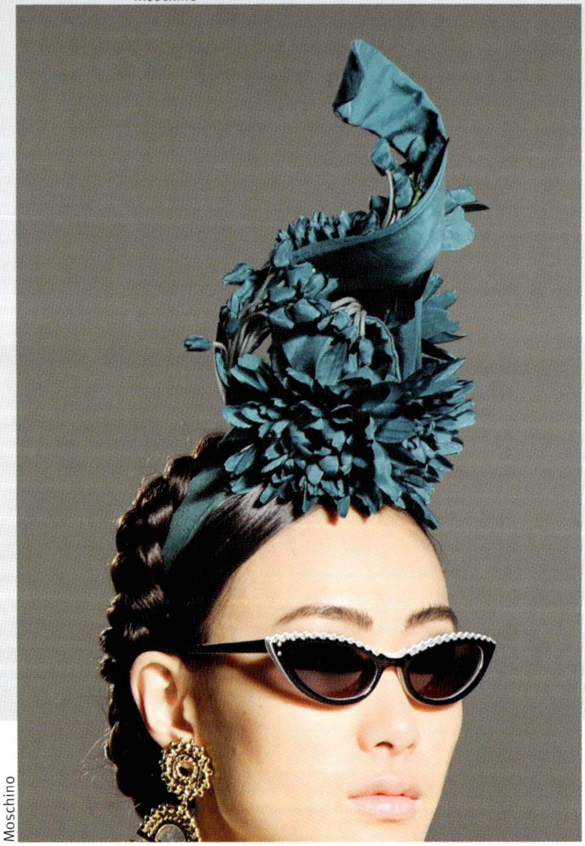
Moschino

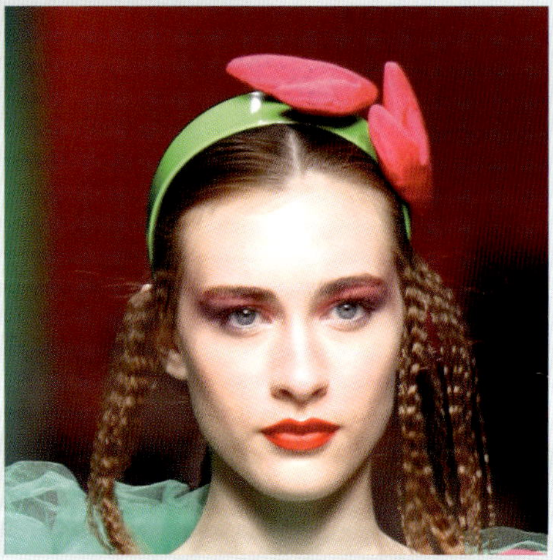
Agatha Ruiz de la Prada

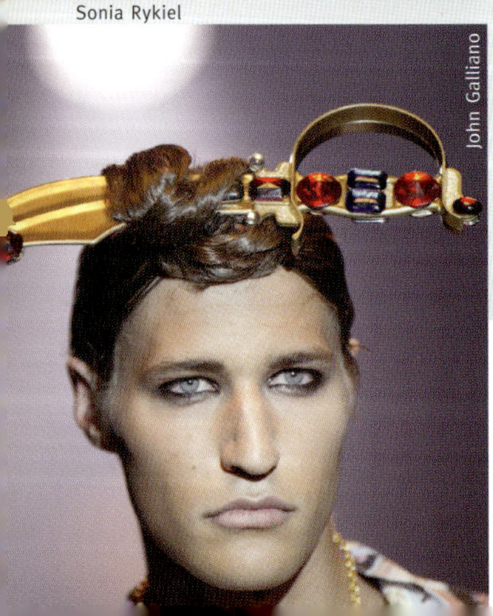
John Galliano

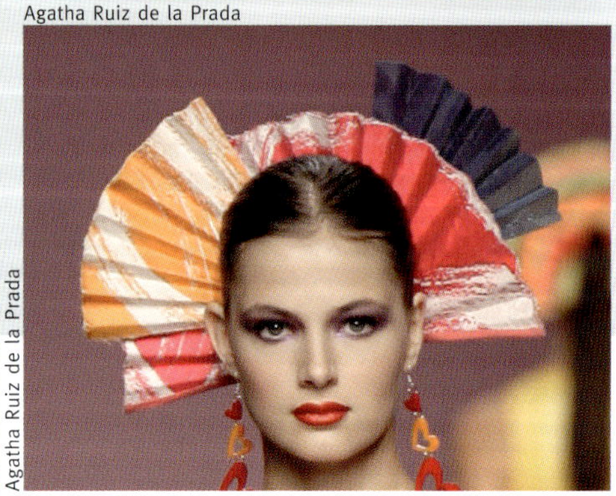
Agatha Ruiz de la Prada

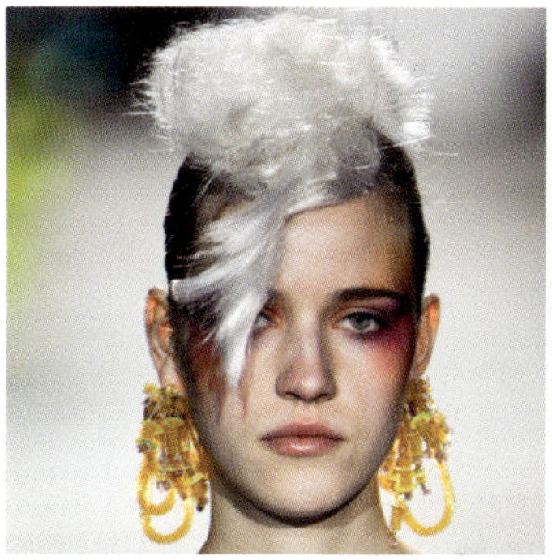

Louise Gray

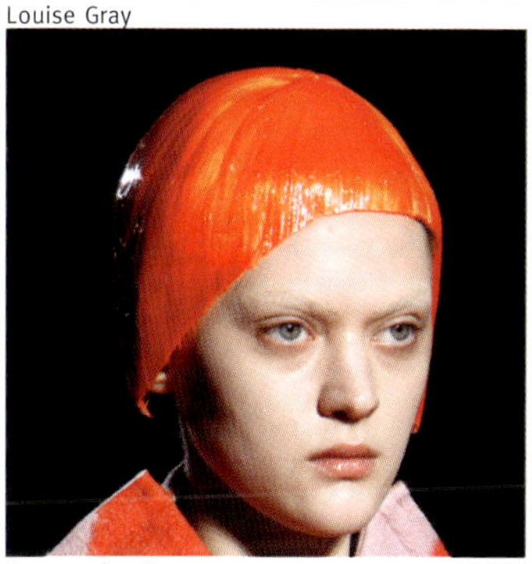

Comme des Garçons

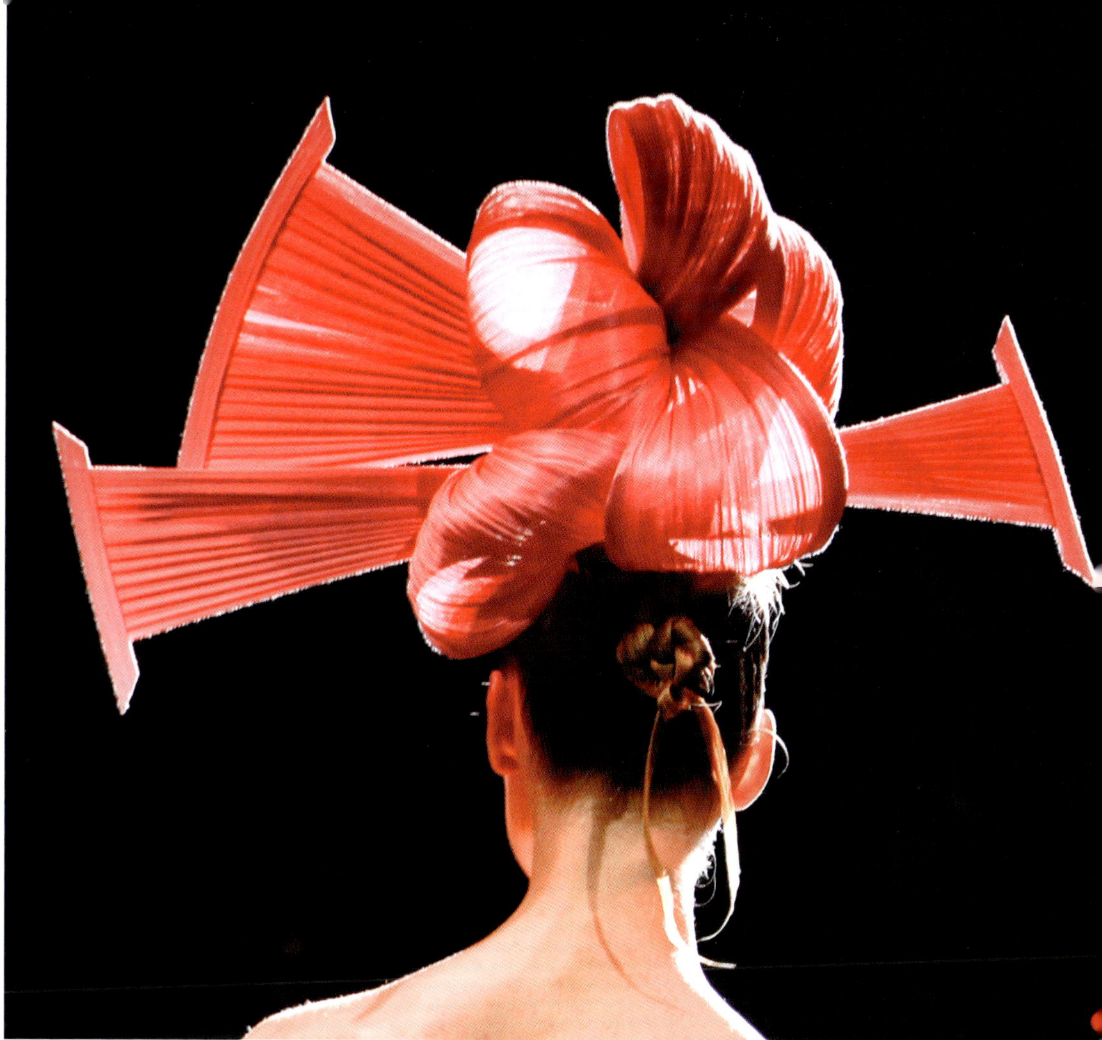

Armani Privè

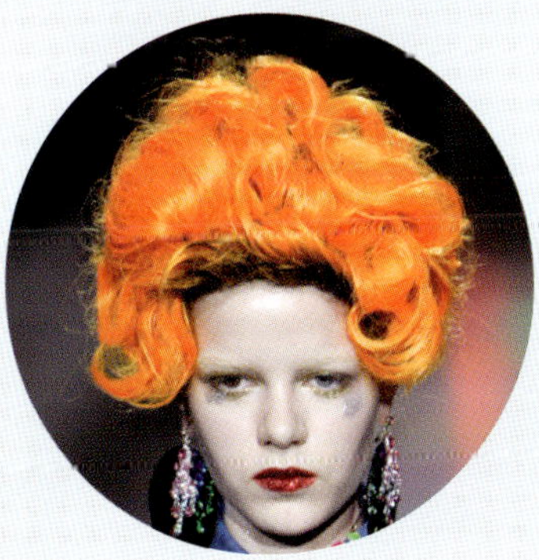

Meadham Kirchhoff

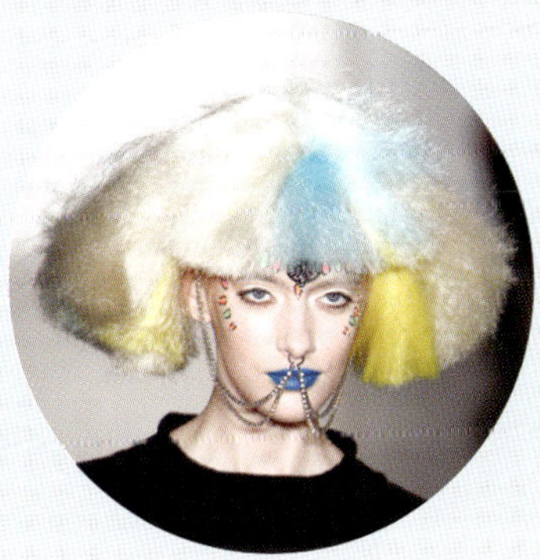

Jeremy Scott

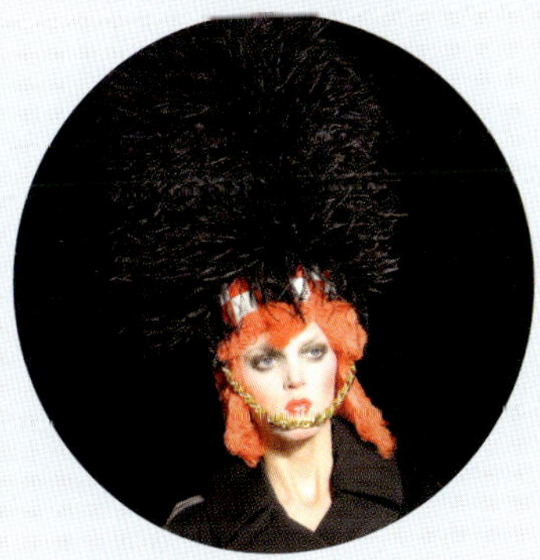

John Galliano

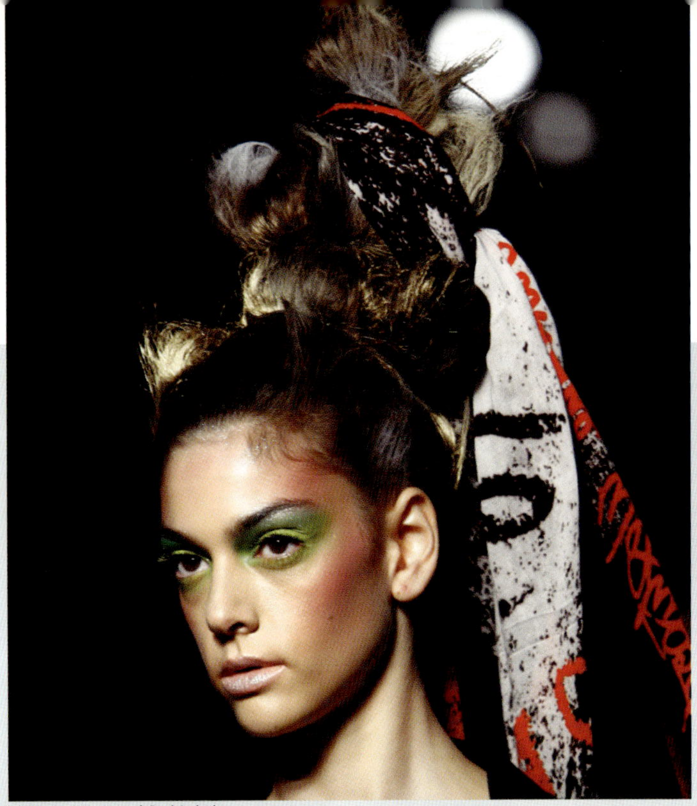
Vivienne Westwood Red Label

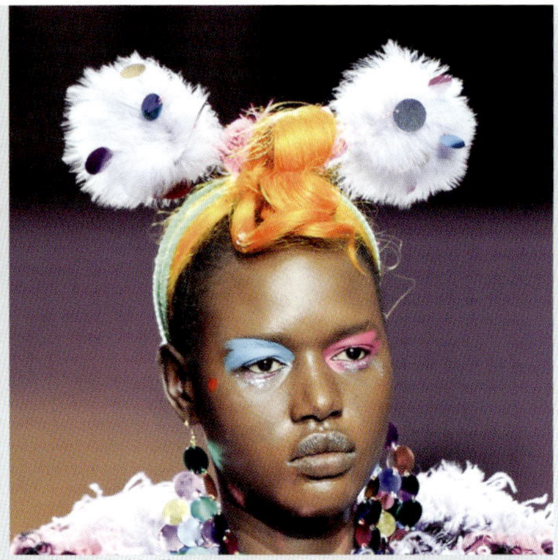
Meadham Kirchhoff

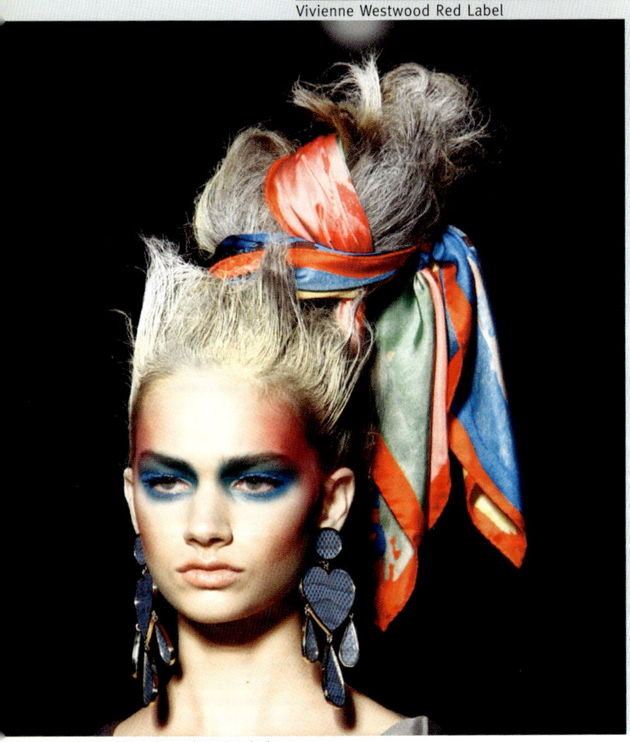
Vivienne Westwood Red Label

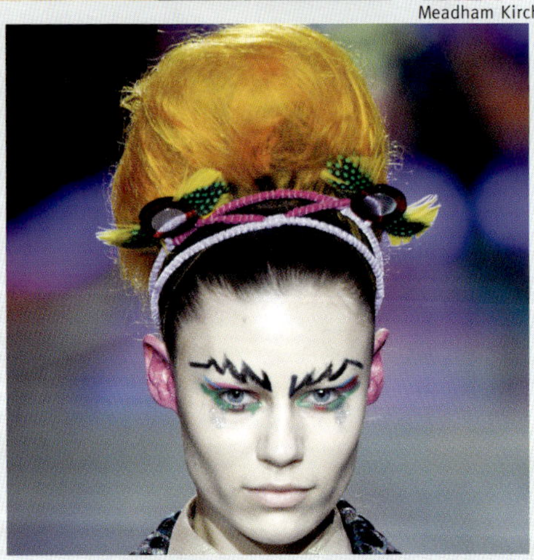
Meadham Kirchhoff

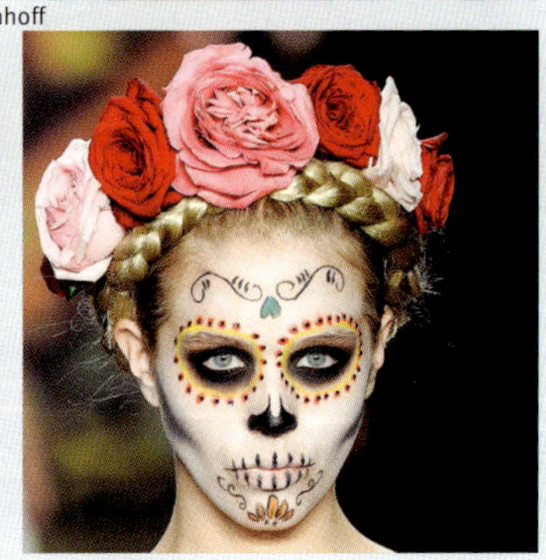
Lena Hoschek

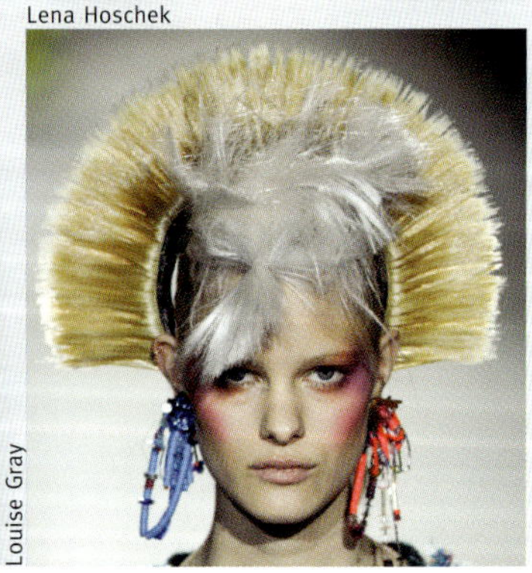
Louise Gray

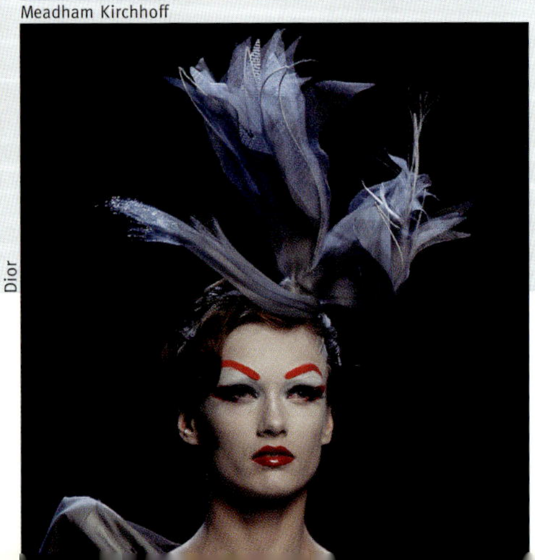
Dior

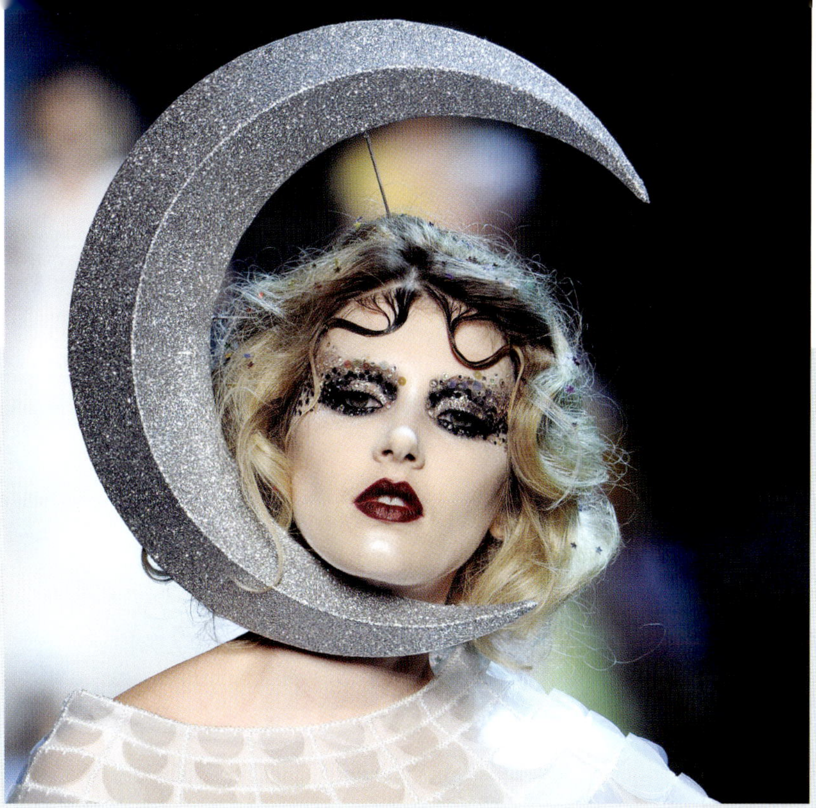

Dior

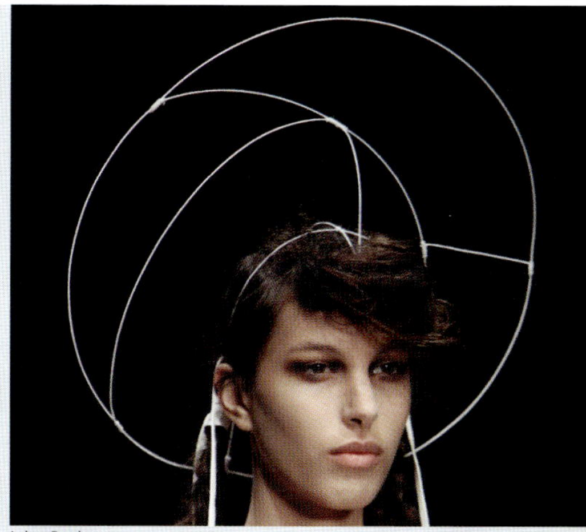

John Rocha

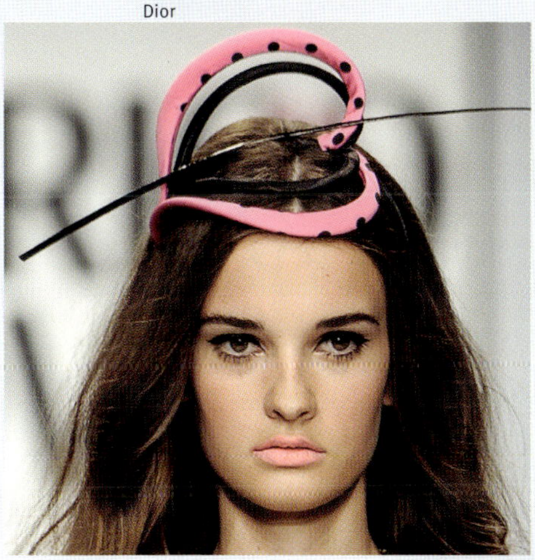

Enrico Coveri

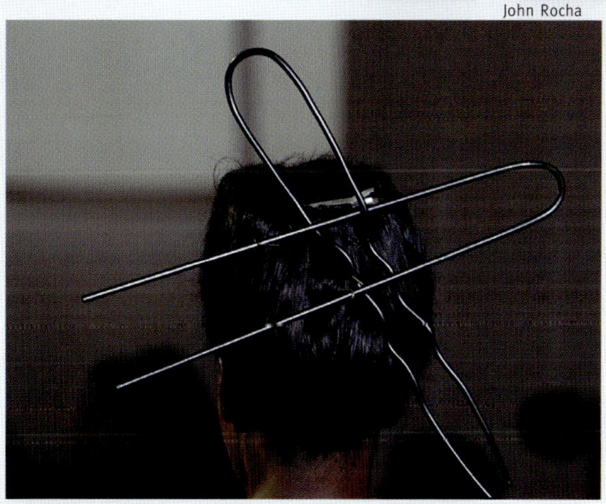

Basso & Brooke

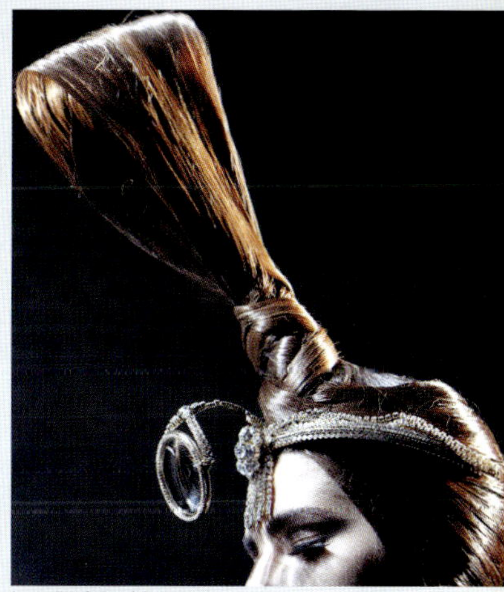

Jean Paul Gaultier

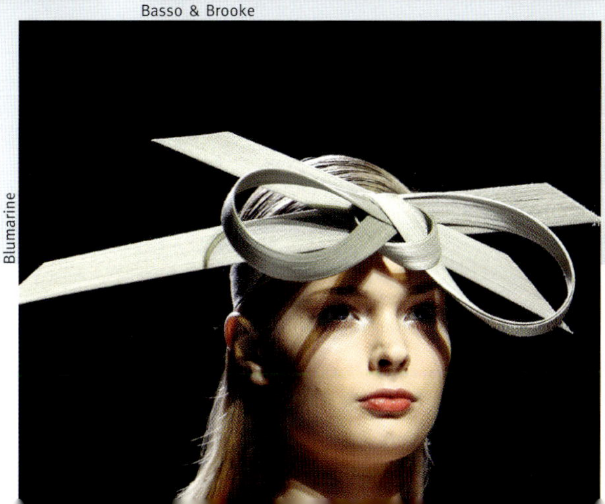

Blumarine

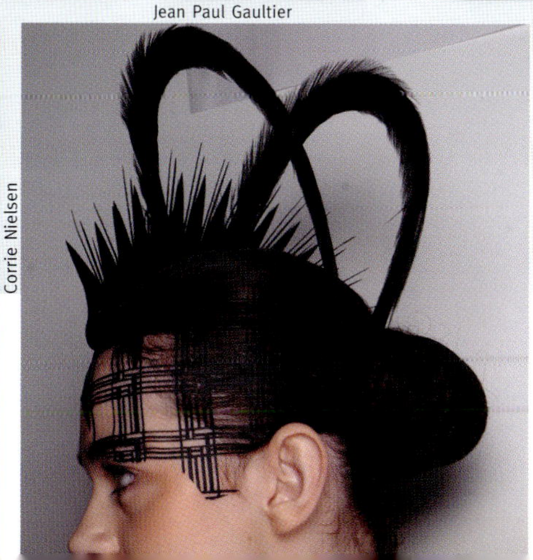

Corrie Nielsen

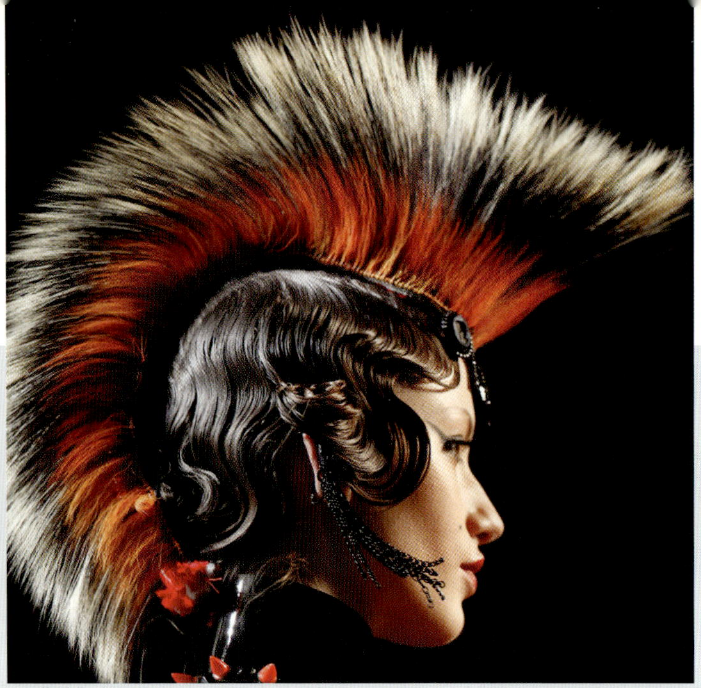

Jean Paul Gaultier

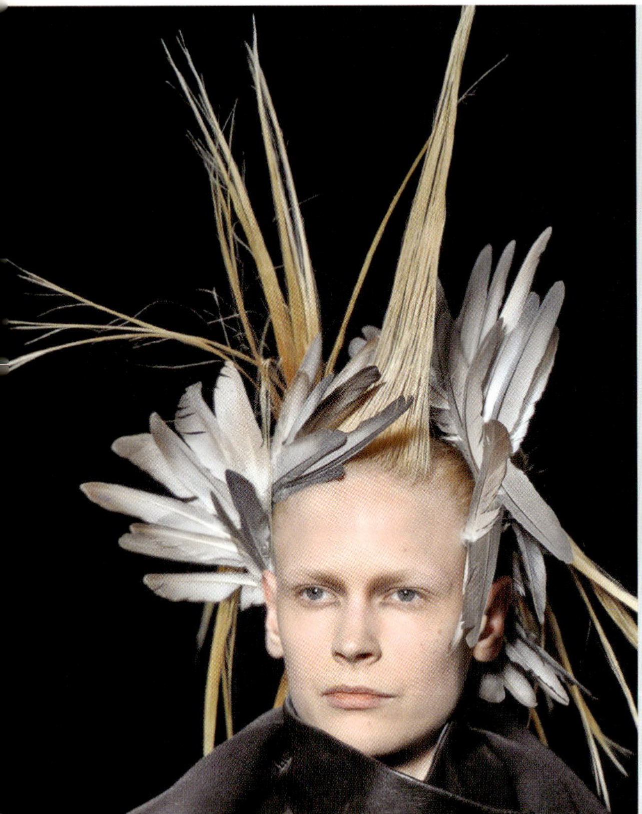

Ann Demeulemeester

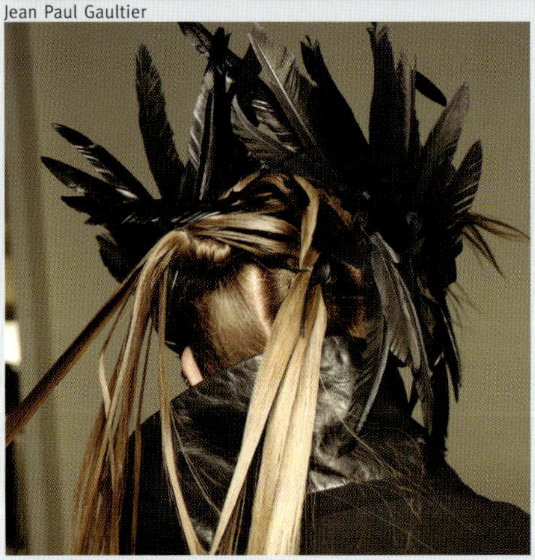

Ann Demeulemeester

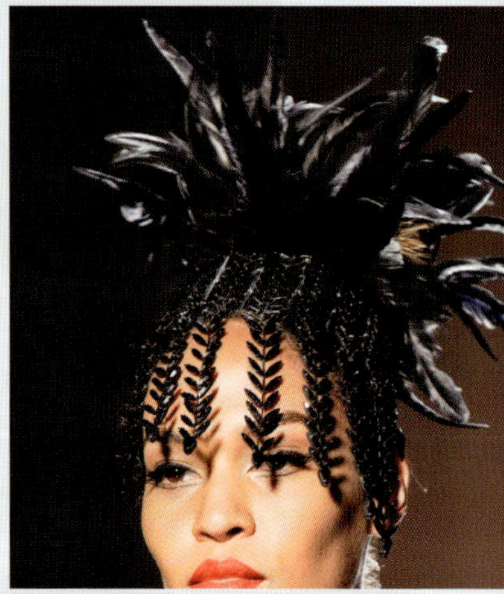

Jean Paul Gaultier

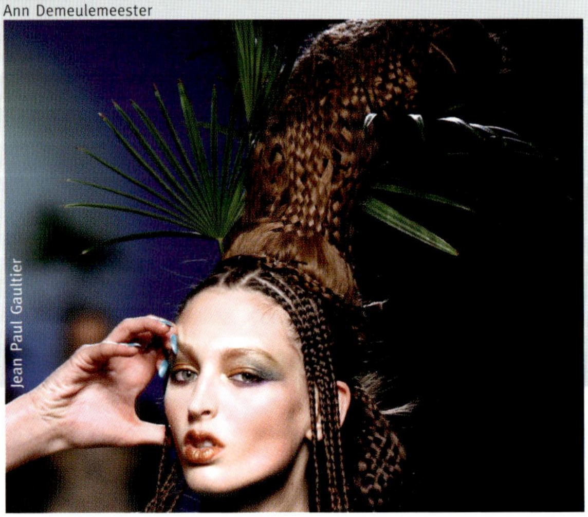

Jean Paul Gaultier

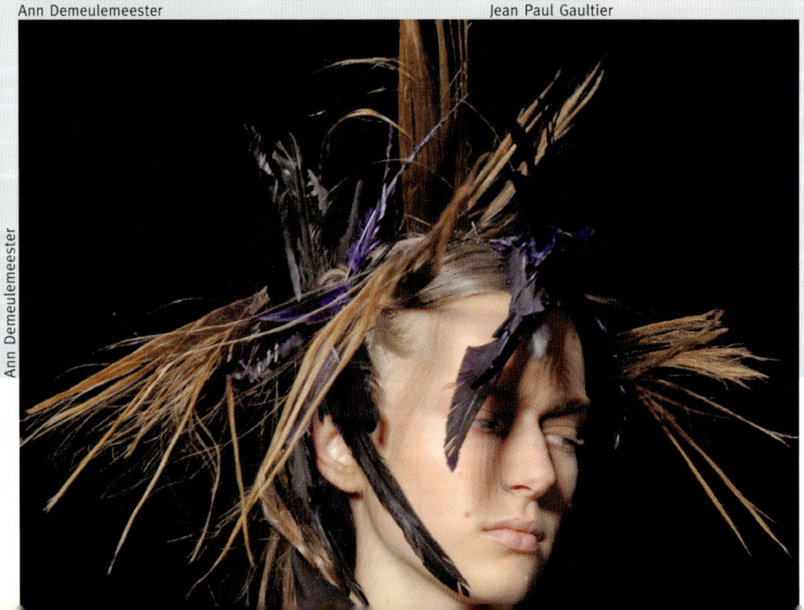

Ann Demeulemeester

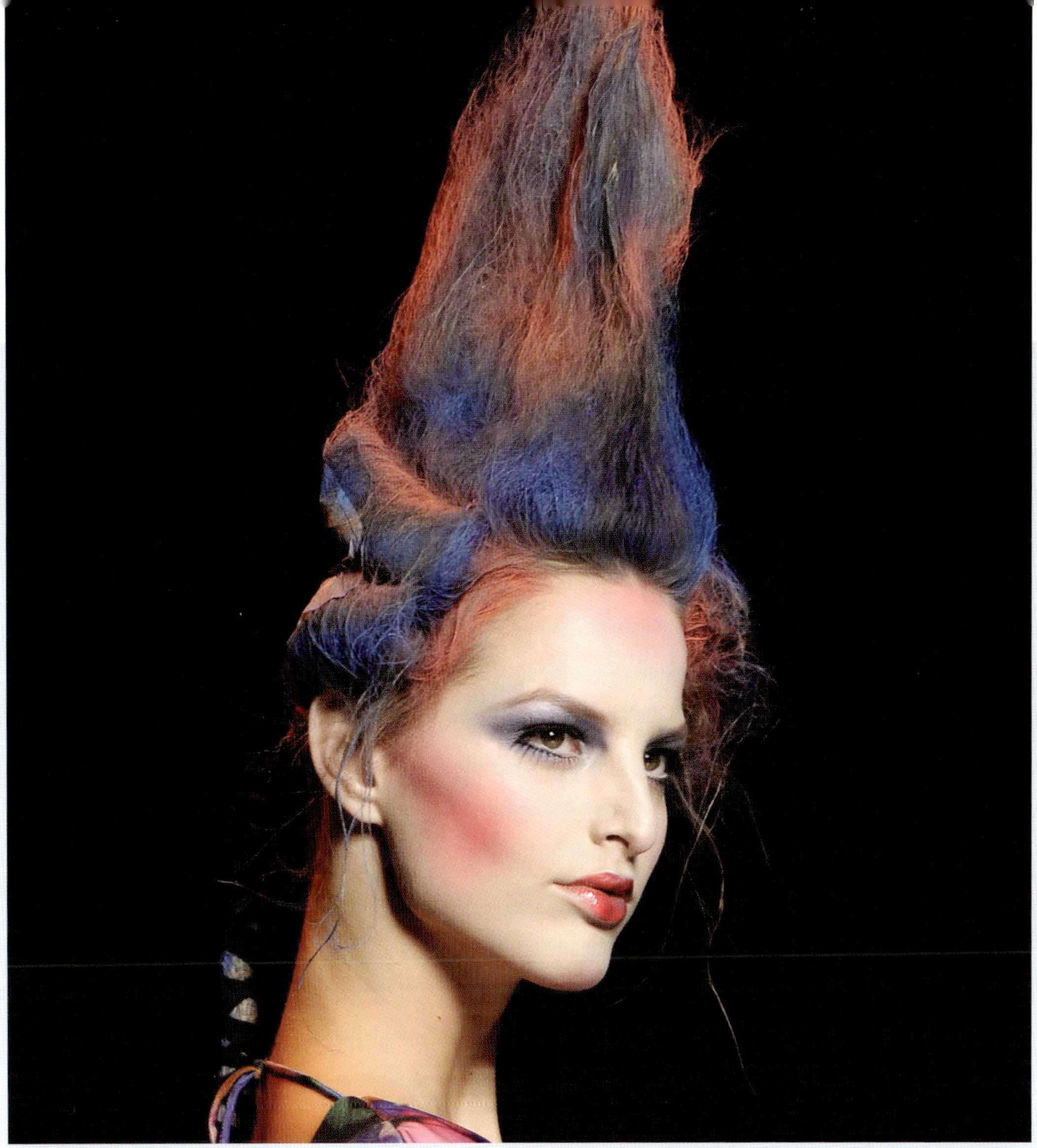

John Galliano

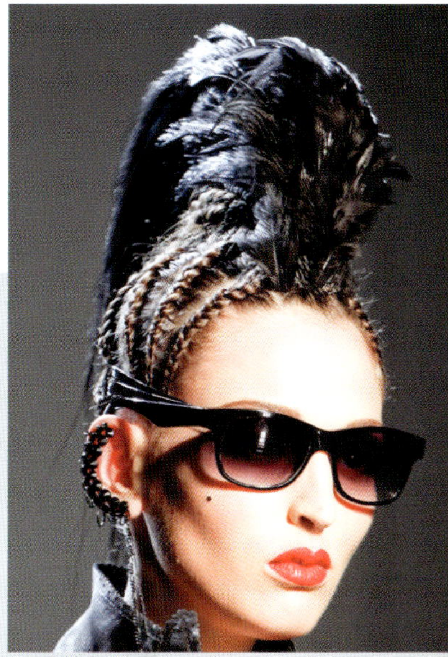

Jean Paul Gaultier

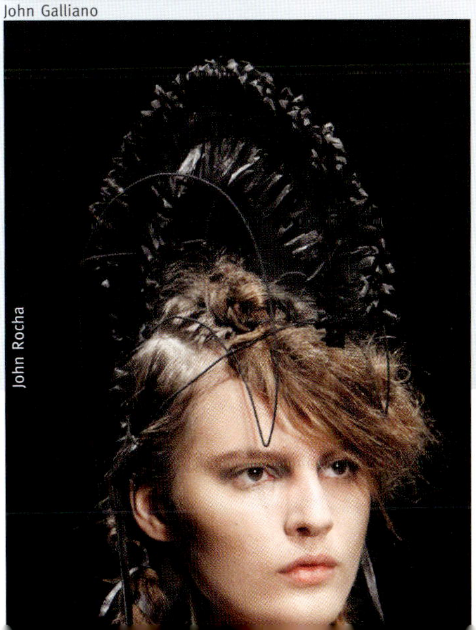

John Rocha

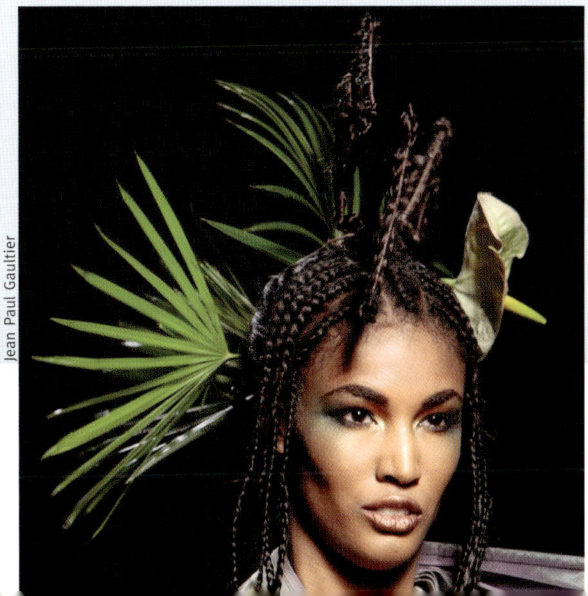

Jean Paul Gaultier

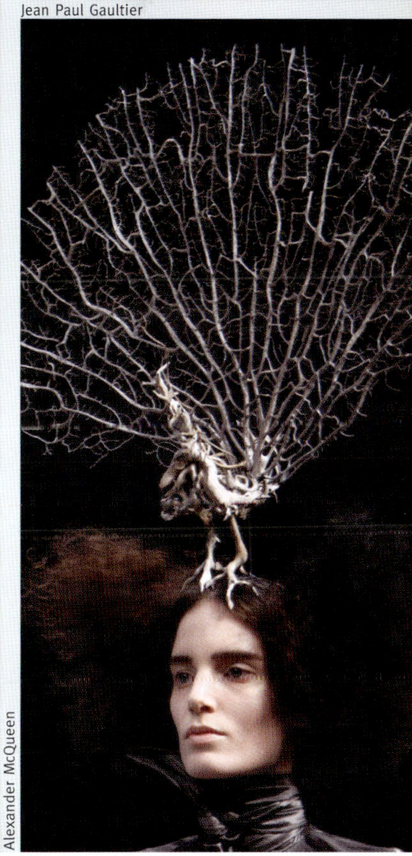

Alexander McQueen

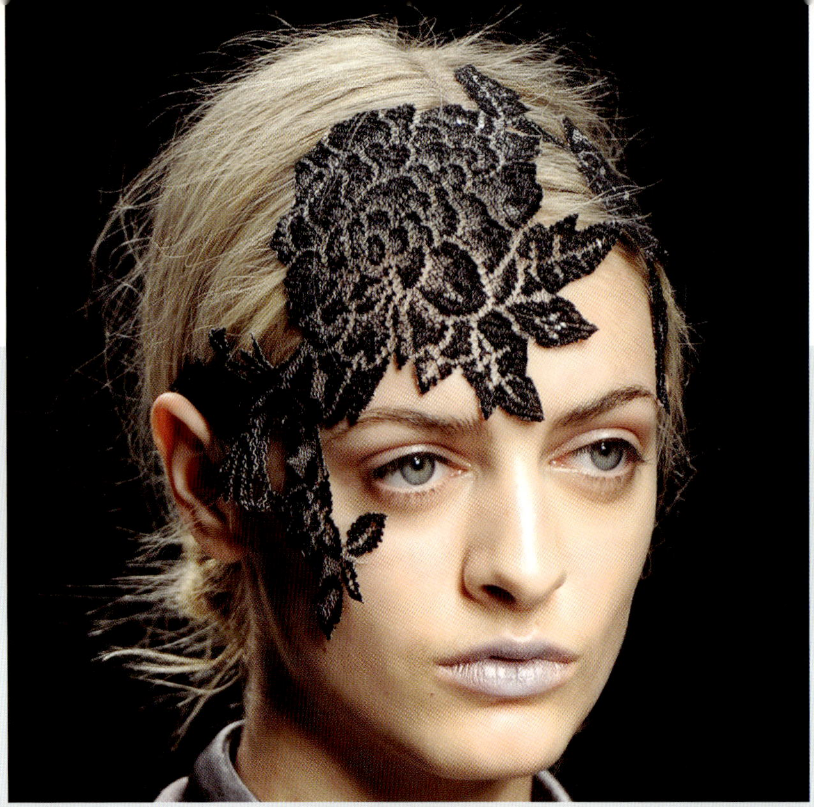

Bora Aksu

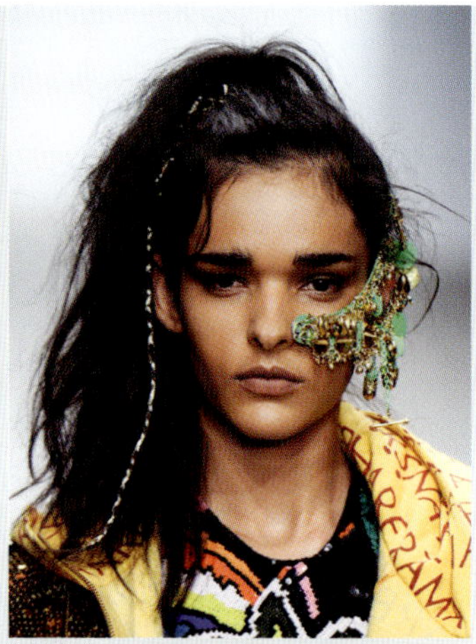

Ashish

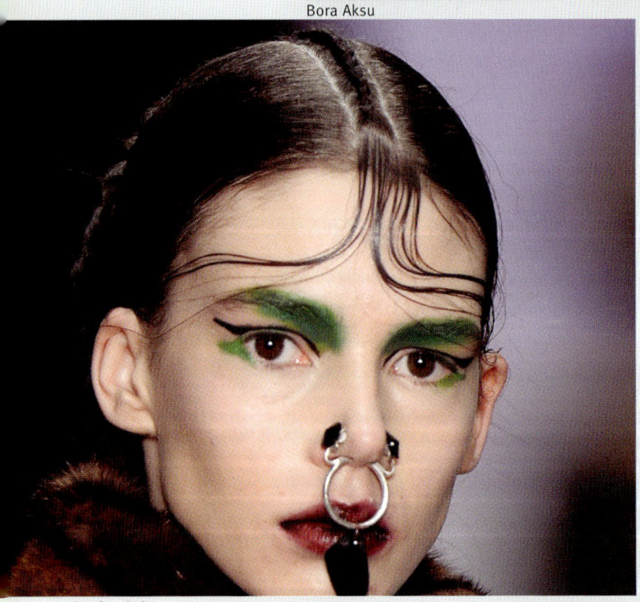

Fyodor Golan

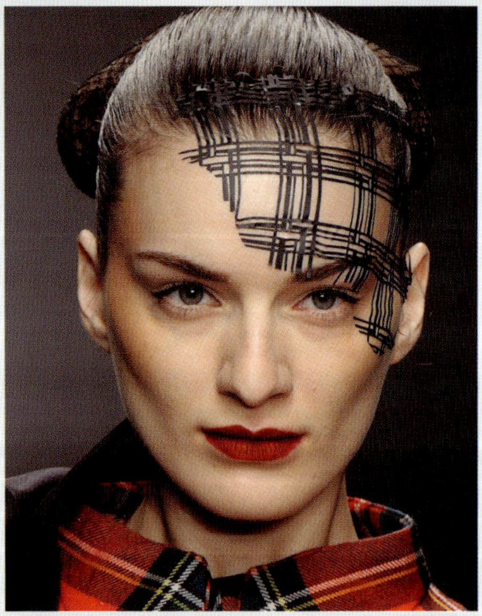

Corrie Nielsen

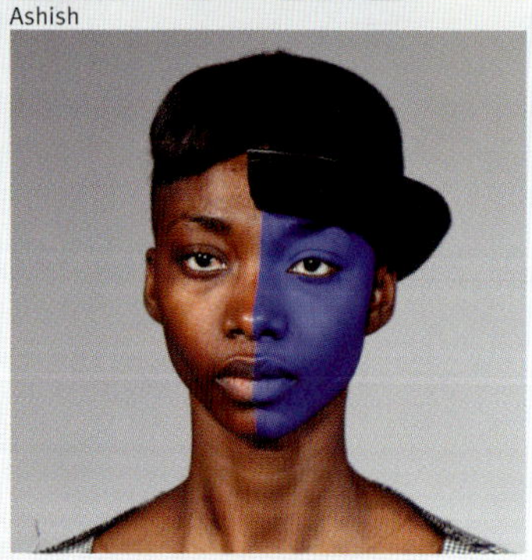

Bernhard Willhelm

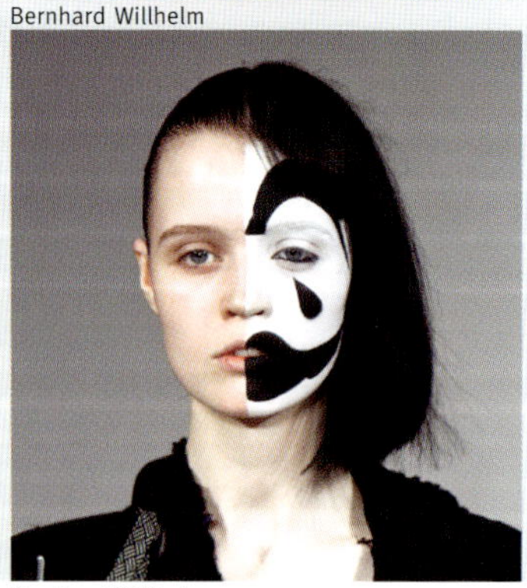

Bernhard Willhelm

Alexander McQueen

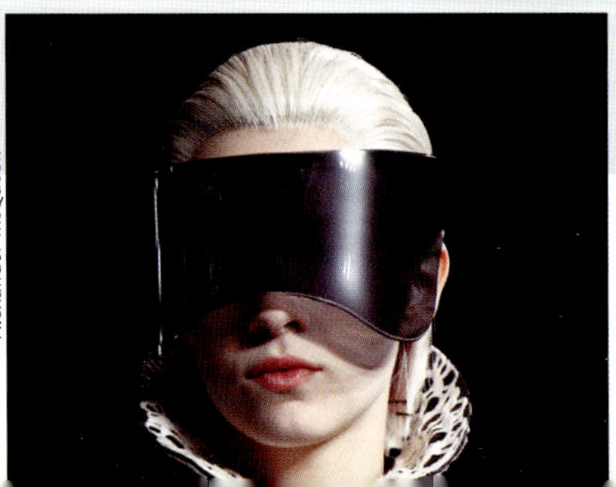

Dior

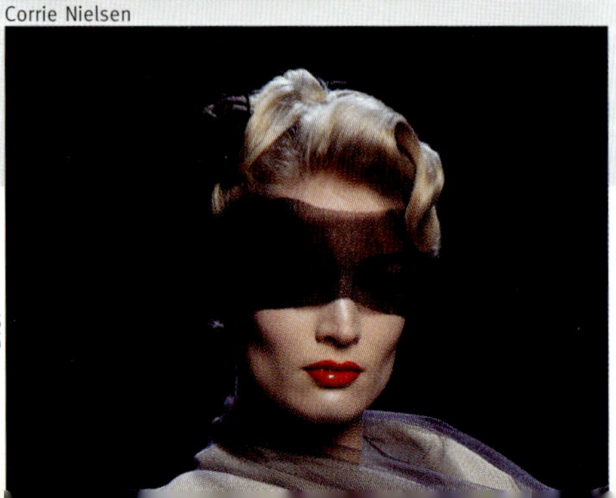

Fyodor Golan

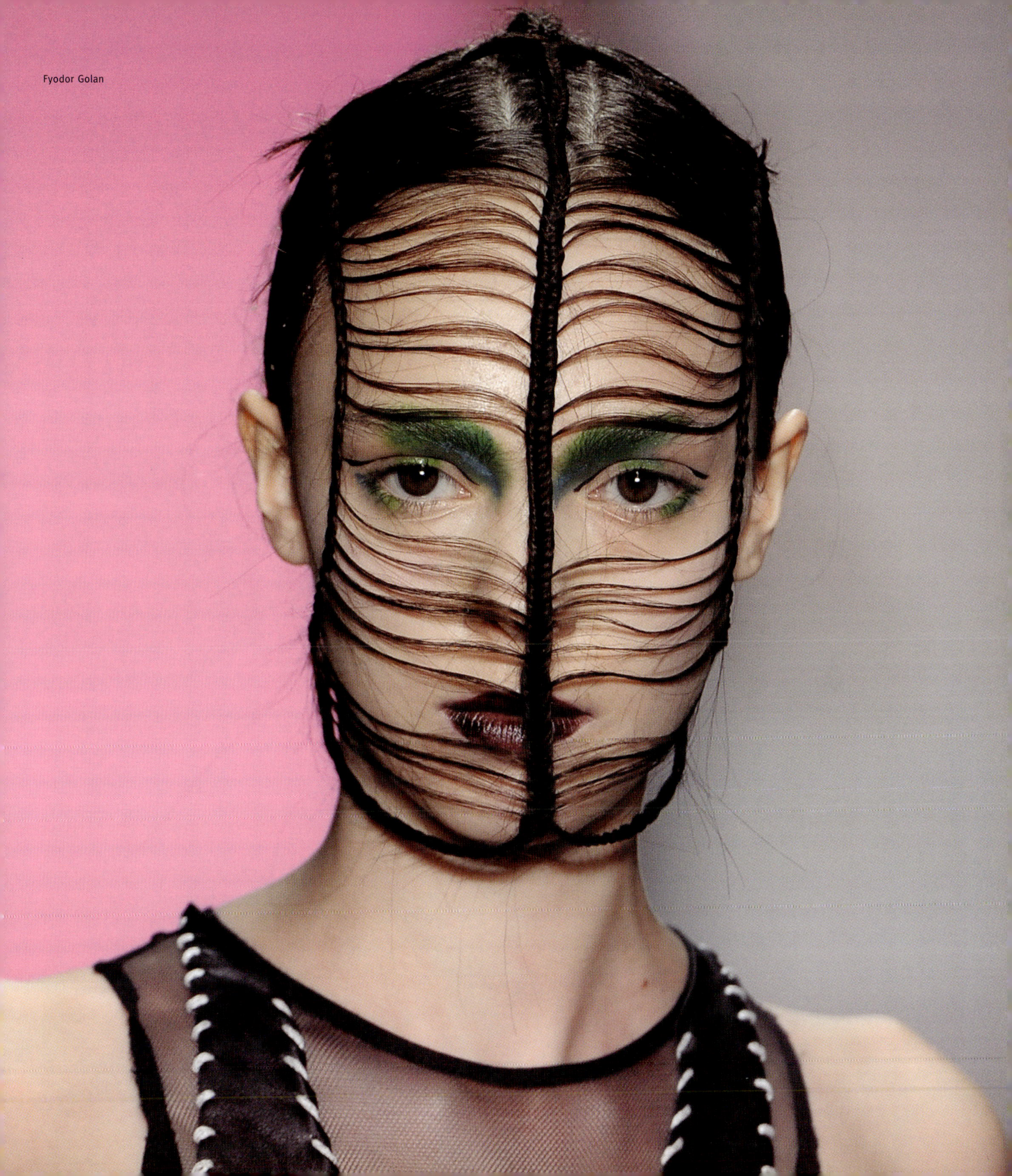

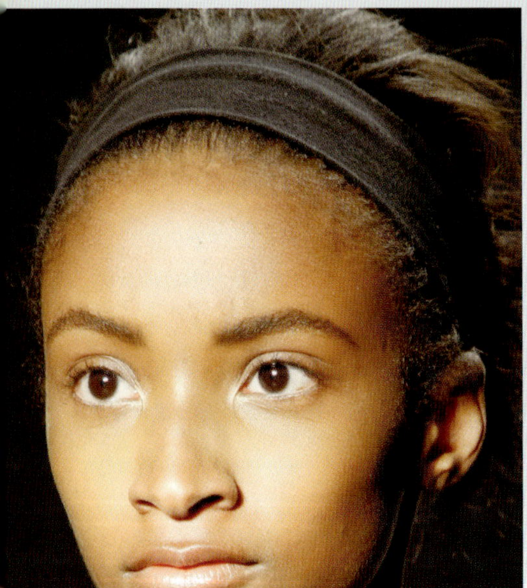
Calvin Klein

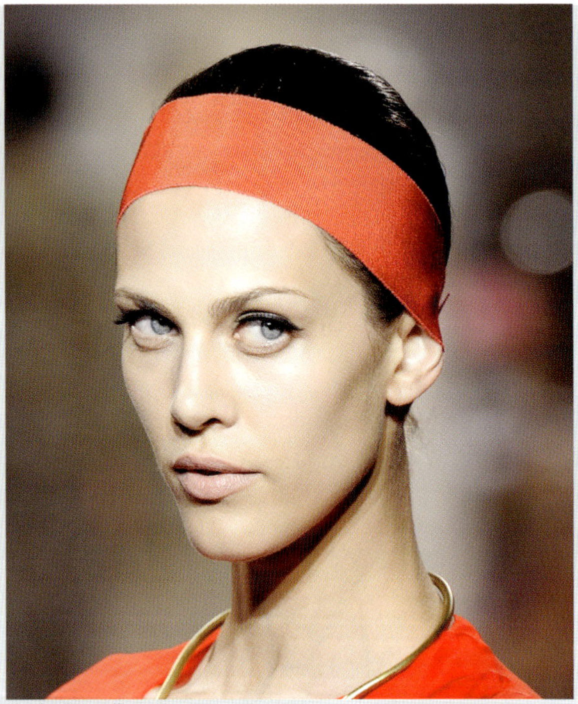
Giambattista Valli

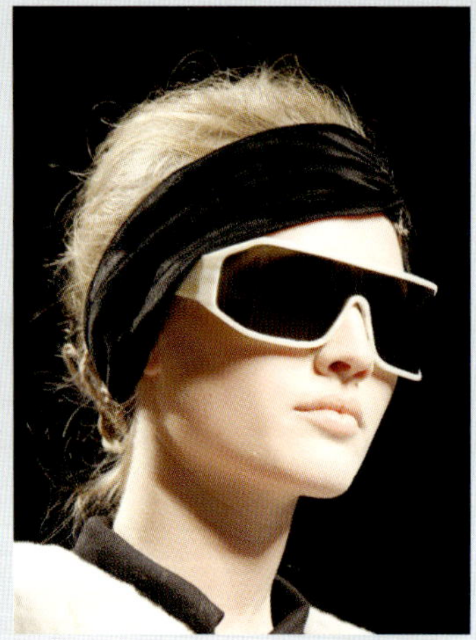
Fendi

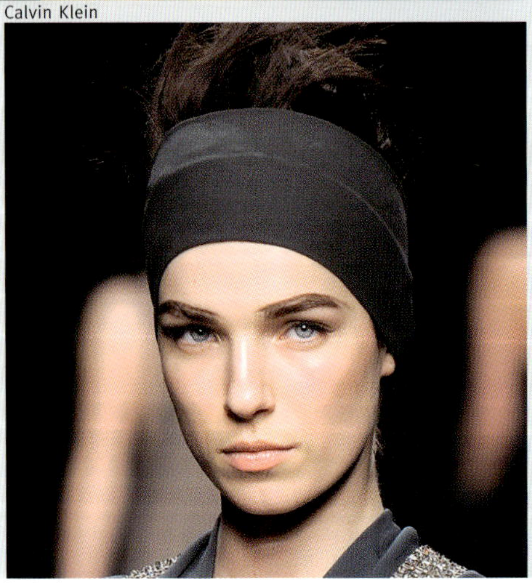
La Perla

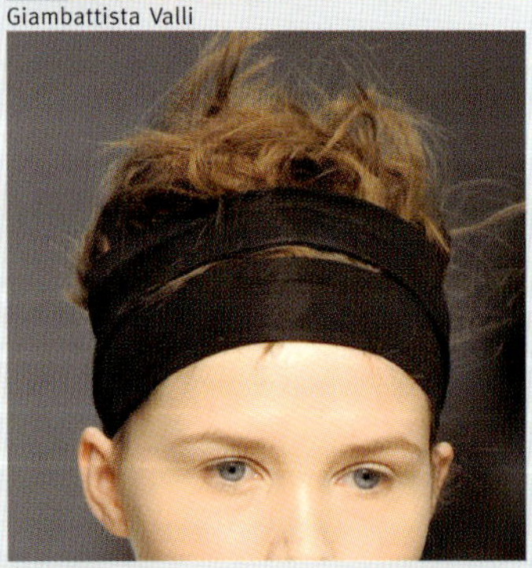
Betty Jackson

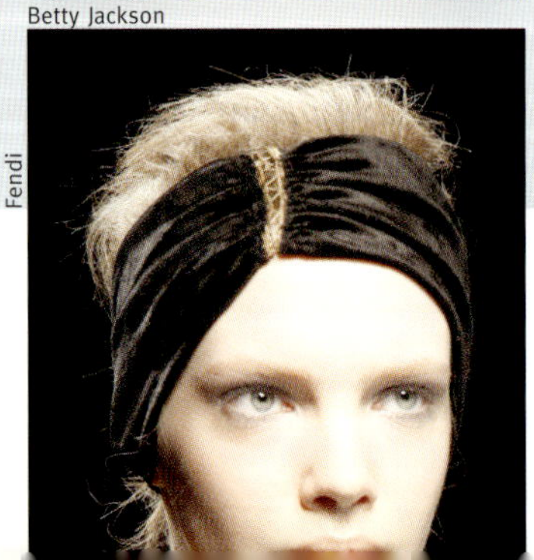
Fendi

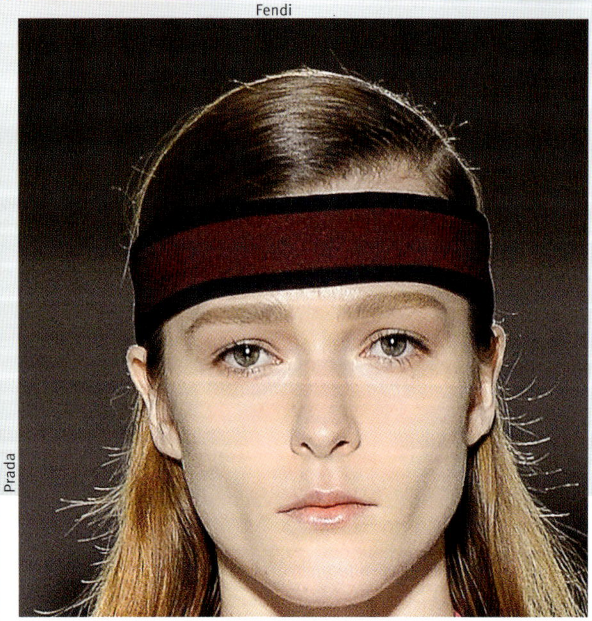
Prada

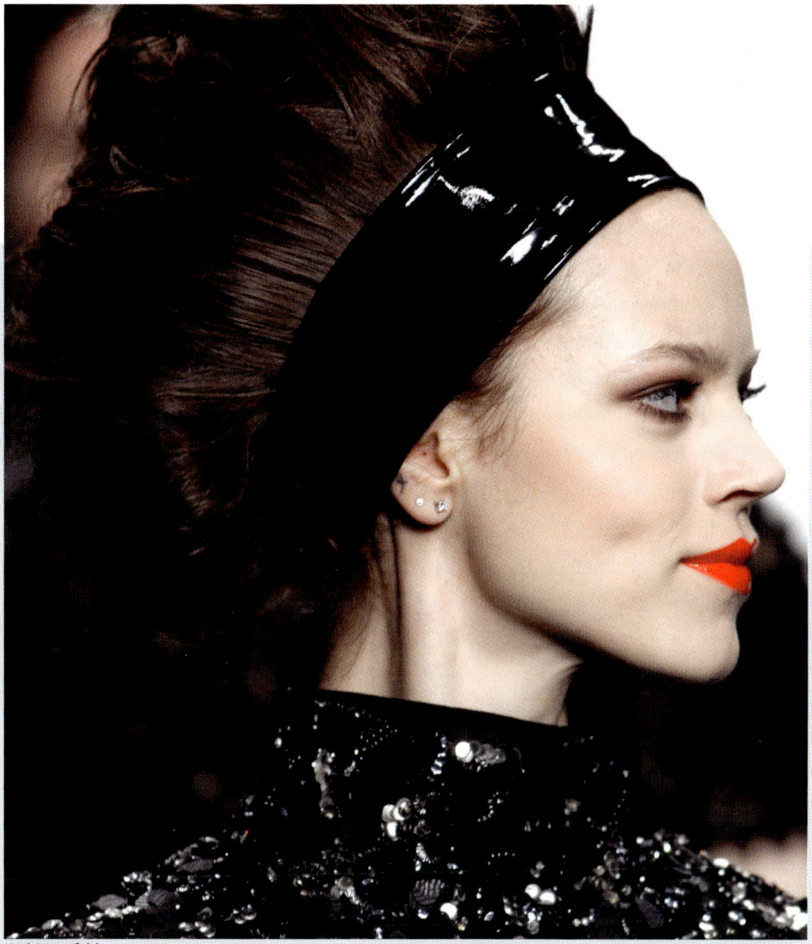
Karl Lagerfeld

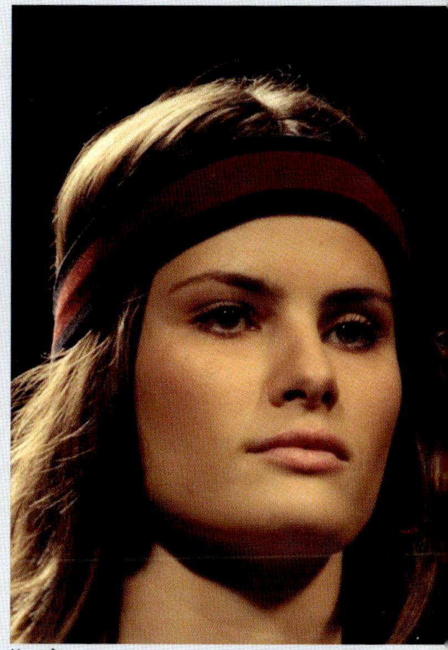
Hermès

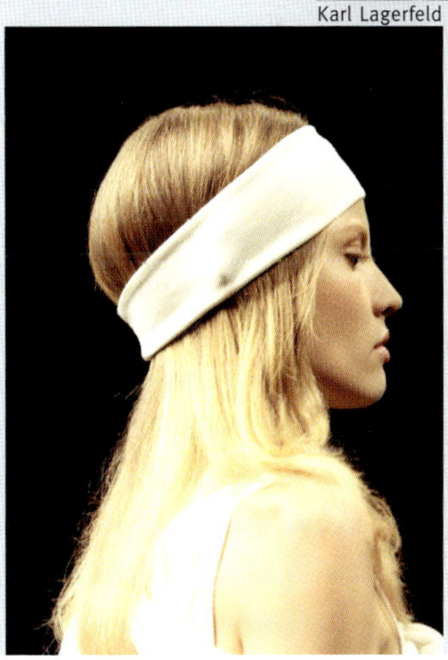
Hermès

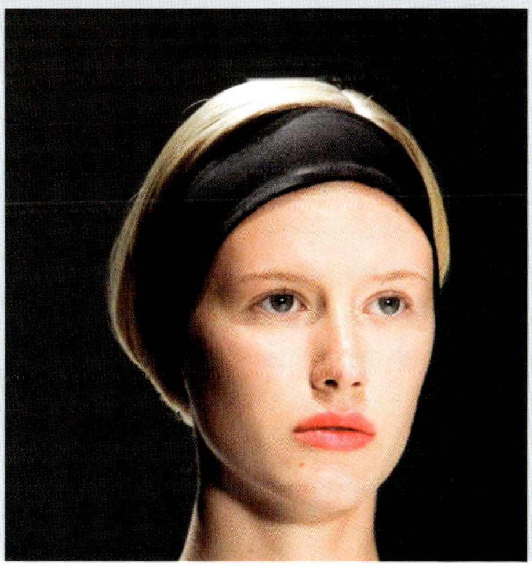
Jasper Conran

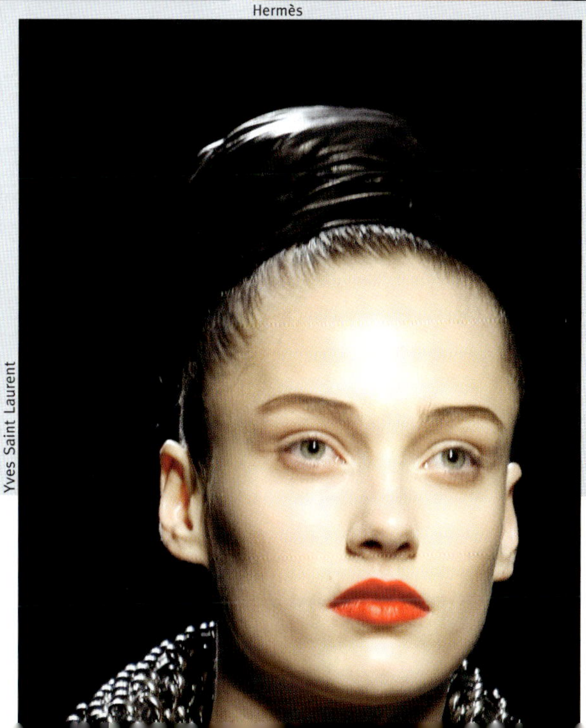
Yves Saint Laurent

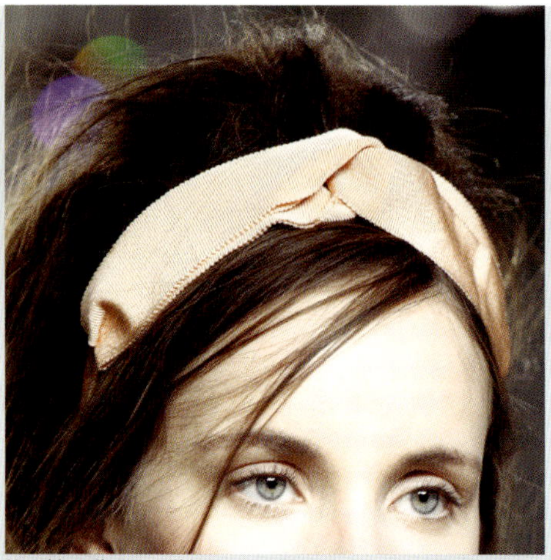
Moschino Cheap & Chic

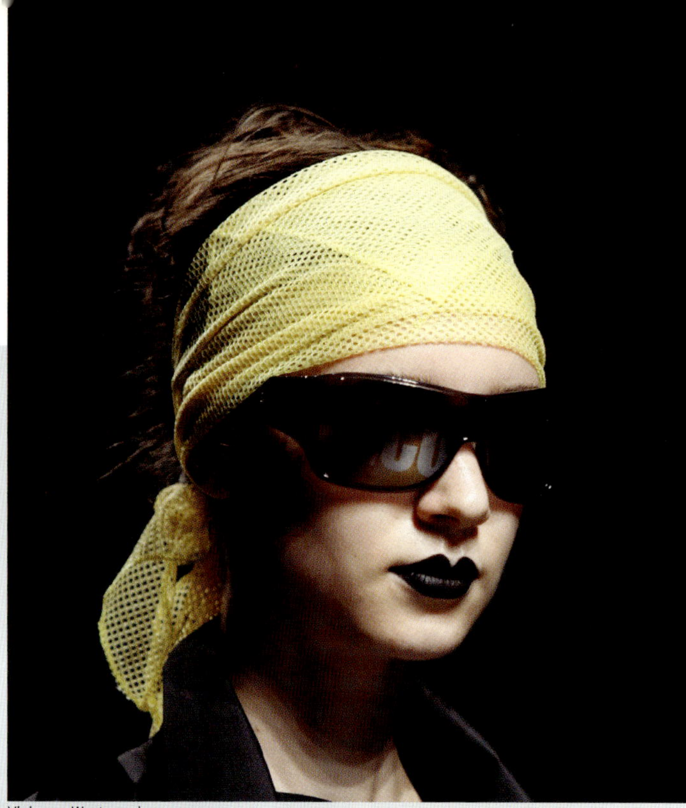
Vivienne Westwood

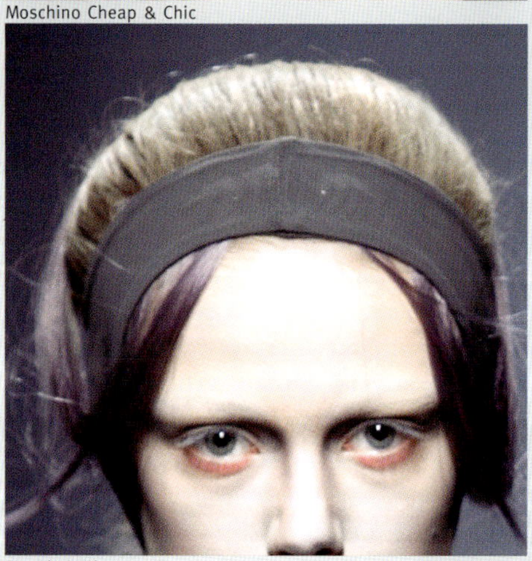
Gareth Pugh

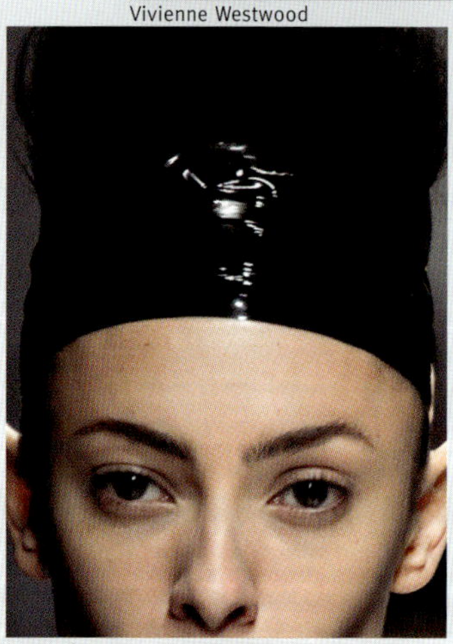
Devastée

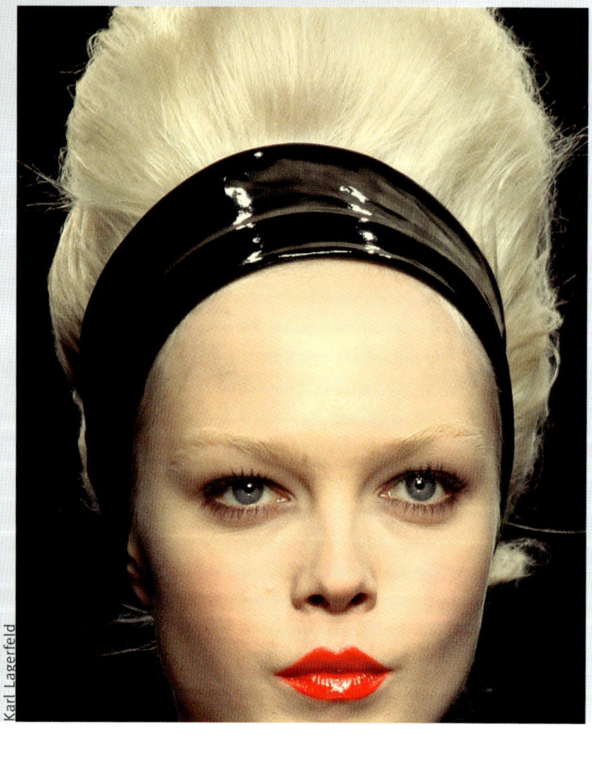
Karl Lagerfeld

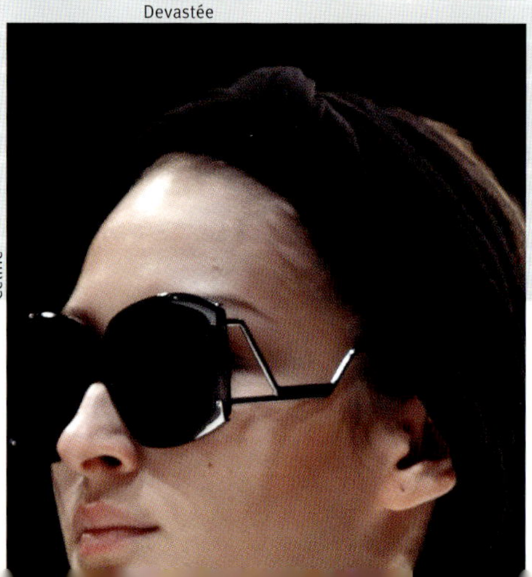
Céline

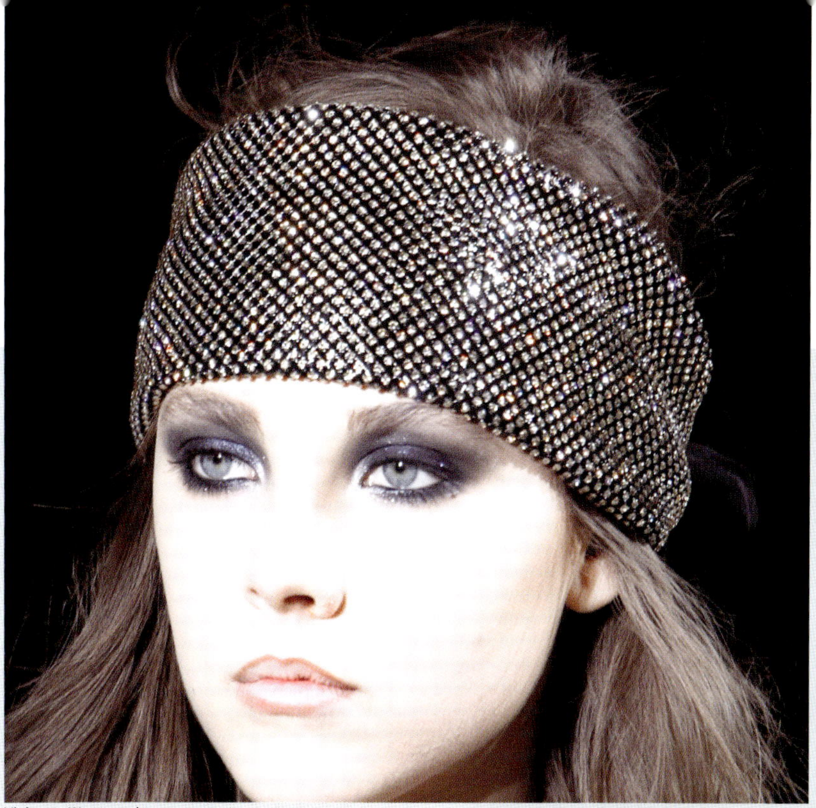

Vivienne Westwood

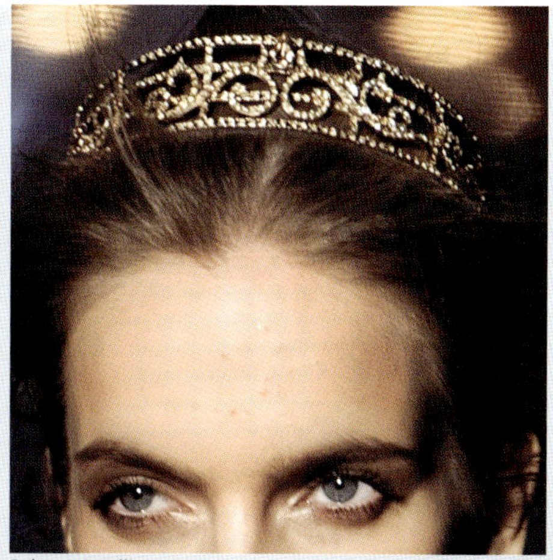

Roberto Cavalli

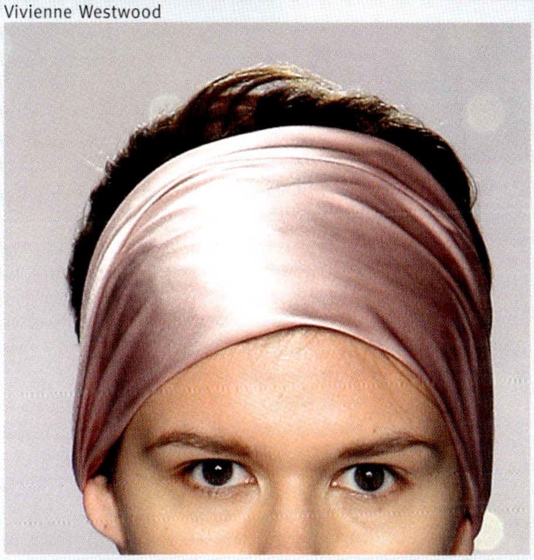

Luisa Beccaria

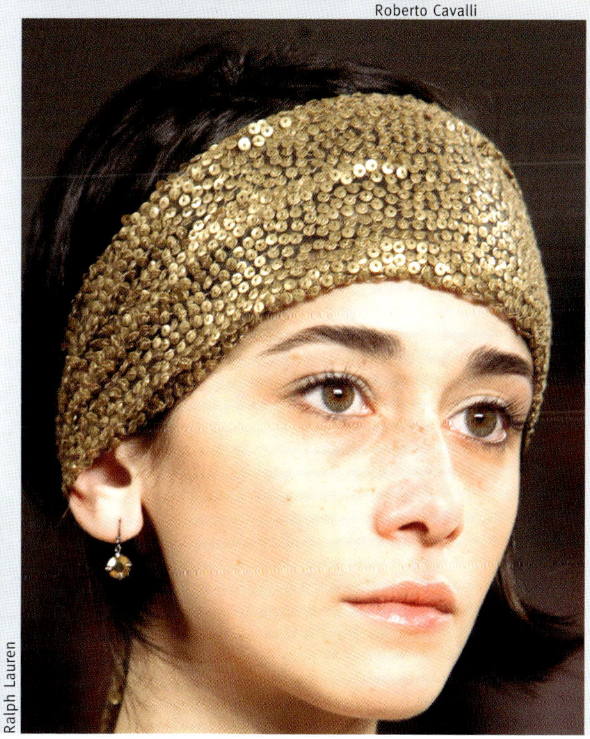

Ralph Lauren

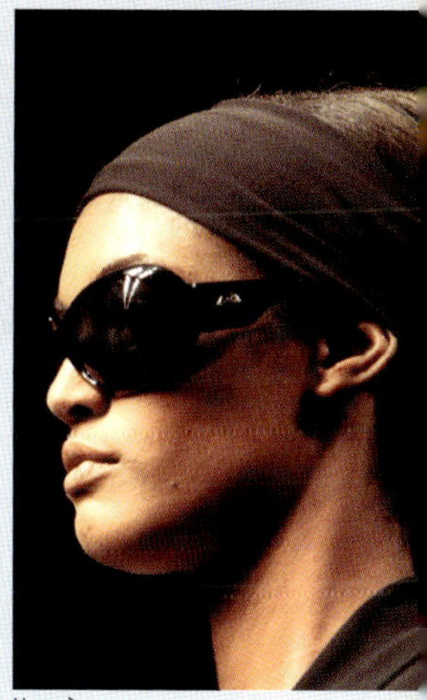

Hermès

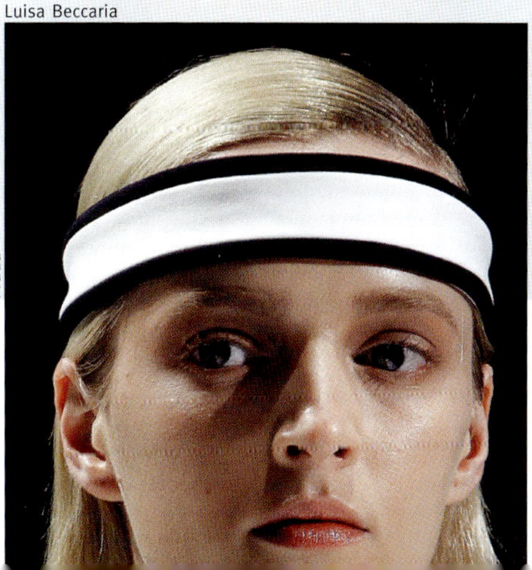

Prada

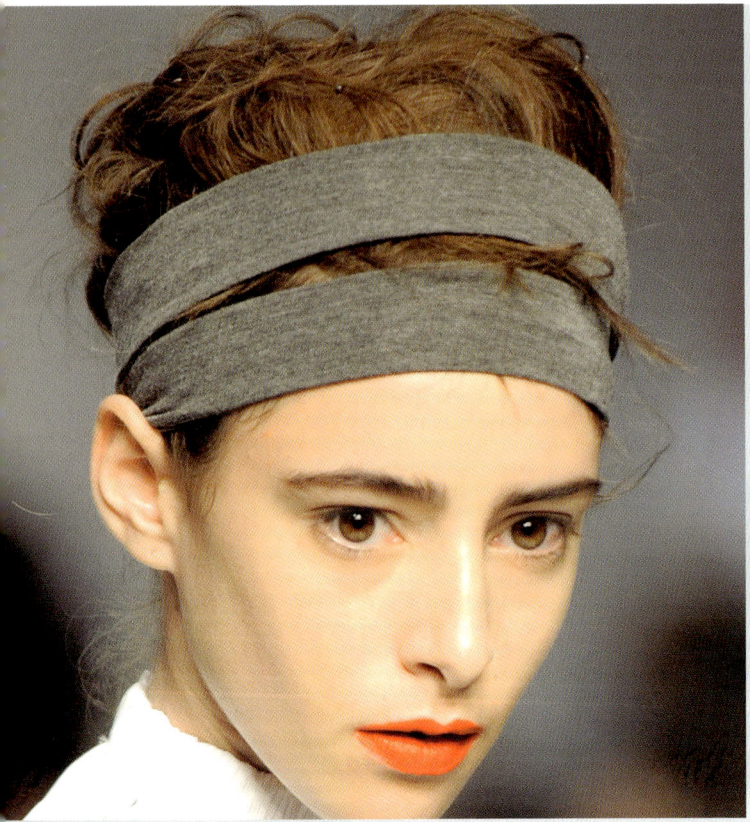

Betty Jackson

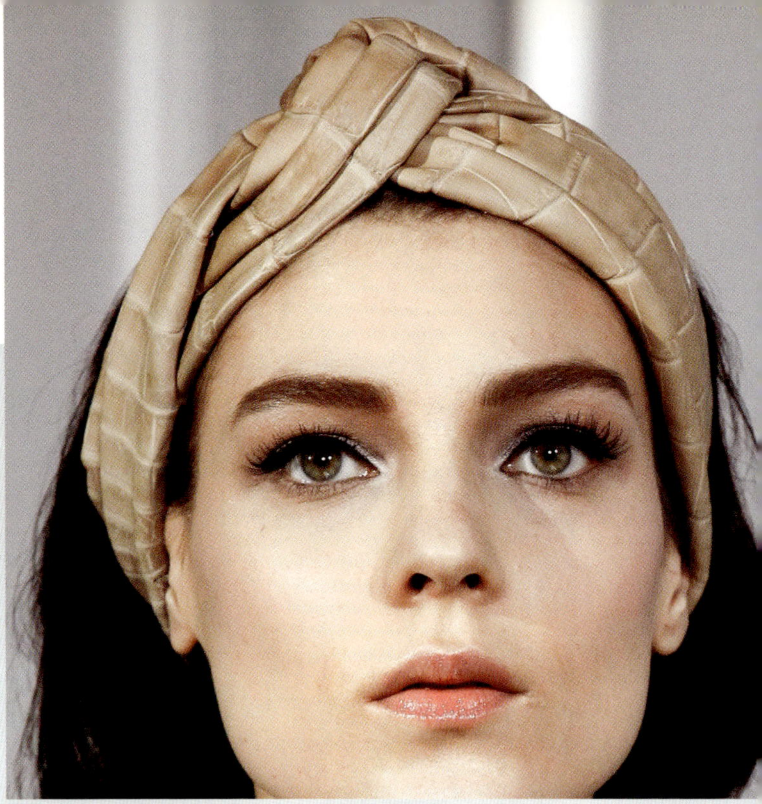

Dior

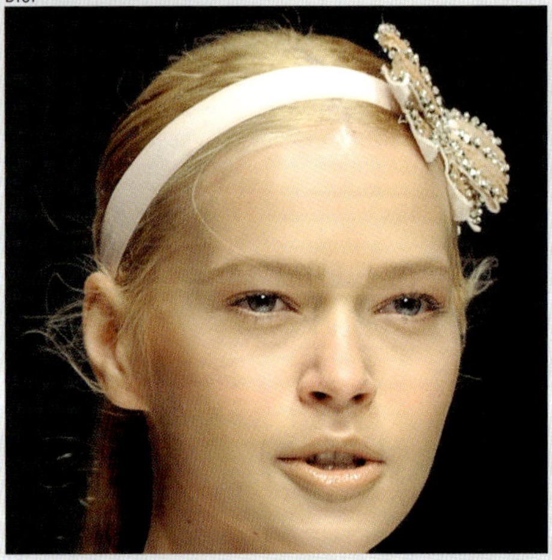

Blugirl

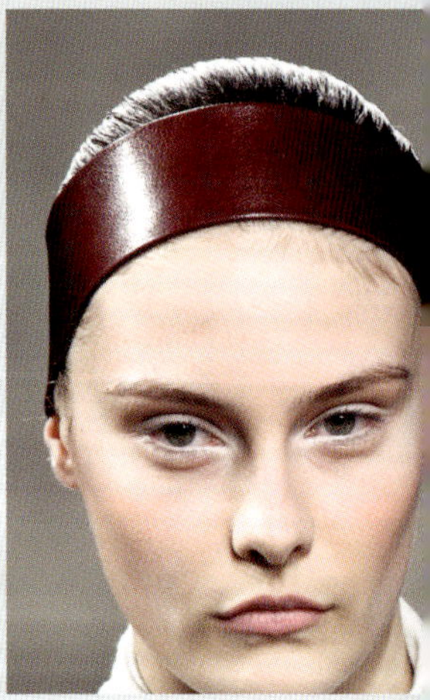

Doo.Ri

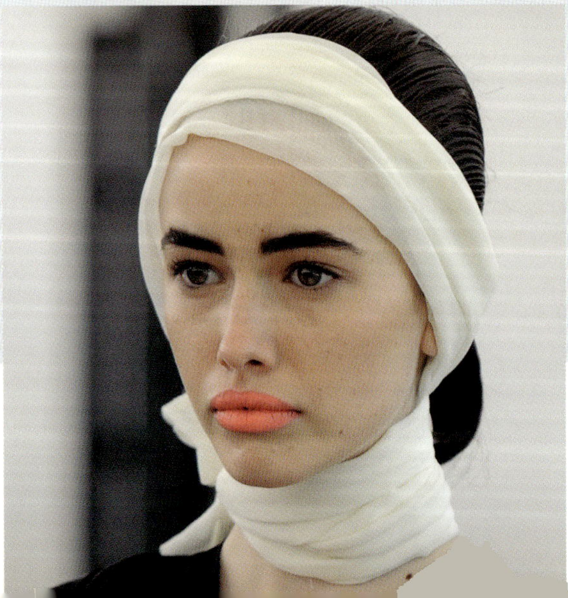

Osman Yousefzada

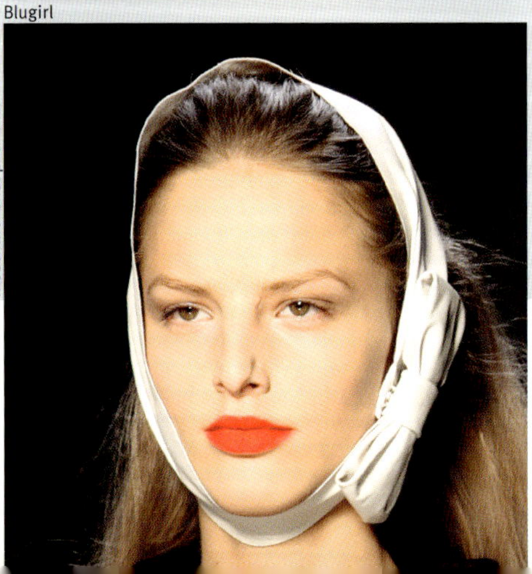

Moschino Cheap & Chic

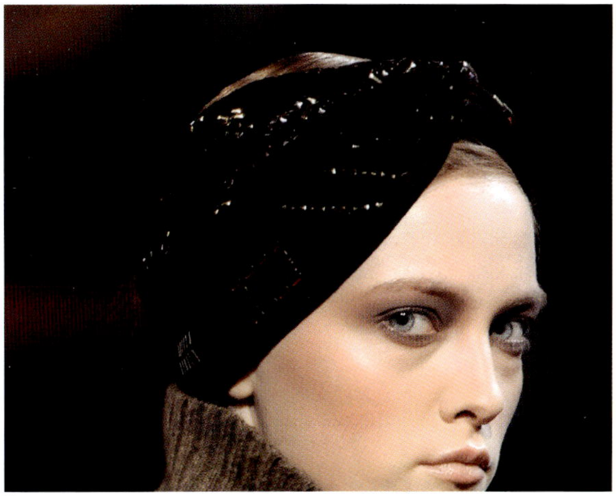
Etro

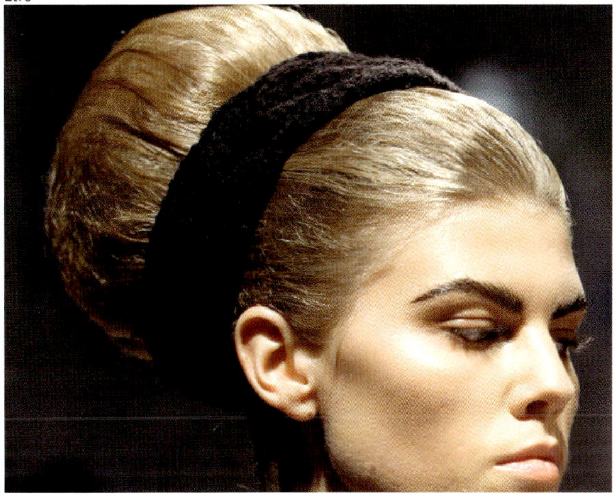
Prada

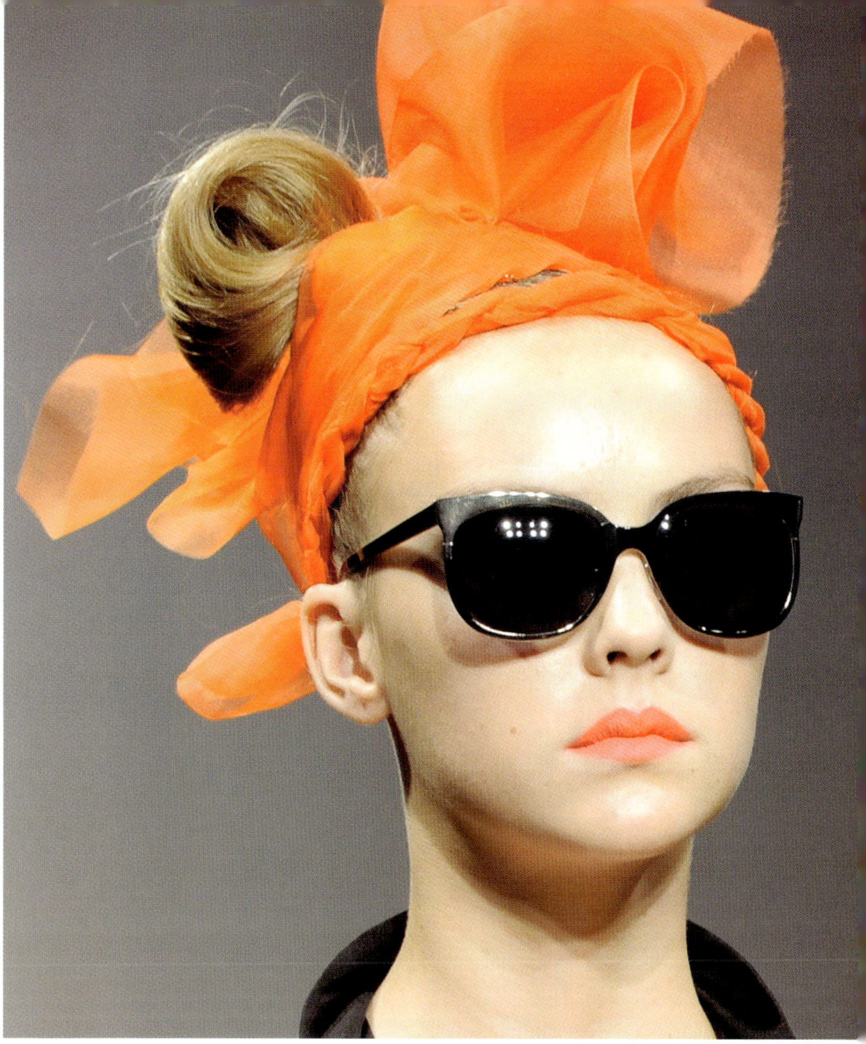
Danielle Scutt

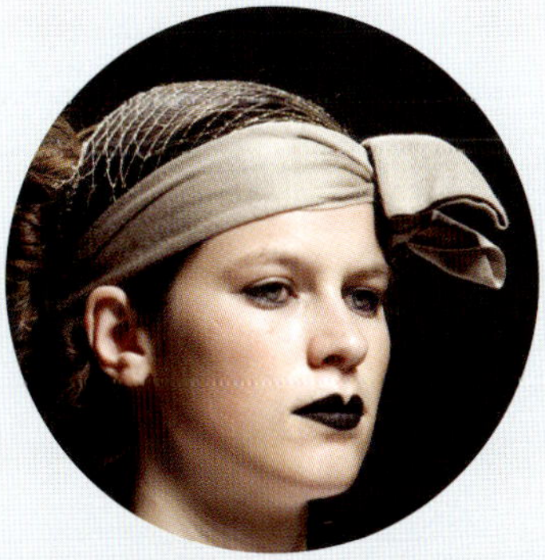
Vivienne Westwood

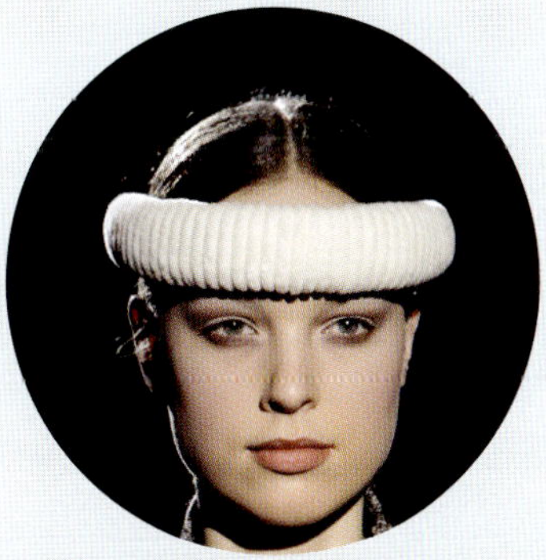
Marc Jacobs

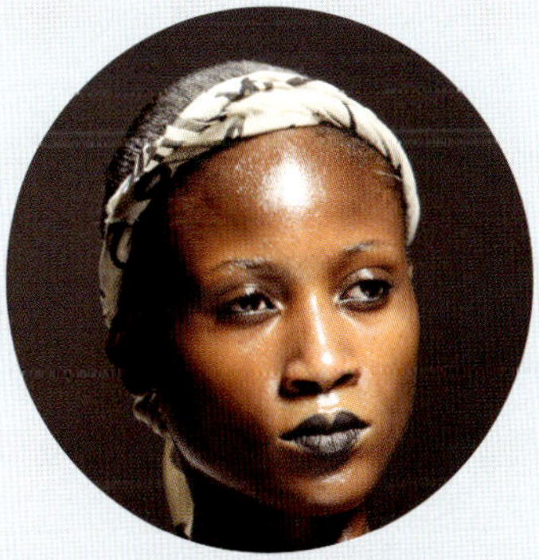
Vivienne Westwood

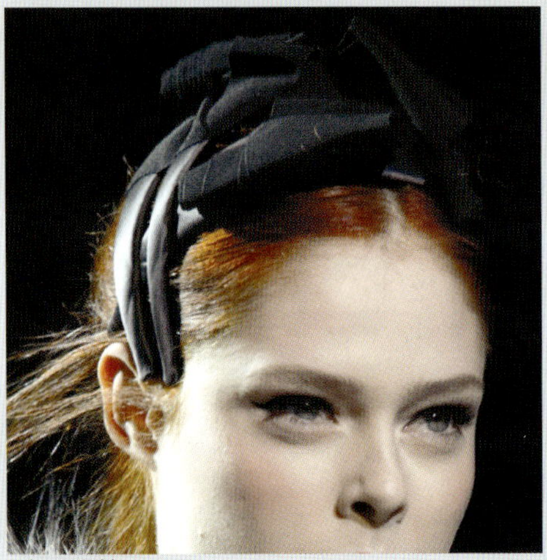
Dolce & Gabbana

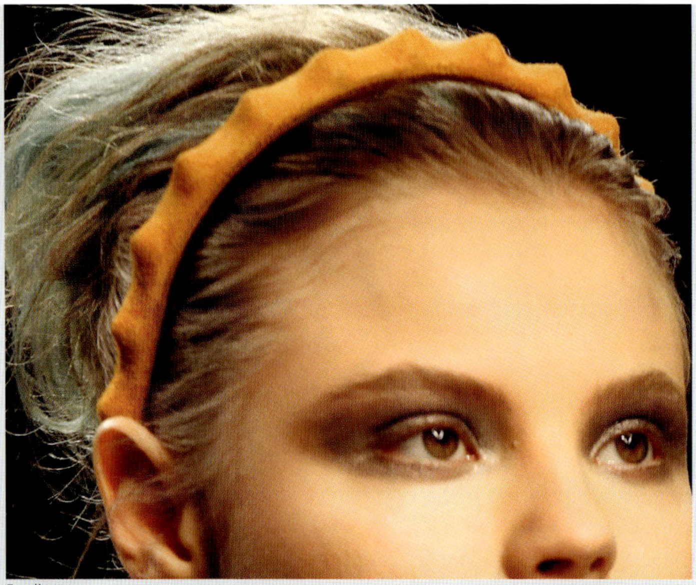
Fendi

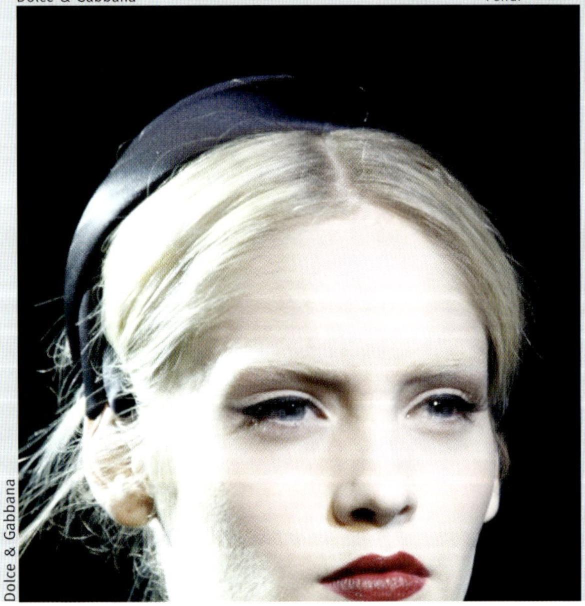
Dolce & Gabbana

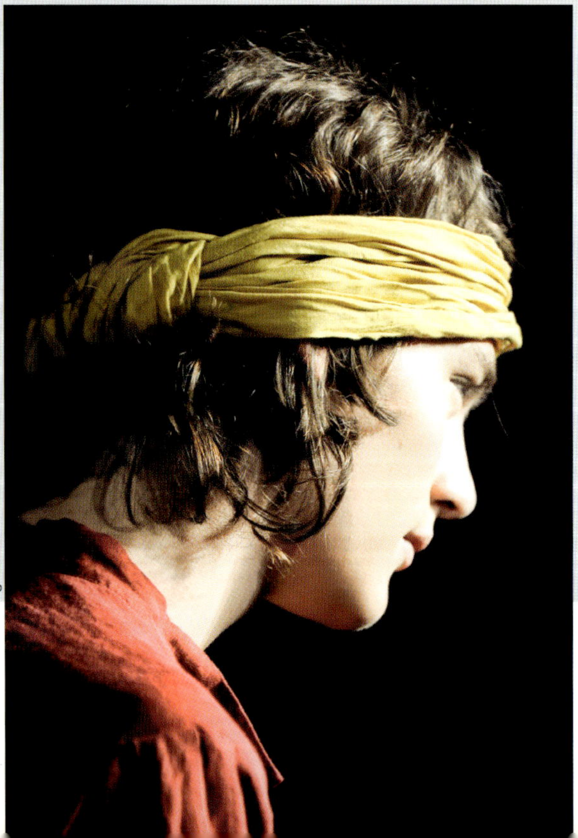
Agnès B.

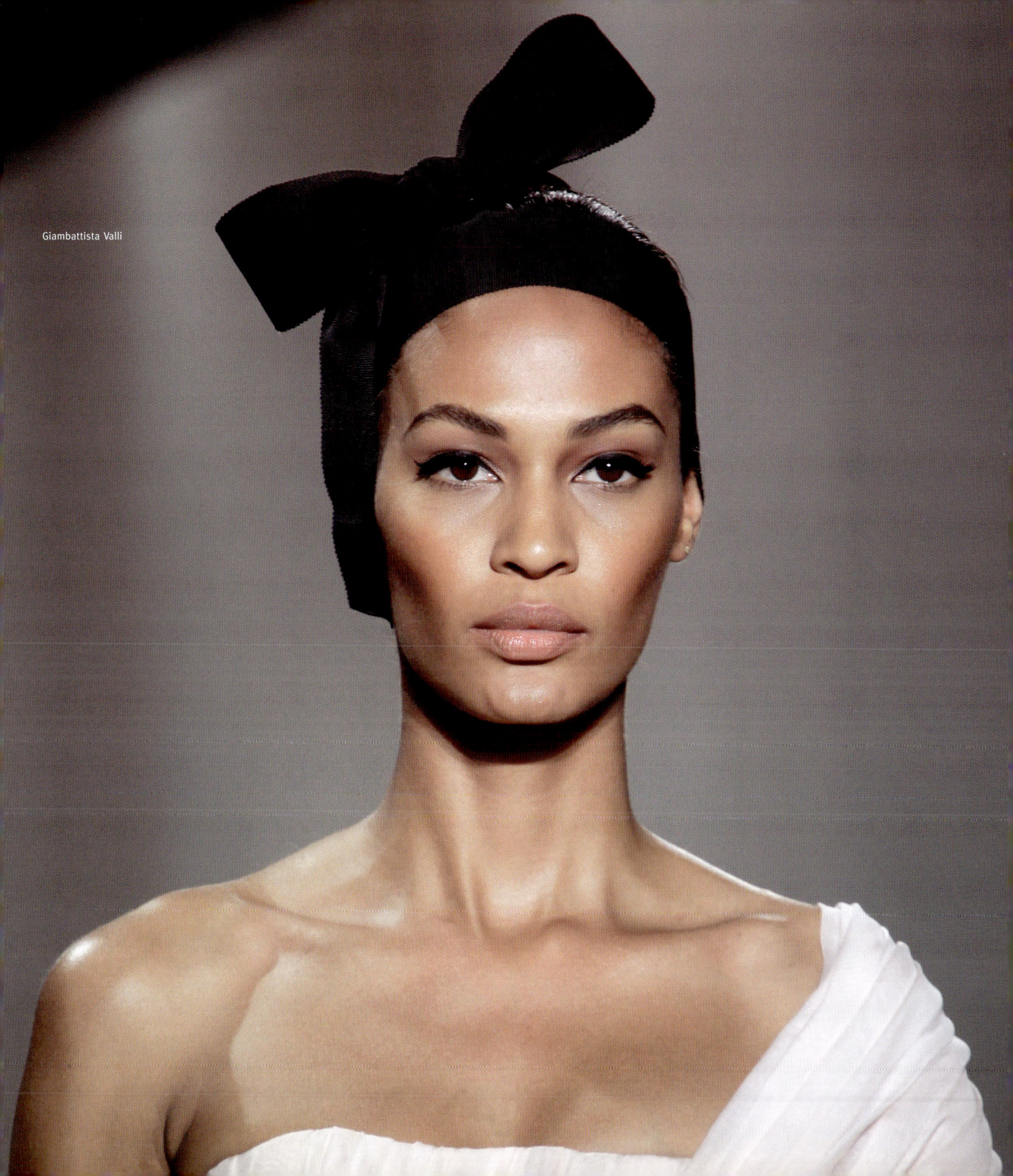

Giambattista Valli

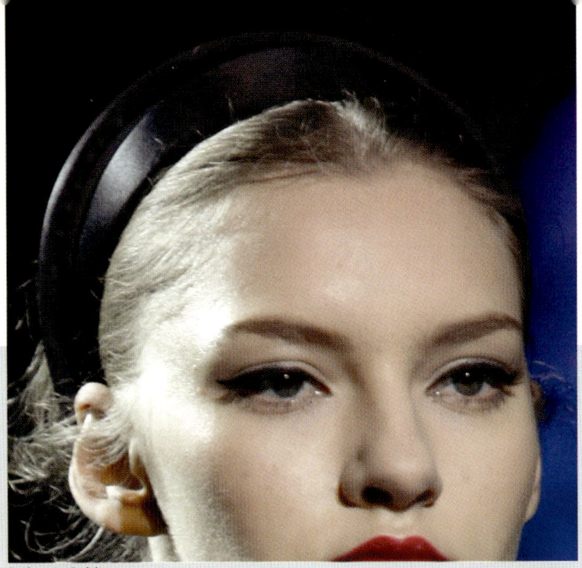

Dolce & Gabbana

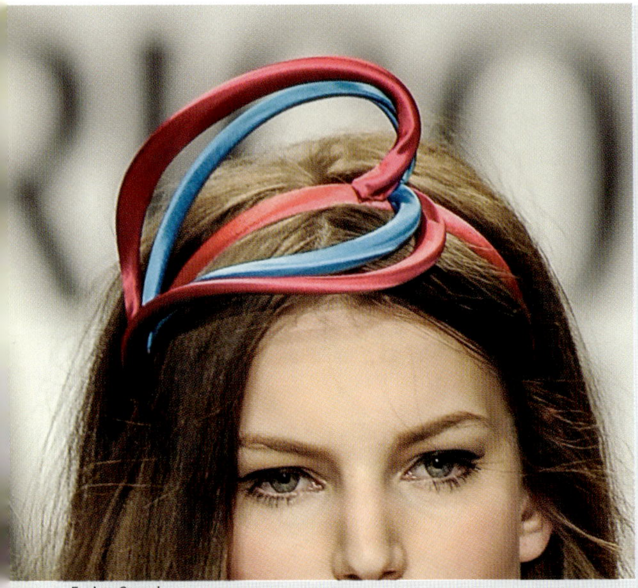

Enrico Coveri

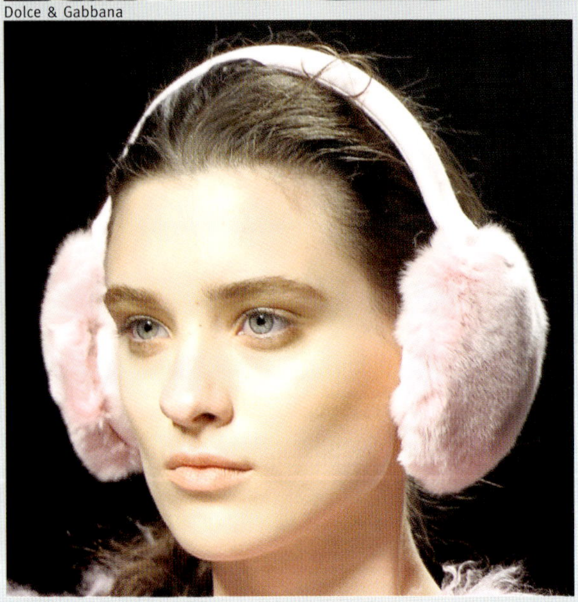

Blugirl

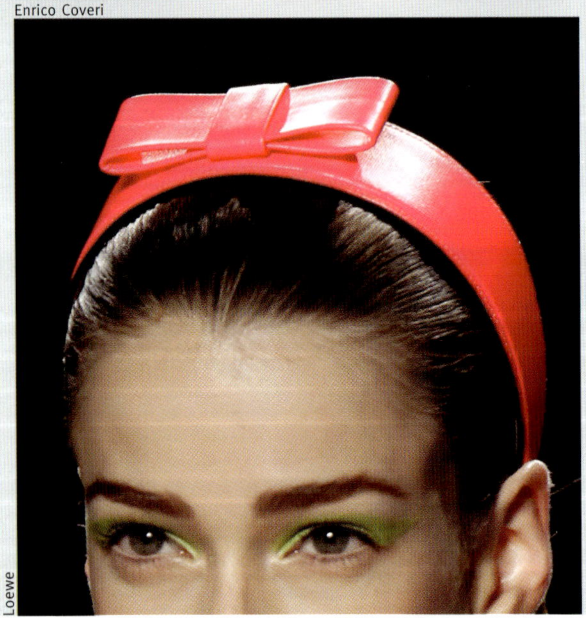

Loewe

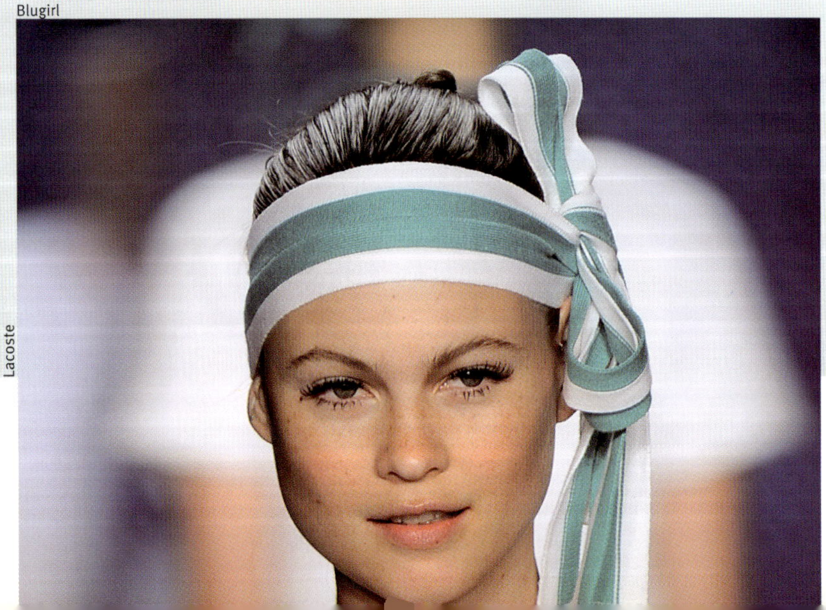

Lacoste

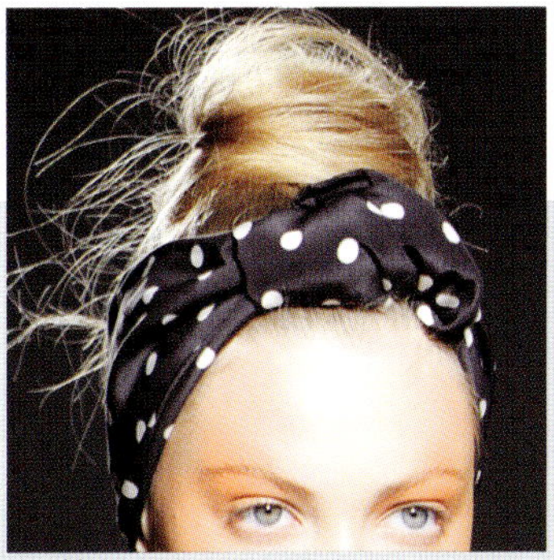

Moschino

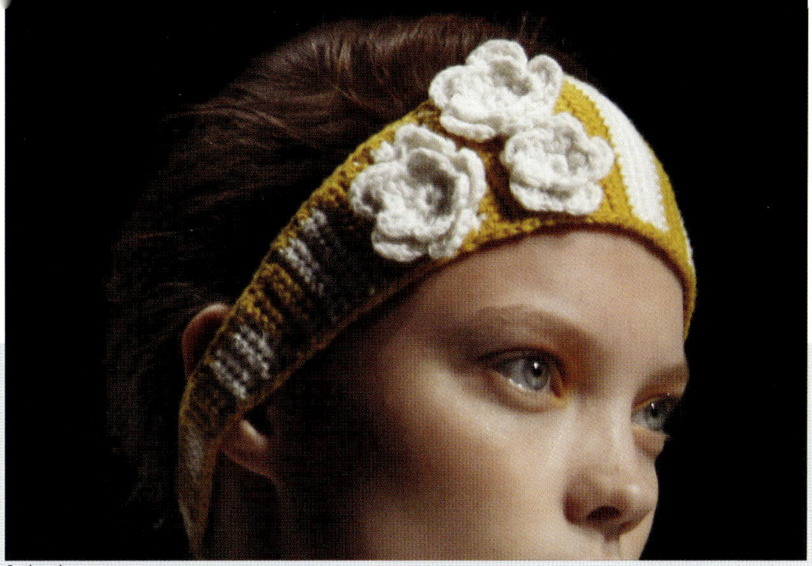

Cacharel

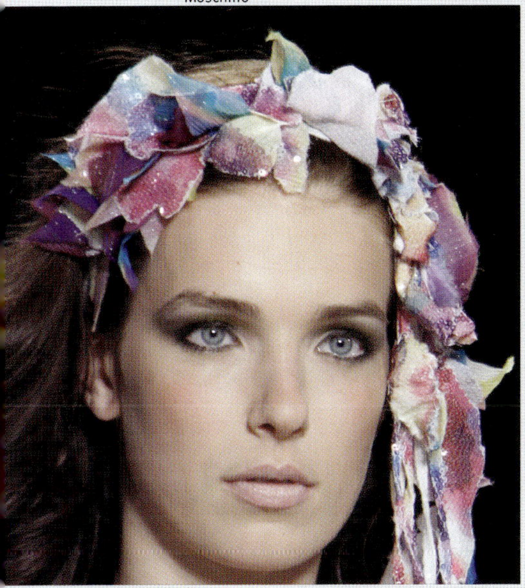

Diane Von Furstenberg

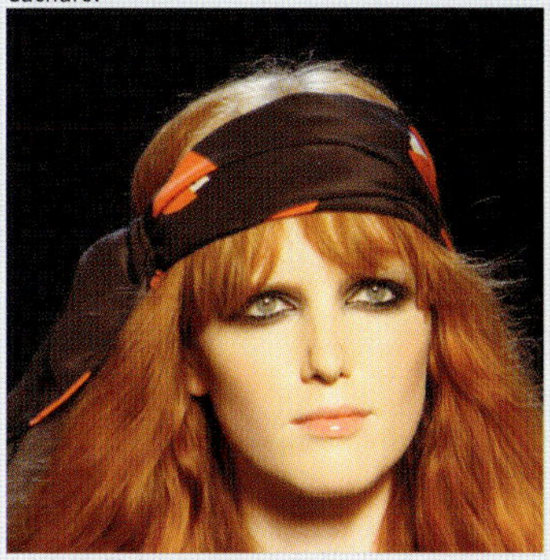

Sonia Rykiel

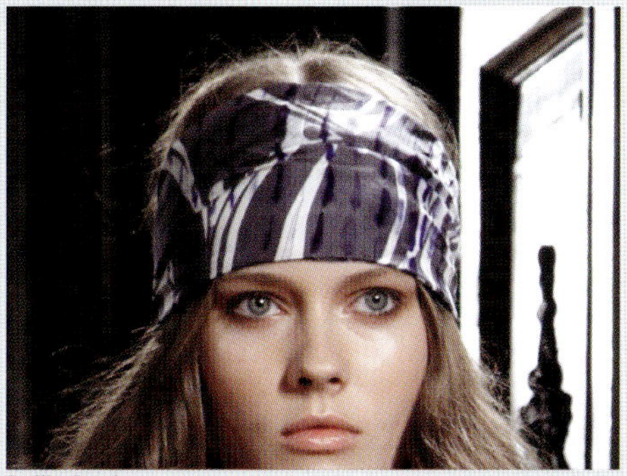

Emilio Pucci

Baby Phat

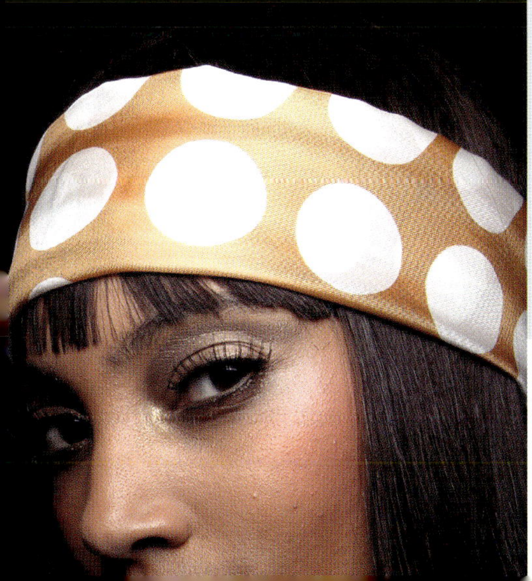

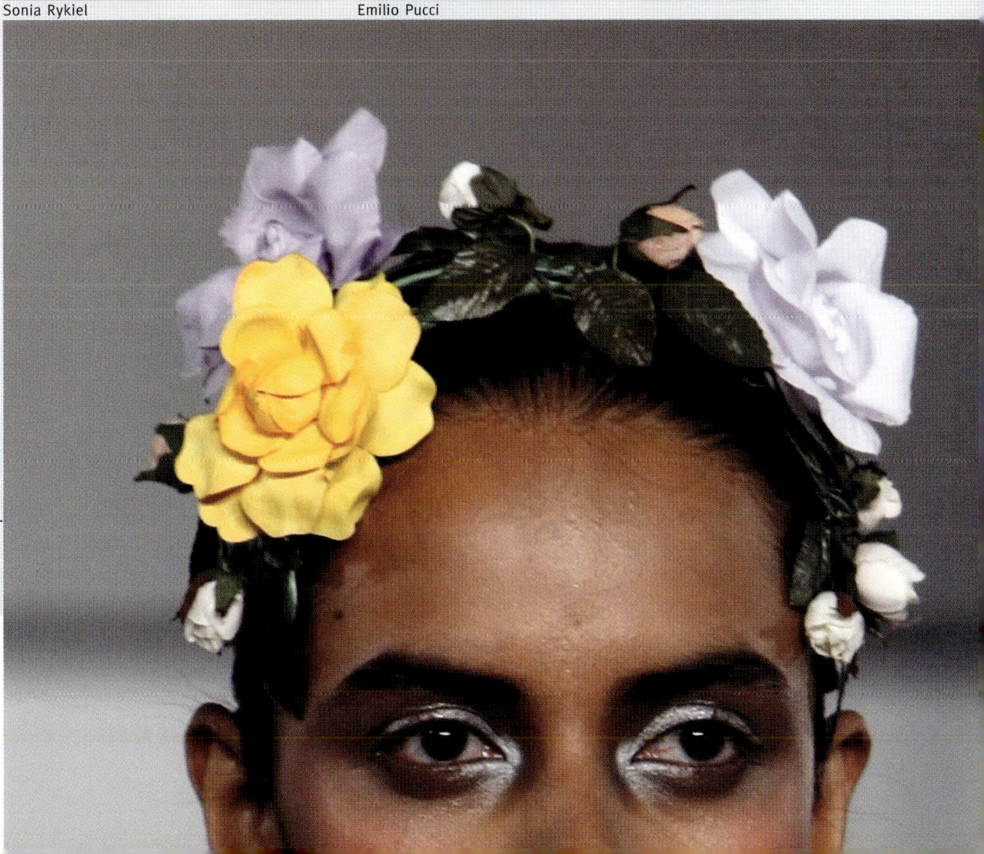

Behnaz Sarafpour

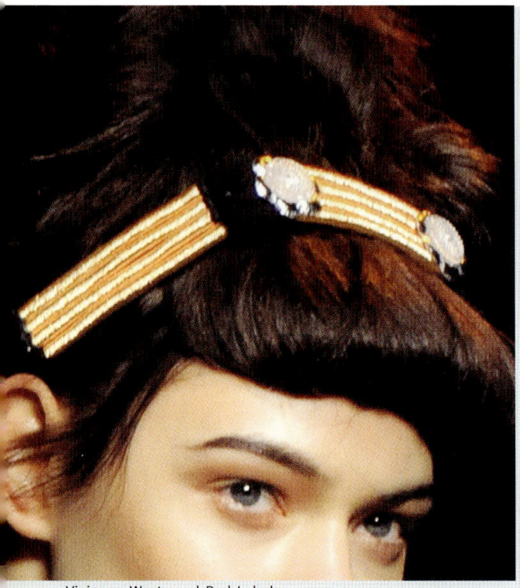

Vivienne Westwood Red Label

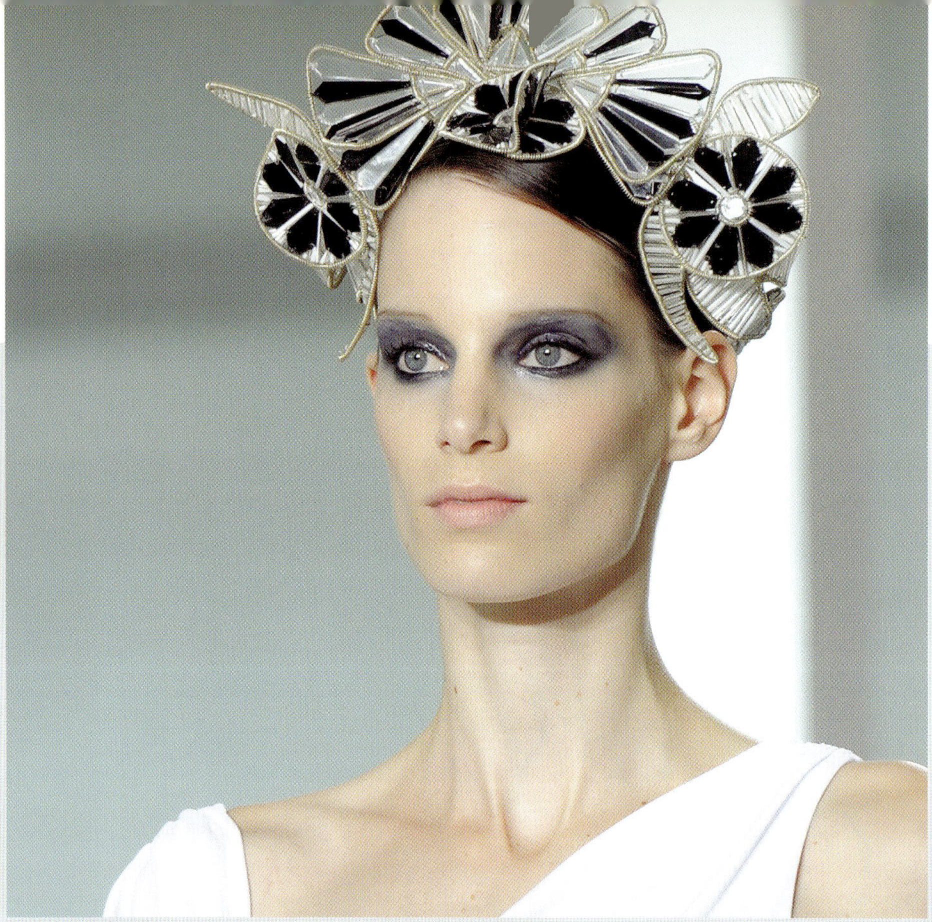

Temperley London

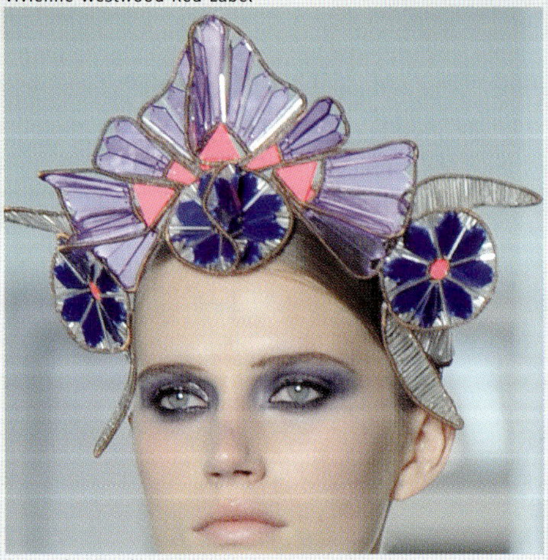

Temperley London

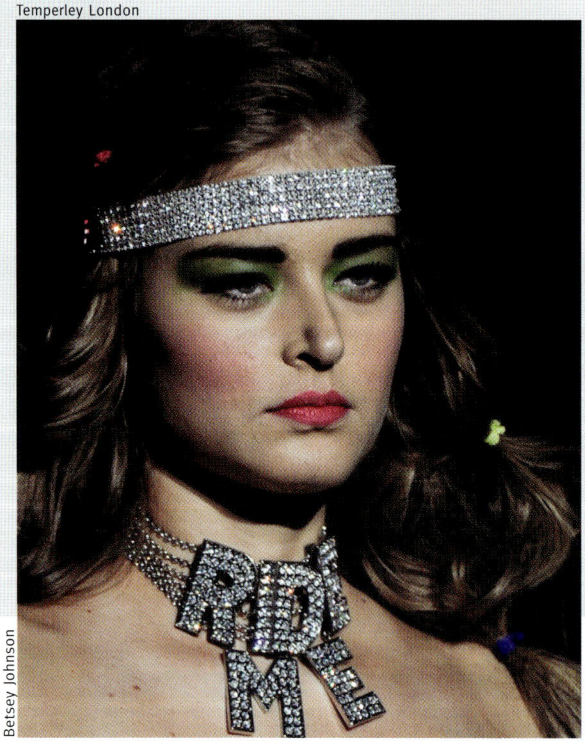


Betsey Johnson

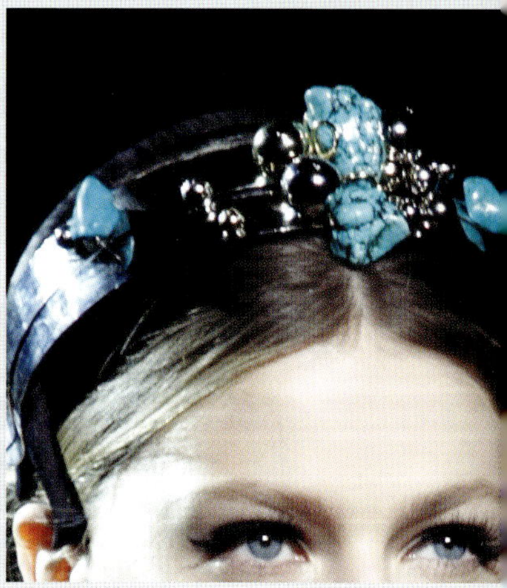

Dolce & Gabbana

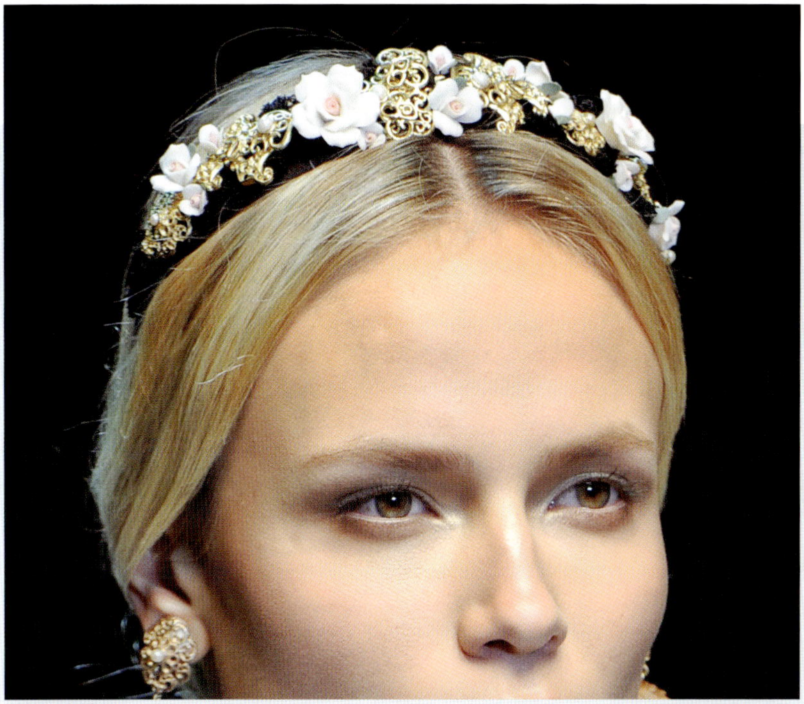
Dolce & Gabbana

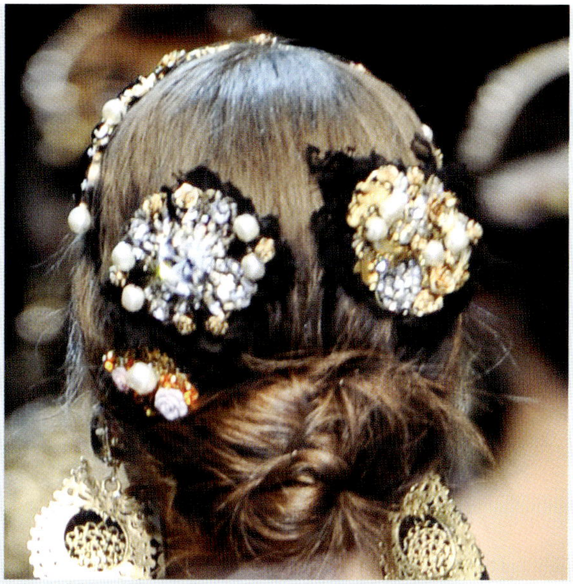
Dolce & Gabbana

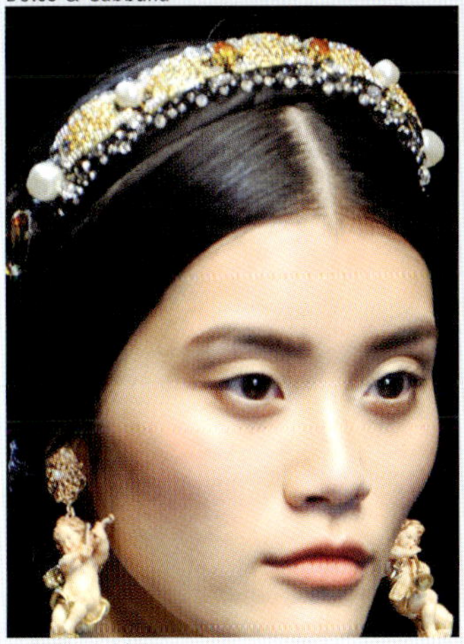
Dolce & Gabbana

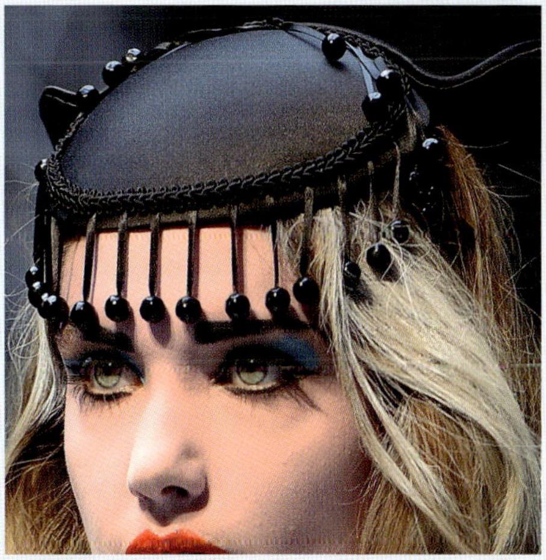
Vivienne Westwood Red Label

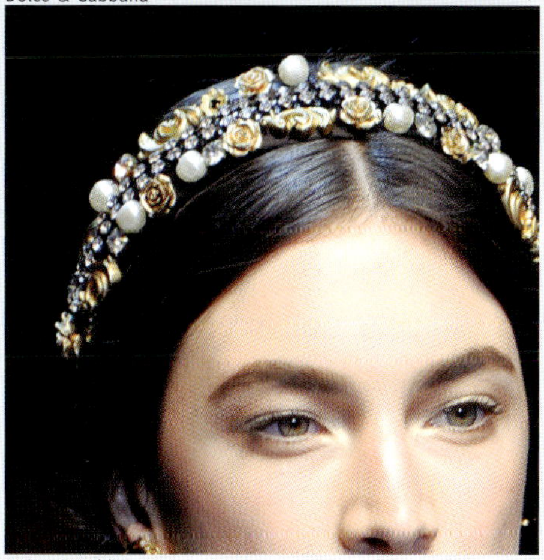
Dolce & Gabbana

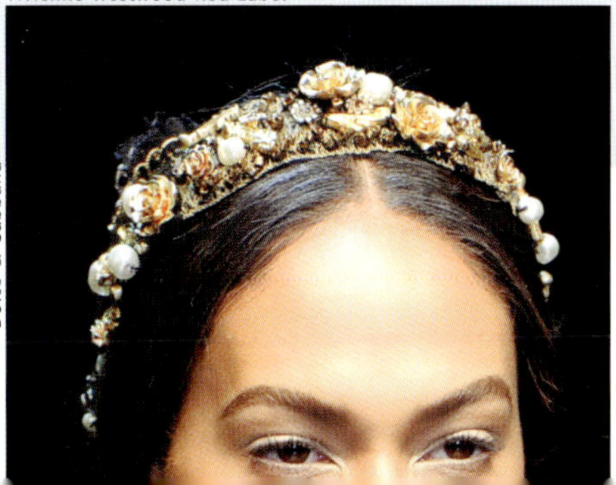
Dolce & Gabbana

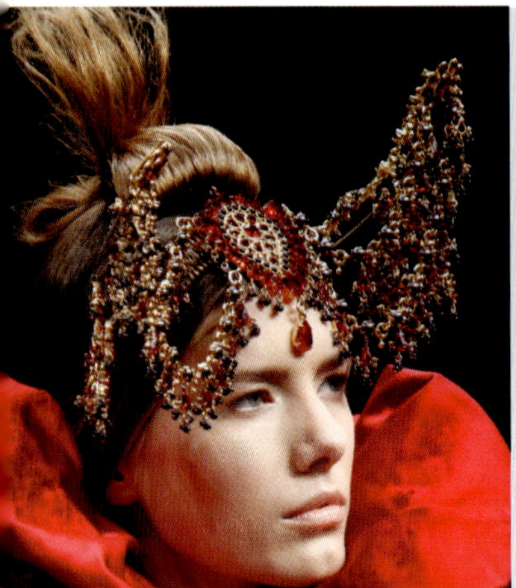
Alexander McQueen

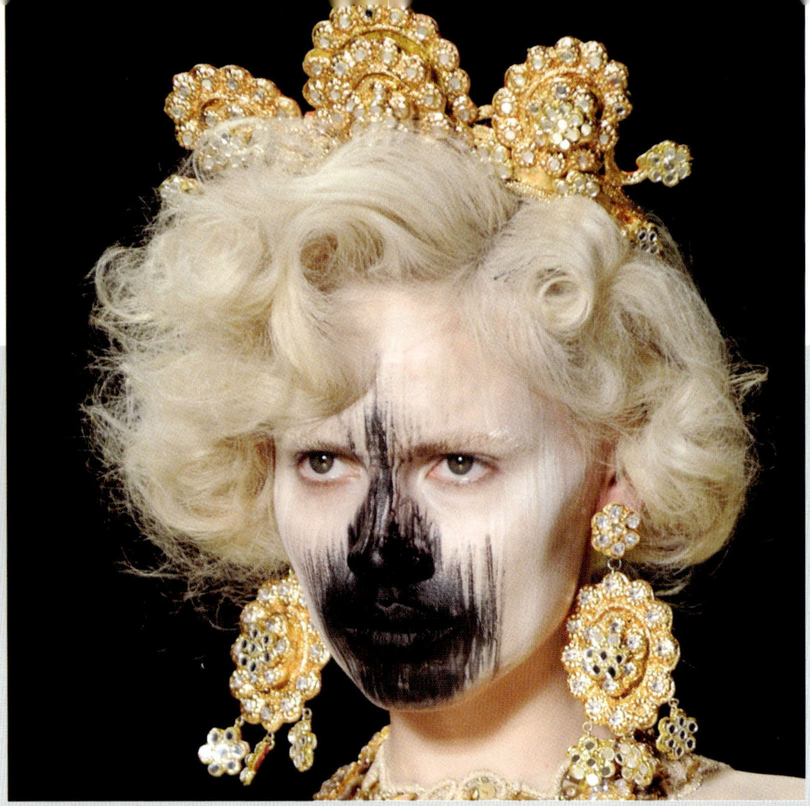
Vivienne Westwood

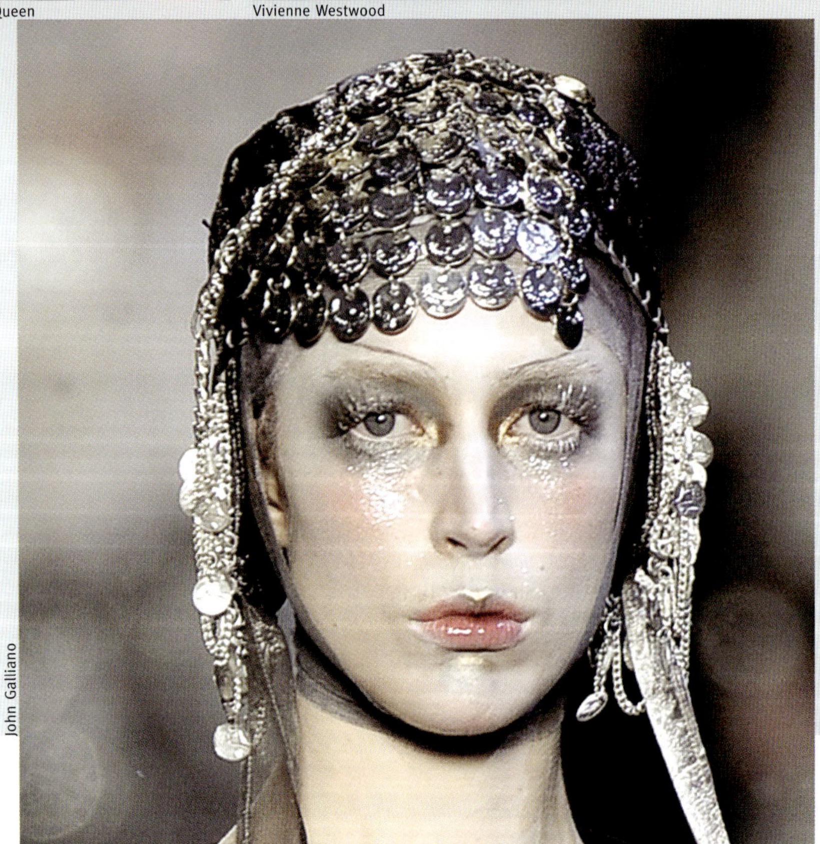
John Galliano

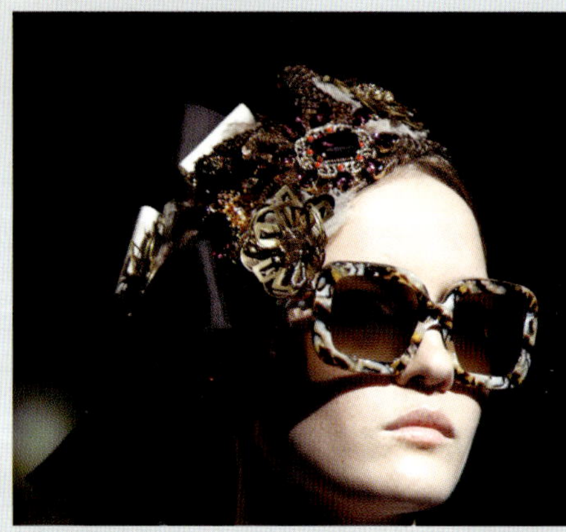
Dolce & Gabbana

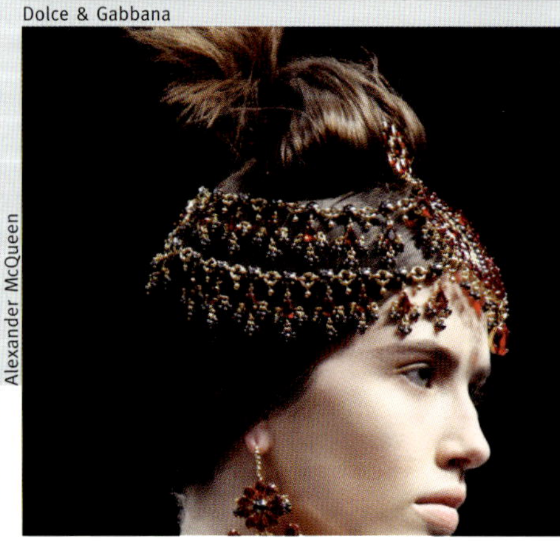
Alexander McQueen

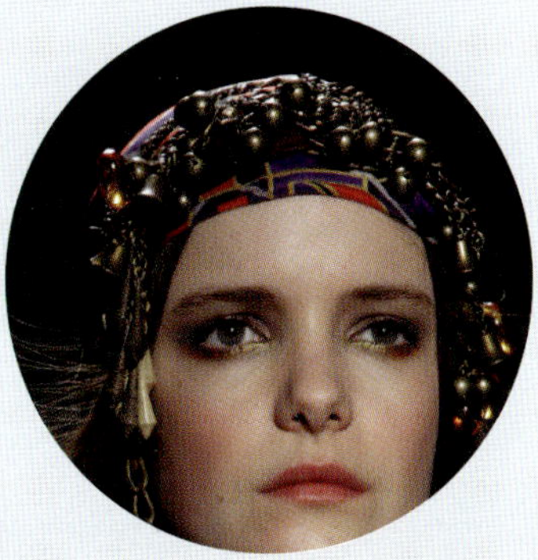
Alexandre Herchcovitch

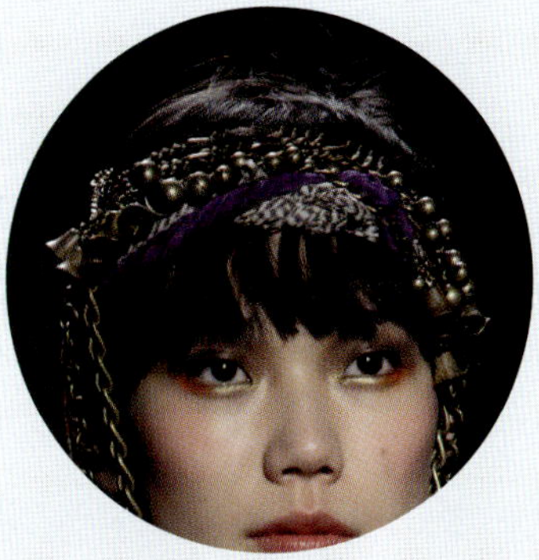
Alexandre Herchcovitch

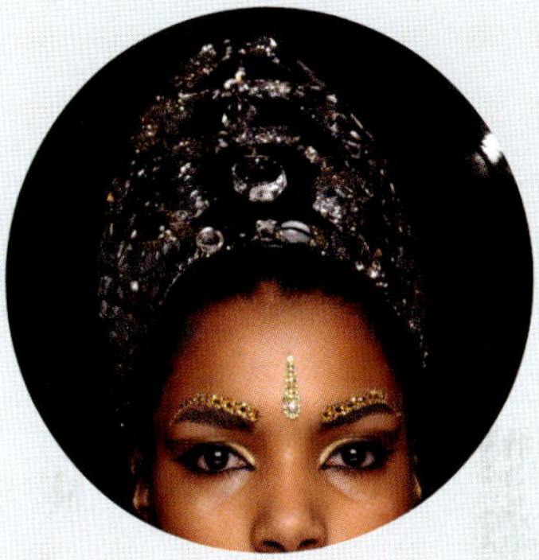
Zandra Rhodes

Comme des Garçons

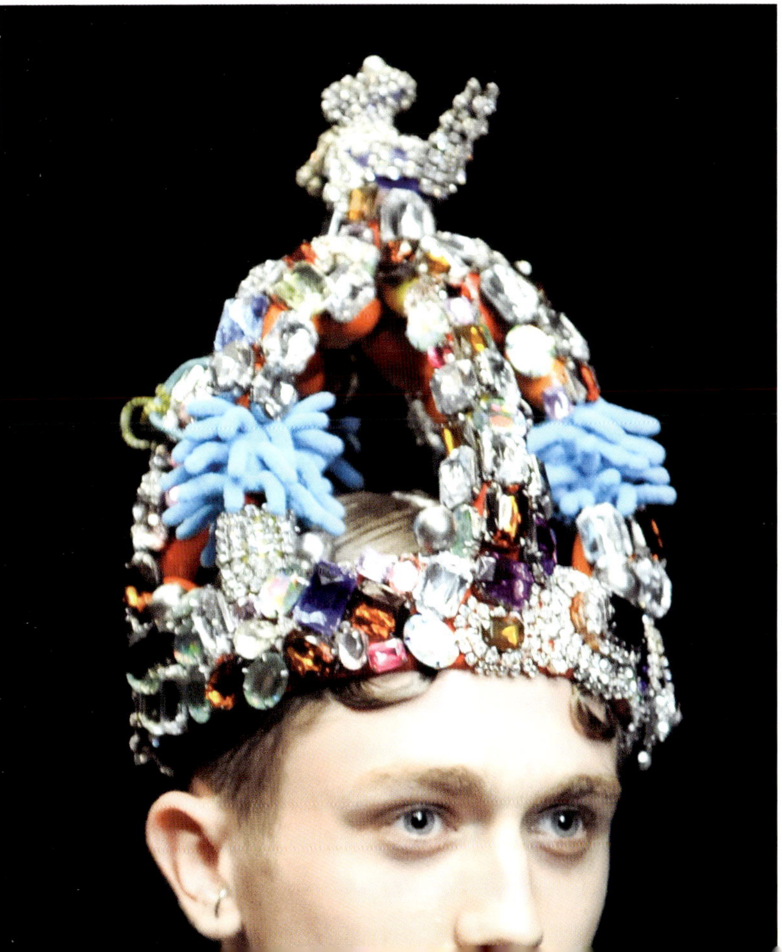

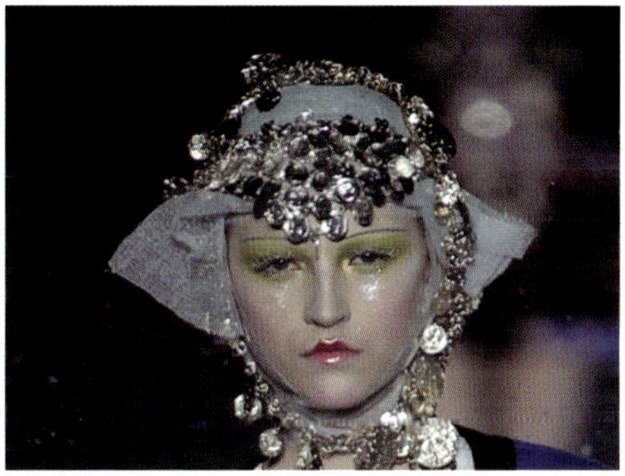
John Galliano

Alexander McQueen

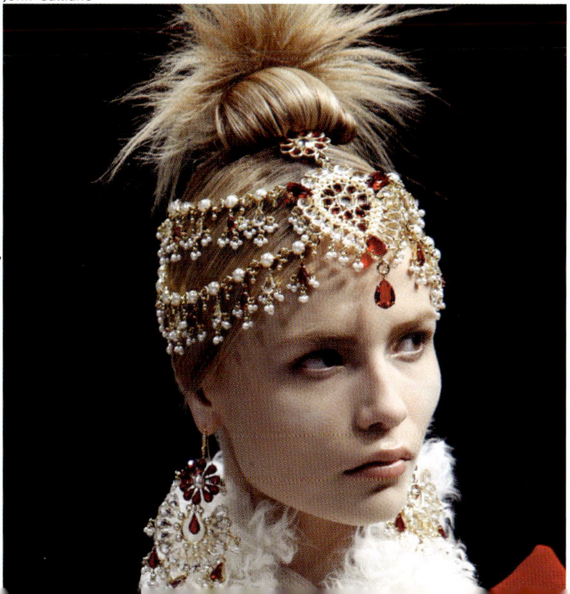

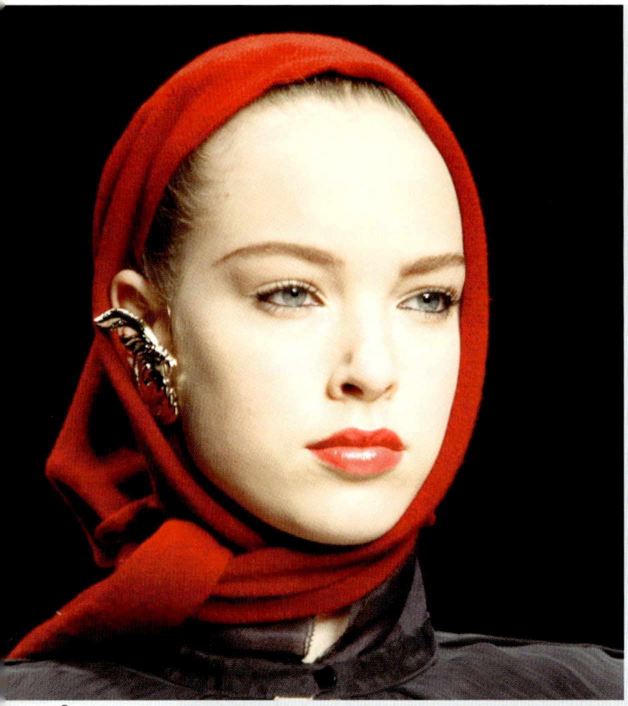

Sportmax

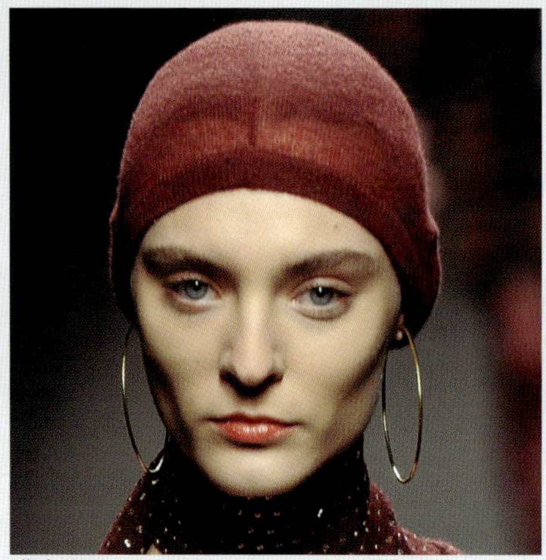

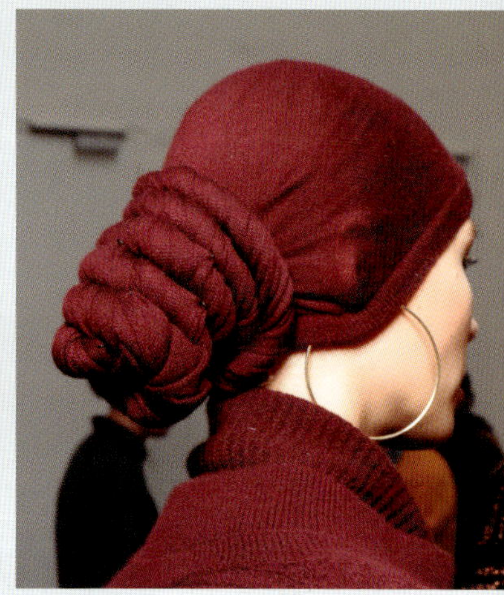

Allude

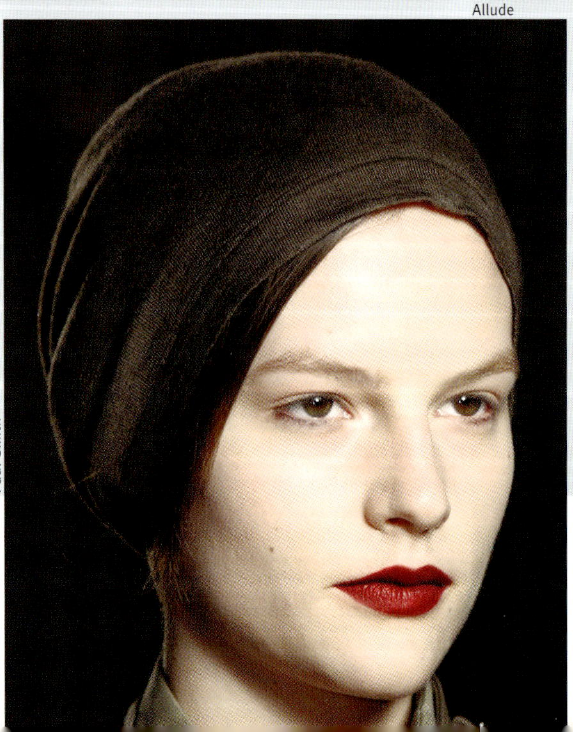

Paul Smith

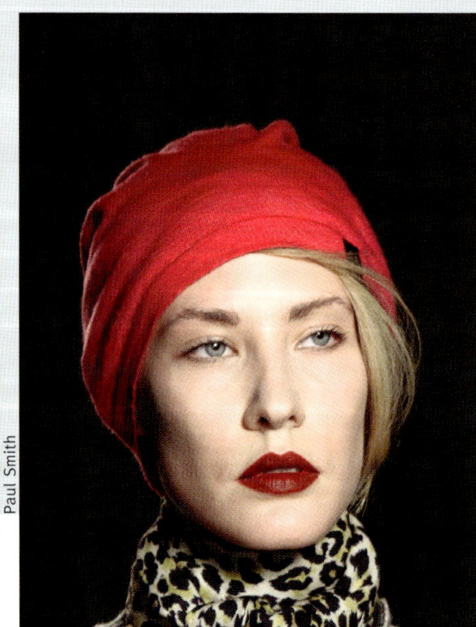

Paul Smith

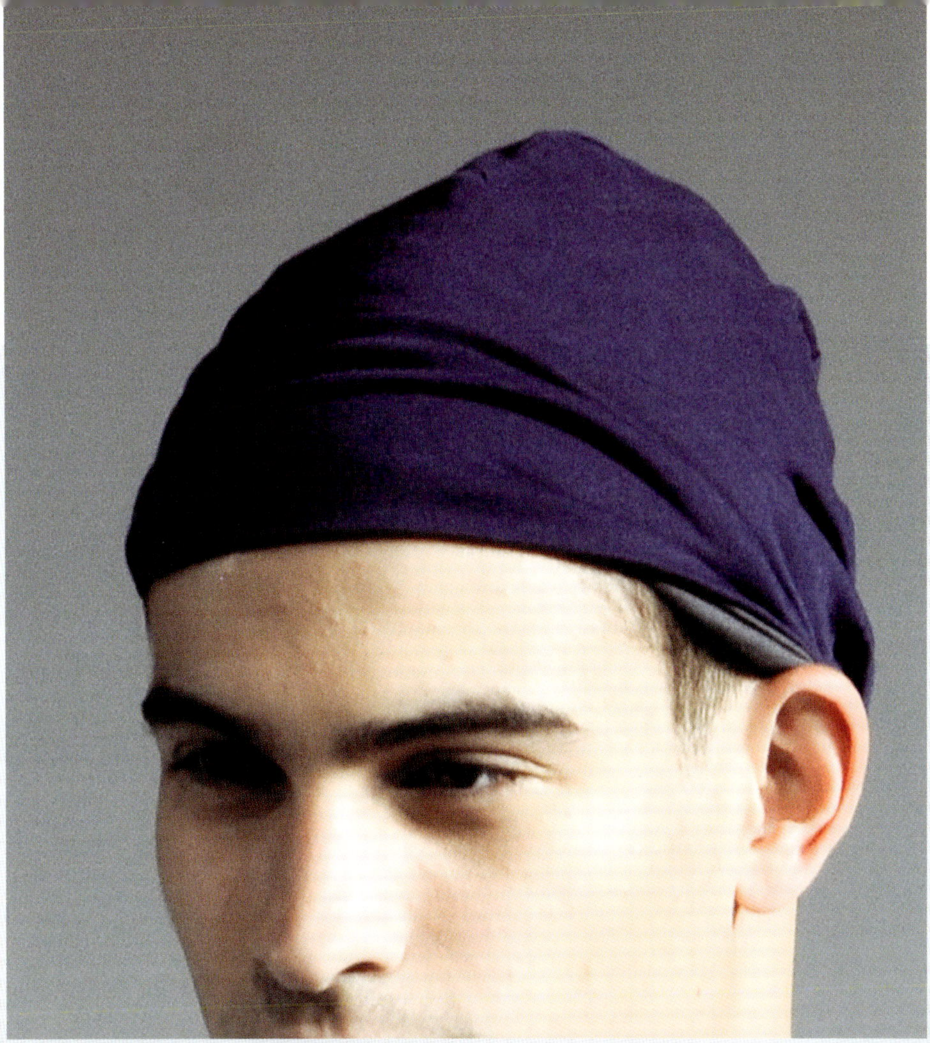

Agnès B.

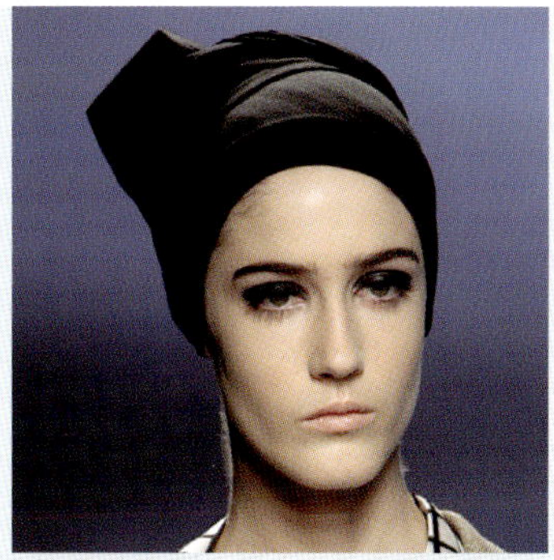

Dries Van Noten

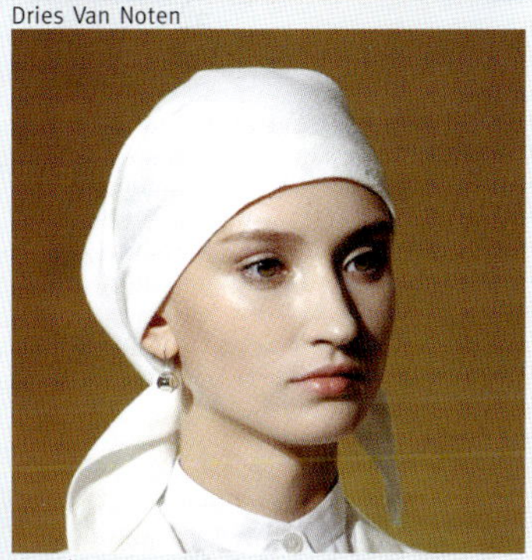

Hermès

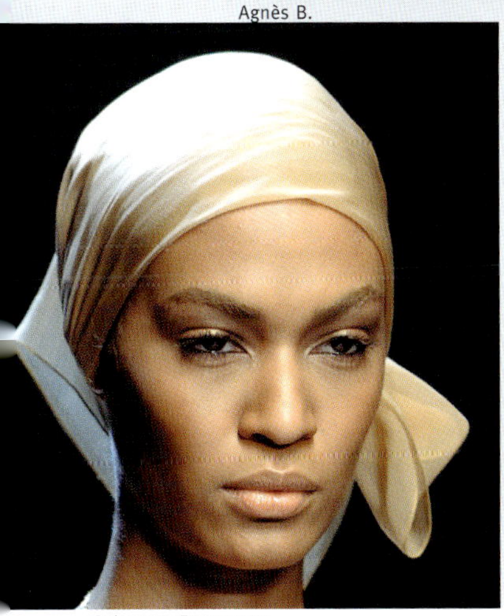

Salvatore Ferragamo

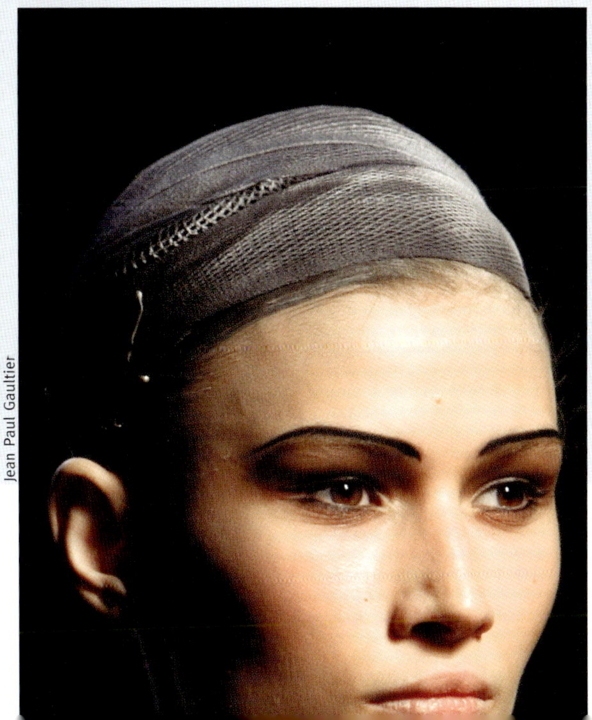

Jean Paul Gaultier

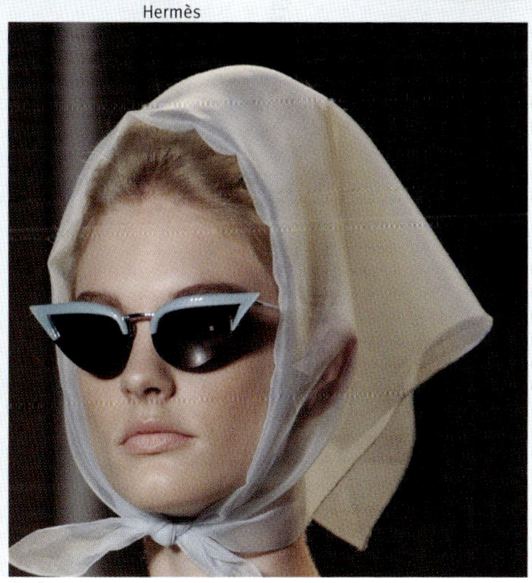

Rochas

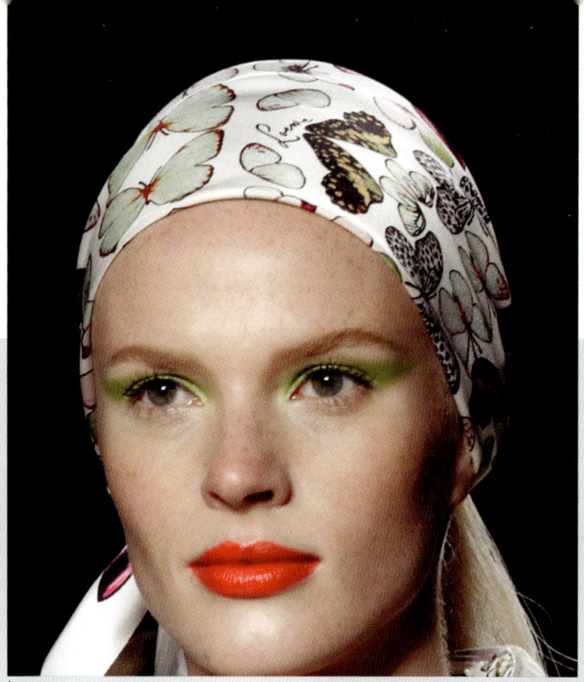
Loewe

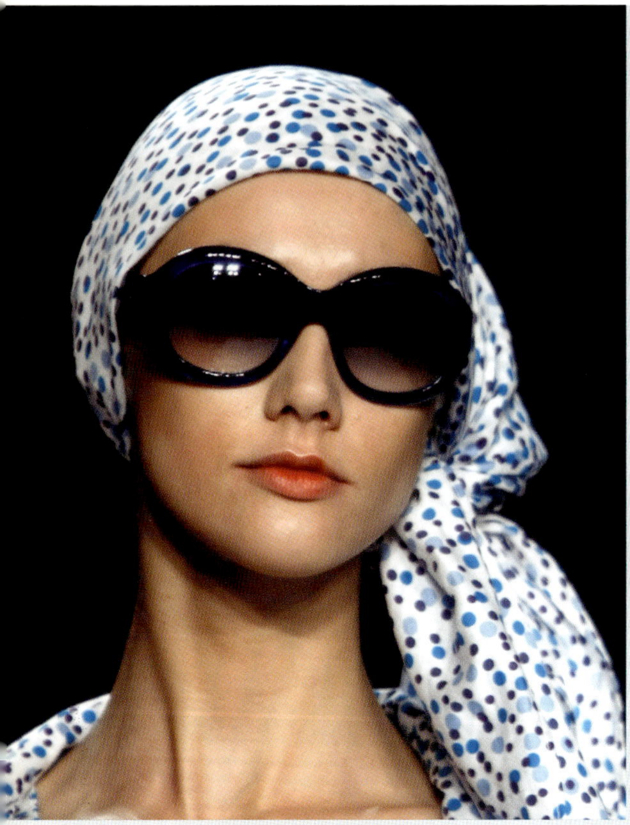
Lacoste

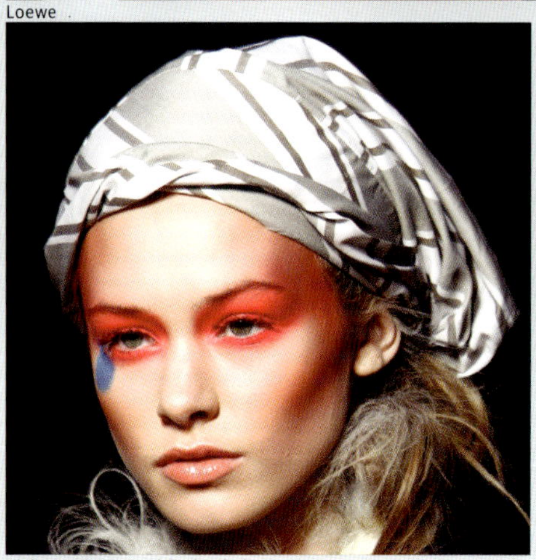
Vivienne Westwood Red Label

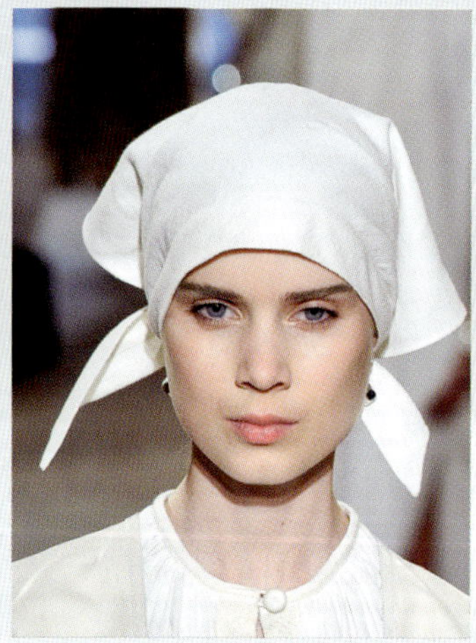
Hermès

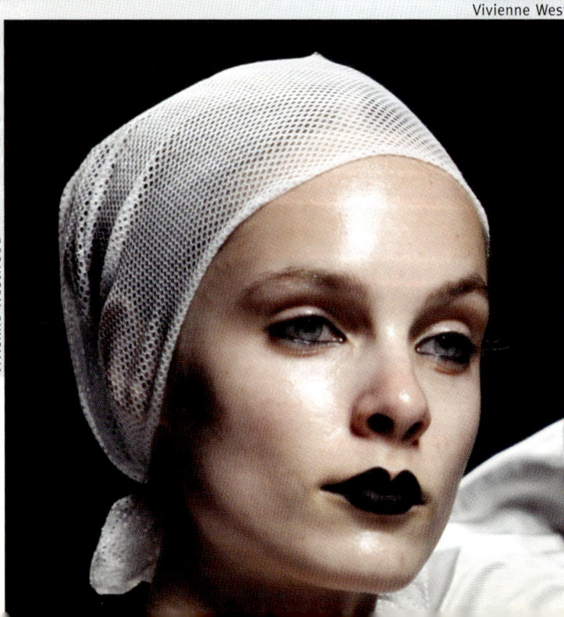
Vivienne Westwood

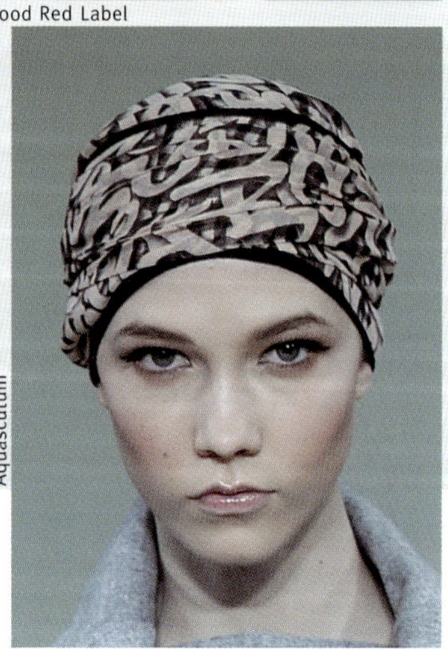
Aquascutum

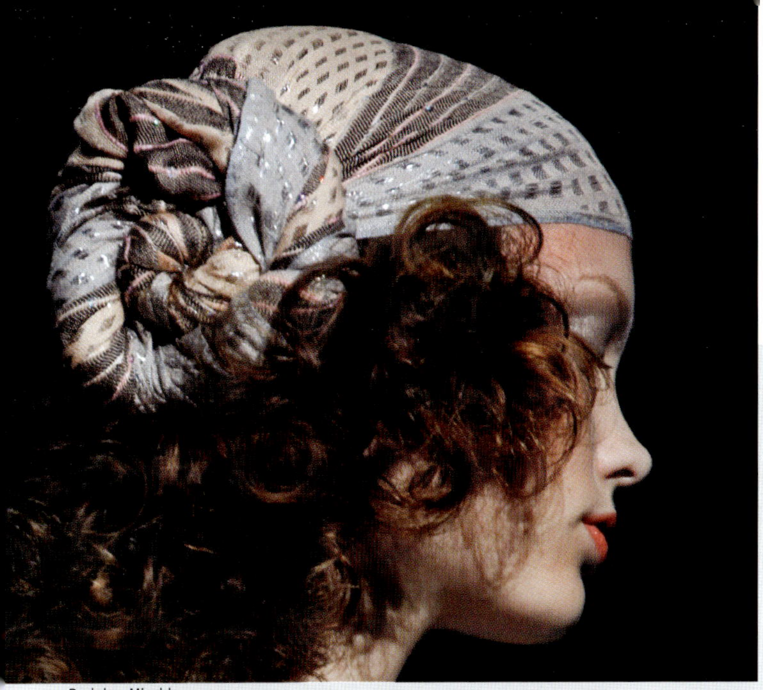
Badgley Mischka

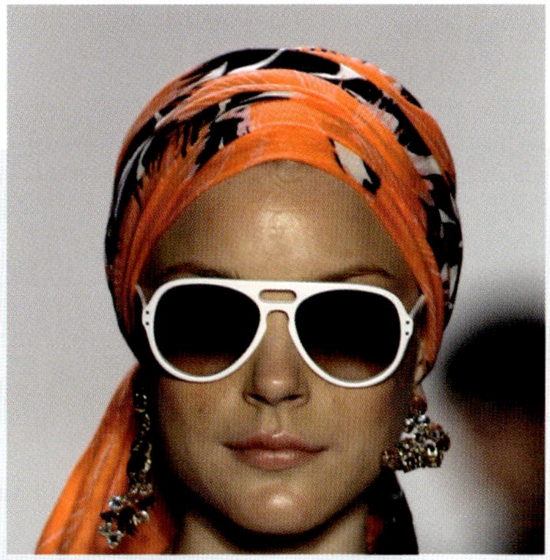
Diane Von Furstenberg

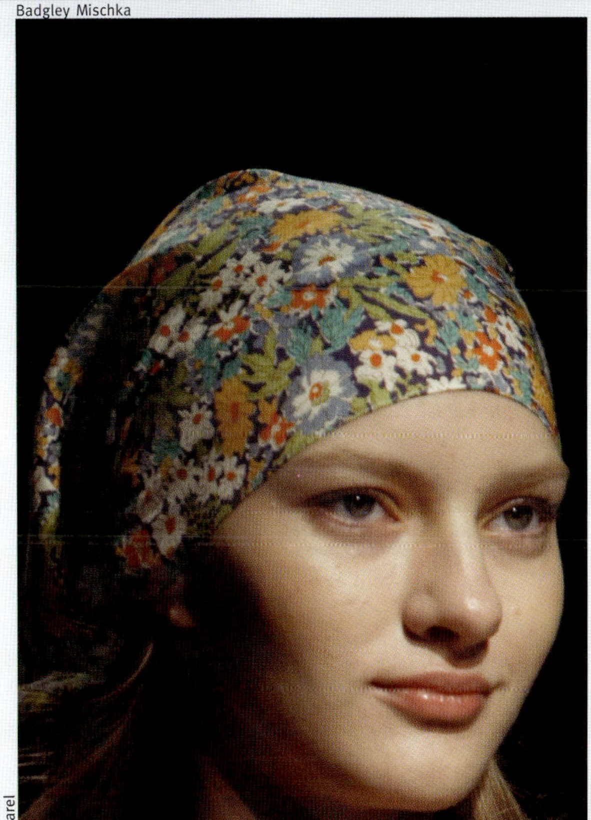
Cacharel

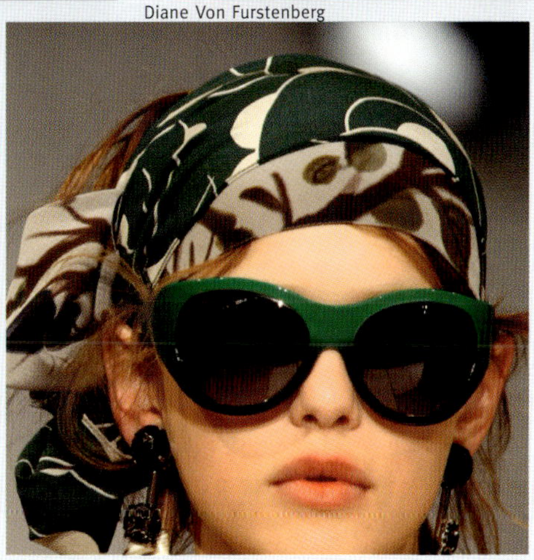
Marni

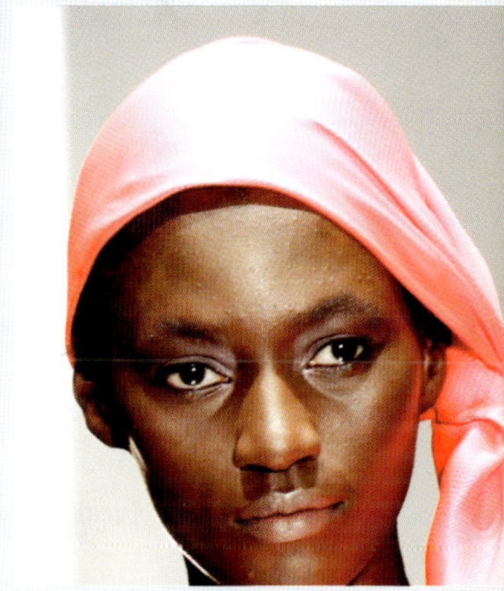
Roksanda Ilincic

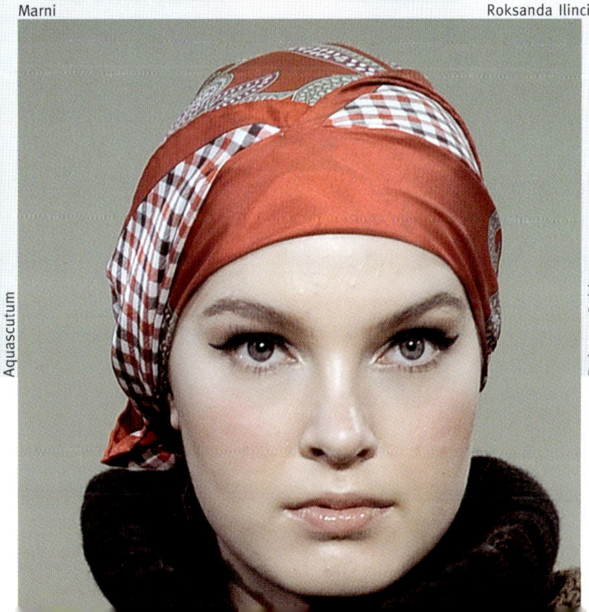
Aquascutum

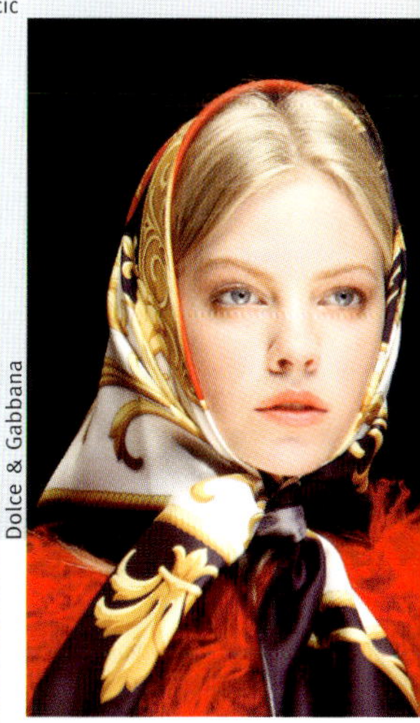
Dolce & Gabbana

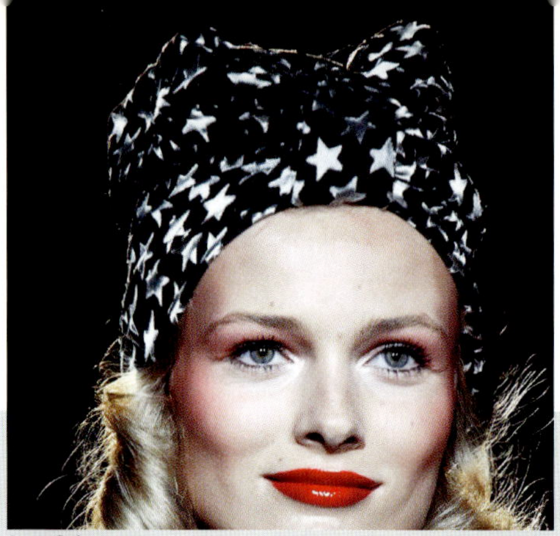

Anna Sui

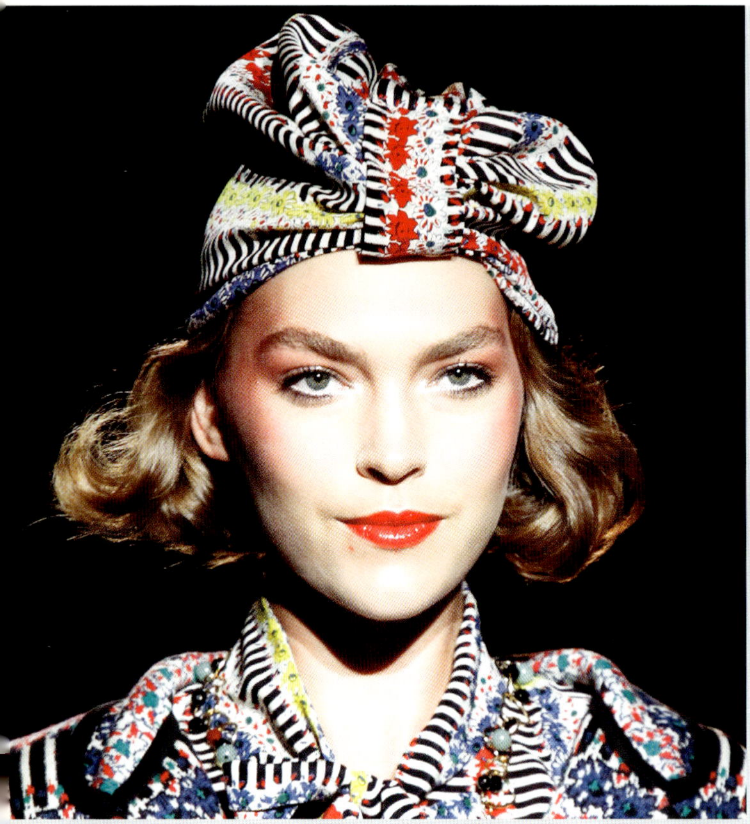

Anna Sui

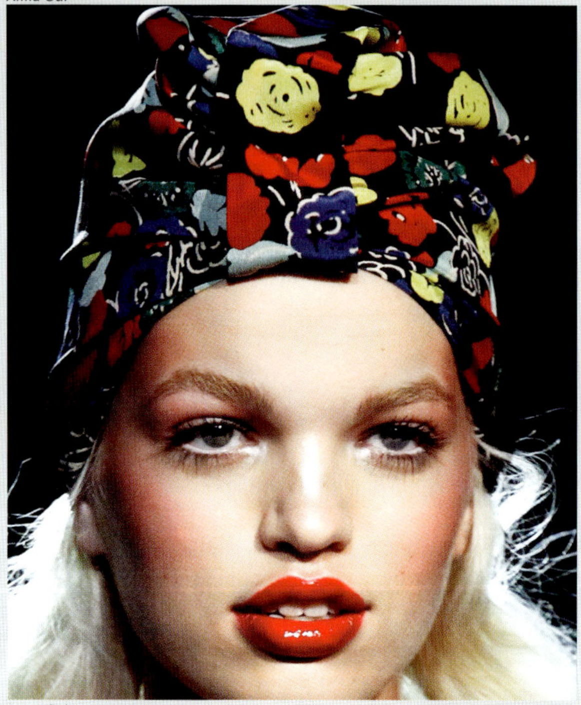

Anna Sui

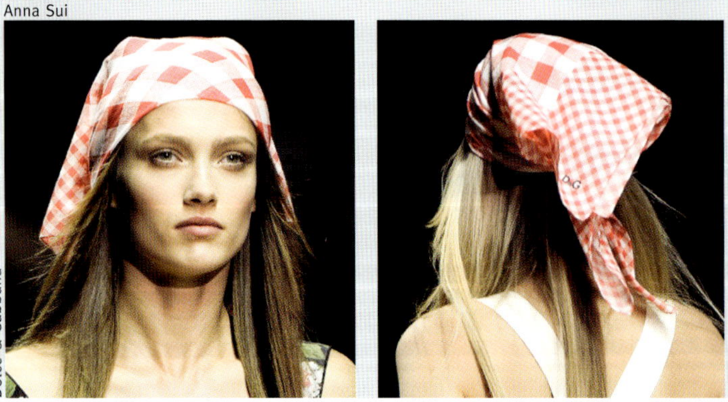

Dolce & Gabbana

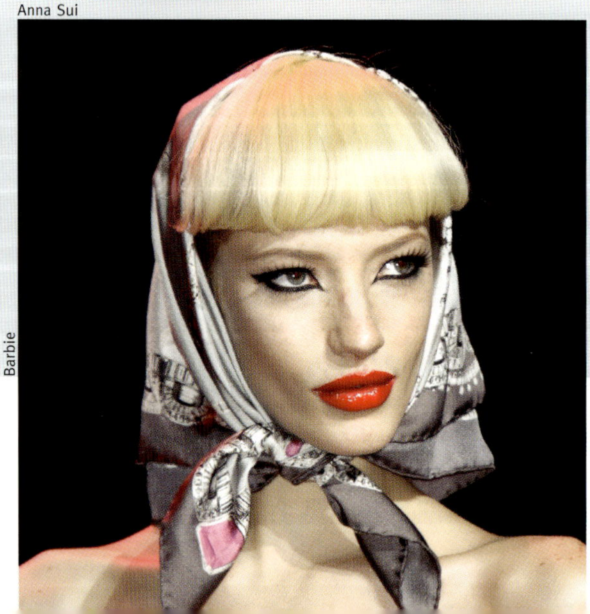

Barbie

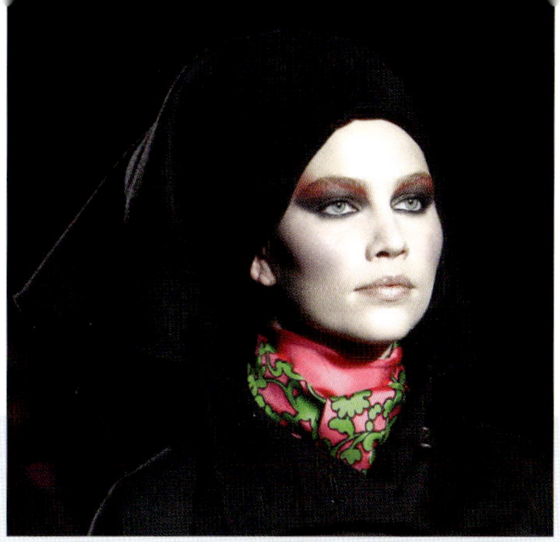

Marc Jacobs

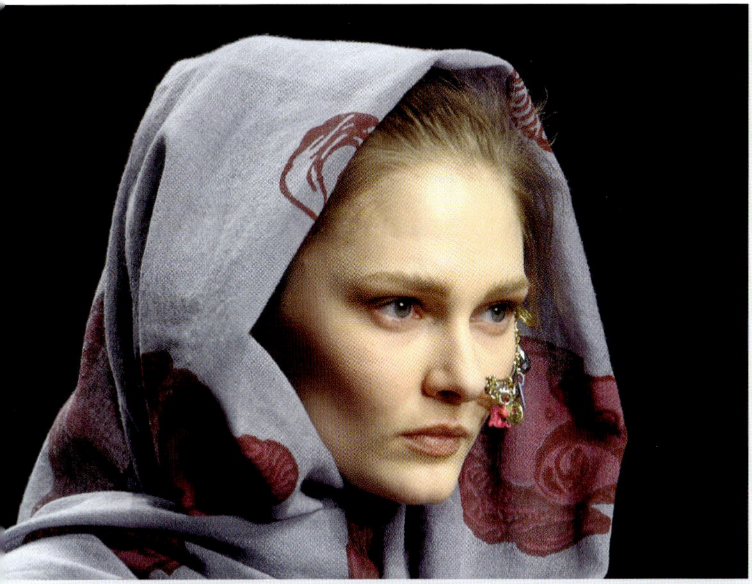

Ashish

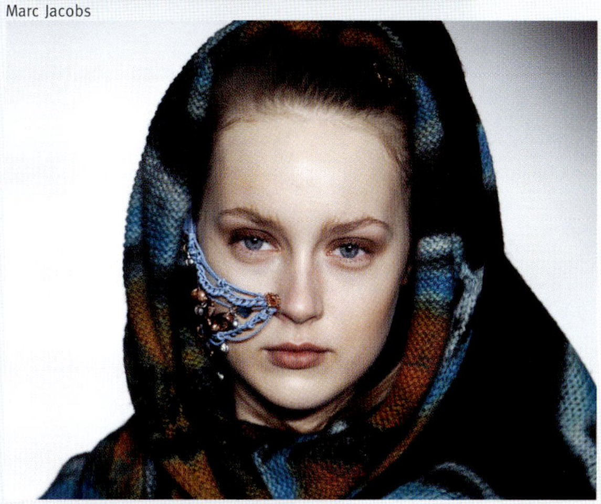

Ashish

Issa

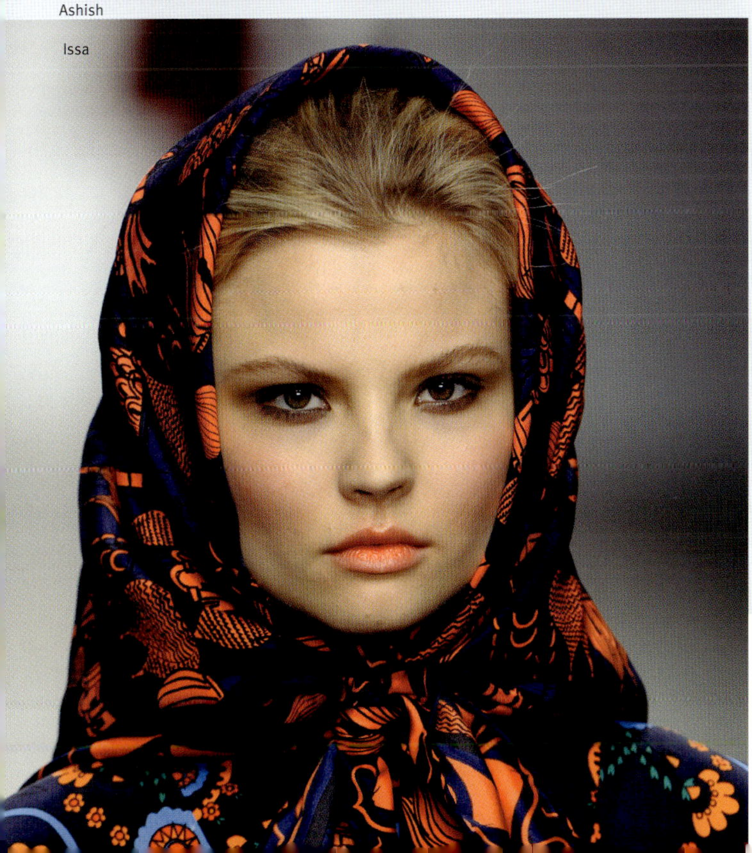

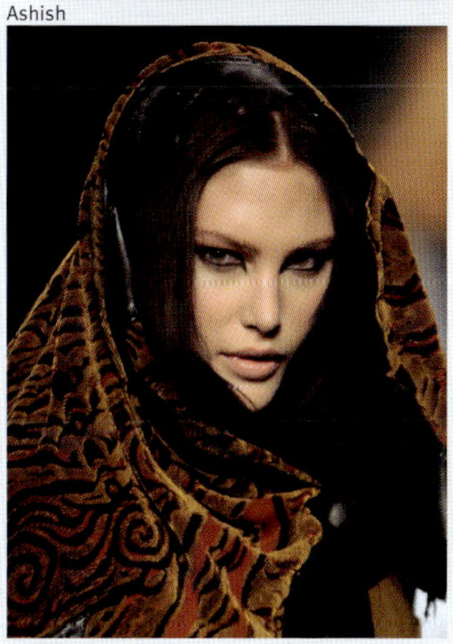

Jean Paul Gaultier

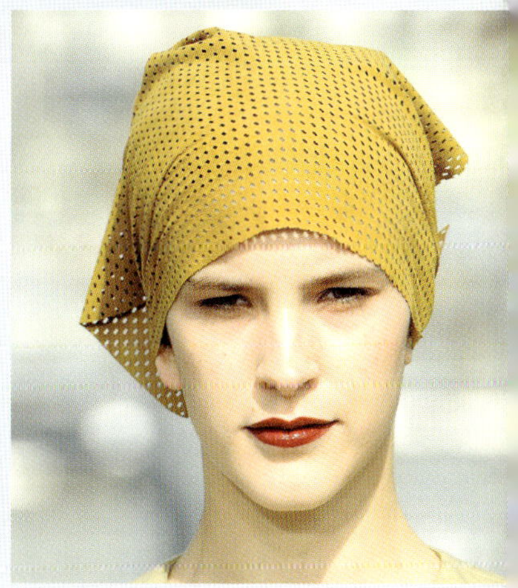

Christophe Lemaire

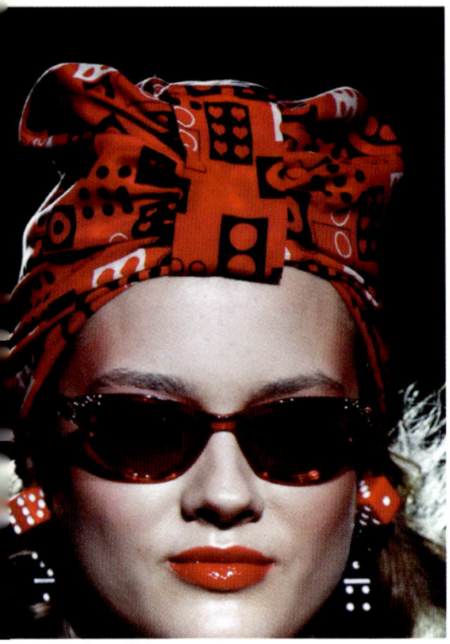

Anna Sui

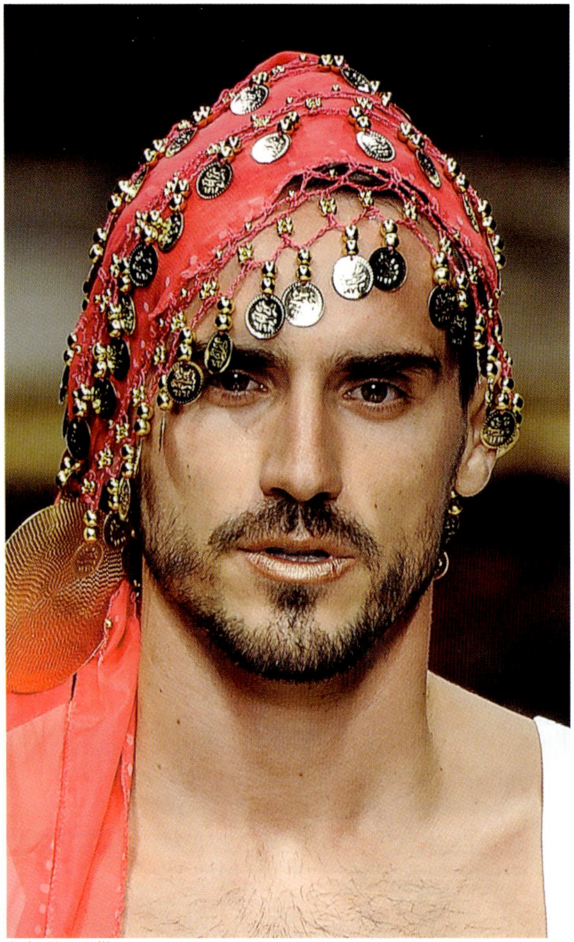

Carlo Pignatelli

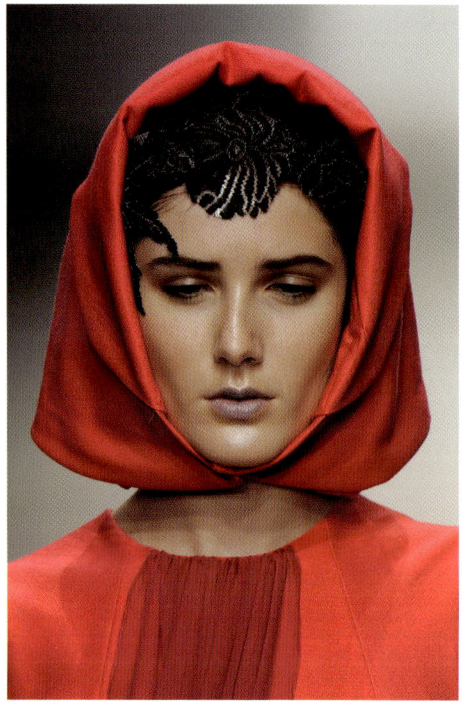

Bora Aksu

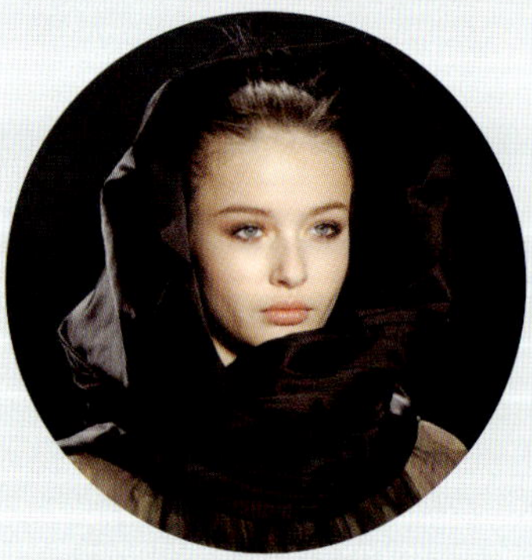

Carlos Miele

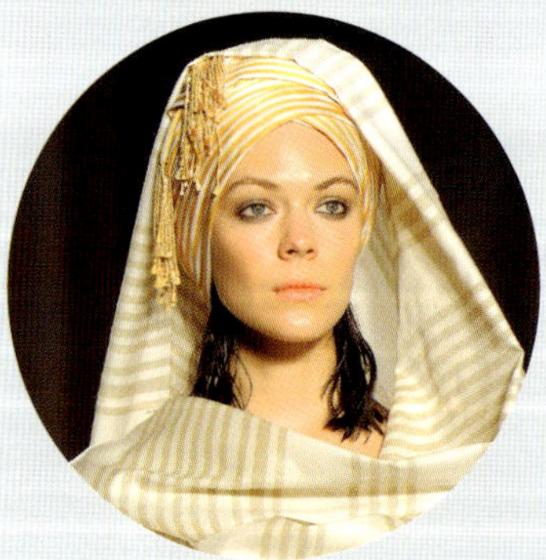

Paul Smith

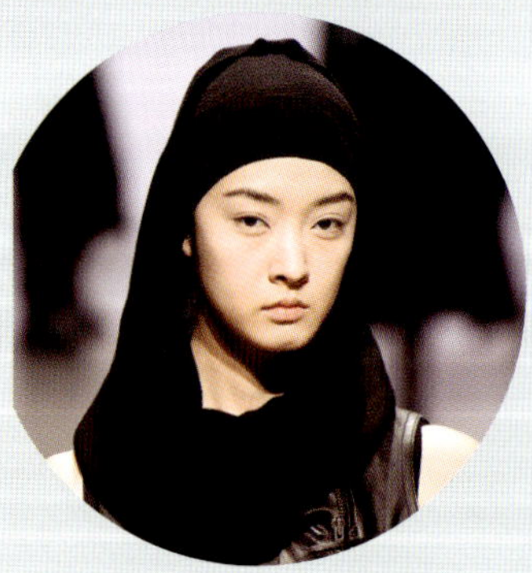

Peachoo + Krejberg

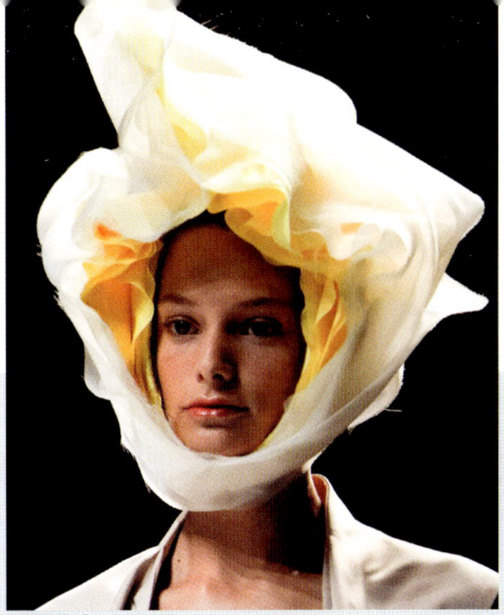

Issey Miyake

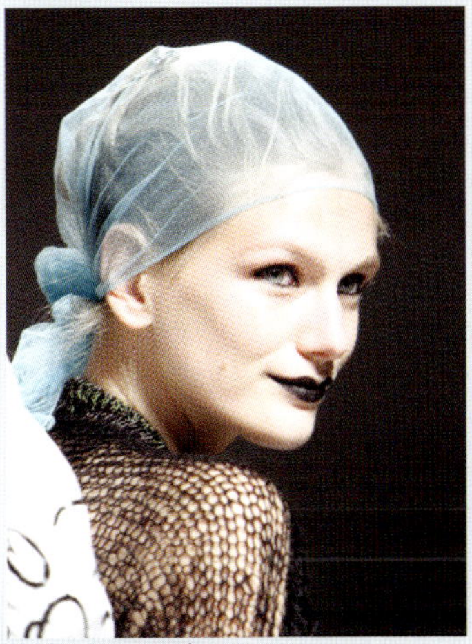

Vivienne Westwood

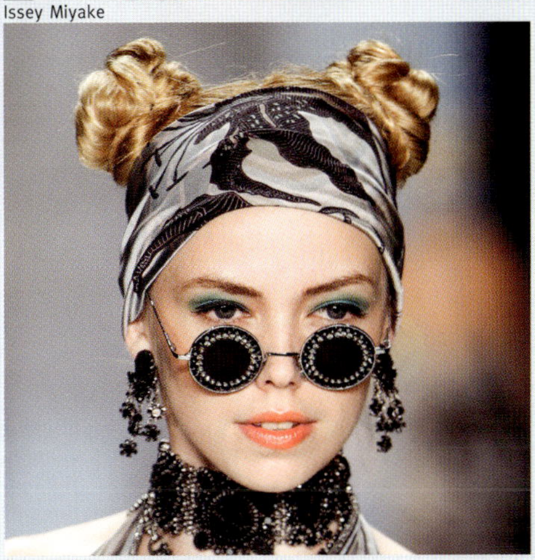

Miranda Konstantinidou

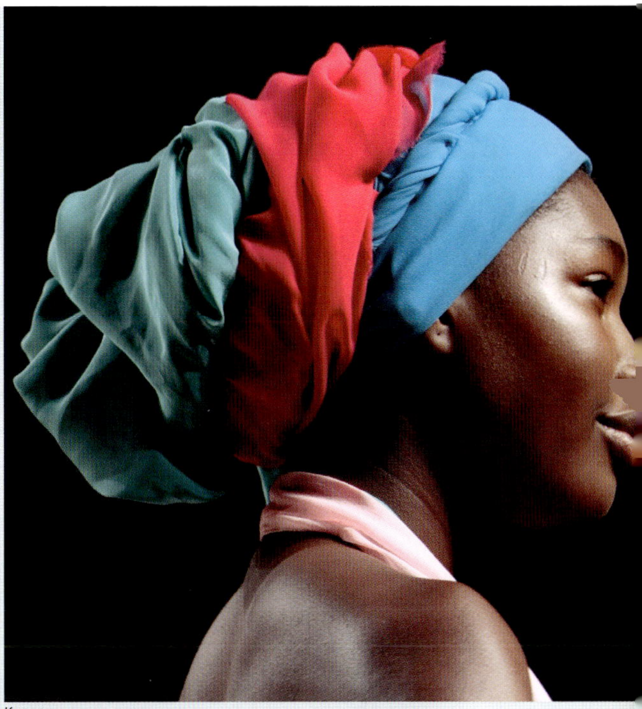

Kenzo

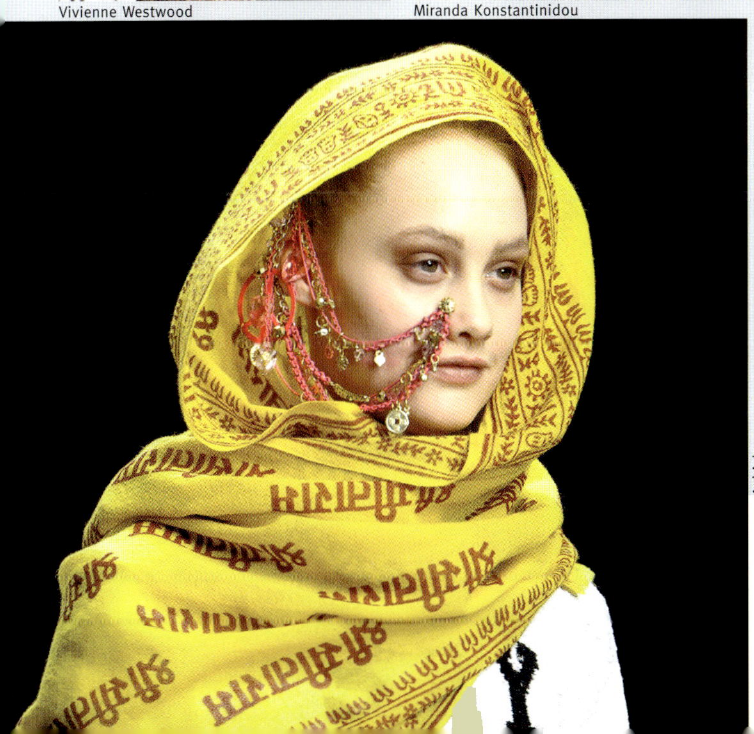

Ashish

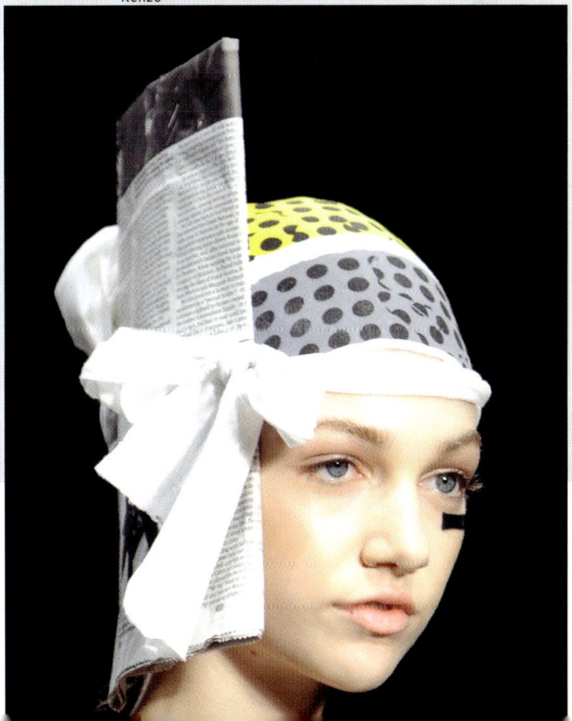

Danielle Scutt

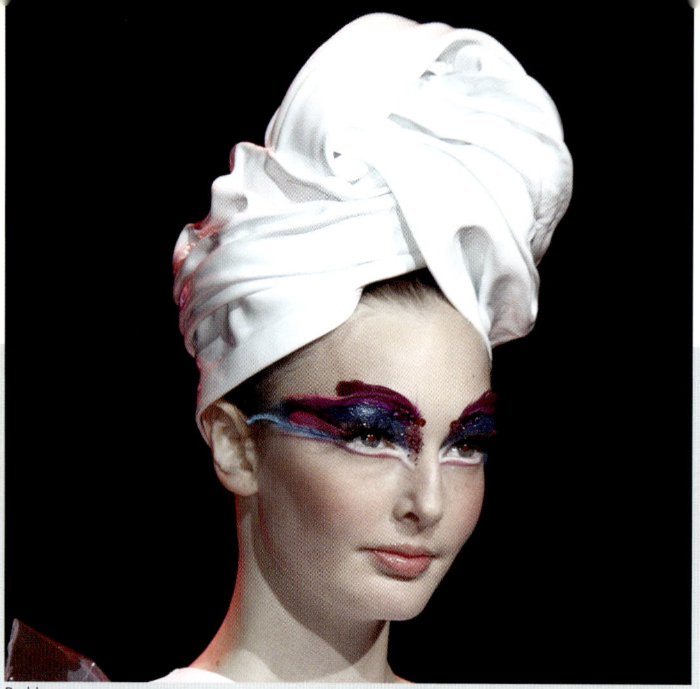

Barbie

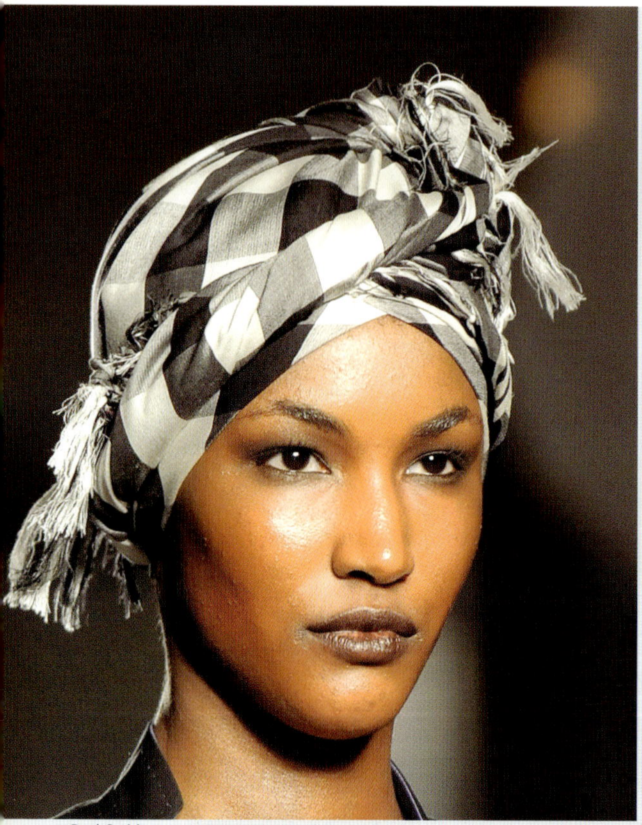

Paul Smith

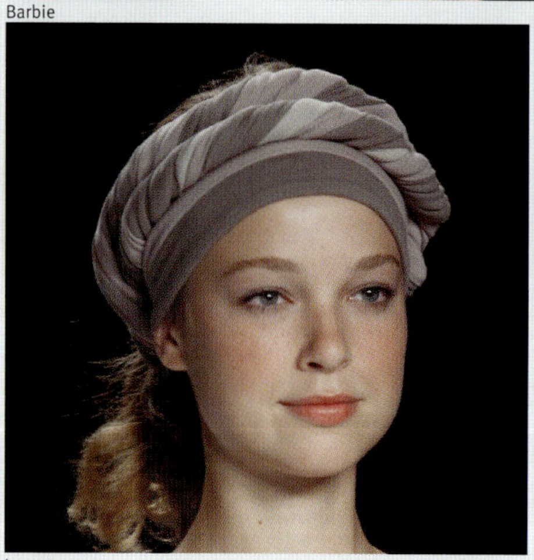

Lacoste

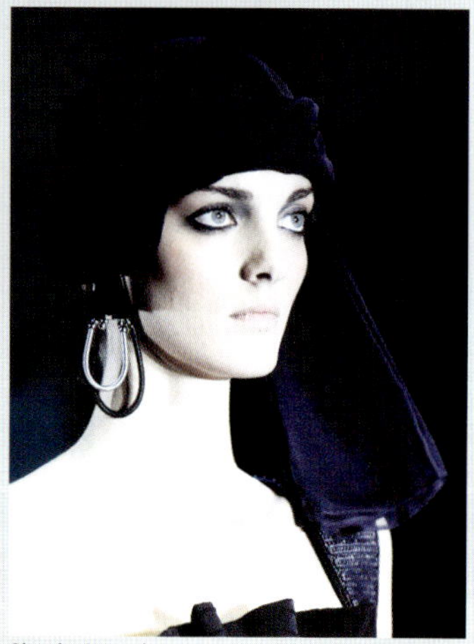

Giorgio Armani

Ralph Lauren

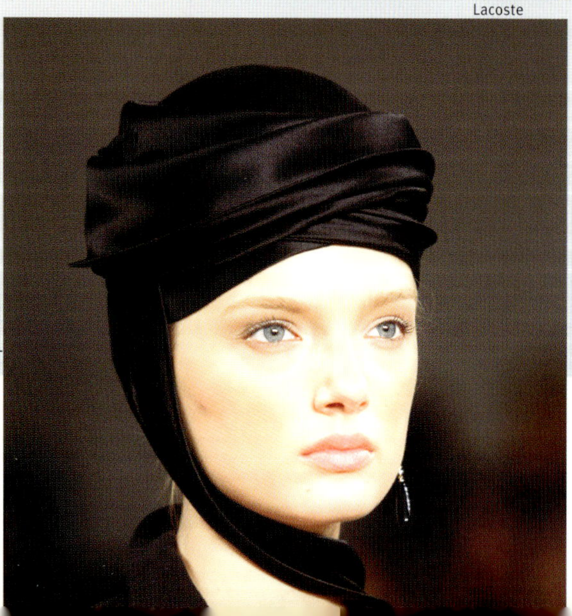

Ralph Lauren

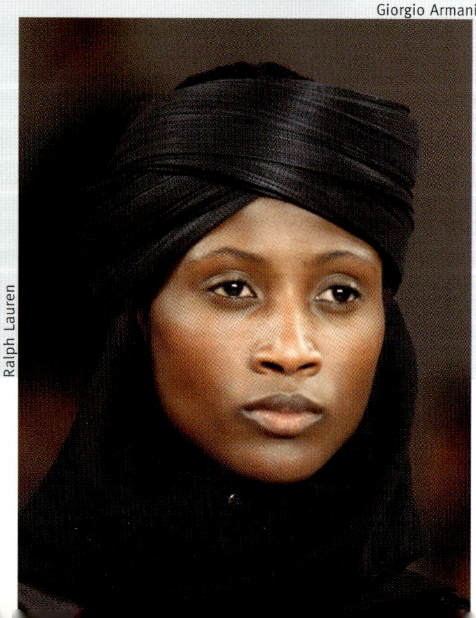

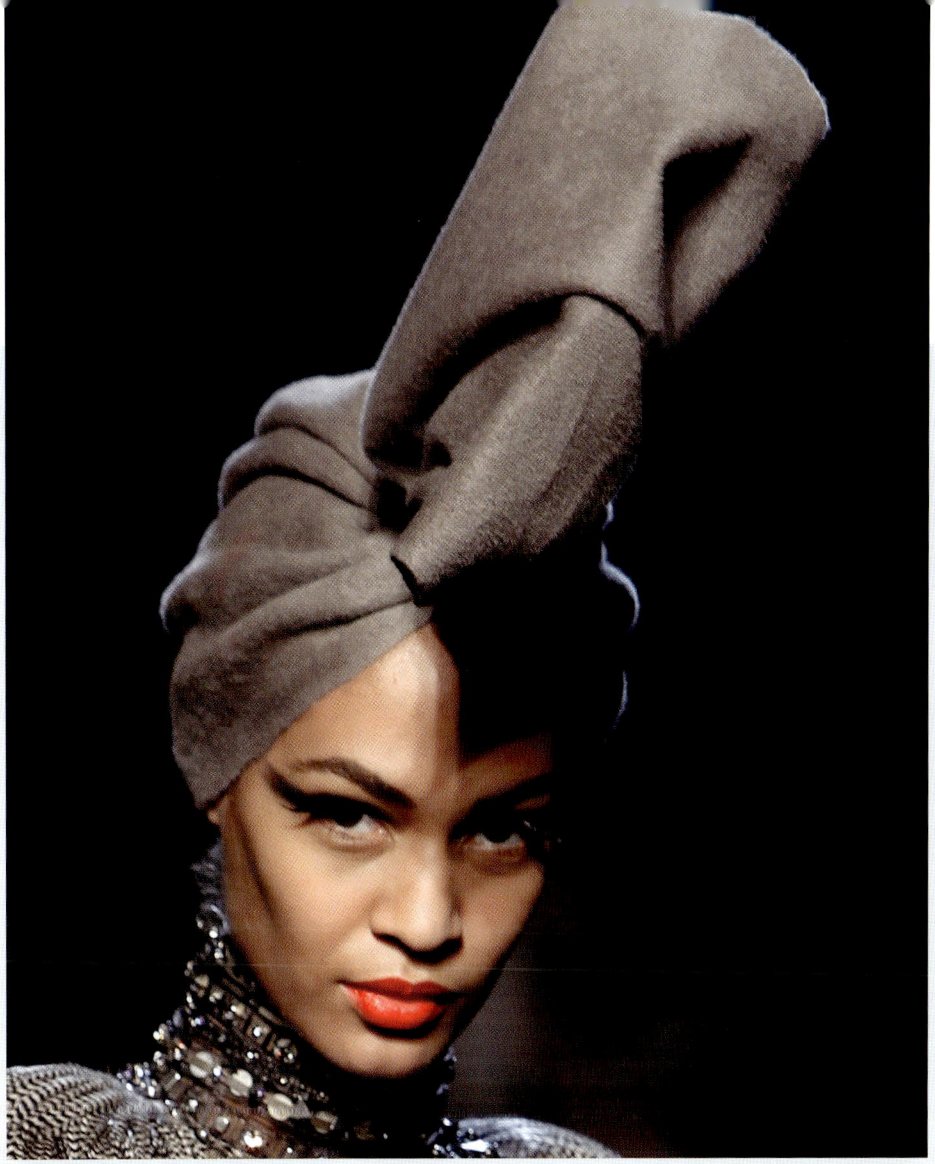

Jean Paul Gaultier

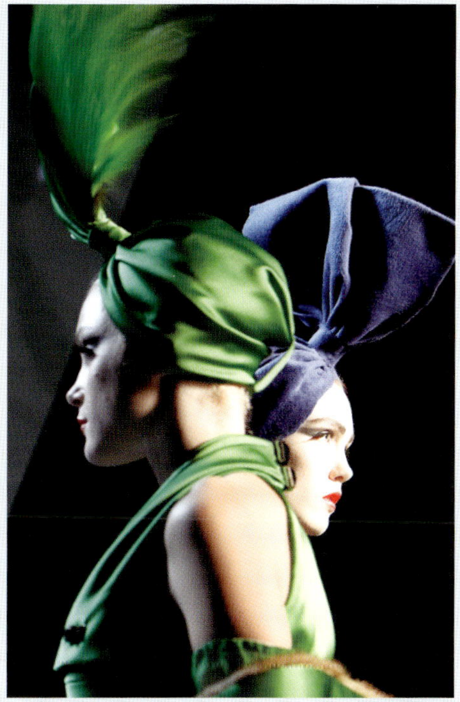

Jean Paul Gaultier

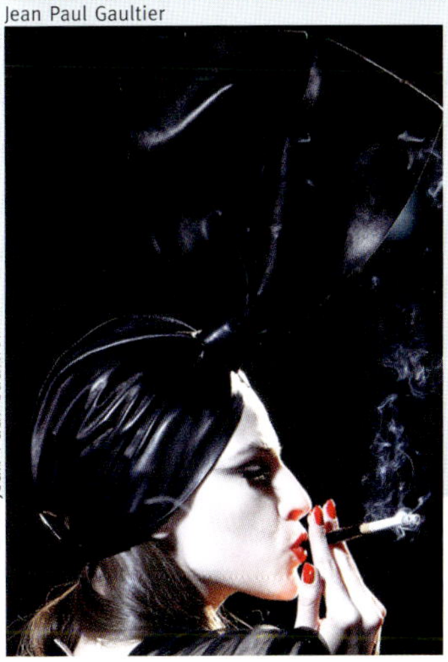

Jean Paul Gaultier

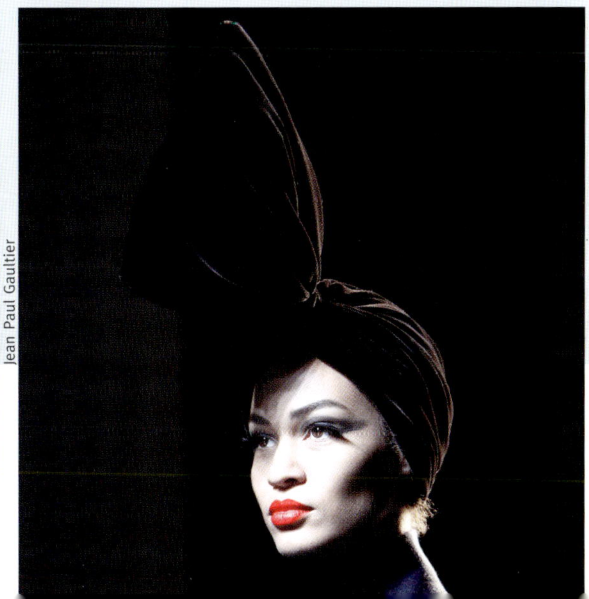

Jean Paul Gaultier

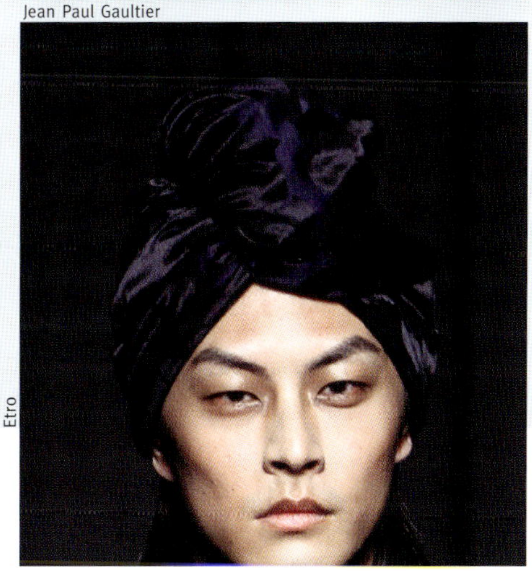

Etro

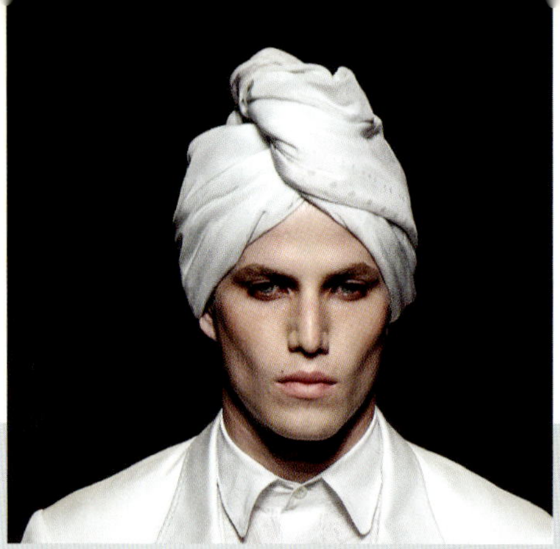

Etro

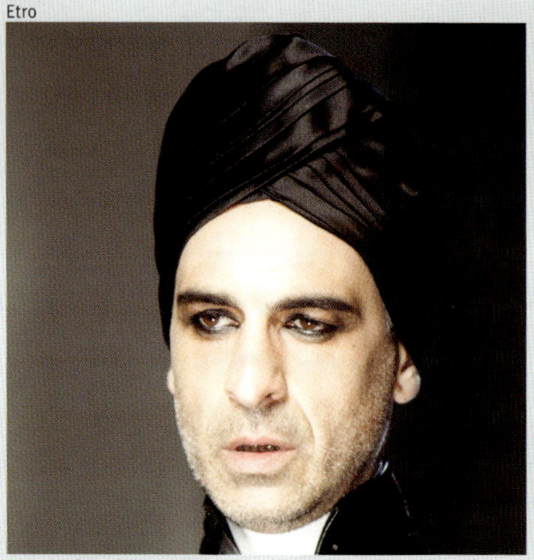

Jean Paul Gaultier

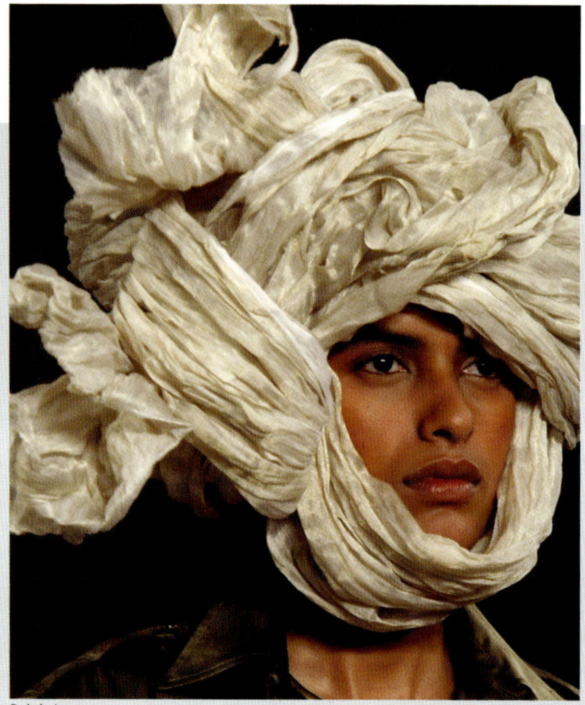

Ralph Lauren

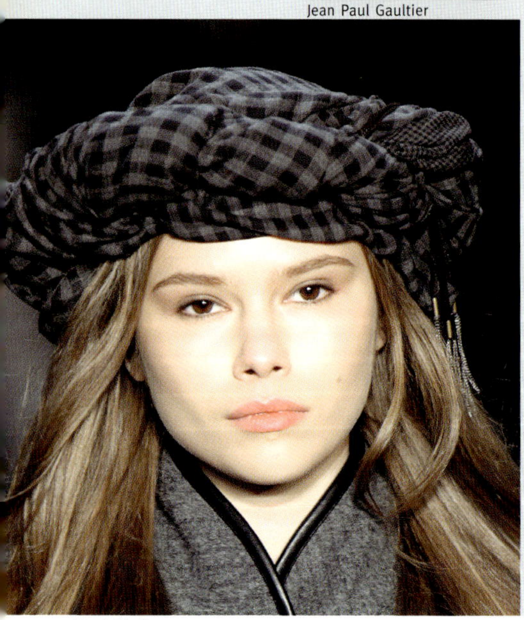

Charlotte Ronson

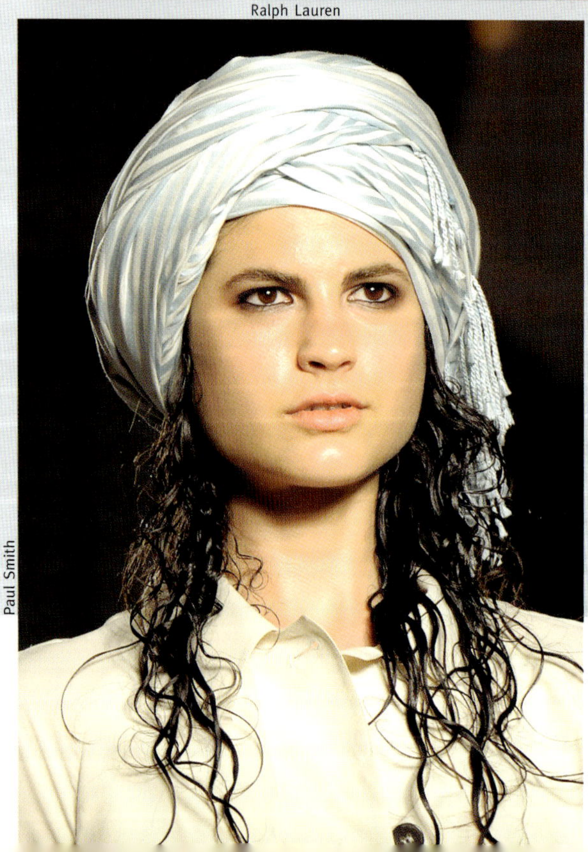

Paul Smith

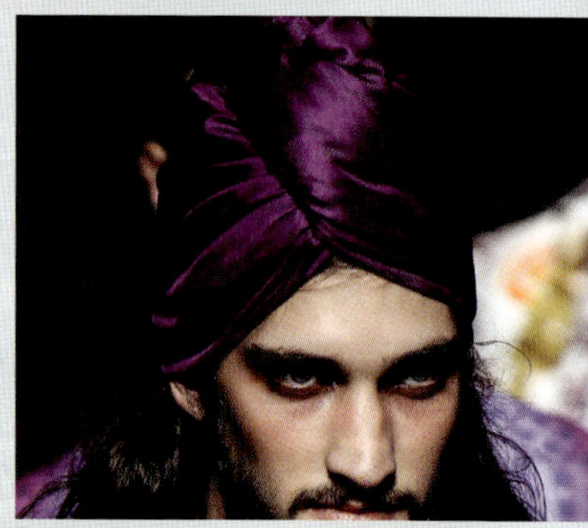

Etro

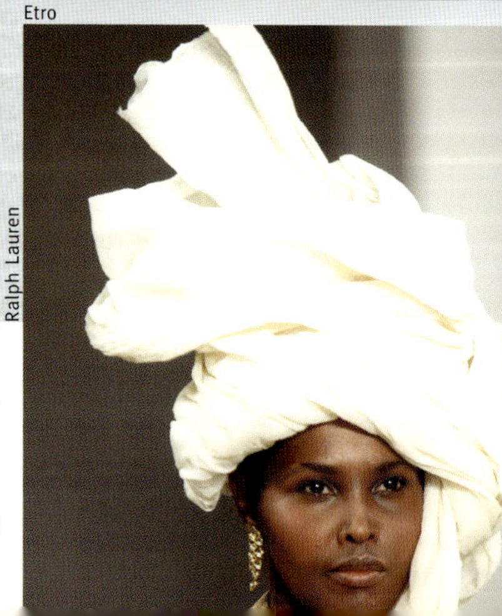

Ralph Lauren

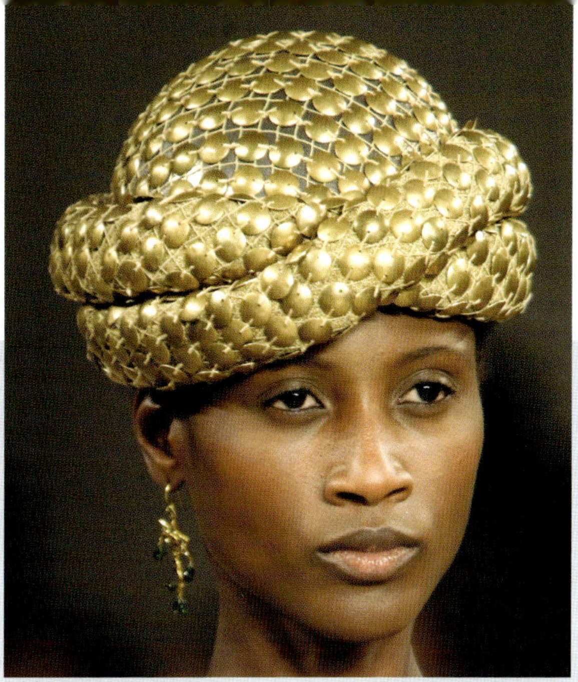
Ralph Lauren

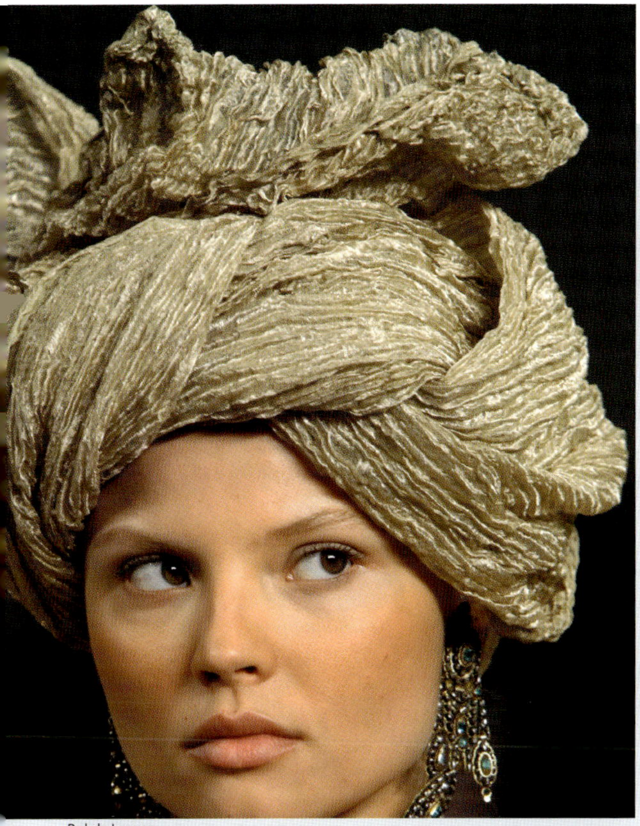
Ralph Lauren

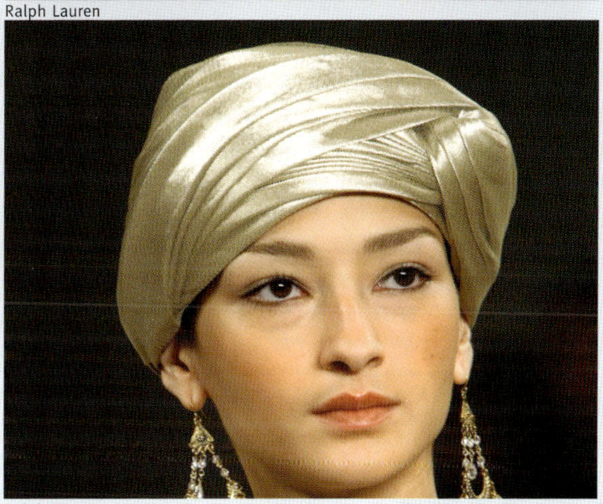
Ralph Lauren

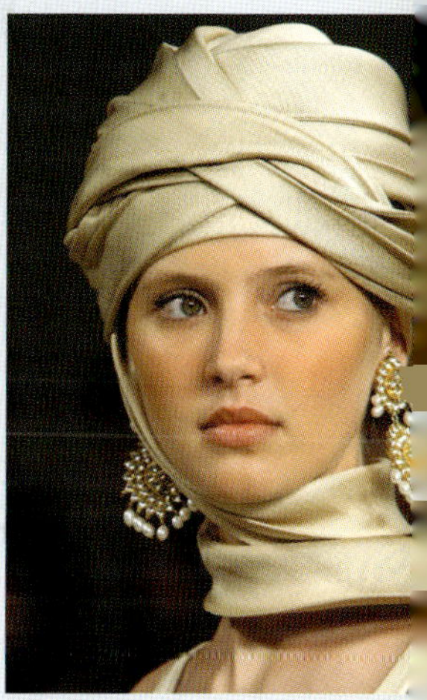
Ralph Lauren

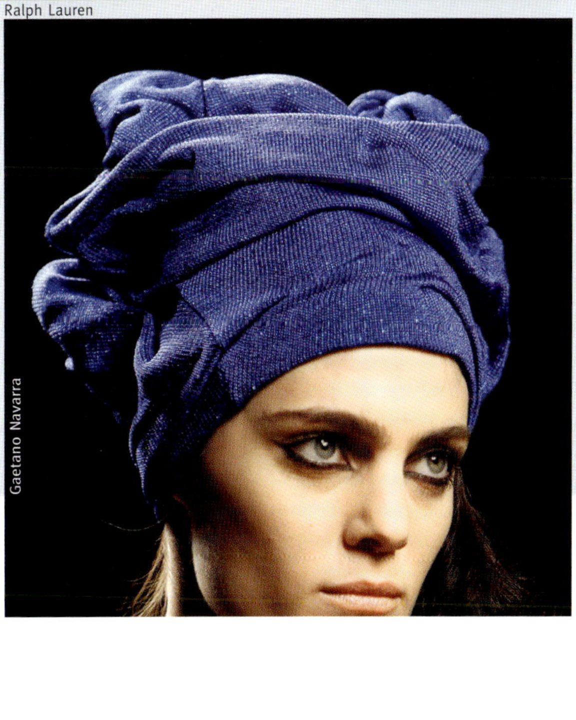
Gaetano Navarra

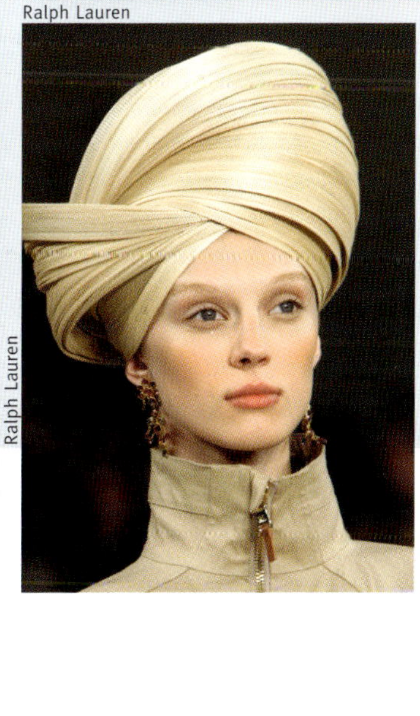
Ralph Lauren

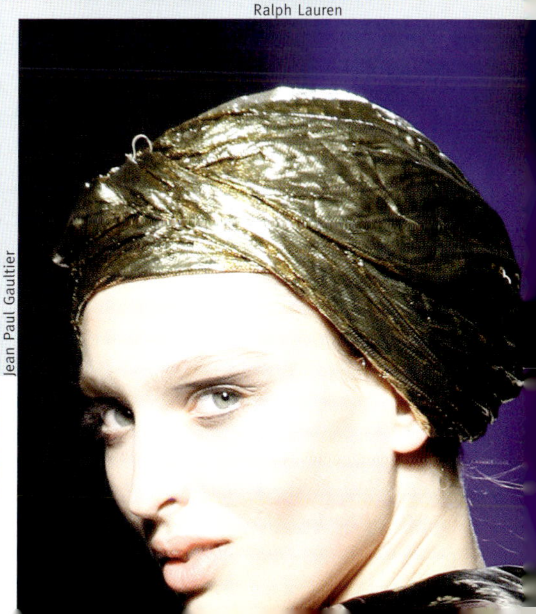
Jean Paul Gaultier

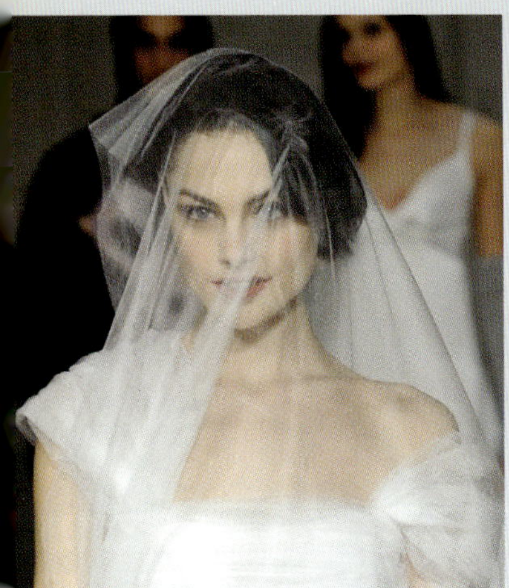

Agnès B.

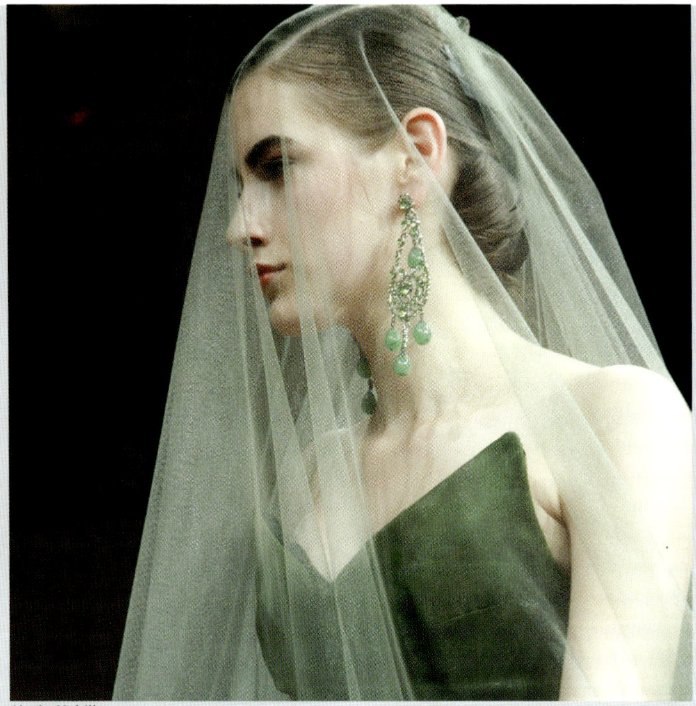

Alexis Mabille

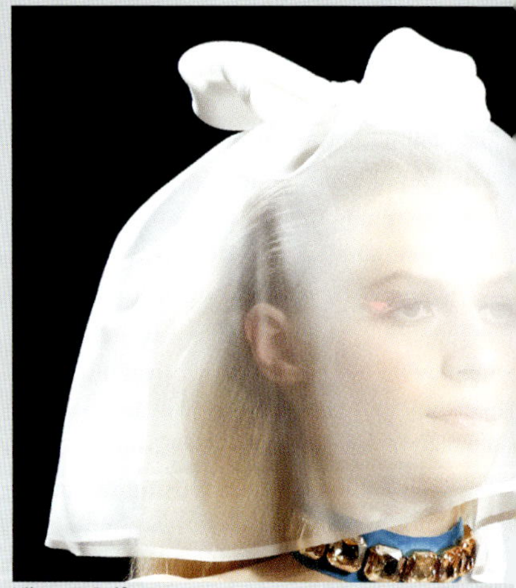

Viktor & Rolf

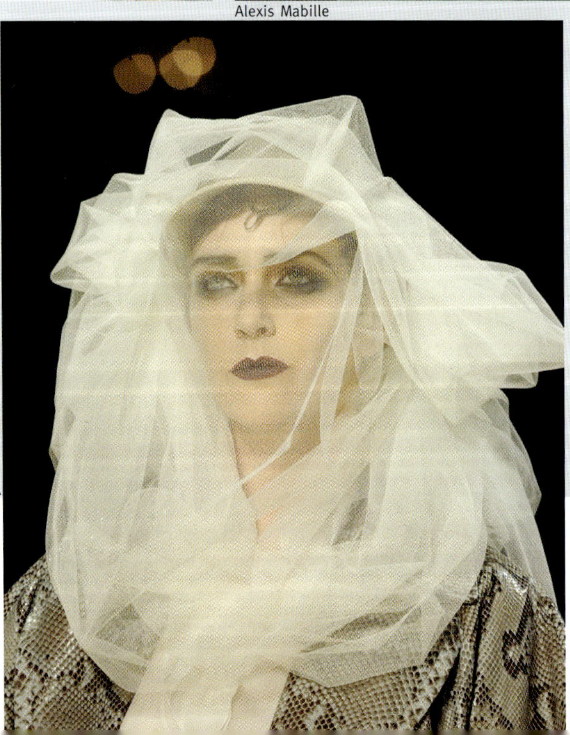

John Galliano

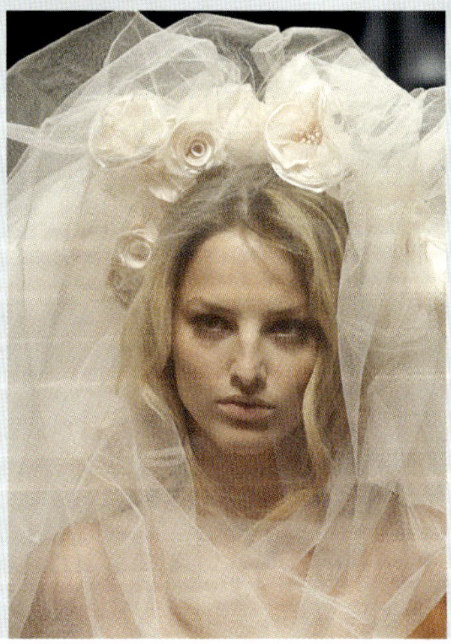

Jean Paul Gaultier

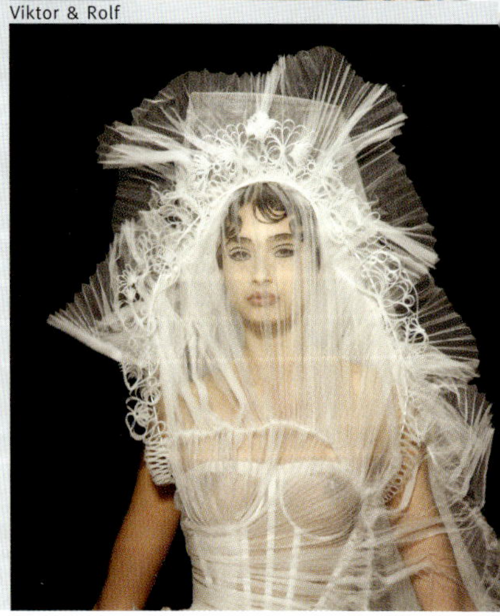

Zuhair Murad

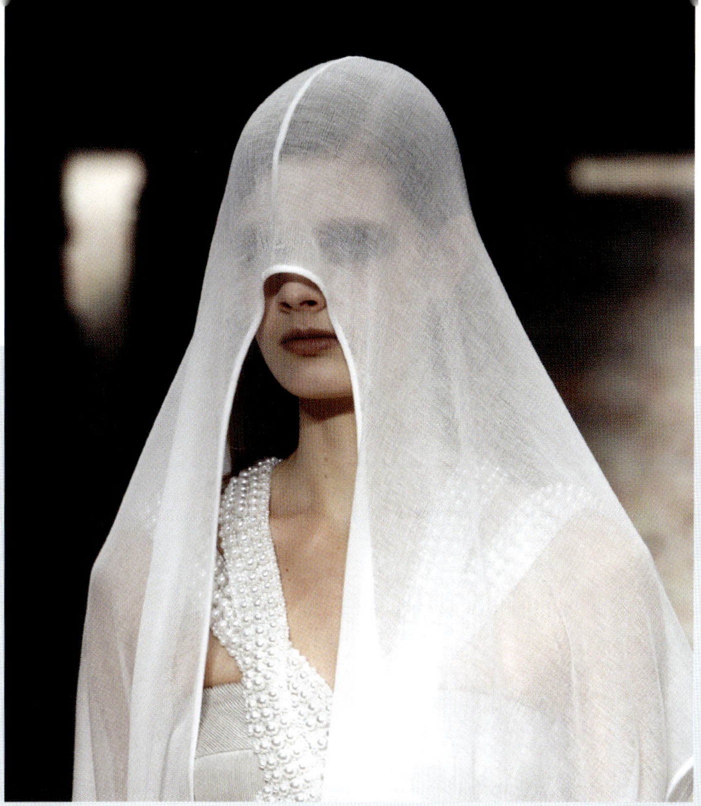

Givenchy

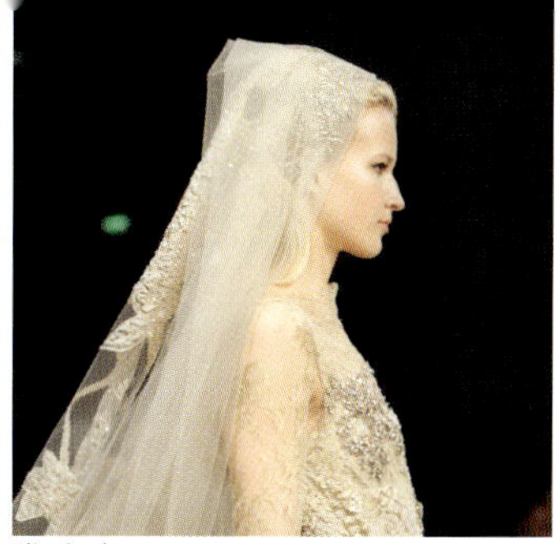

Elie Saab

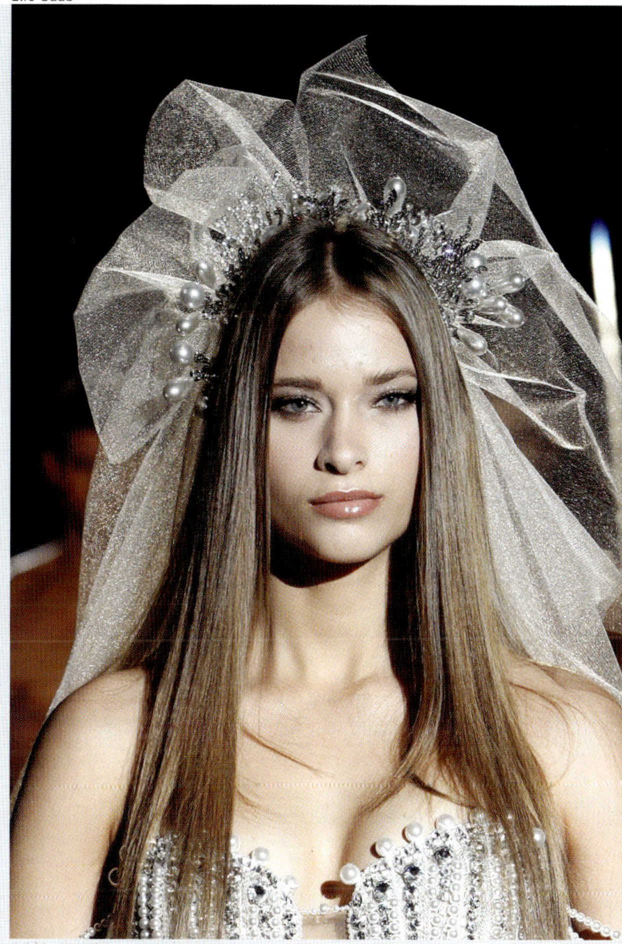

Zuhair Murad

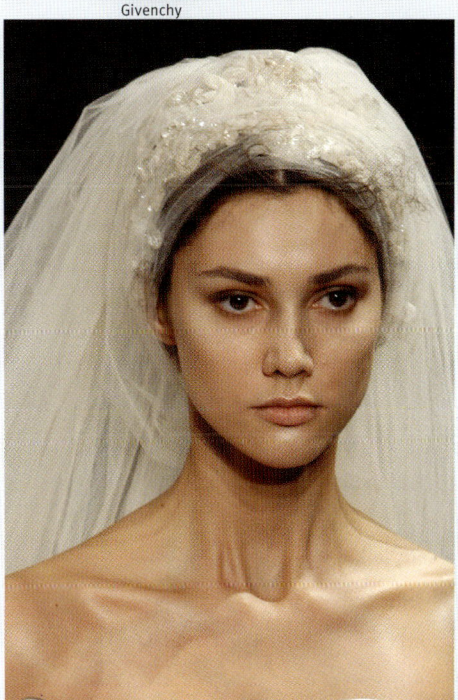

Elie Saab

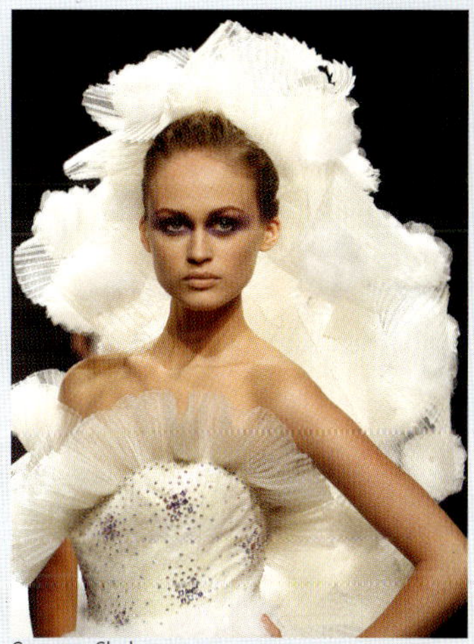

Georges Chakra

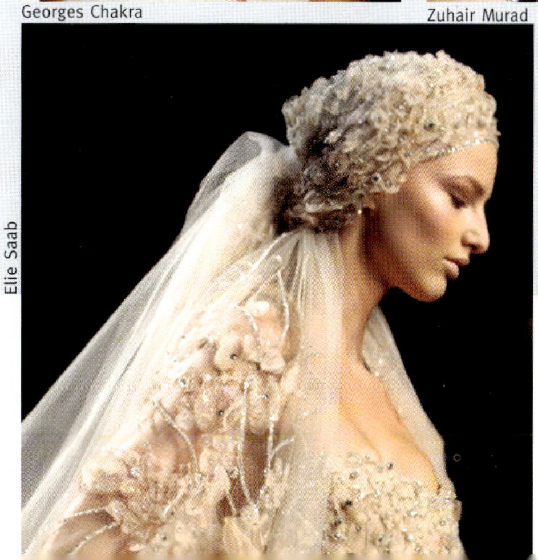

Elie Saab

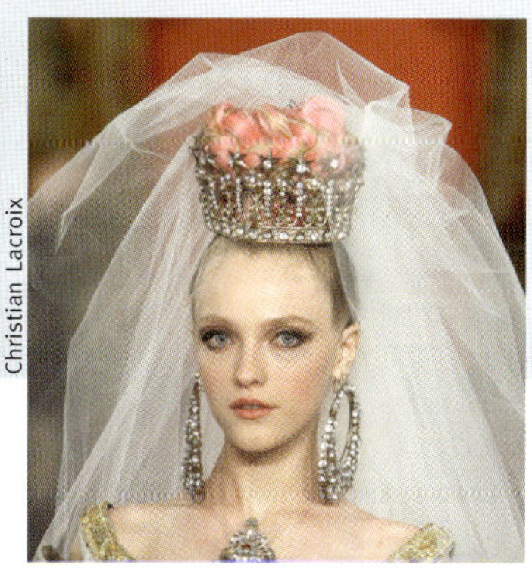

Christian Lacroix

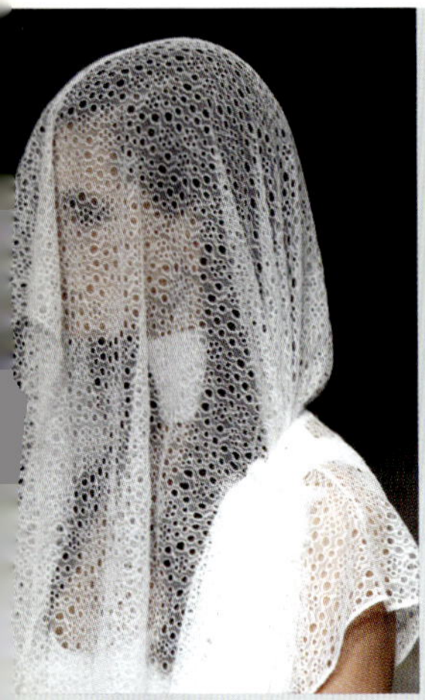
Givenchy

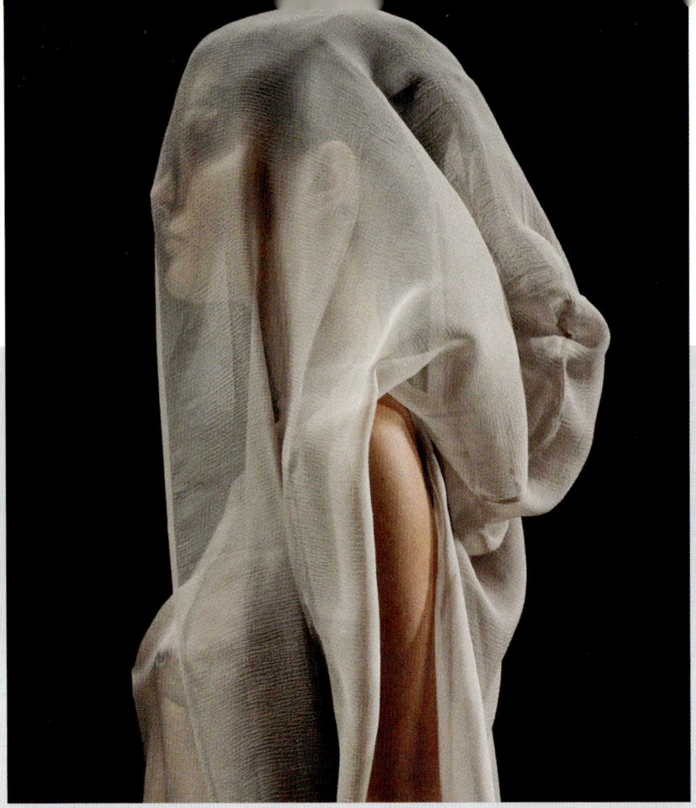
Haider Ackermann

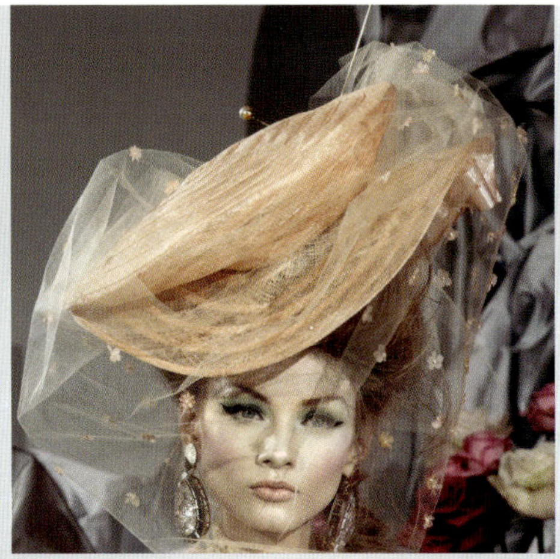
Dior

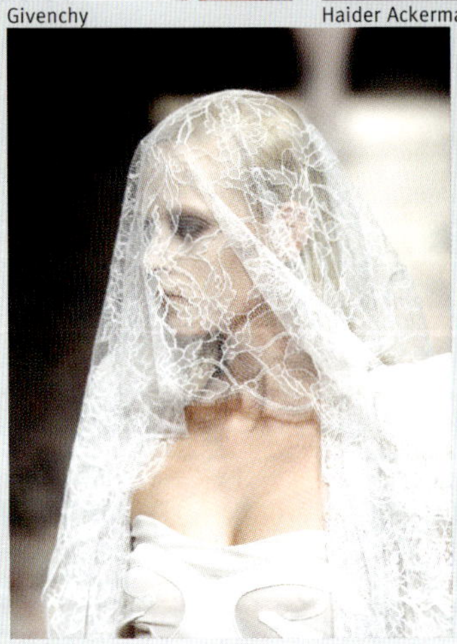
Givenchy

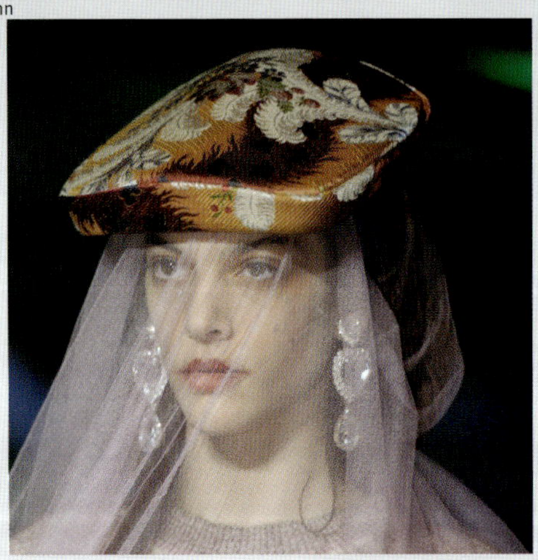
Vivienne Westwood

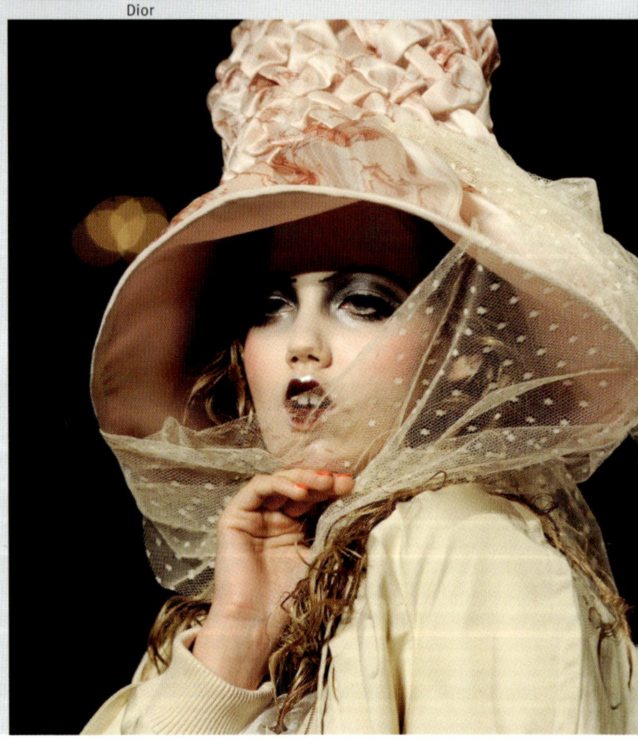
John Galliano

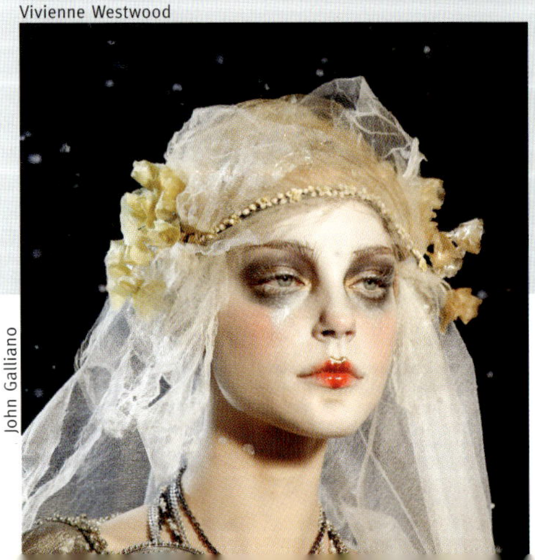
John Galliano

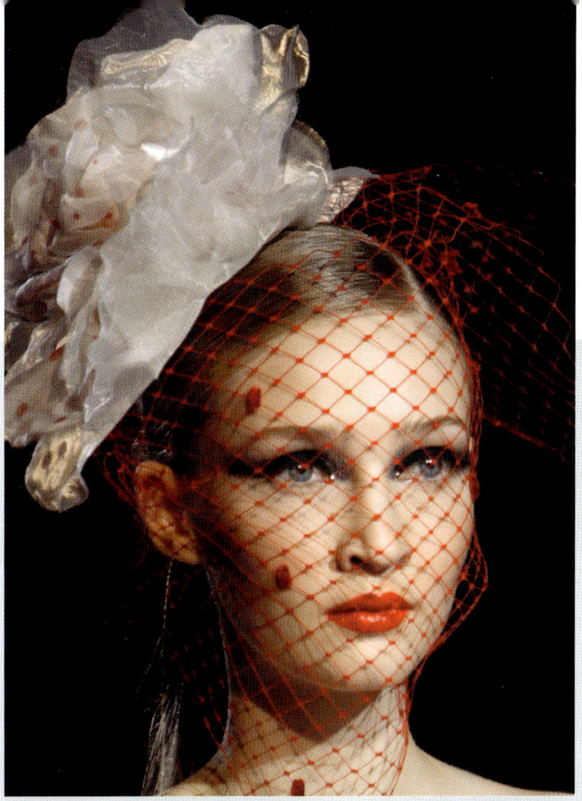
Roccobarocco

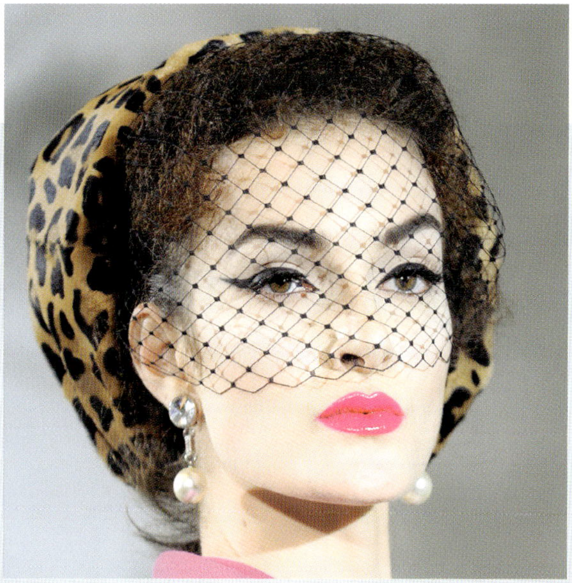
Dior

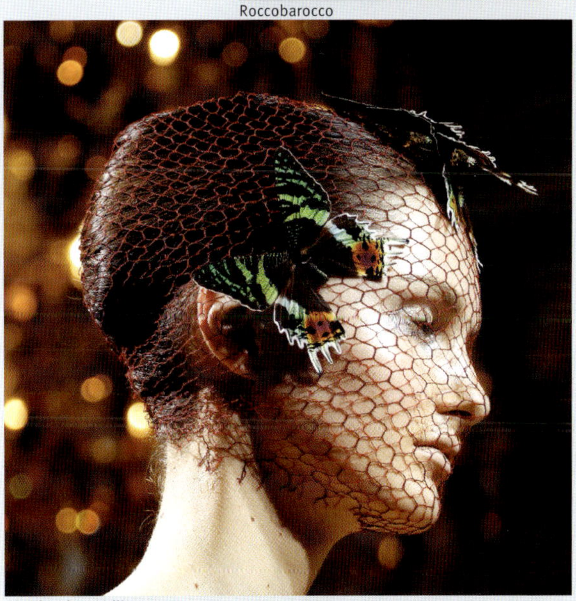
Giambattista Valli

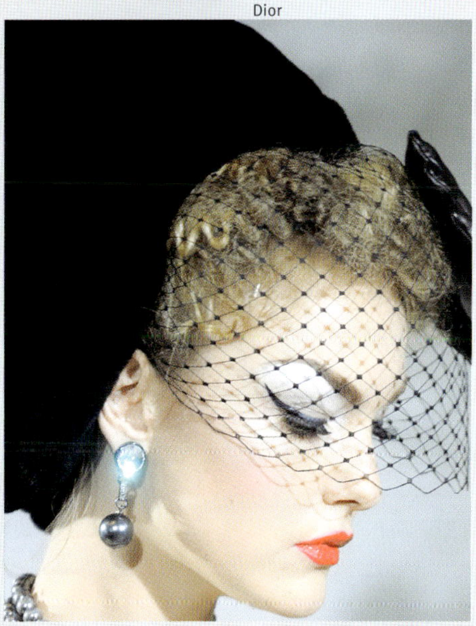
Dior

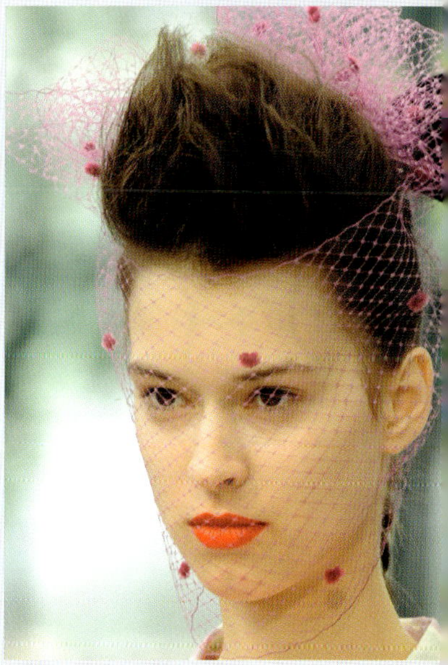
Luella

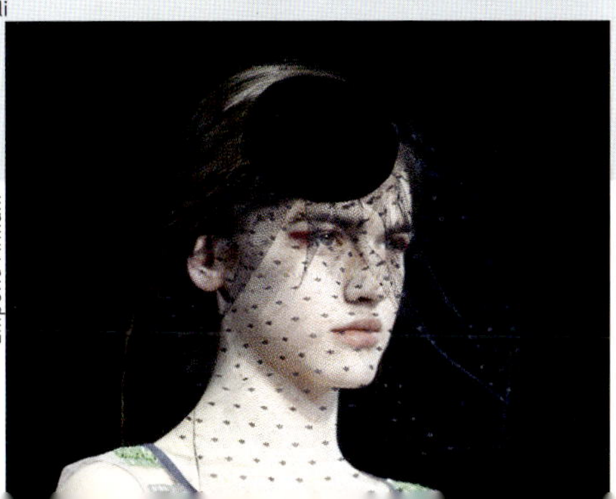
Emporio Armani

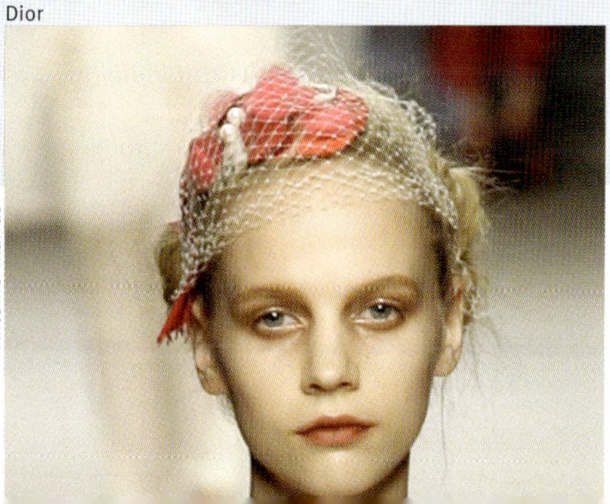
Antonio Marras

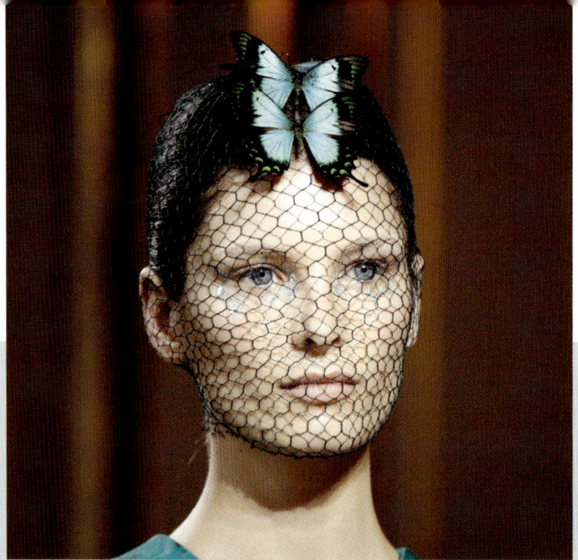

Giambattista Valli

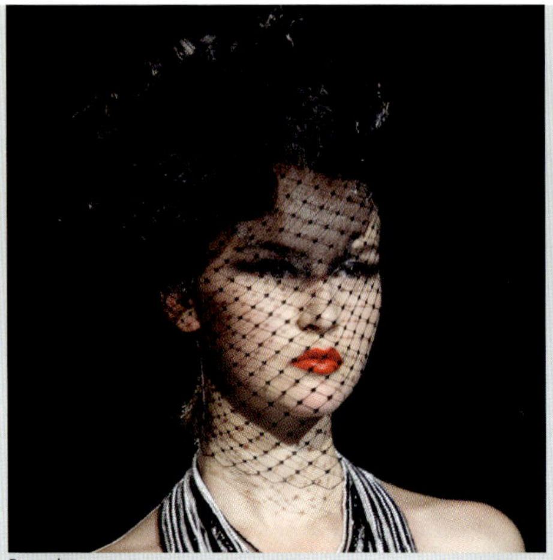

Roccobarocco

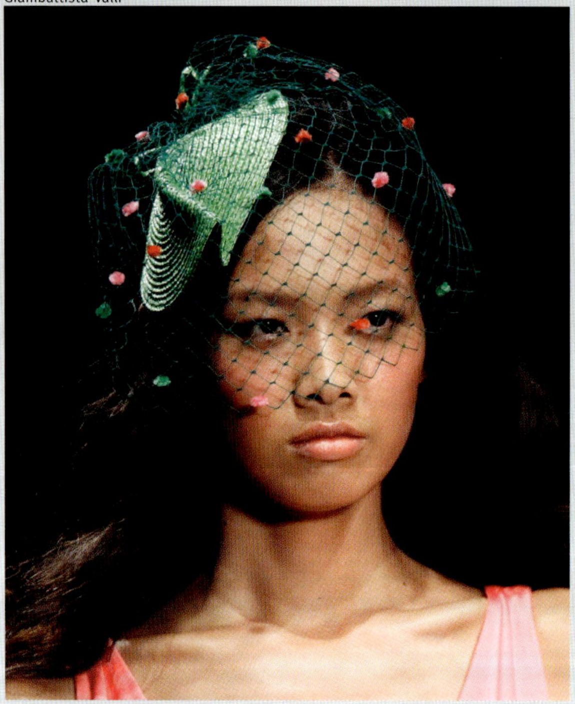

Issa

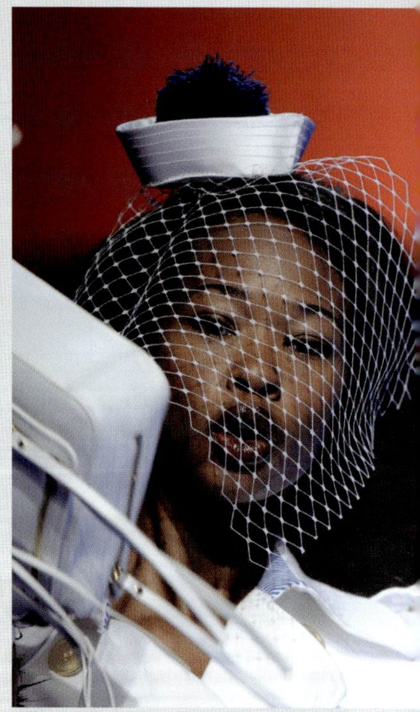

JC de Castelbajac

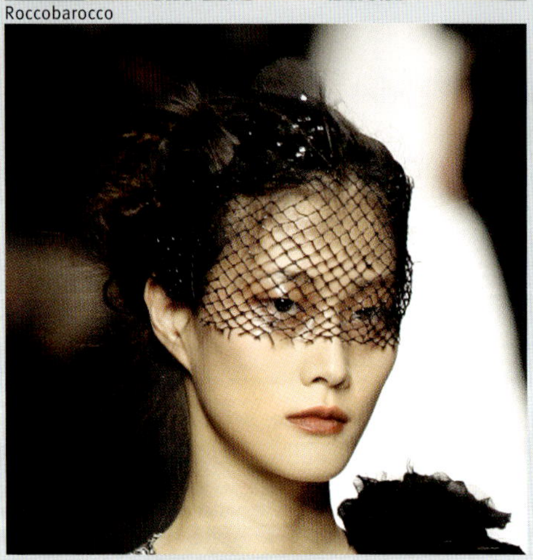

Antonio Marras

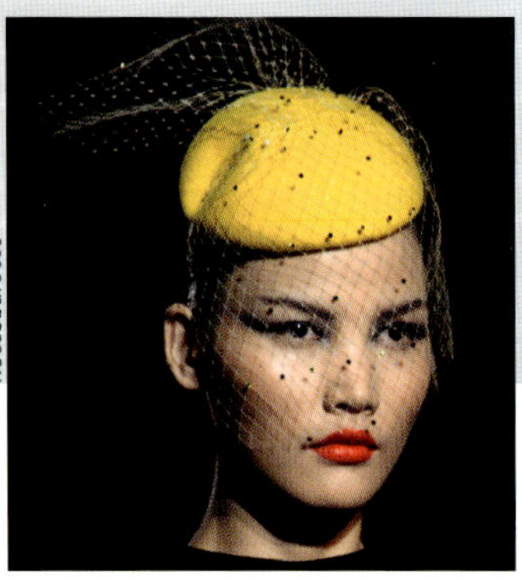

Roccobarocco

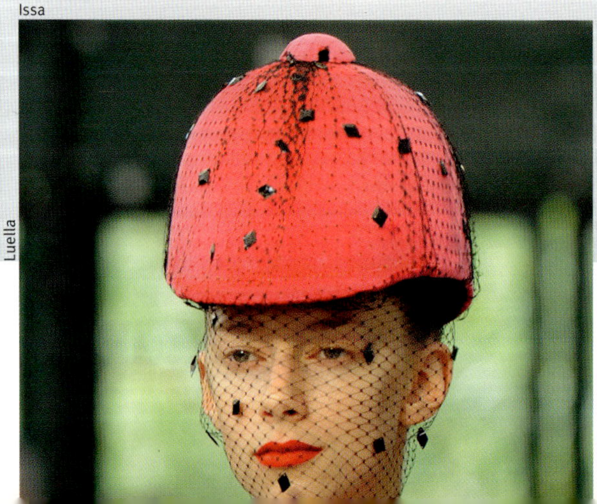

Luella

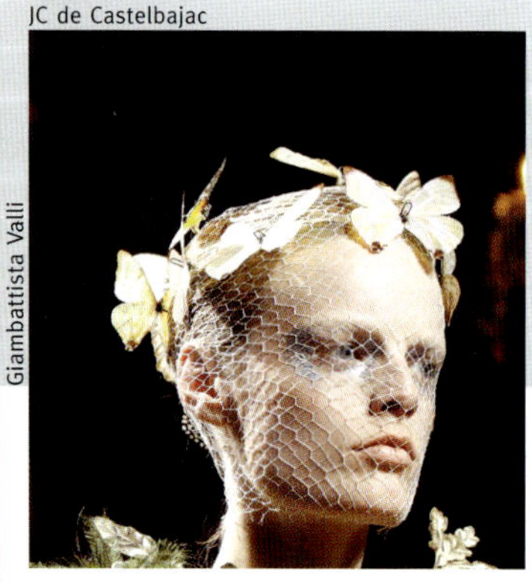

Giambattista Valli

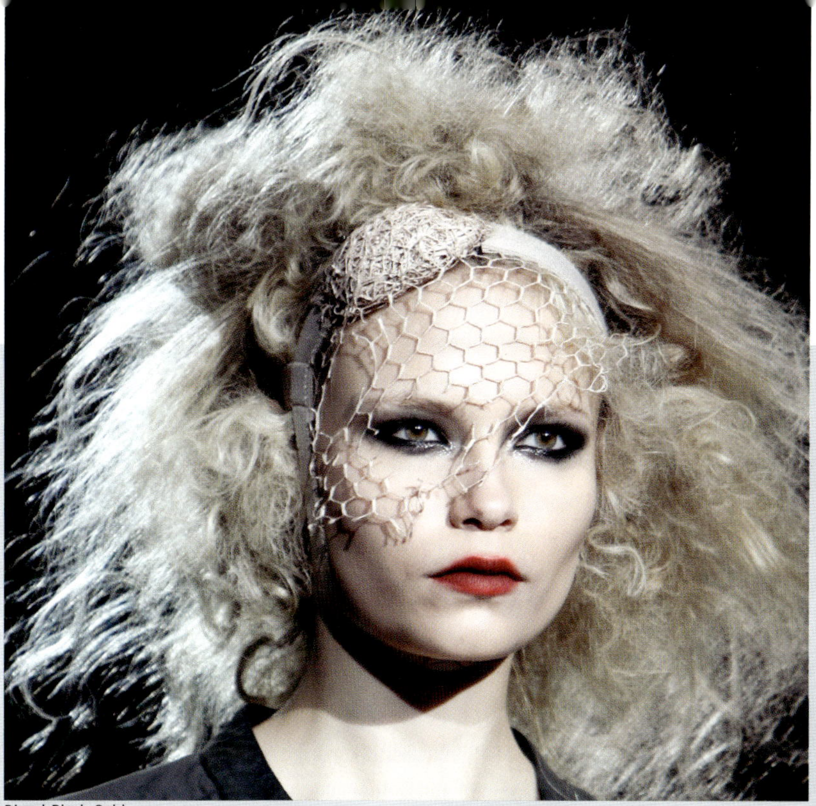

Diesel Black Gold

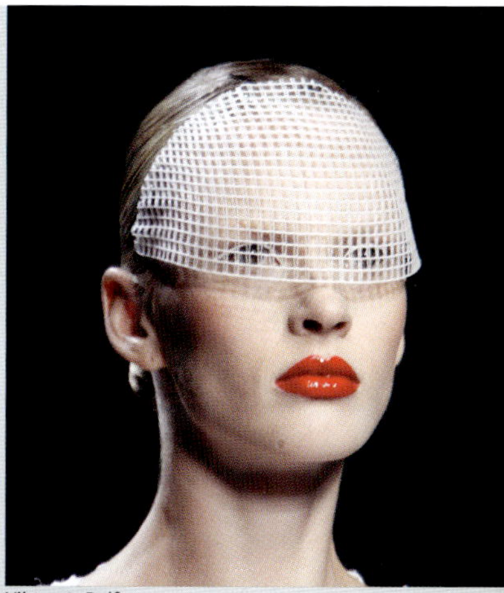

Viktor & Rolf

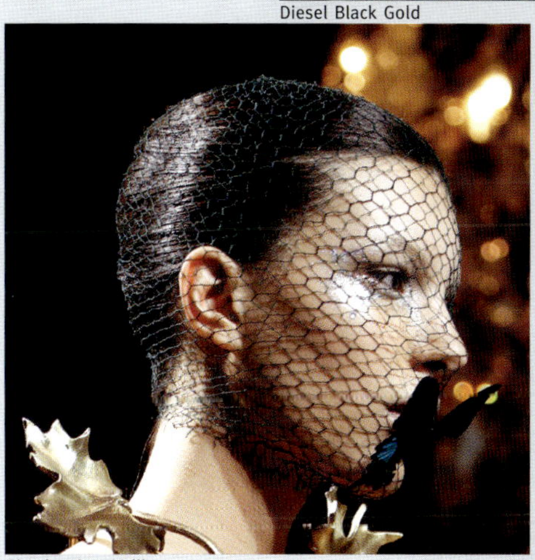

Giambattista Valli

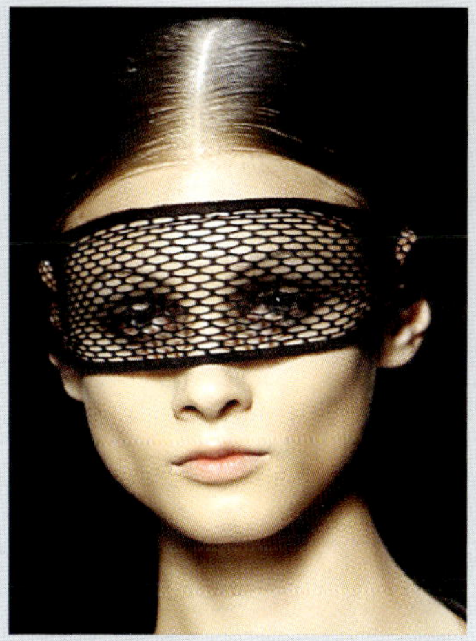

Jean Paul Gaultier

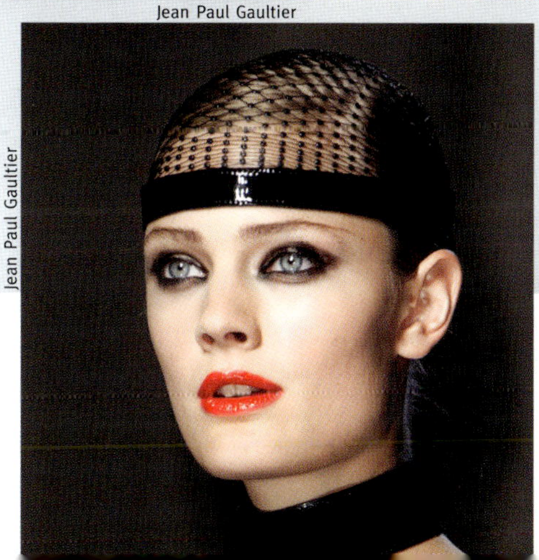

Jean Paul Gaultier

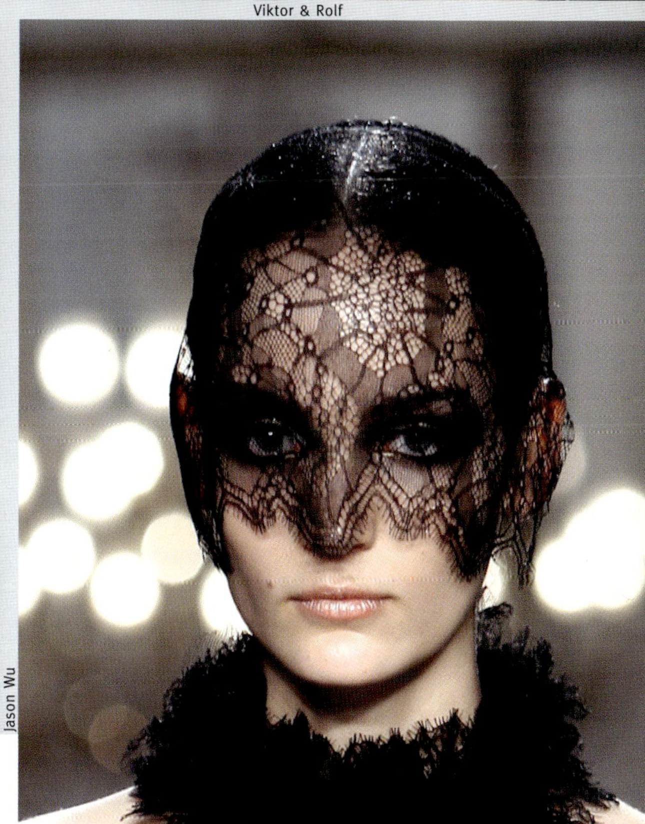

Jason Wu

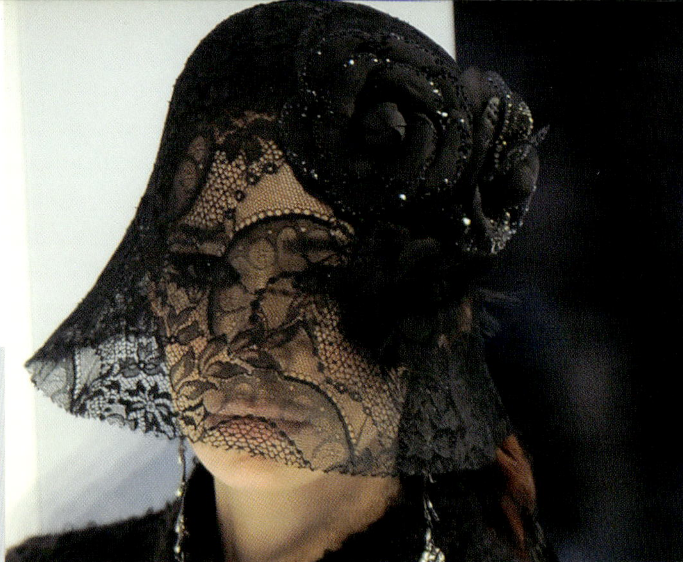

Chanel

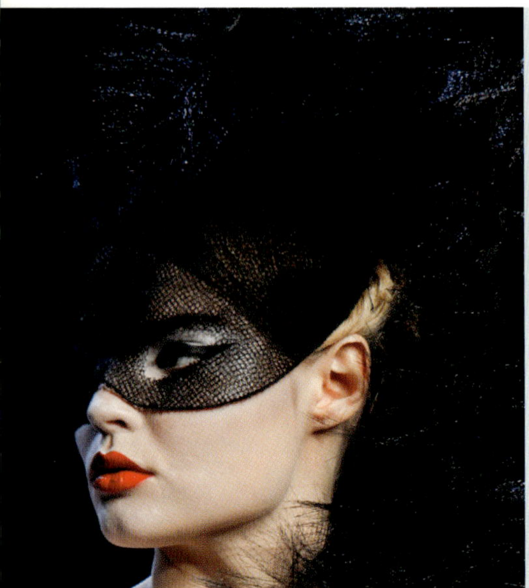

Dior

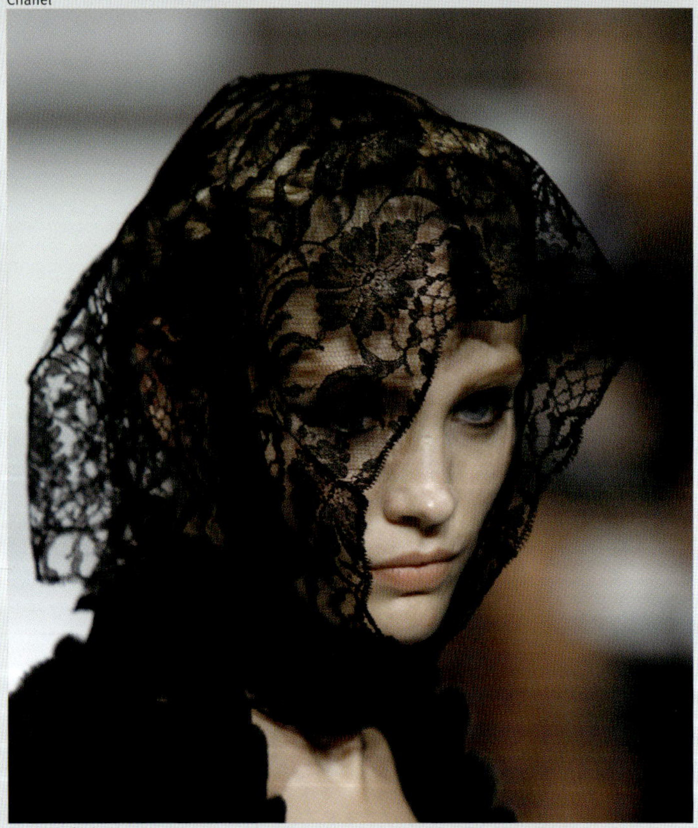

Oscar de la Renta

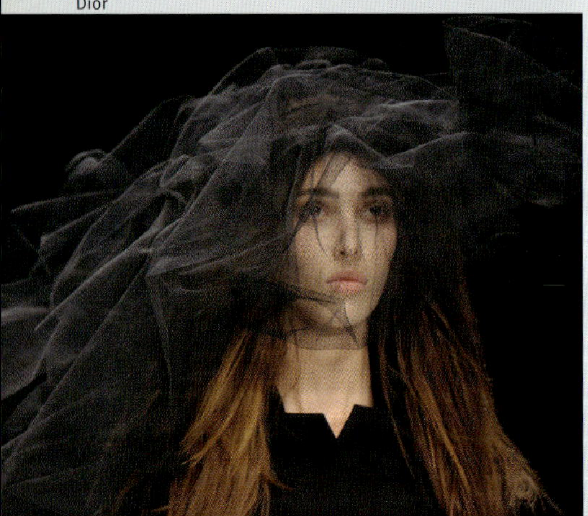

John Rocha

Armani Privè

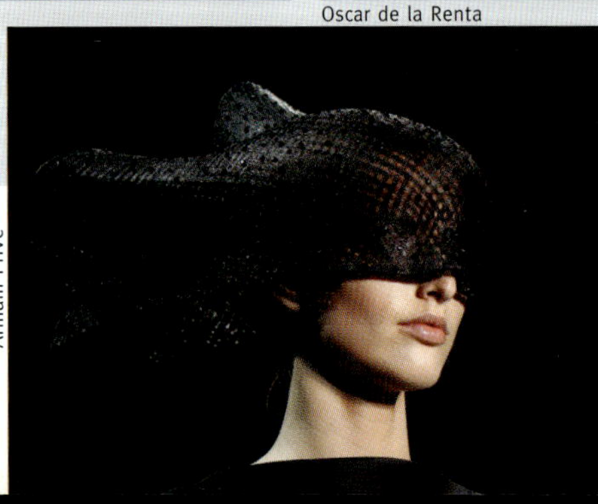

Chanel

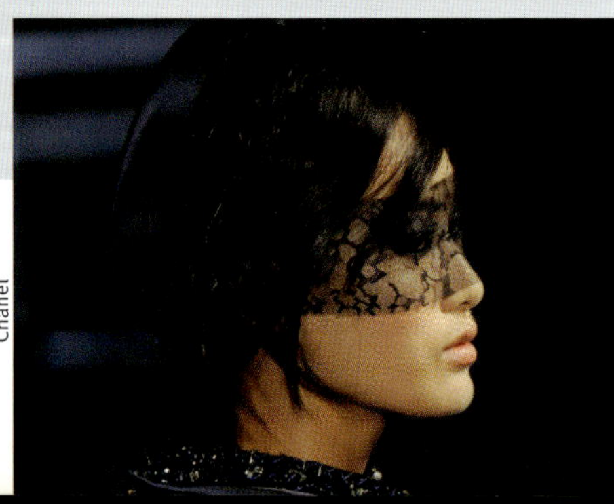

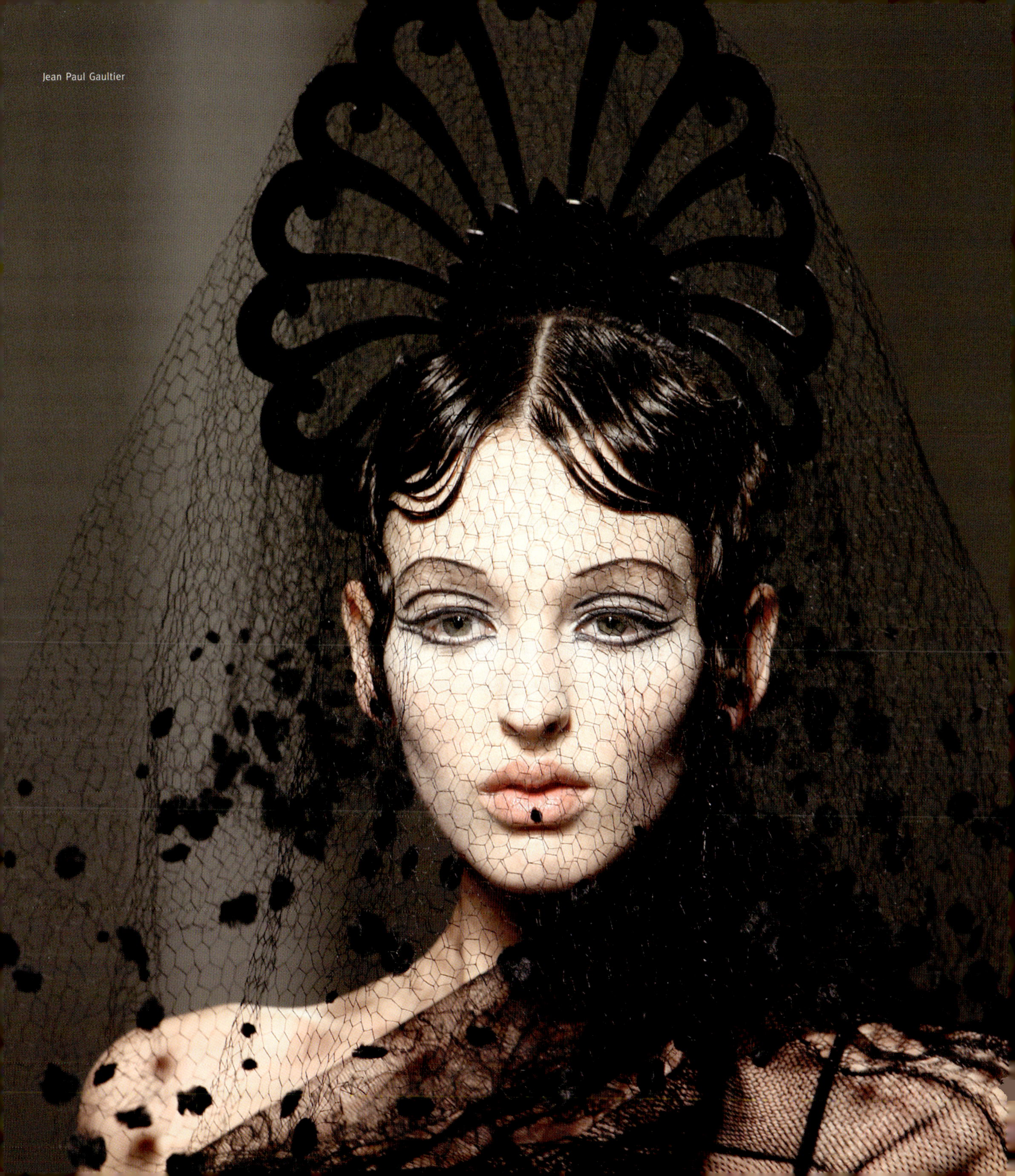

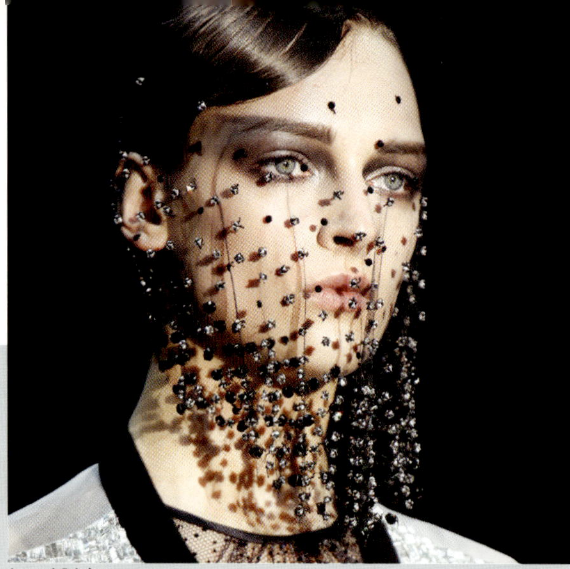

Armani Privè

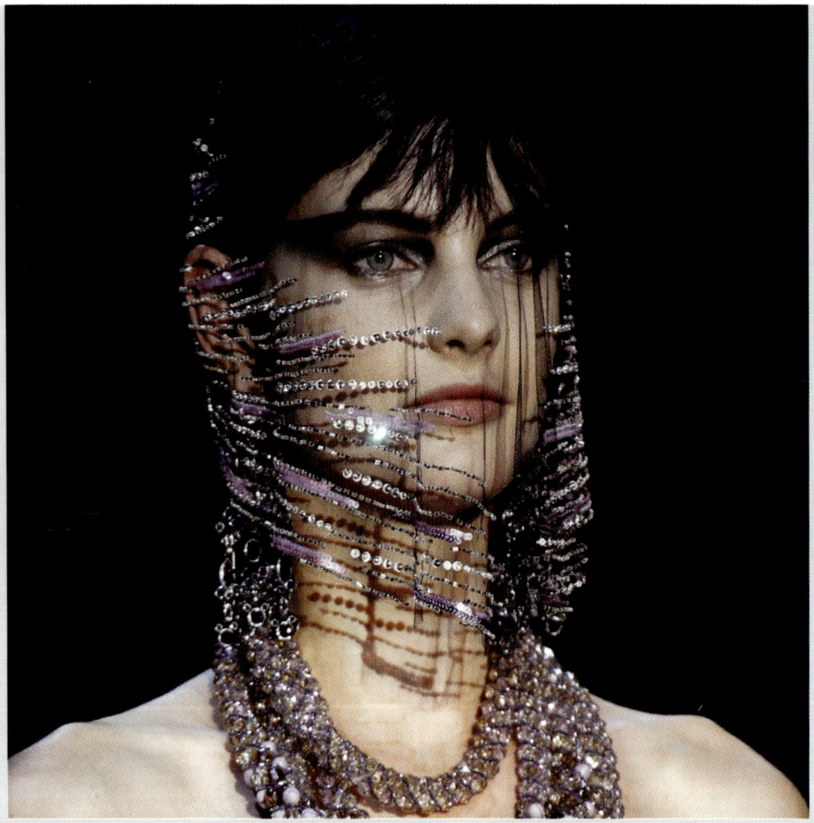

Armani Privè

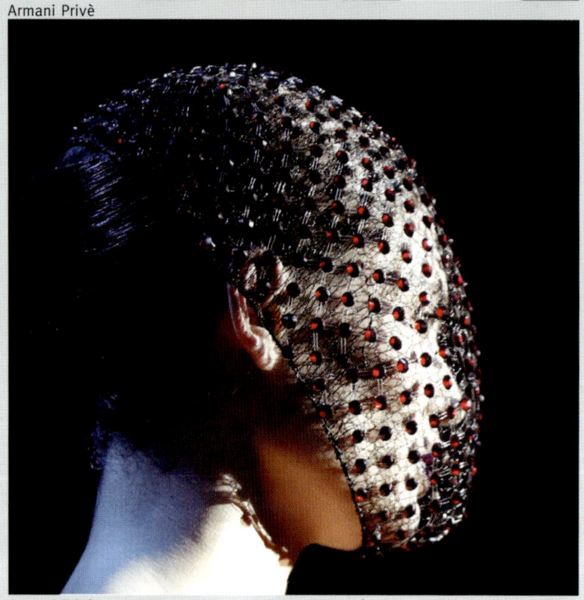

Armani Privè

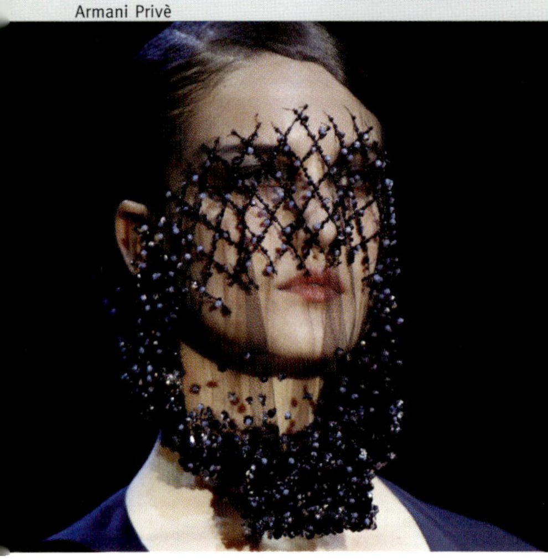

Armani Privè

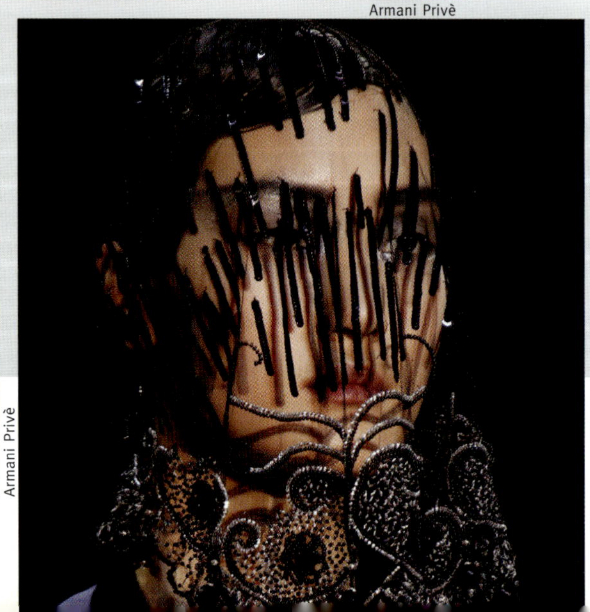

Armani Privè

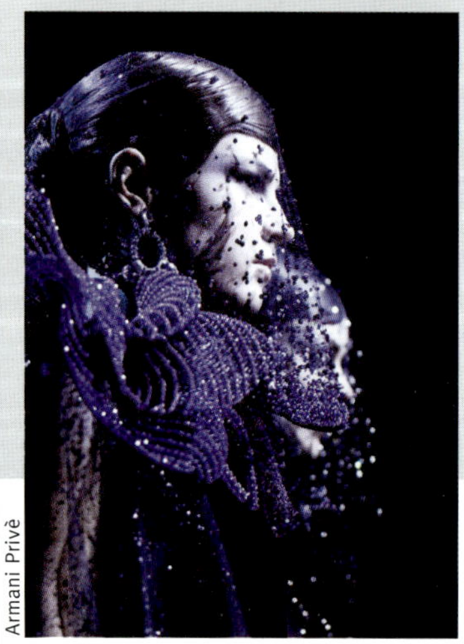

Armani Privè

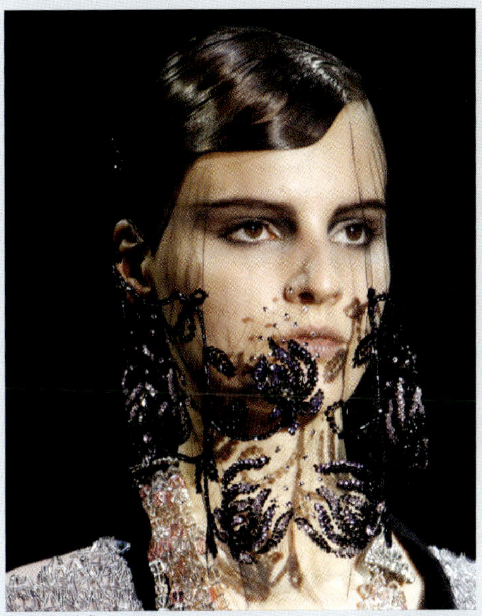

Armani Privè

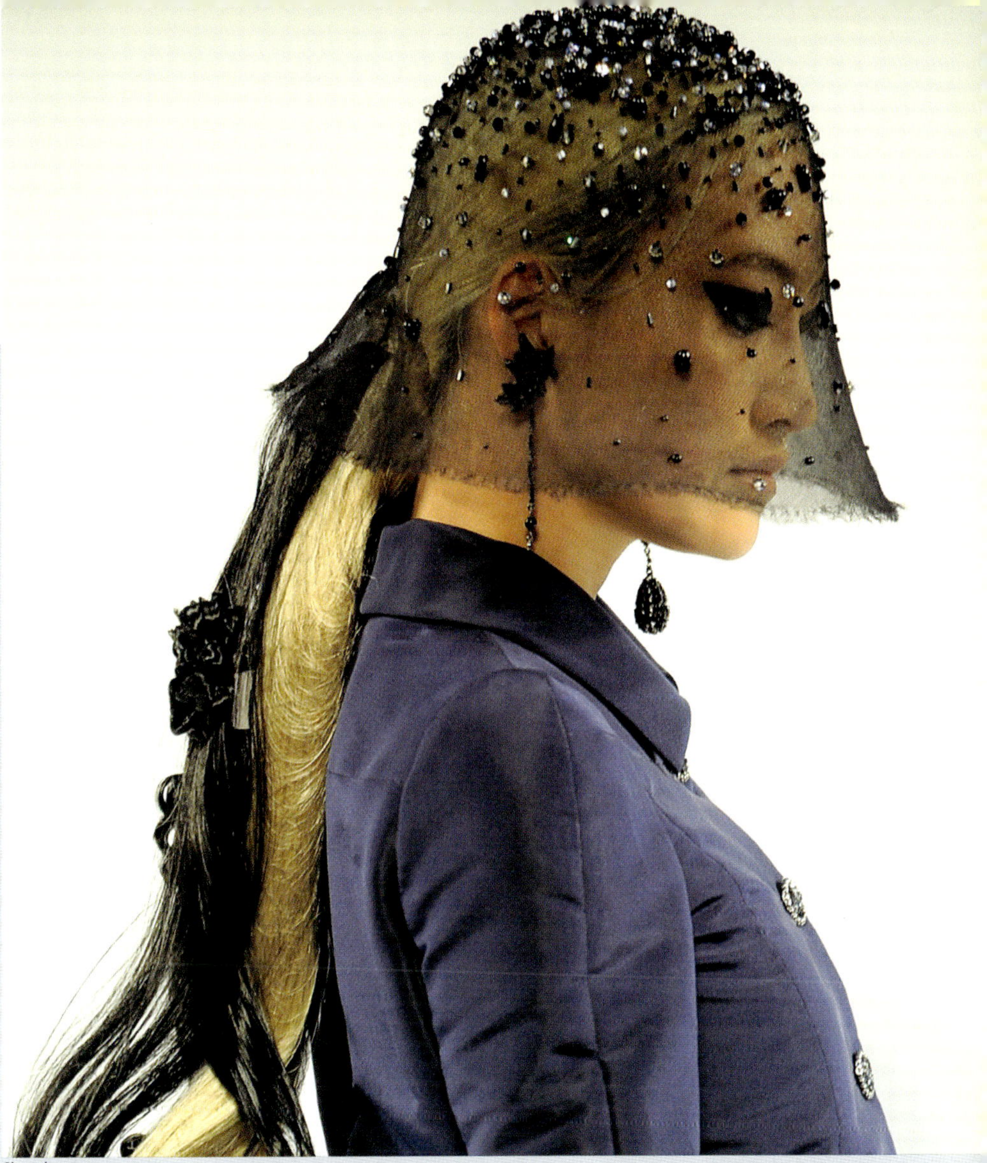

Chanel

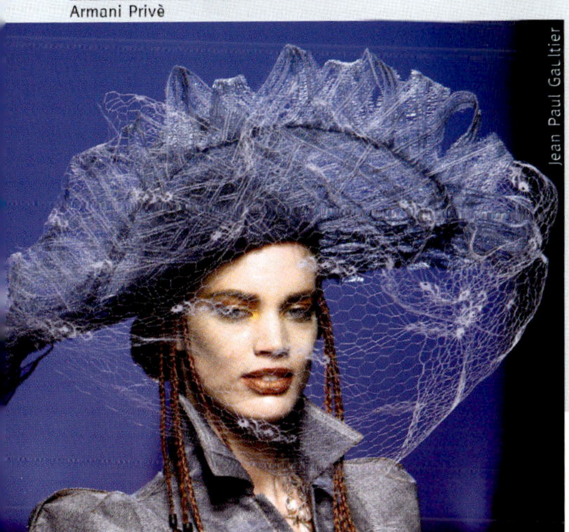

Jean Paul Gaultier

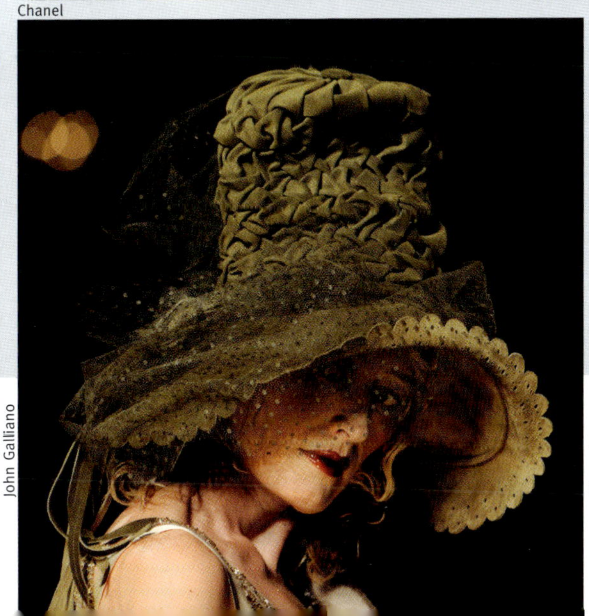

John Galliano

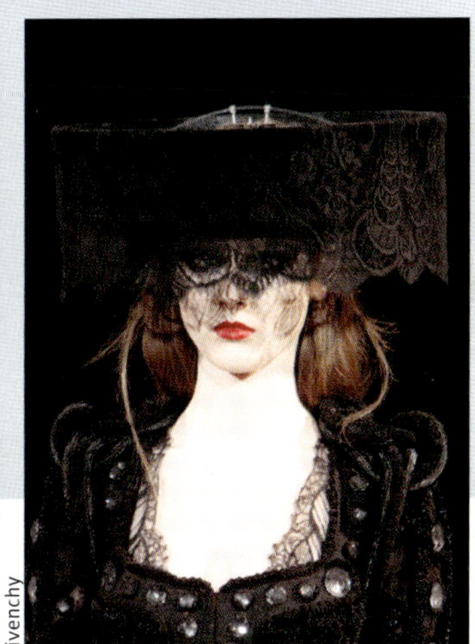

Givenchy

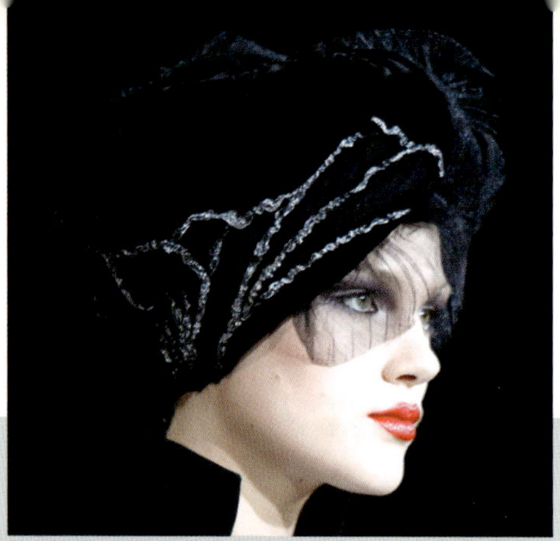

Giorgio Armani

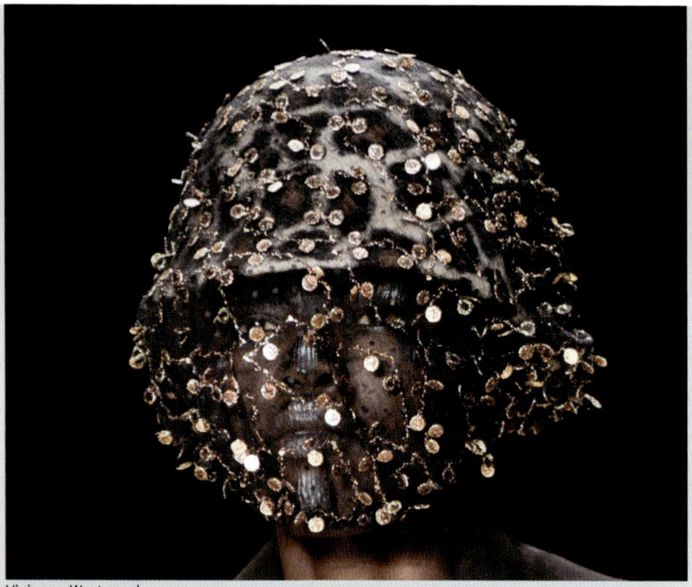

Vivienne Westwood

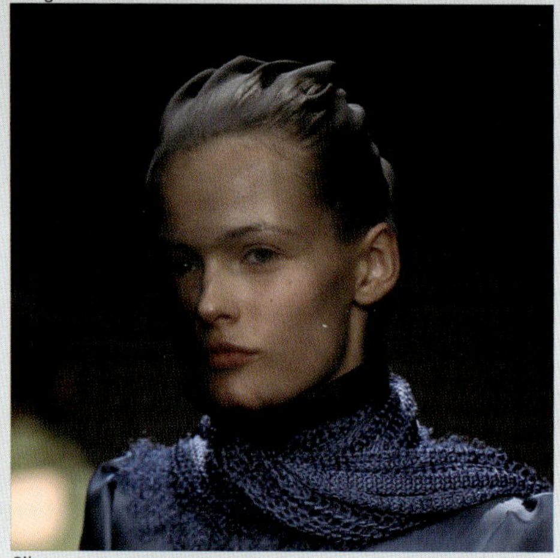

Giles

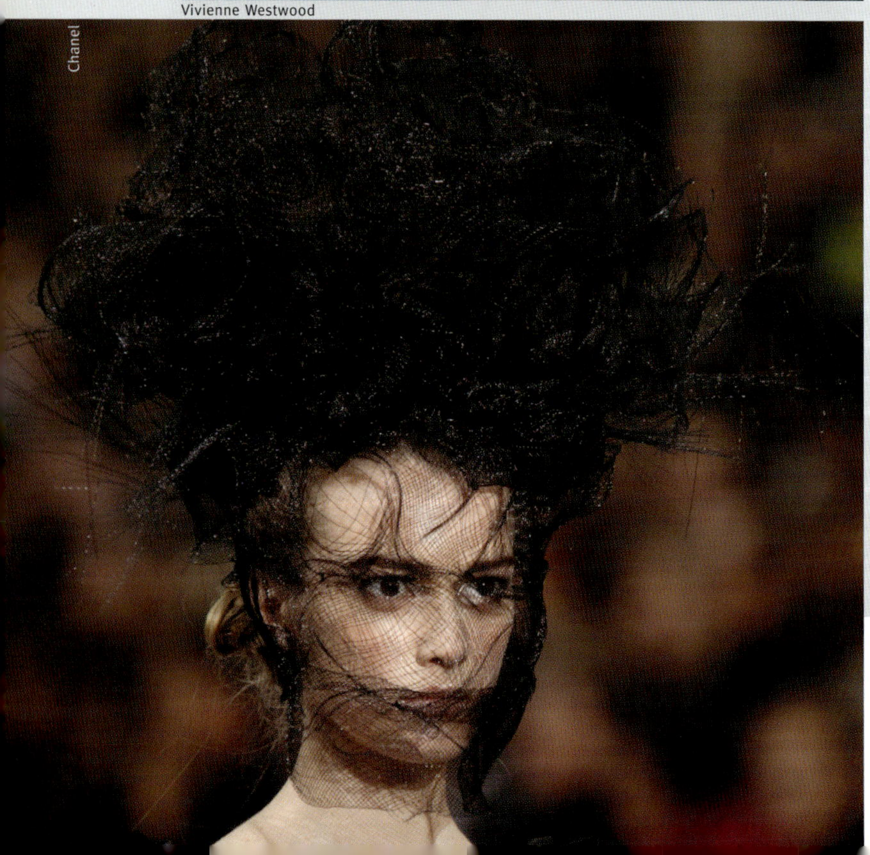

Chanel

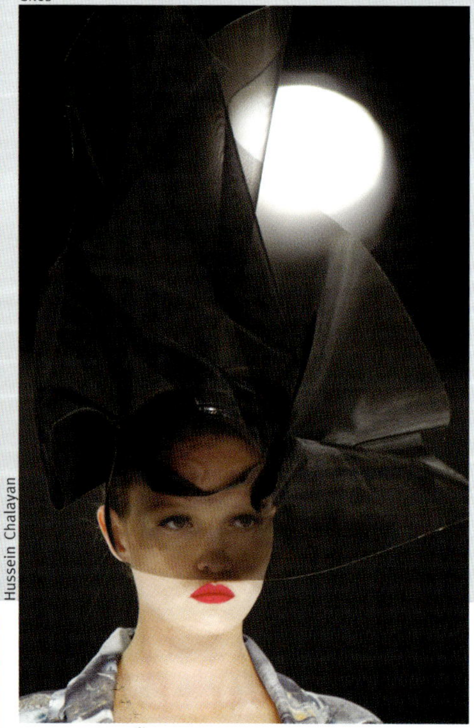

Hussein Chalayan

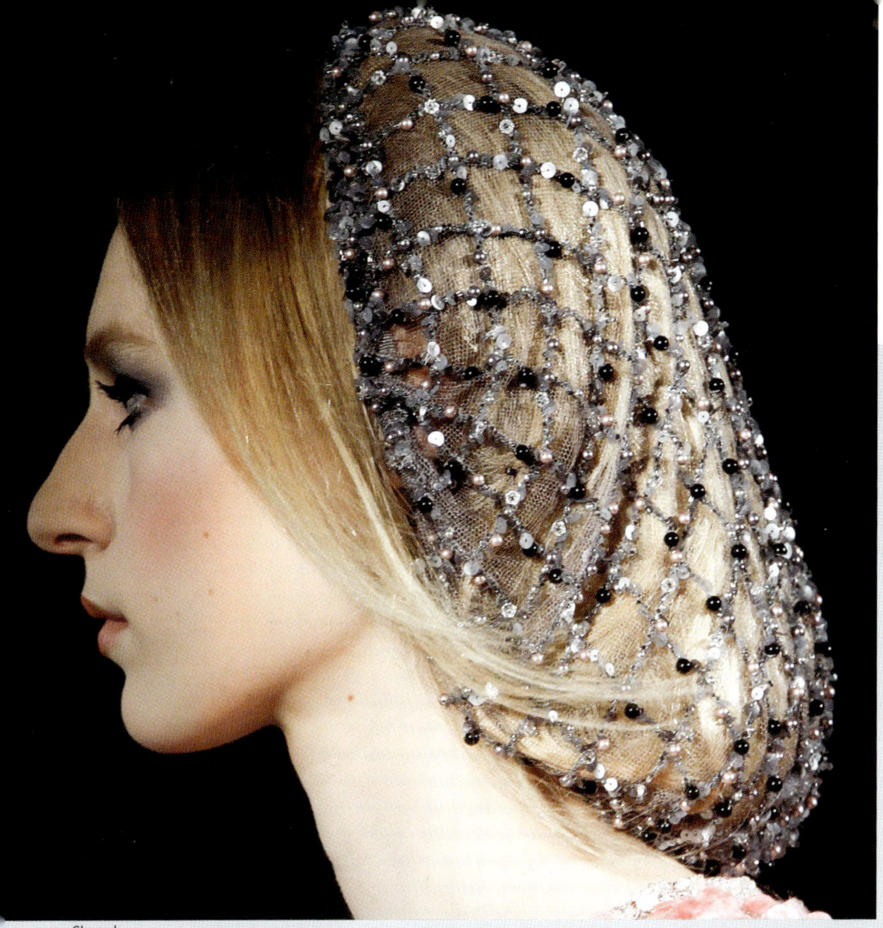

Chanel

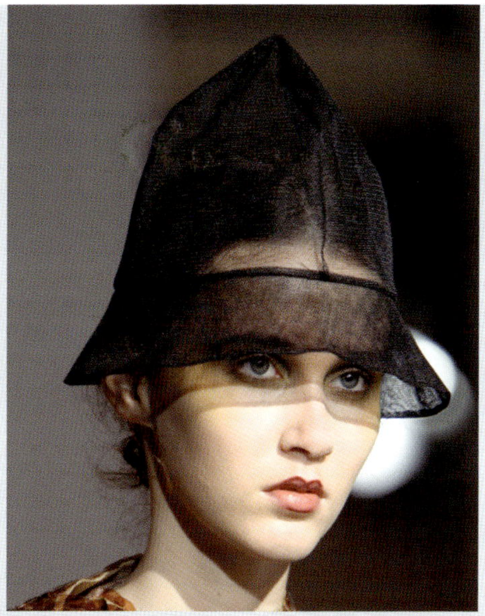

Marni

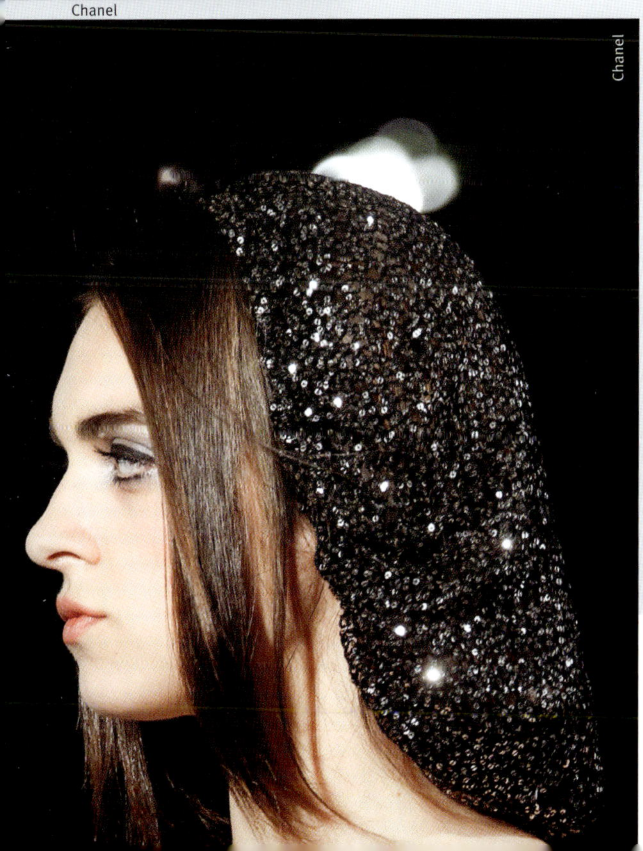

Chanel

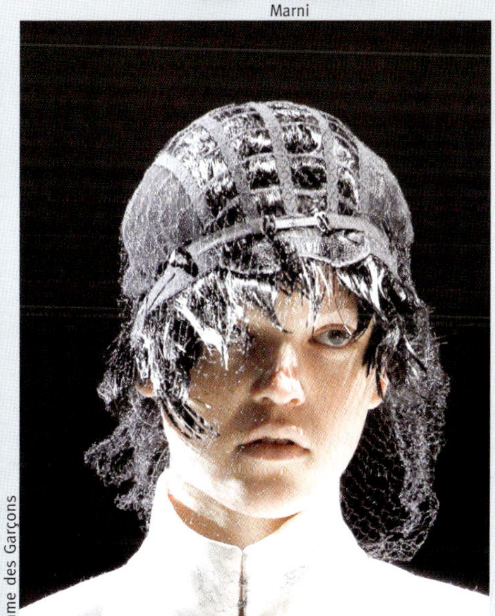

Comme des Garçons

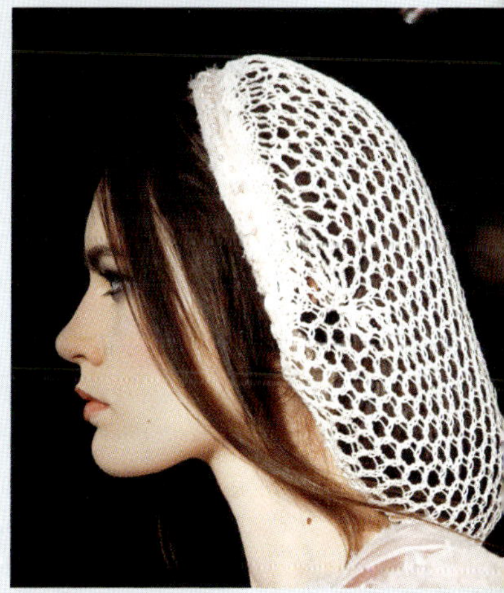

Chanel

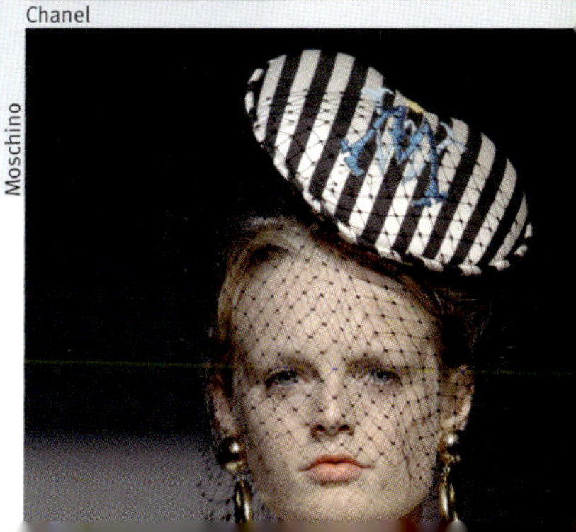

Moschino

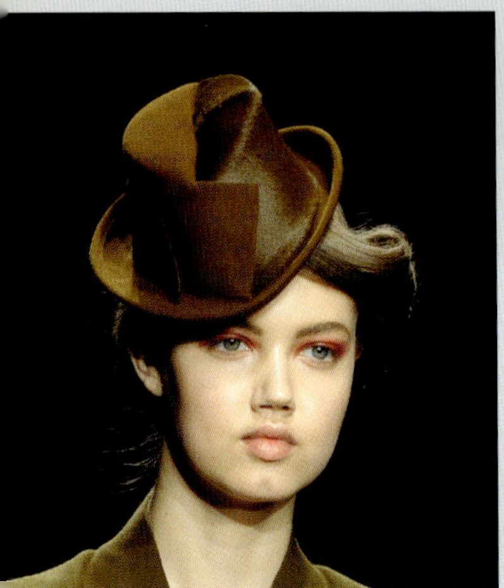

Donna Karan

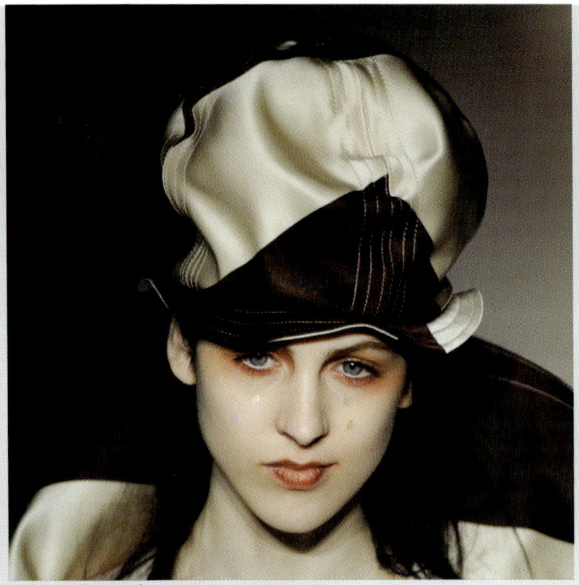

Vivienne Westwood

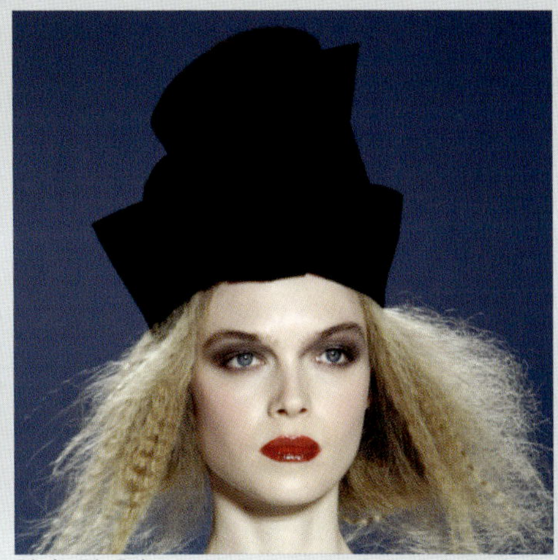

Erin by Erin Fetherston

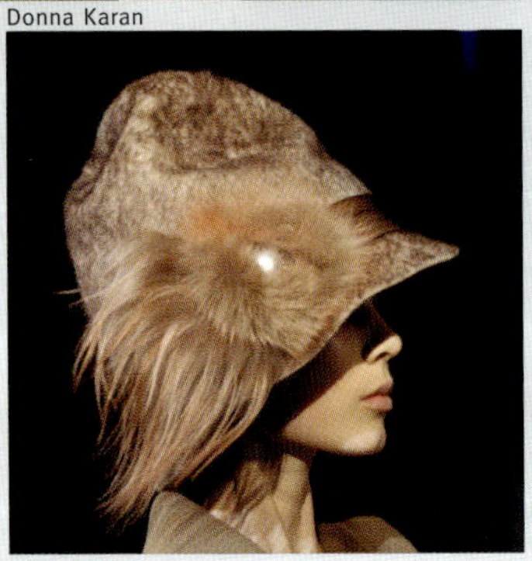

Louis Vuitton

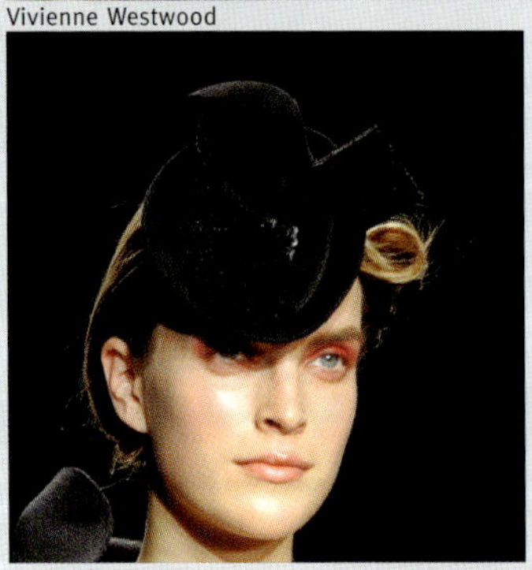

Donna Karan

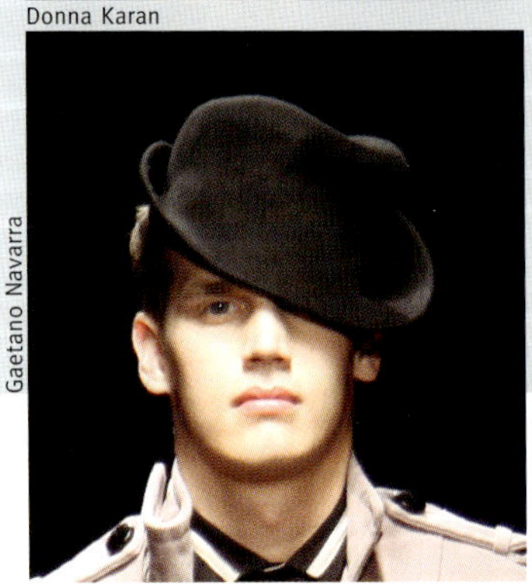

Gaetano Navarra

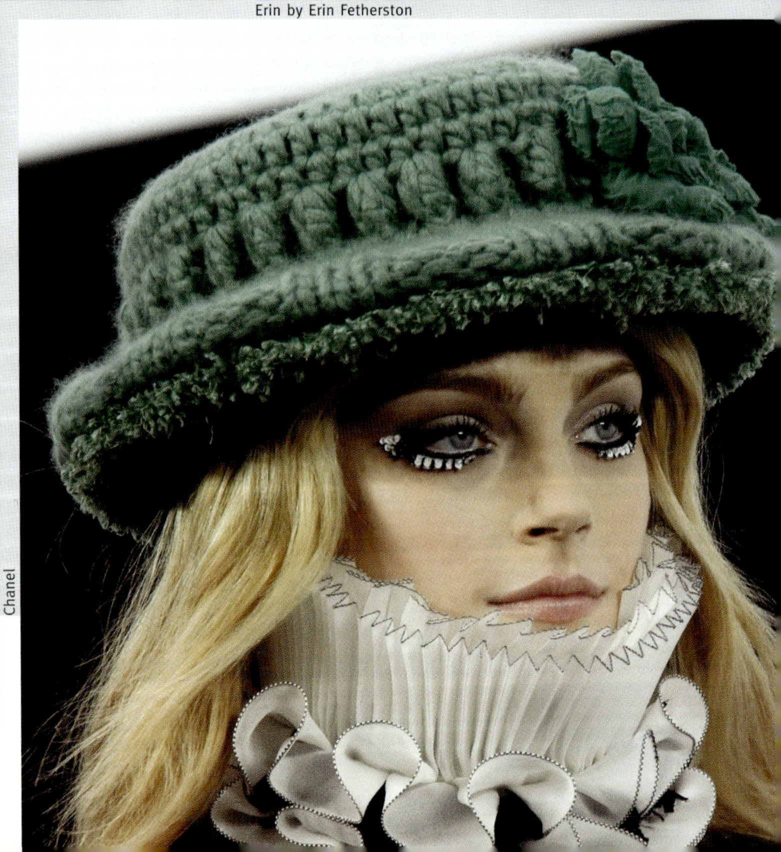

Chanel

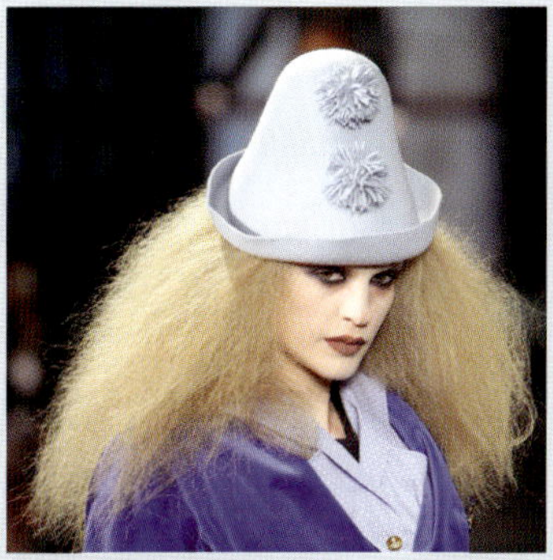
Vivienne Westwood Red Label

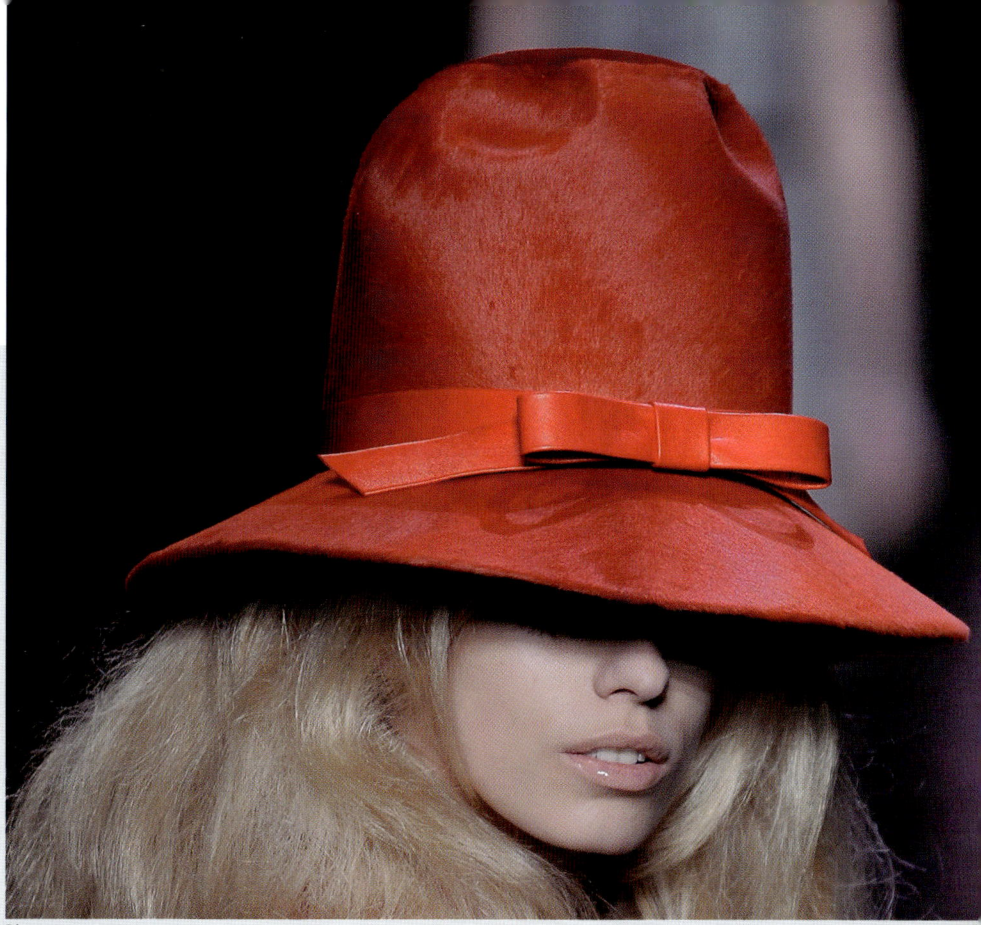
Dior

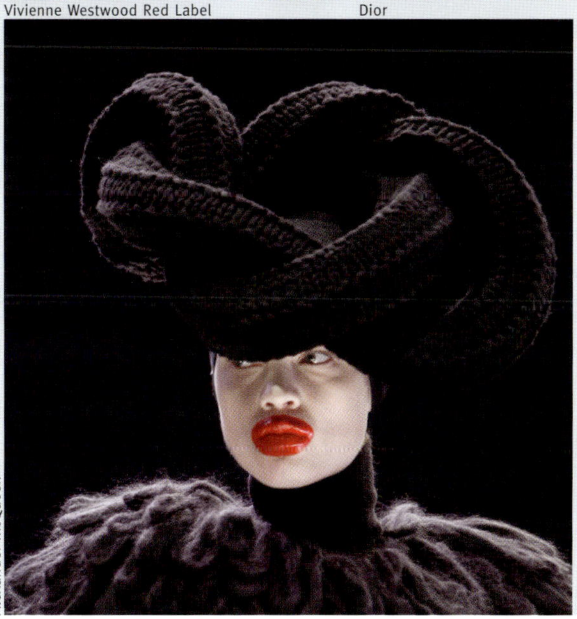
Alexander McQueen

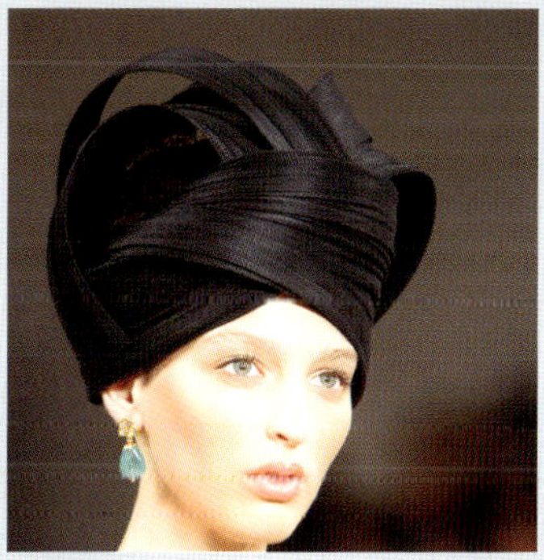
Ralph Lauren

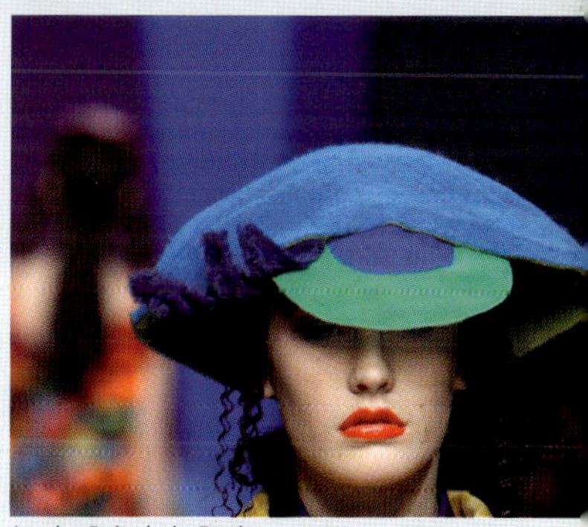
Agatha Ruiz de la Prada

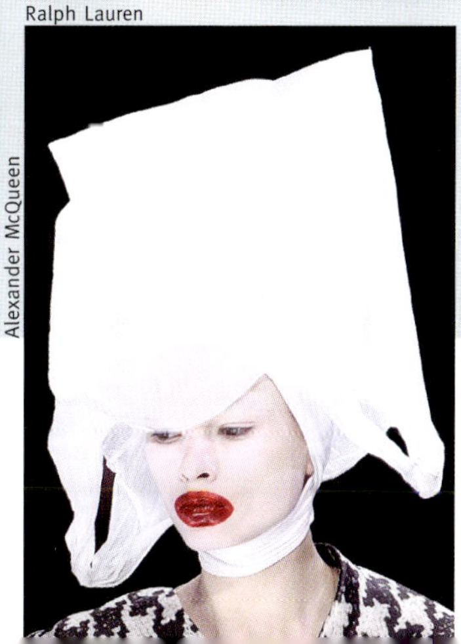
Alexander McQueen

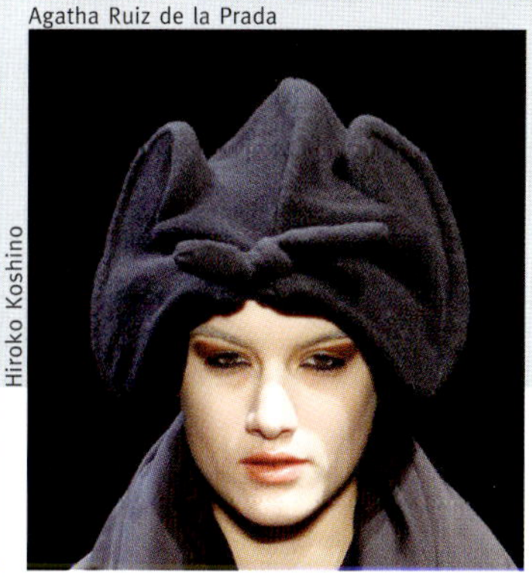
Hiroko Koshino

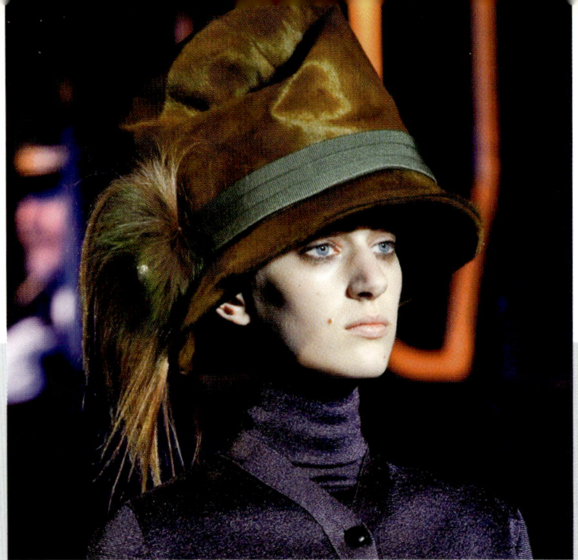

Louis Vuitton

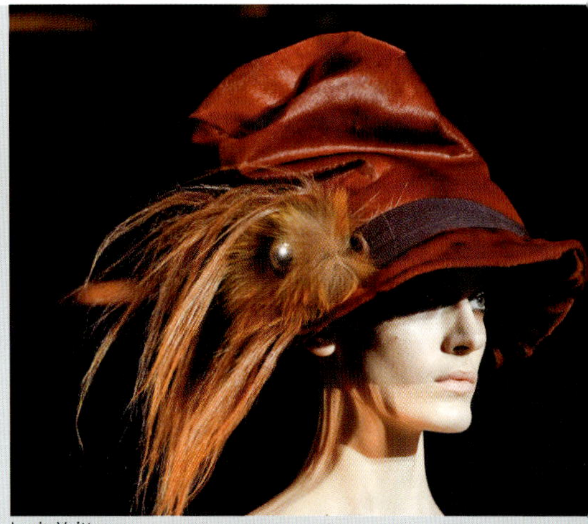

Louis Vuitton

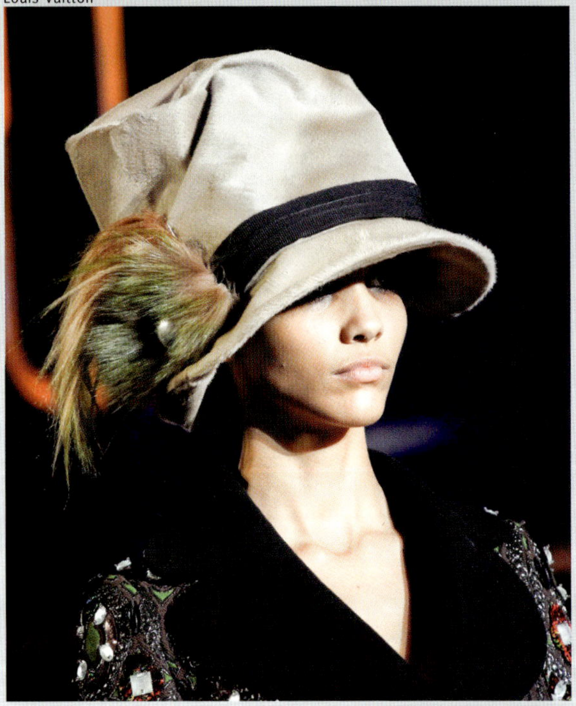

Louis Vuitton

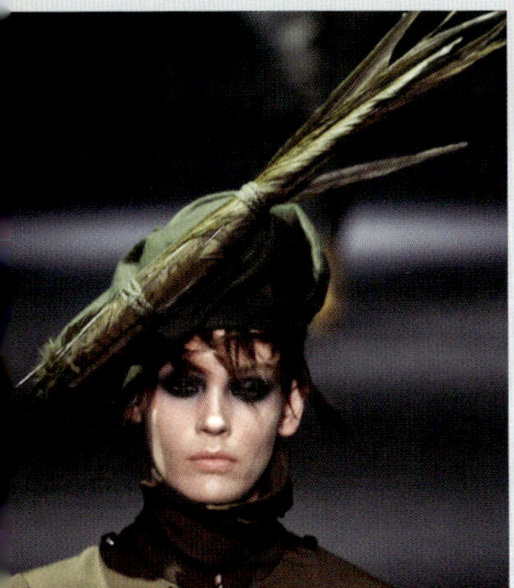

John Galliano

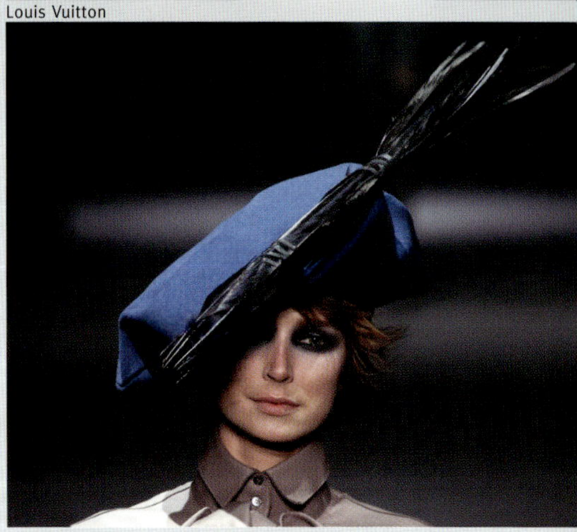

John Galliano

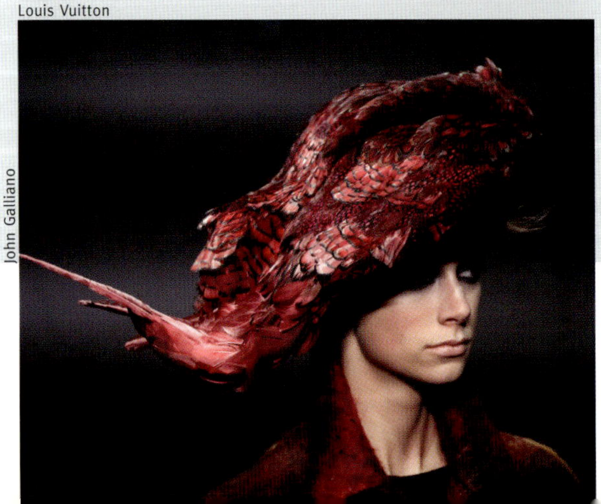

John Galliano

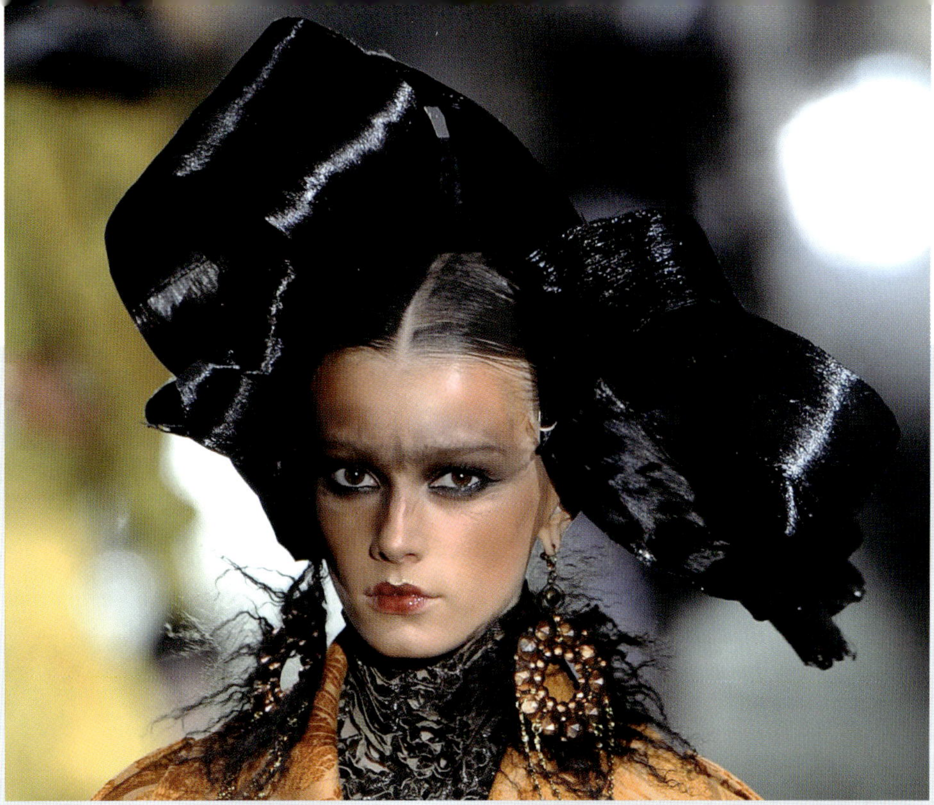

John Galliano

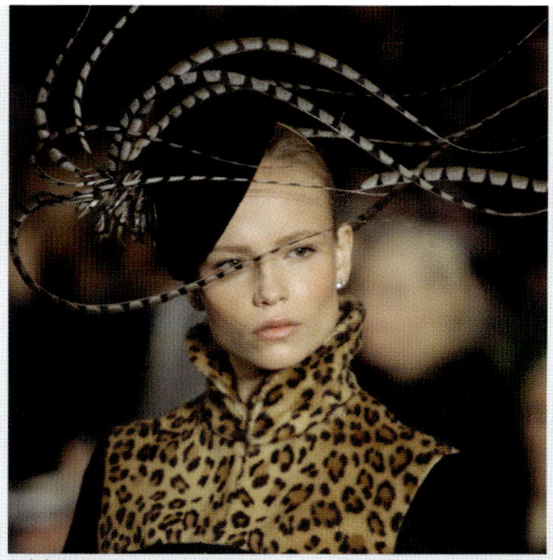

Ralph Lauren

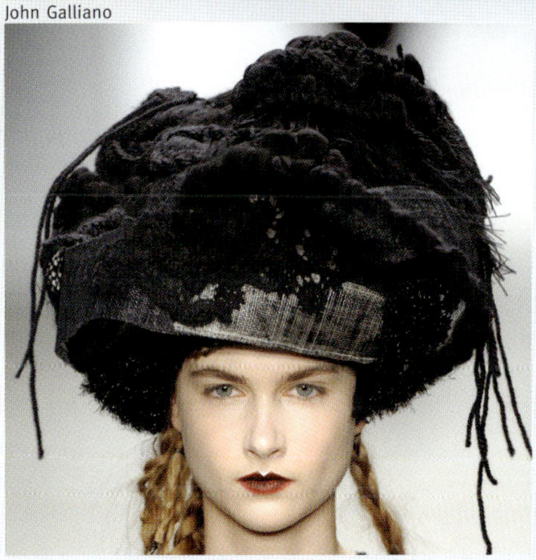

John Rocha

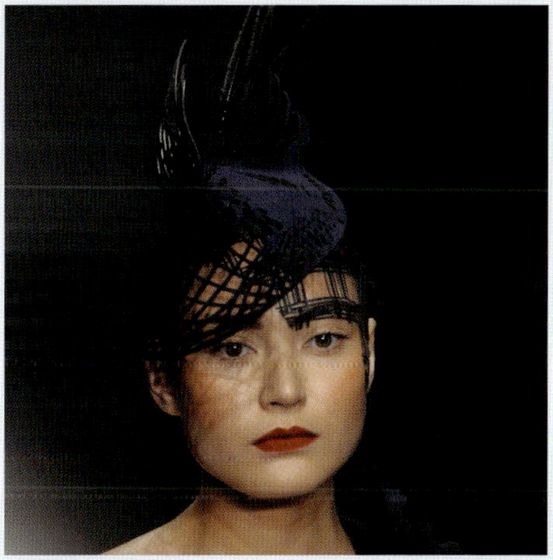

Corrie Nielsen

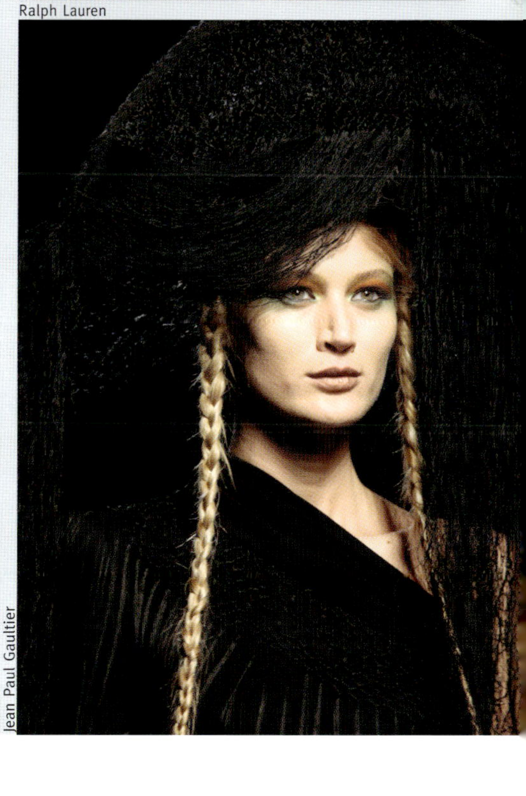

Jean Paul Gaultier

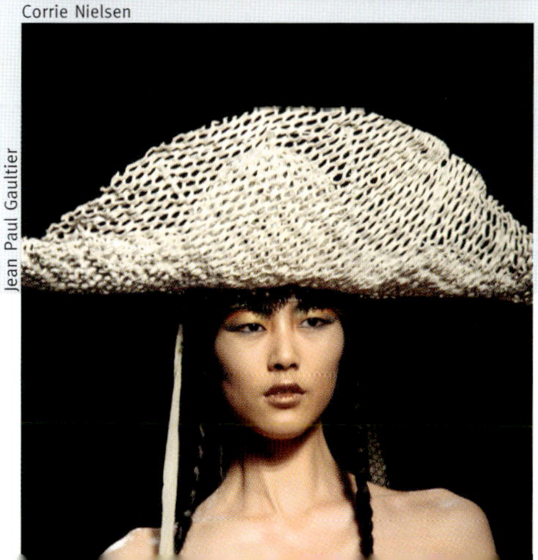

Jean Paul Gaultier

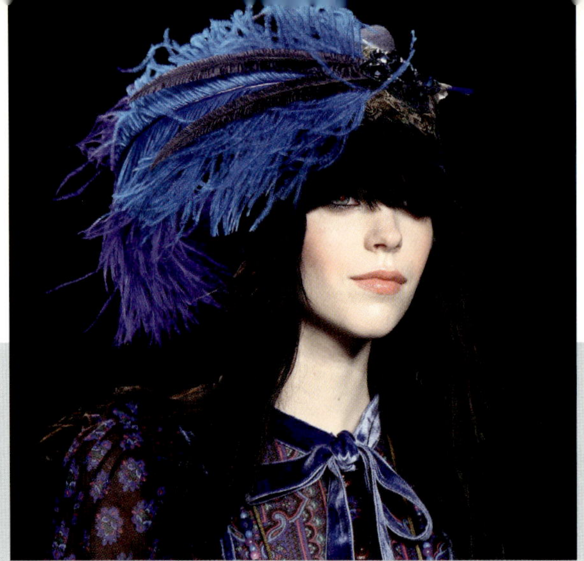

Anna Sui

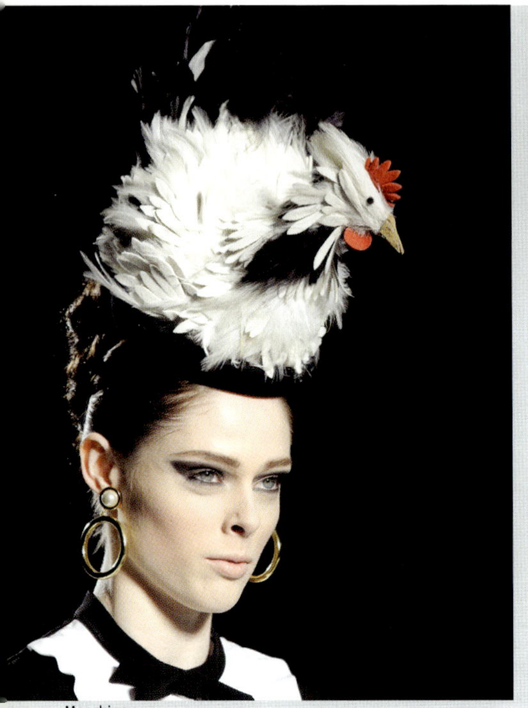

Moschino

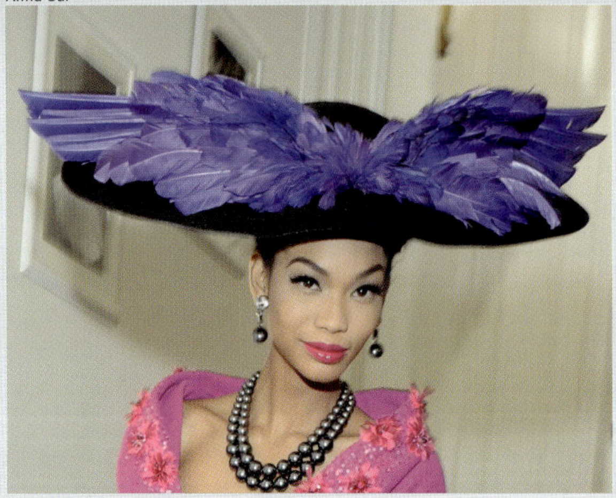

Dior

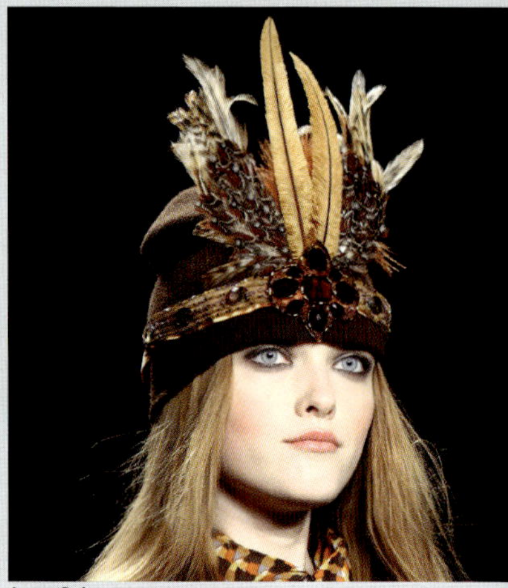

Anna Sui

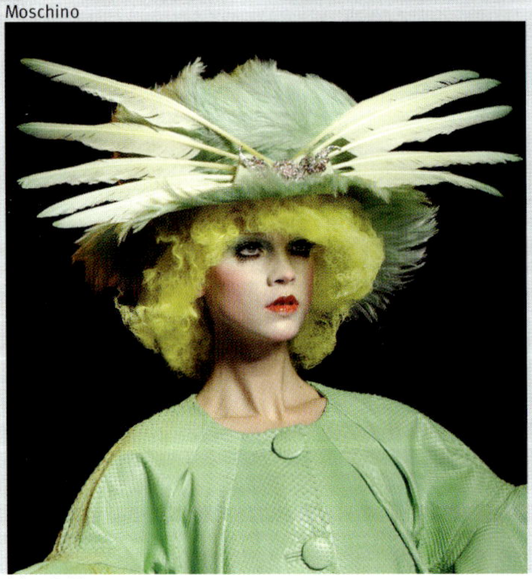

John Galliano

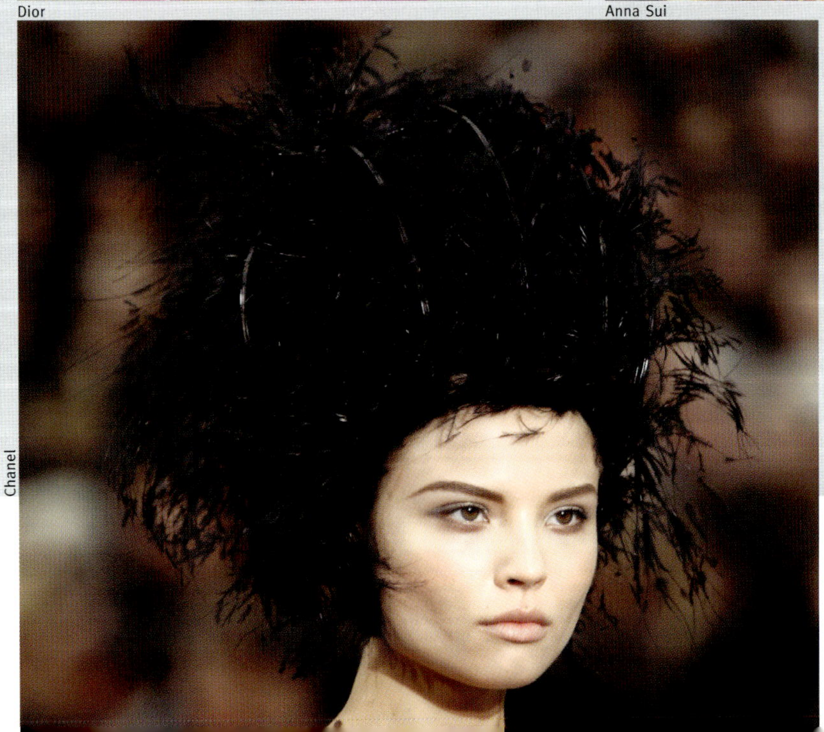

Chanel

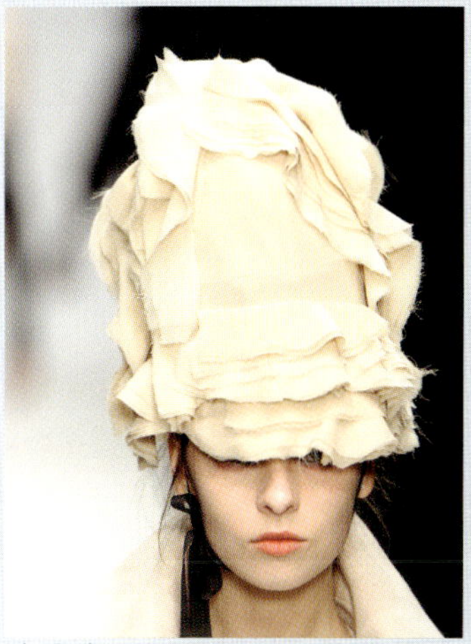

John Rocha

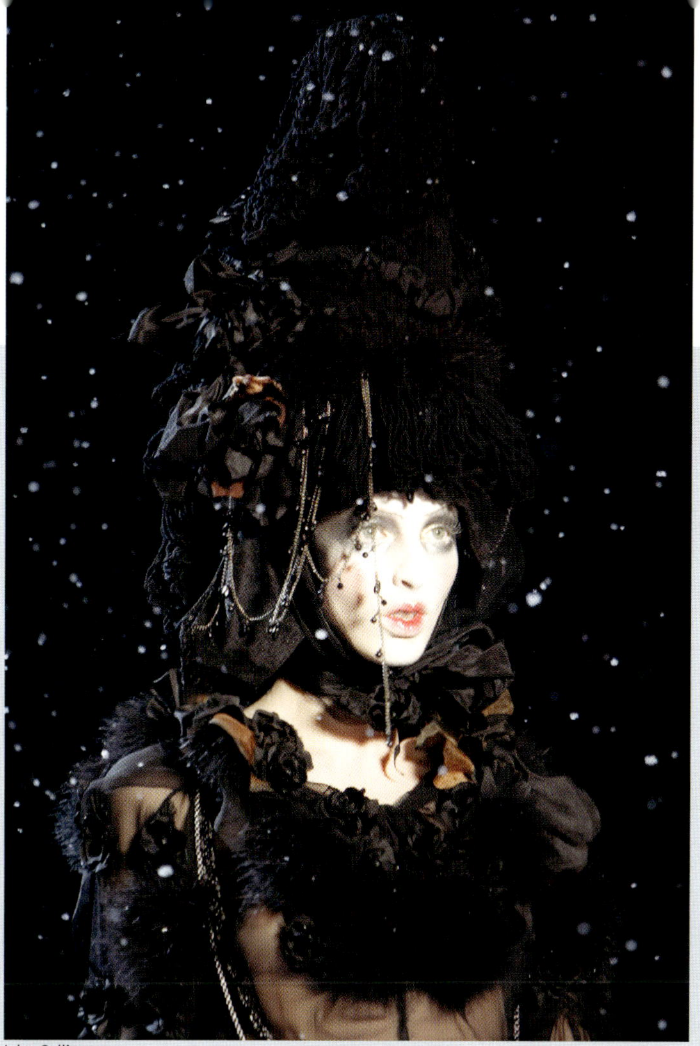

John Galliano

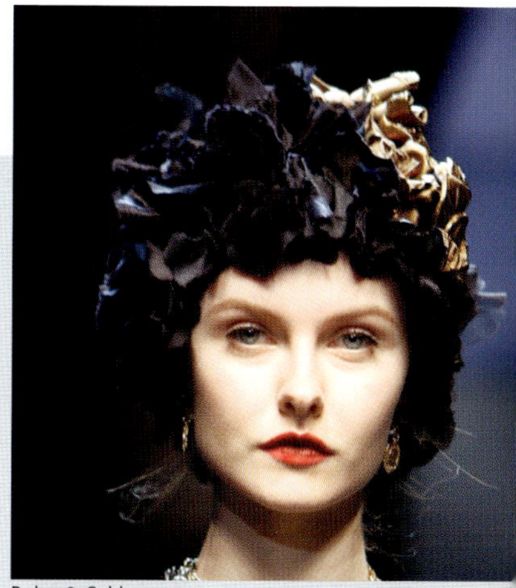

Dolce & Gabbana

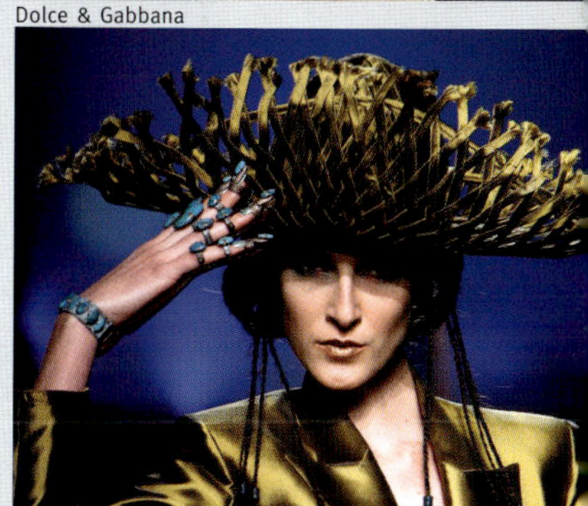

Jean Paul Gaultier

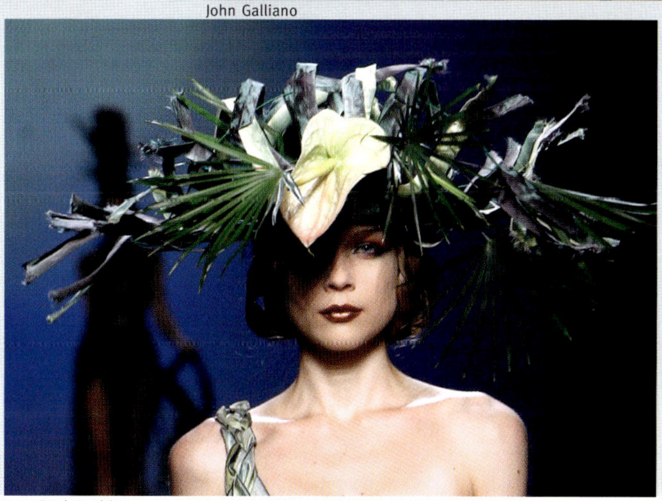

Jean Paul Gaultier

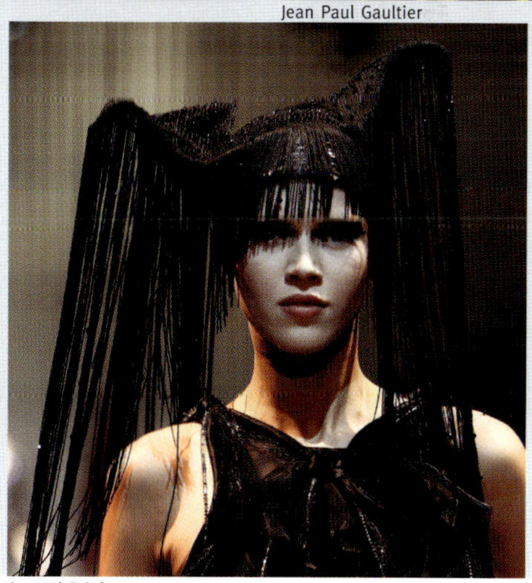

Armani Privè

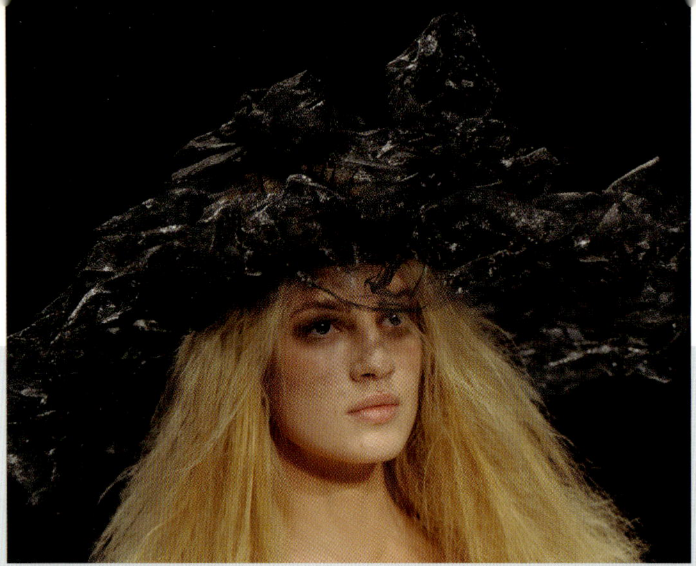
John Rocha

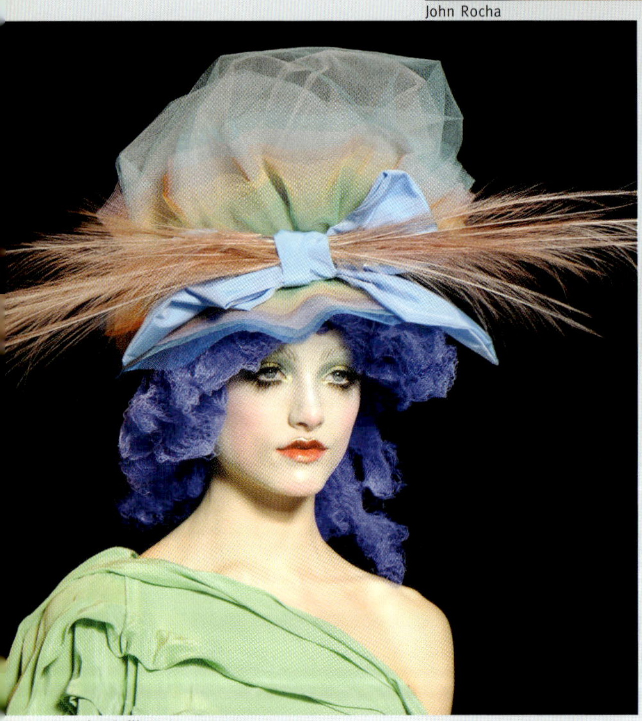
John Galliano

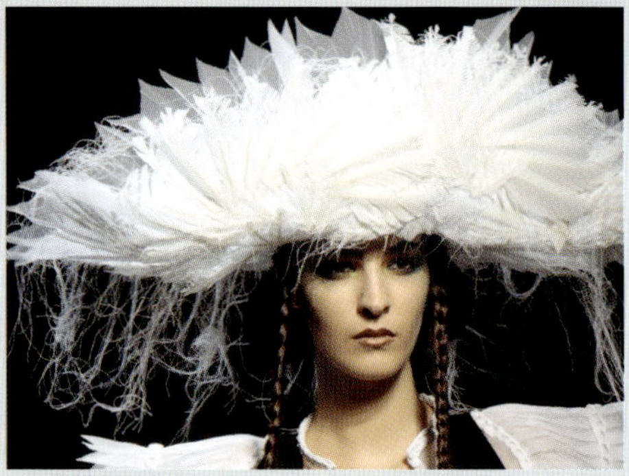
Jean Paul Gaultier

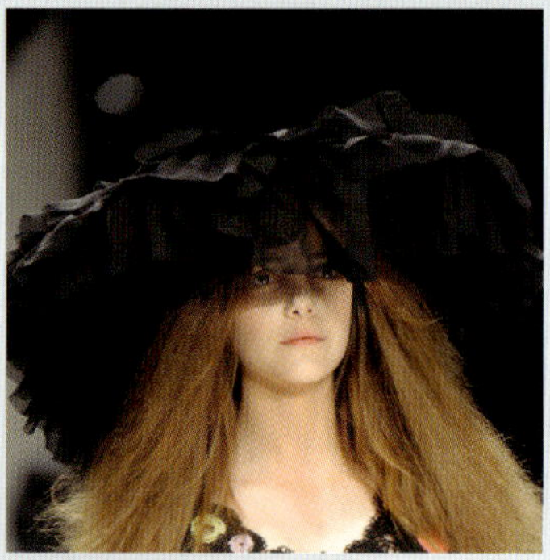
John Rocha

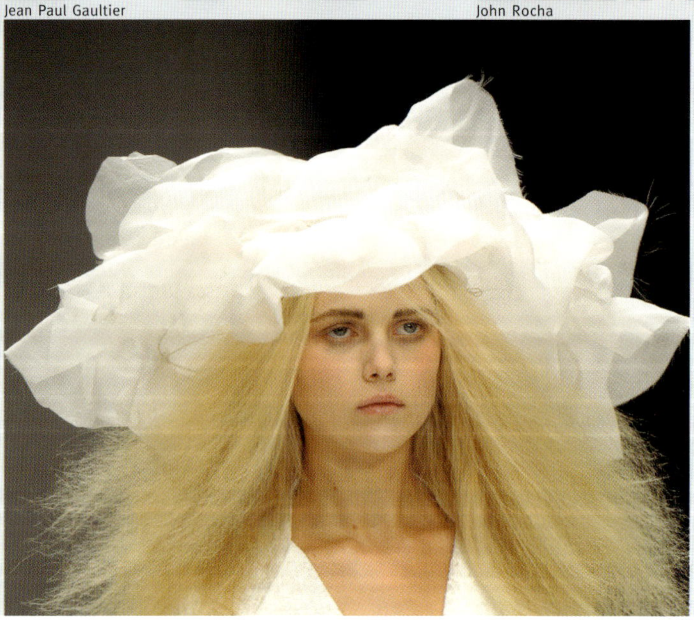
John Rocha

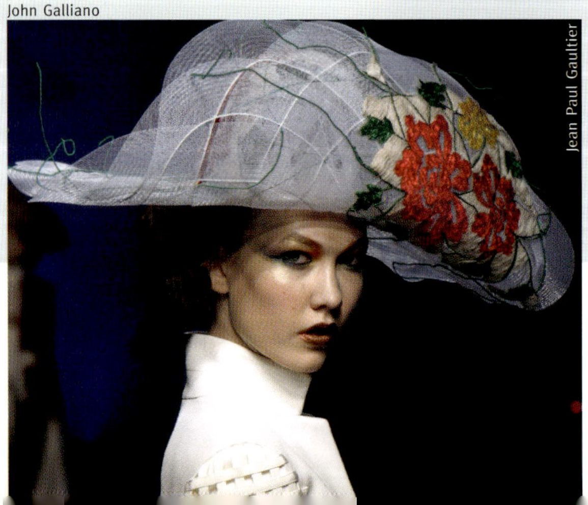
Jean Paul Gaultier

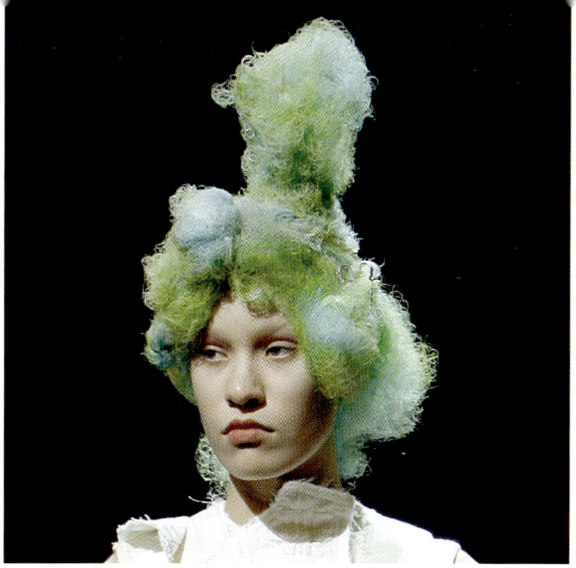

Comme des Garçons

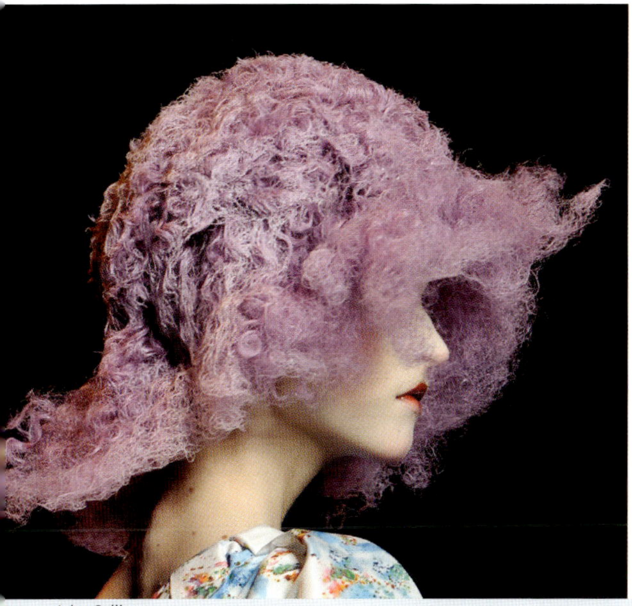

John Galliano

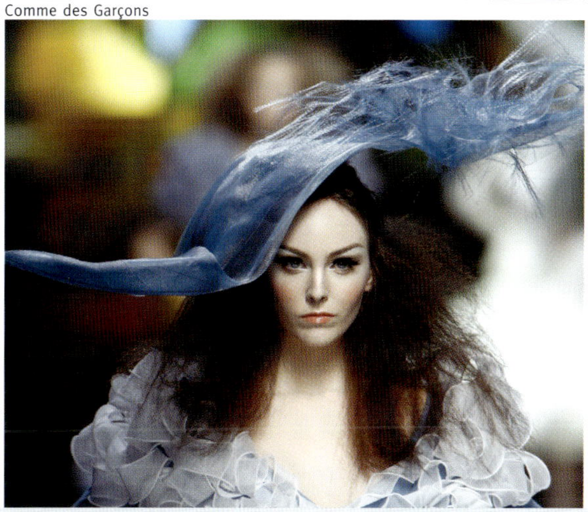

Dior

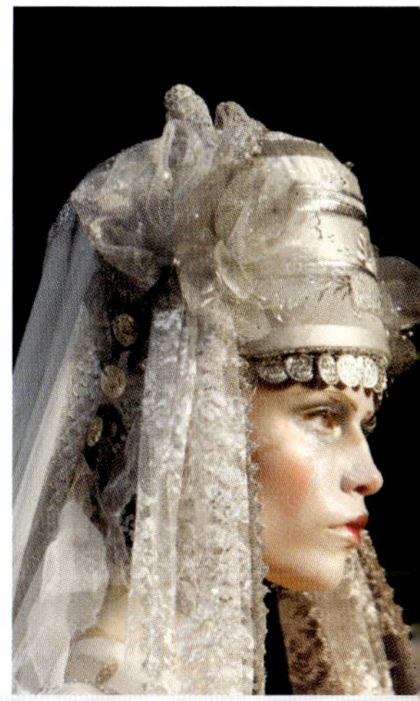

John Galliano

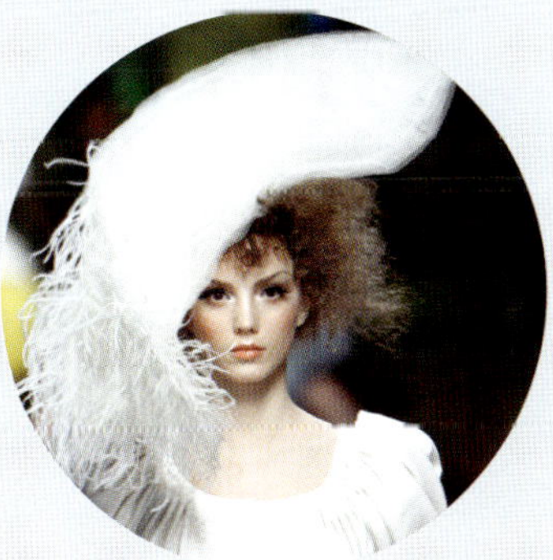

Dior

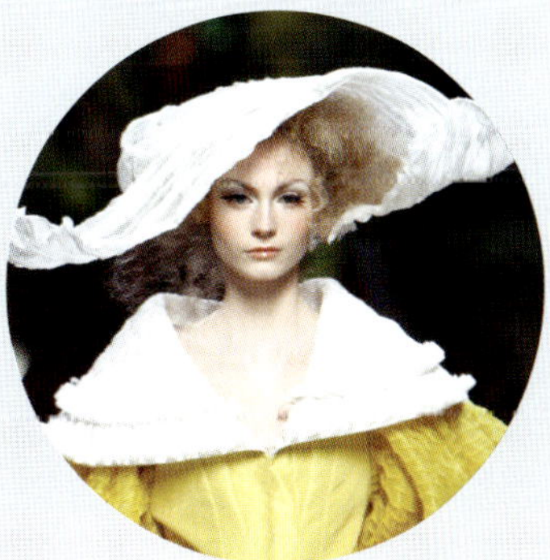

Dior

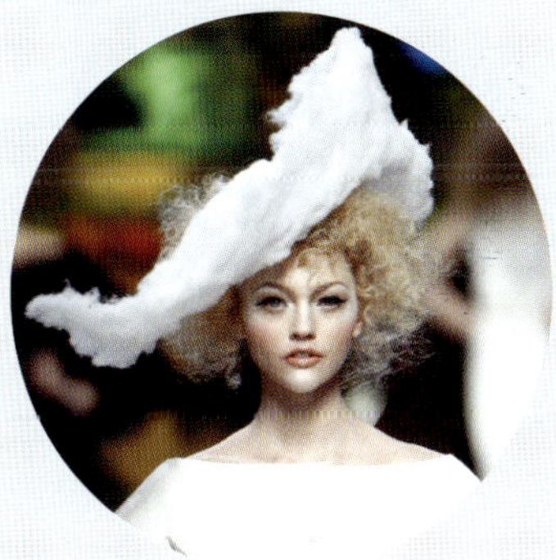

Dior

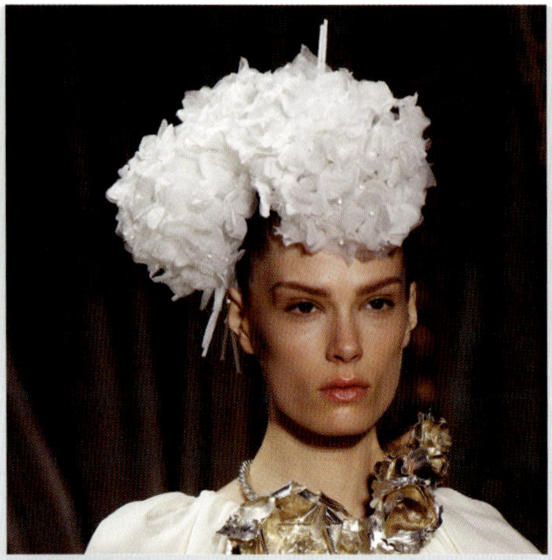

Giambattista Valli

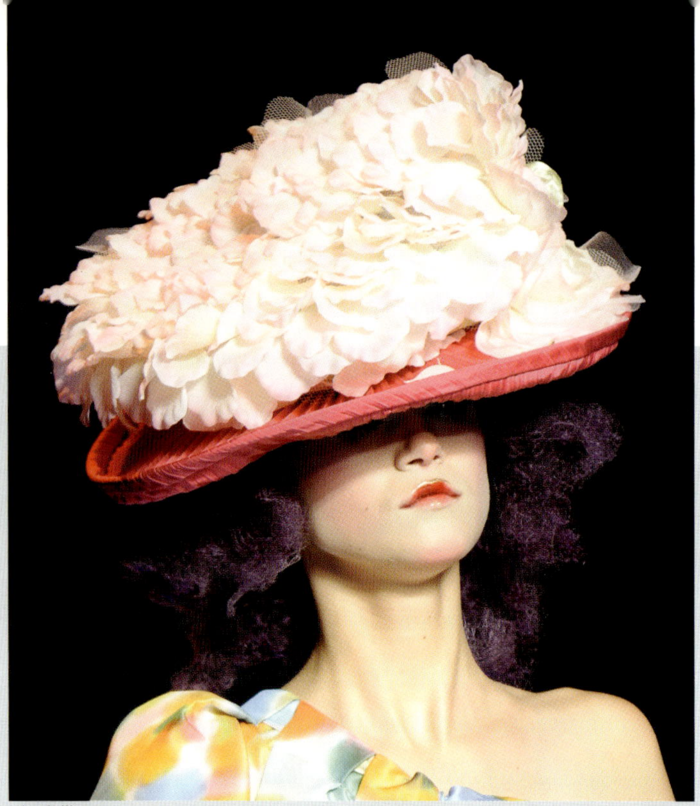

John Galliano

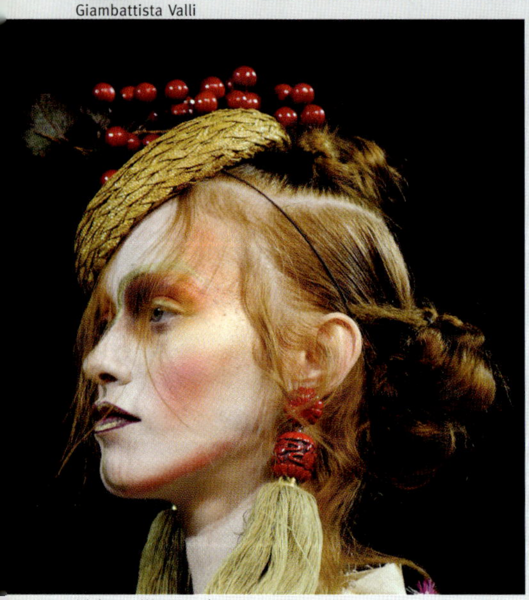

Vivienne Westwood

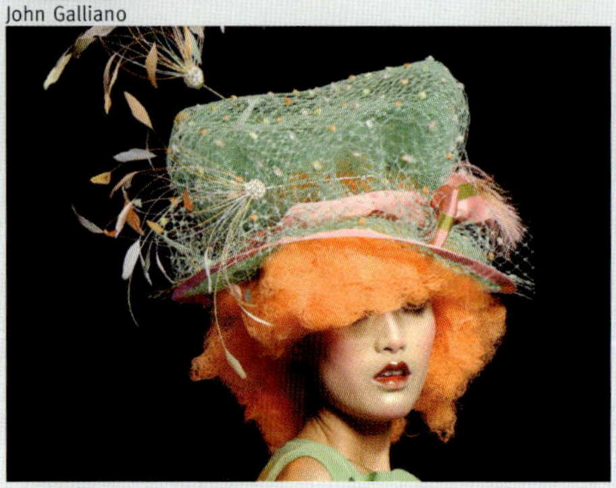

John Galliano

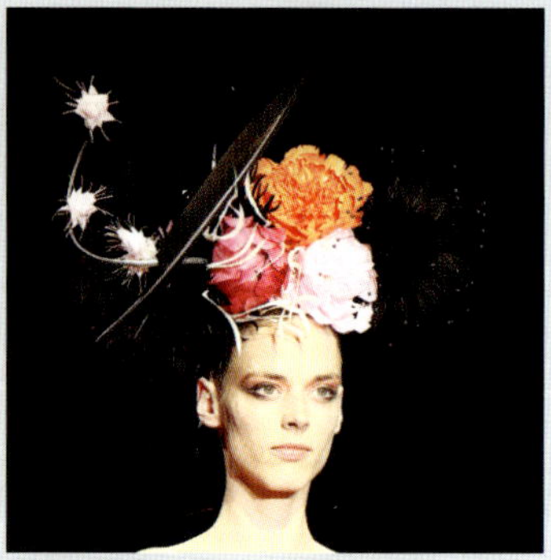

Armani Privè

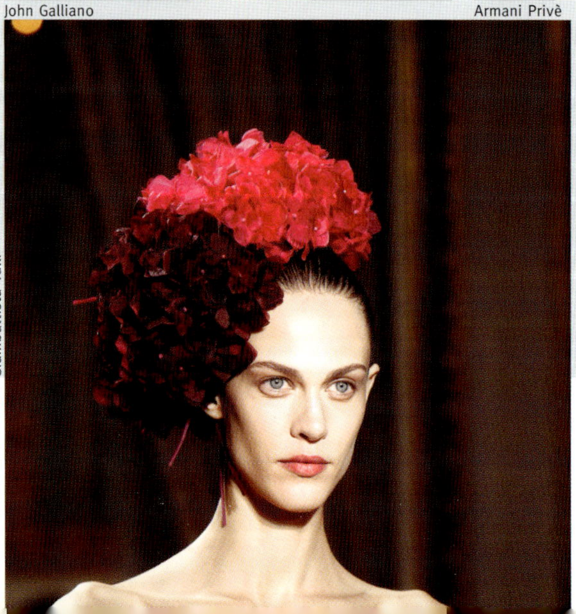

Giambattista Valli

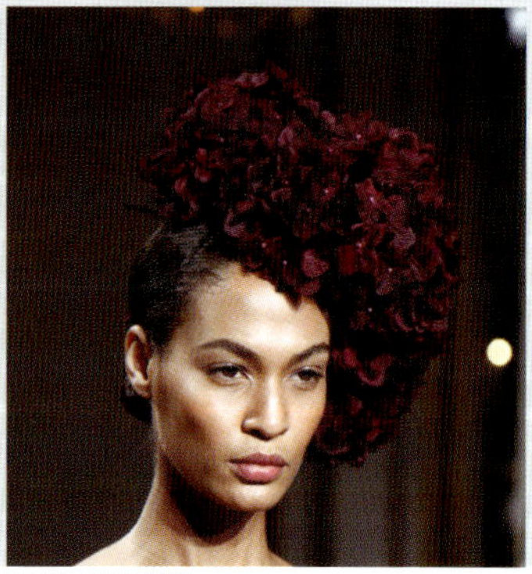

Giambattista Valli

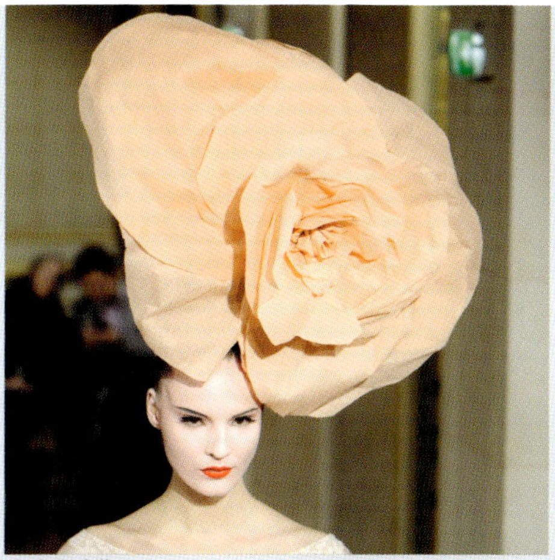

Alexis Mabille

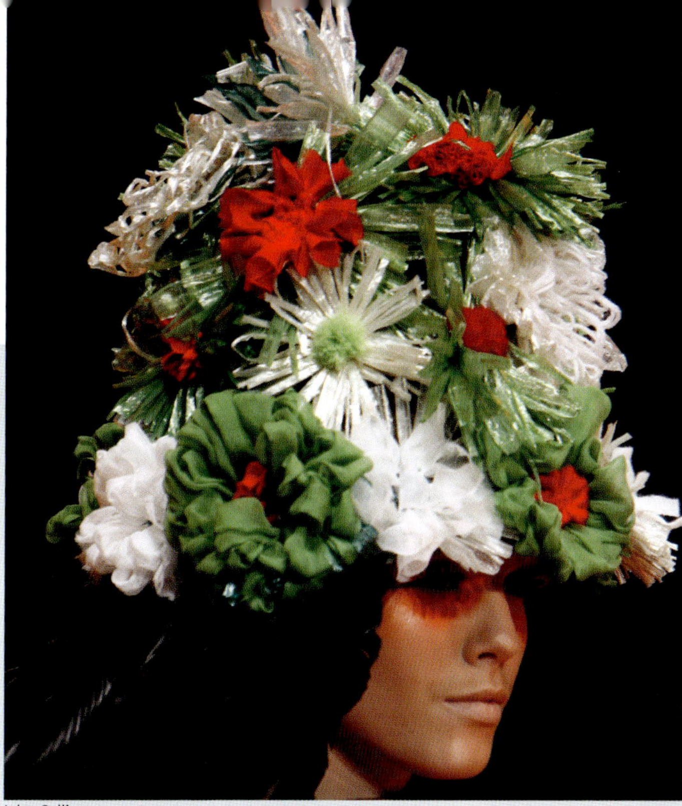

John Galliano

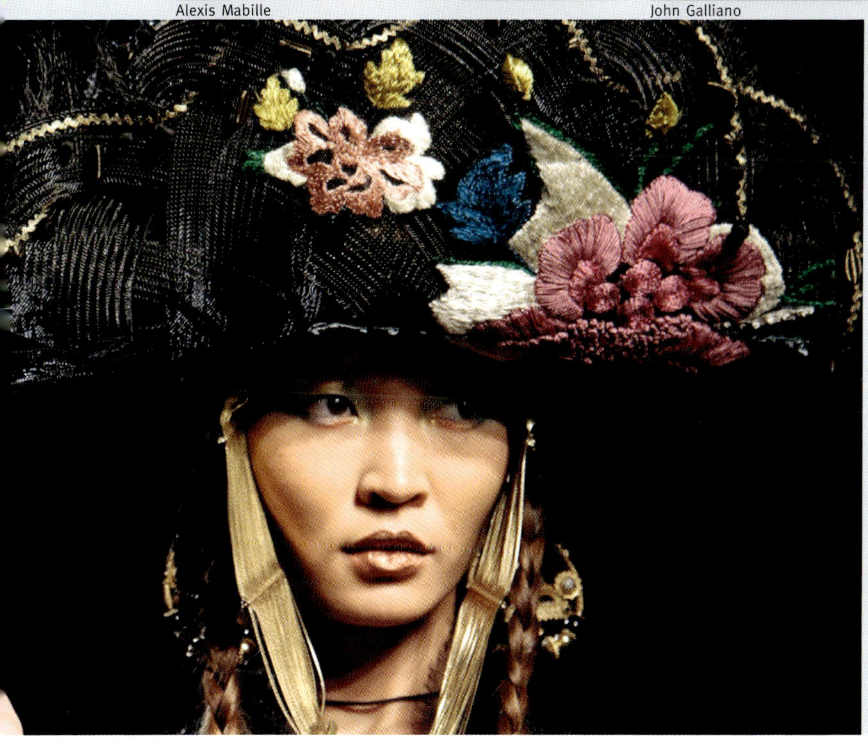

Jean Paul Gaultier

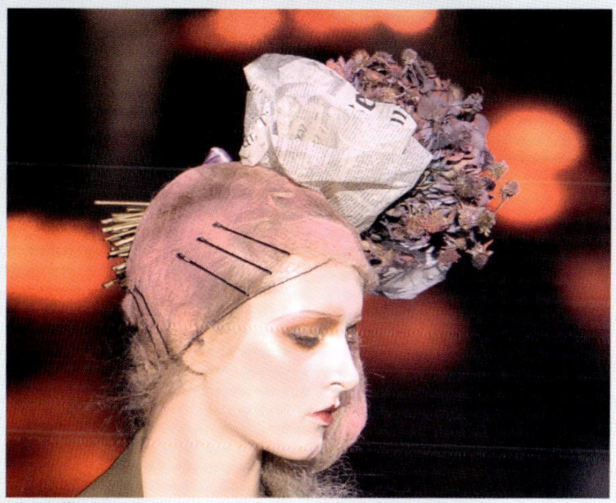

John Galliano

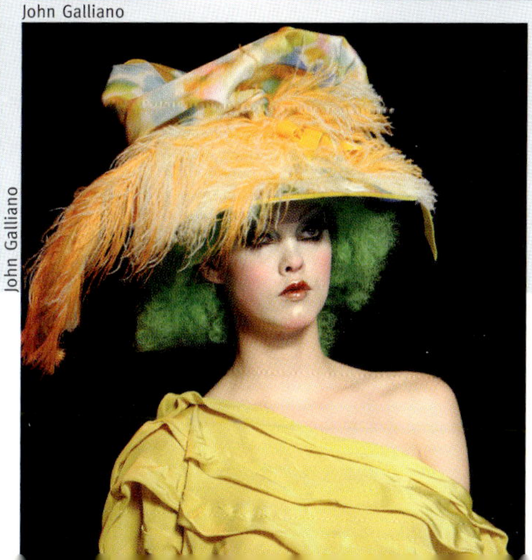

John Galliano

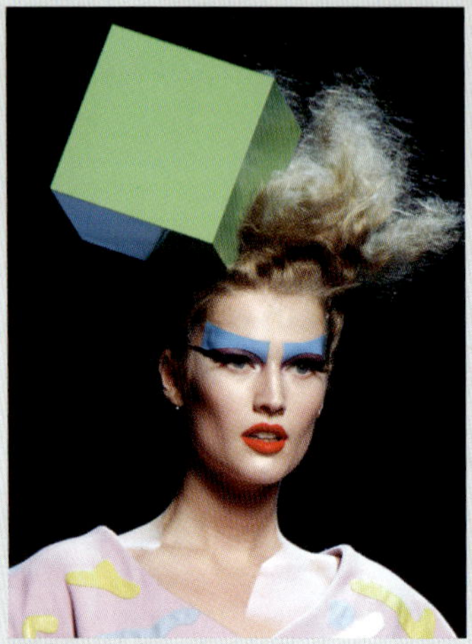

Dior

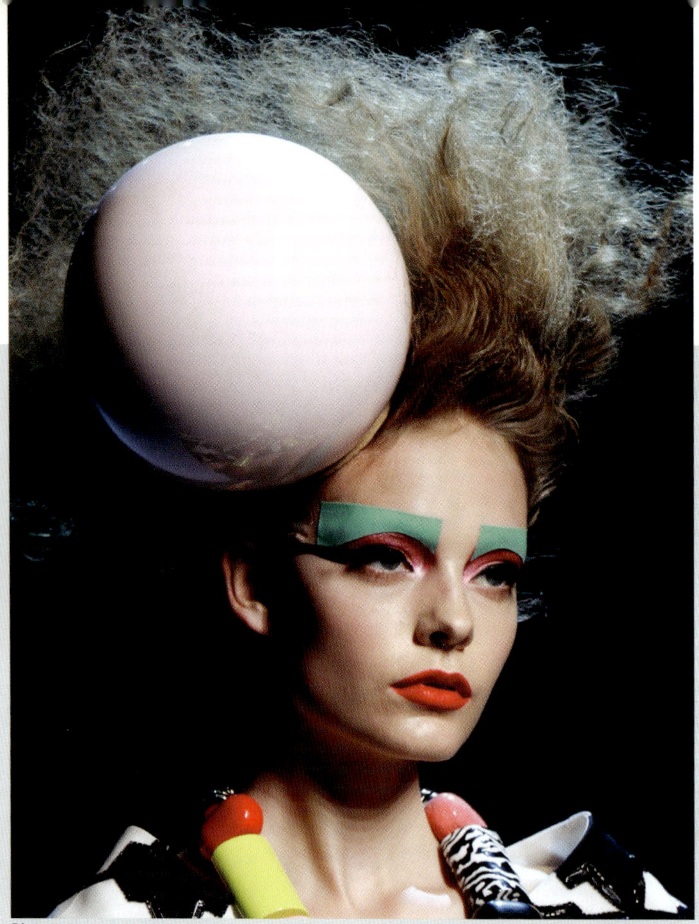

Dior

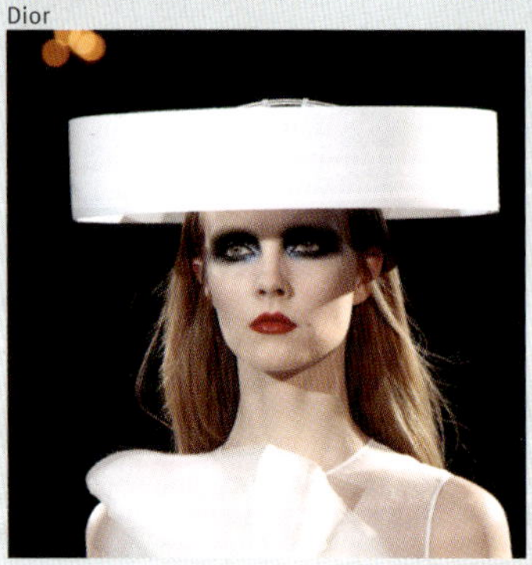

Givenchy

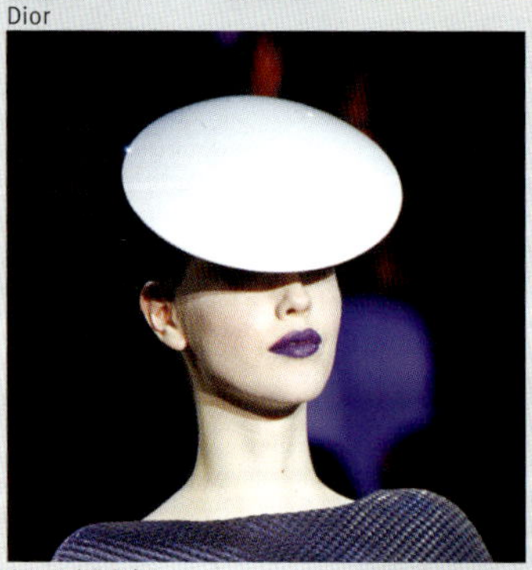

Armani Privè

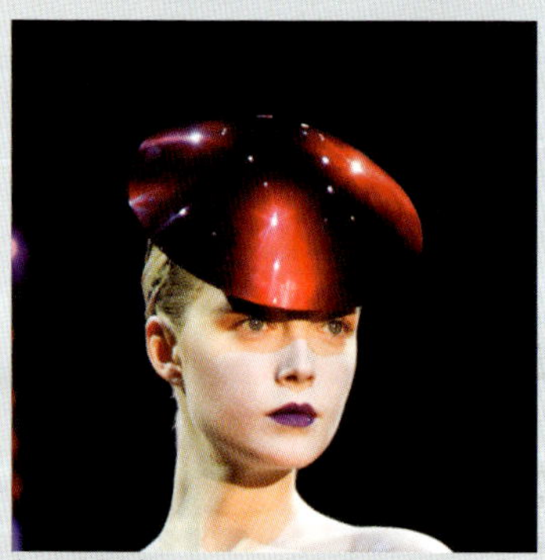

Armani Privè

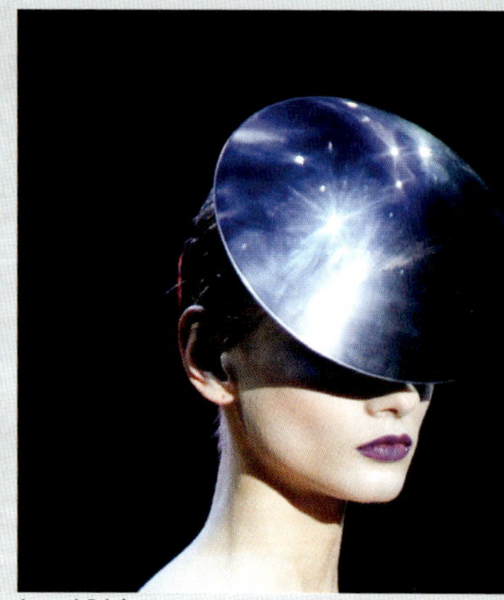

Armani Privè

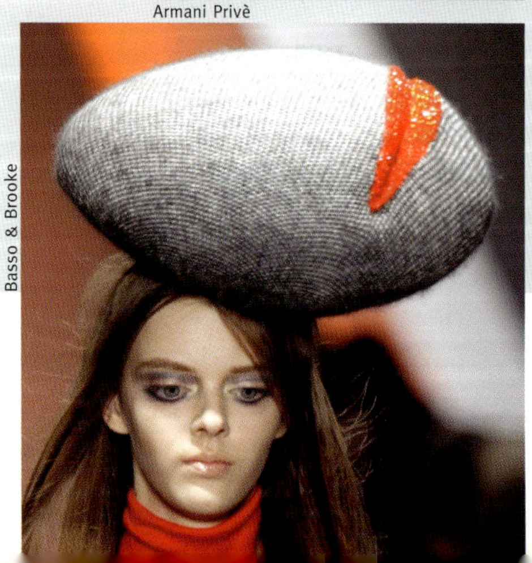

Basso & Brooke

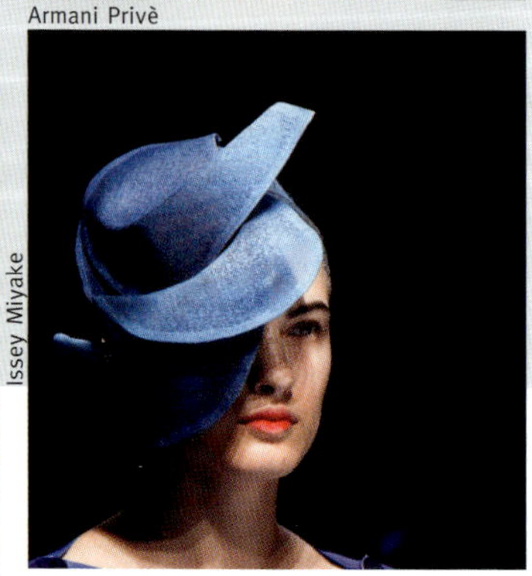

Issey Miyake

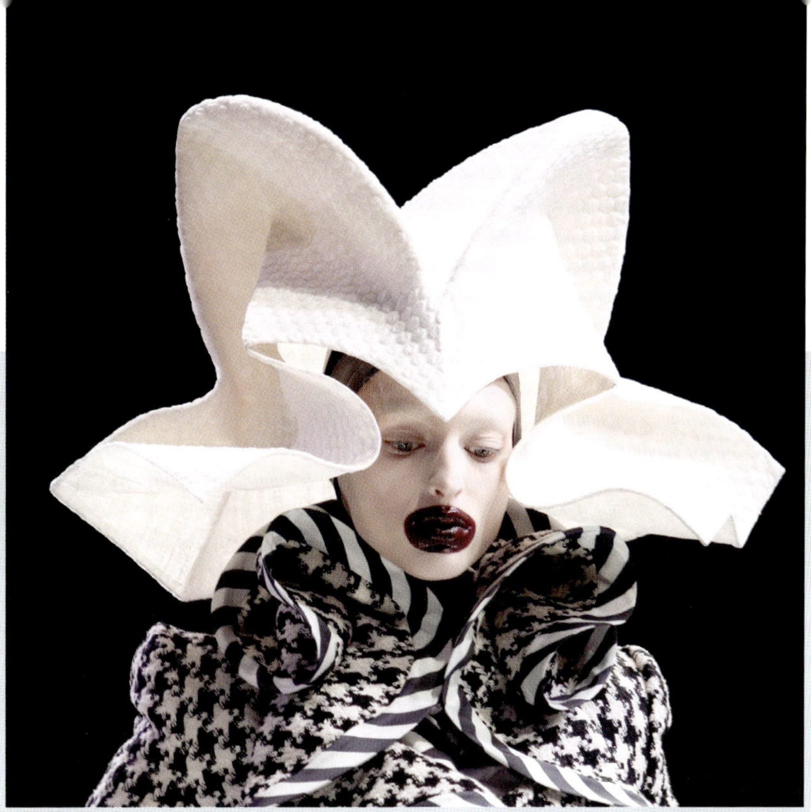

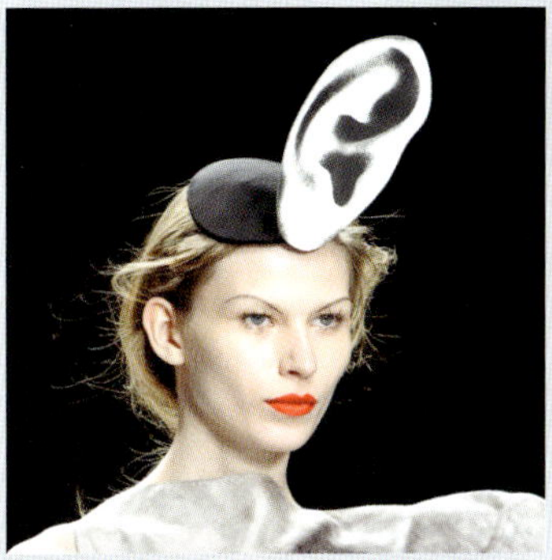

JC de Castelbajac

Alexander McQueen

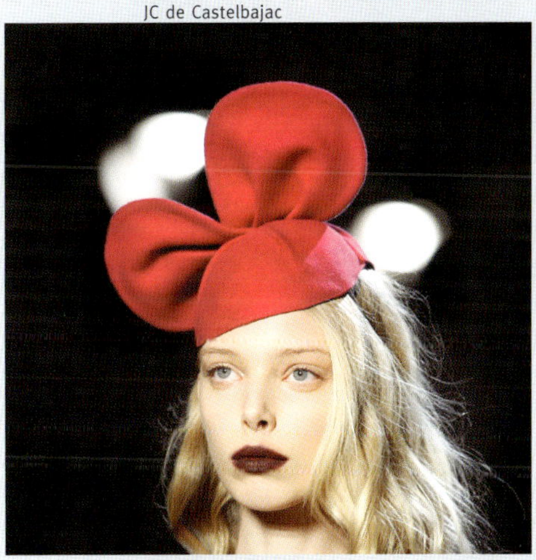

Moschino Cheap & Chic

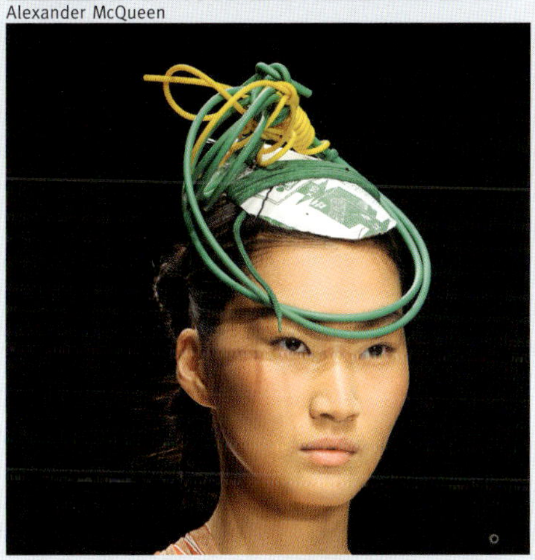

Kinder Aggugini

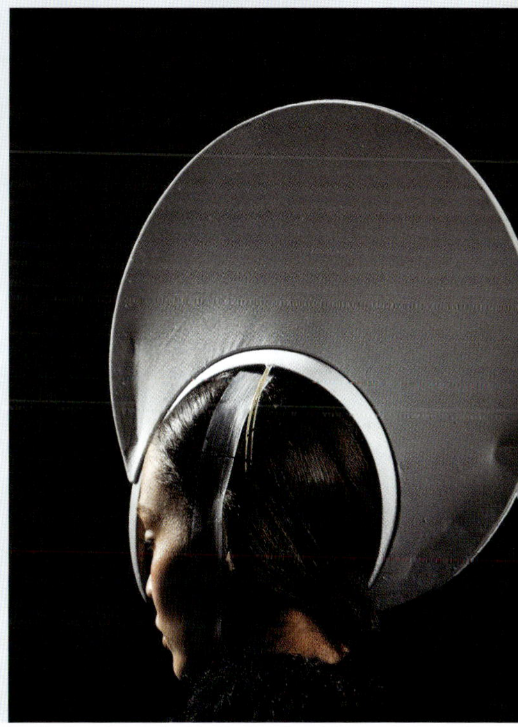

Gareth Pugh

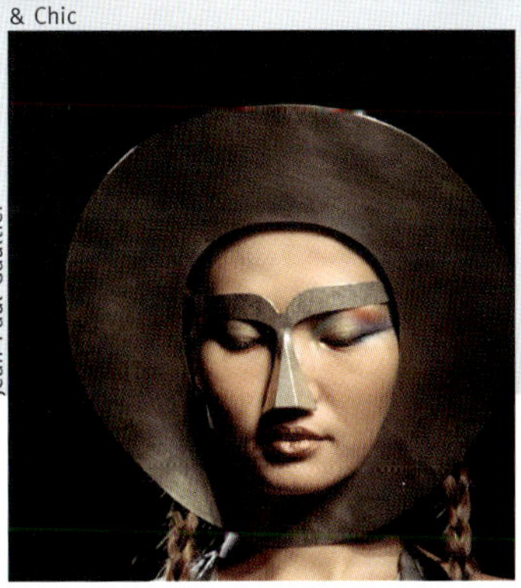

Jean Paul Gaultier

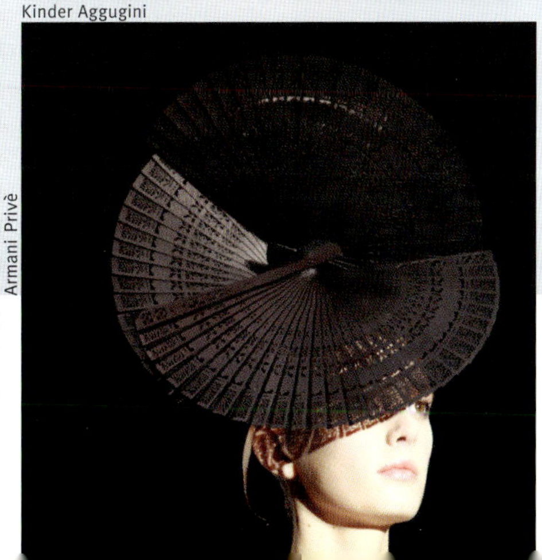

Armani Privè

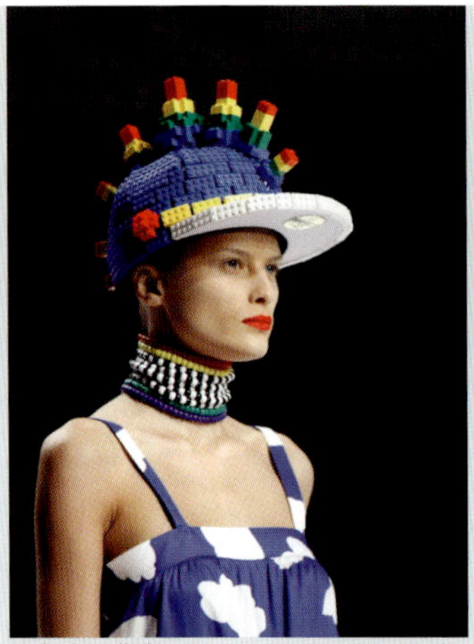
JC de Castelbajac

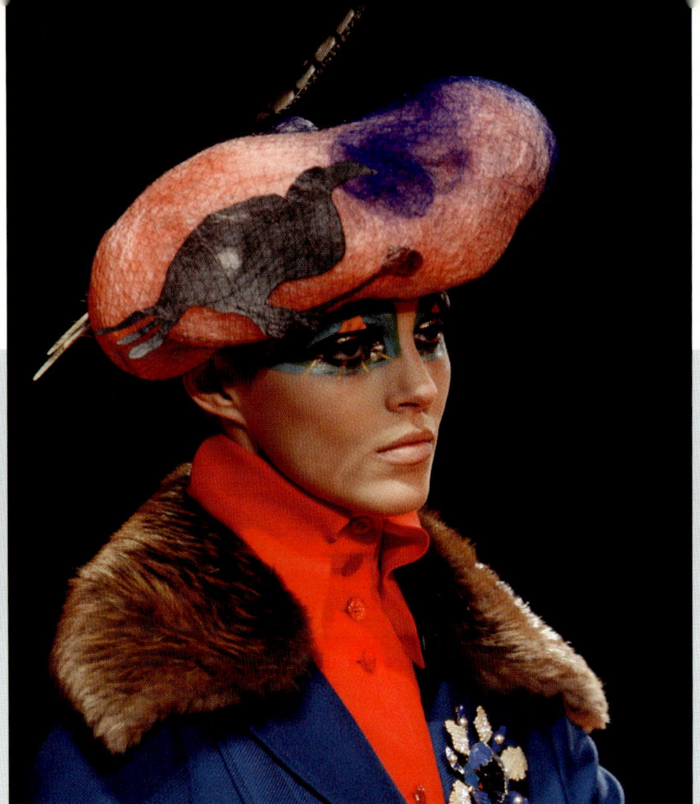
John Galliano

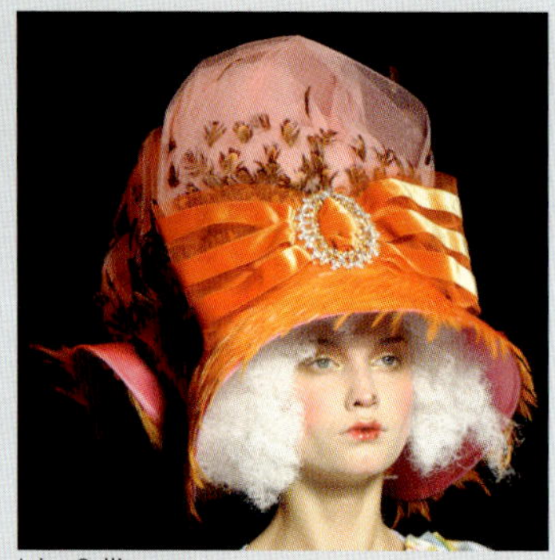
John Galliano

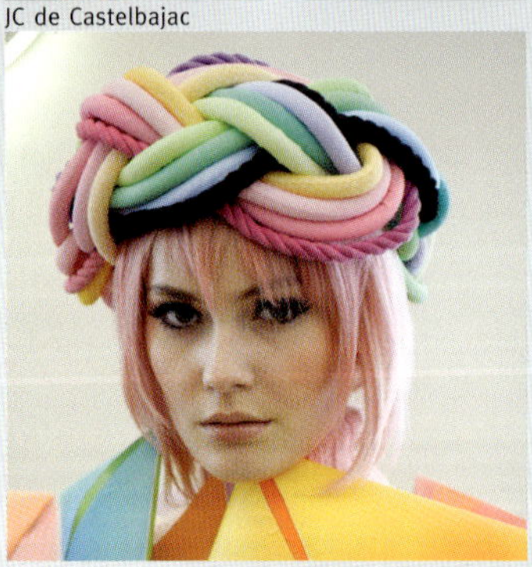
Fred Butler

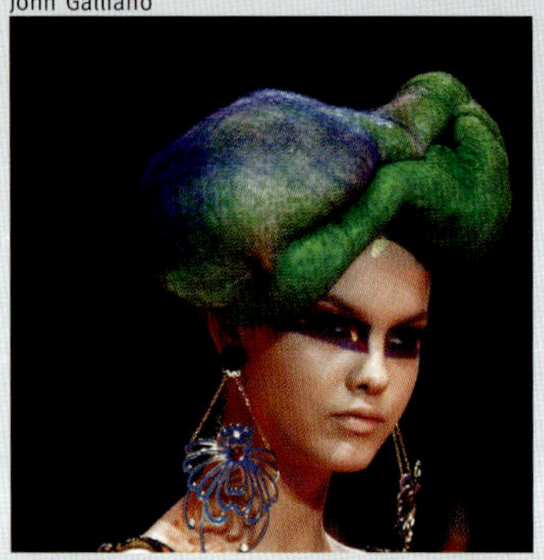
John Galliano

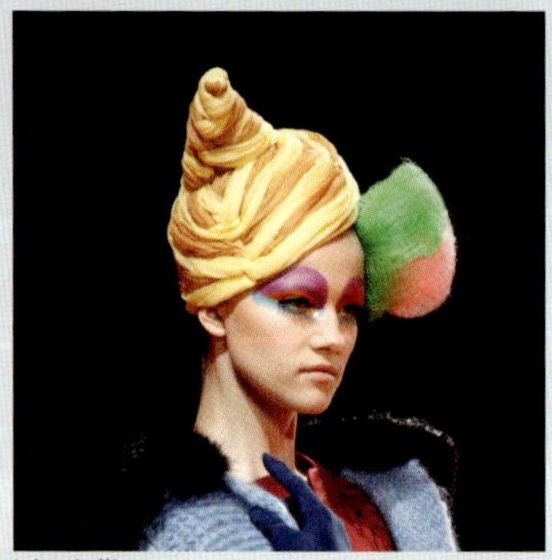
John Galliano

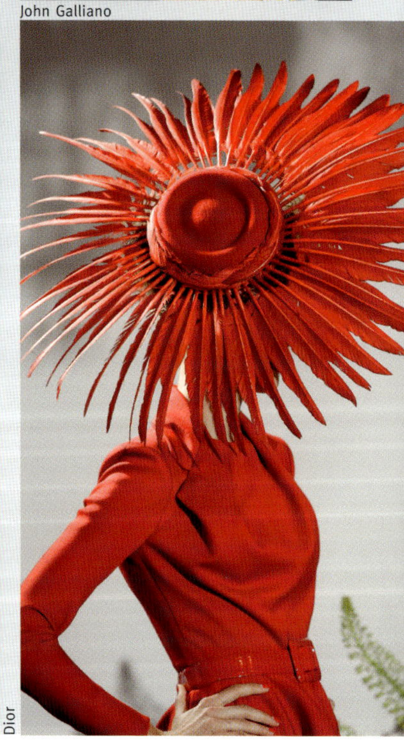
Dior

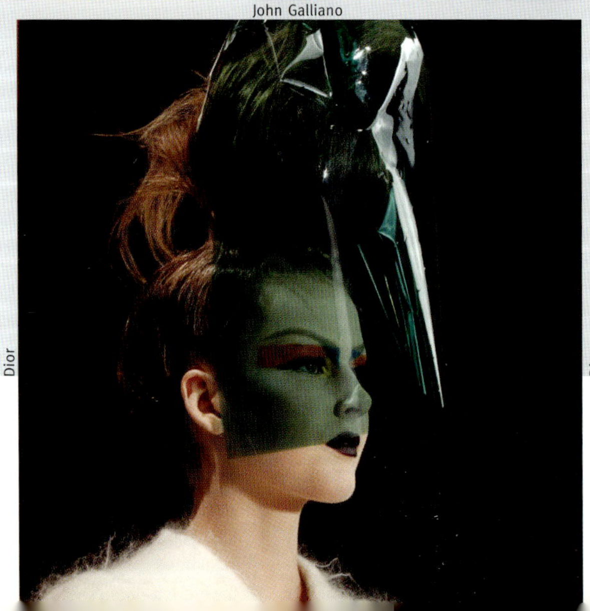
Dior

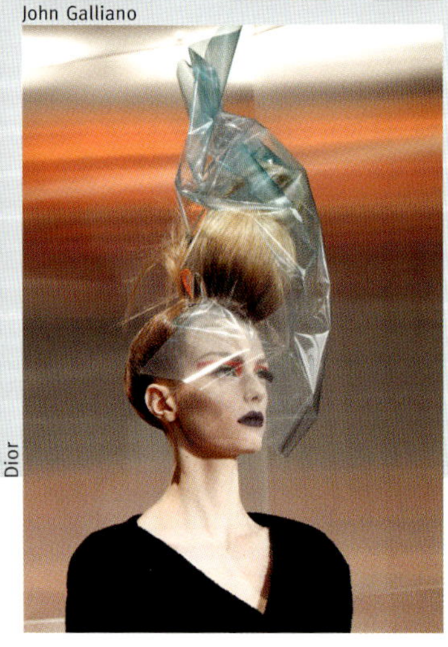
Dior

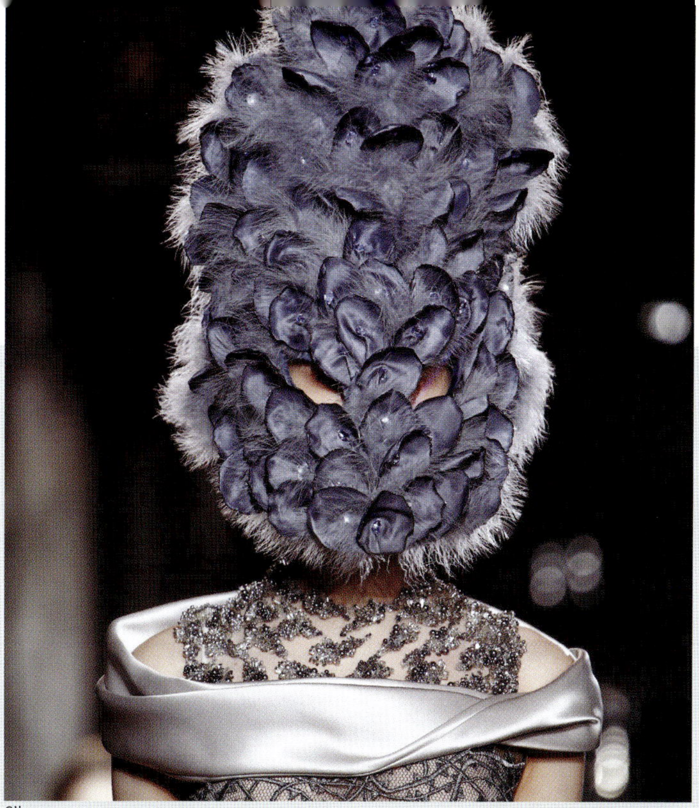
Giles

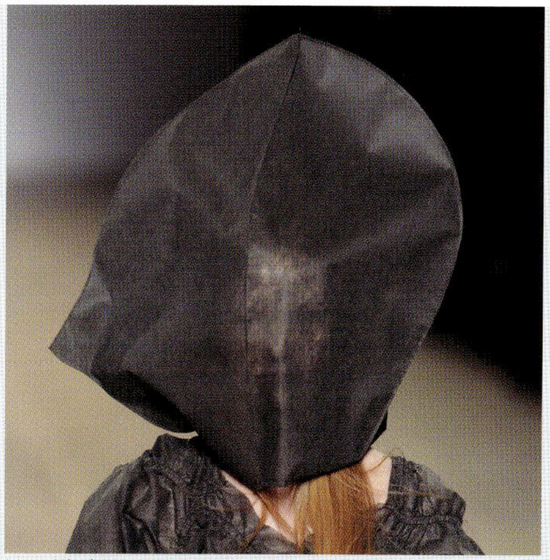
Issey Miyake

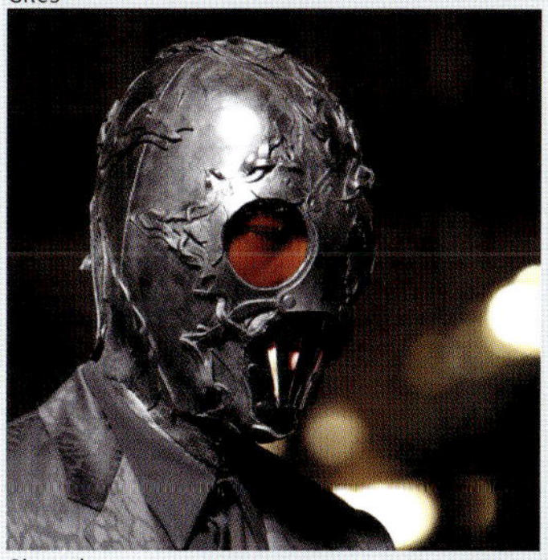
Givenchy

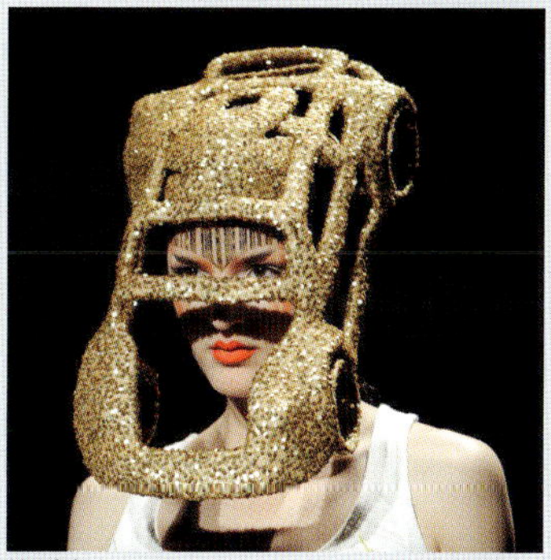
Manish Arora

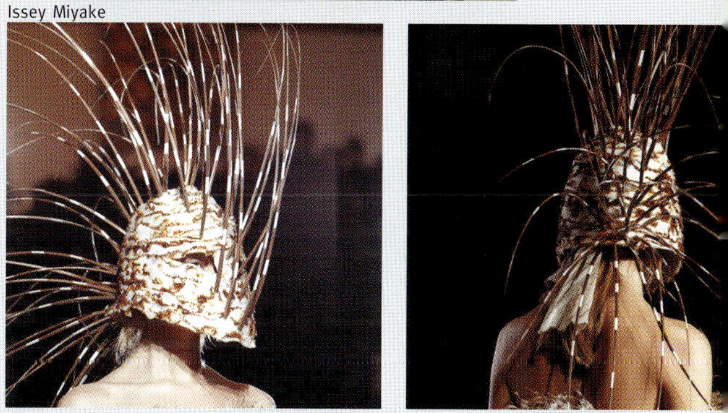
Giles

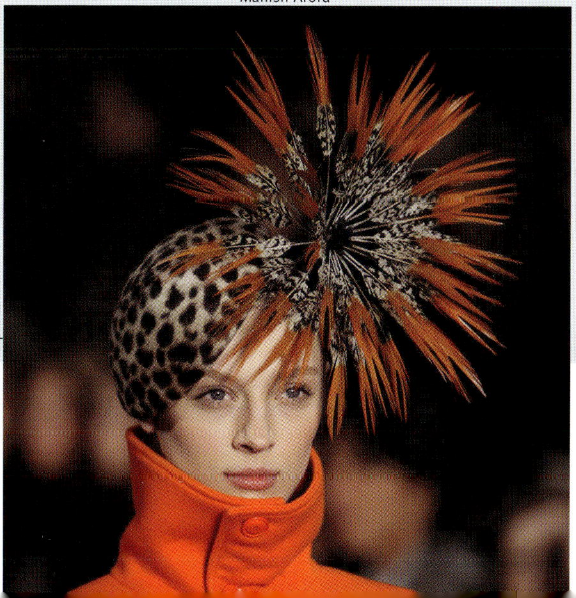
Ralph Lauren

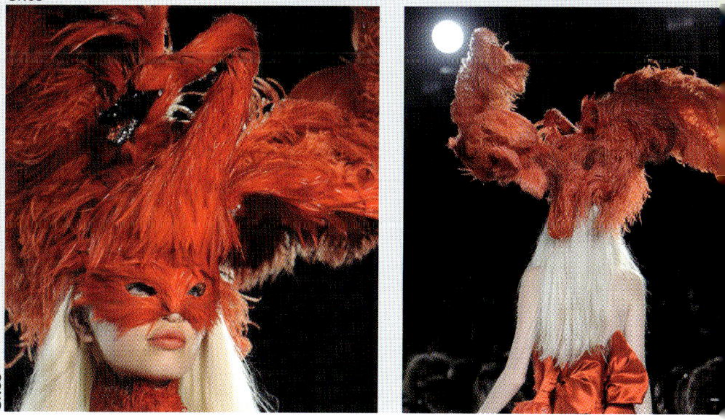
Giles

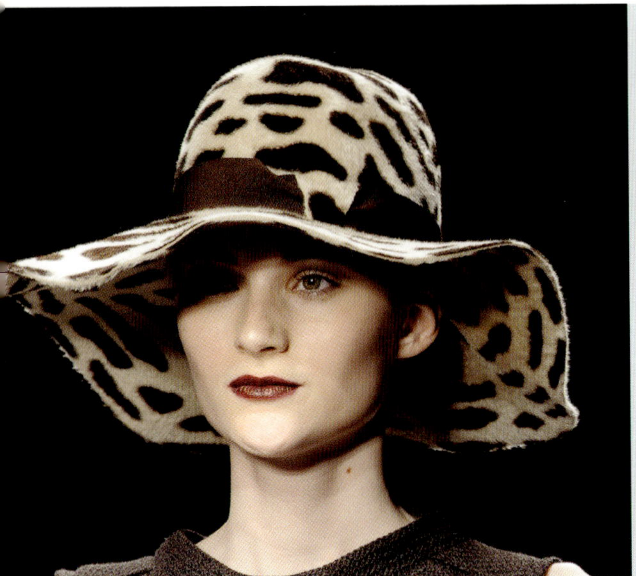

Caroline Charles

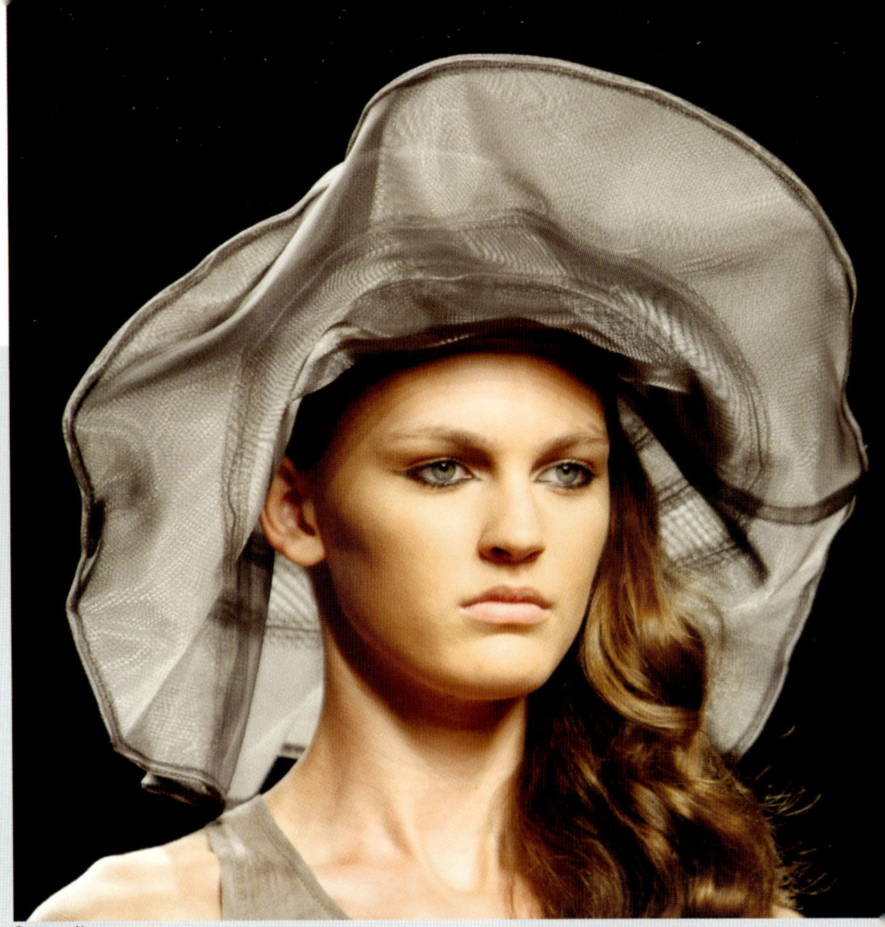

Gaetano Navarra

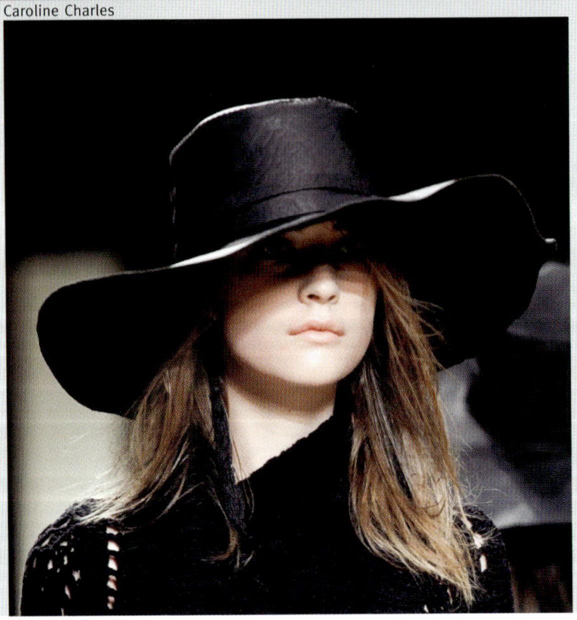

Ann Demeulemeester

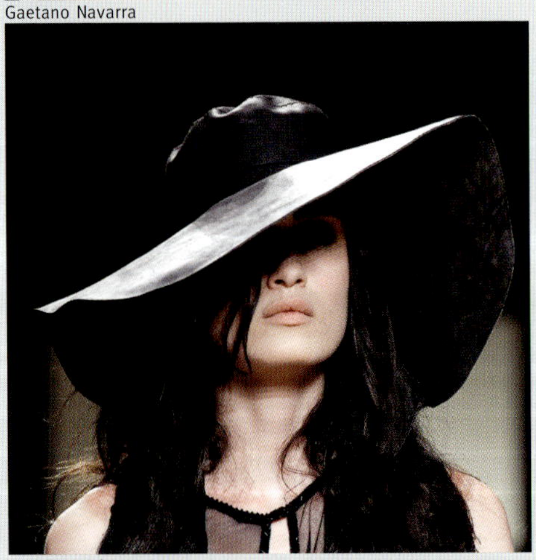

Ann Demeulemeester

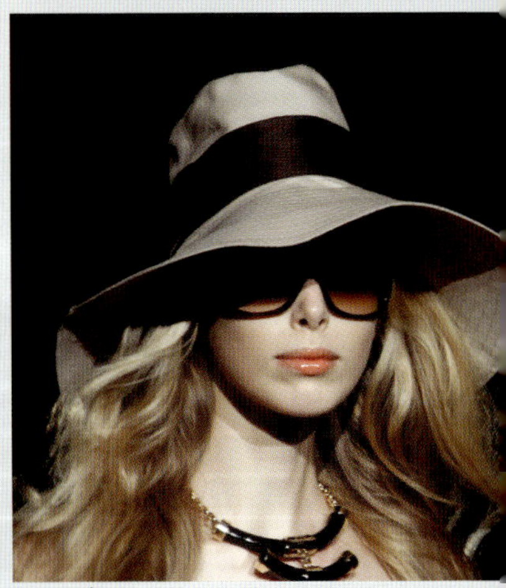

Dsquared2

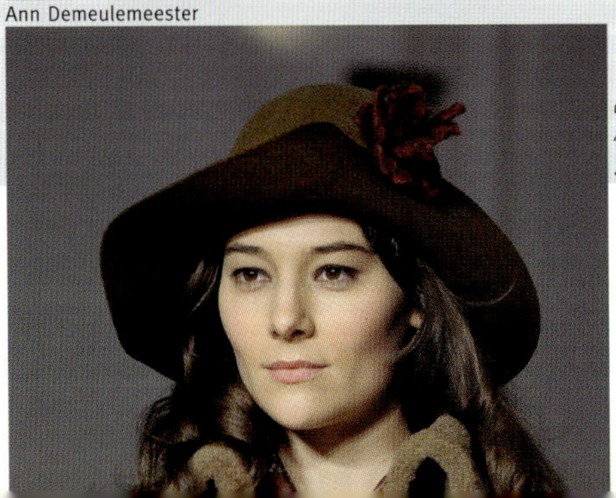

Agnès B.

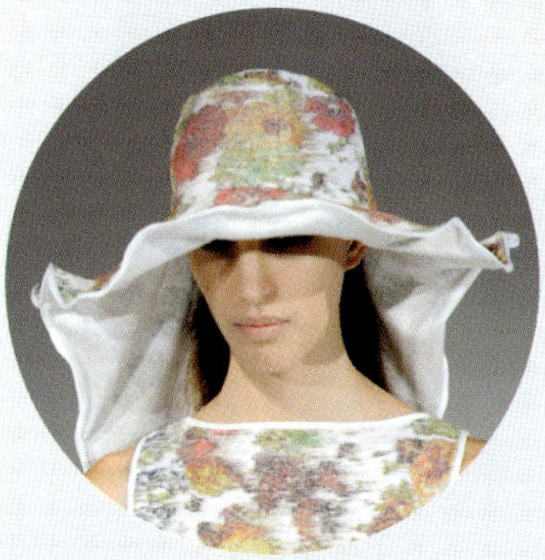

Hussein Chalayan

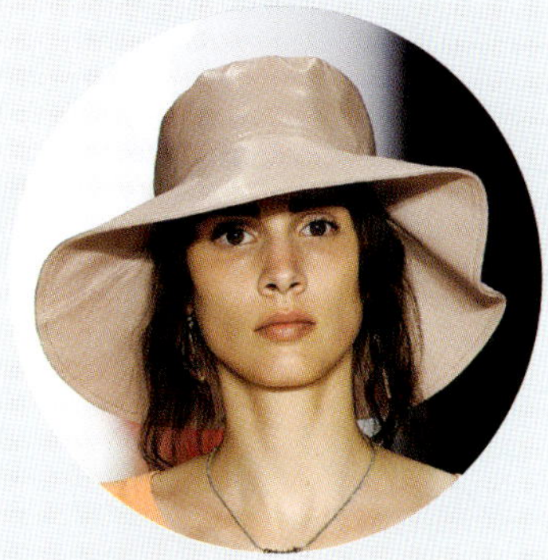

Escada Sport

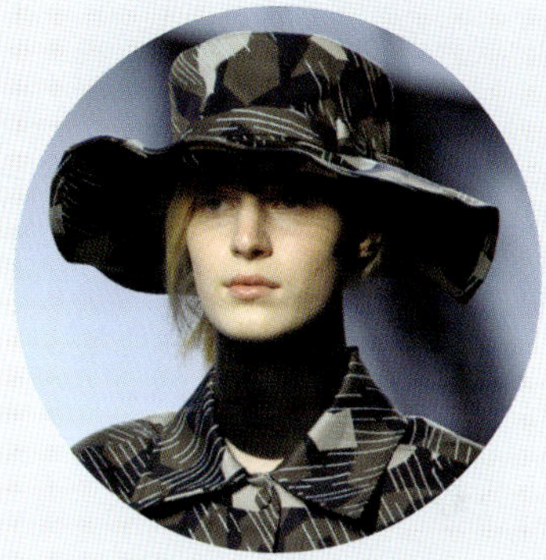

Acne

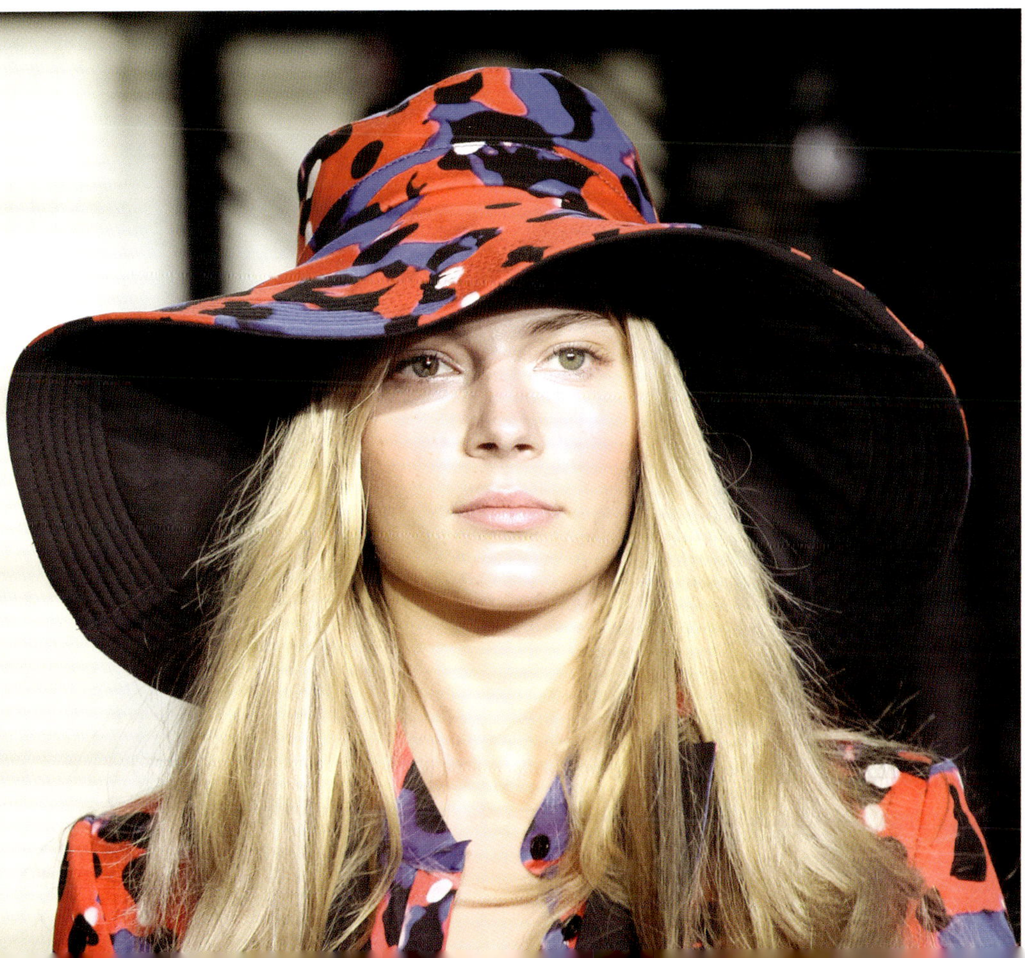

DKNY

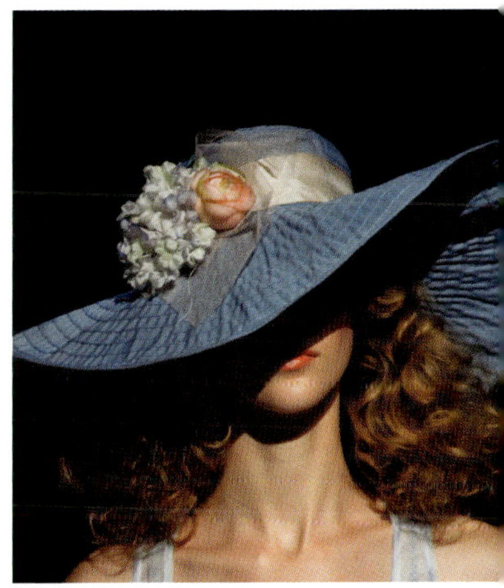

Badgley Mischka

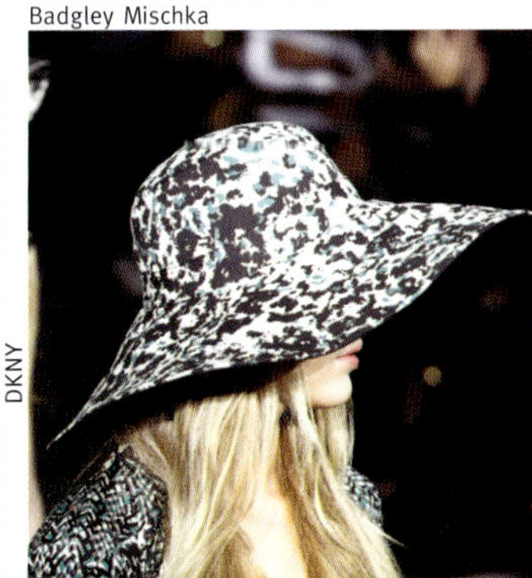

DKNY

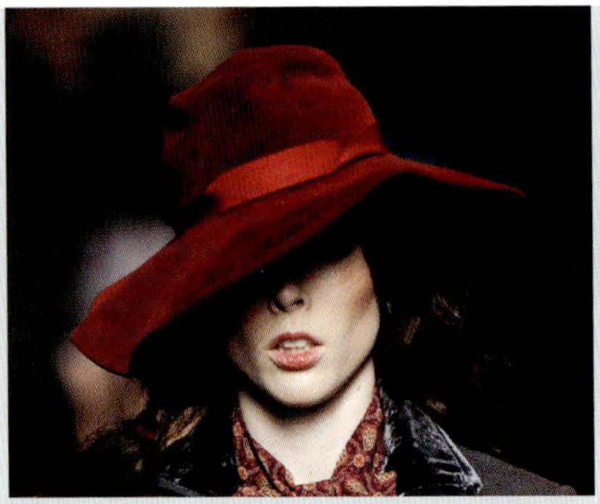
Dior

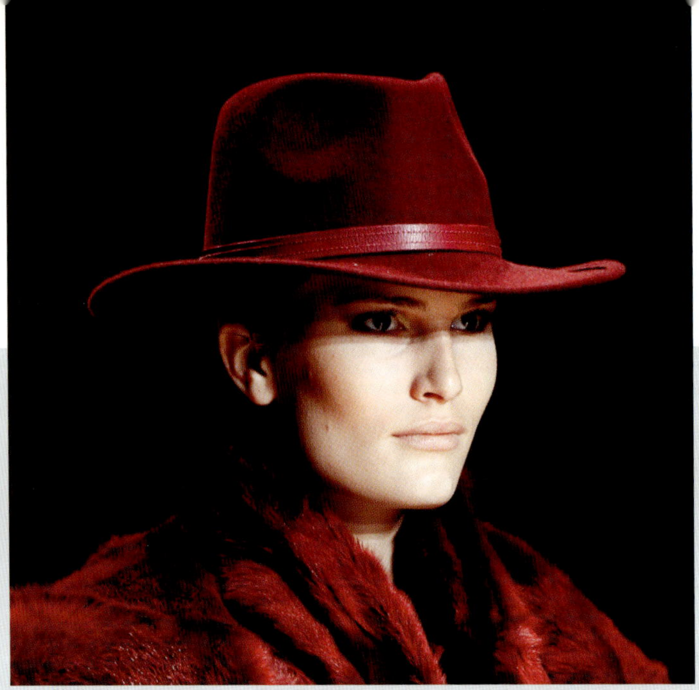
Laura Biagiotti

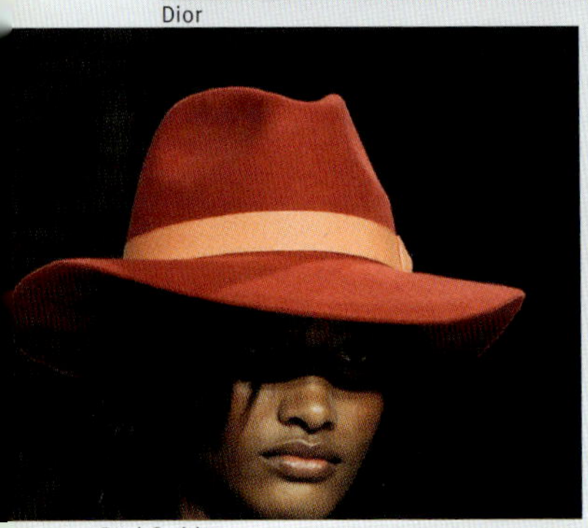
Paul Smith

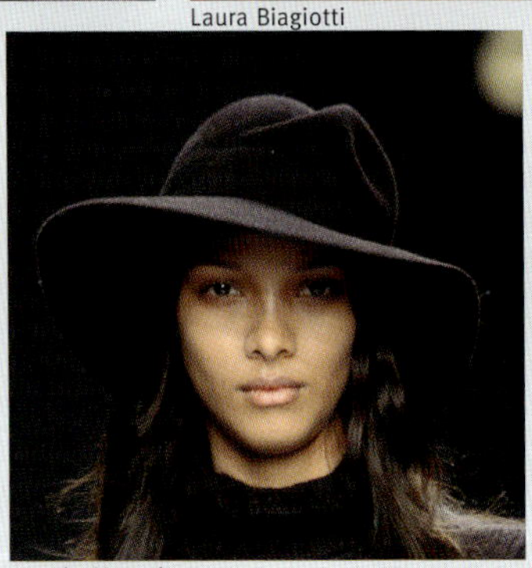
Angelo Marani

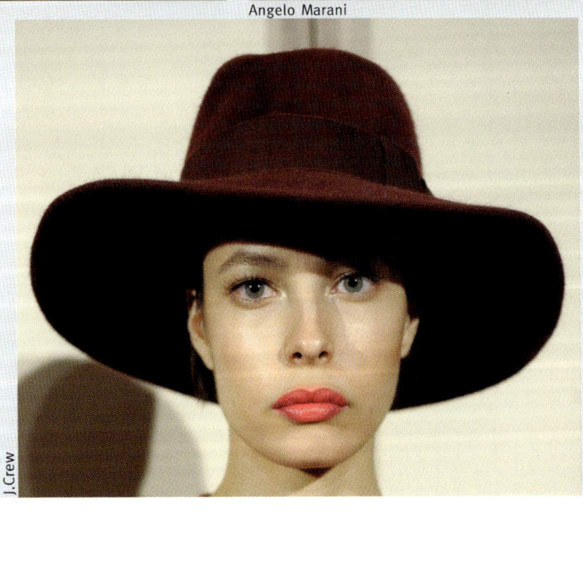
J.Crew

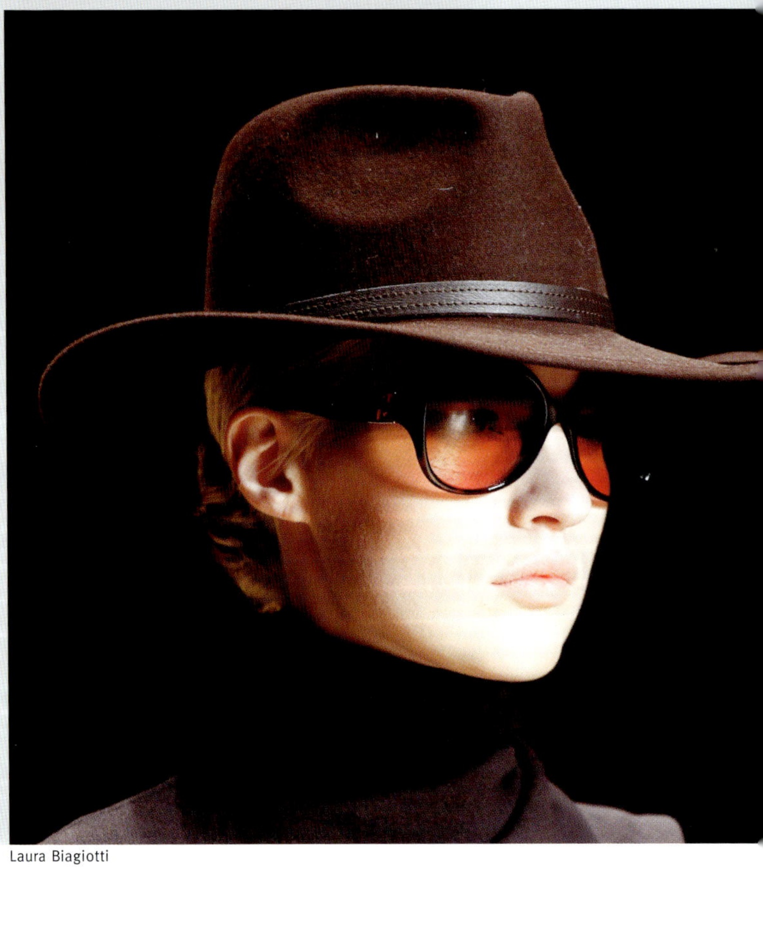
Laura Biagiotti

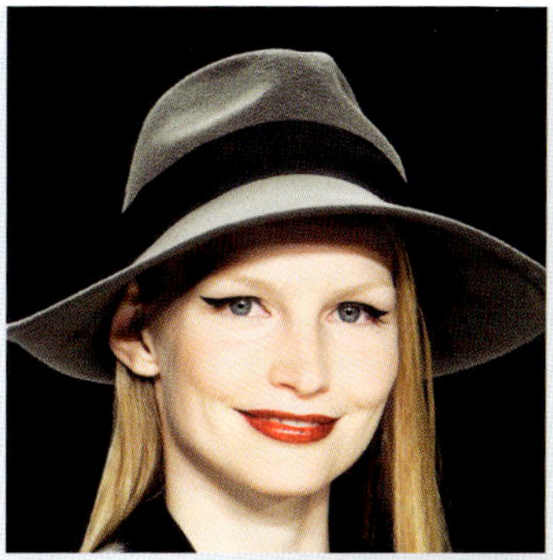

Minx

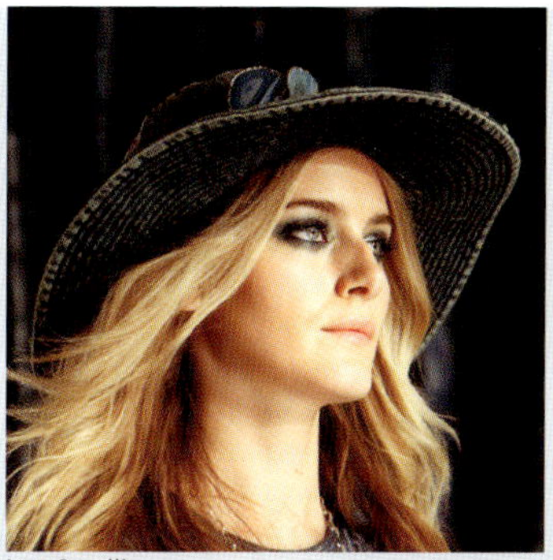

Just Cavalli

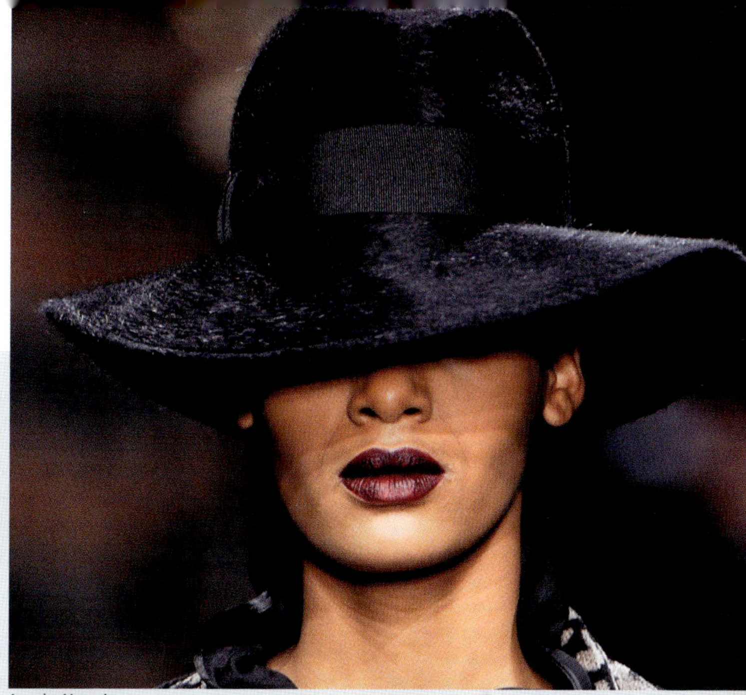

Angelo Marani

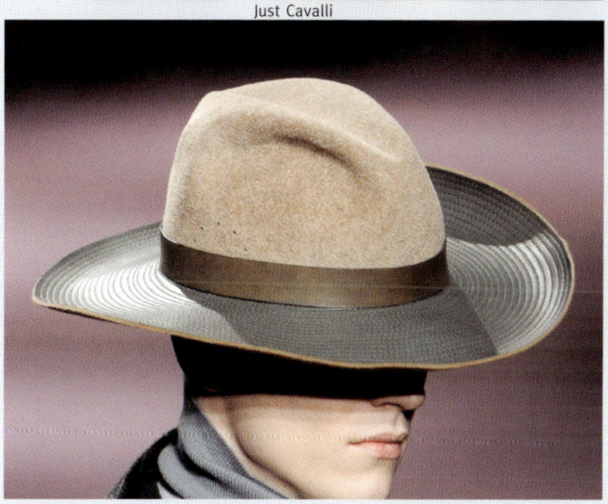

Lanvin

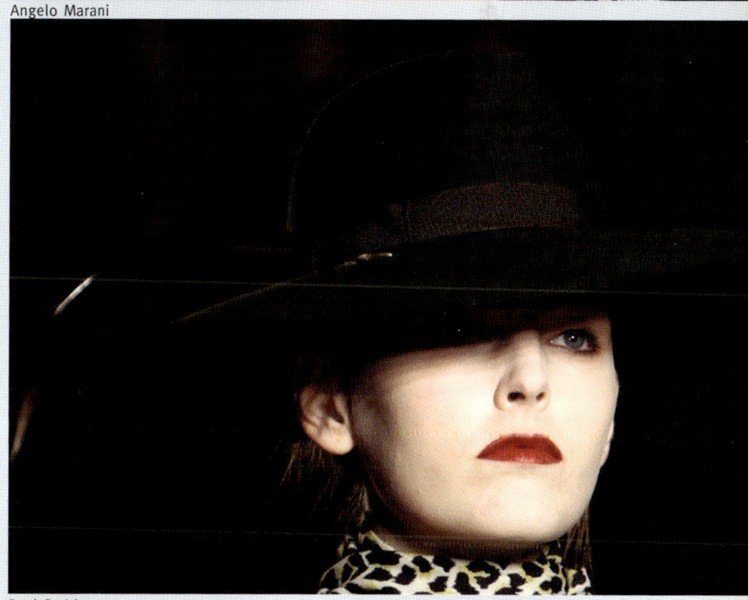

Paul Smith

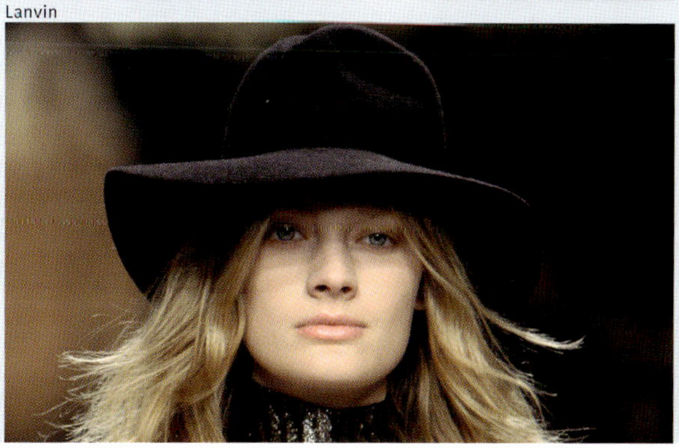

Angelo Marani

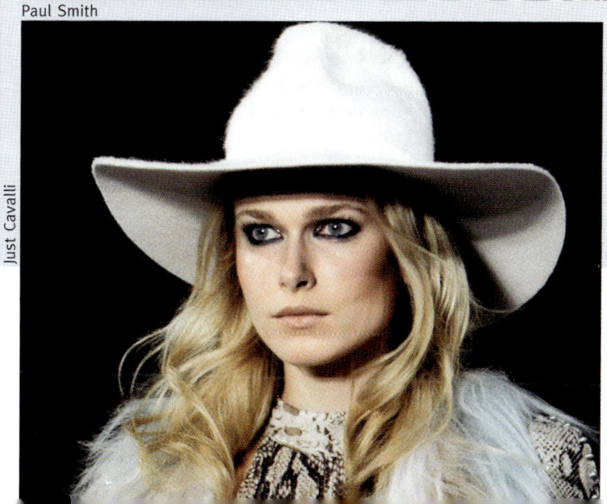

Just Cavalli

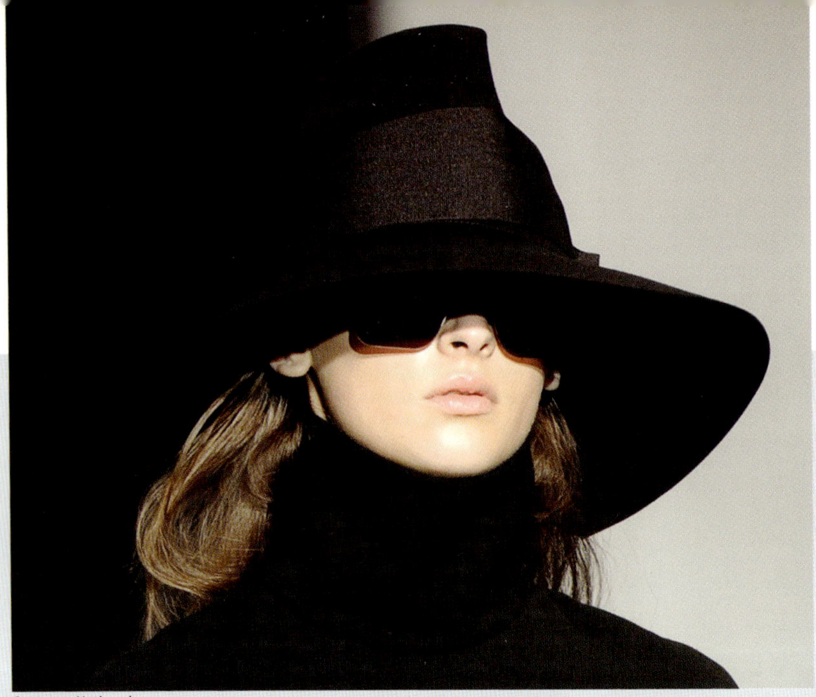

Costume National

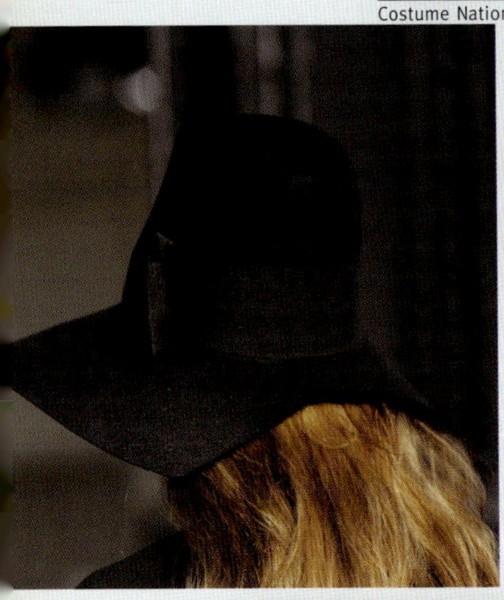

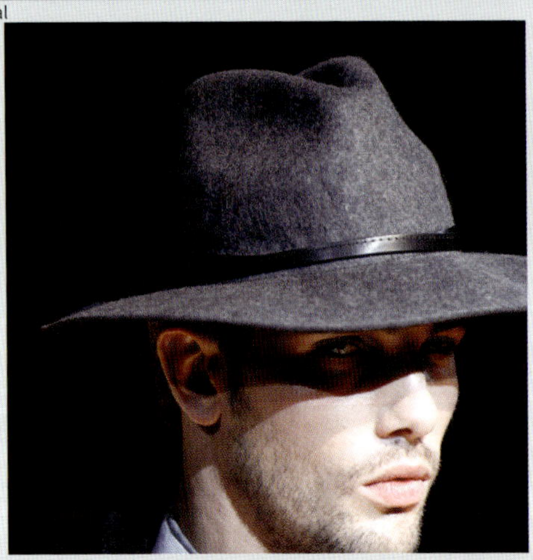

Emporio Armani

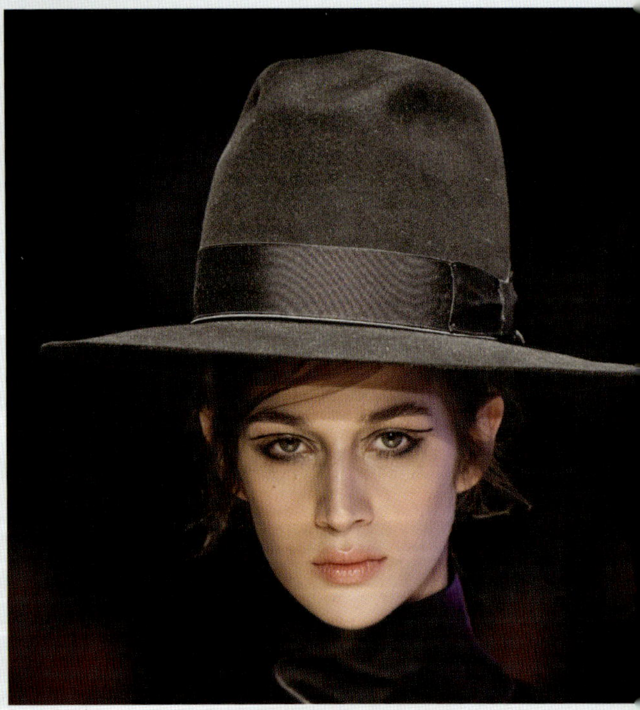

Ter et Bantine

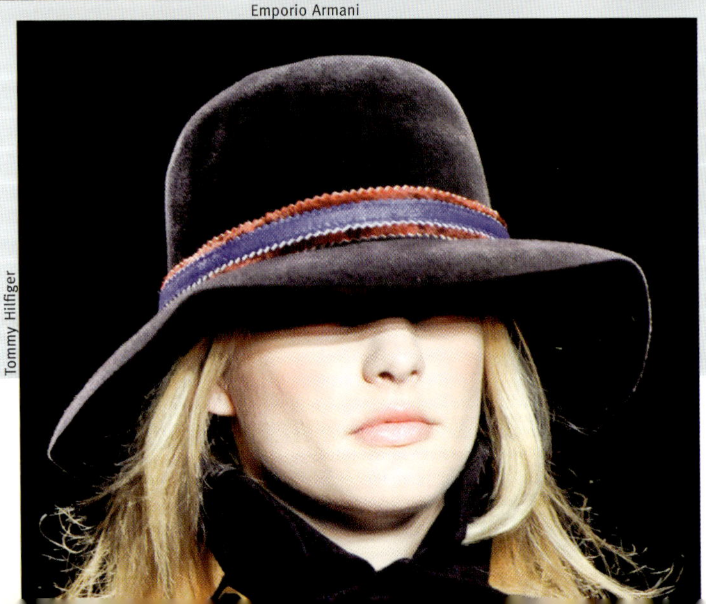

Tommy Hilfiger

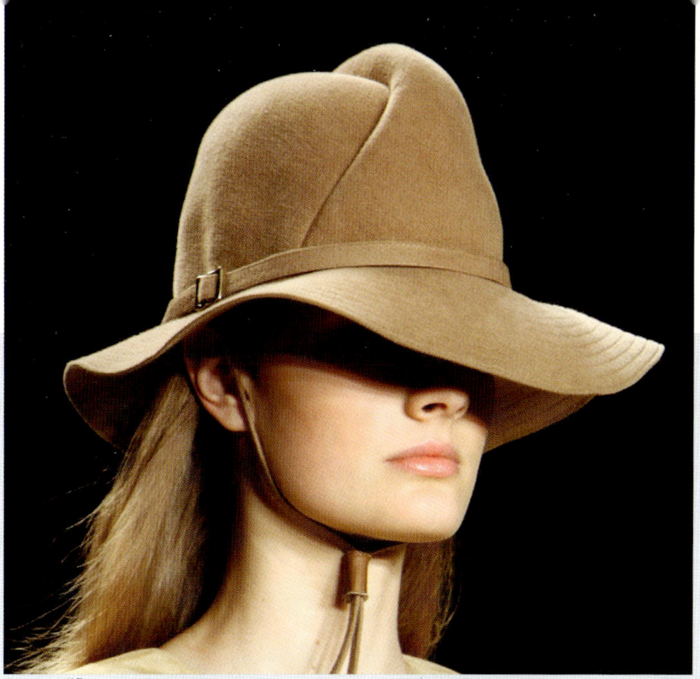
Tommy Hilfiger

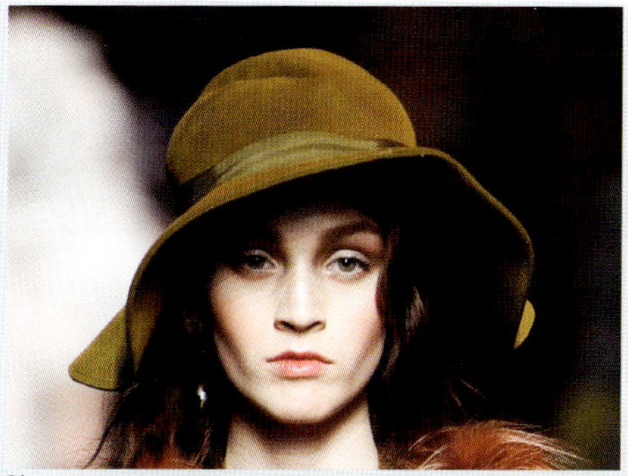
Dior

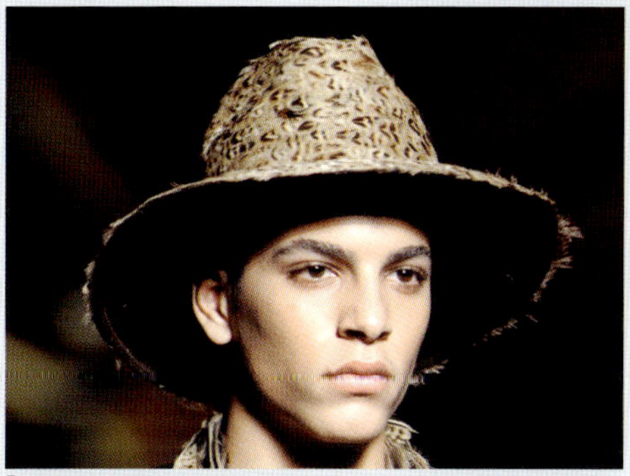
Etro

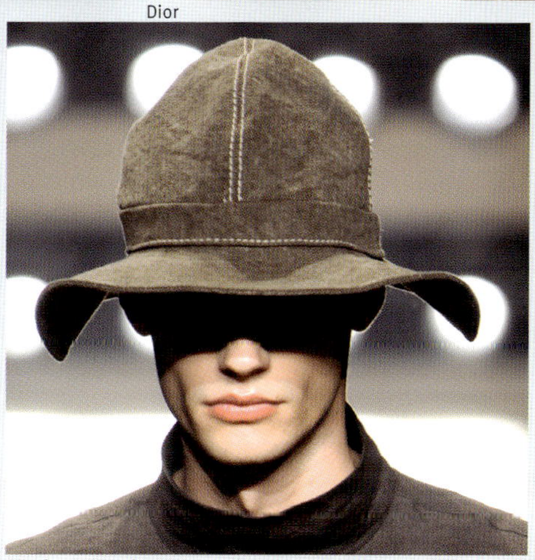
Gianfranco Ferré

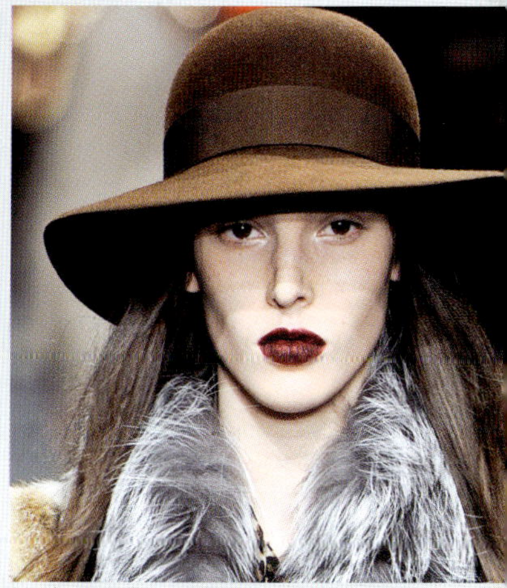
Angelo Marani

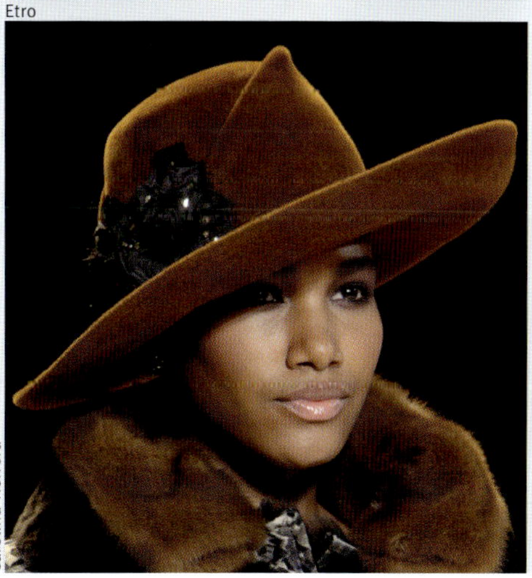
Carolina Herrera

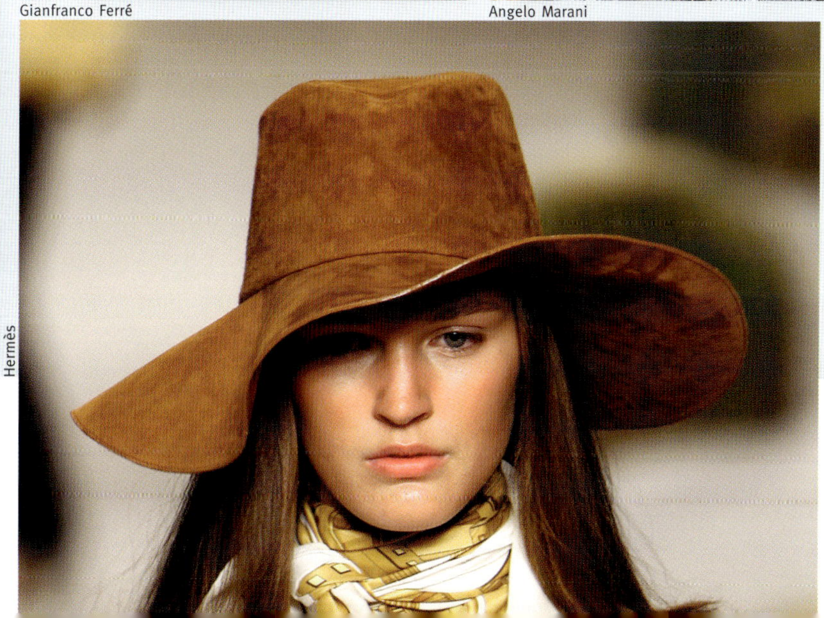
Hermès

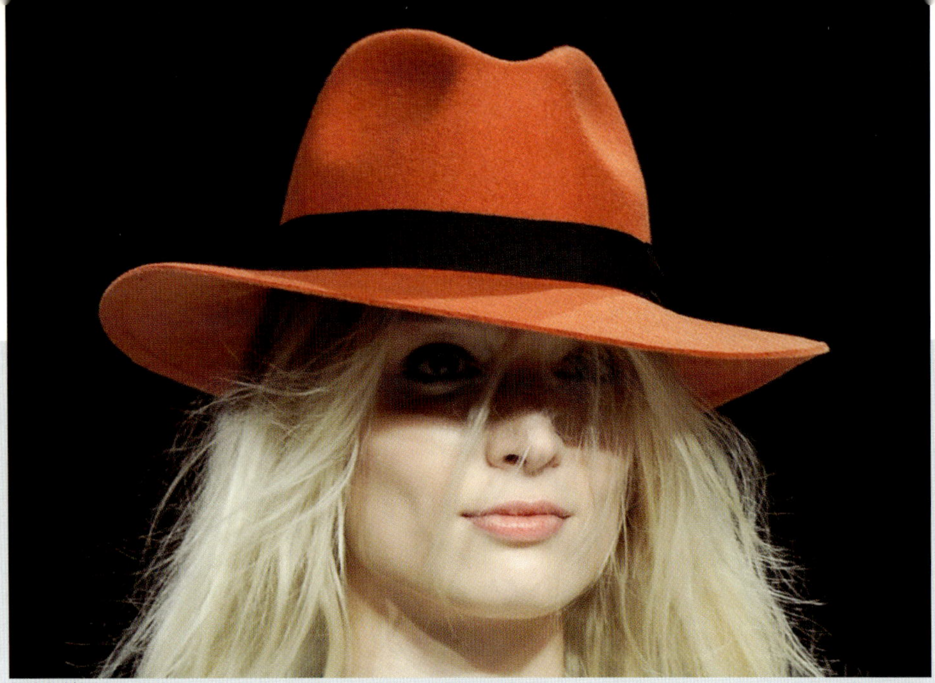

Paul Smith

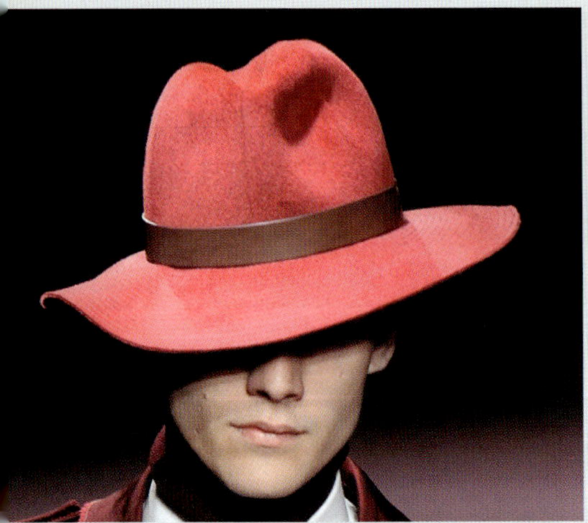

Lanvin

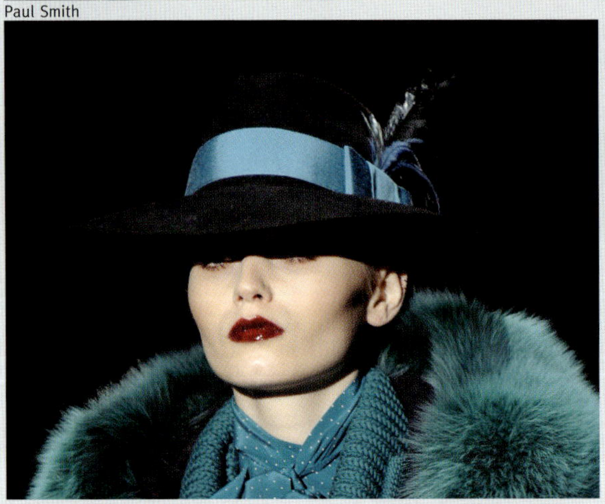

Gucci

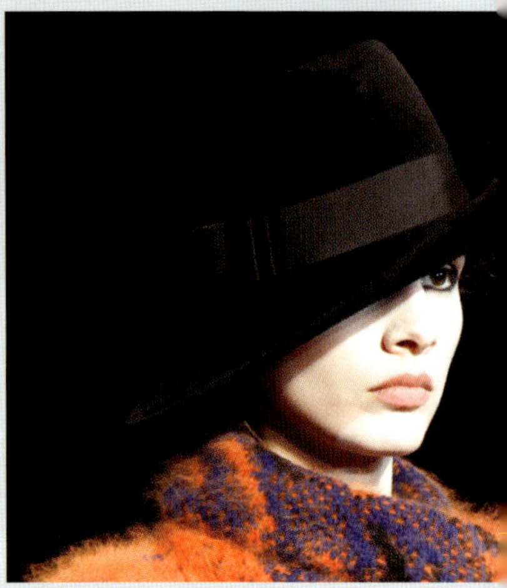

Giorgio Armani

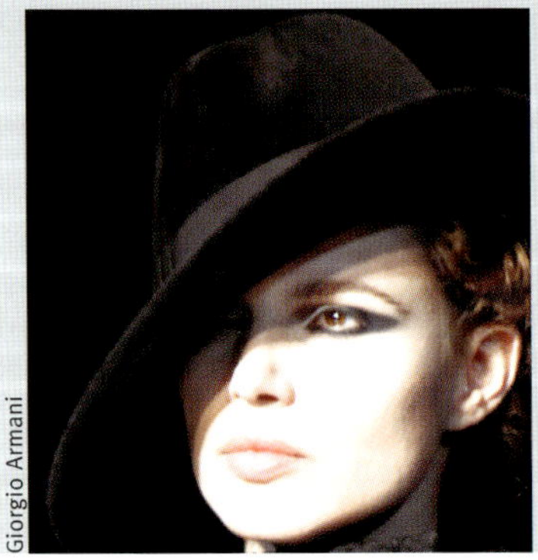

Giorgio Armani

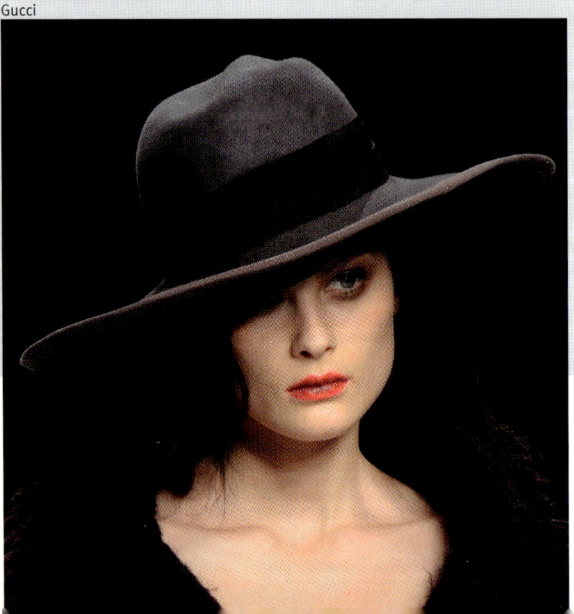

Mariella Burani

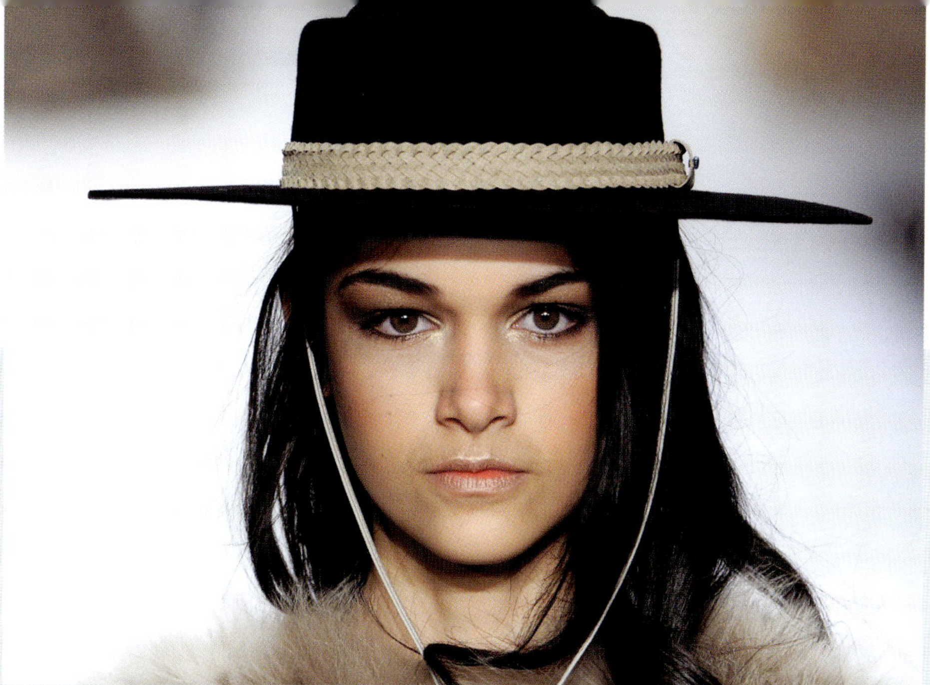

Carlos Miele

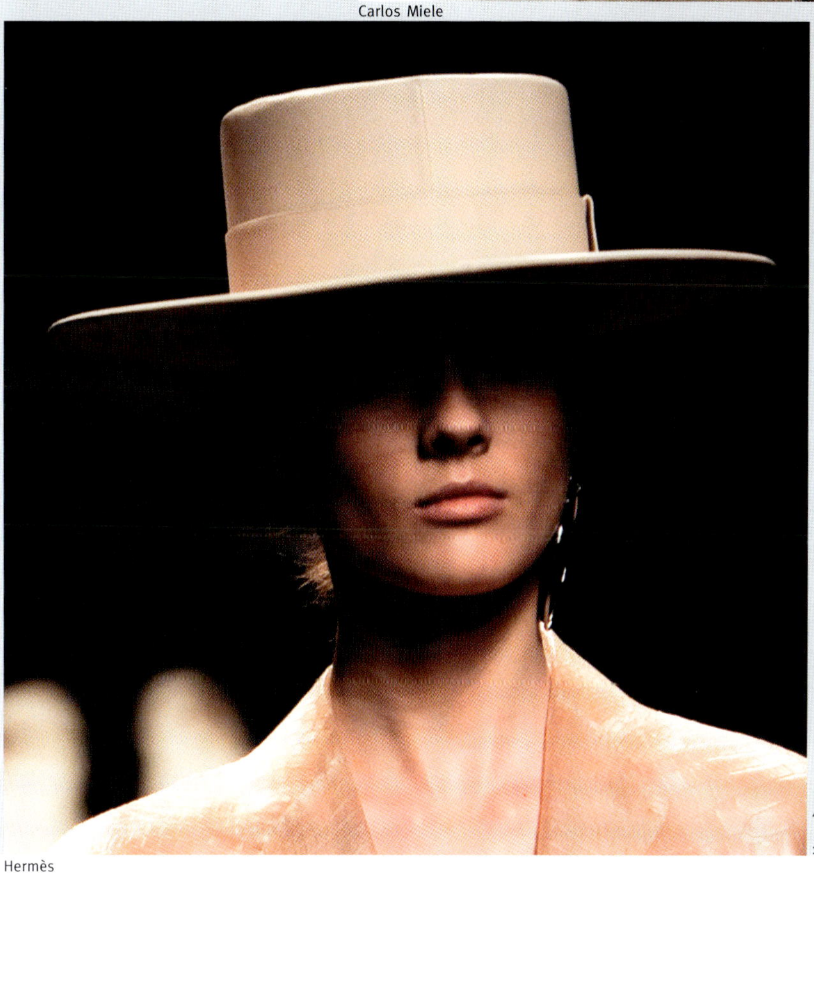

Hermès

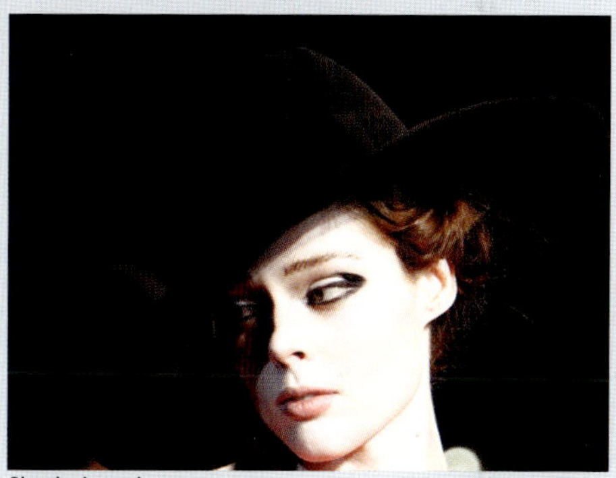

Giorgio Armani

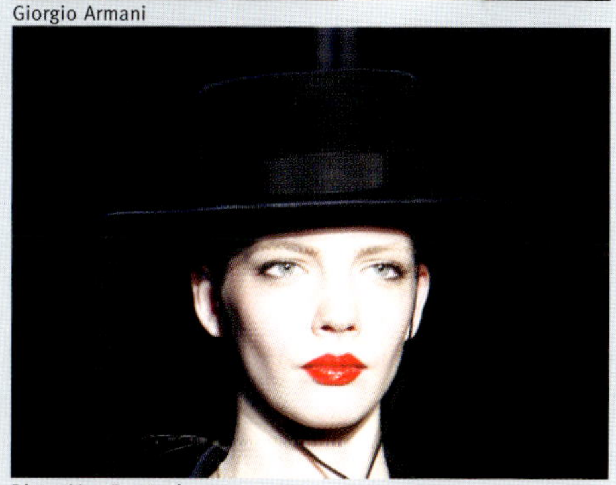

Diane Von Furstenberg

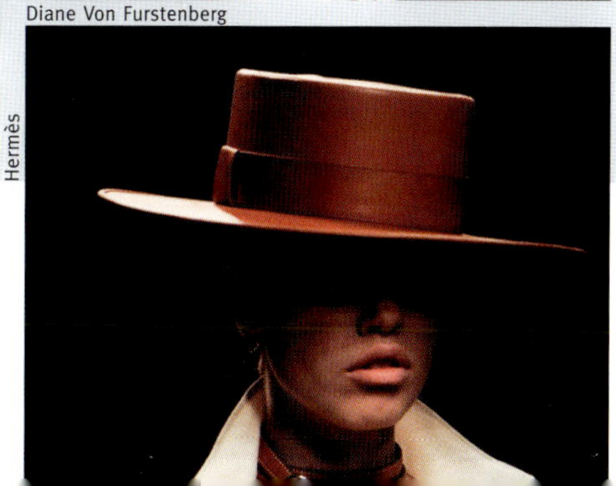

Hermès

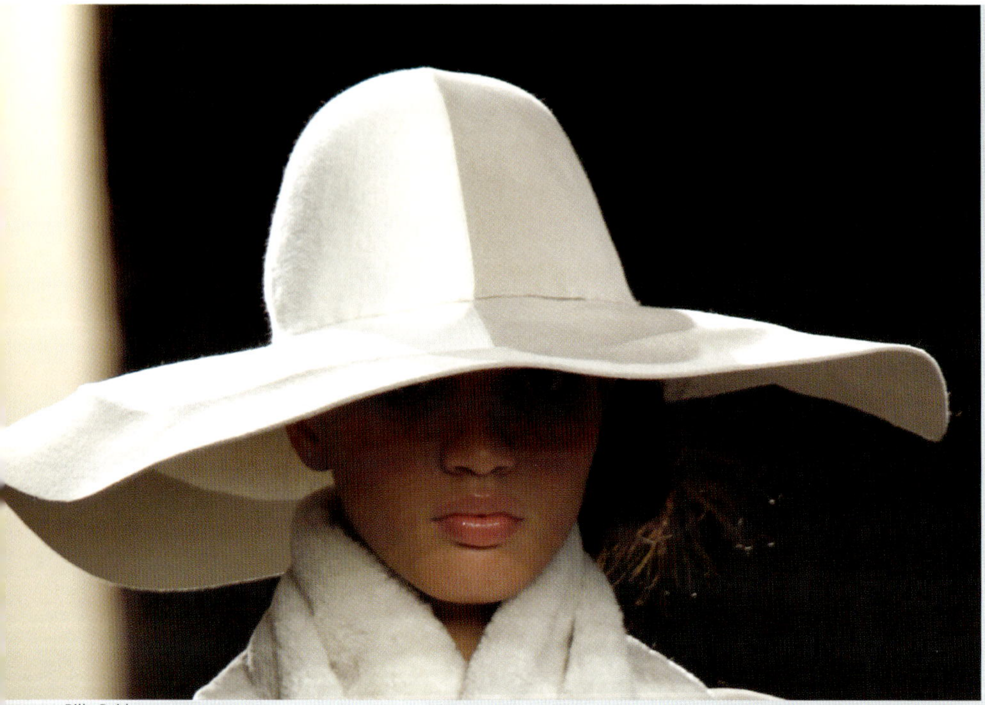

Billy Reid

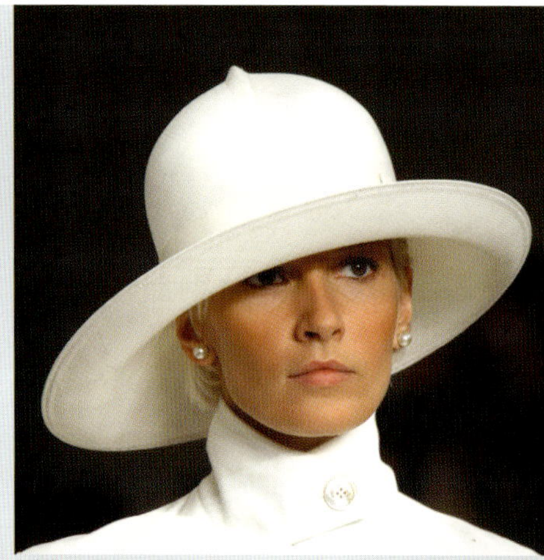

Ralph Lauren

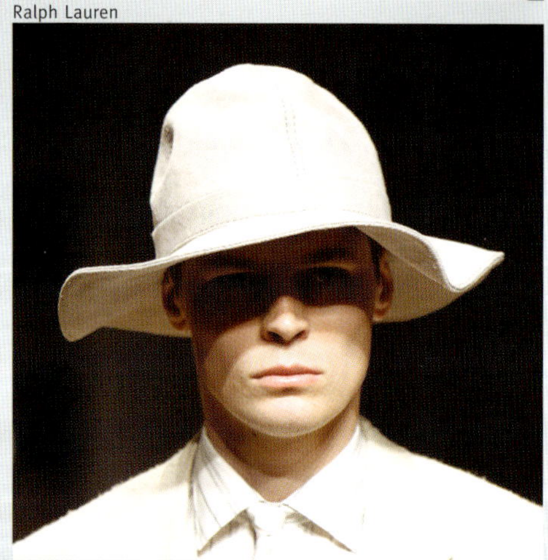

Gianfranco Ferré

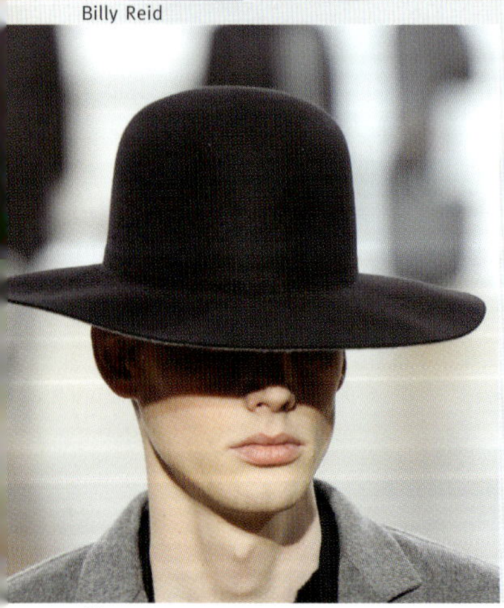

Dior

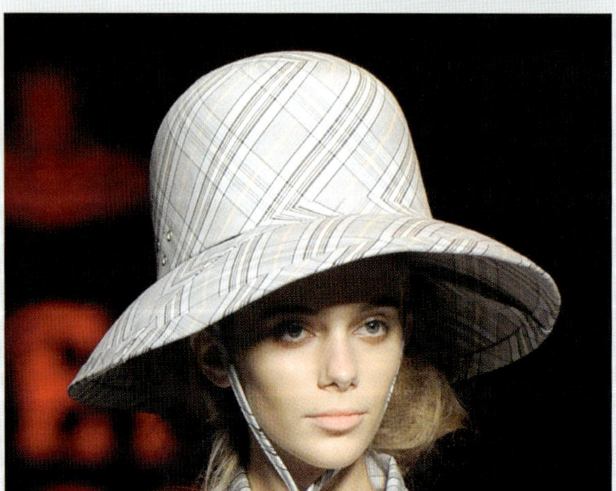

Vivienne Westwood Red Label

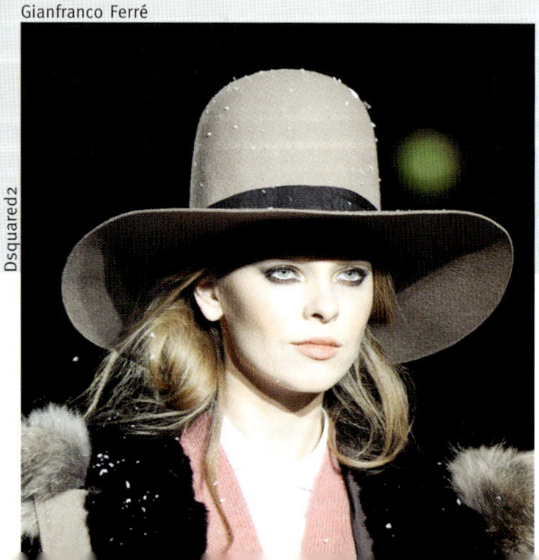

Dsquared2

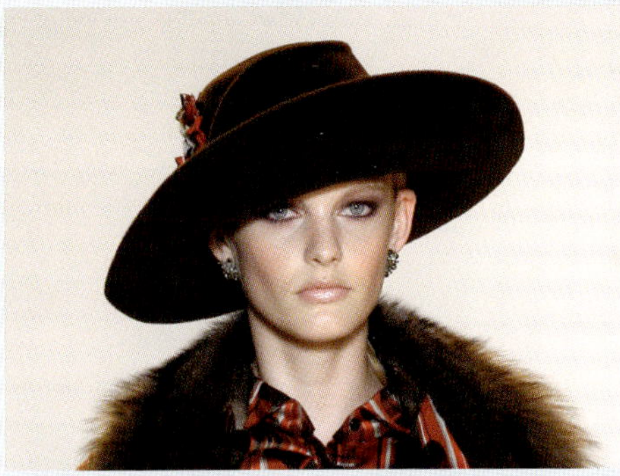
Carolina Herrera

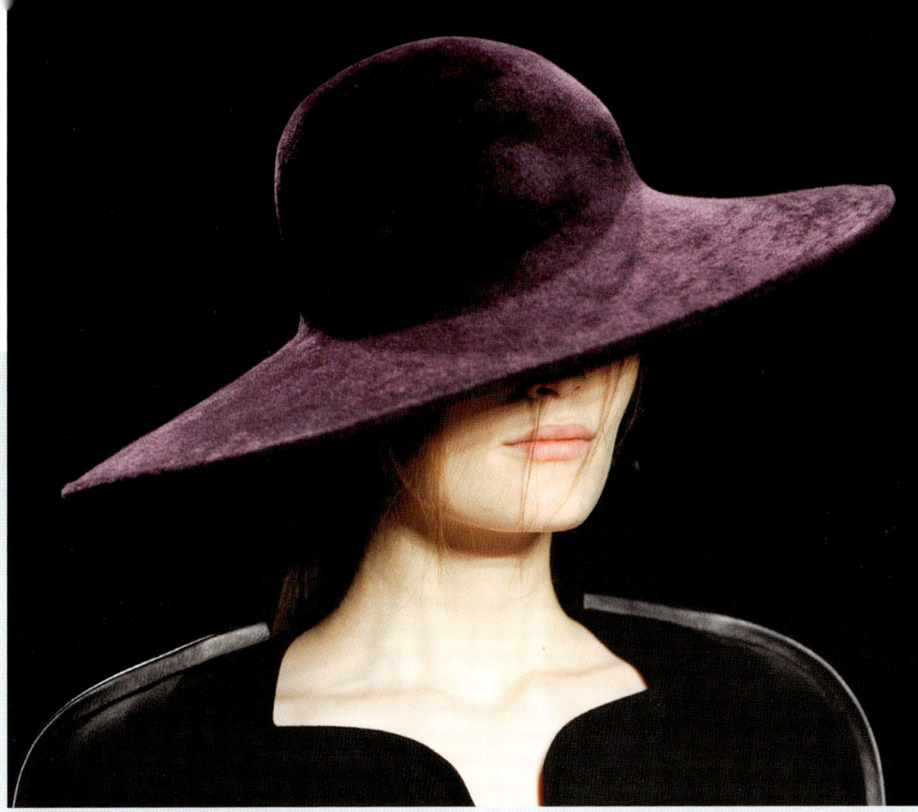
Marios Schwab

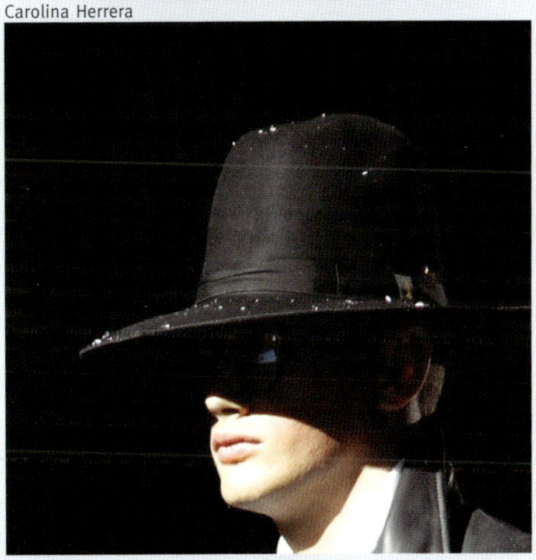
Dsquared2

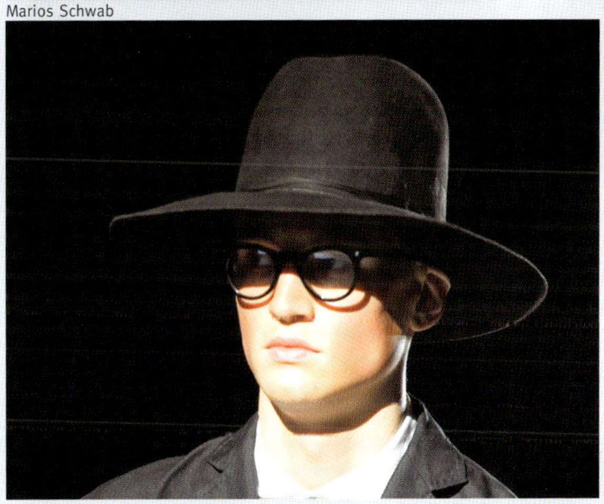
Dsquared2

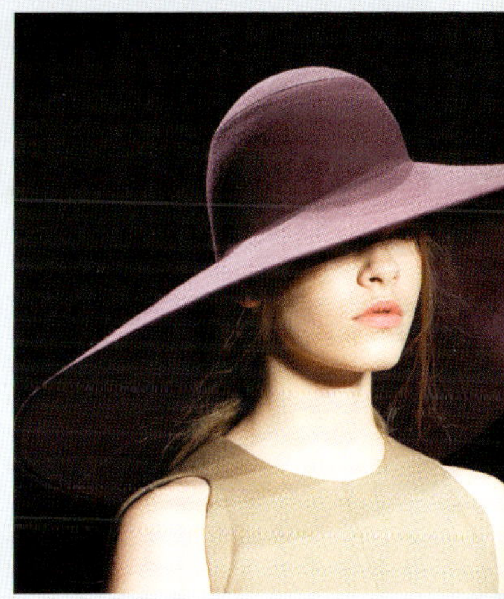
Marios Schwab

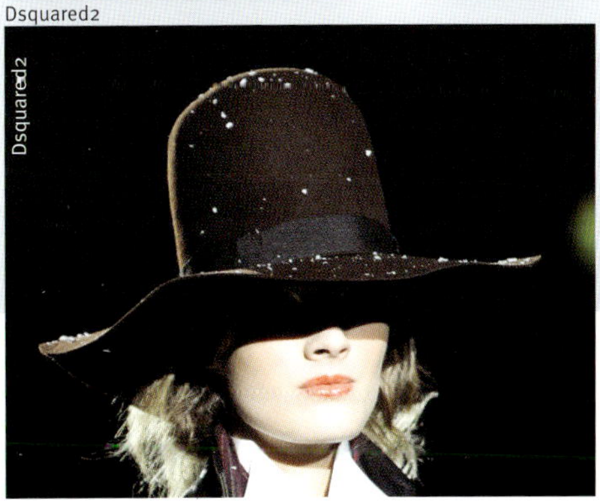
Dsquared2

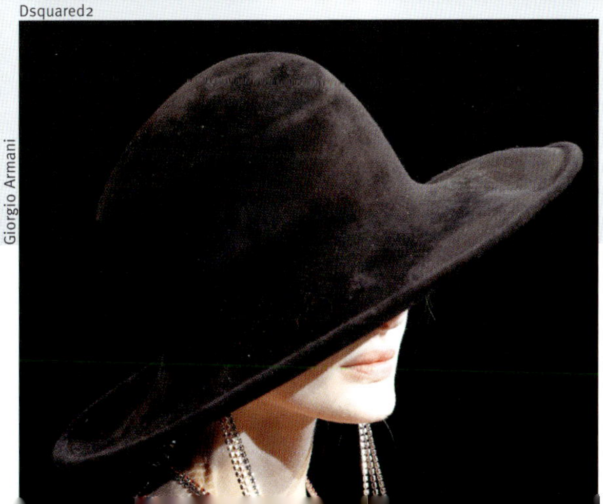
Giorgio Armani

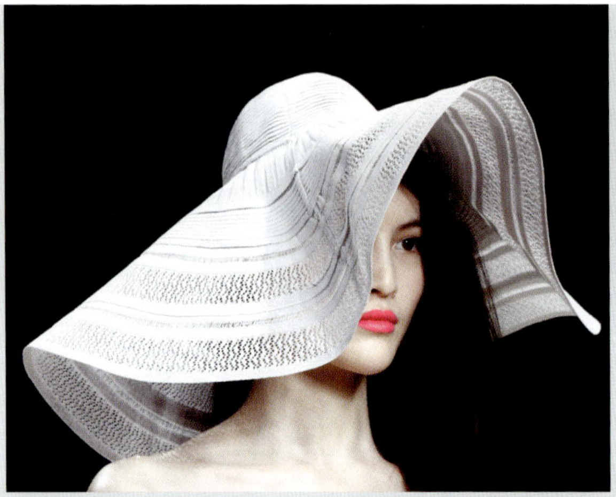

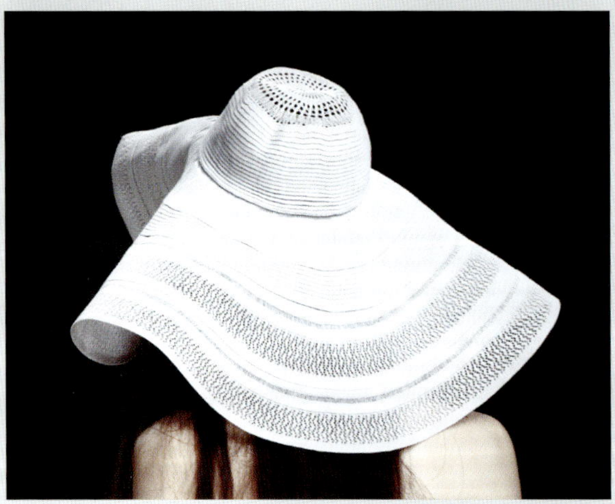

Les Copains

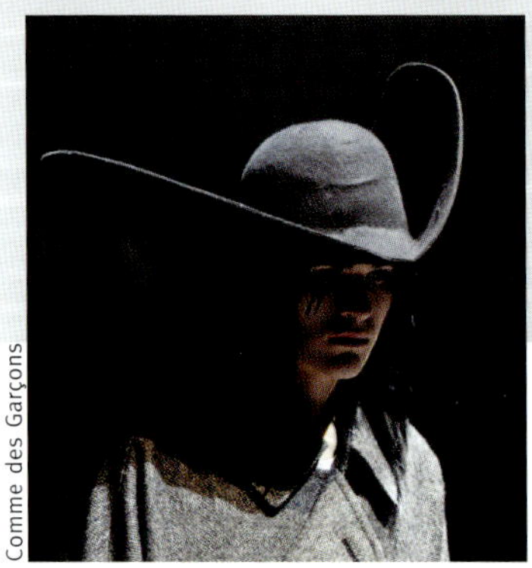

Comme des Garçons

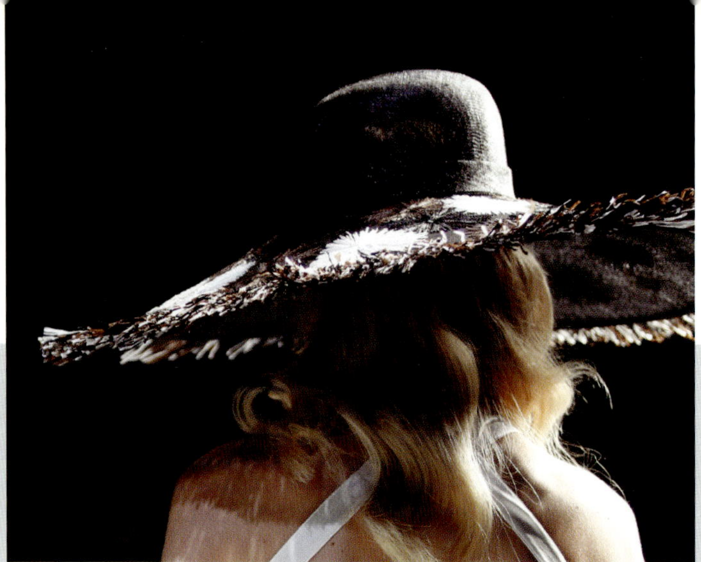

Roccobarocco

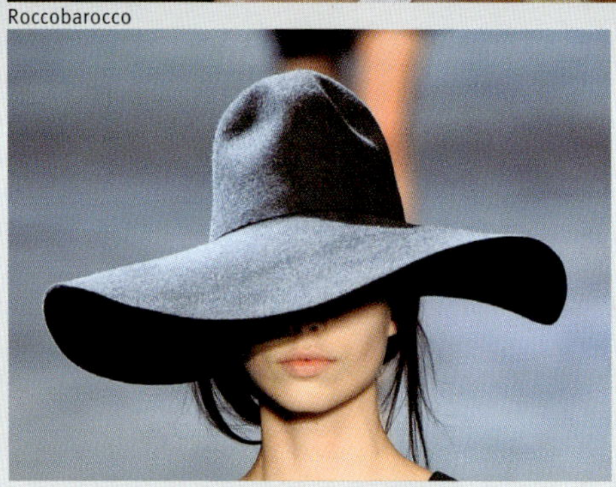

Lanvin

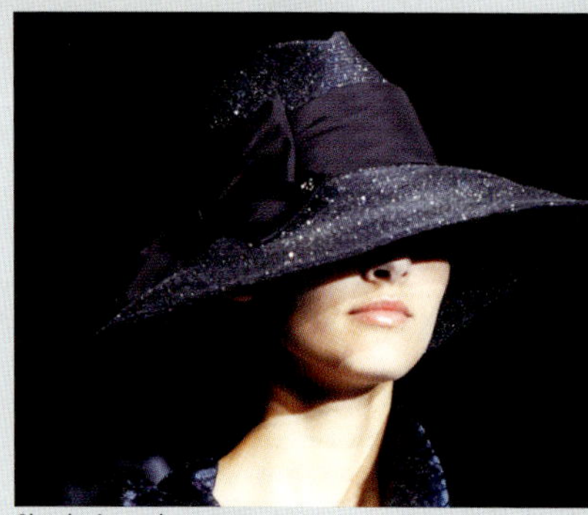

Giorgio Armani

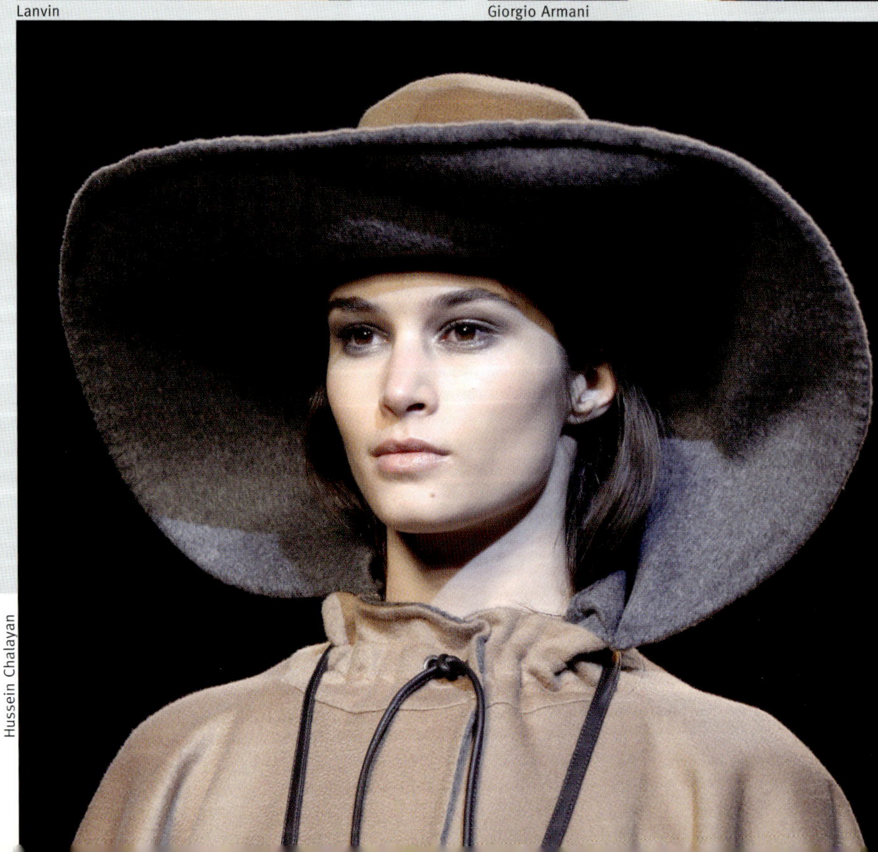

Hussein Chalayan

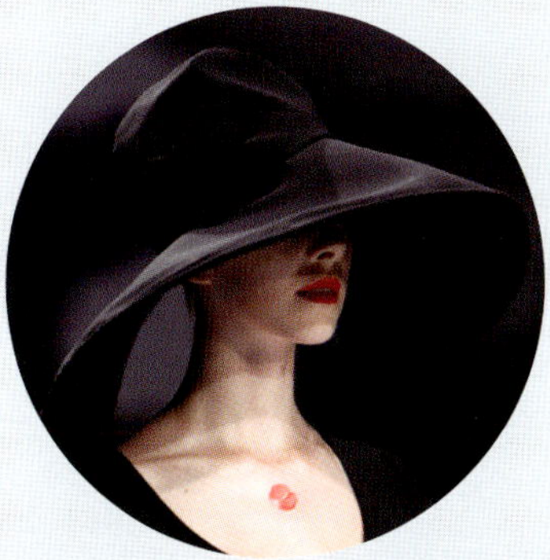
JC de Castelbajac

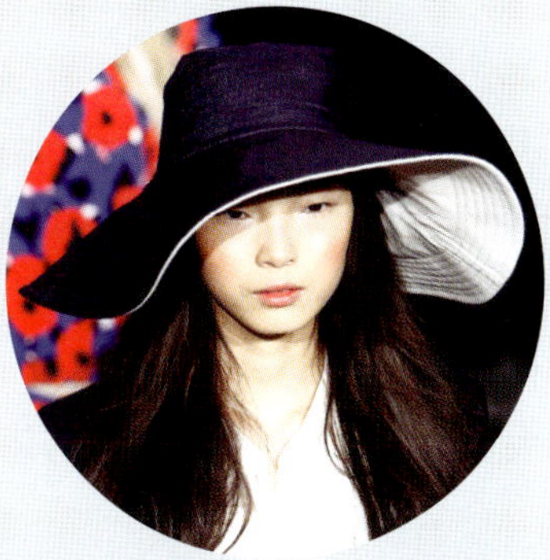
DKNY

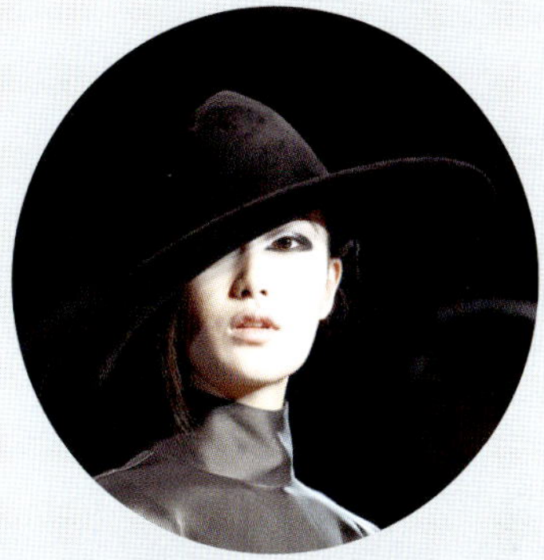
Giorgio Armani

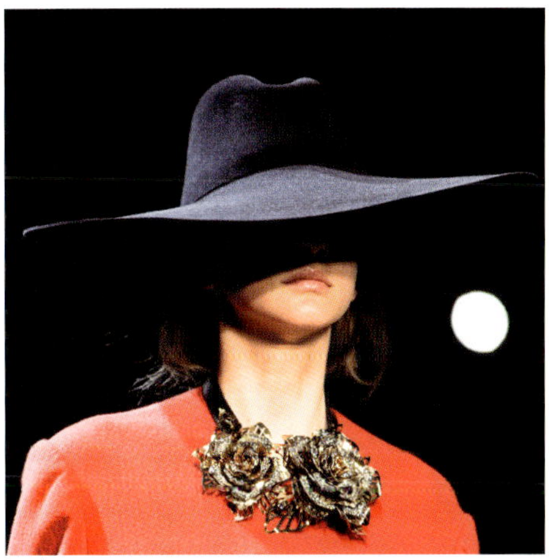
Lanvin

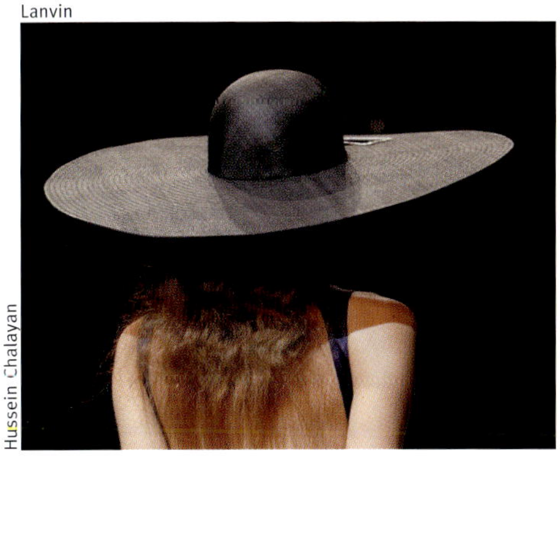
Hussein Chalayan

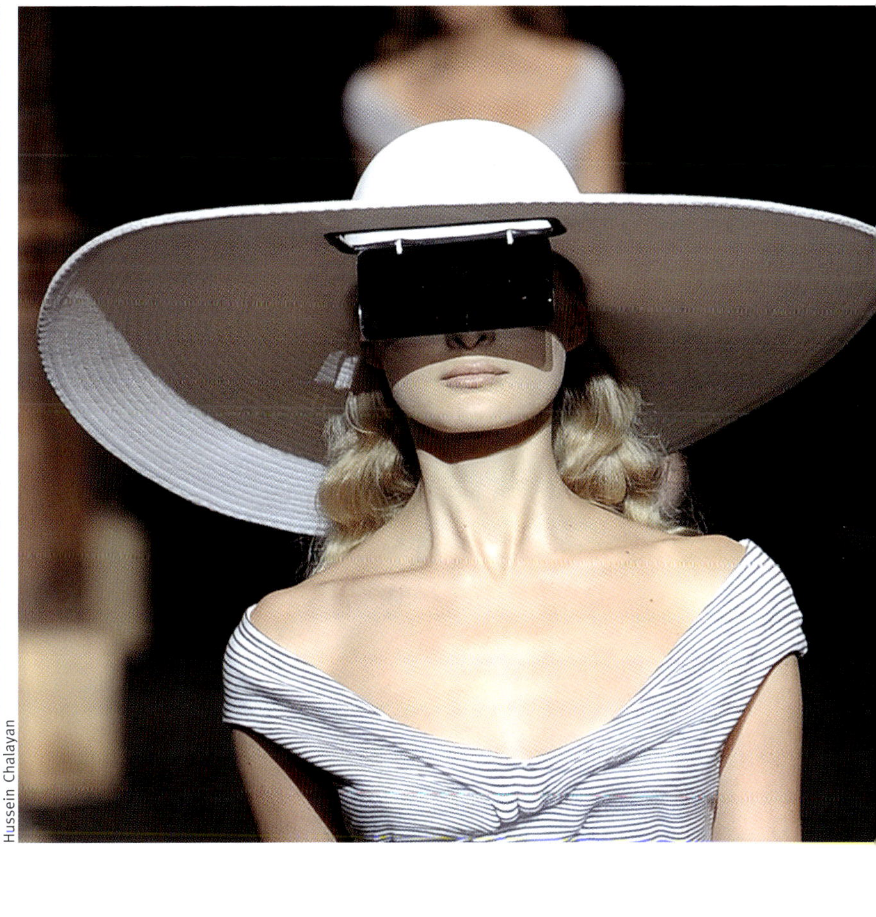
Hussein Chalayan

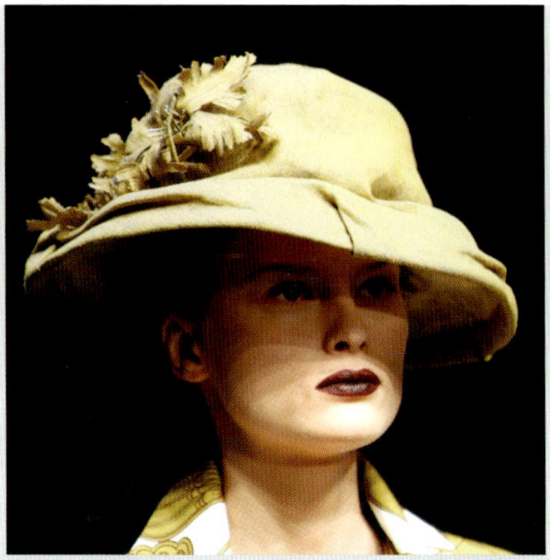

Mariella Burani

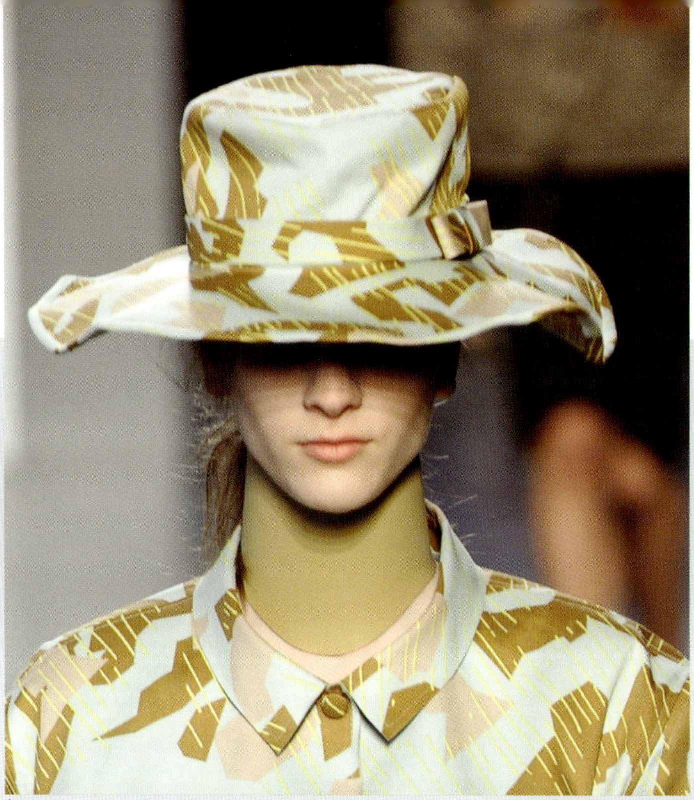

Acne

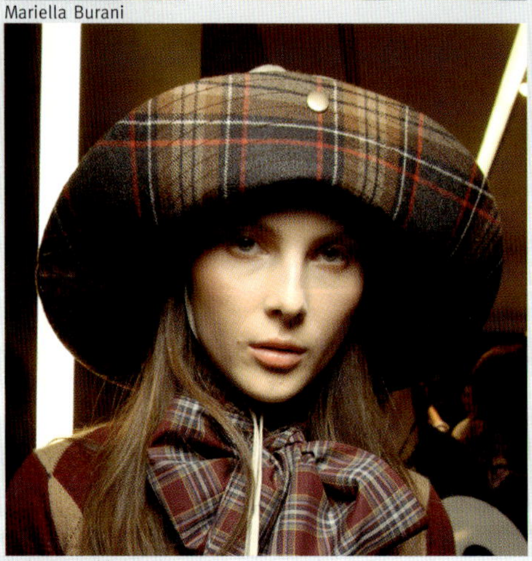

Dolce & Gabbana

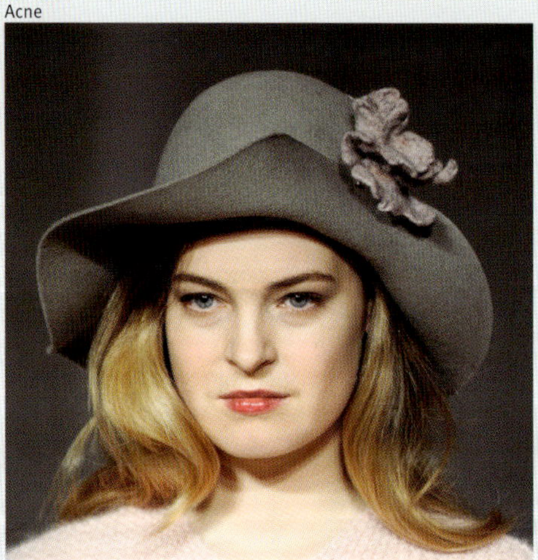

Agnès B.

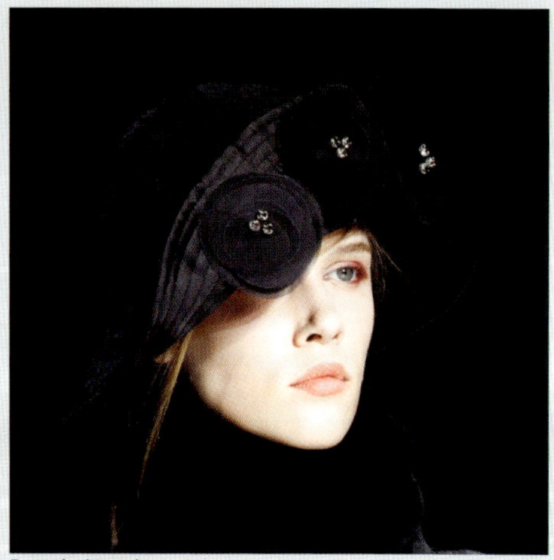

Emporio Armani

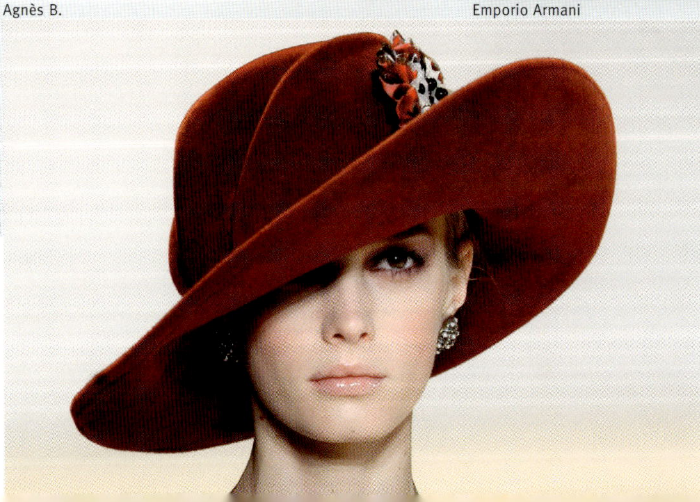

Carolina Herrera

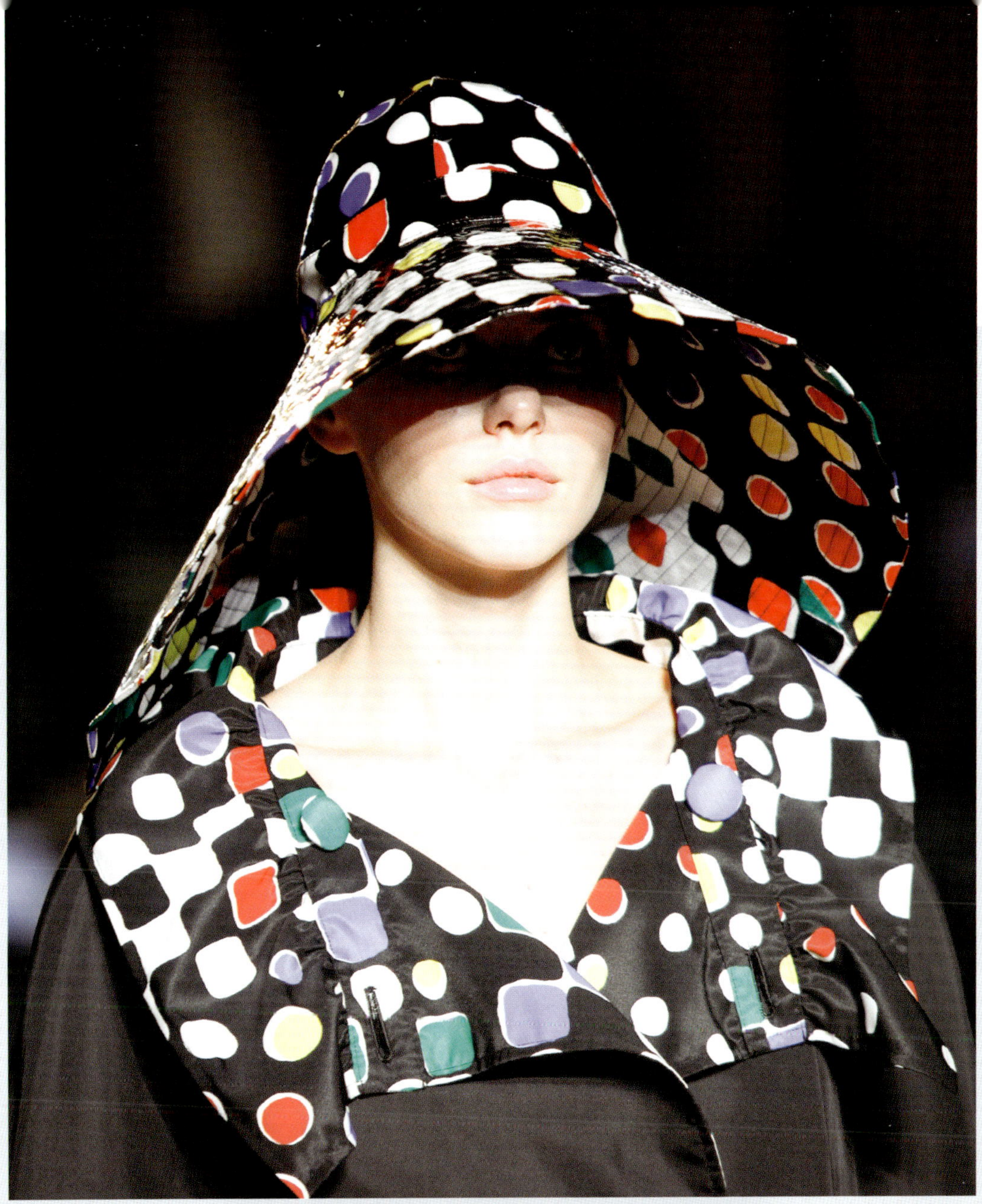
Tsumori Chisato

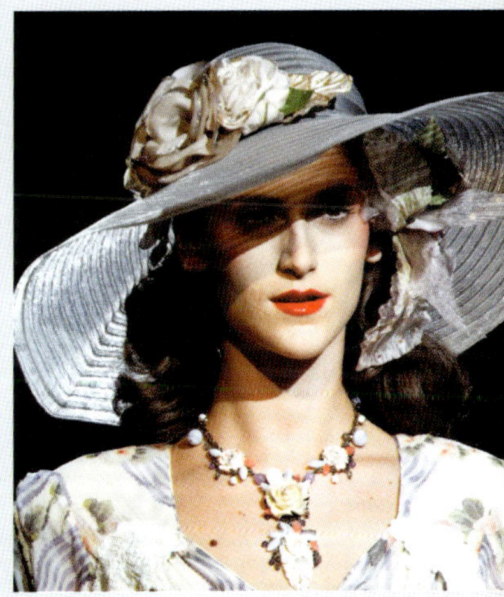
Anna Sui

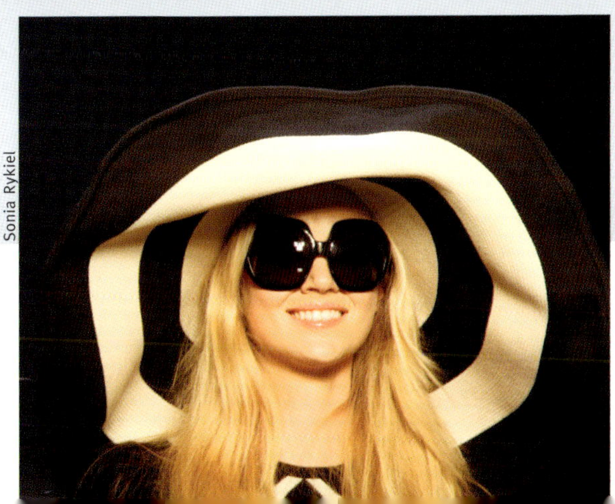
Sonia Rykiel

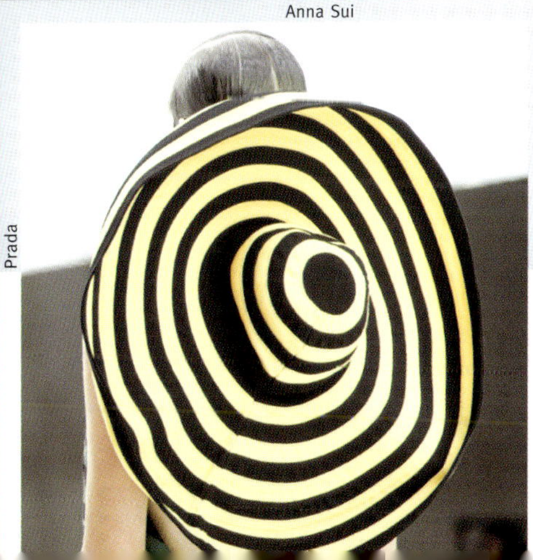
Prada

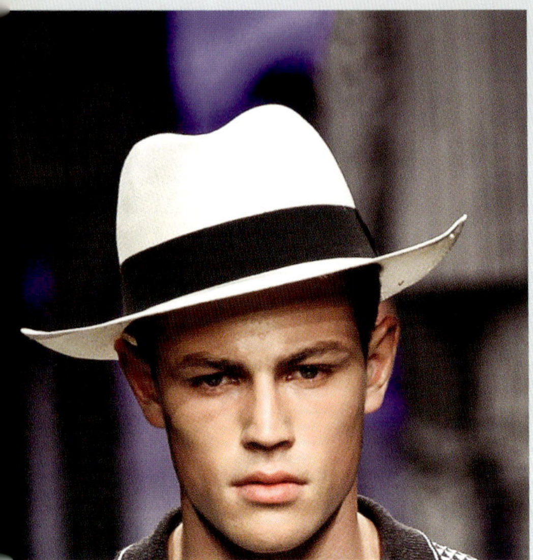

Canali

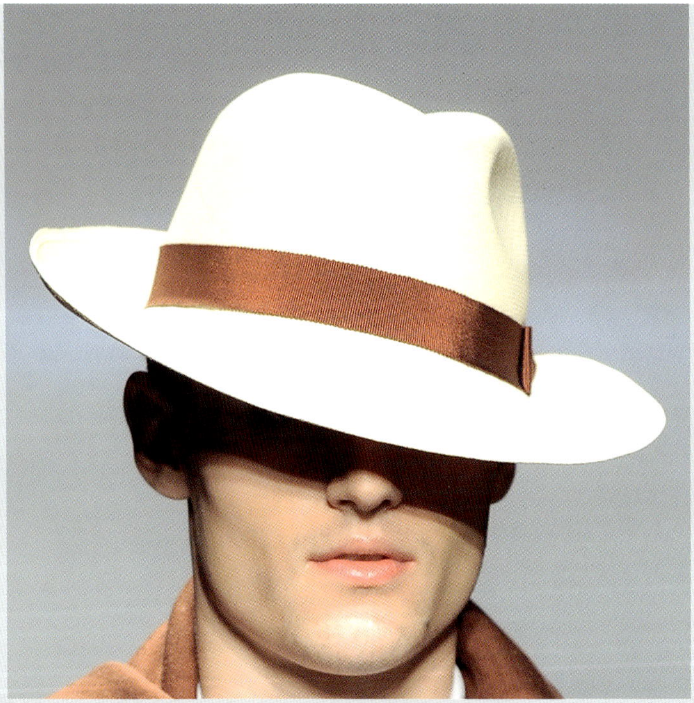

Salvatore Ferragamo

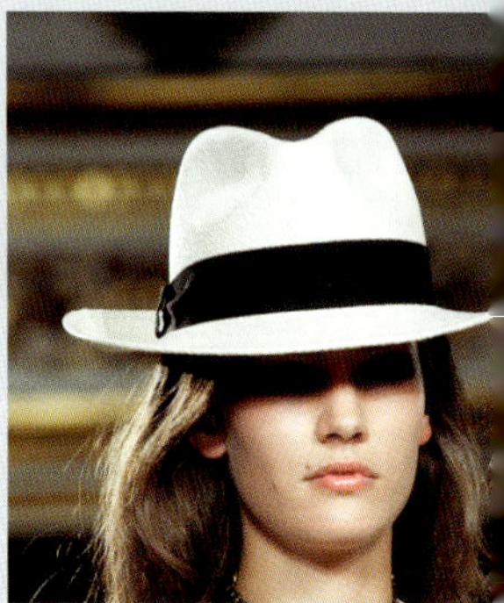

Emilio Pucci

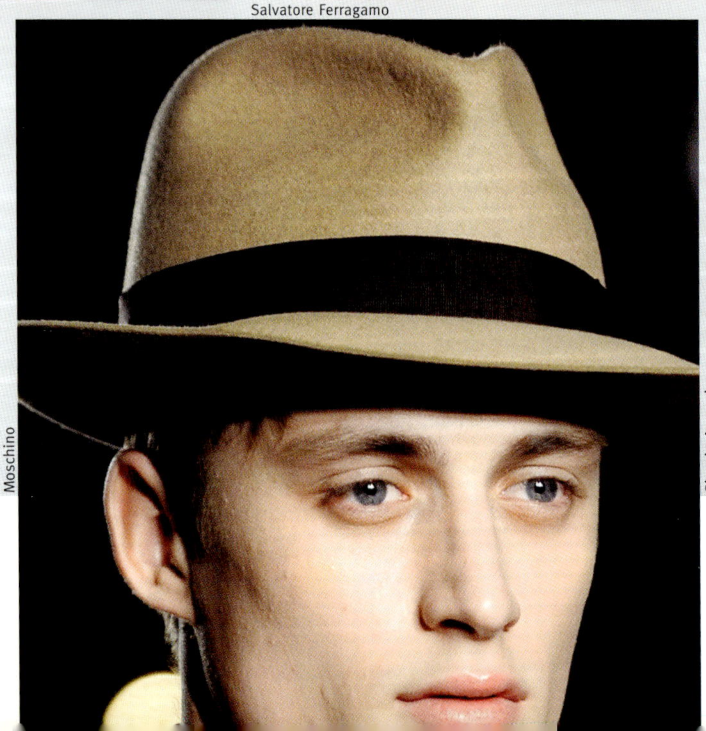

Moschino

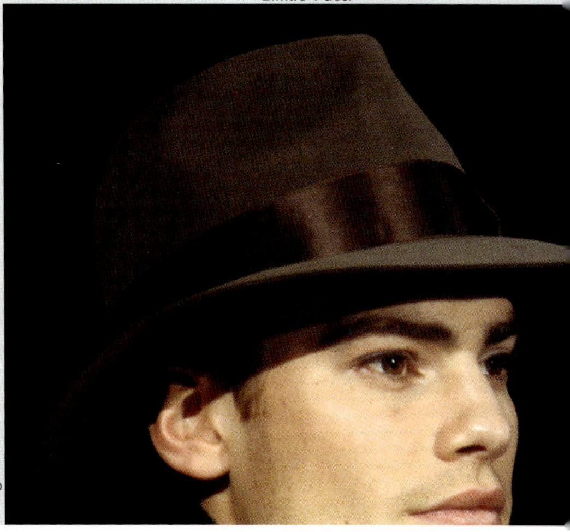

Giorgio Armani

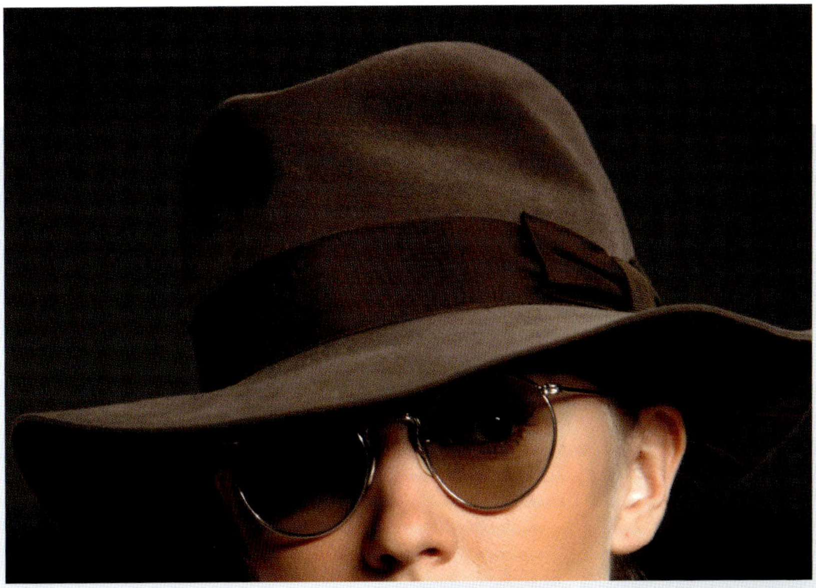

Ralph Lauren

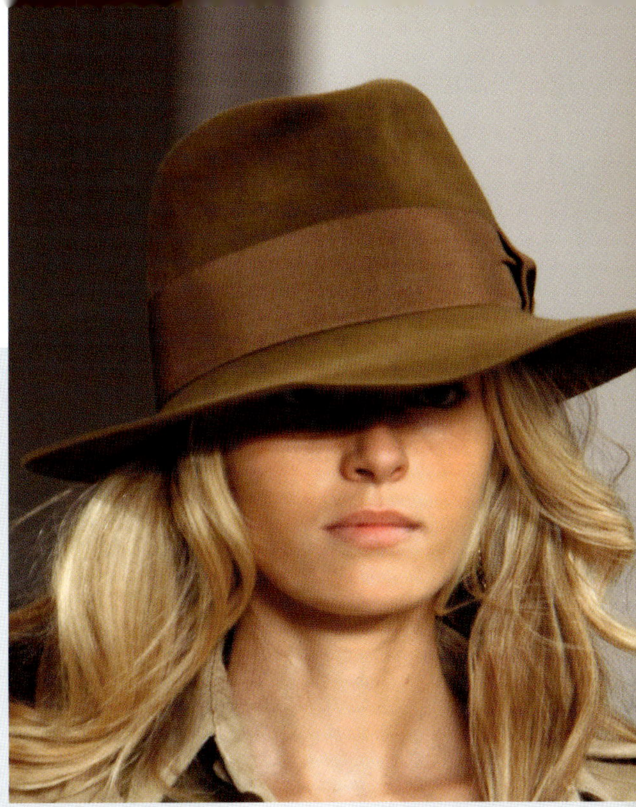

Ralph Lauren

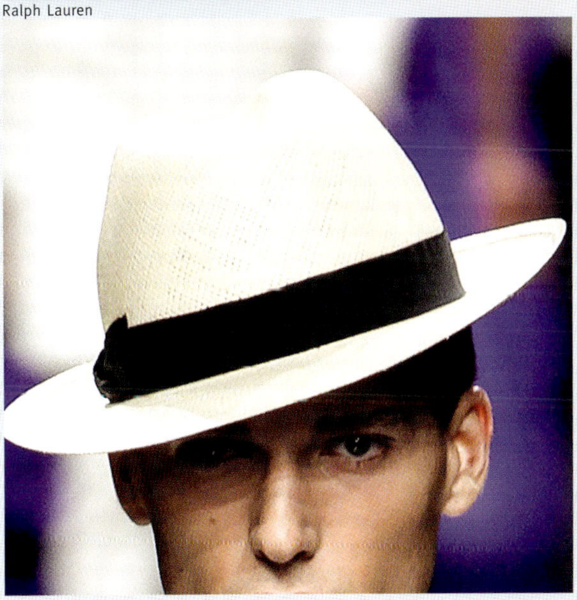

Canali

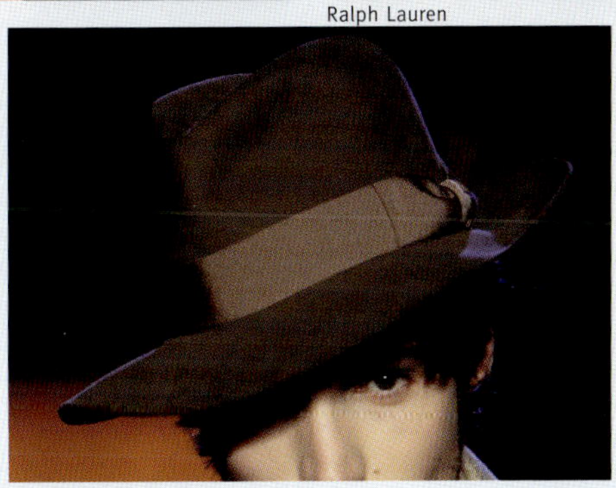

Emanuel Ungaro

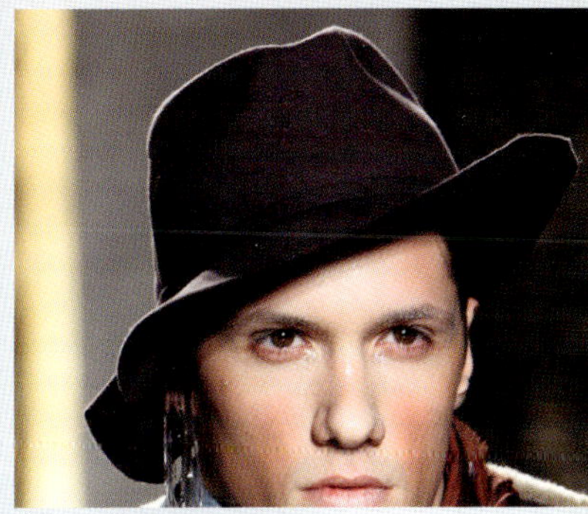

Vivienne Westwood

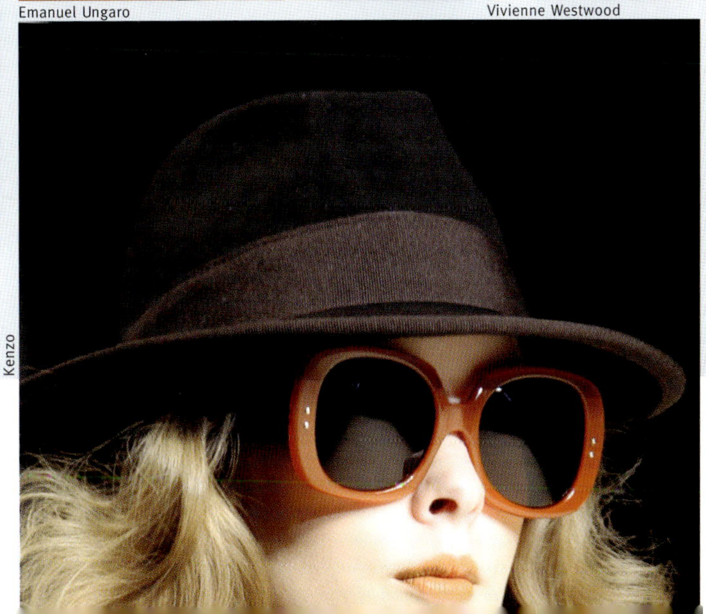

Kenzo

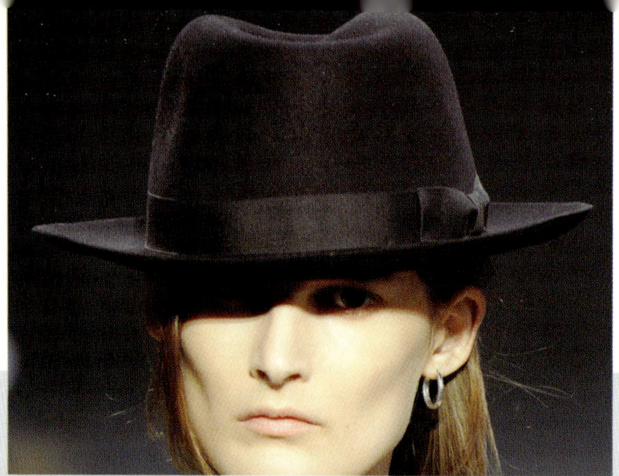

Hermès

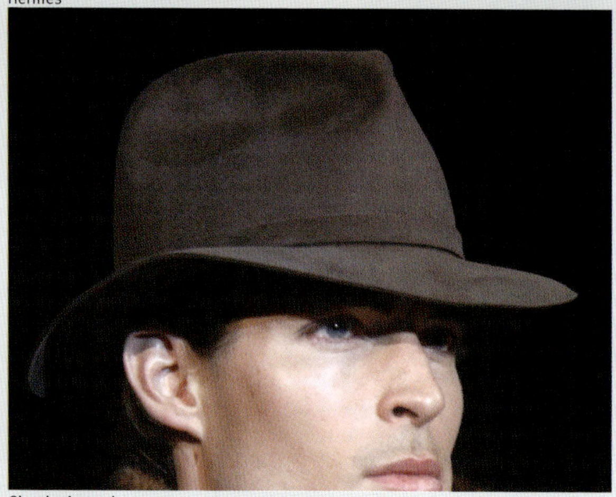

Giorgio Armani

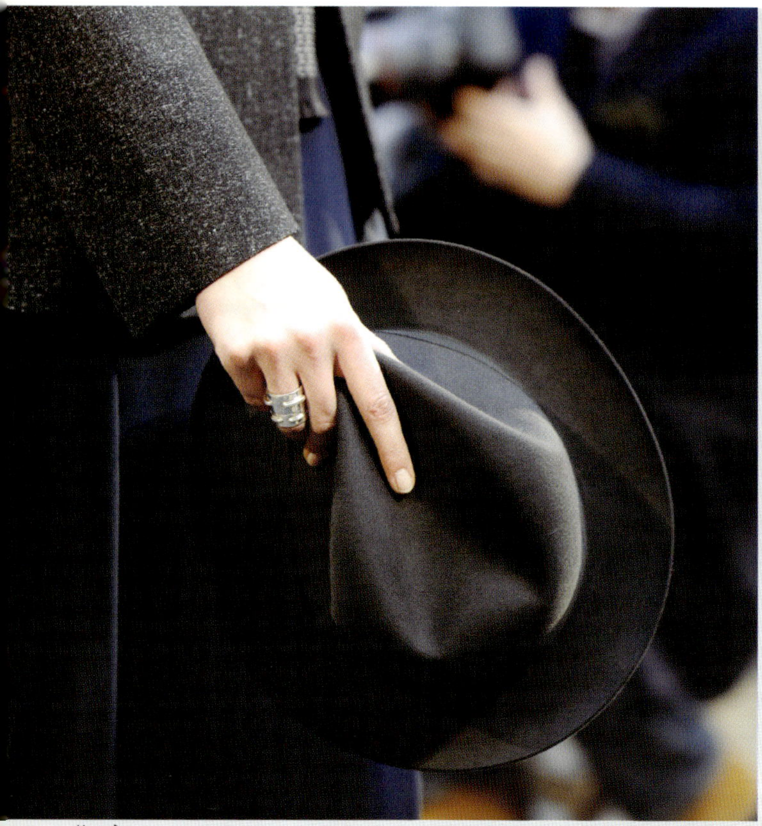

Hermès

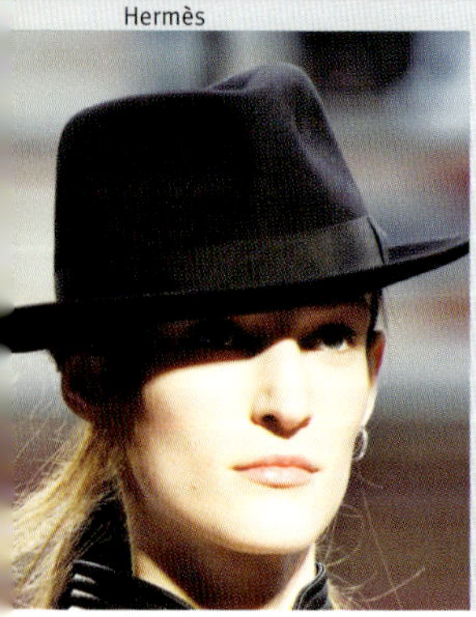

Hermès

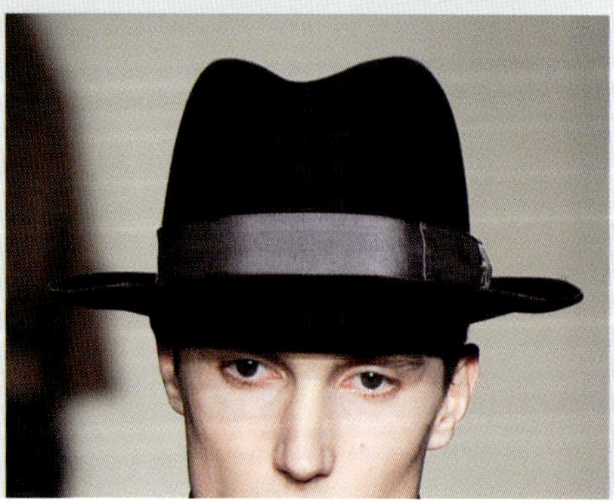

Moschino

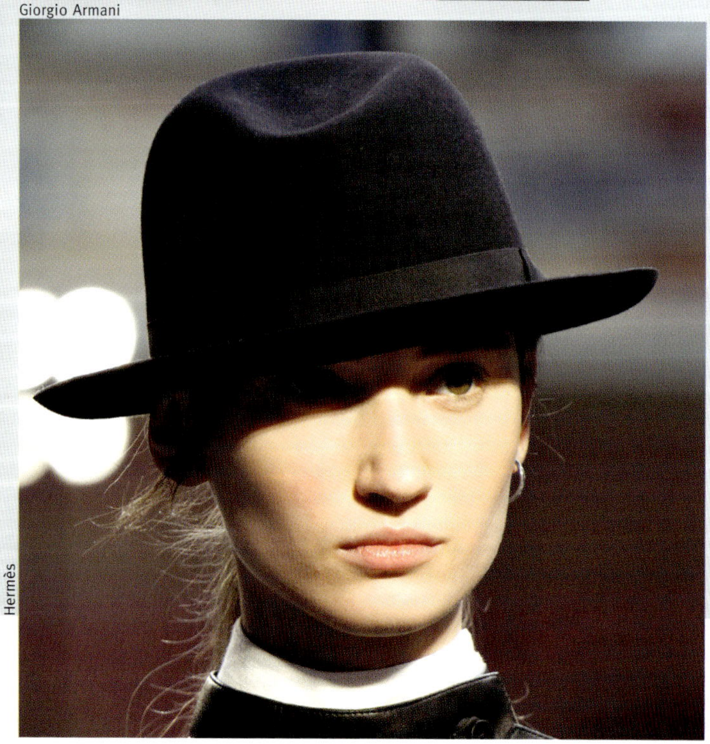

Hermès

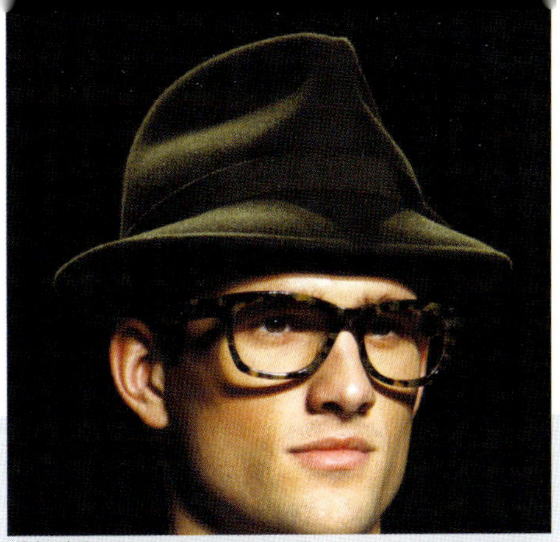

Michael Kors

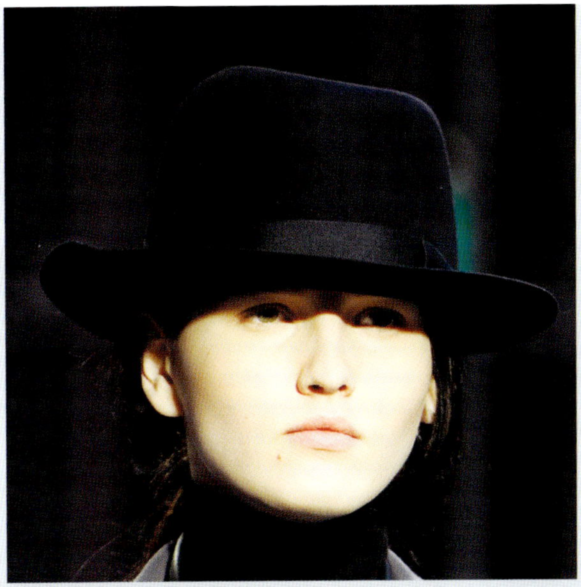

Hermès

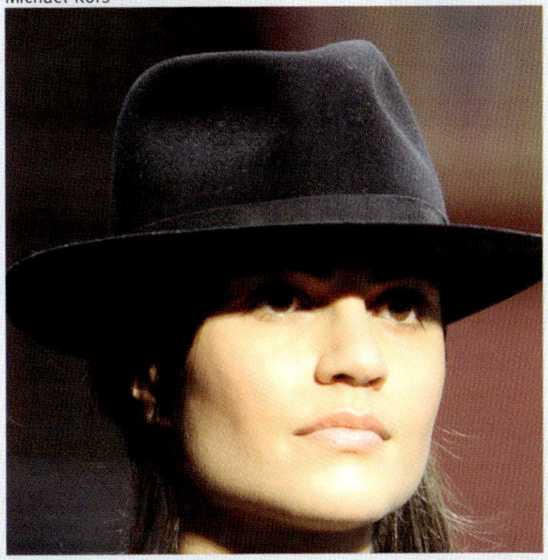

Hermès

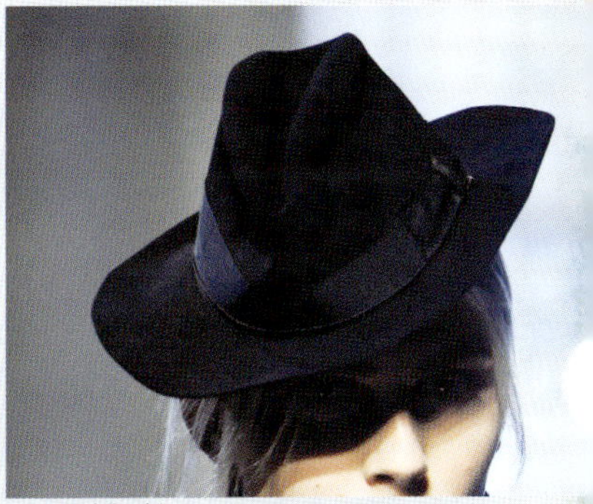

Jean Paul Gaultier

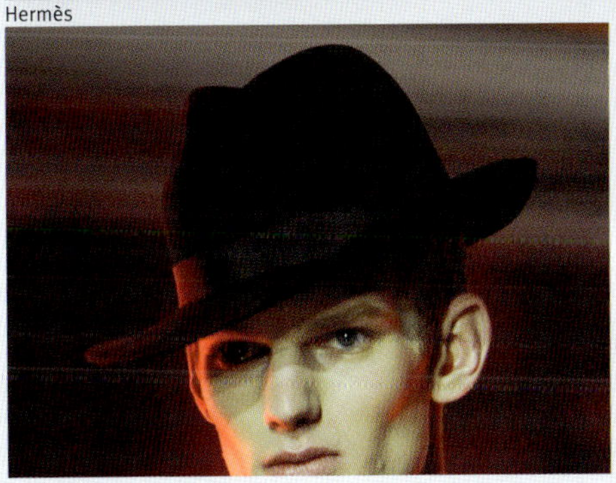

John Galliano

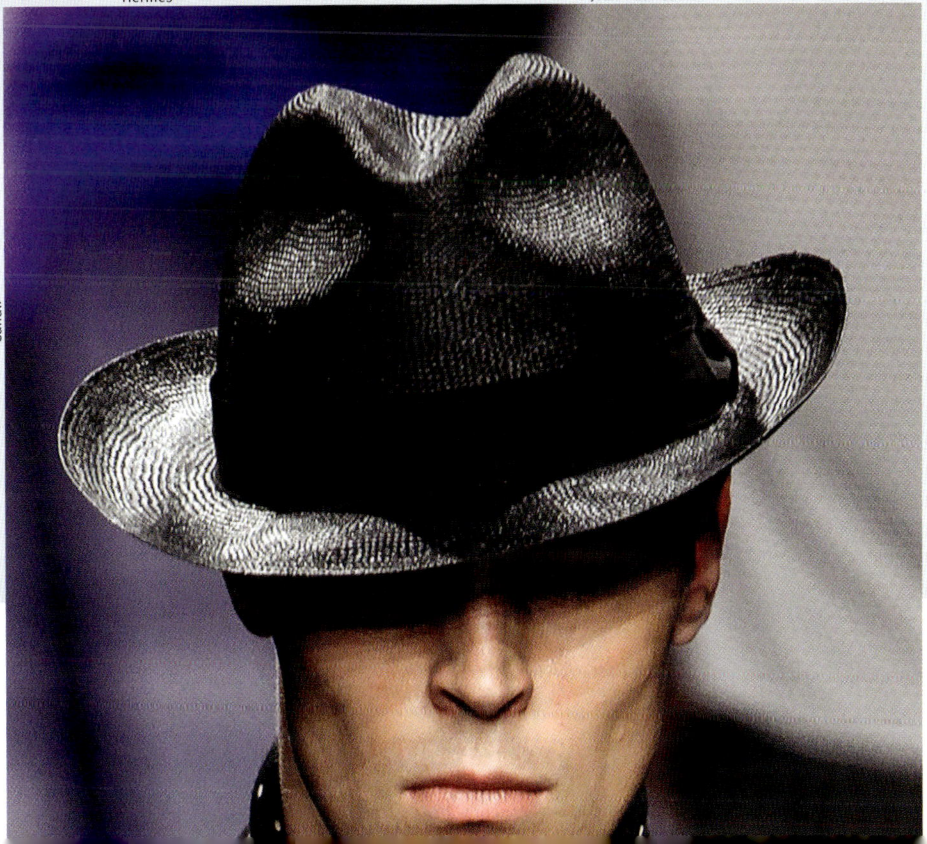

Canali

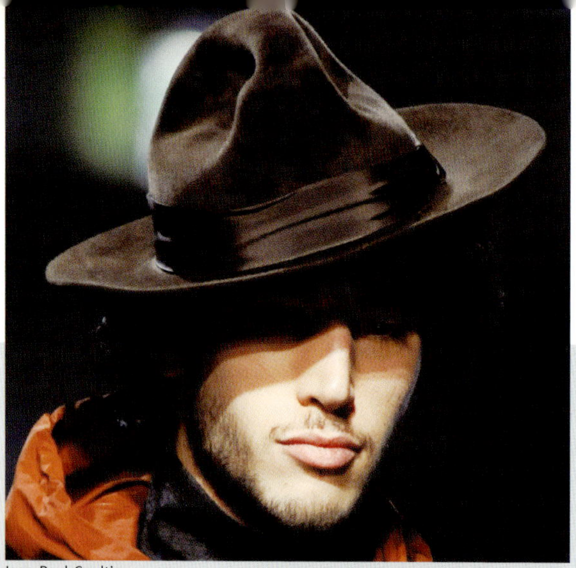

Jean Paul Gaultier

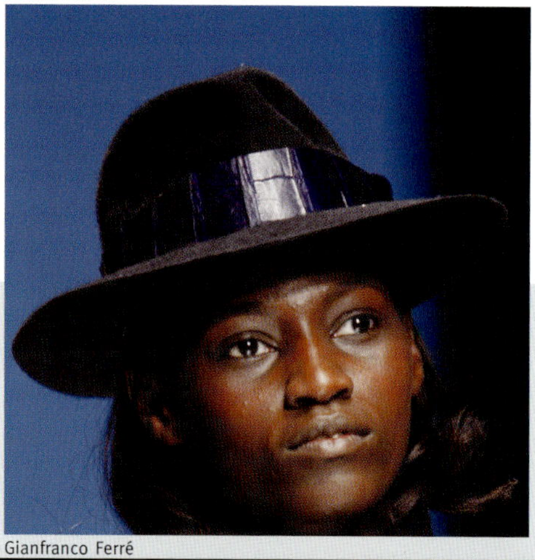

Gianfranco Ferré

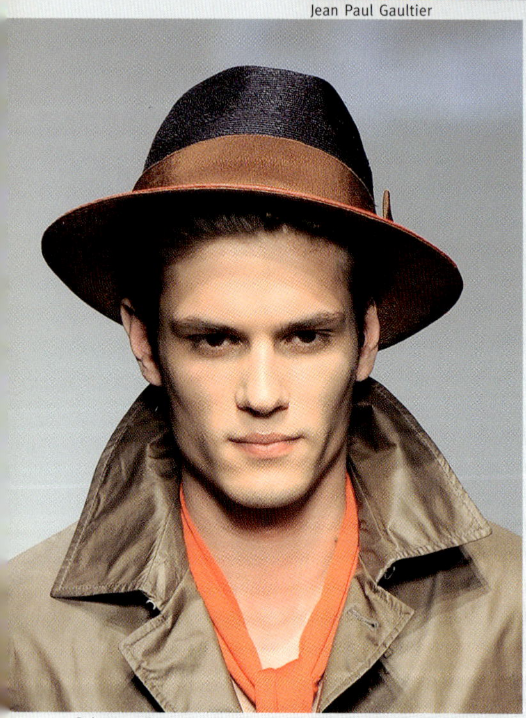

Salvatore Ferragamo

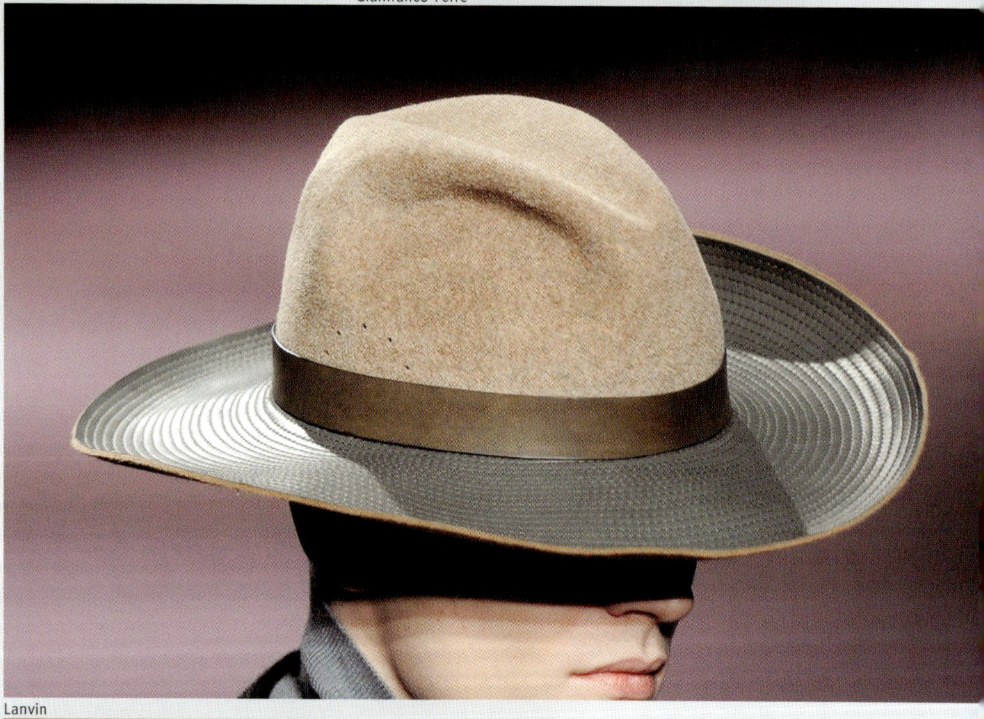

Lanvin

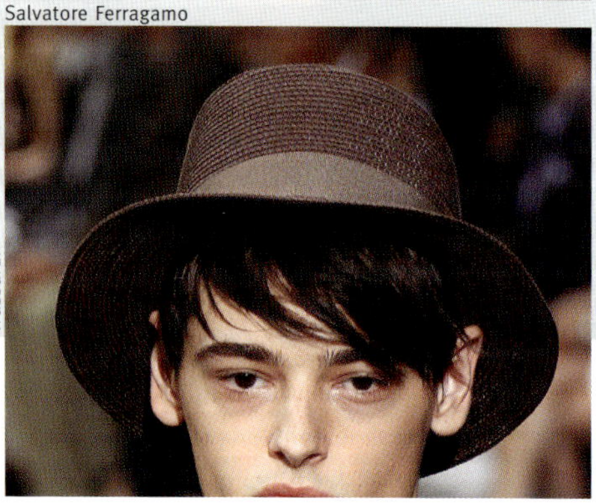

Trussardi

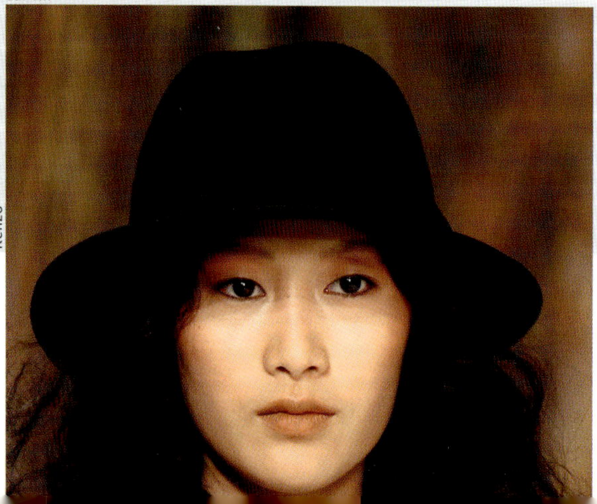

Kenzo

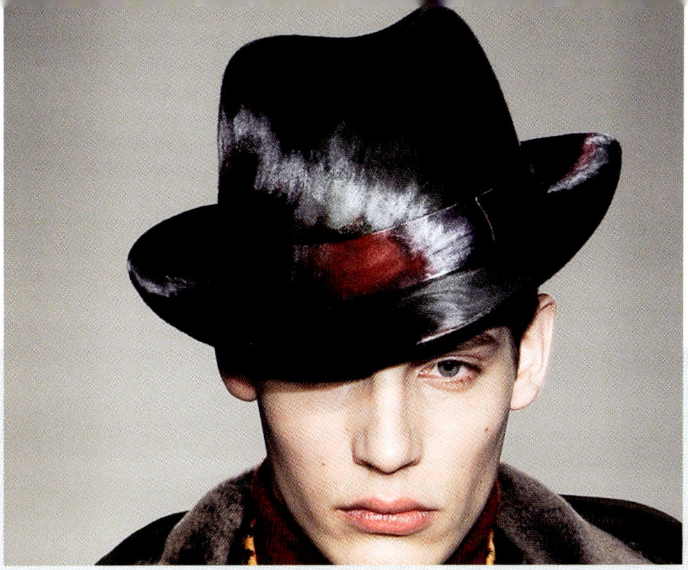
Moschino

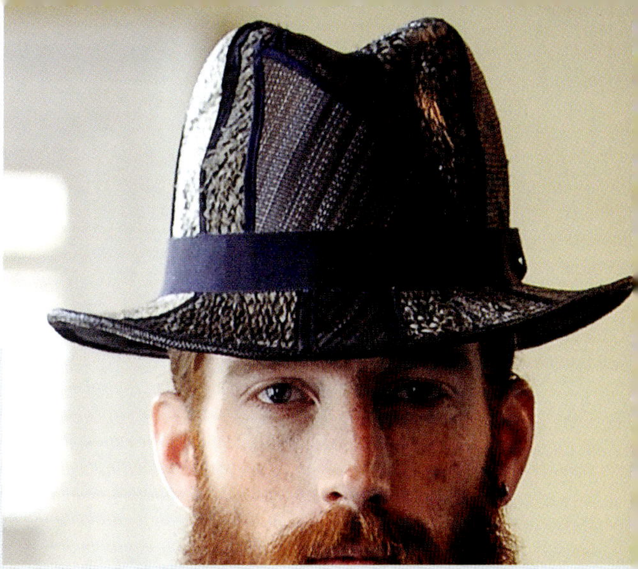
Omar Kashoura

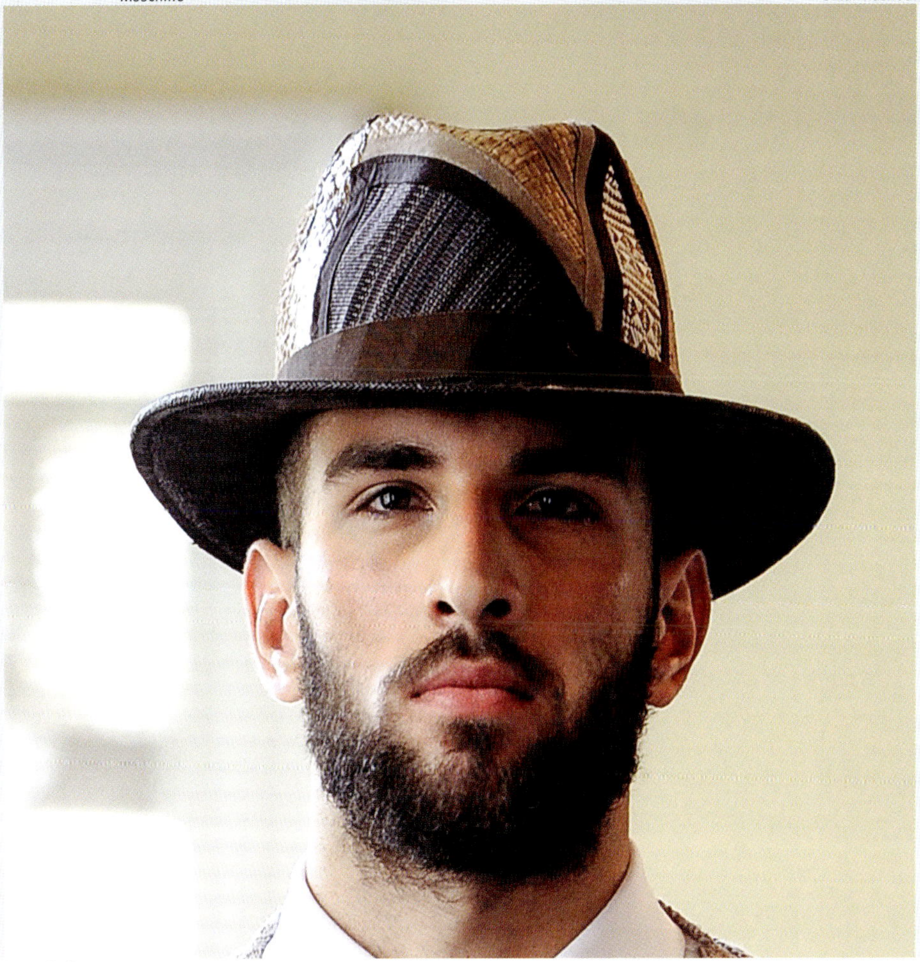
Omar Kashoura

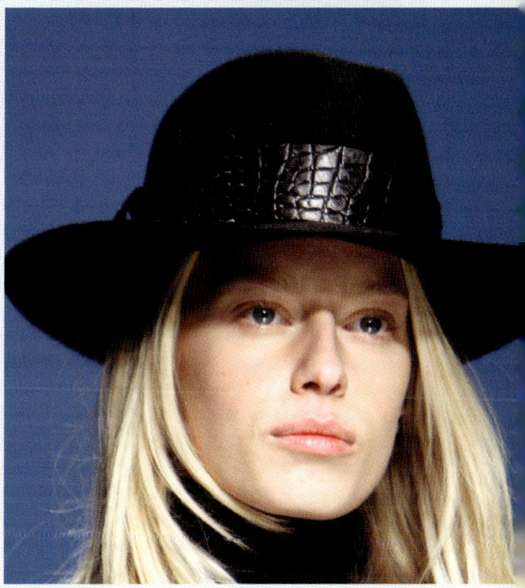
Gianfranco Ferré

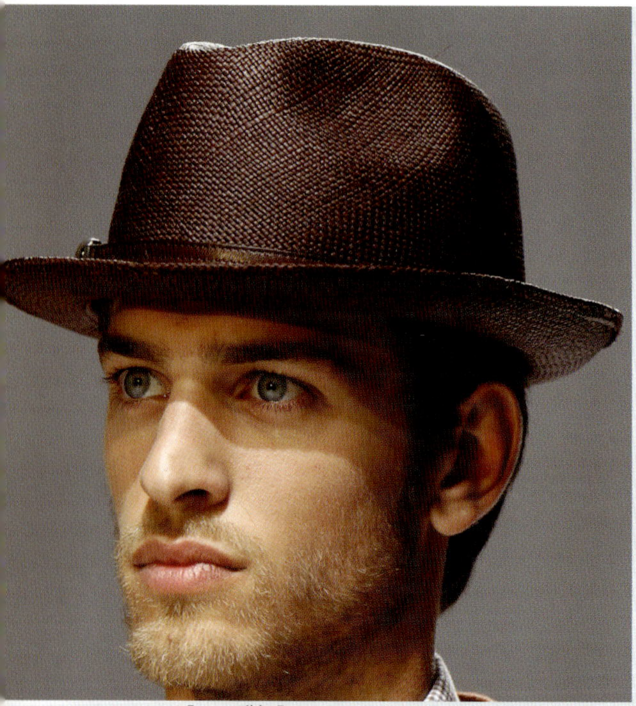

Ermenegildo Zegna

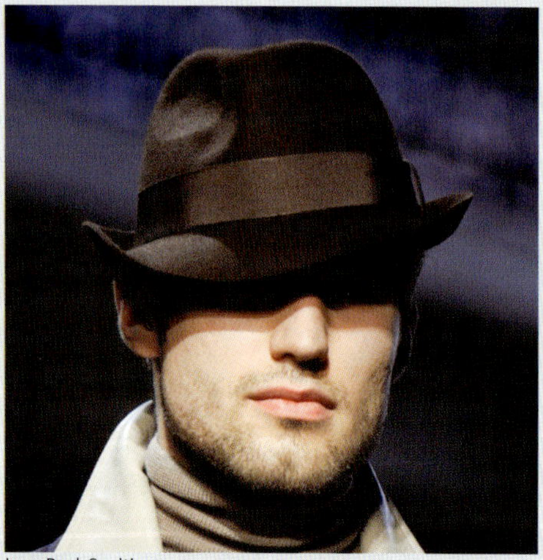

Jean Paul Gaultier

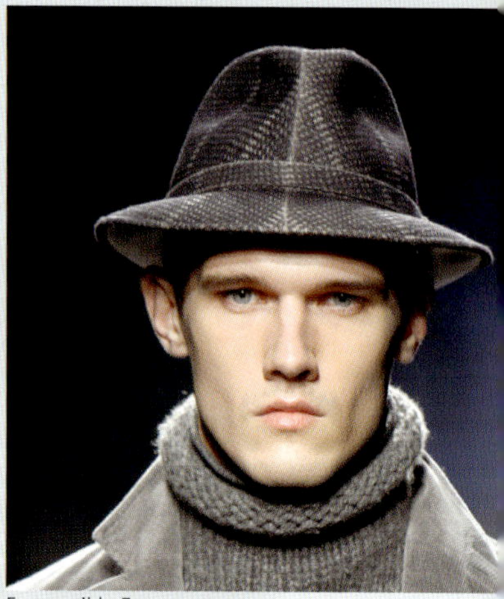

Ermenegildo Zegna

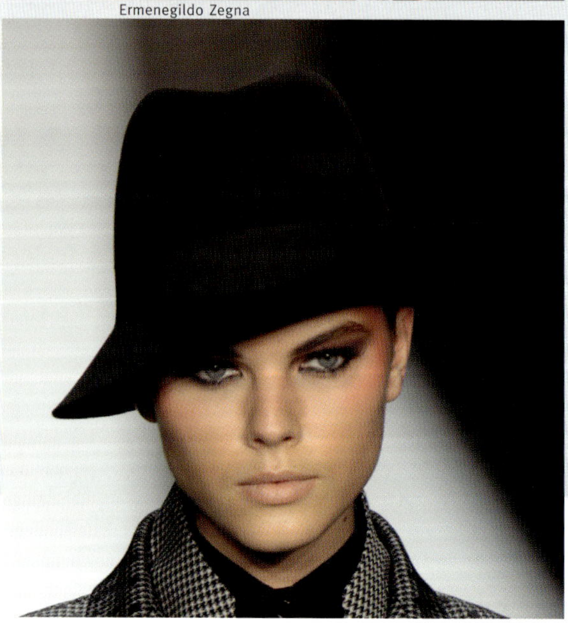

Bill Blass

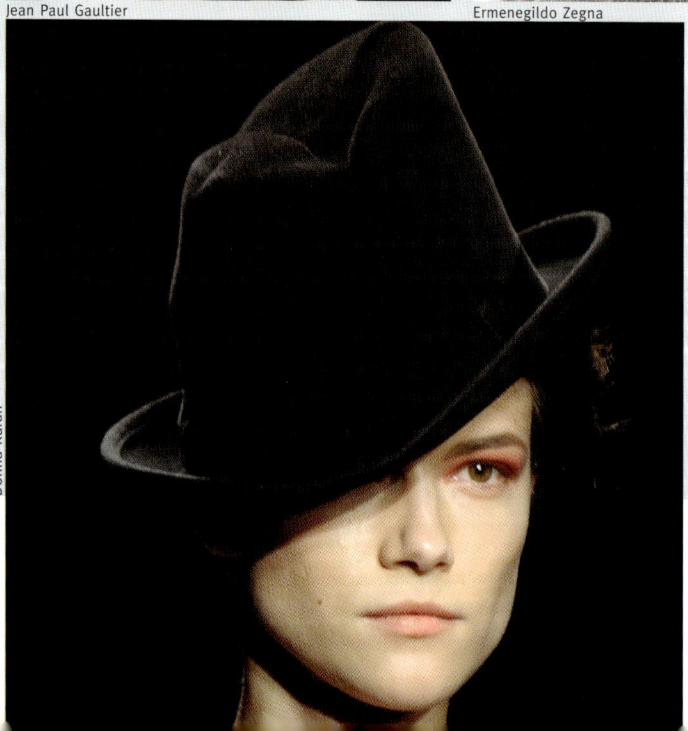

Donna Karan

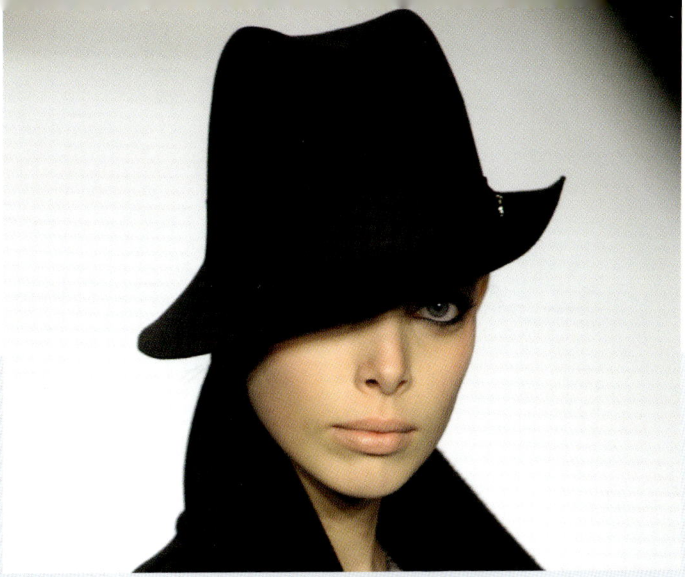

Bill Blass

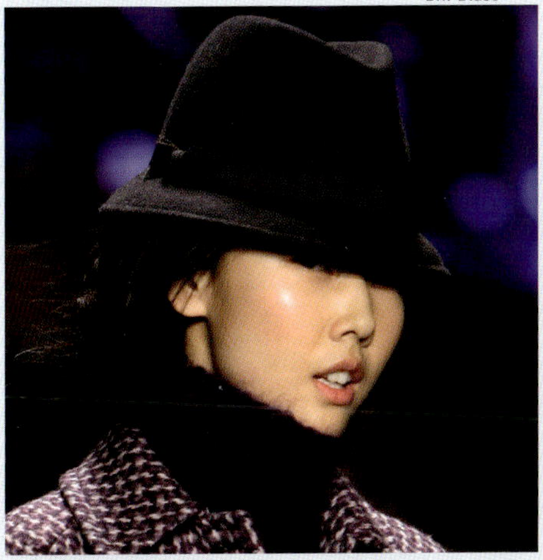

Michael Kors

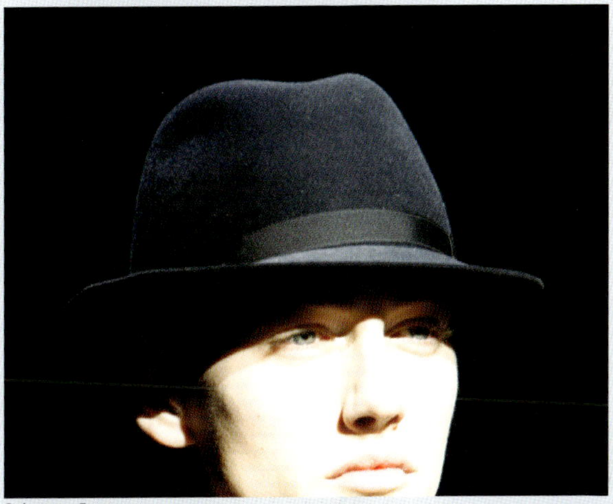

Salvatore Ferragamo

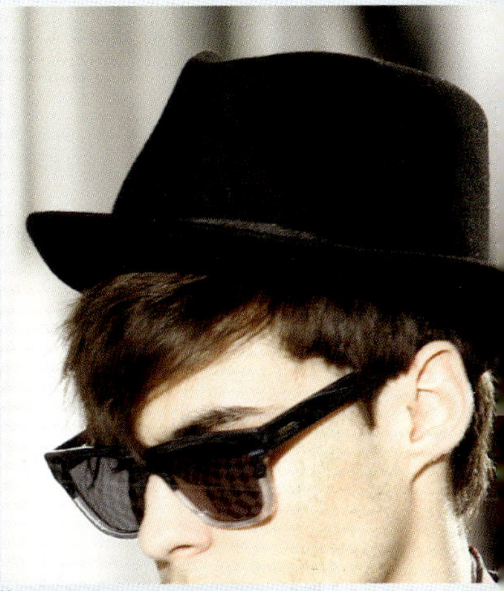

Kenzo

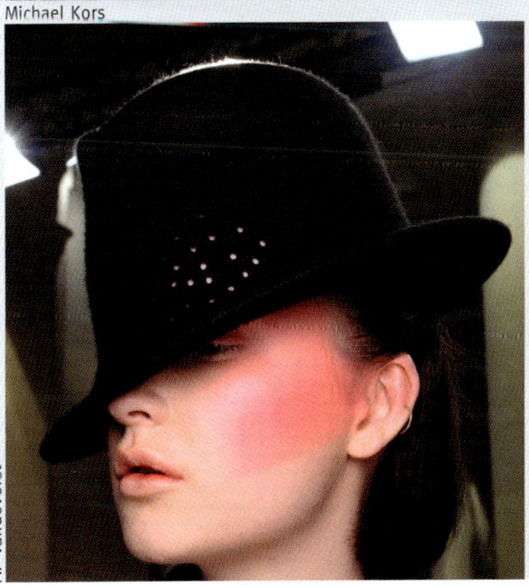

AF Vandevorst

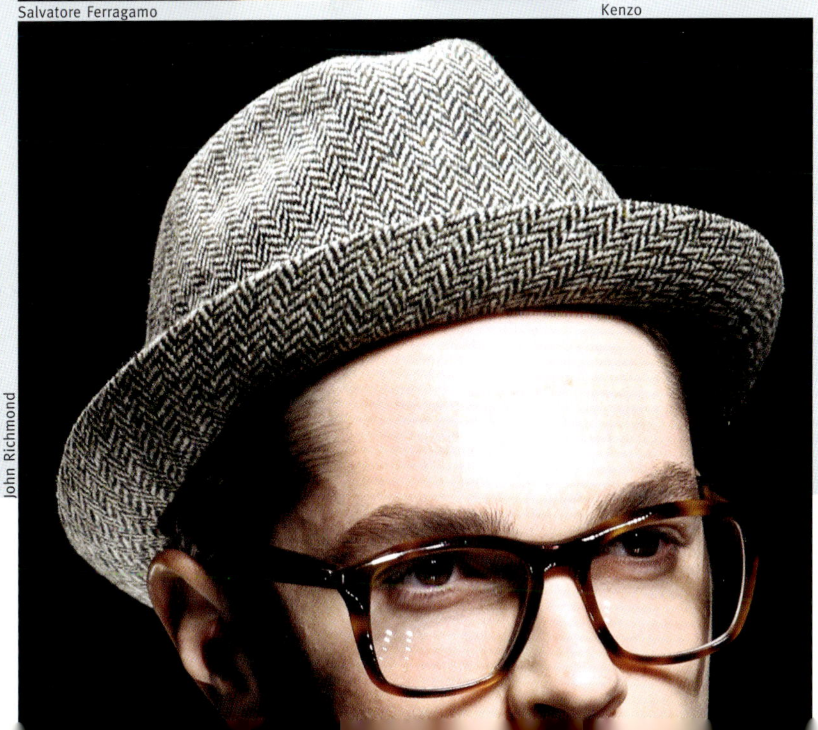

John Richmond

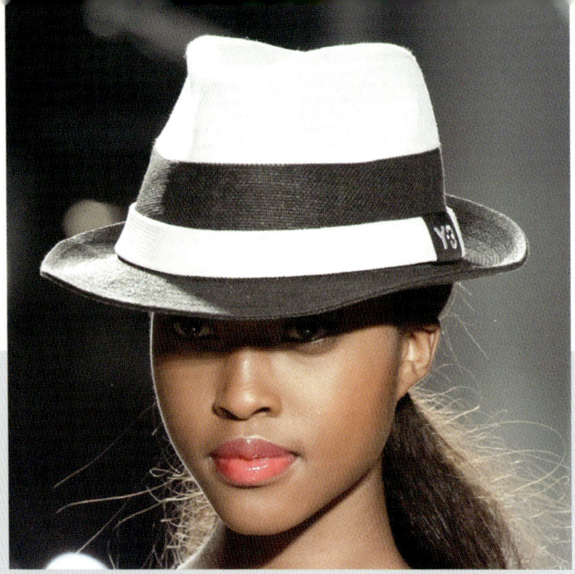

Y3

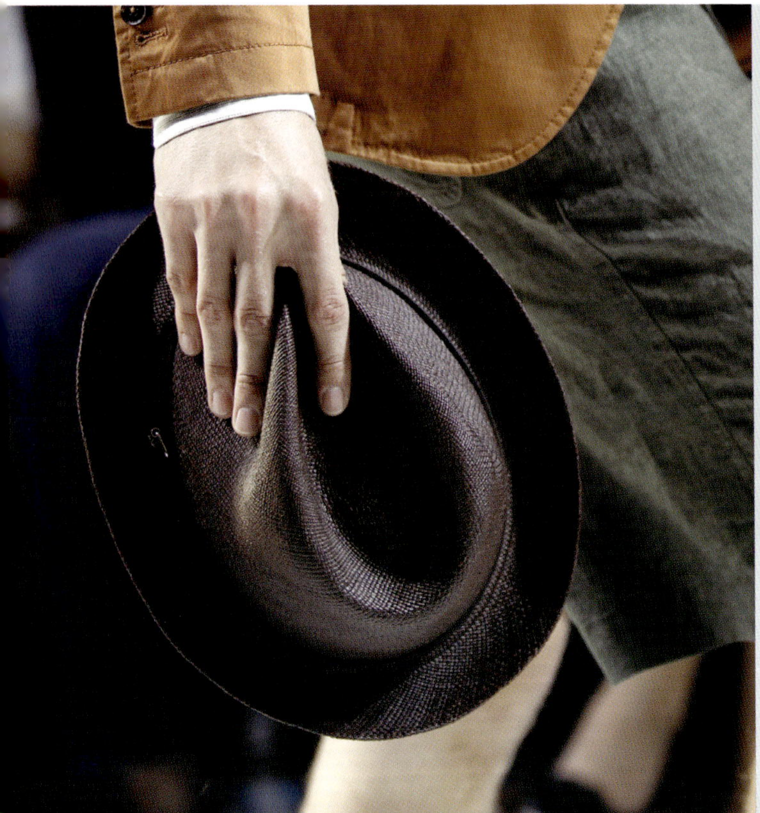

Ermenegildo Zegna

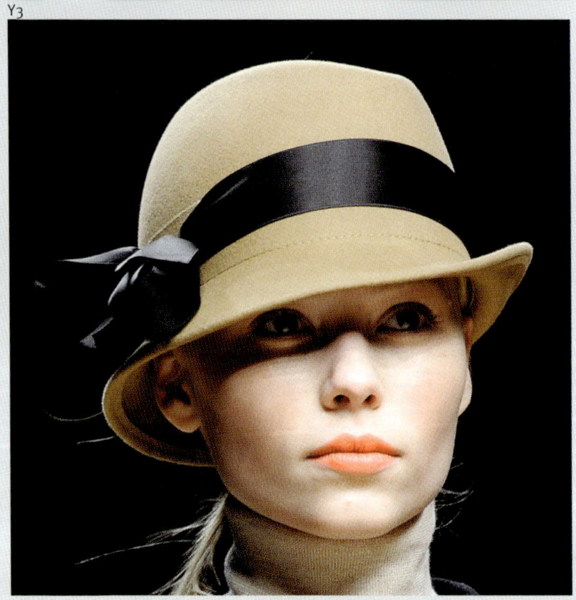

Blugirl

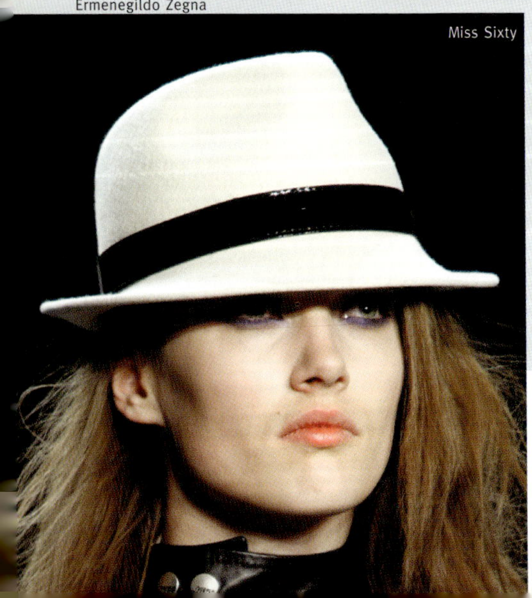

Miss Sixty

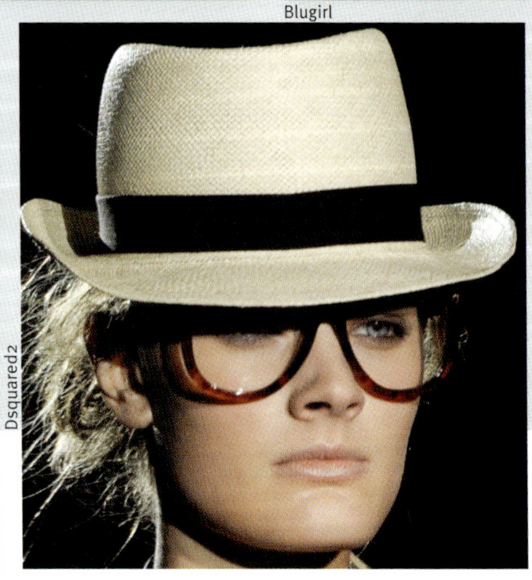

Dsquared2

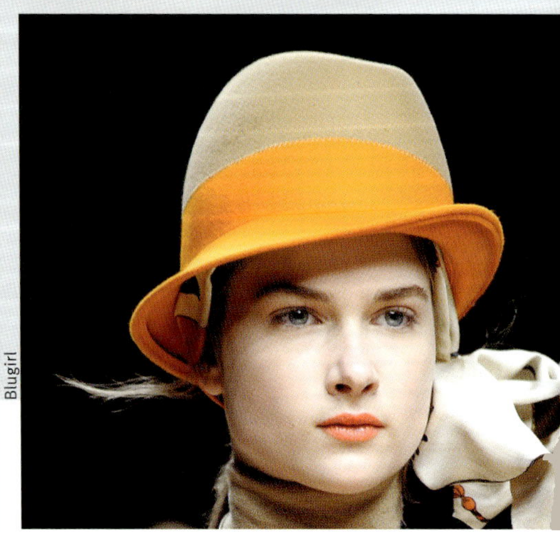

Blugirl

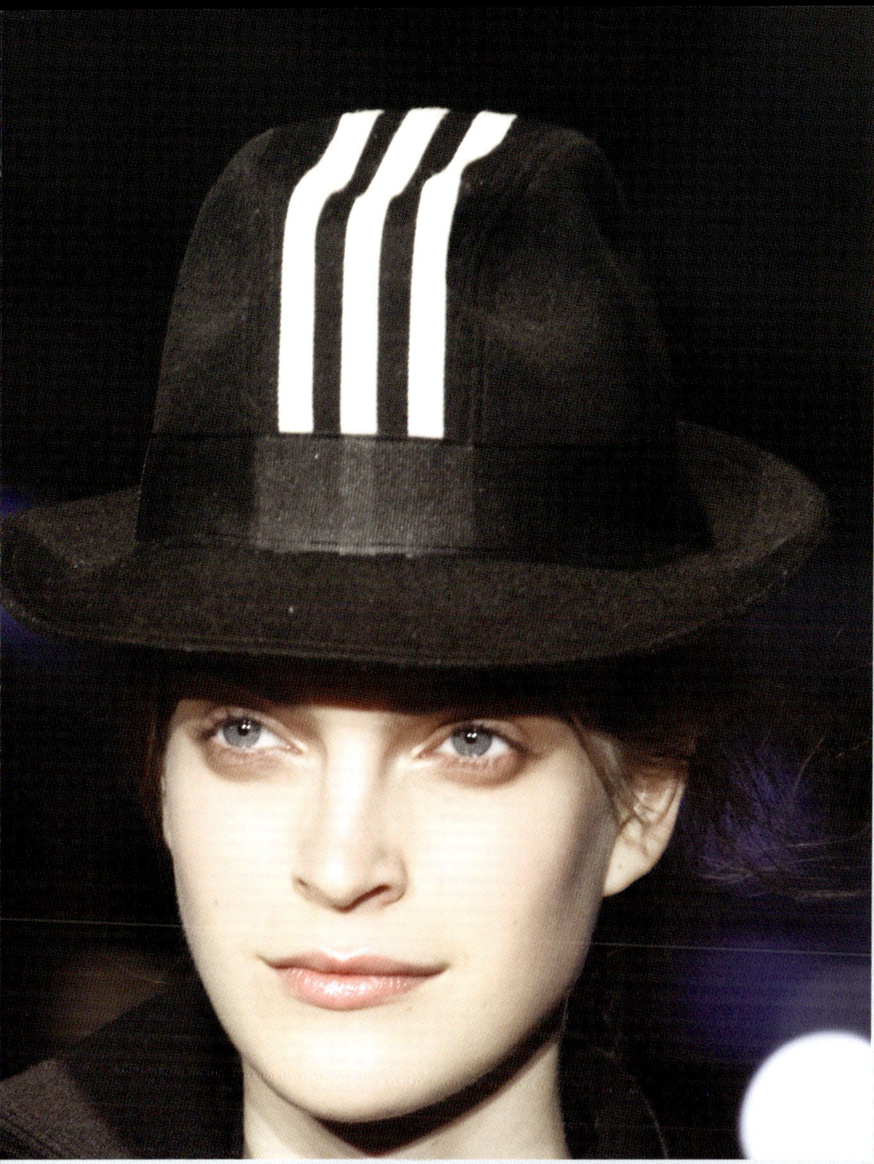

Y3

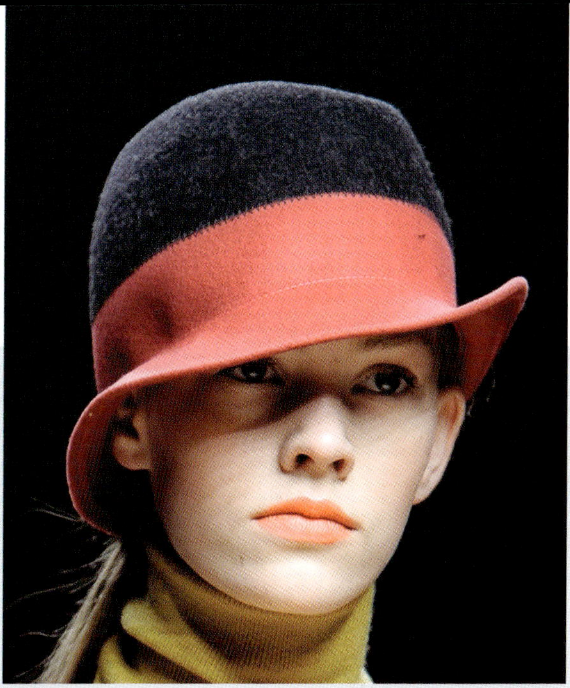

Blugirl

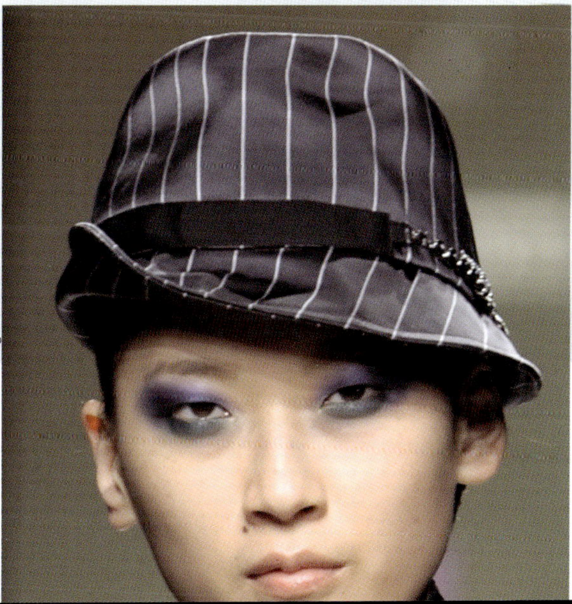

Angelo Marani

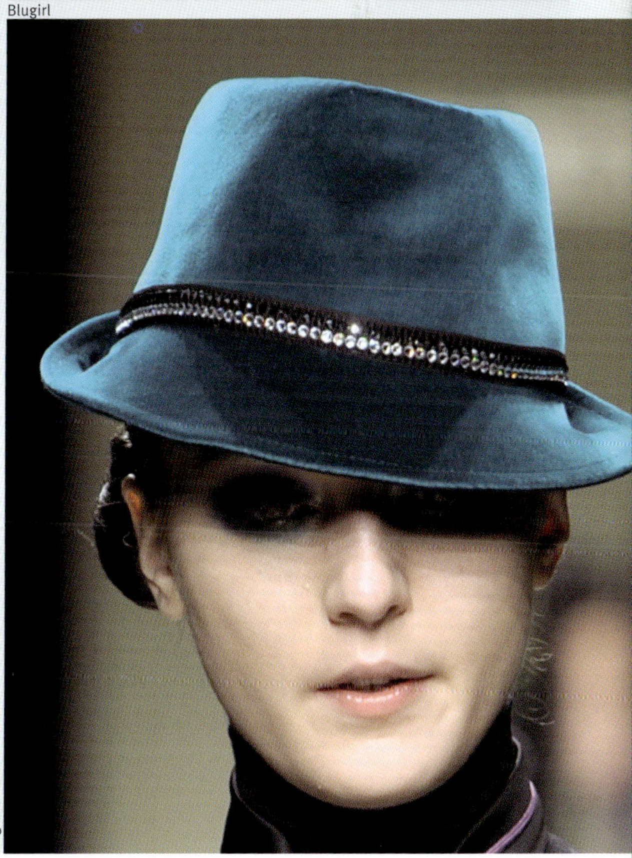

Angelo Marani

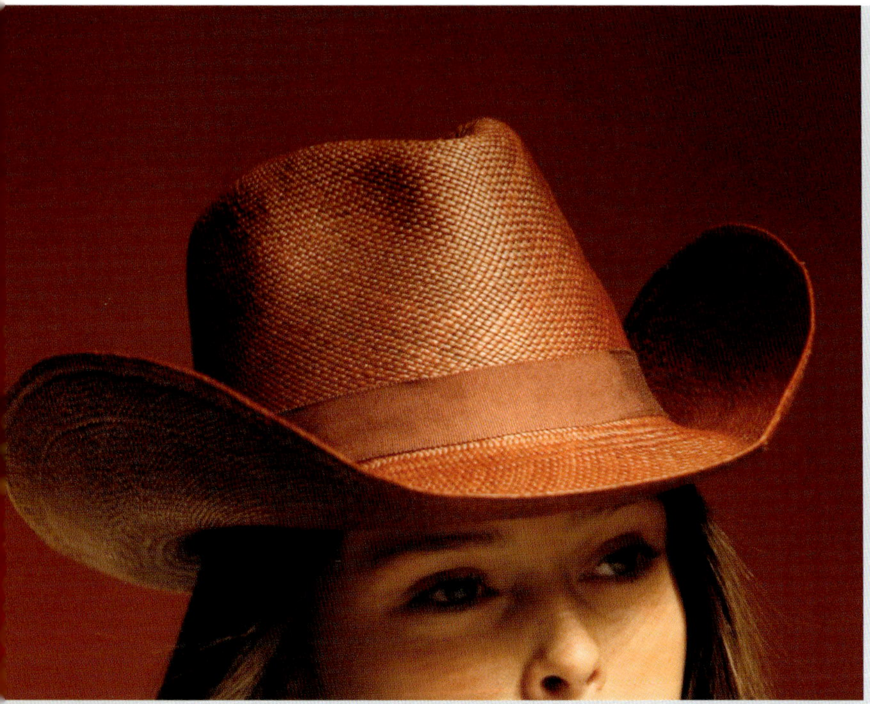
Hermès

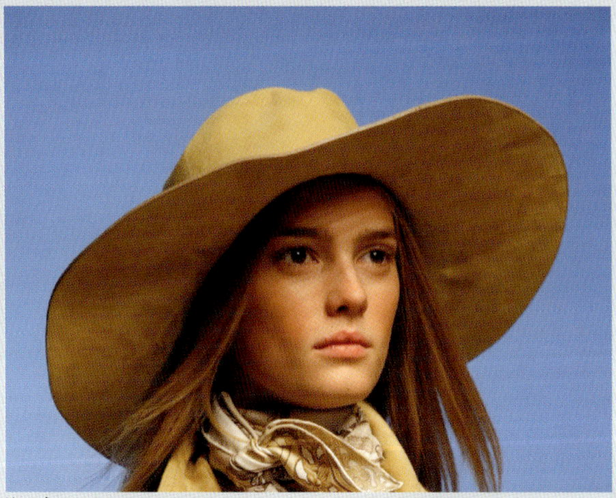
Hermès

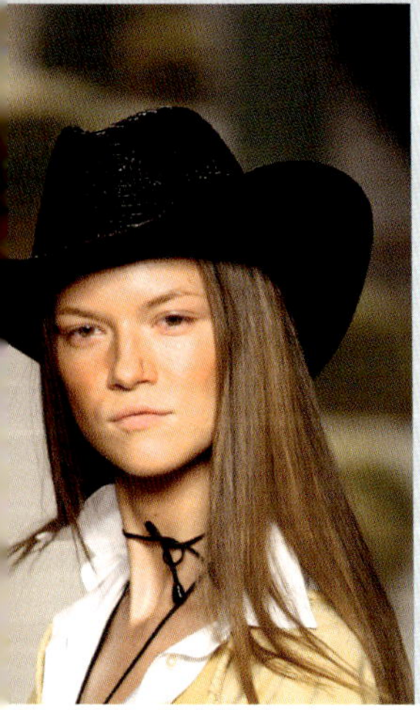
Hermès

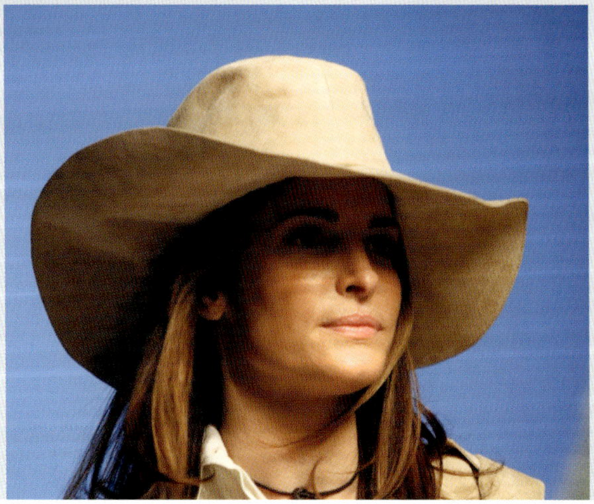
Hermès

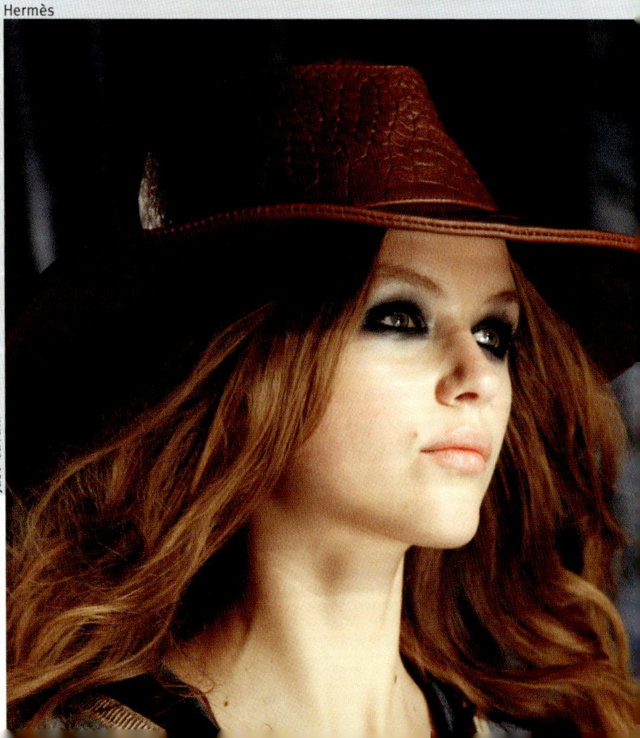
Just Cavalli

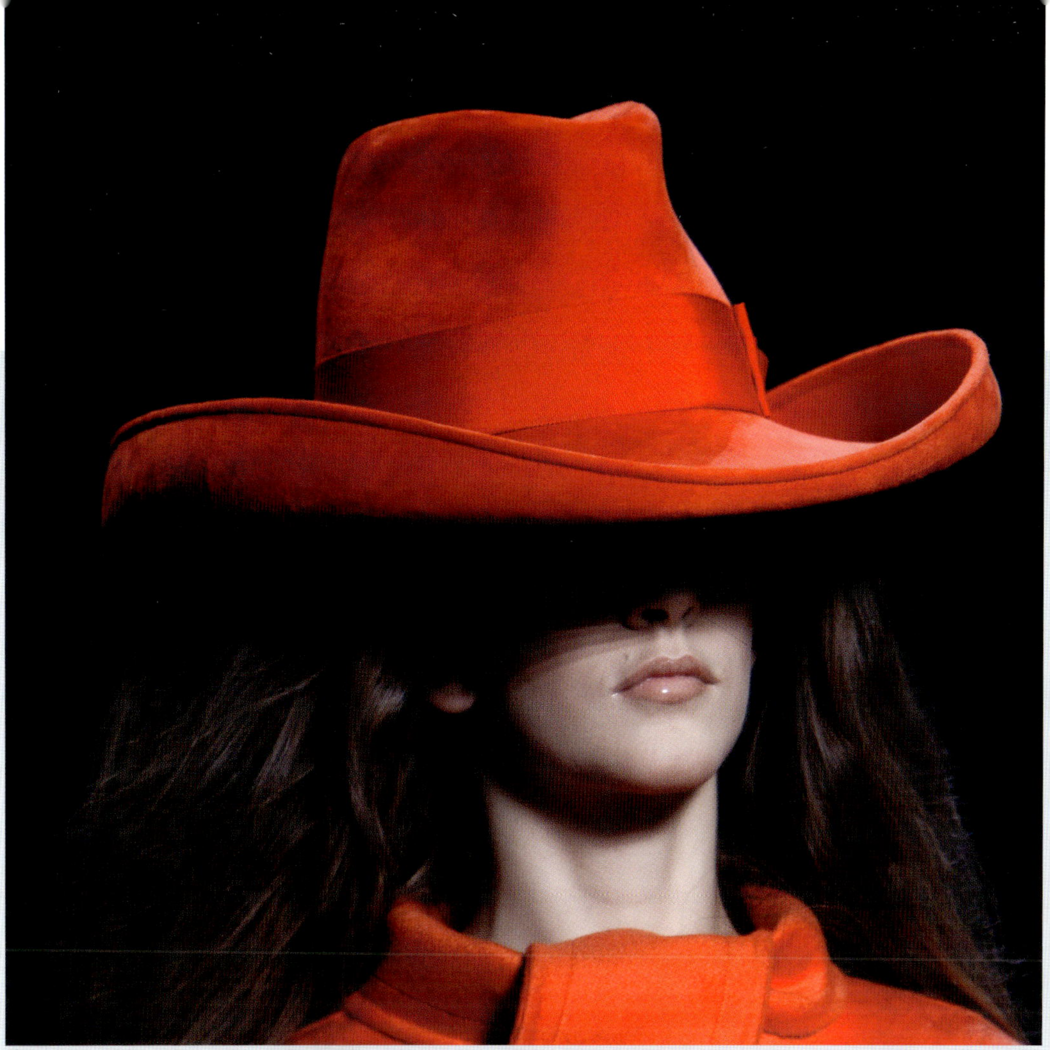

Dior

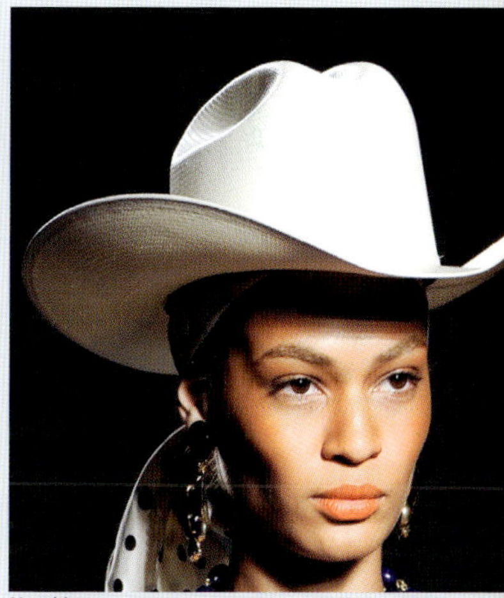

Moschino

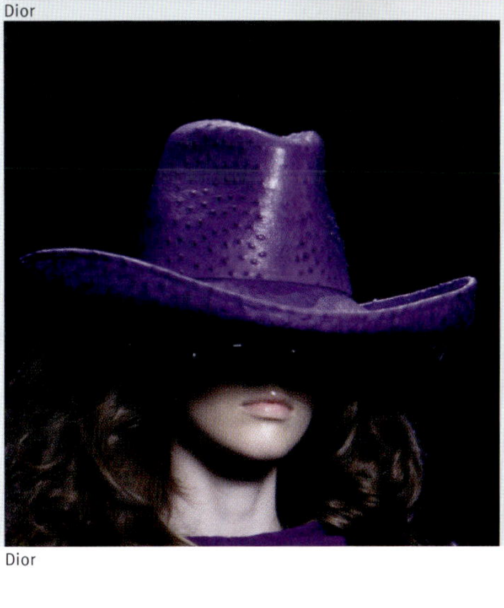

Dior

Moschino

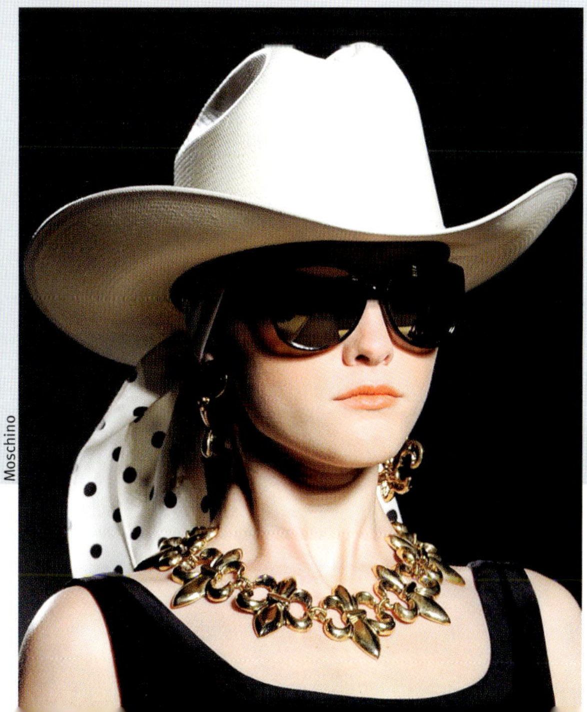

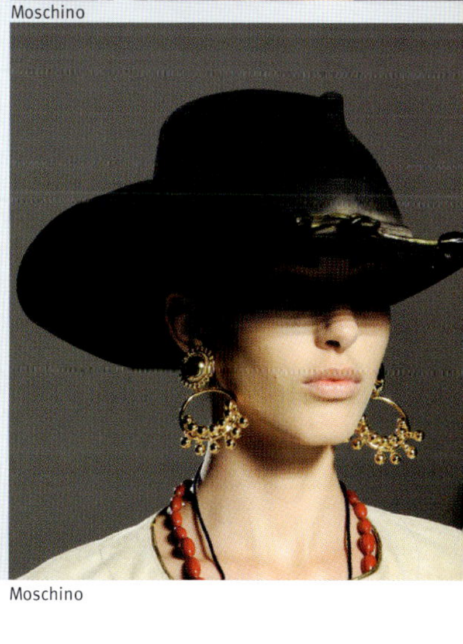

Moschino

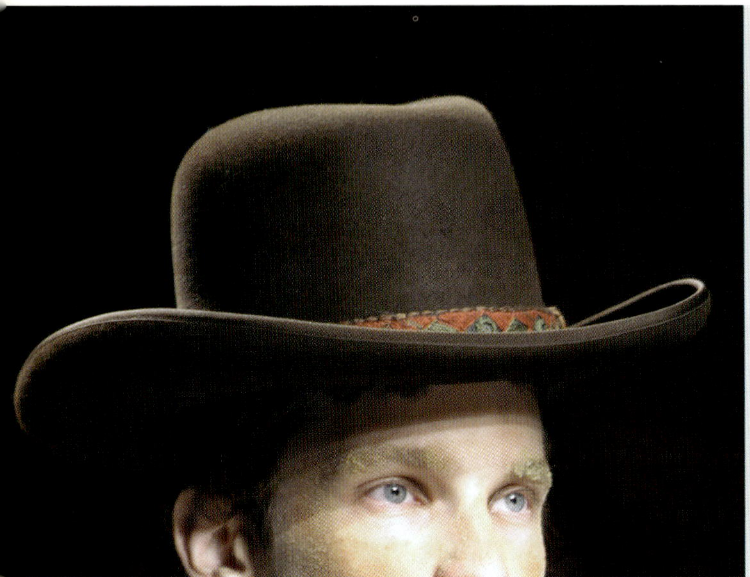

Alexander McQueen

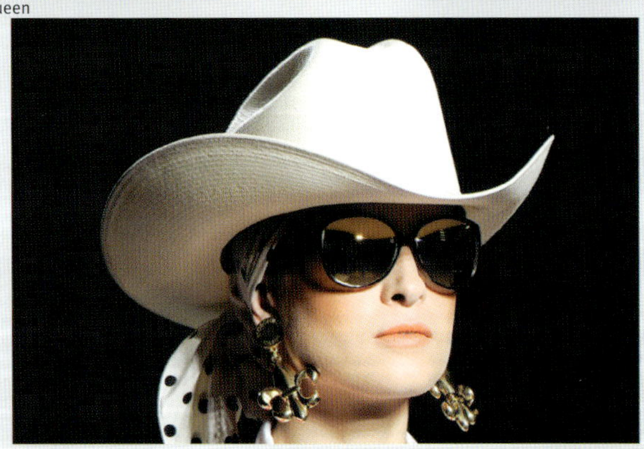

Moschino

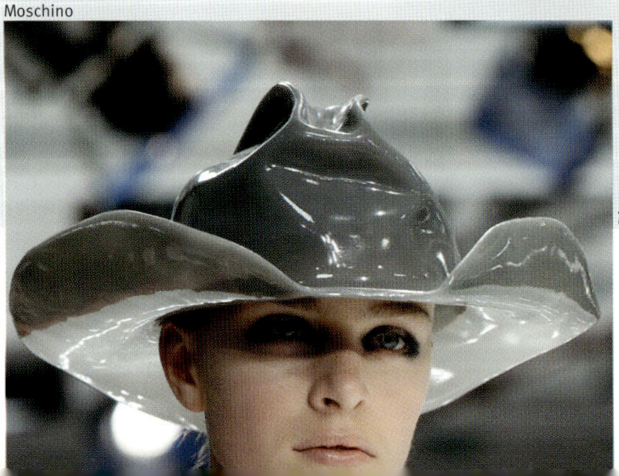

Acne

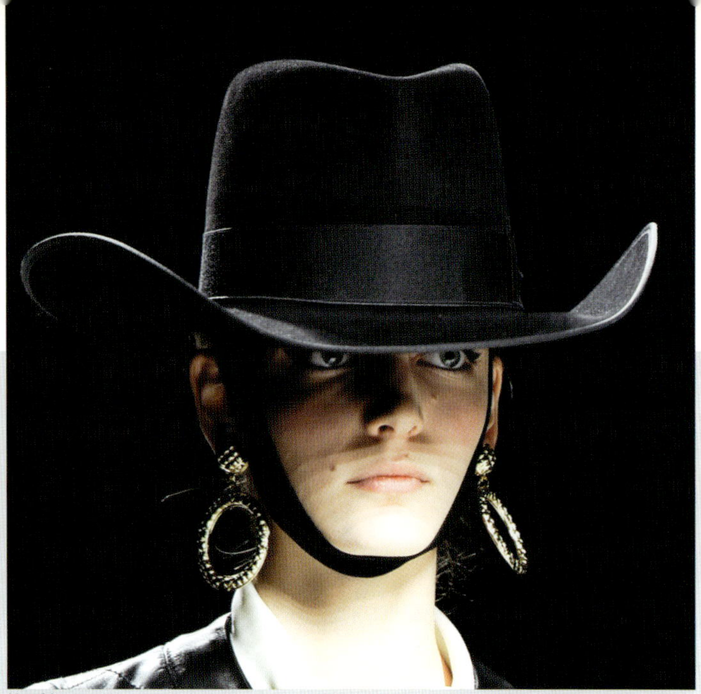

Moschino

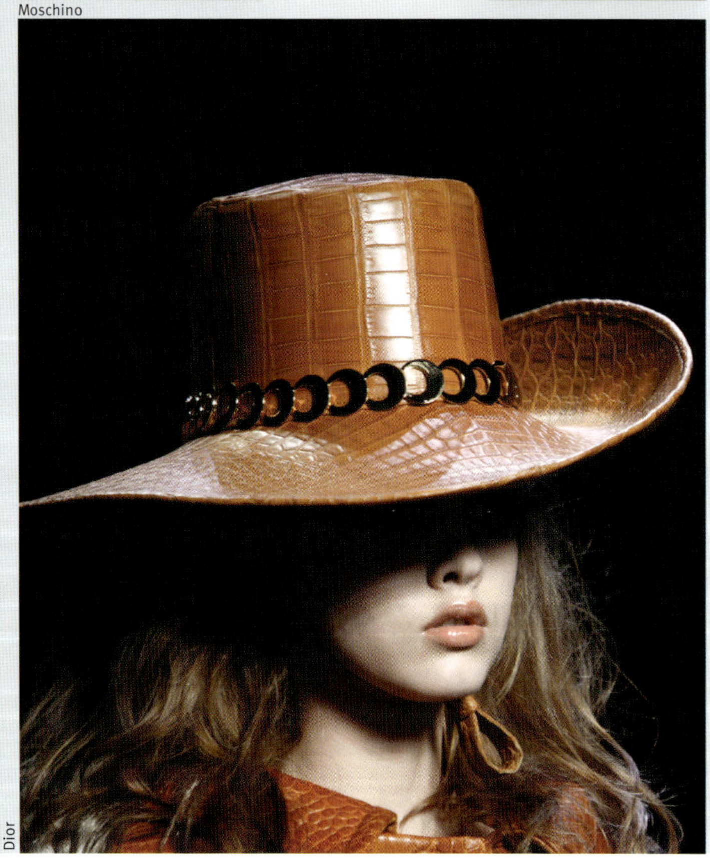

Dior

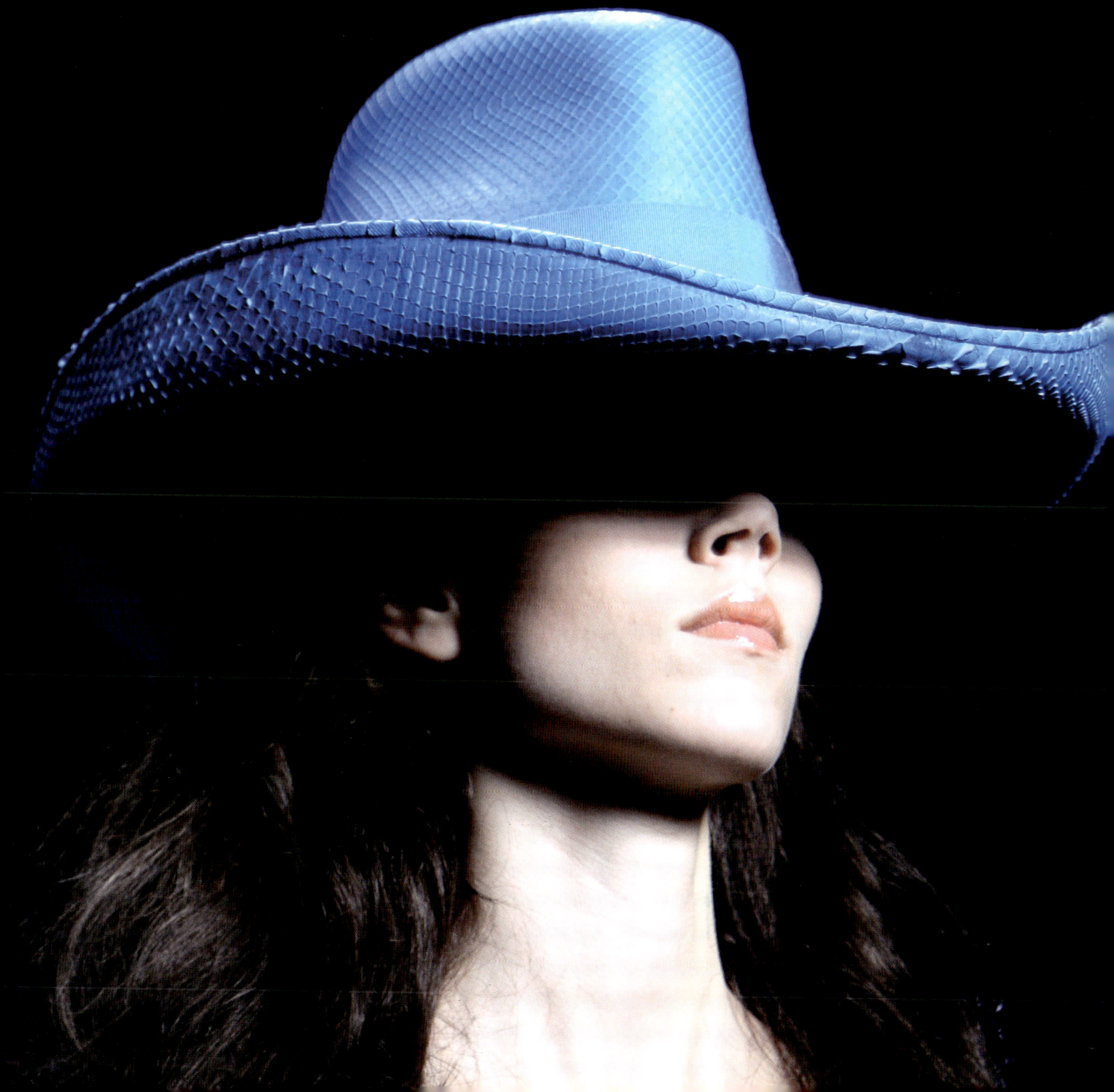

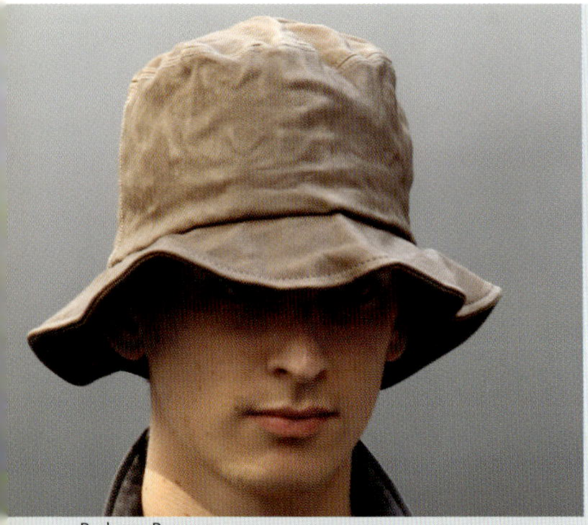

Burberry Prorsum

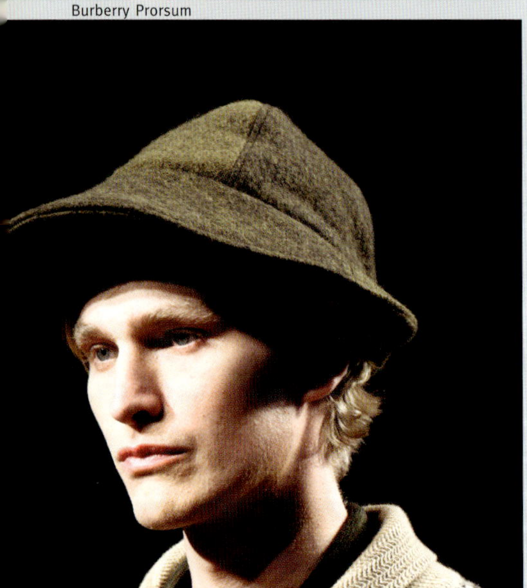

Missoni

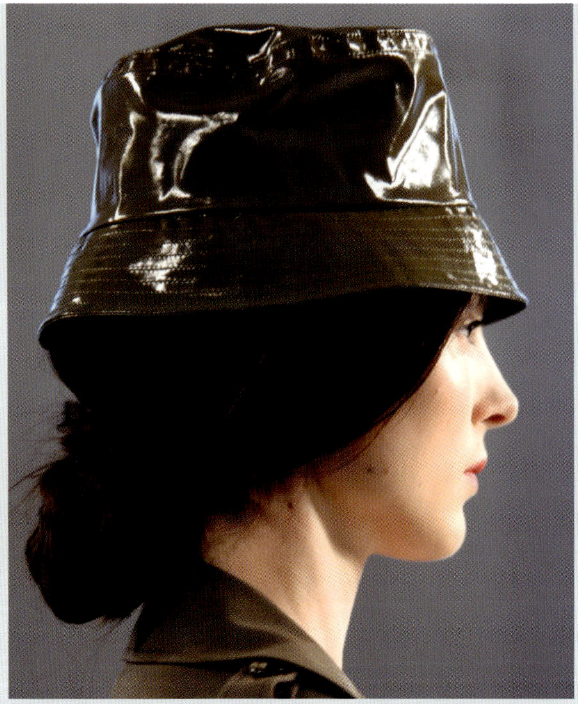

Aquascutum

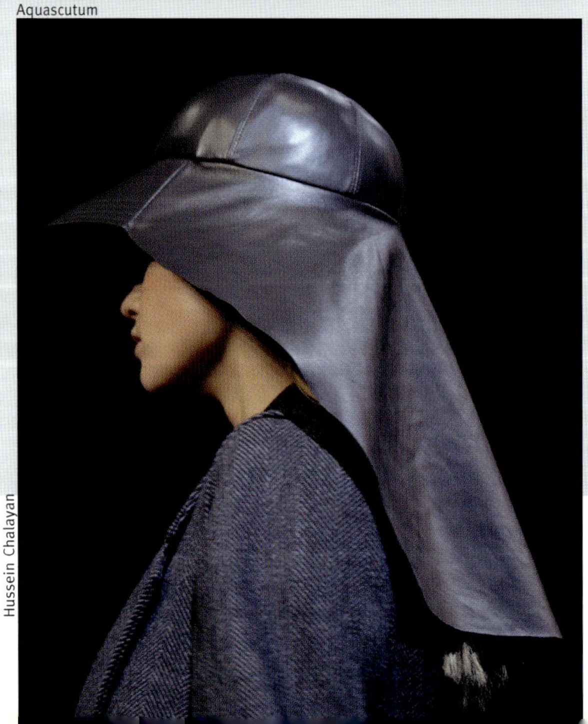

Hussein Chalayan

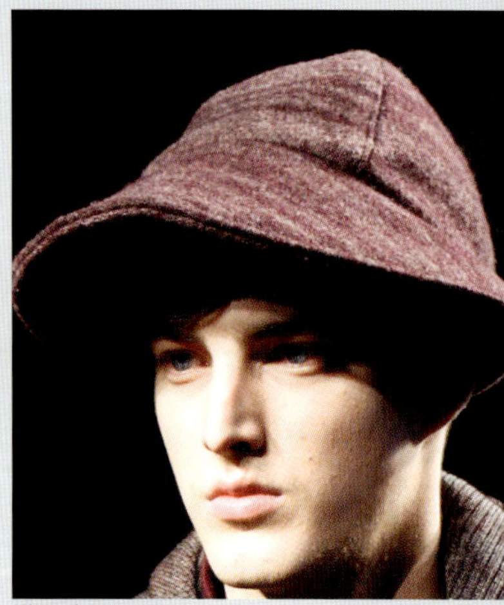

Missoni

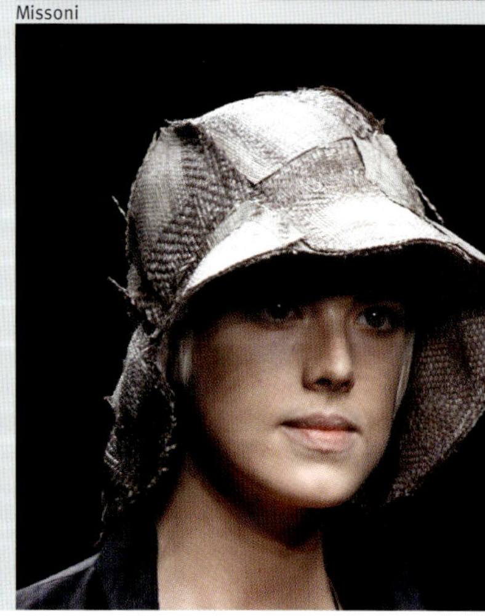

Burberry Prorsum

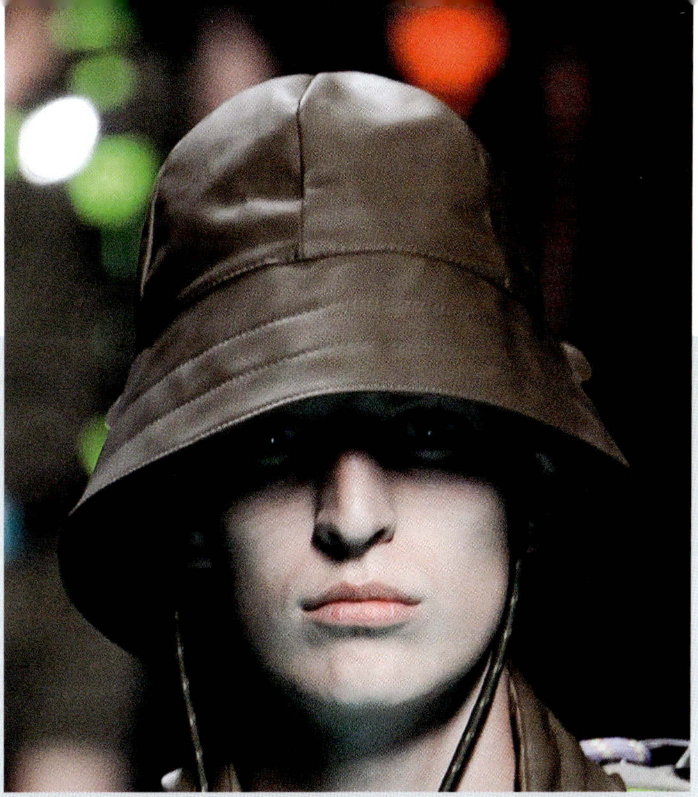

Louis Vuitton

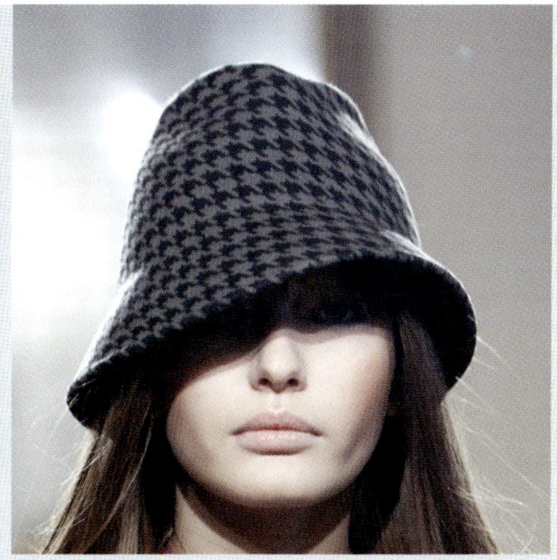

Massimo Rebecchi

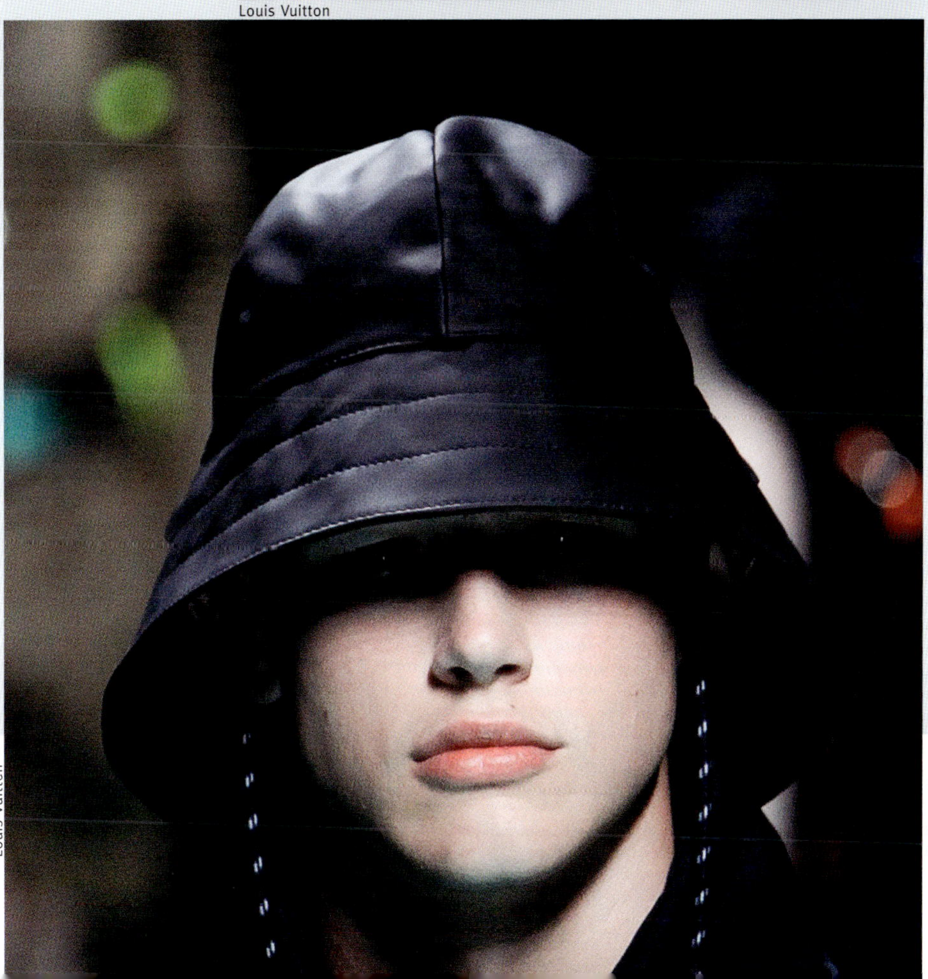

Louis Vuitton

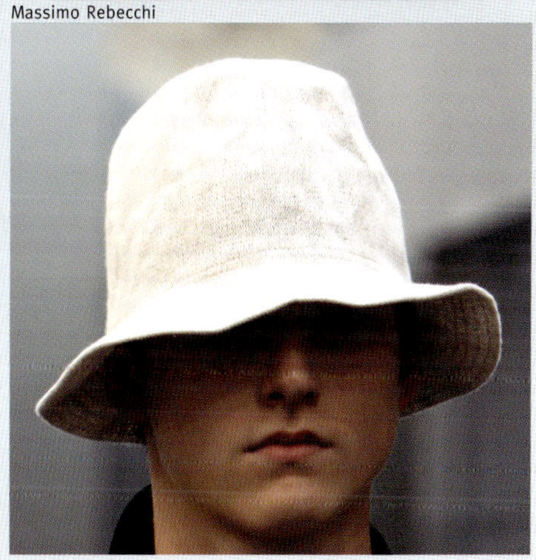

Burberry Prorsum

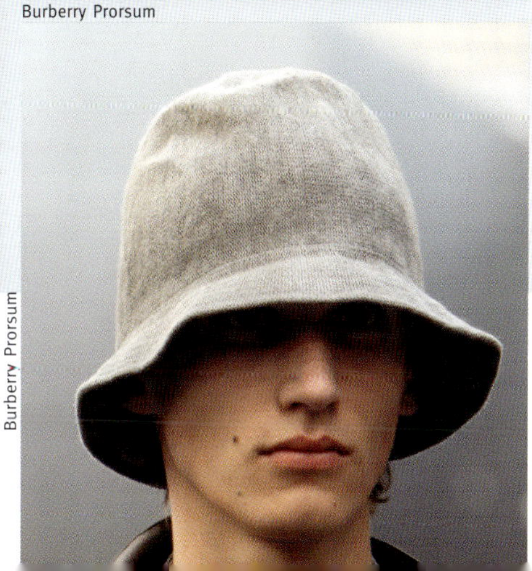

Burberry Prorsum

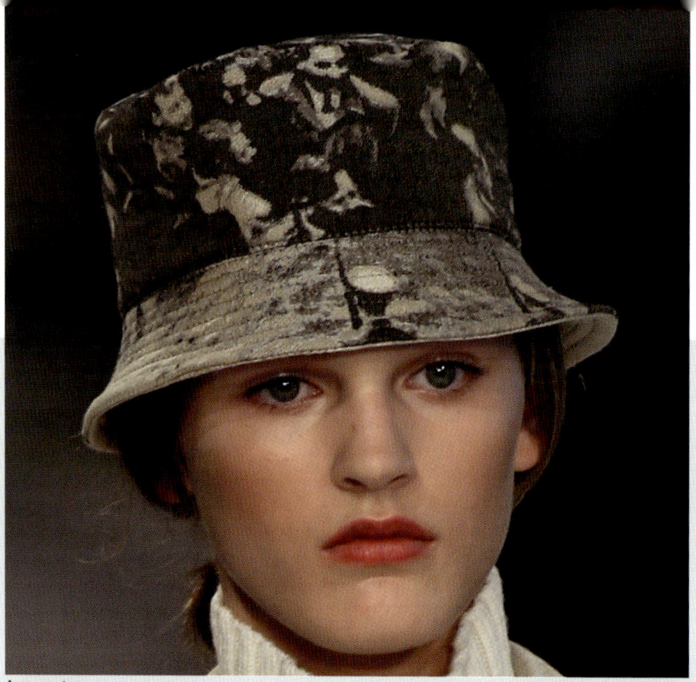

Aquascutum

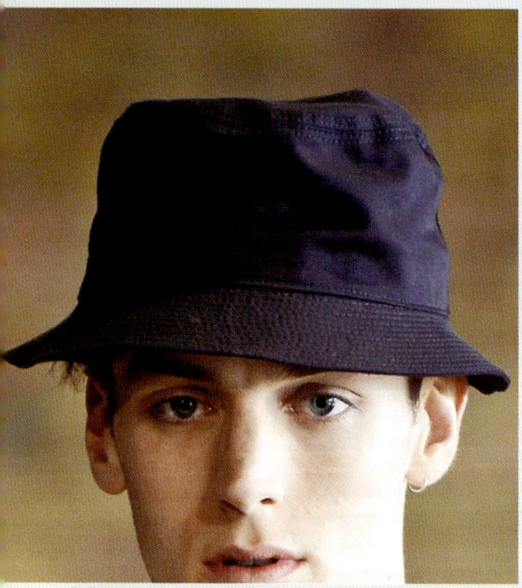

E. Tautz

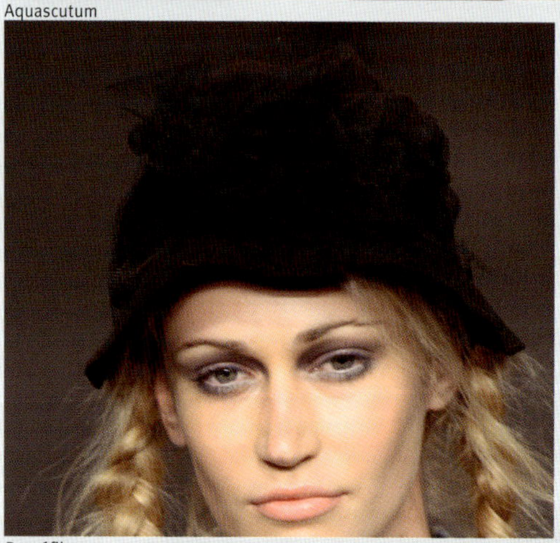

Drosófila

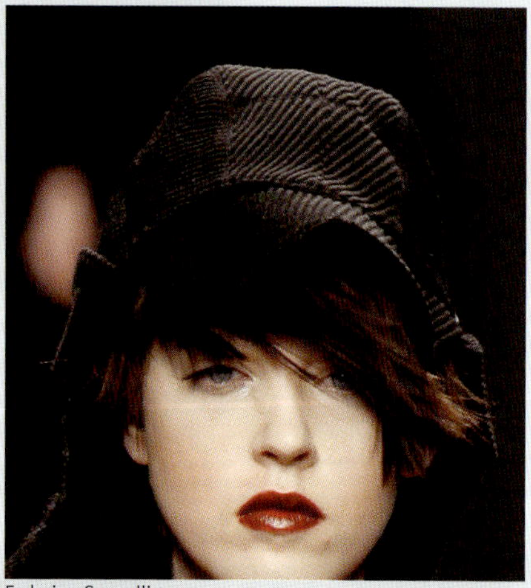

Federico Sangalli

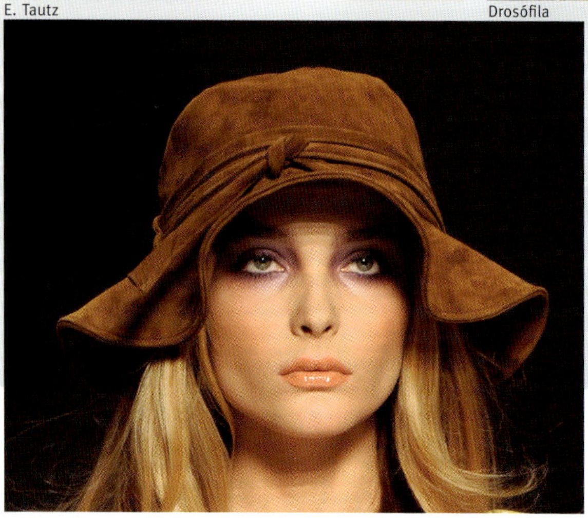

Etro

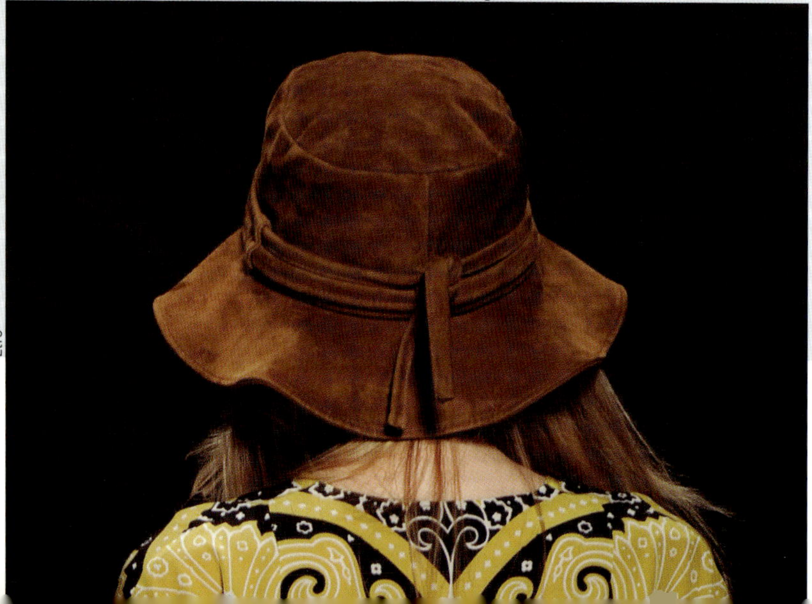

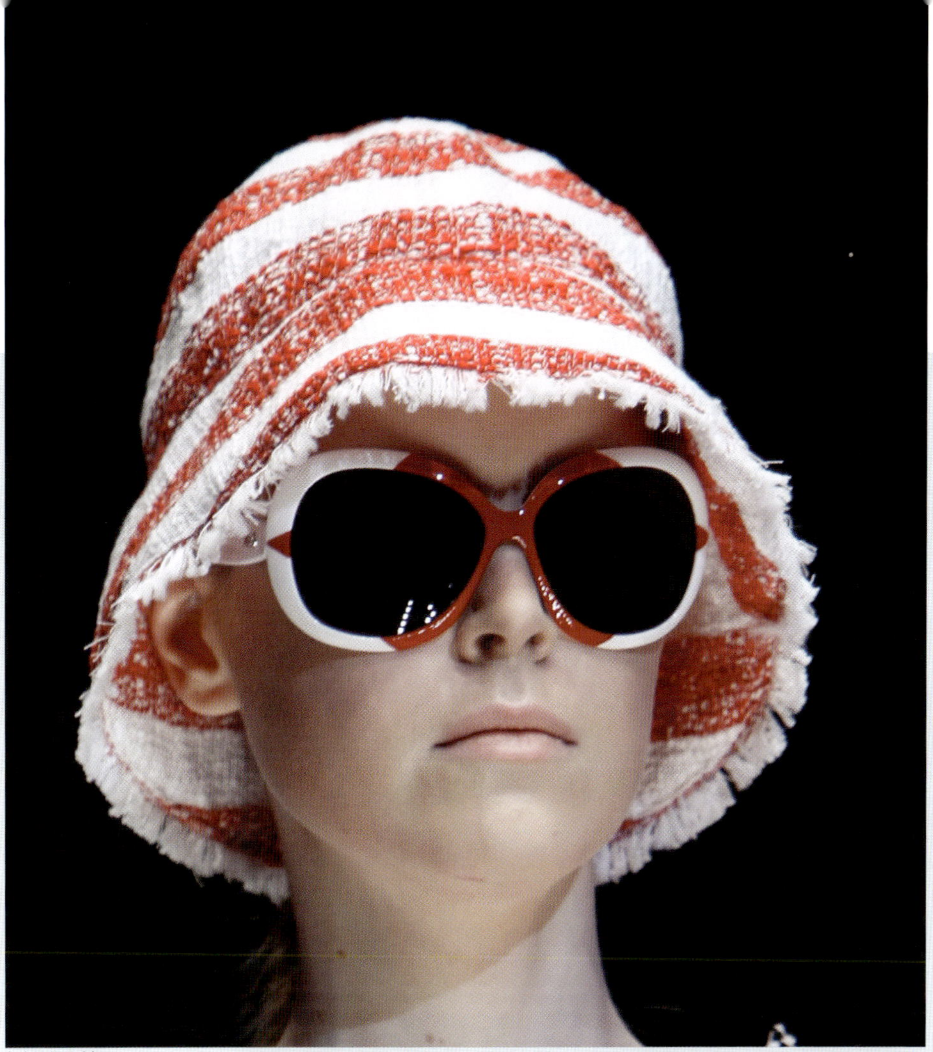
Dolce & Gabbana

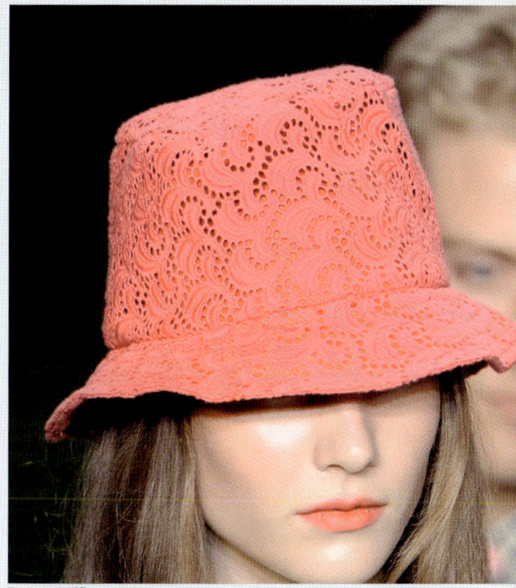
Tommy Hilfiger

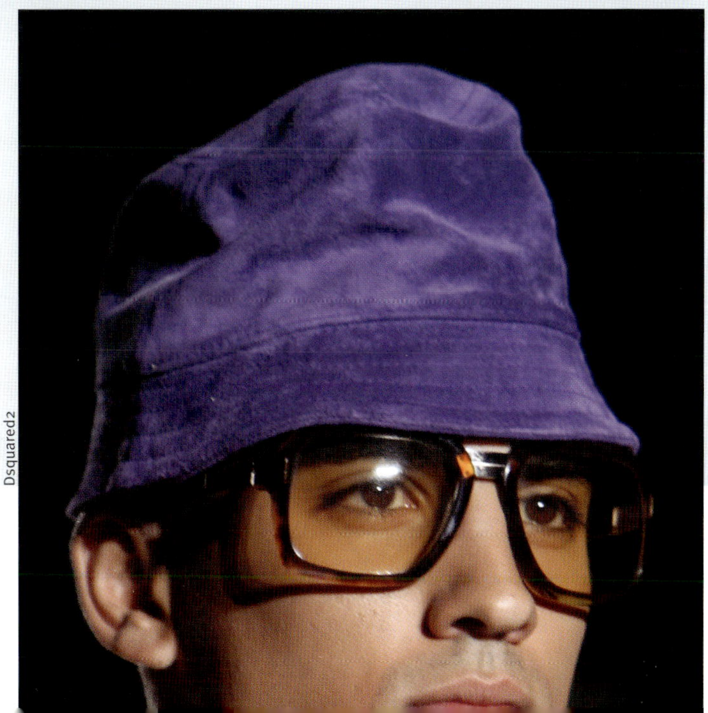
Dsquared2

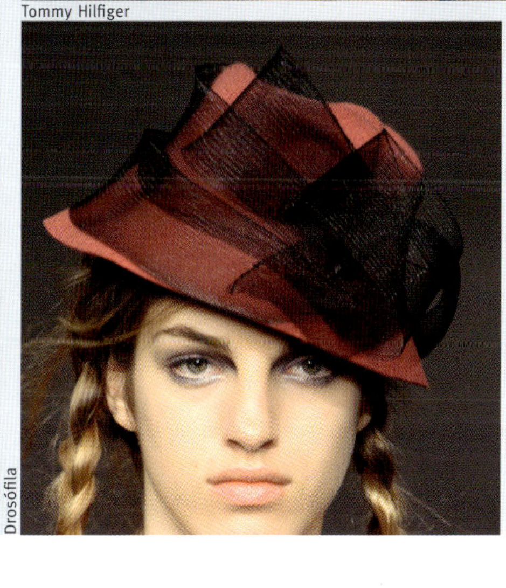
Drosófila

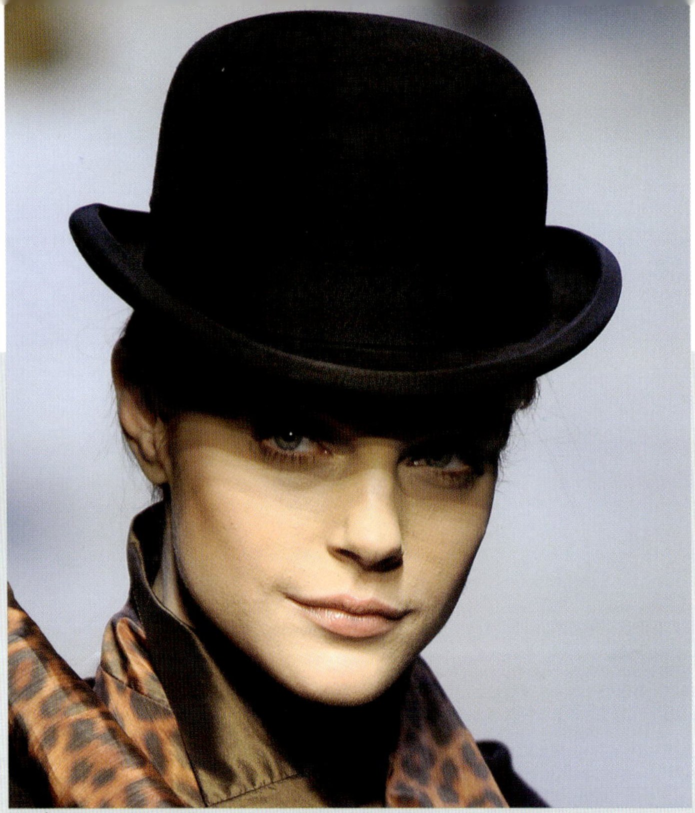

Hermès

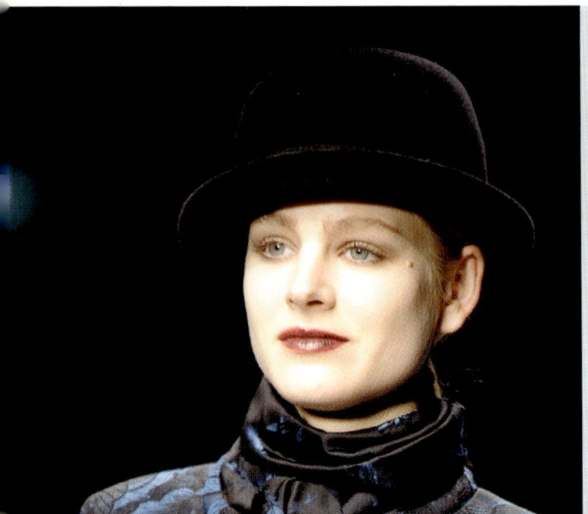

Caroline Charles

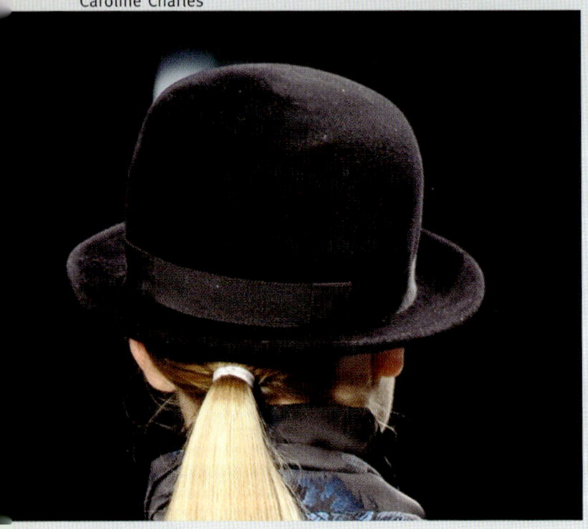

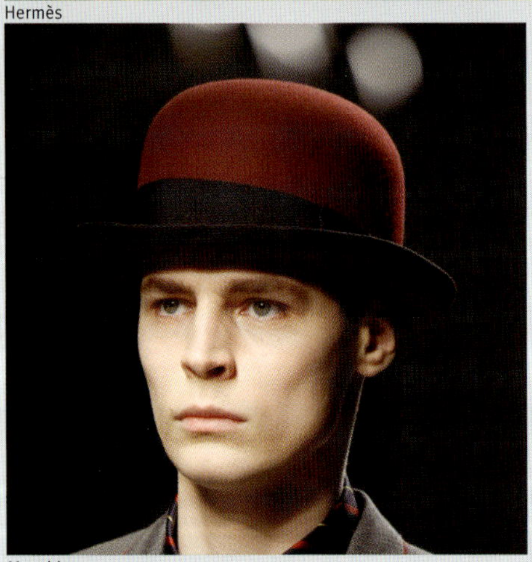

Moschino

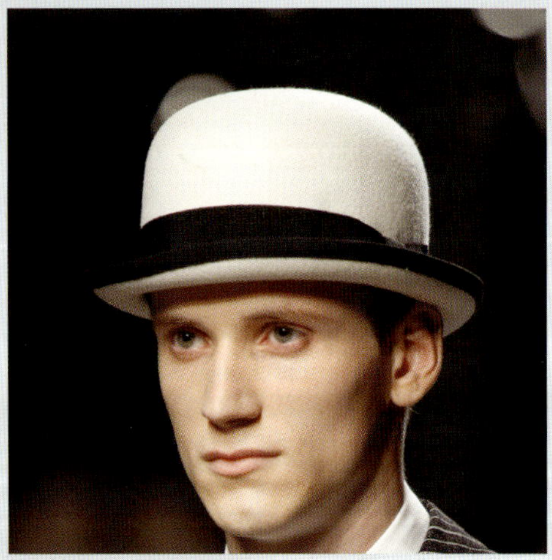

Moschino

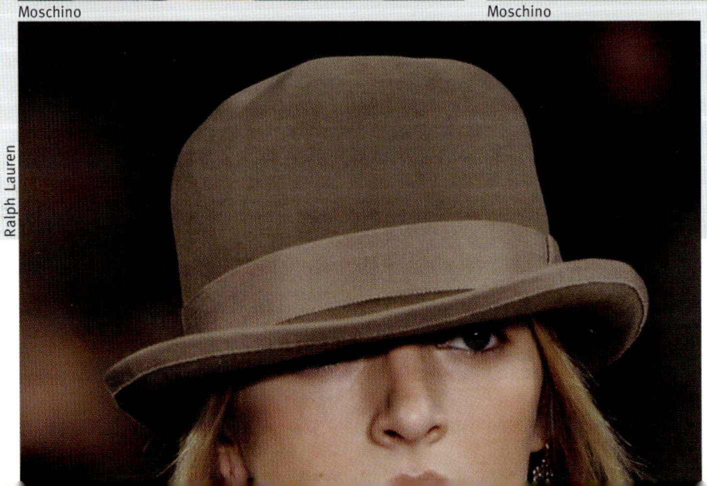

Ralph Lauren

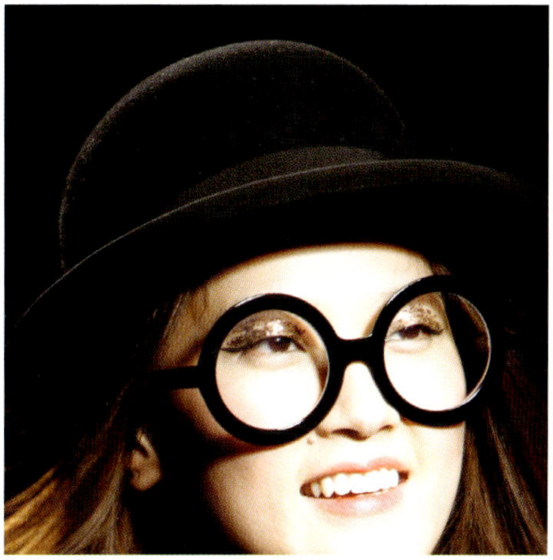
Sonia Rykiel

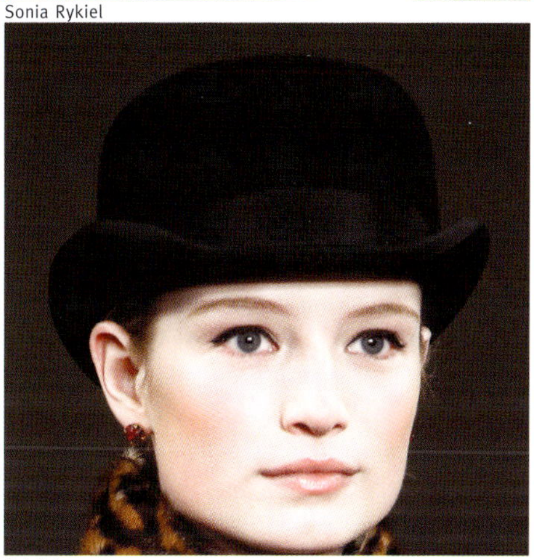
Ralph Lauren

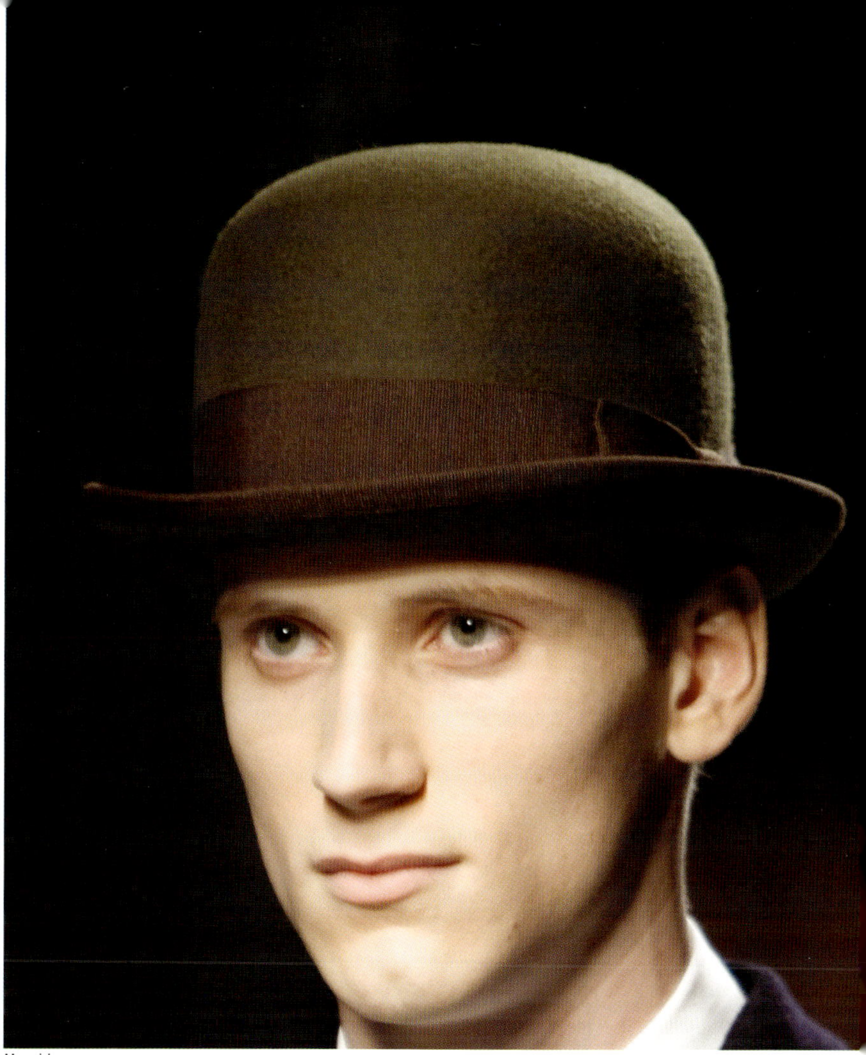
Moschino

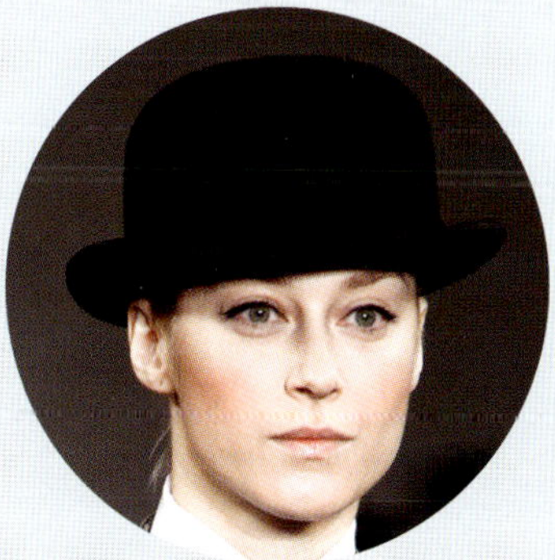
Ralph Lauren

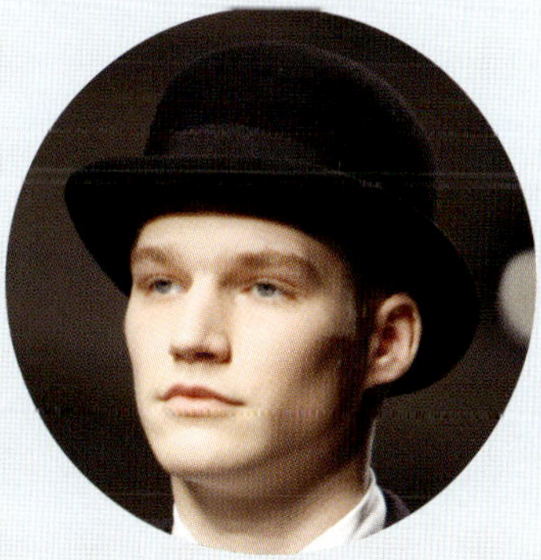
Moschino

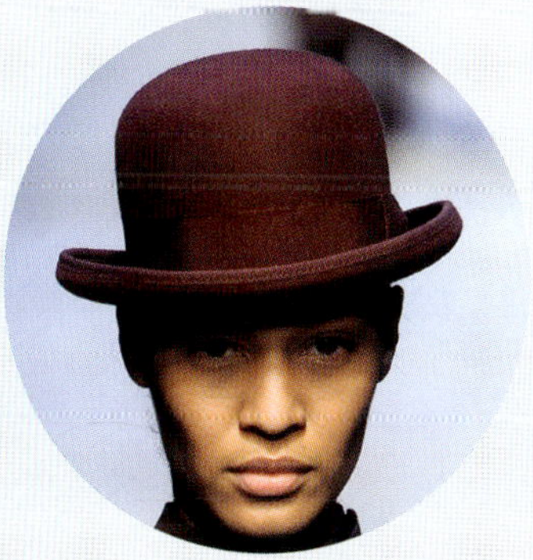
Hermès

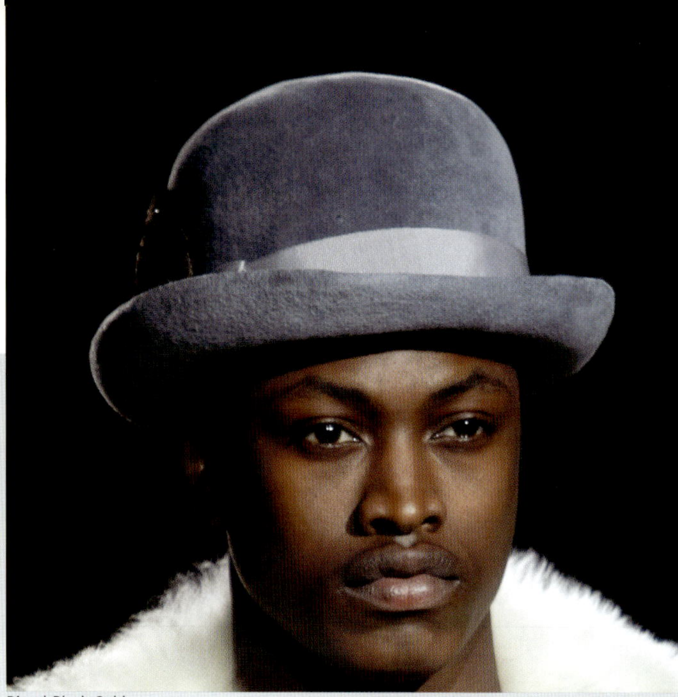

Diesel Black Gold

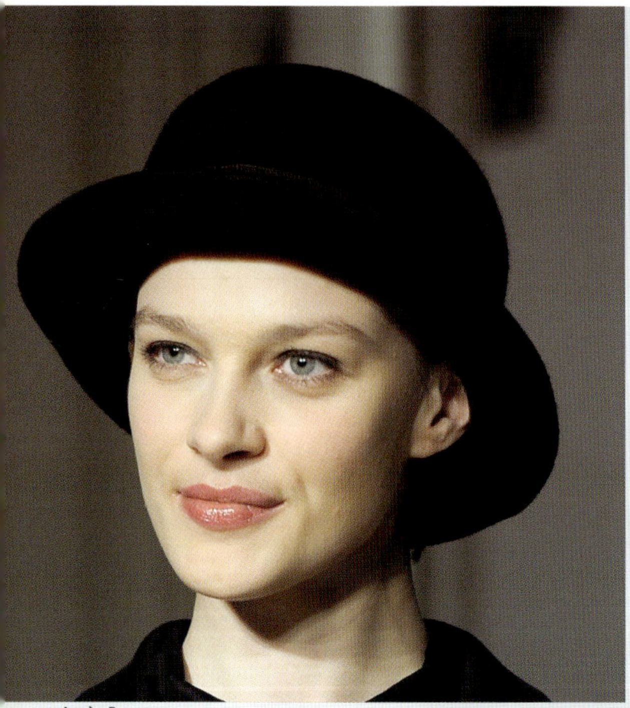

Agnès B.

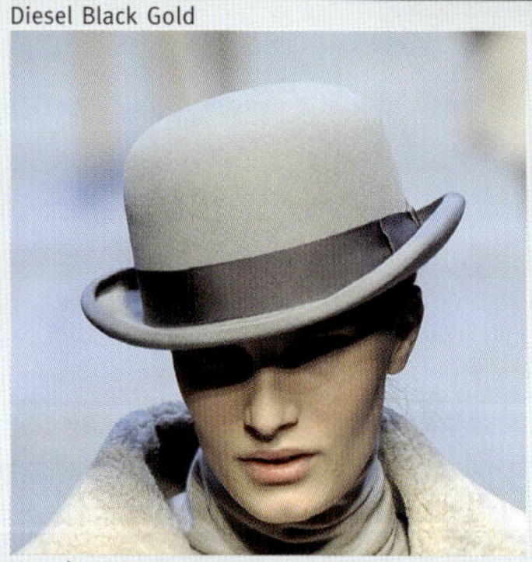

Hermès

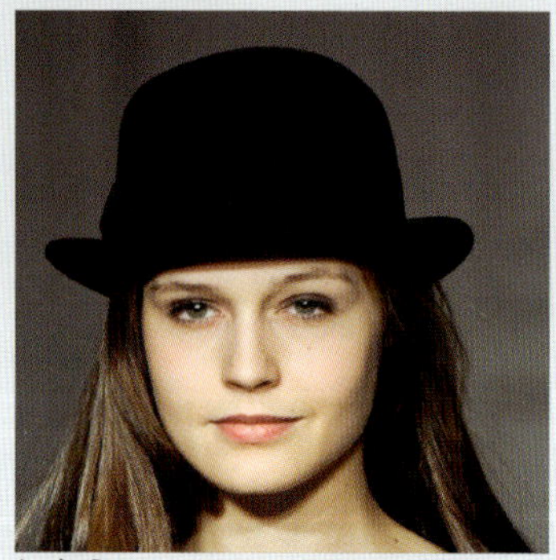

Agnès B.

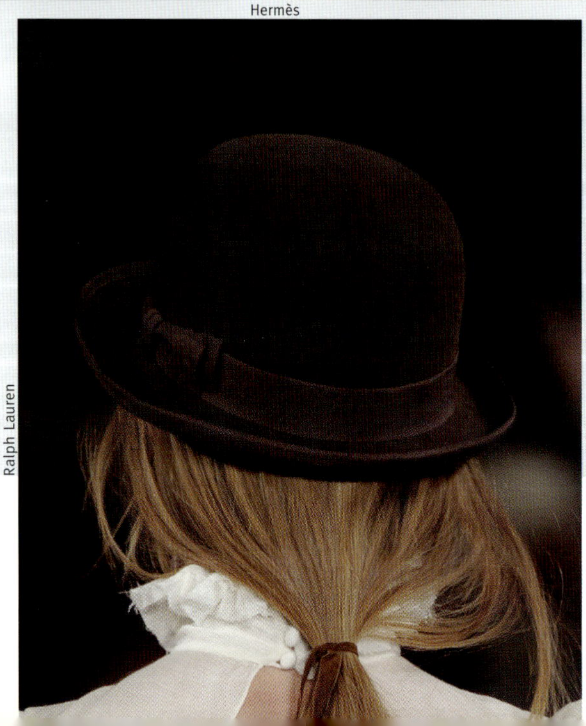

Ralph Lauren

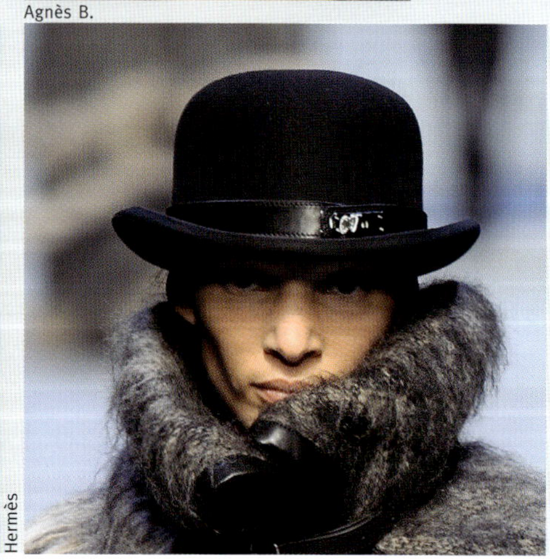

Hermès

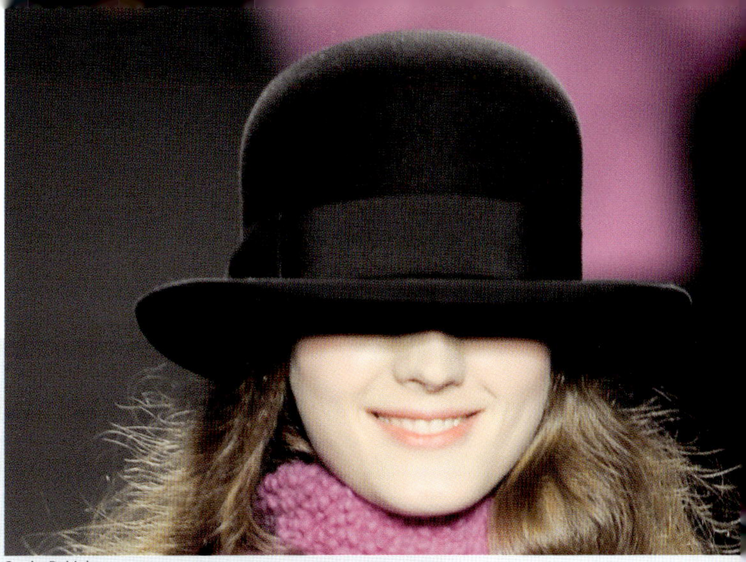
Sonia Rykiel

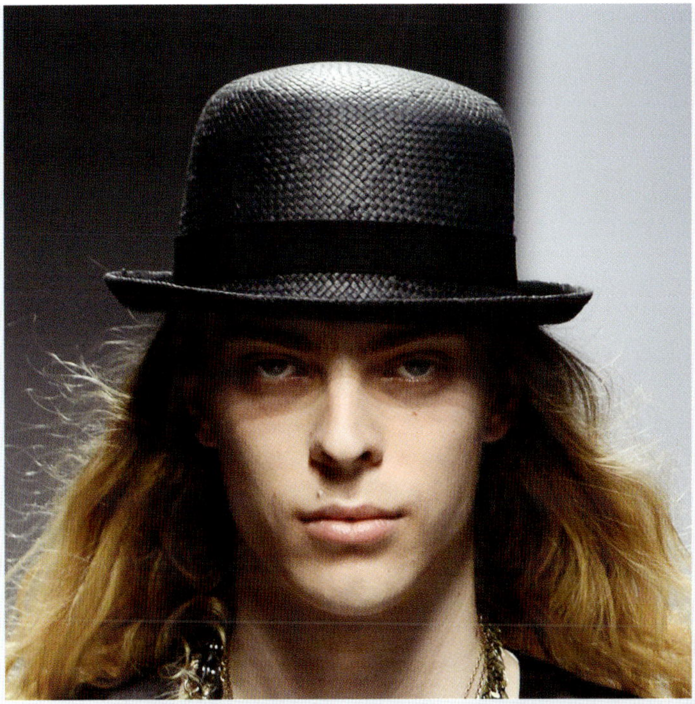
Diesel Black Gold

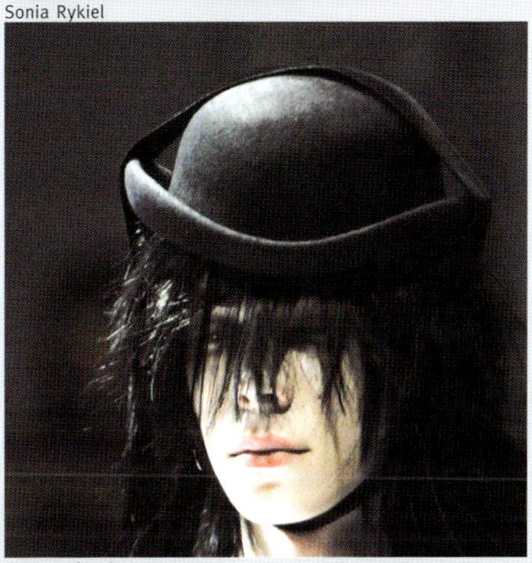
Comme des Garçons

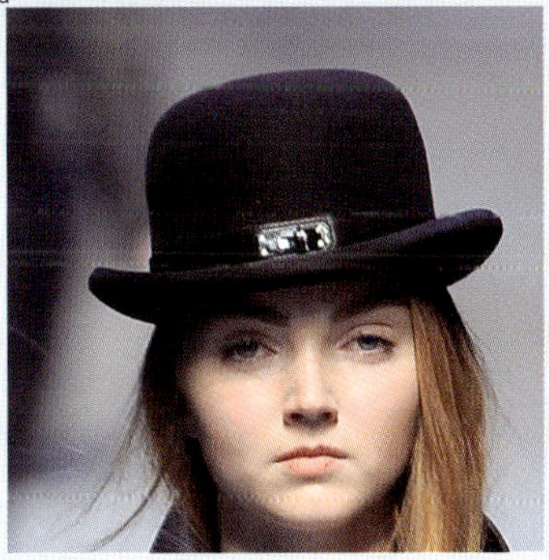
Hermès

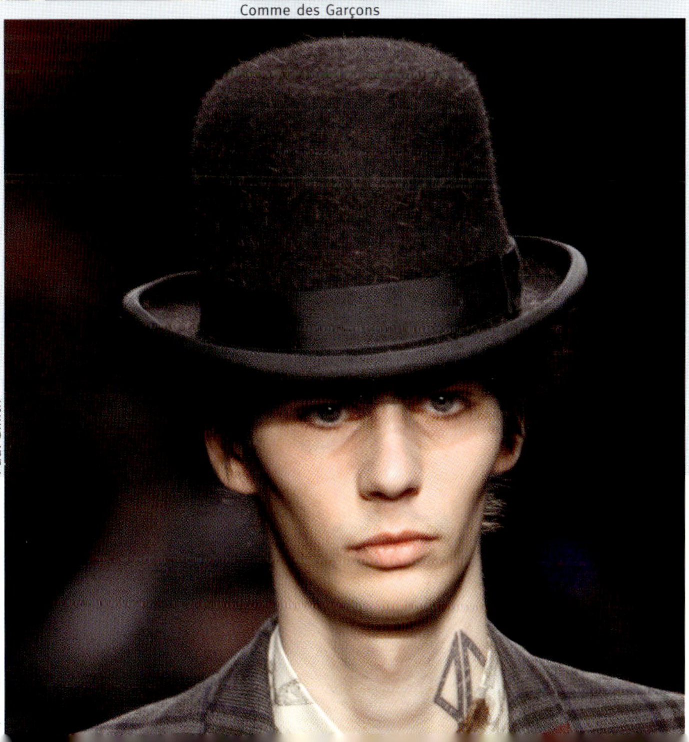
Paul Smith

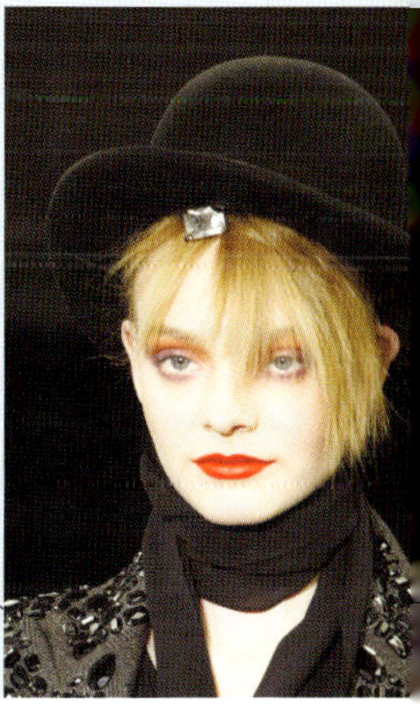
Sonia Rykiel

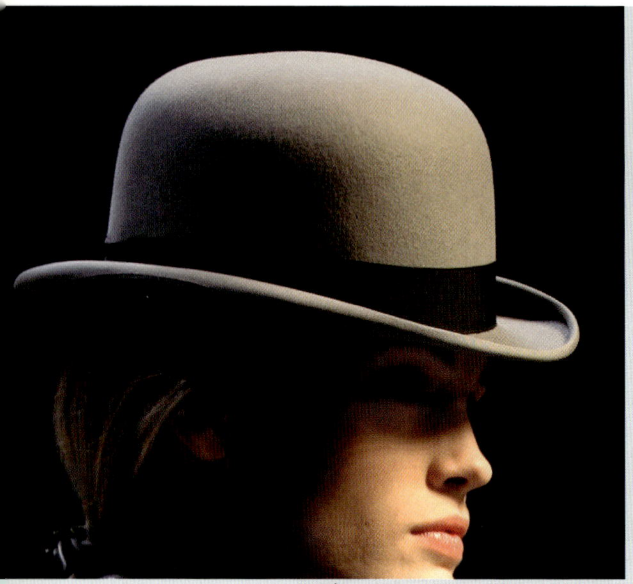
Hermès

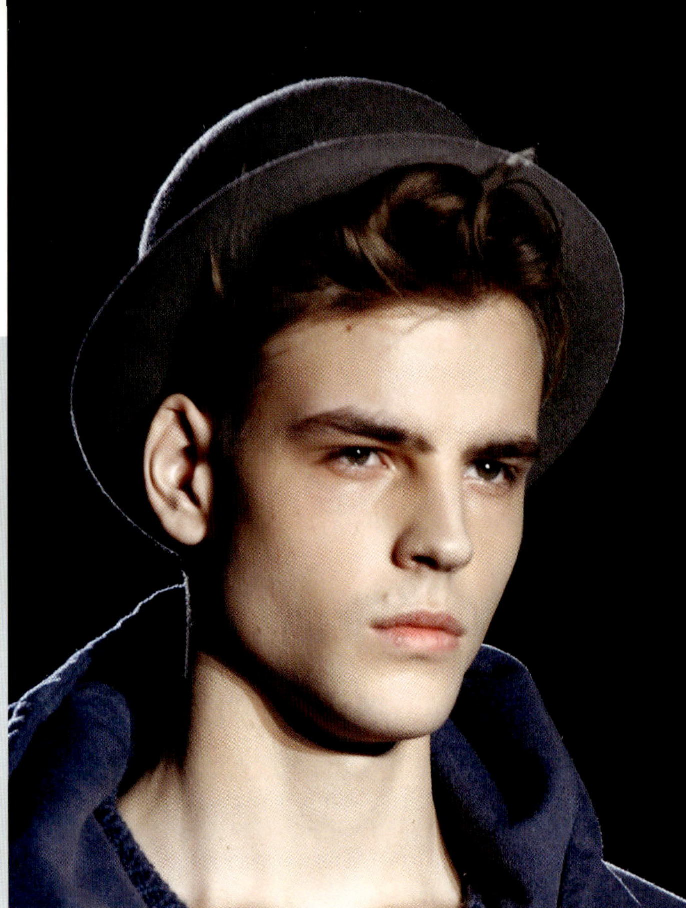
Iceberg

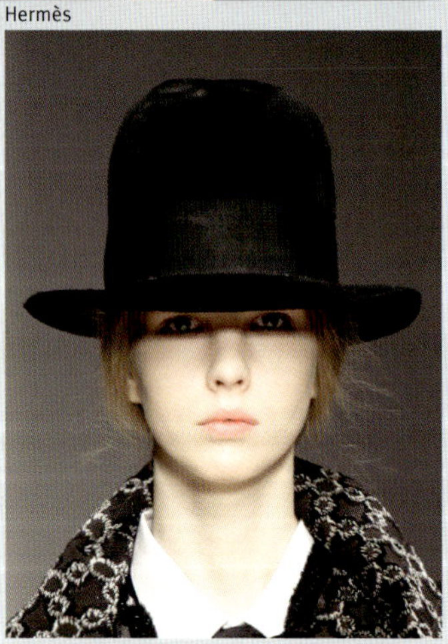
Antonio Marras

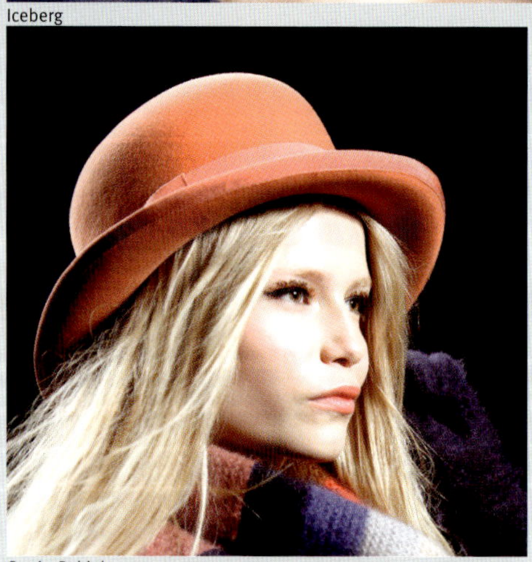
Sonia Rykiel

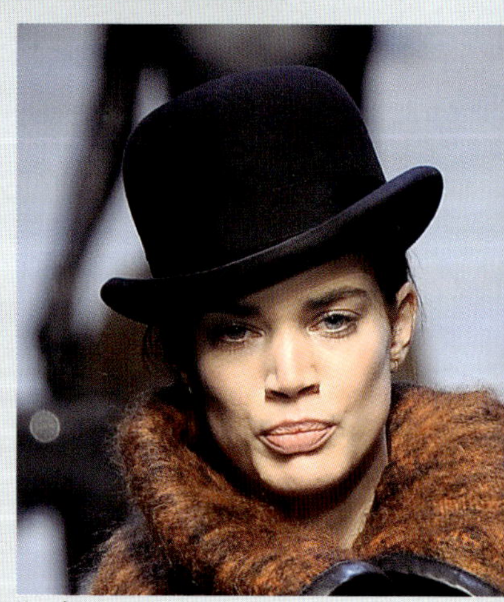
Hermès

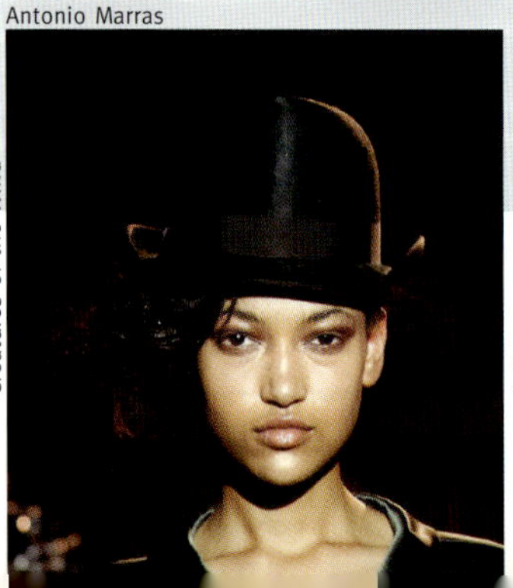
Creatures of the Wind

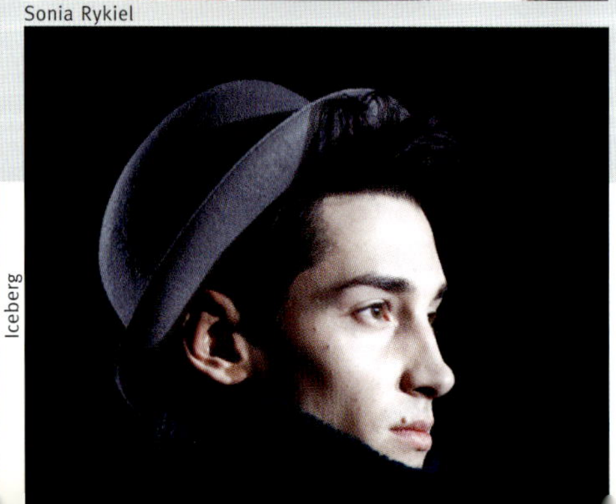
Iceberg

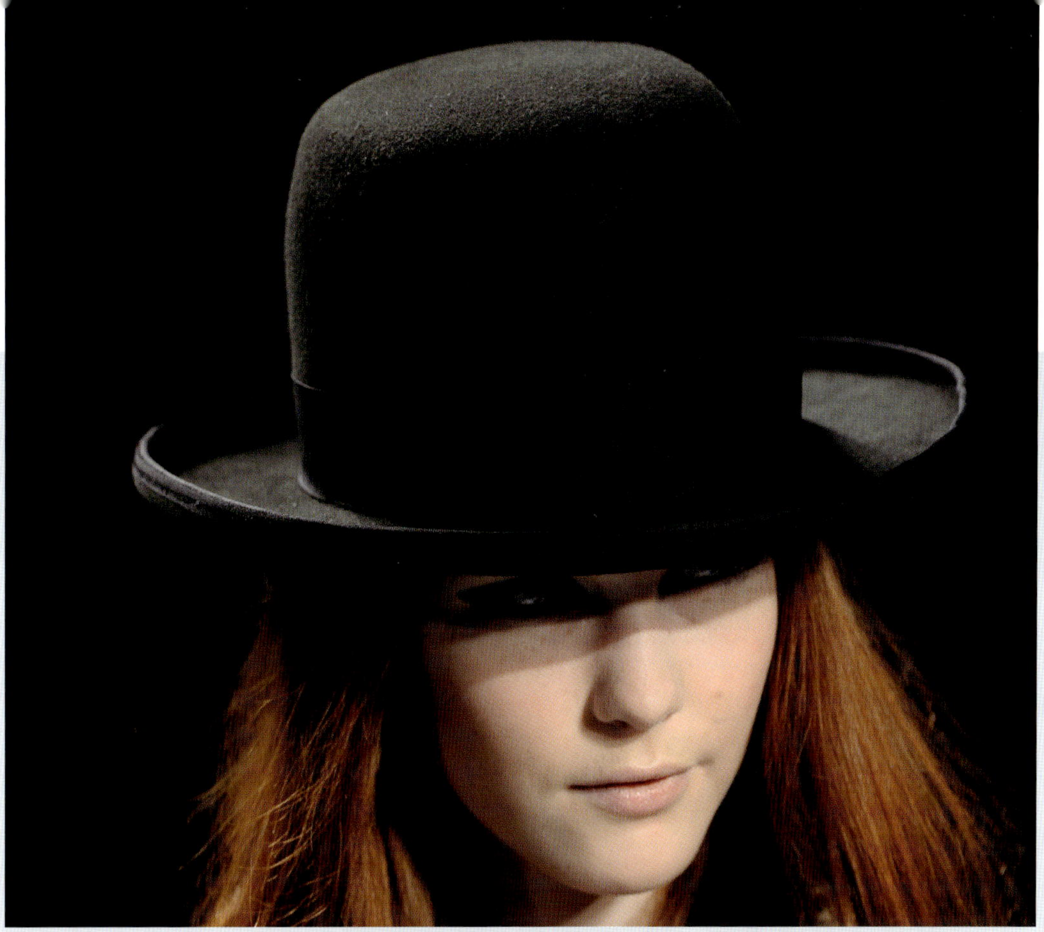

Rebecca Taylor

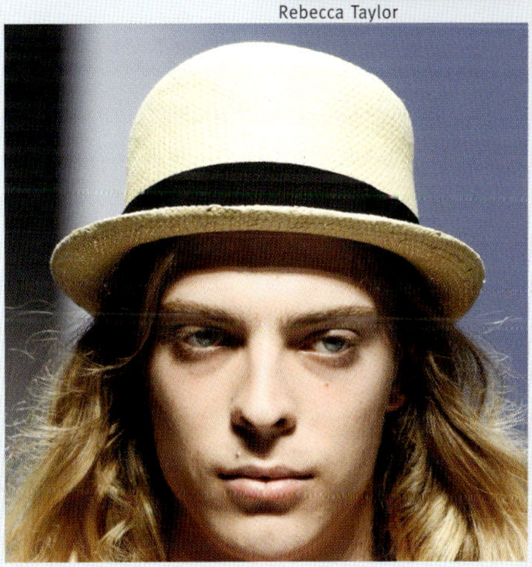

Diesel Black Gold

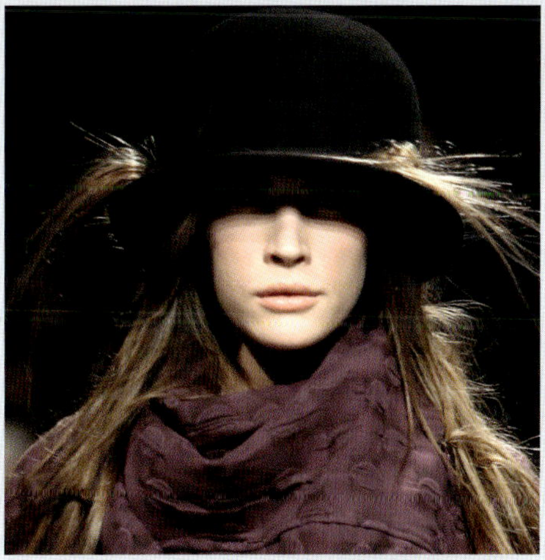

Ann Demeulemeester

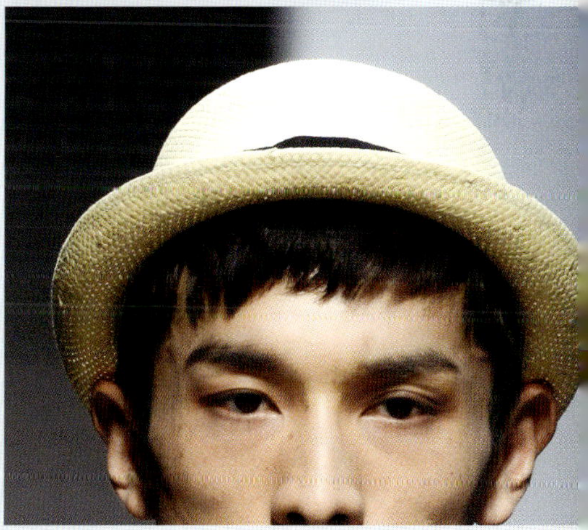

Diesel Black Gold

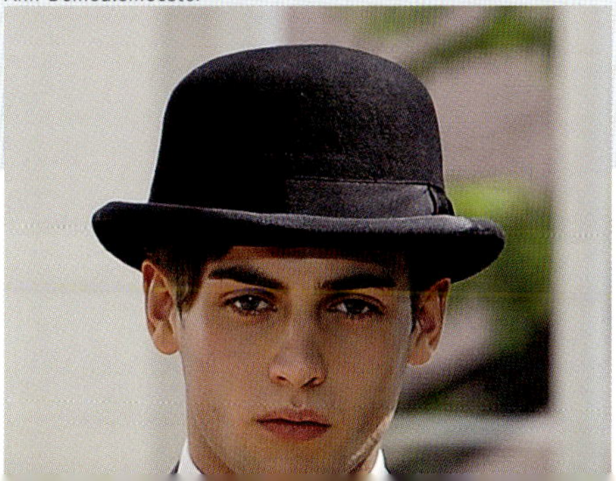

Hackett London

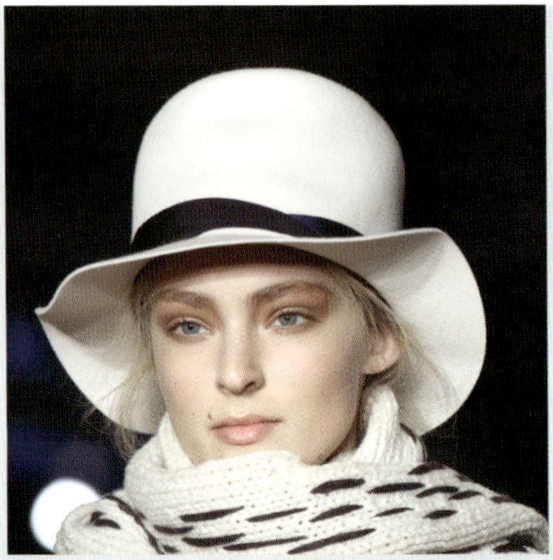

Y3

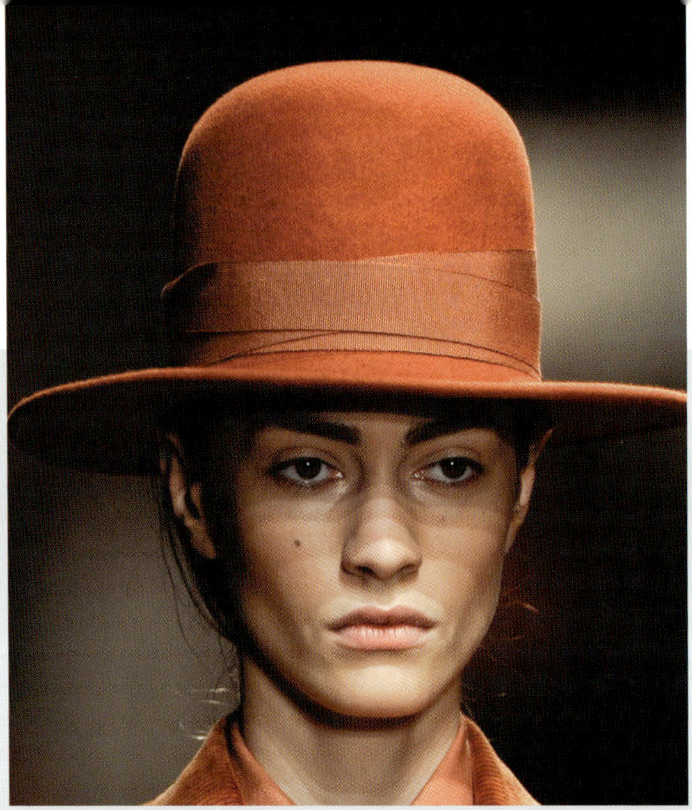

Trussardi

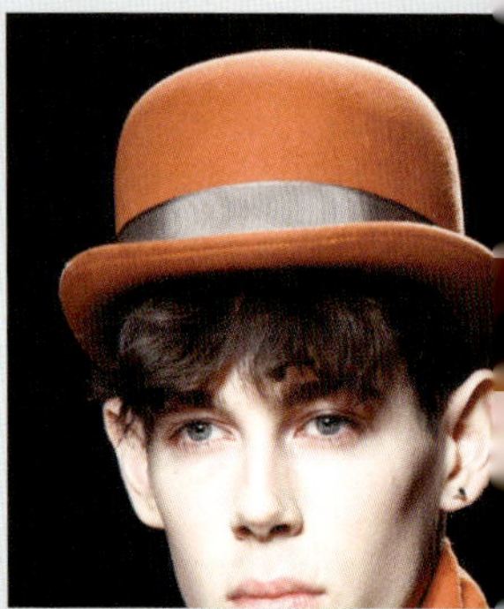

Rag & Bone

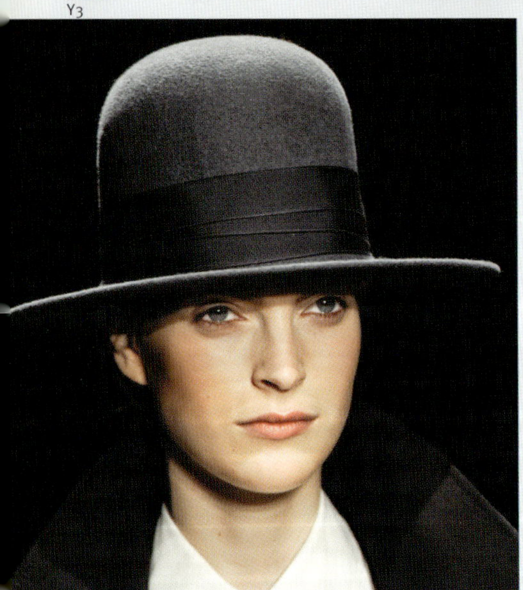

Trussardi

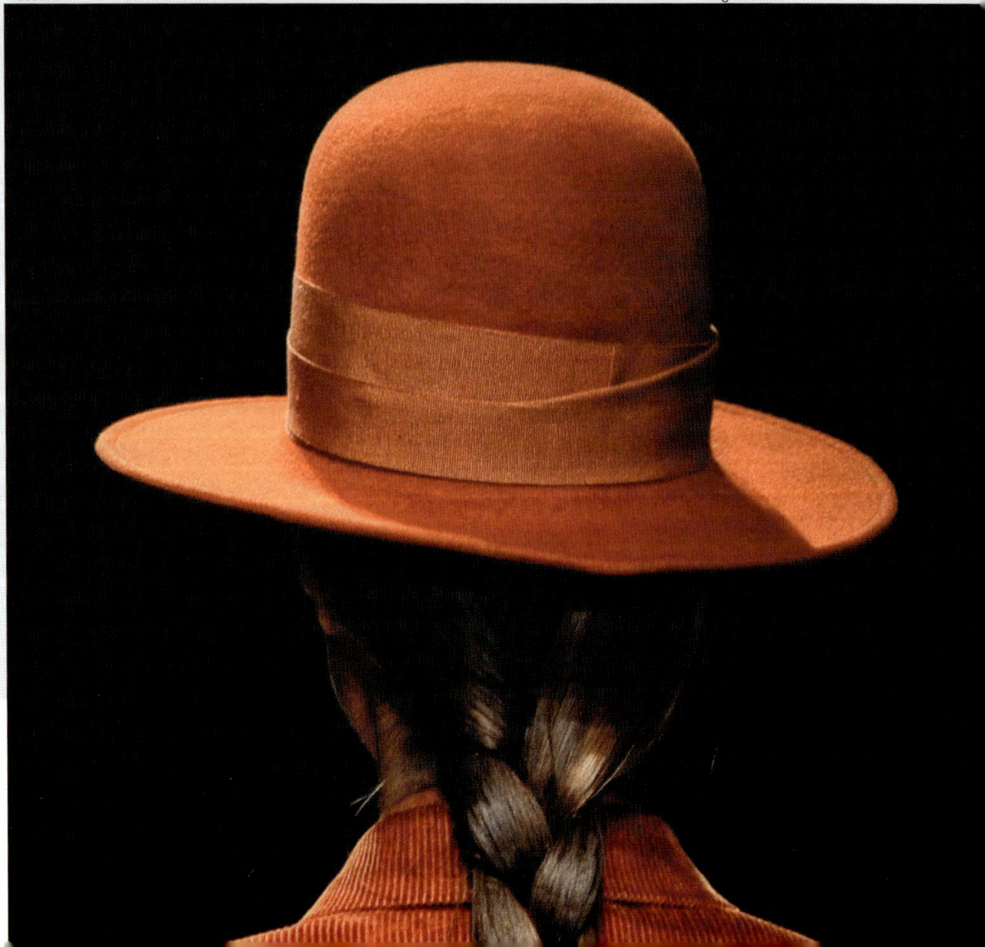

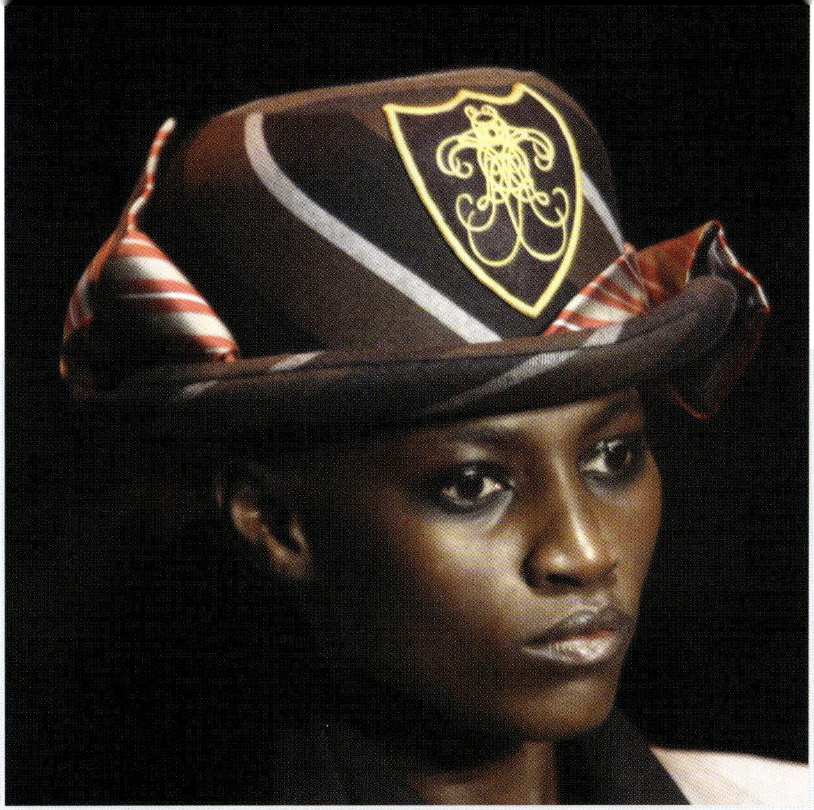

Vivienne Westwood Red Label

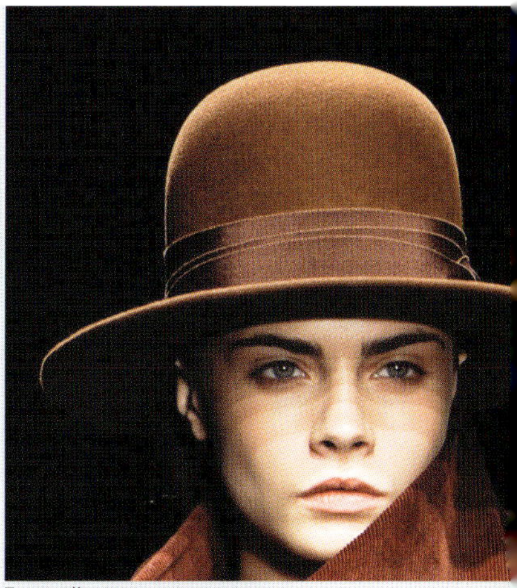

Trussardi

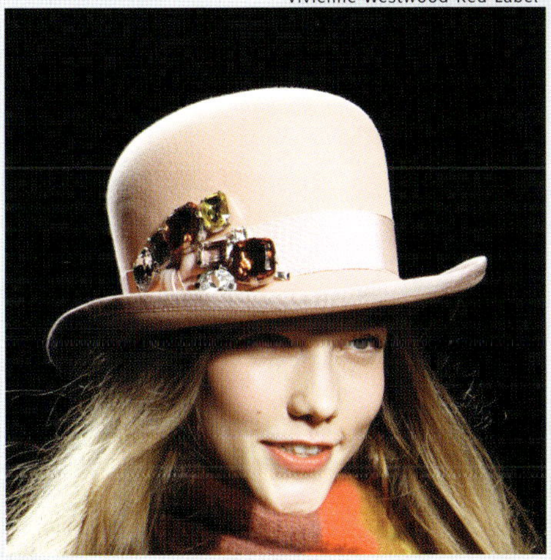

Sonia Rykiel

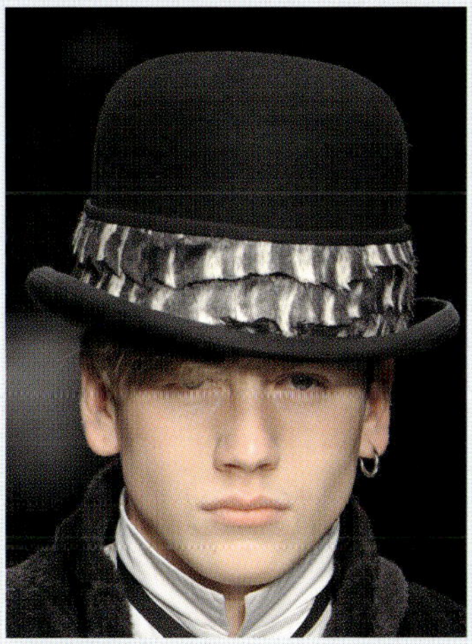

John Rocha

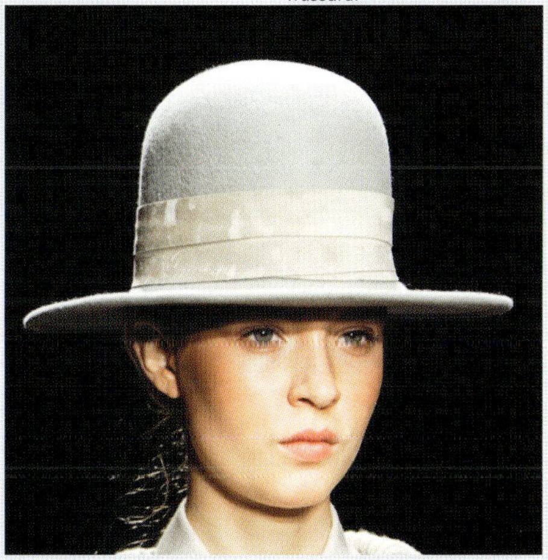

Trussardi

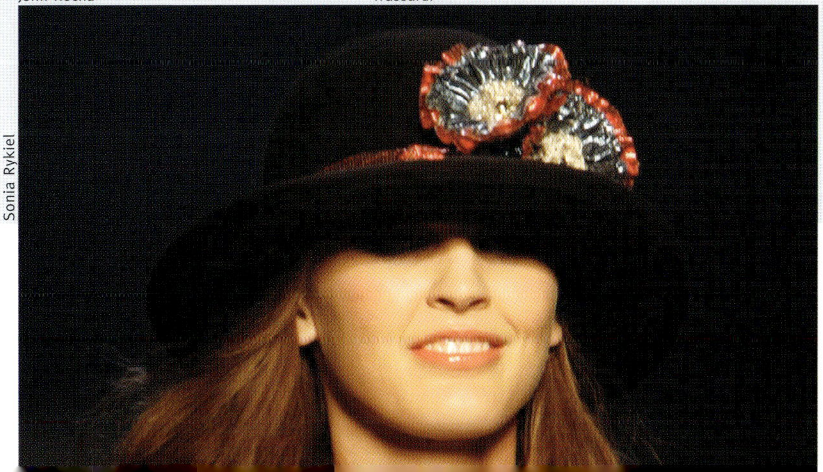

Sonia Rykiel

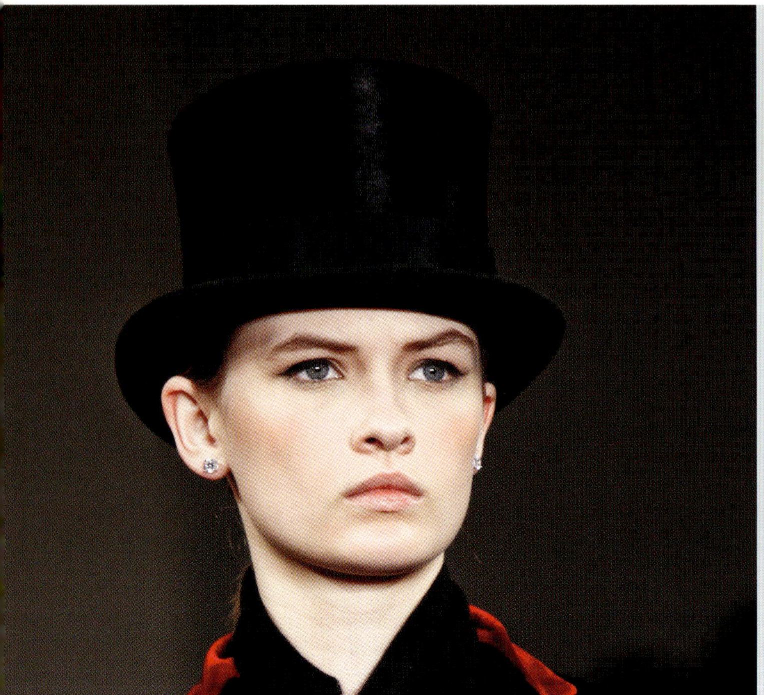

Ralph Lauren

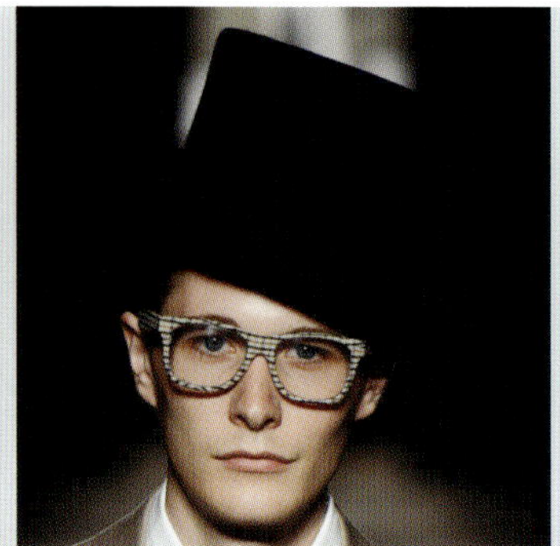

Daks

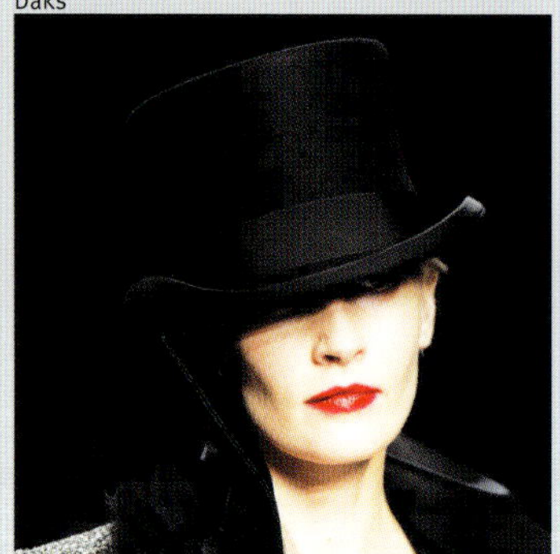

Mariella Burani

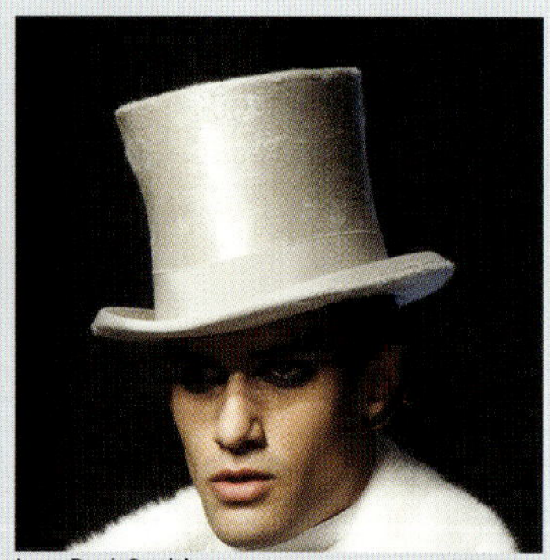

Jean Paul Gaultier

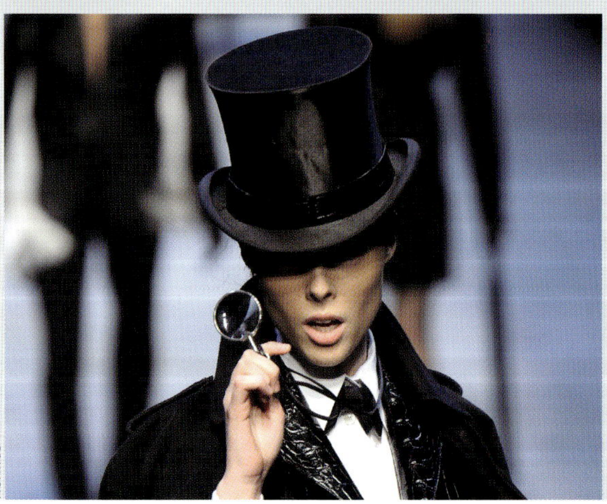

Hermès

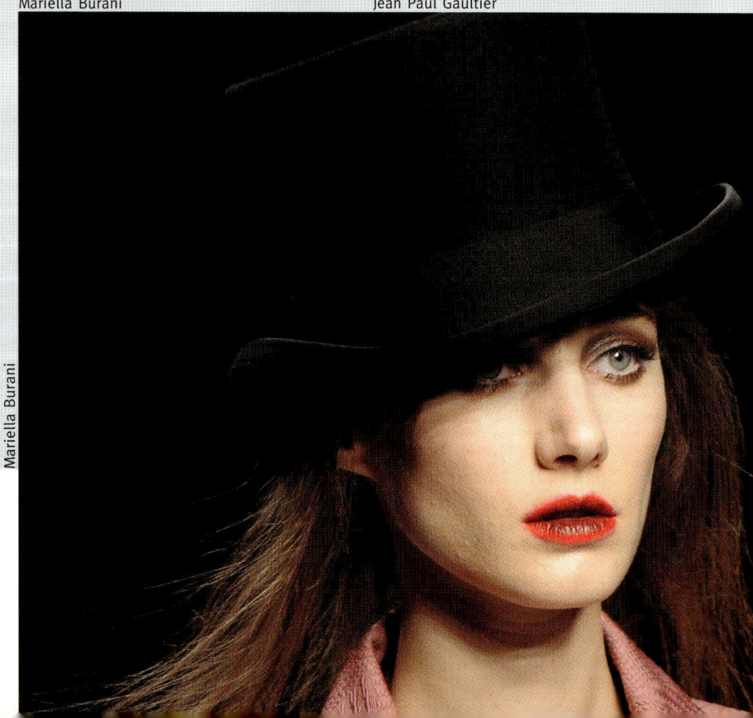

Mariella Burani

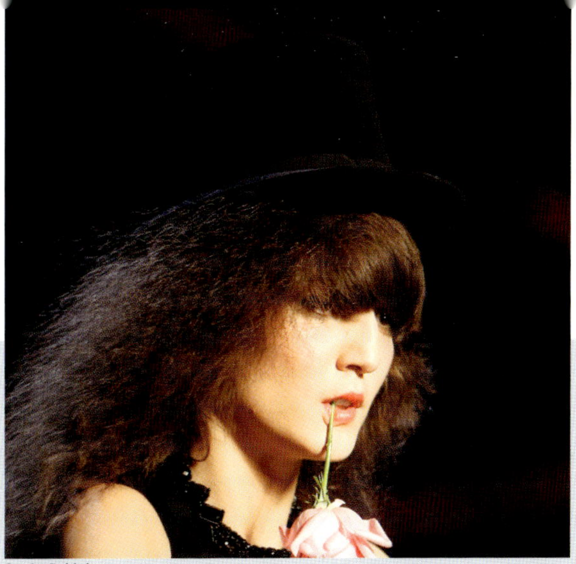

Sonia Rykiel

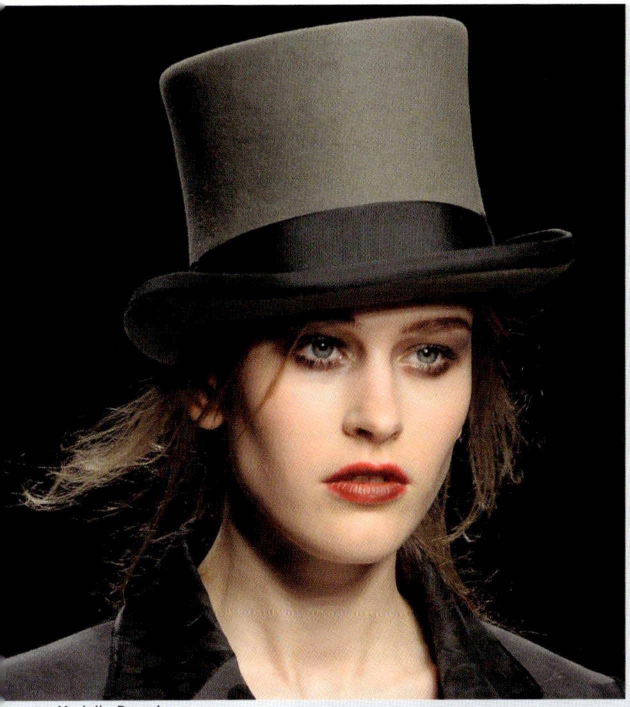

Mariella Burani

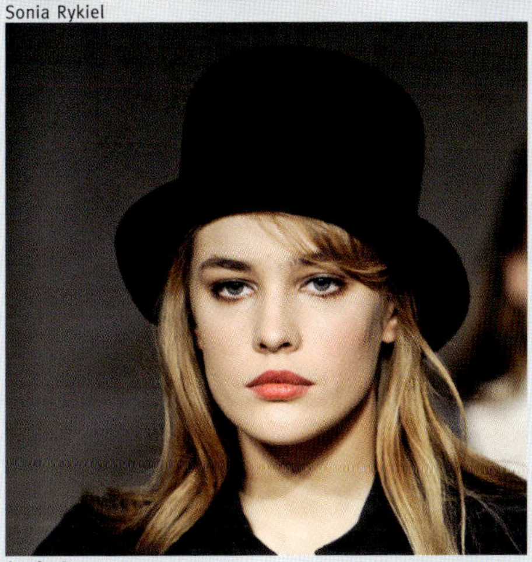

Agnès B.

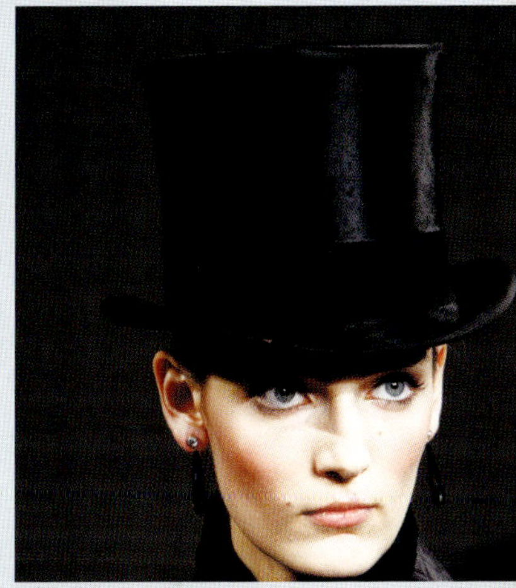

Ralph Lauren

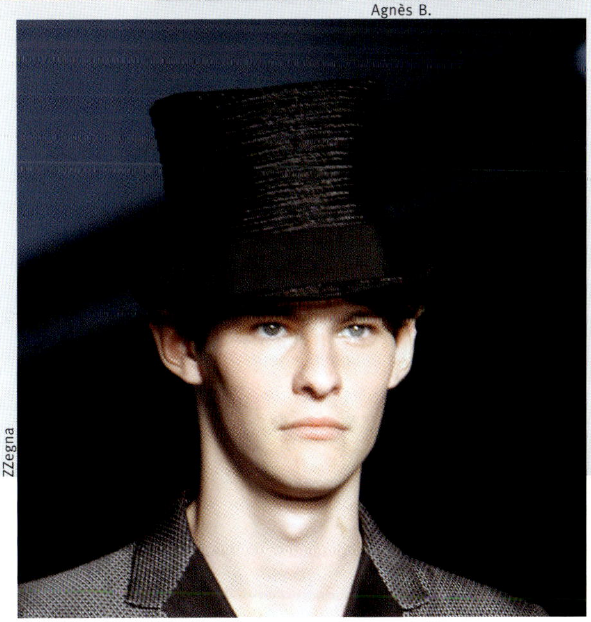

ZZegna

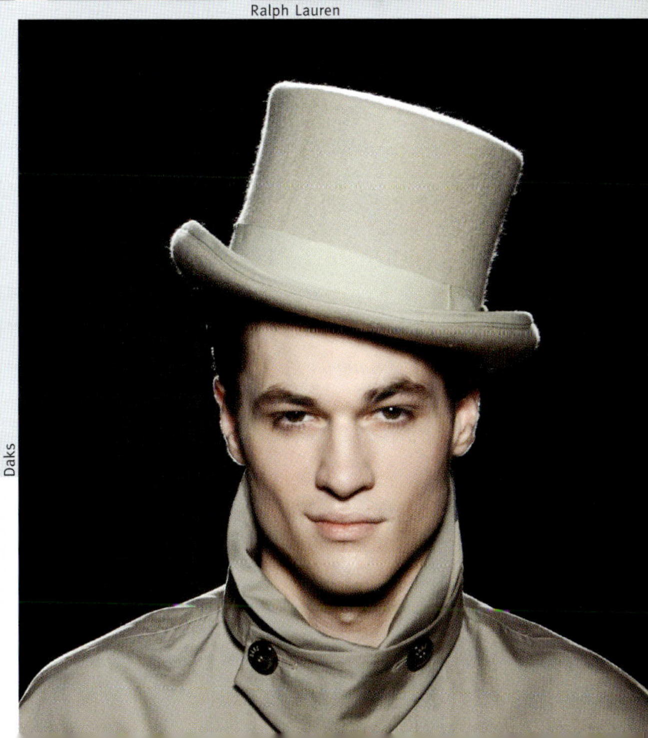

Daks

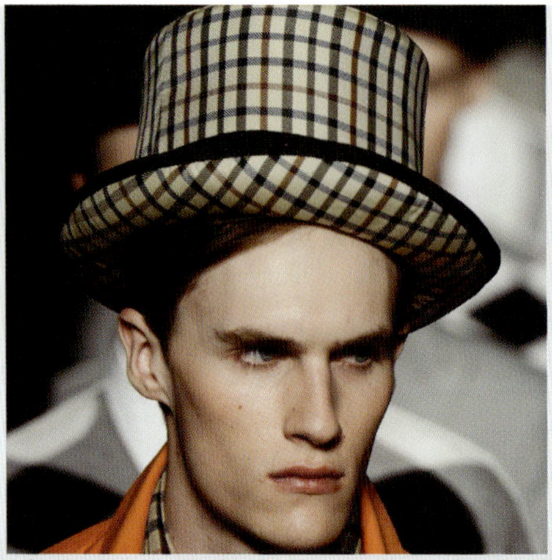

Daks

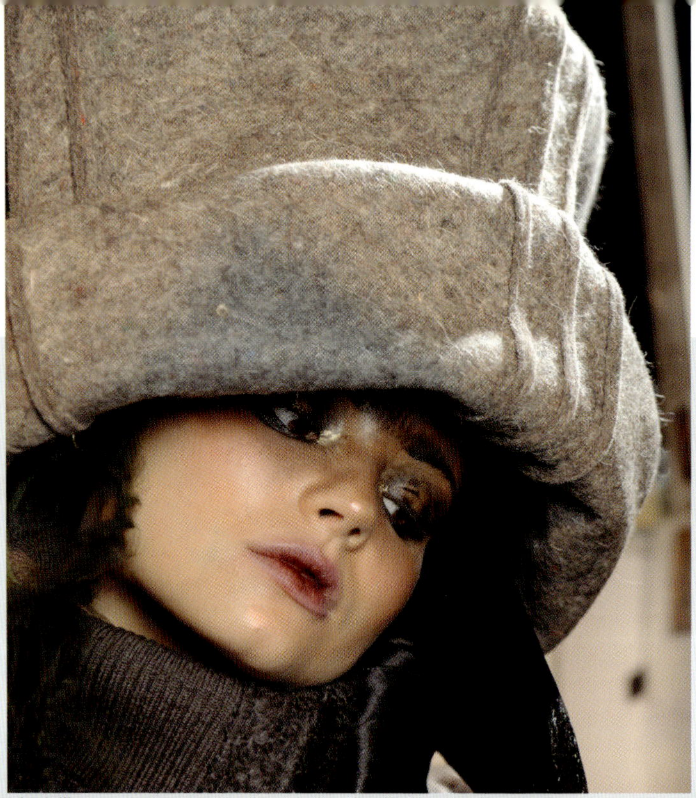

John Galliano

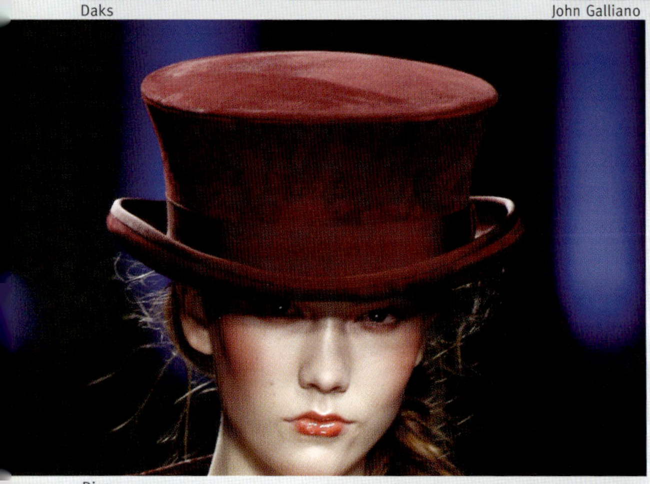

Dior

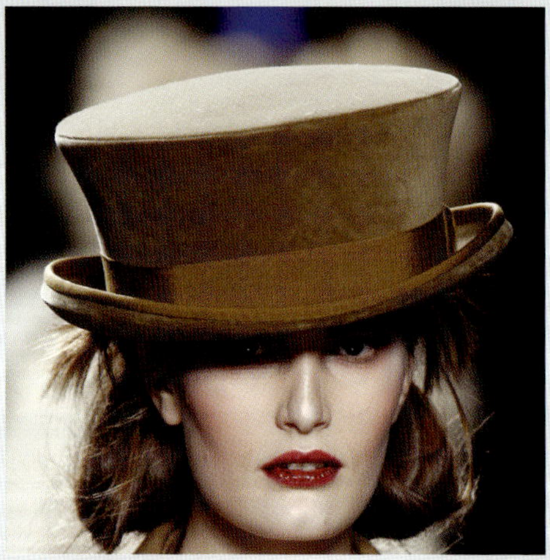

Dior

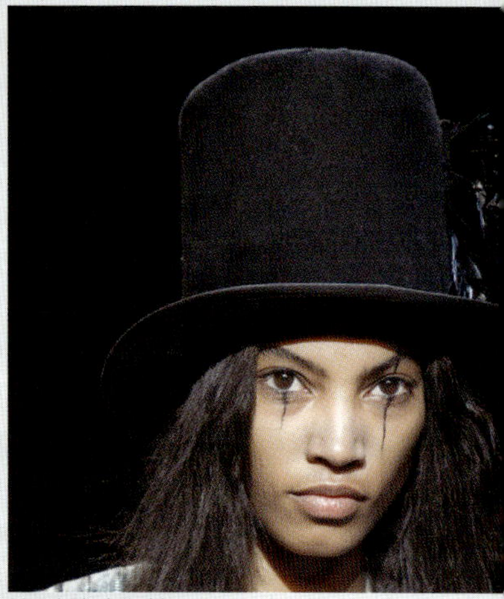

Diesel Black Gold

Dior

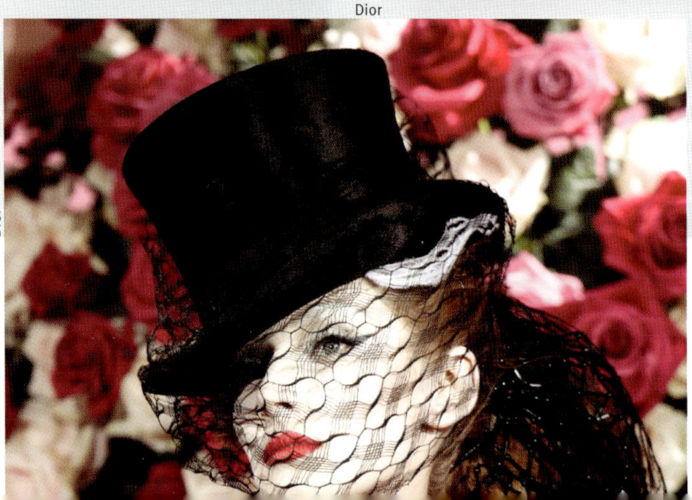

Dior

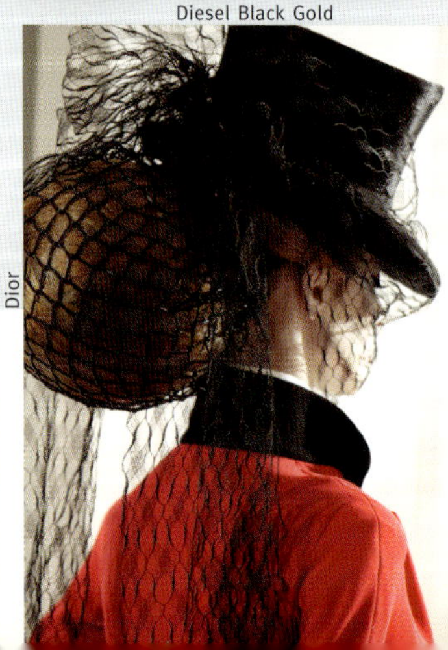

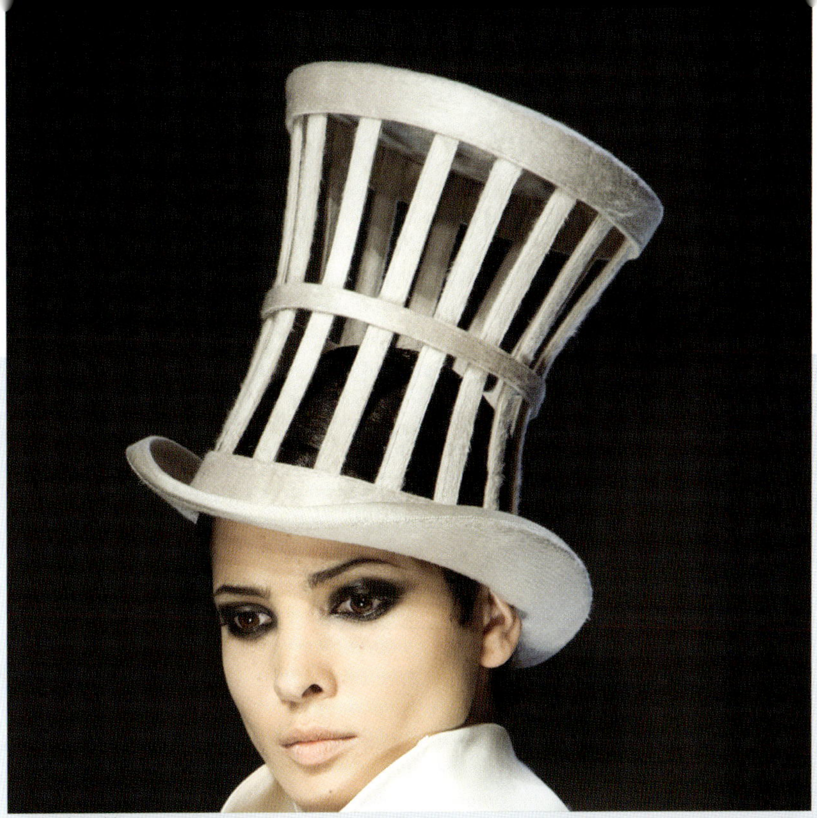

Jean Paul Gaultier

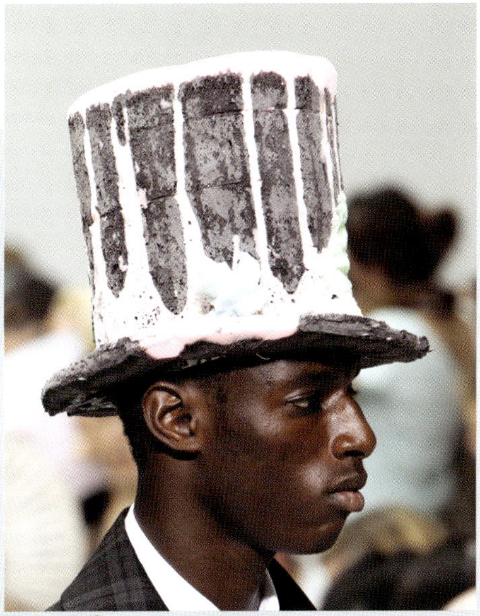

Viktor & Rolf

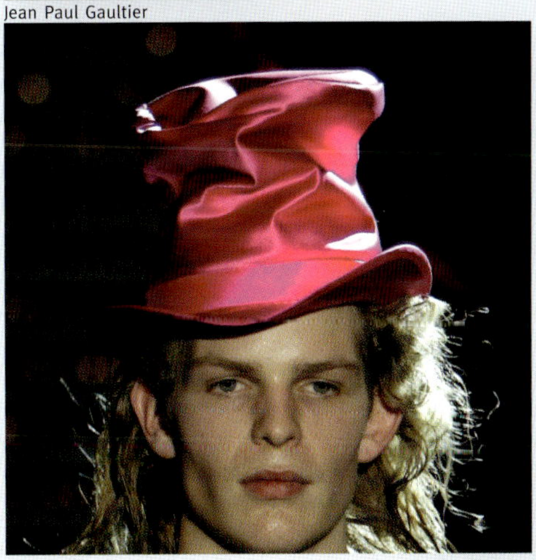

Comme des Garçons

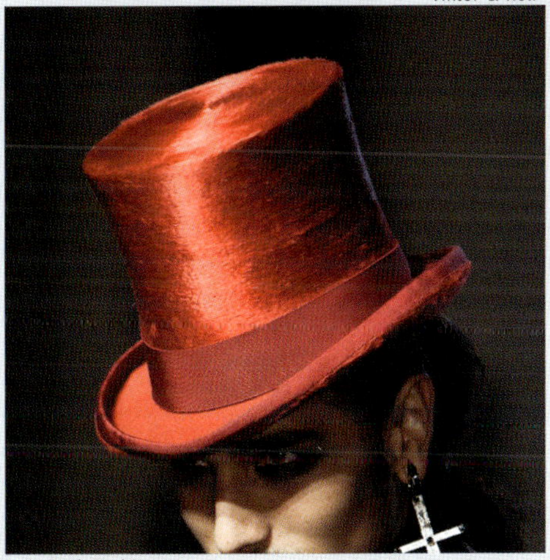

Jean Paul Gaultier

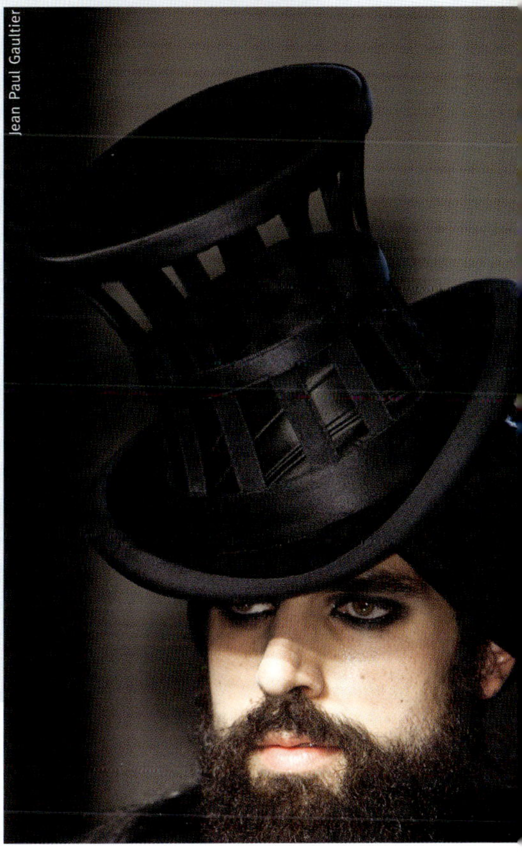

Jean Paul Gaultier

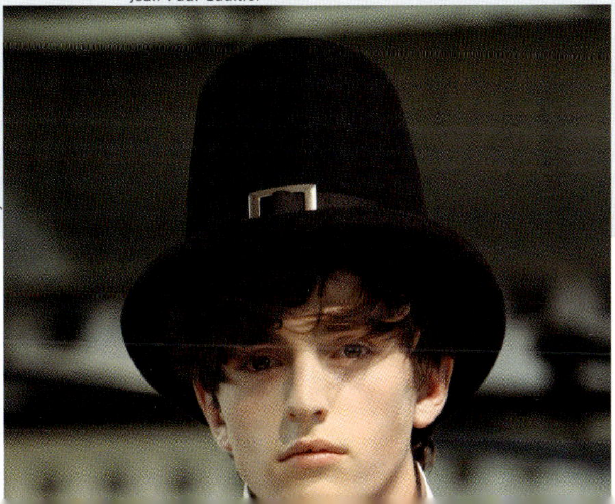

Yohji Yamamoto

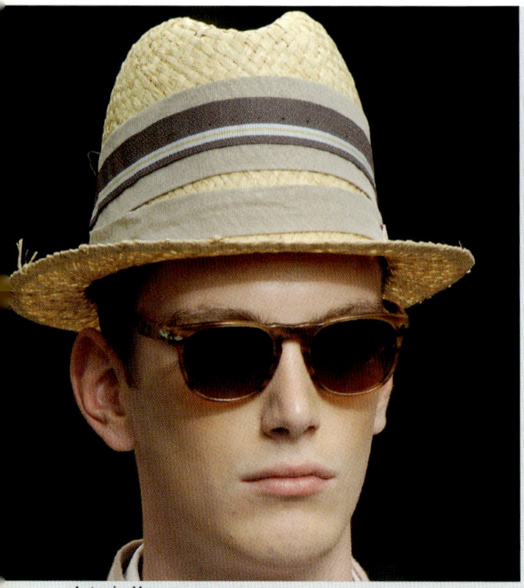
Antonio Marras

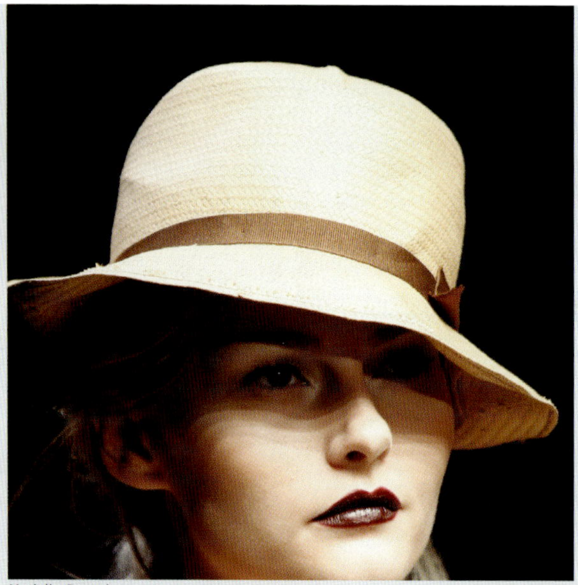
Mariella Burani

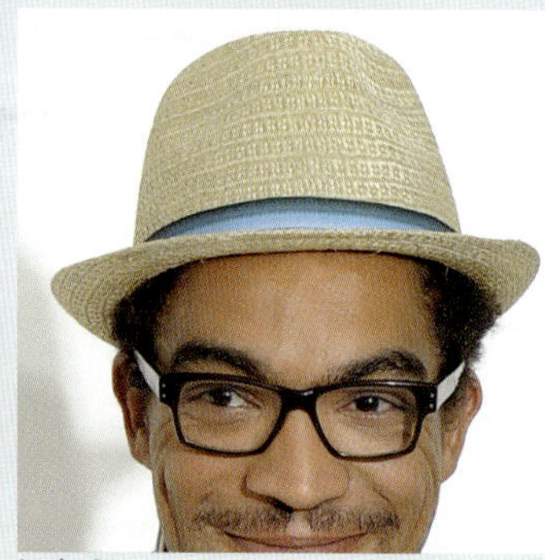
Agnès B.

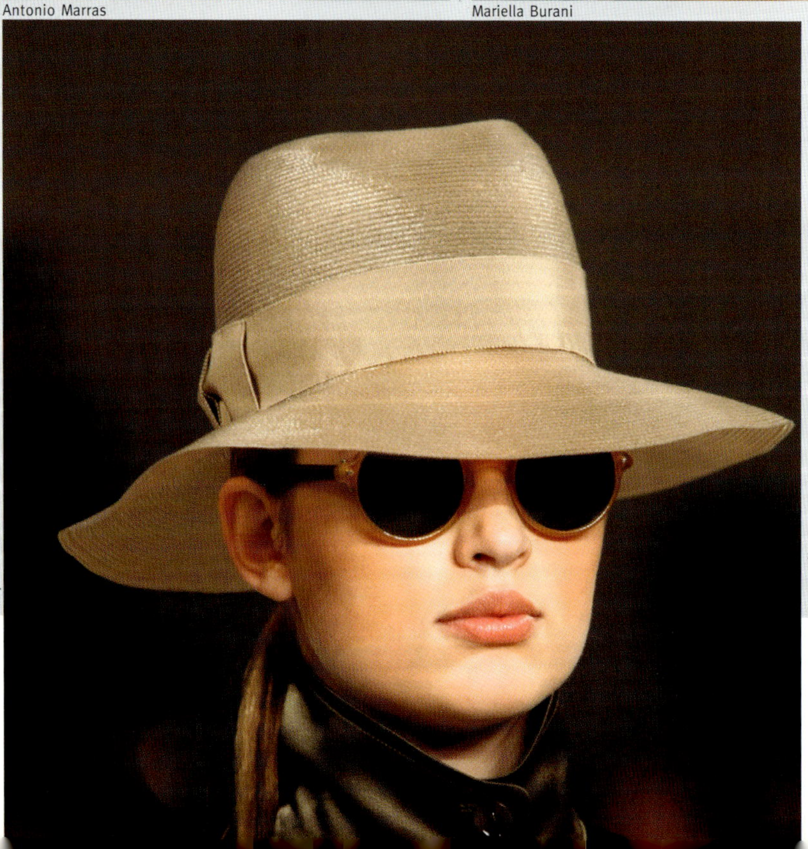
Ralph Lauren

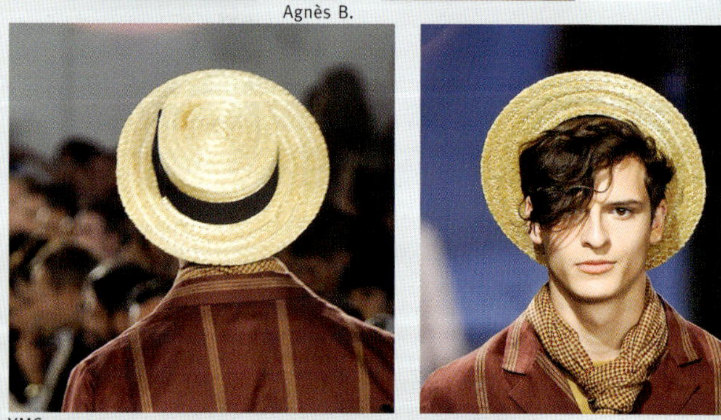
YMC

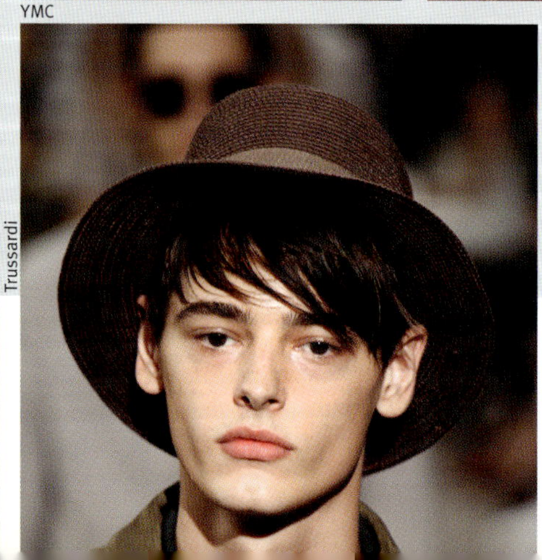
Trussardi

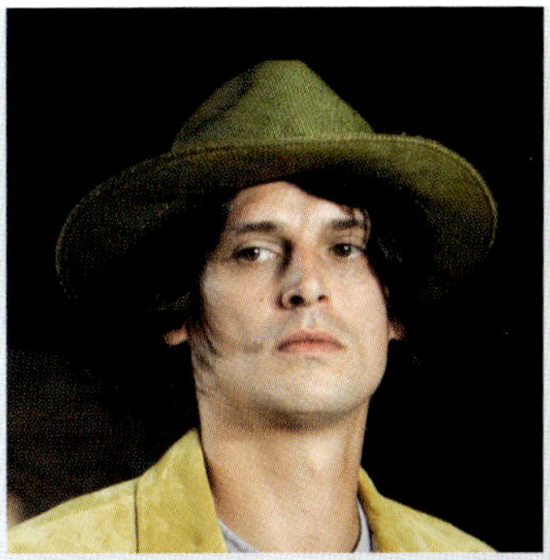
Agnès B.

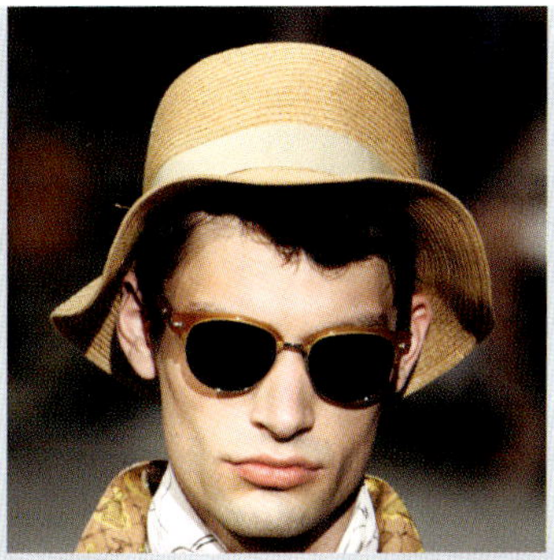
Trussardi

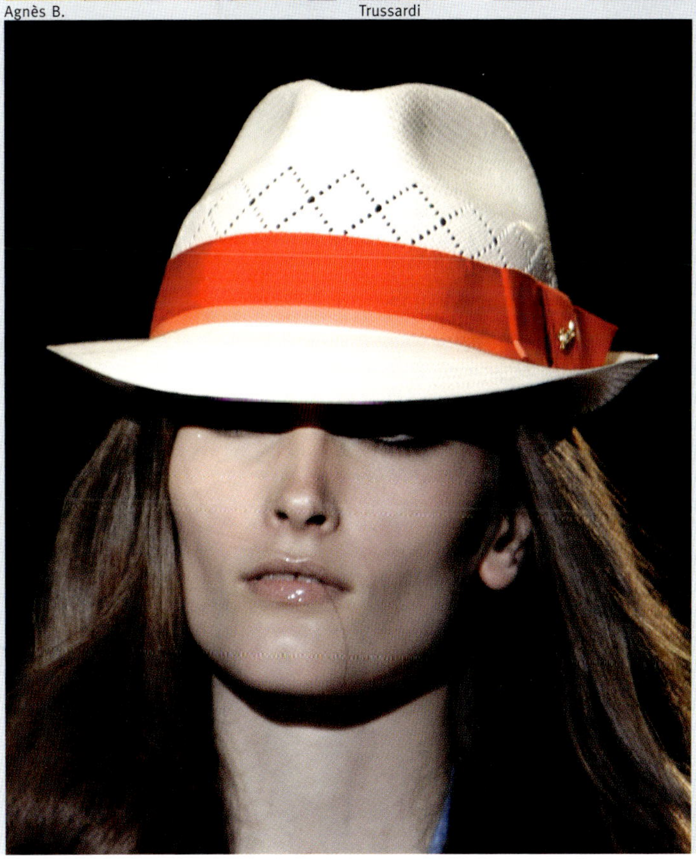
Gucci

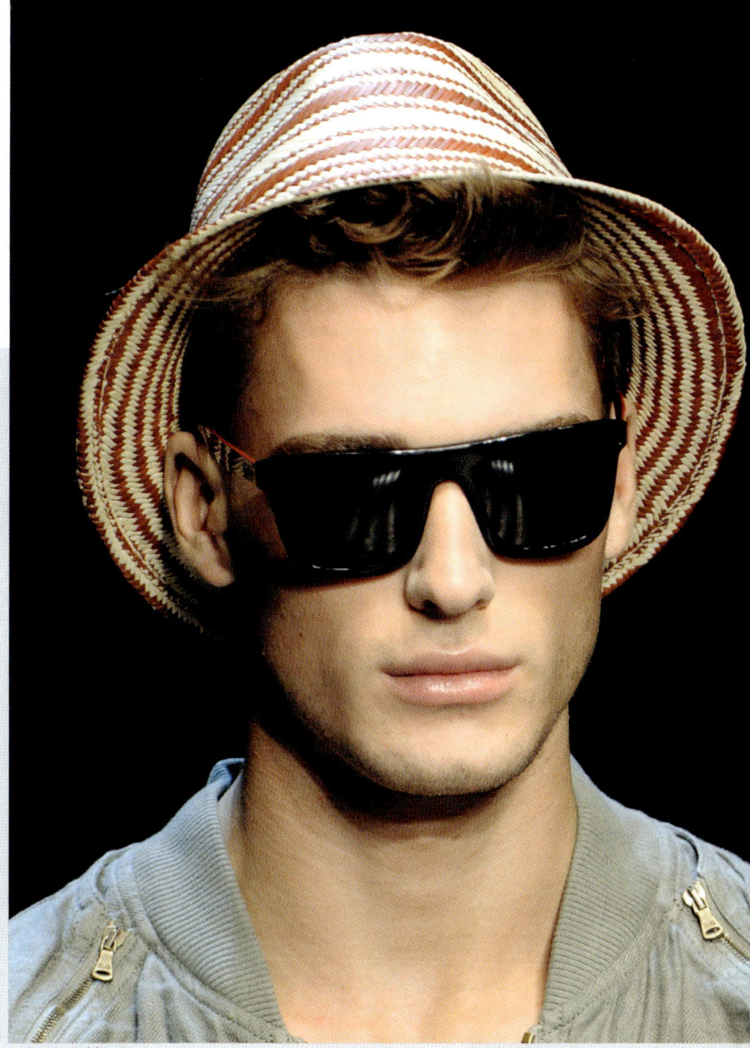
Dolce & Gabbana

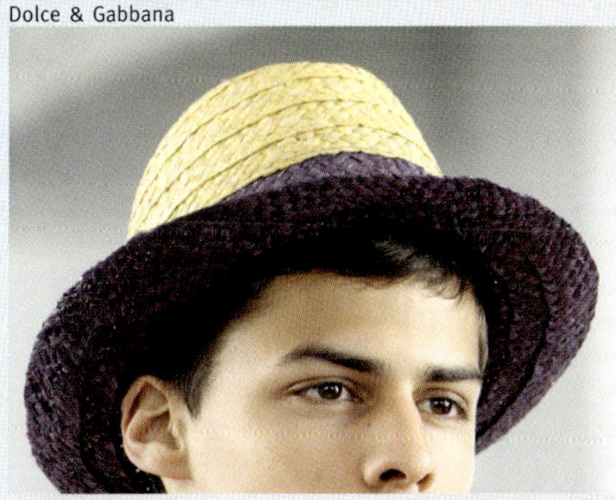
Issey Miyake

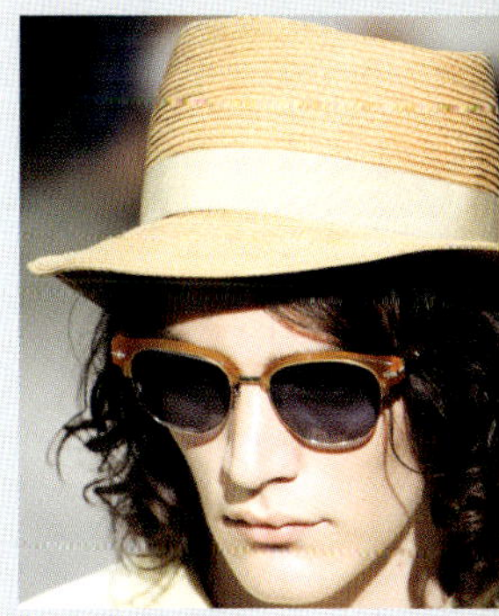
Trussardi

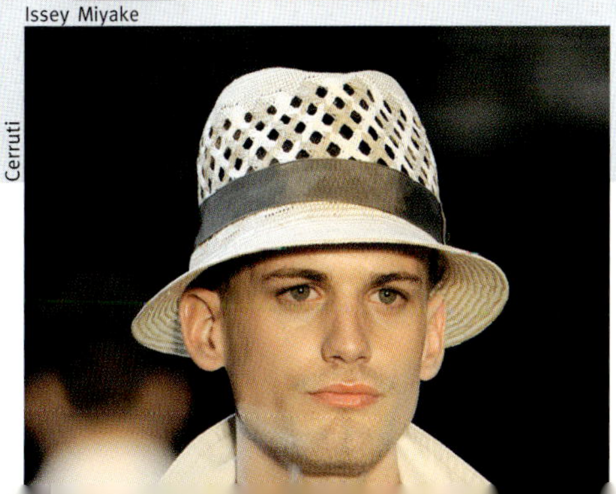
Cerruti

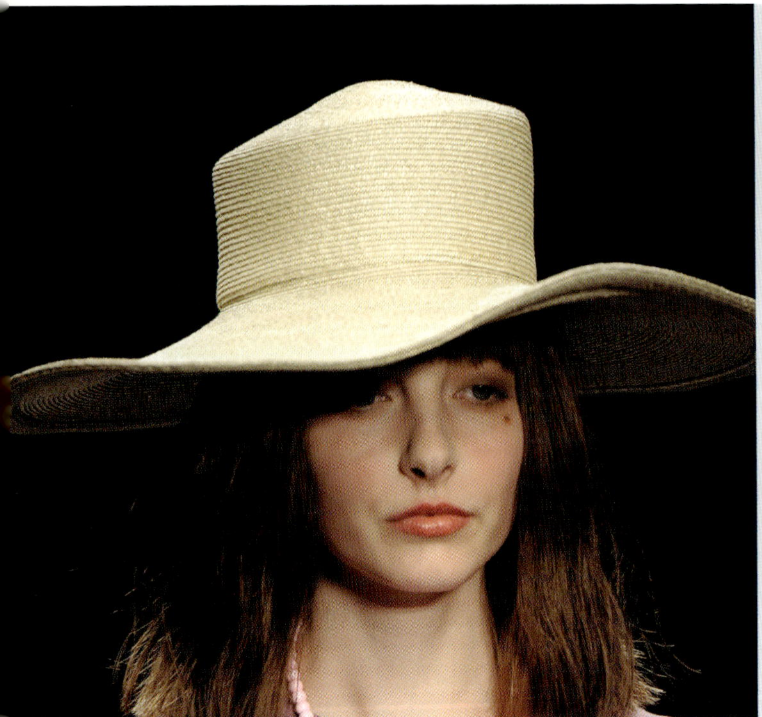
Charles Anastase

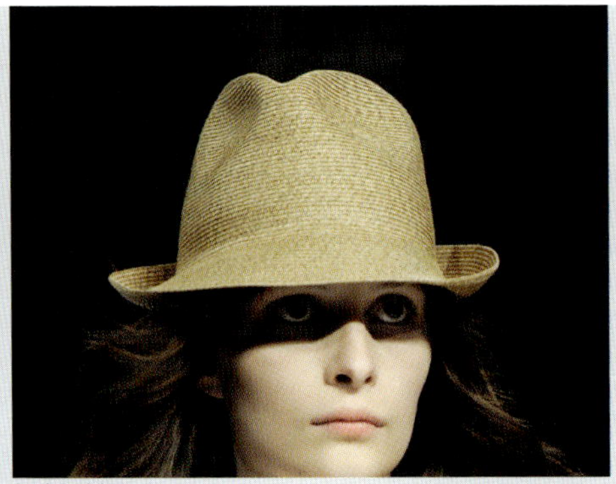
Paul Smith

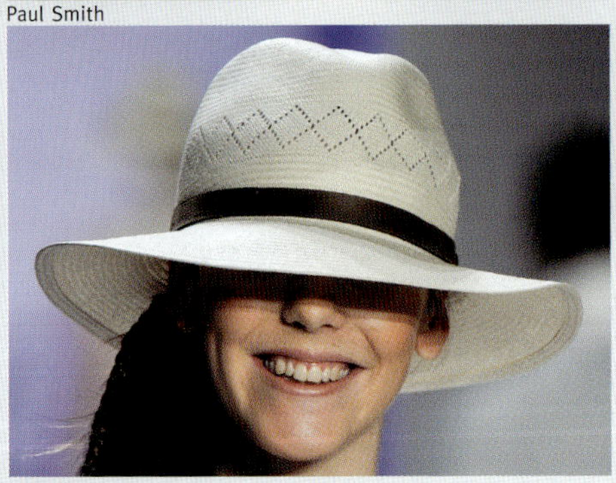
Lacoste

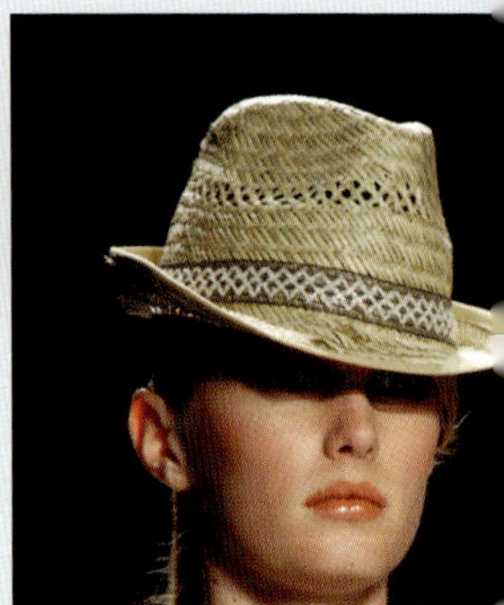
Nicole Miller

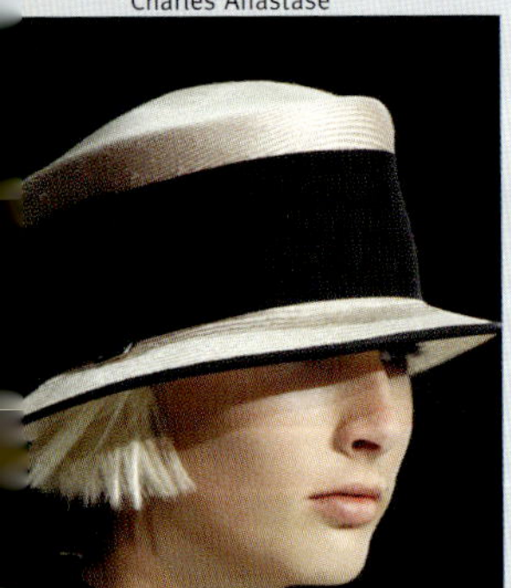
Emporio Armani

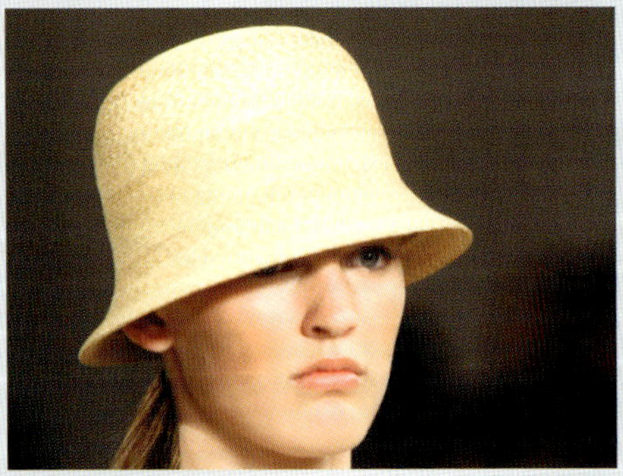
Ralph Lauren

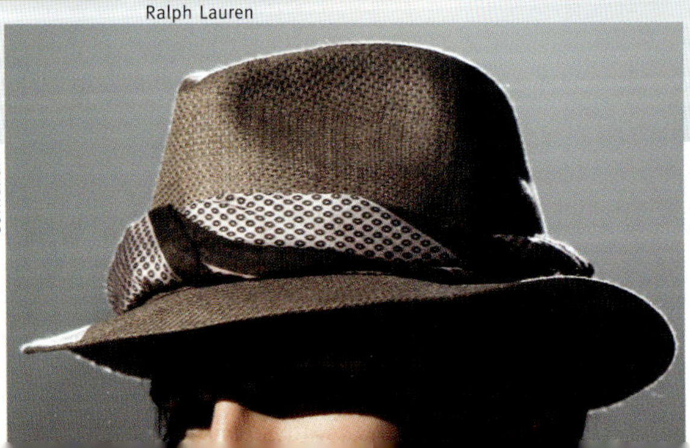
Corneliani

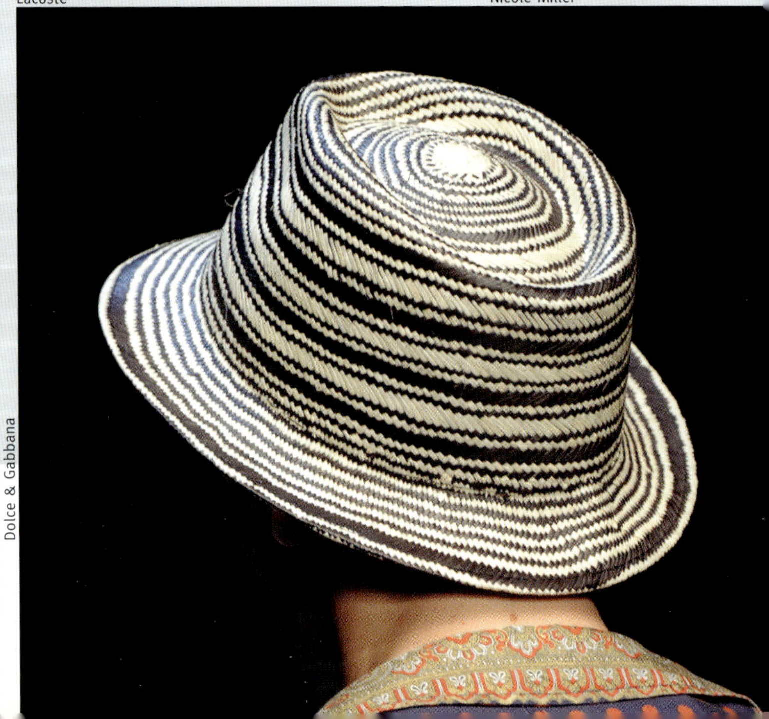
Dolce & Gabbana

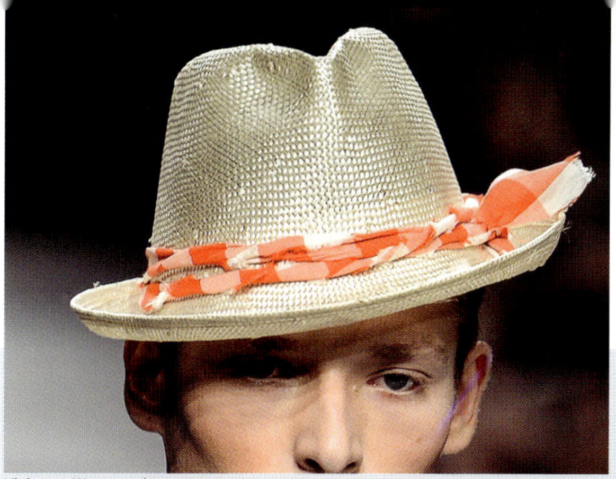

Vivienne Westwood

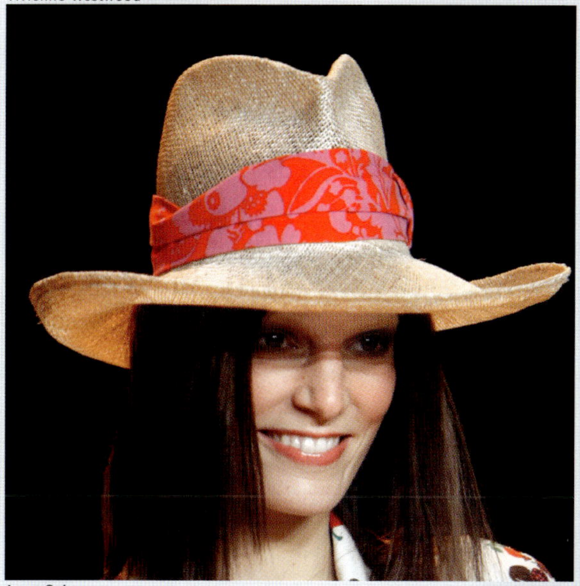

Anna Sui

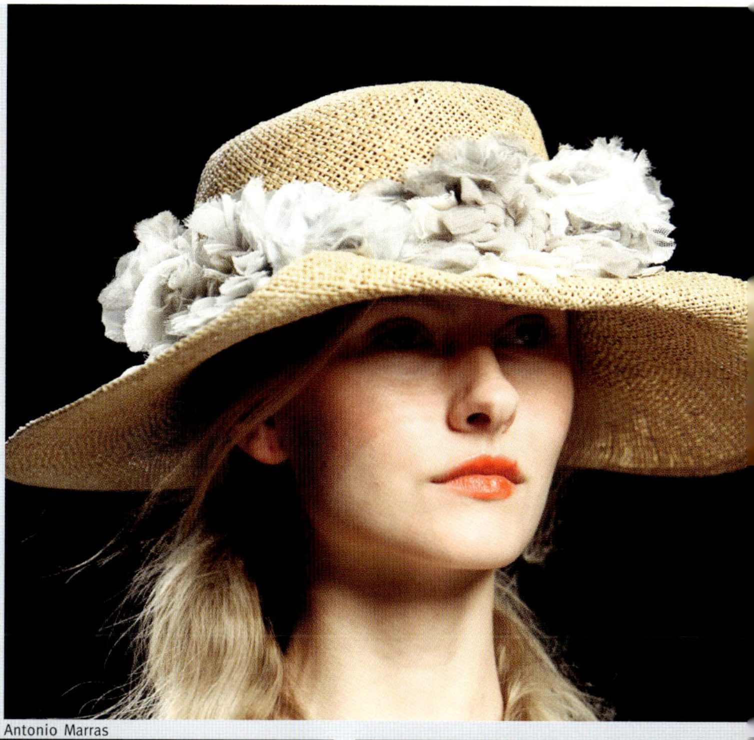

Antonio Marras

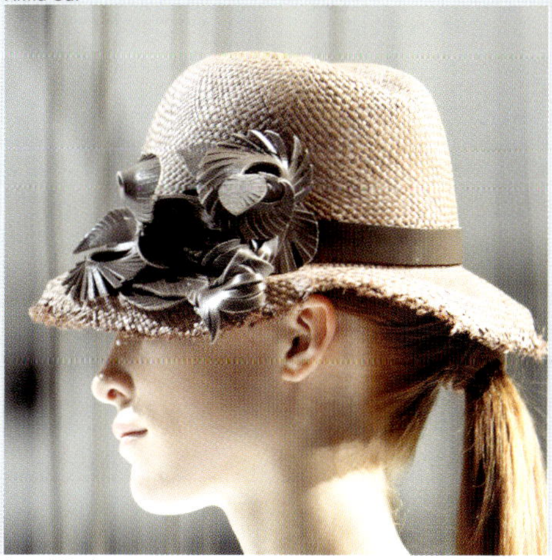

Issey Miyake

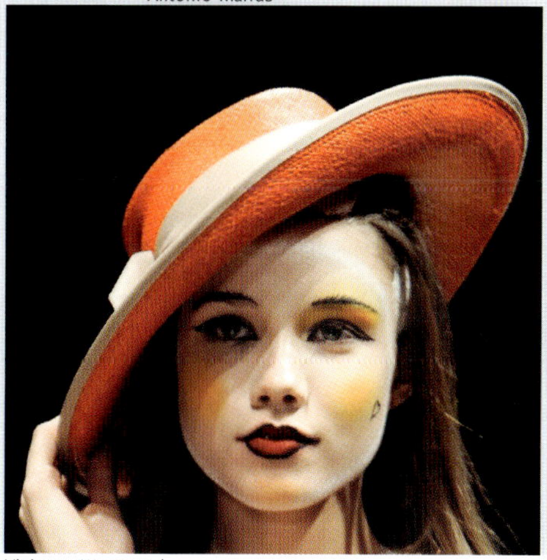

Vivienne Westwood

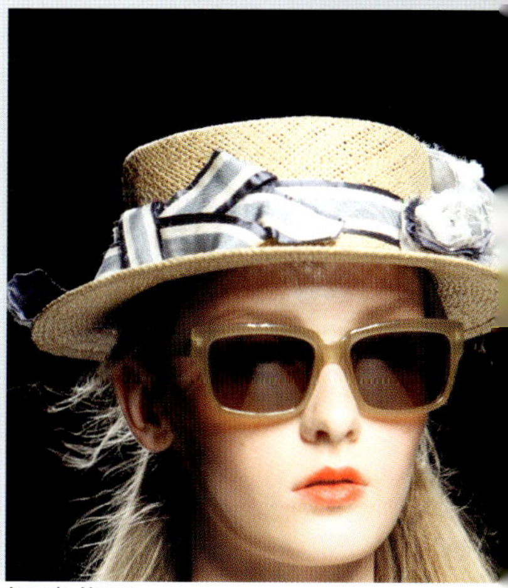

Antonio Marras

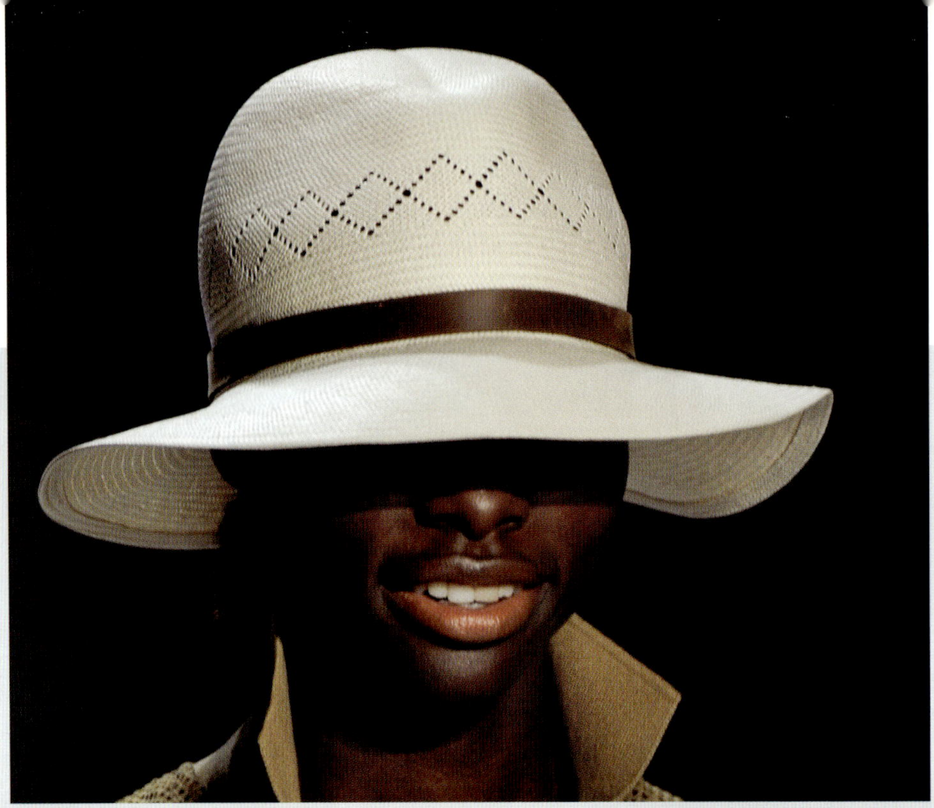

Lacoste

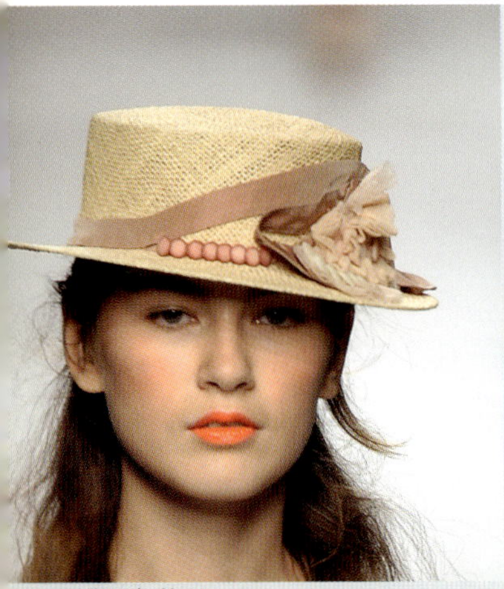

Antonio Marras

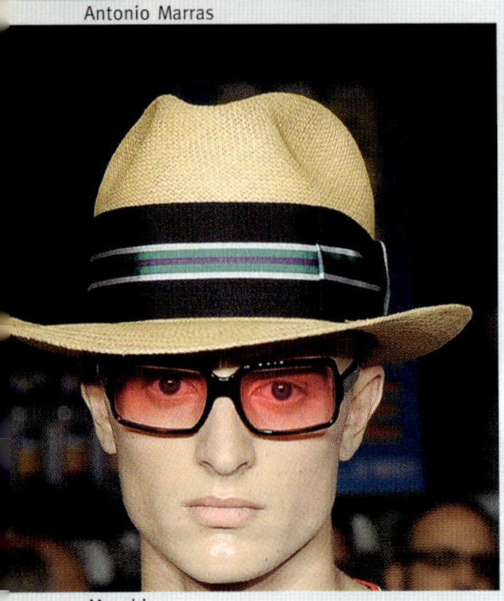

Moschino

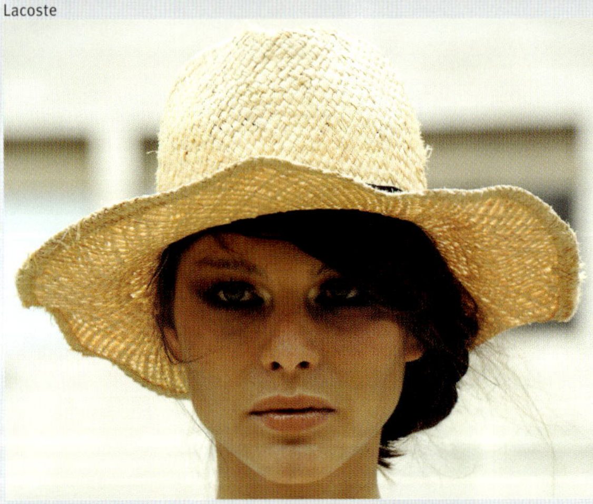

Catherine Malandrino

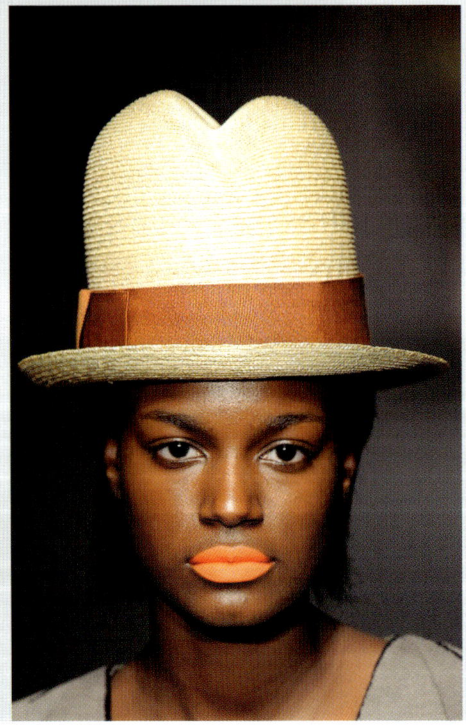

JC de Castelbajac

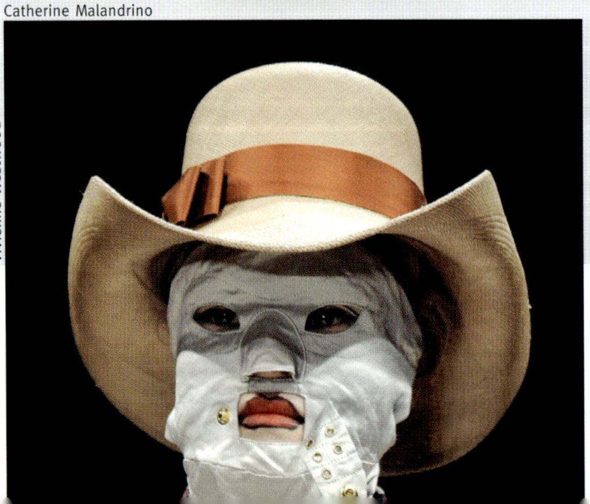

Vivienne Westwood

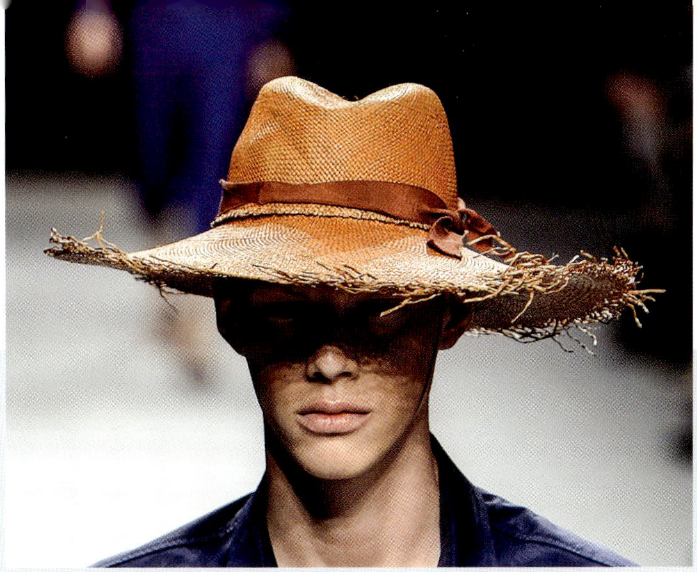

Vivienne Westwood

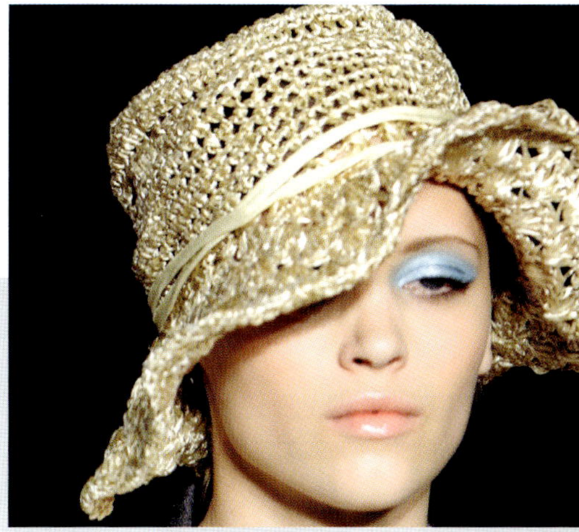

Moschino Cheap & Chic

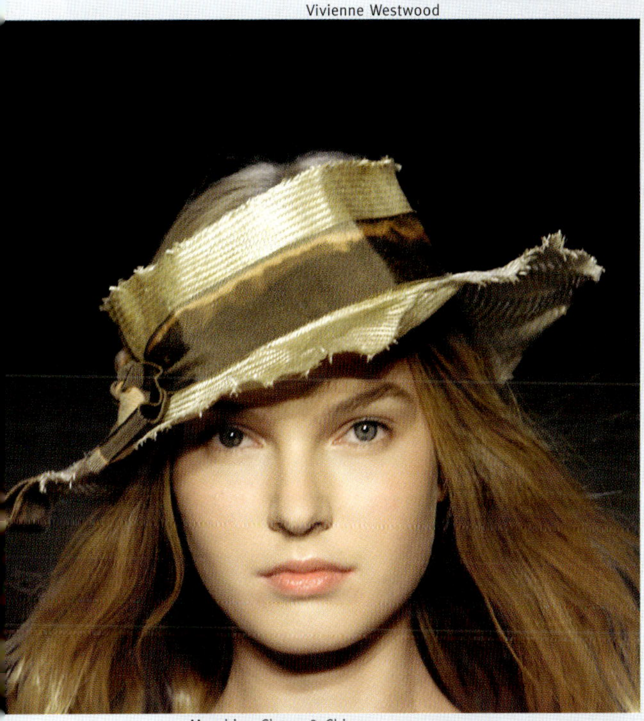

Moschino Cheap & Chic

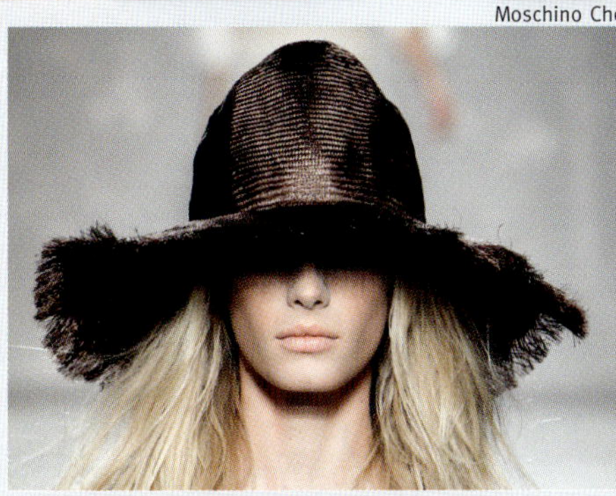

Alberta Ferretti

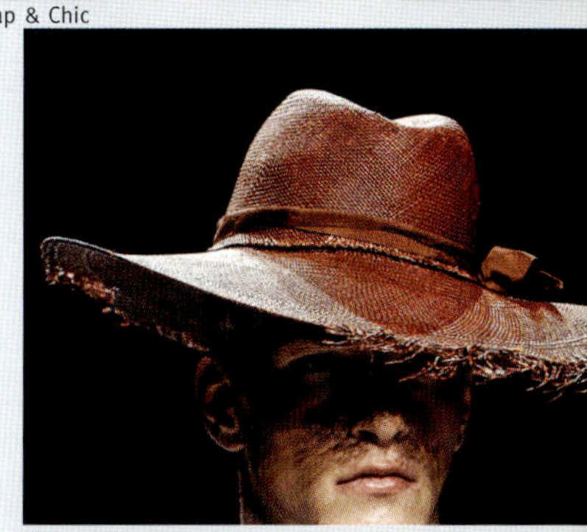

Vivienne Westwood

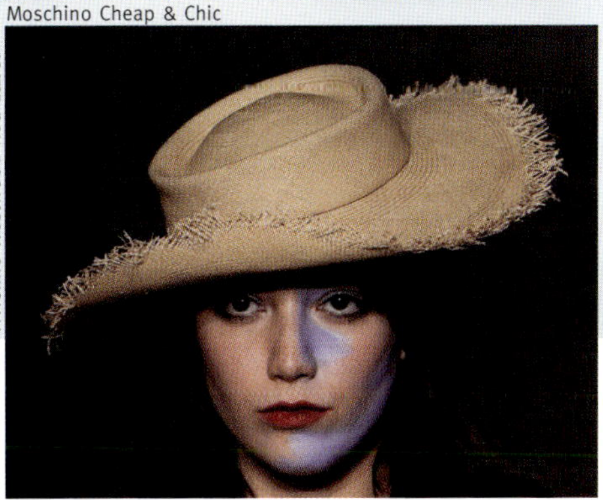

Vivienne Westwood Red Label

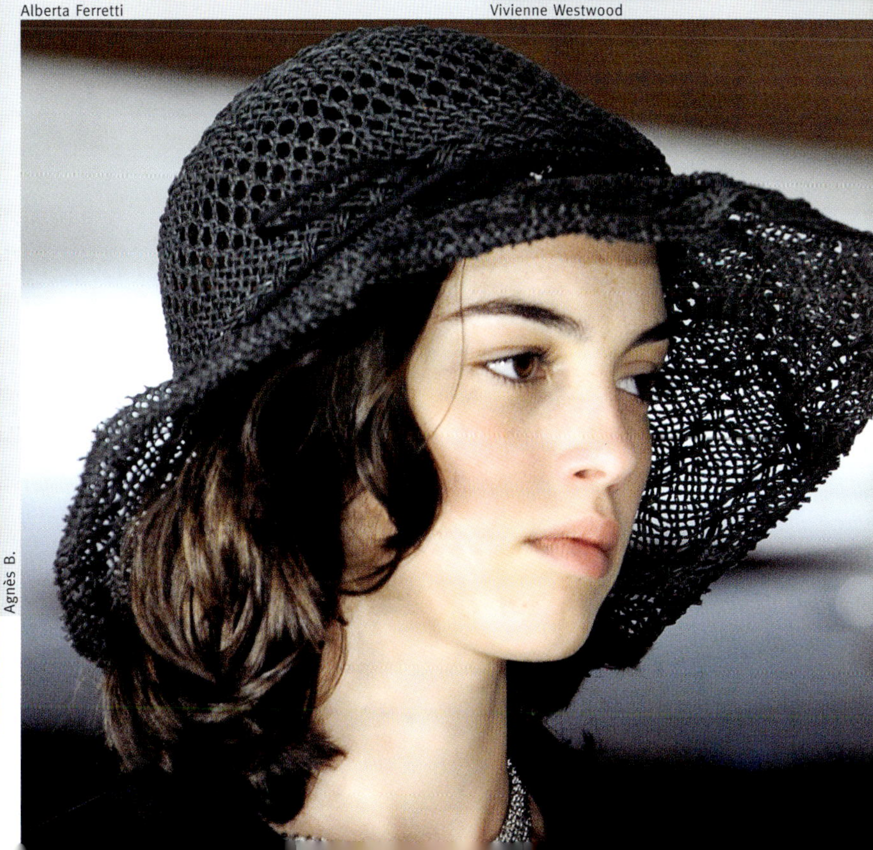

Agnès B.

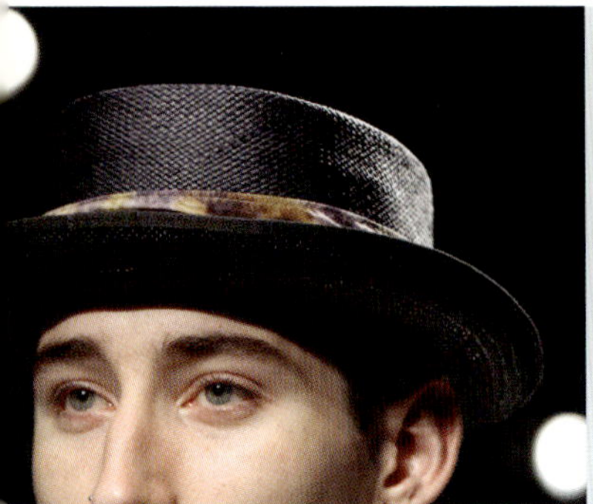
Paul Smith

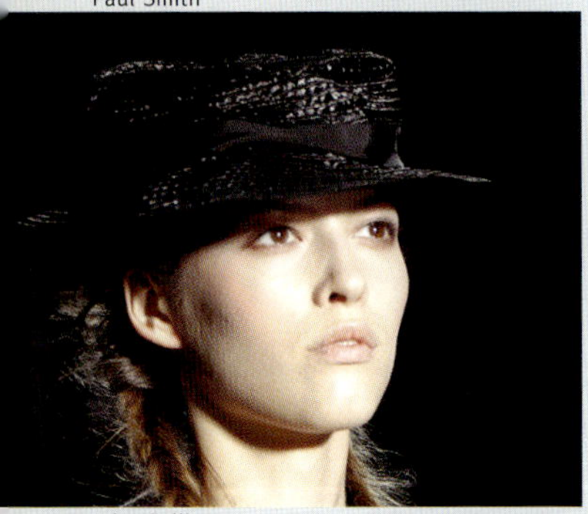
John Galliano

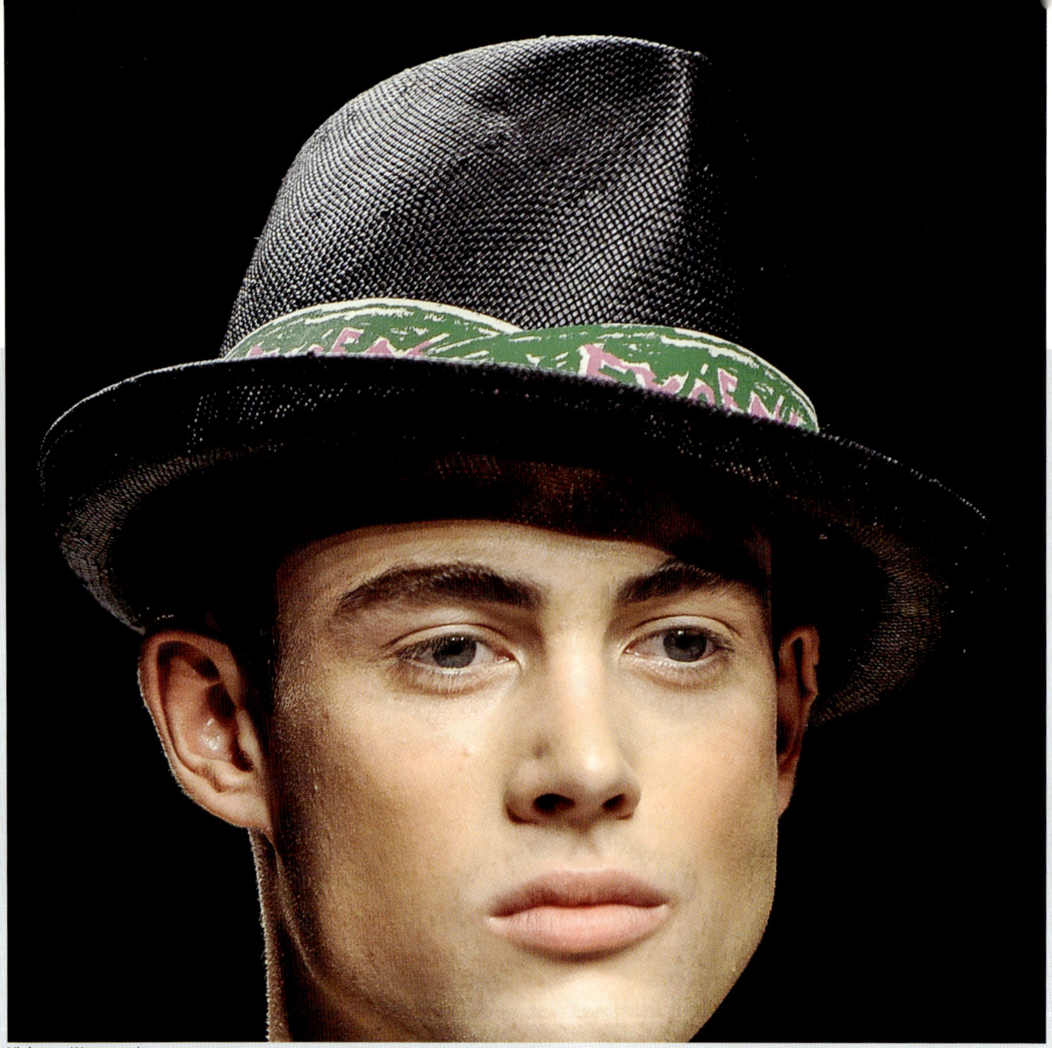
Vivienne Westwood

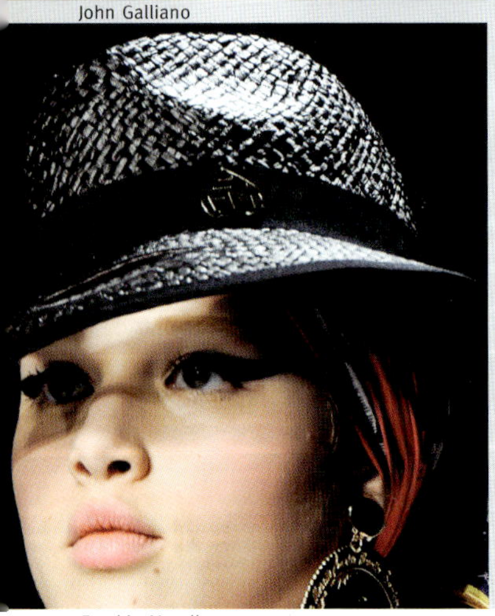
Frankie Morello

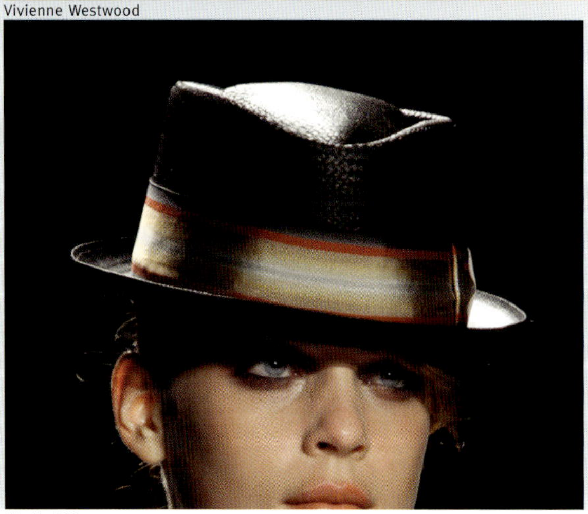
Nicole Miller

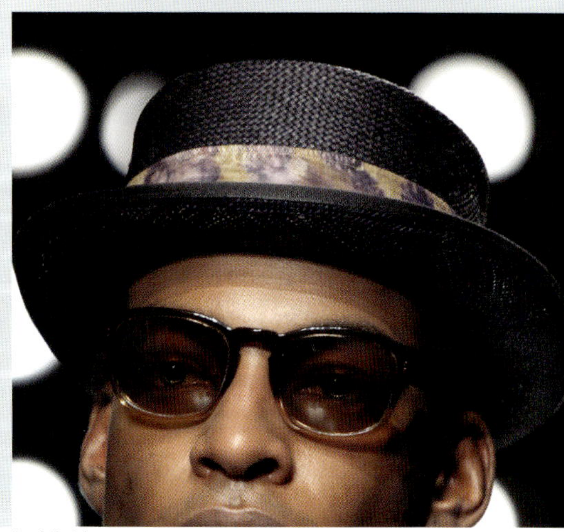
Paul Smith

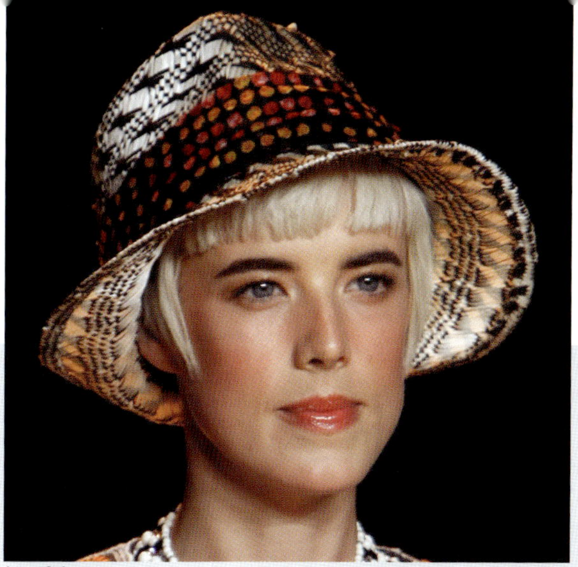

Anna Sui

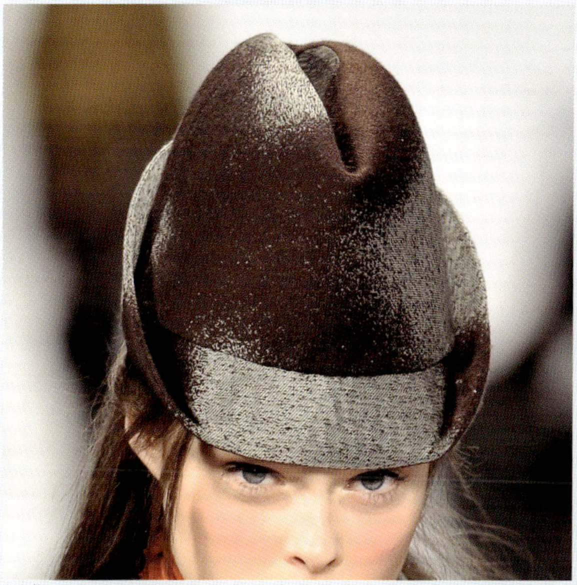

Carolina Herrera

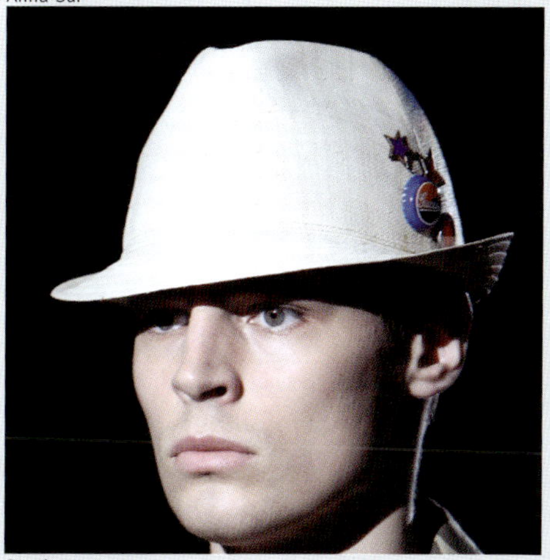

Gucci

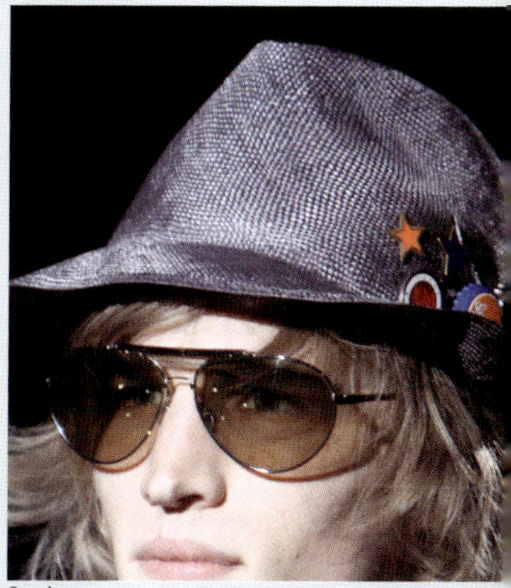

Gucci

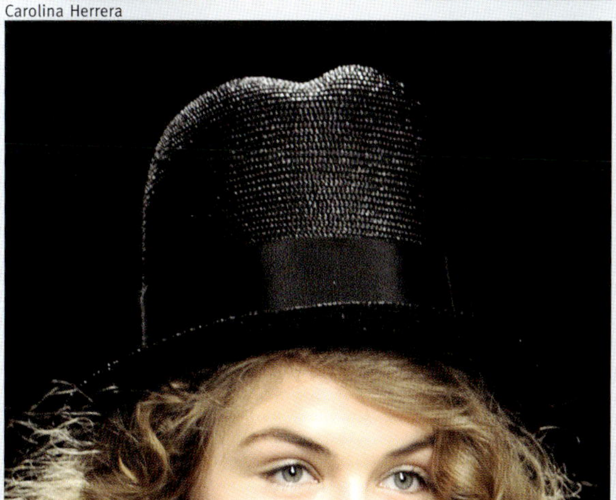

JC de Castelbajac

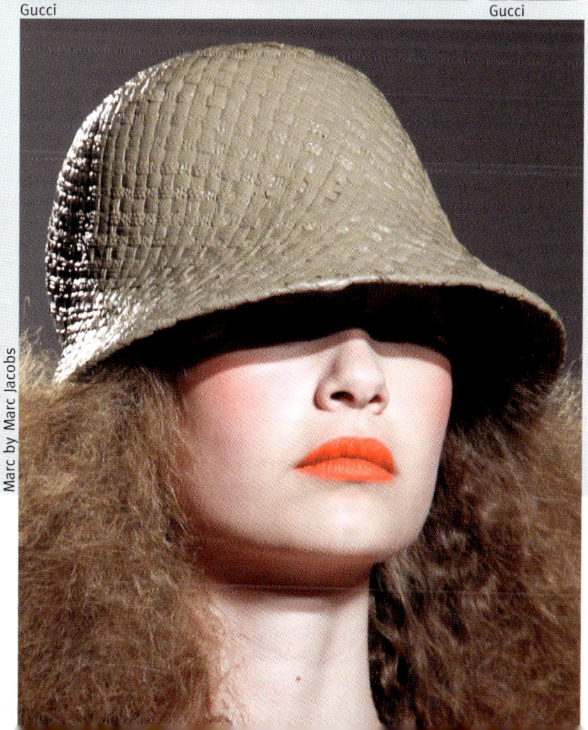

Marc by Marc Jacobs

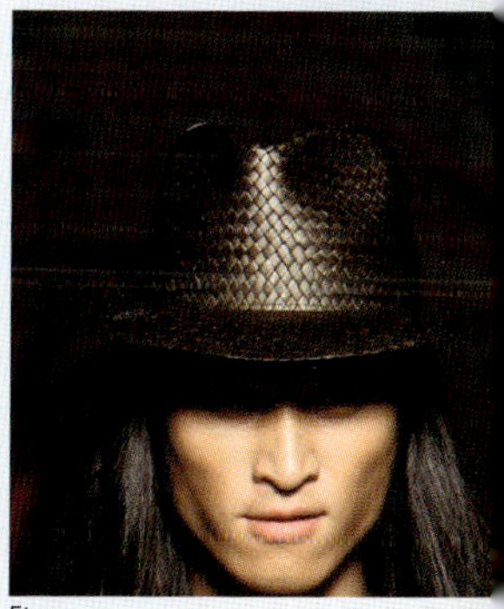

Etro

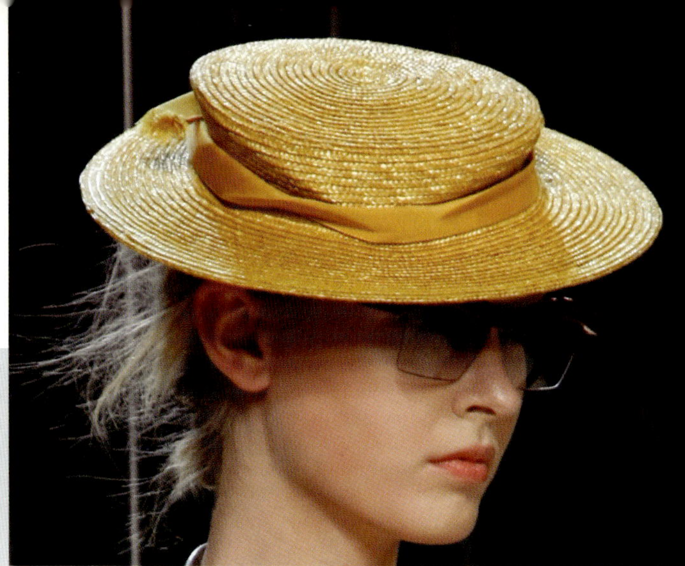

Marc Jacobs

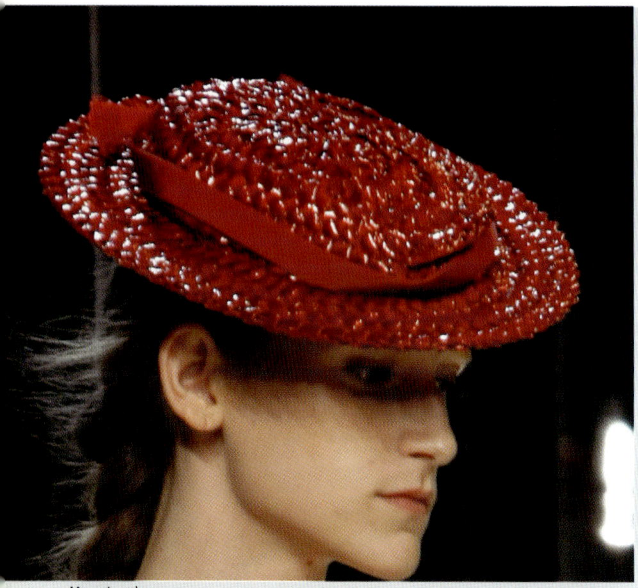

Marc Jacobs

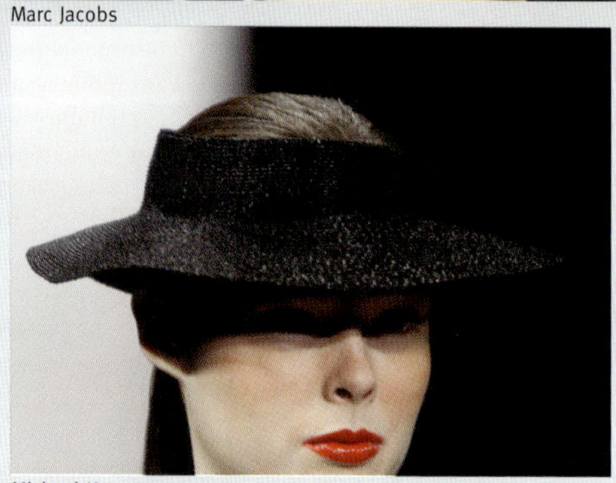

Michael Kors

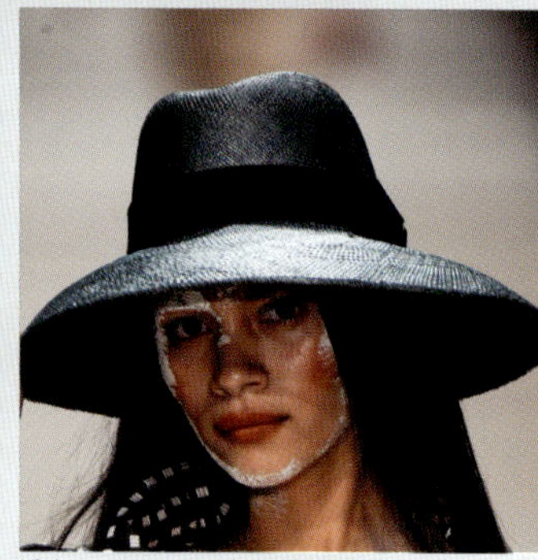

Vivienne Westwood

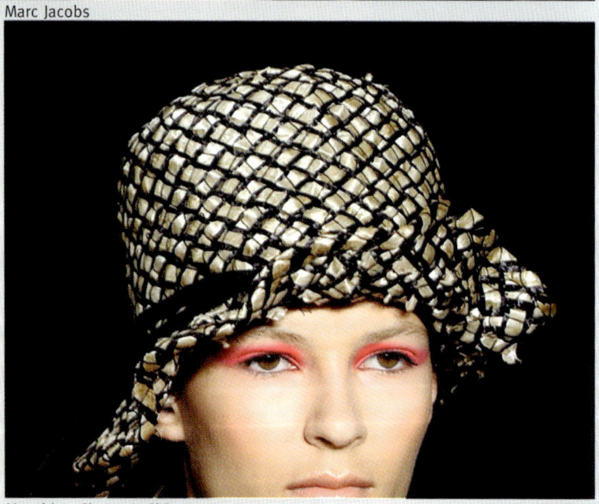

Moschino Cheap & Chic

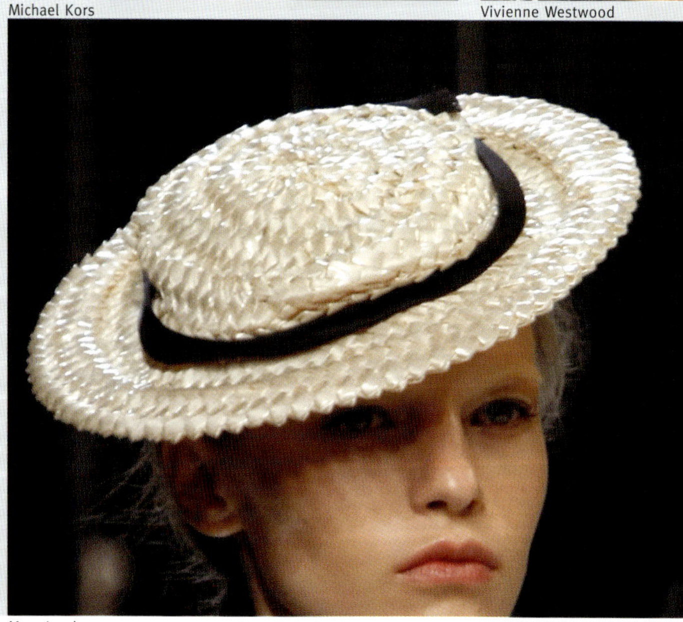

Marc Jacobs

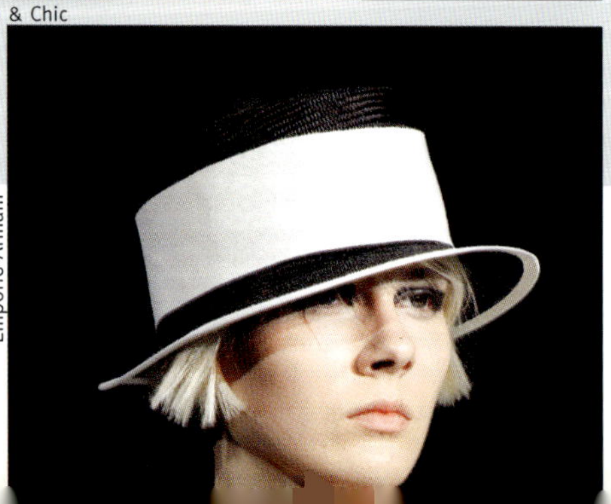

Emporio Armani

Burberry Prorsum

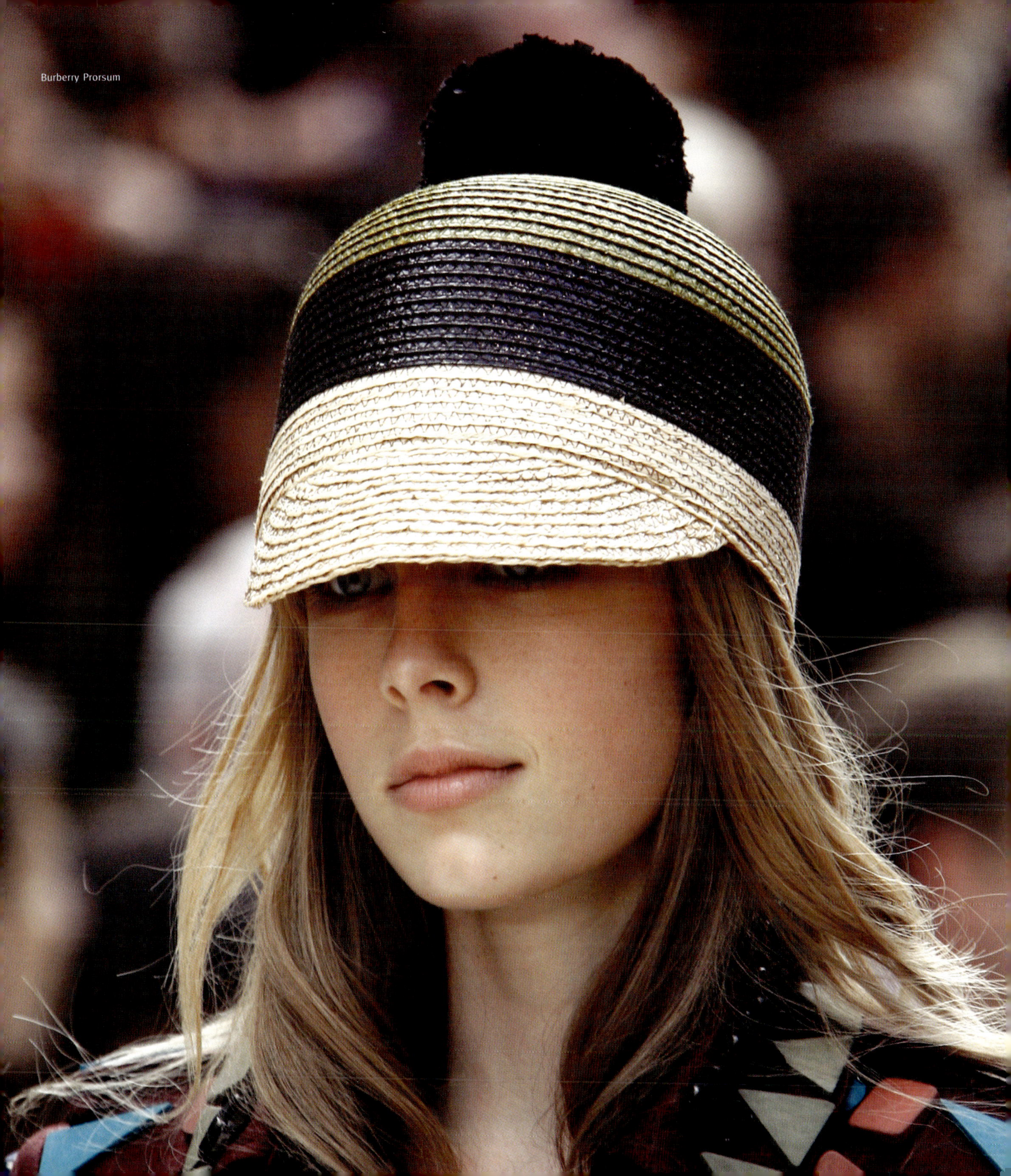

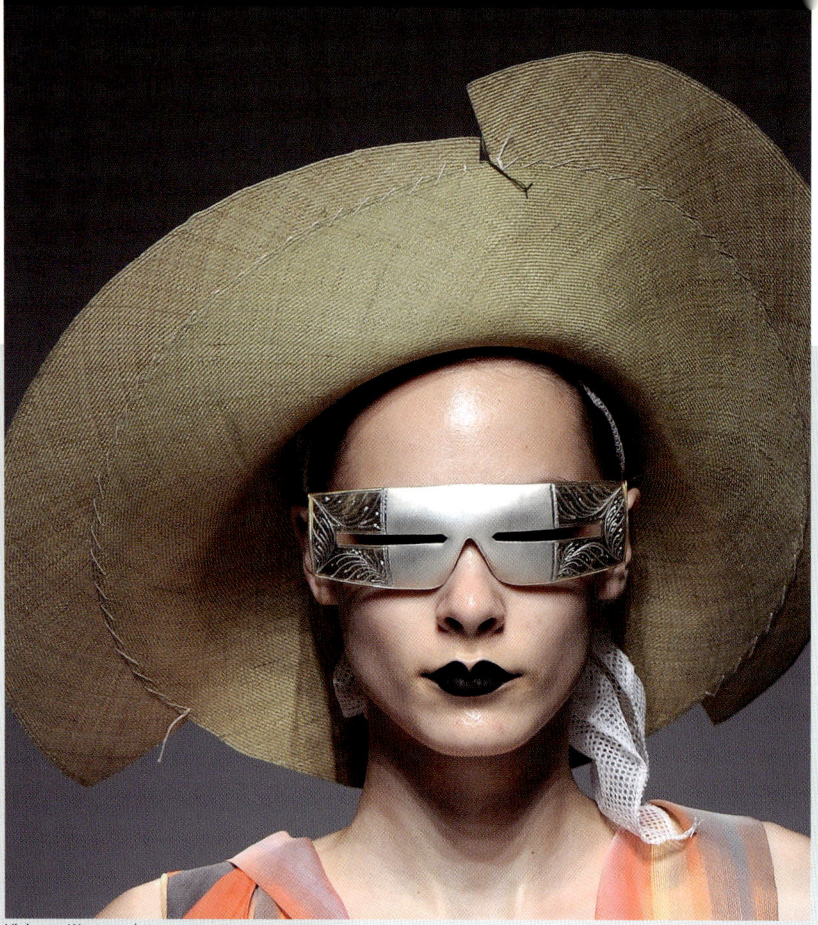

Vivienne Westwood

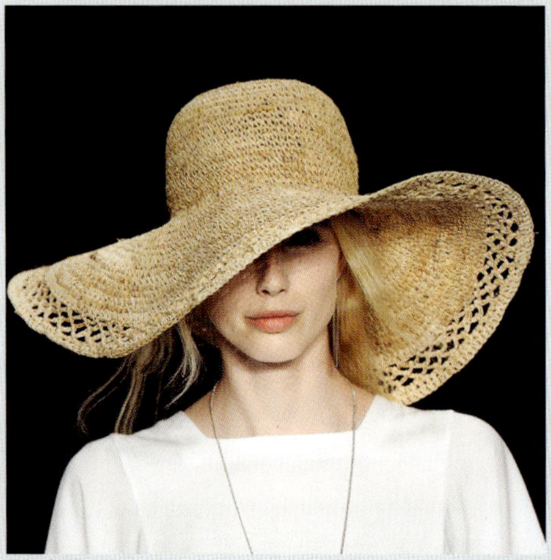

Escada Sport

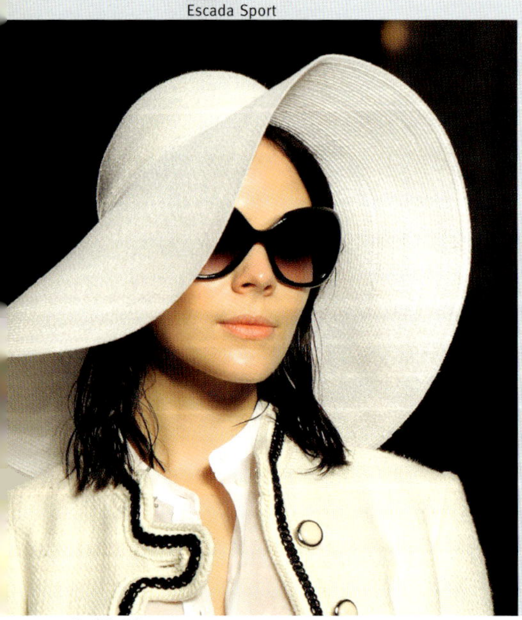

Paul Smith

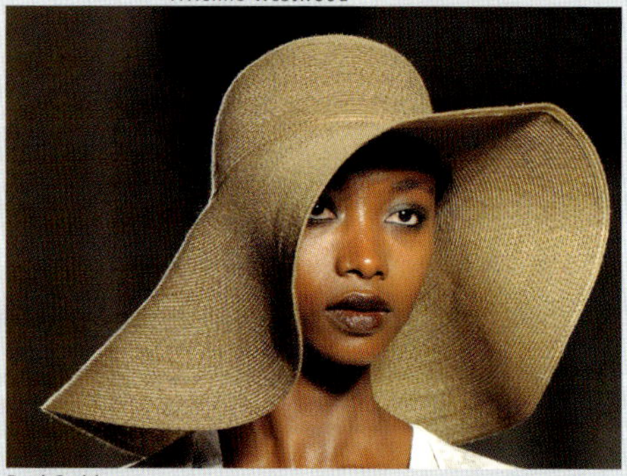

Paul Smith

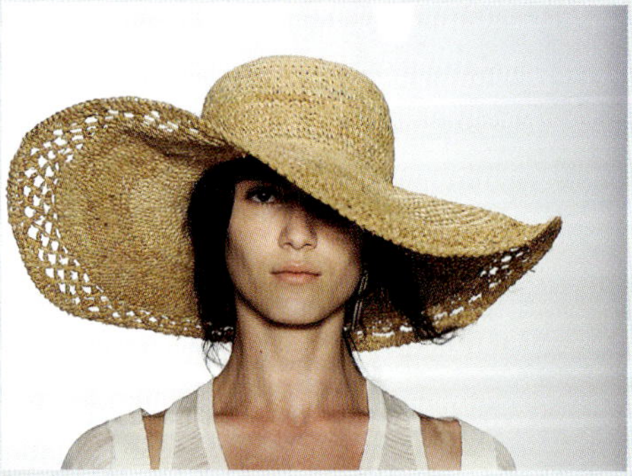

Escada Sport

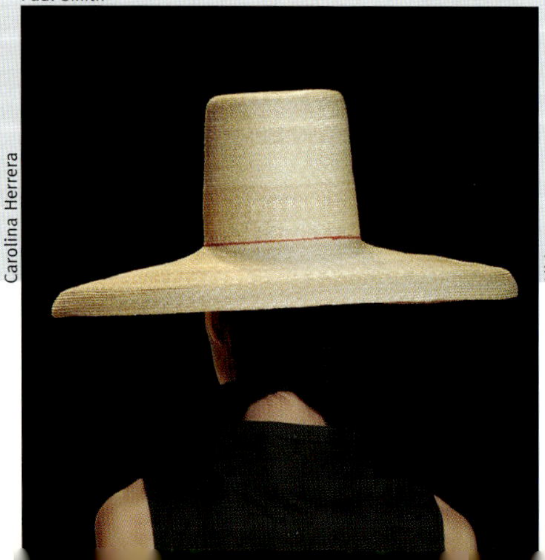

Carolina Herrera

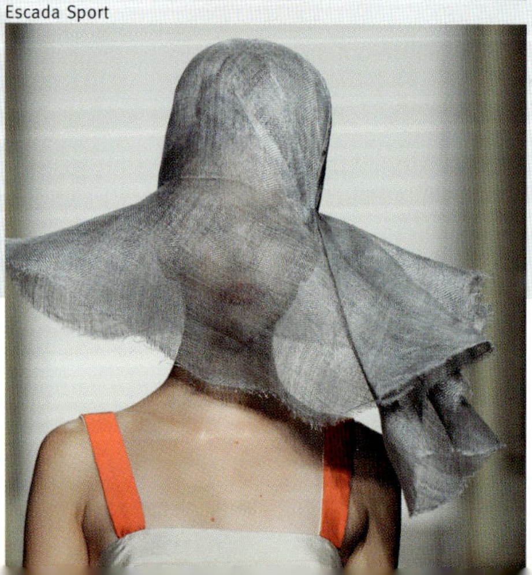

Albino

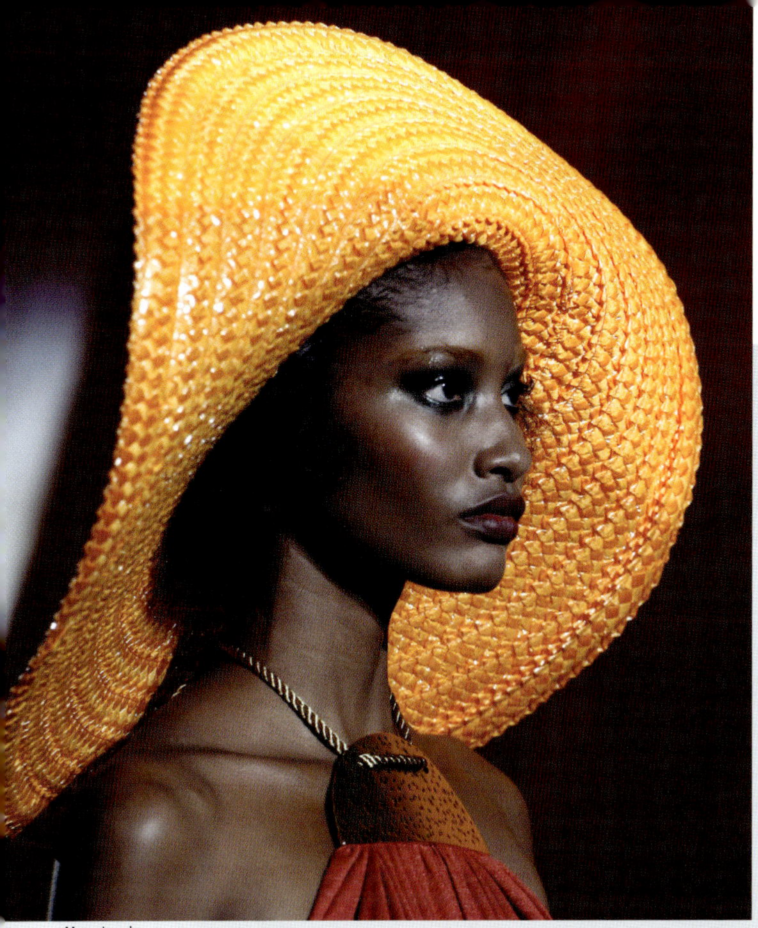
Marc Jacobs

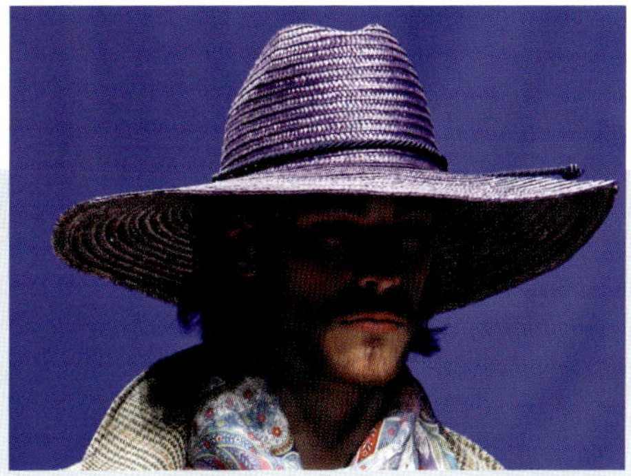
Etro

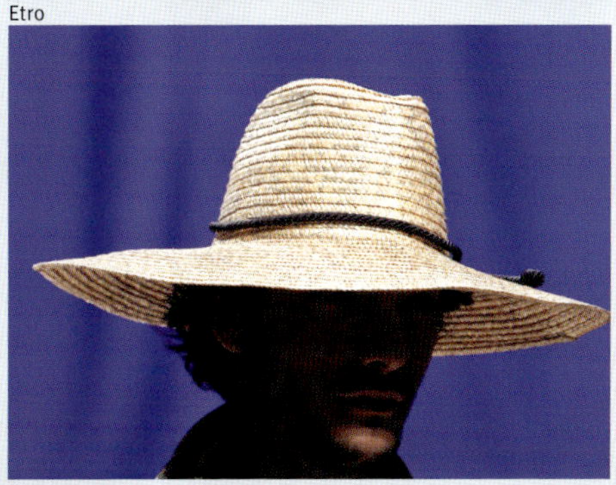
Etro

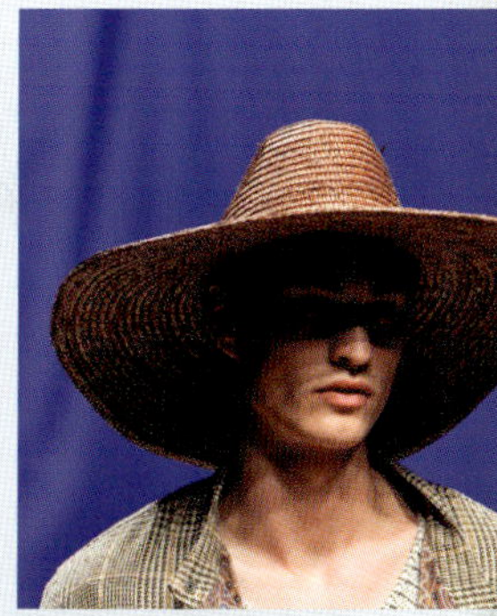
Etro

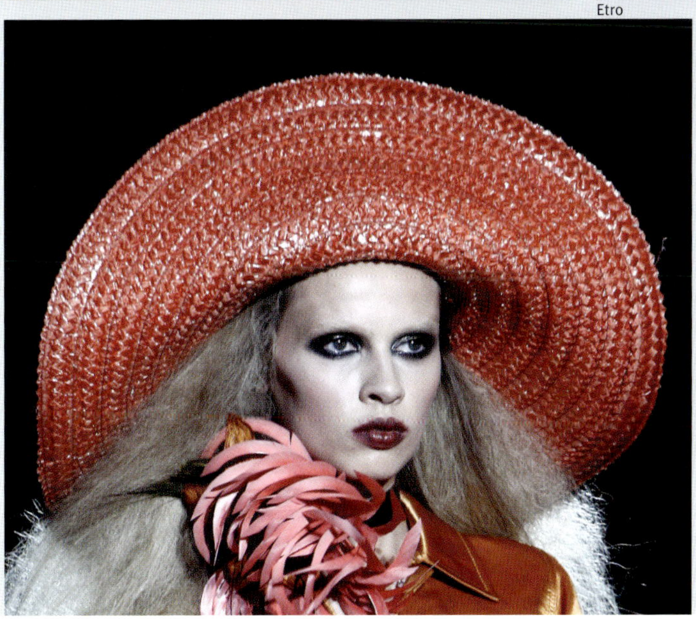
Marc Jacobs

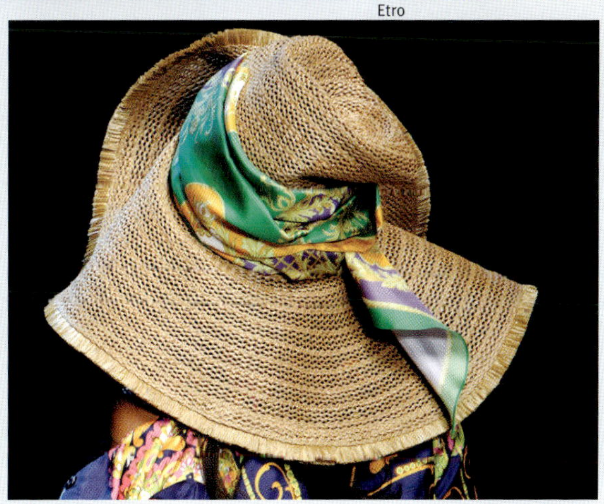
Dolce & Gabbana

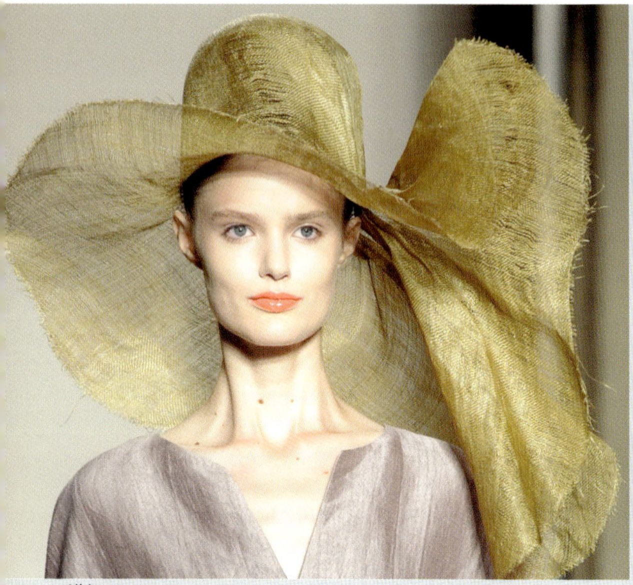

Albino

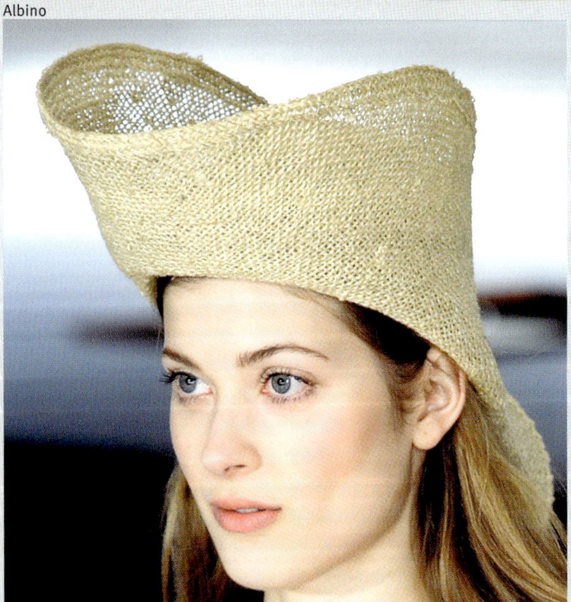

Agnès B.

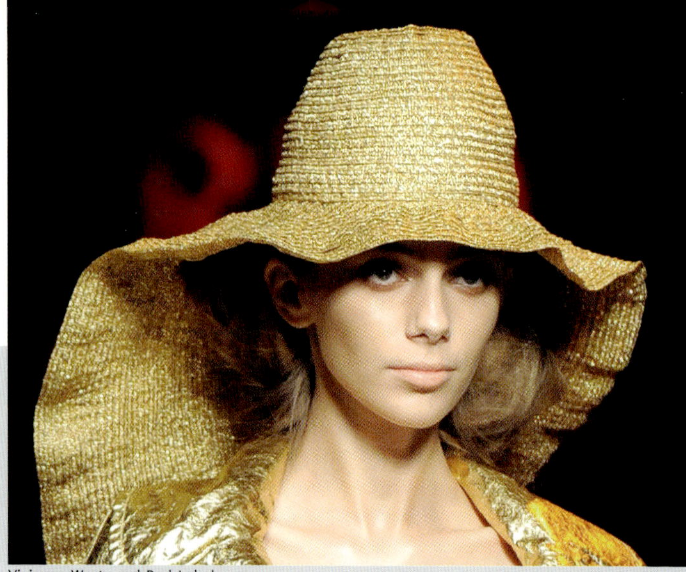

Vivienne Westwood Red Label

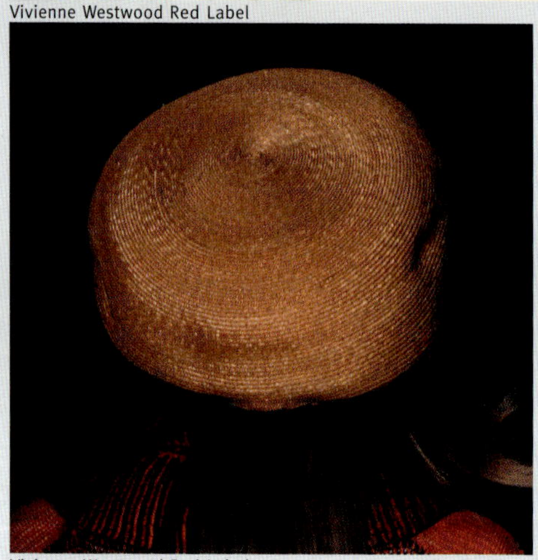

Vivienne Westwood Red Label

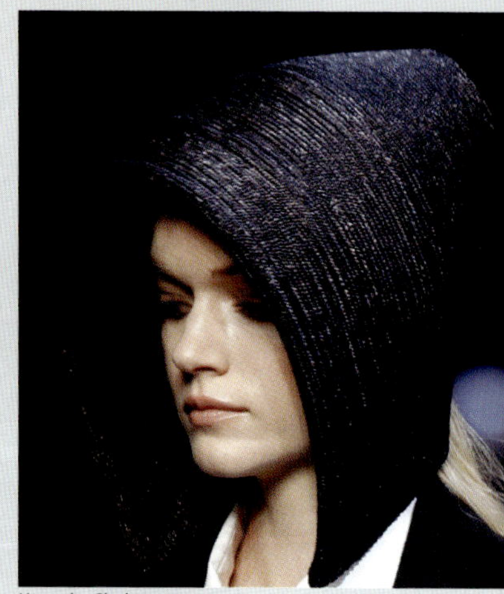

Hussein Chalayan

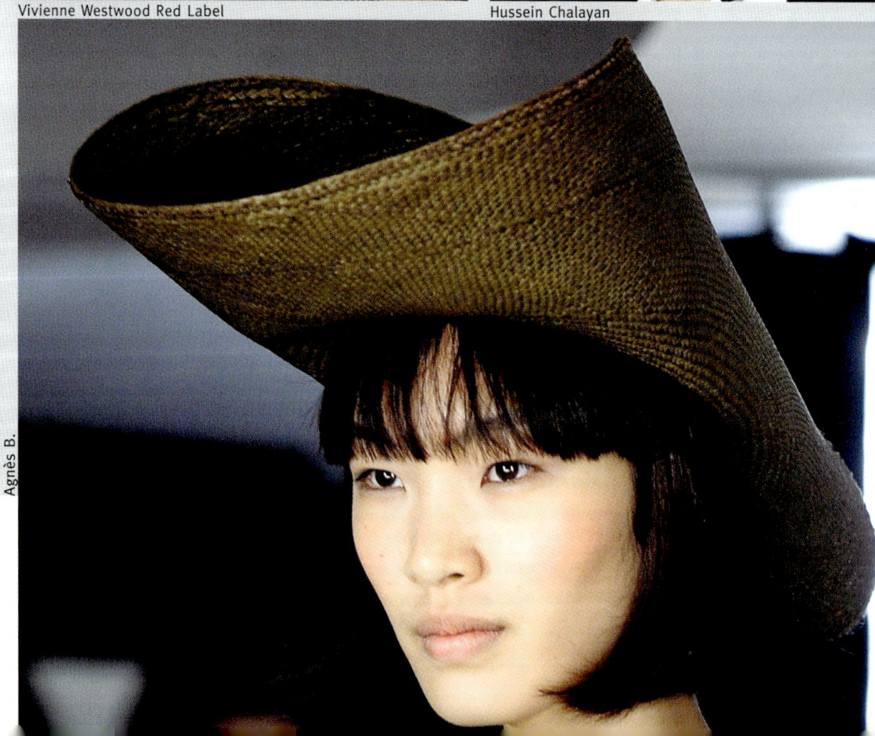

Agnès B.

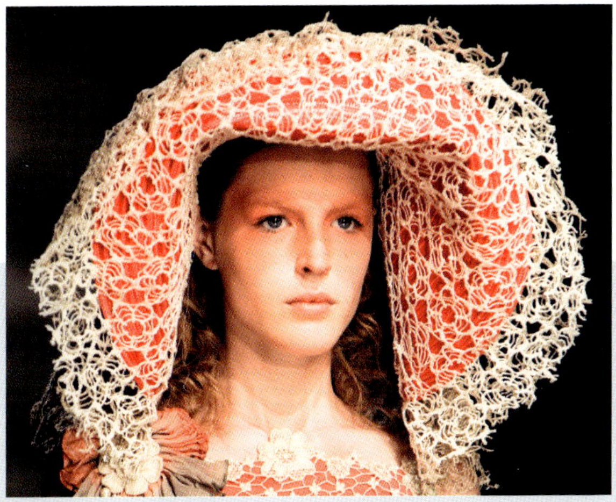

Maurizio Pecoraro

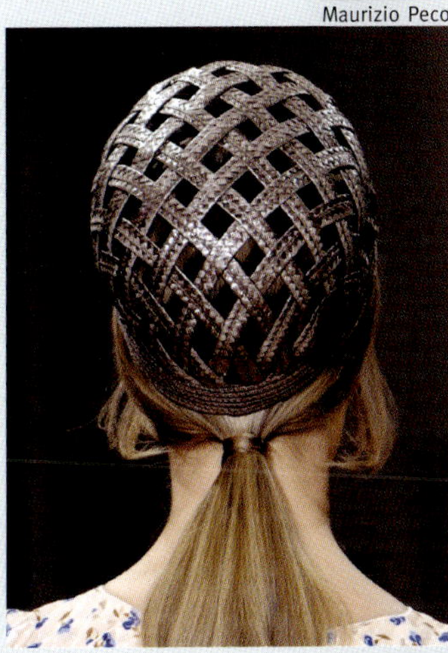

Nina Ricci

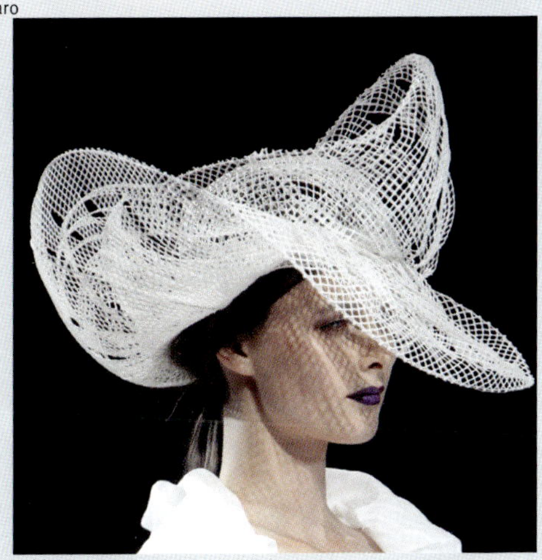

Yohji Yamamoto

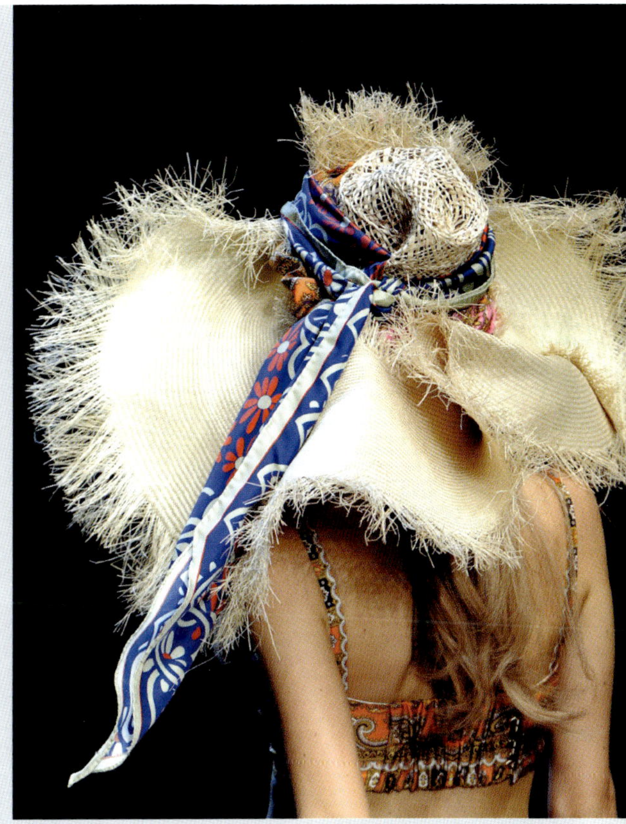

Dolce & Gabbana

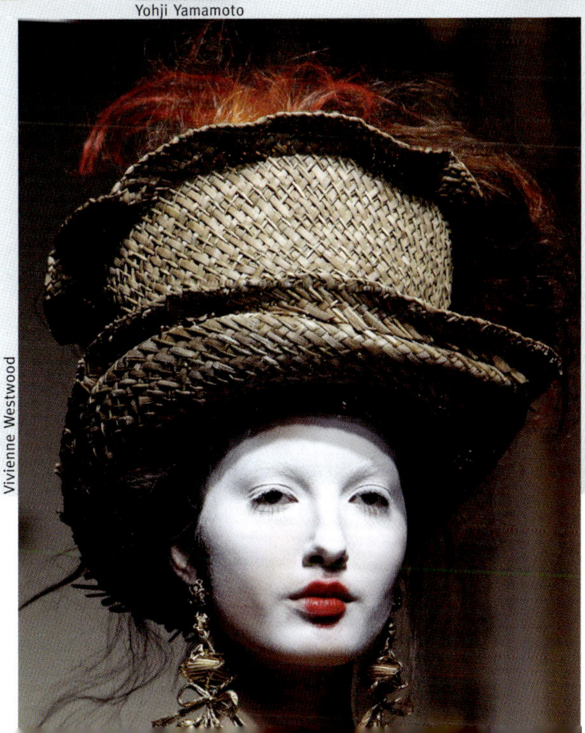

Vivienne Westwood

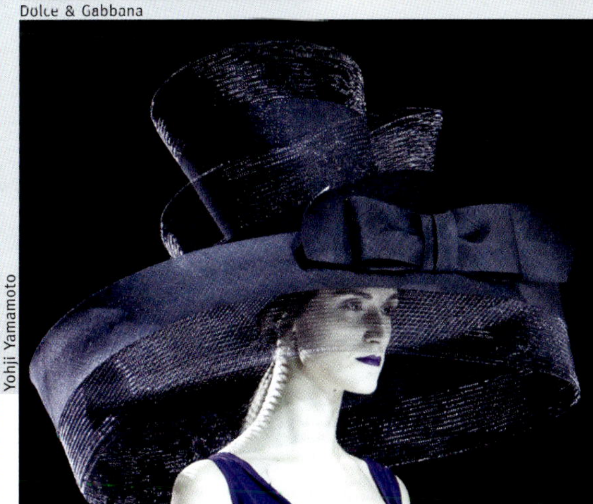

Yohji Yamamoto

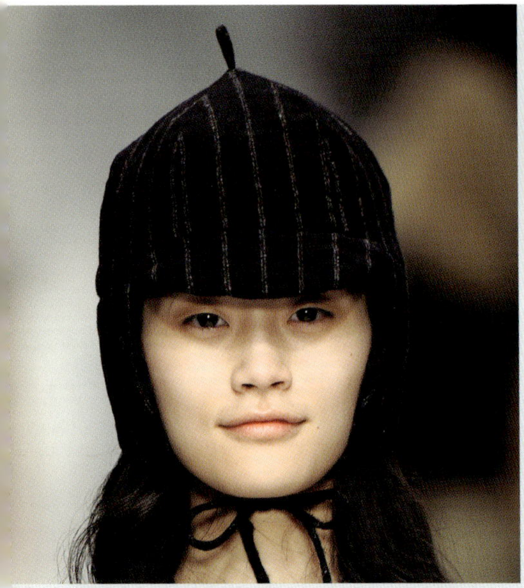

Daks

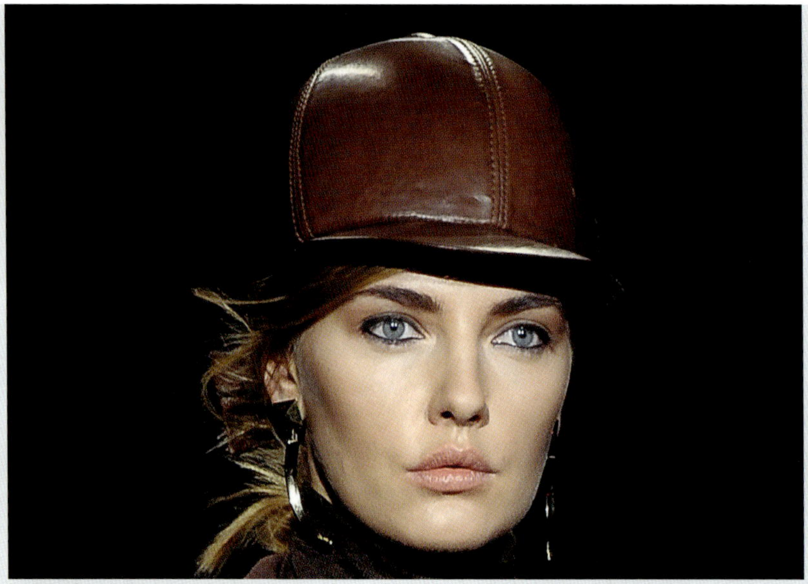

Ermanno Scervino

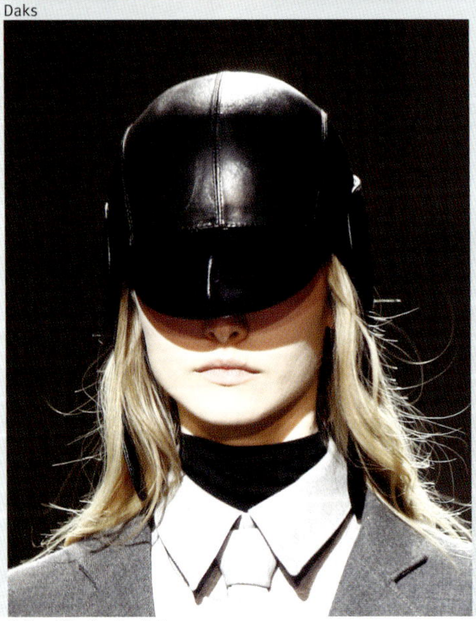

Felipe Oliveira Baptista

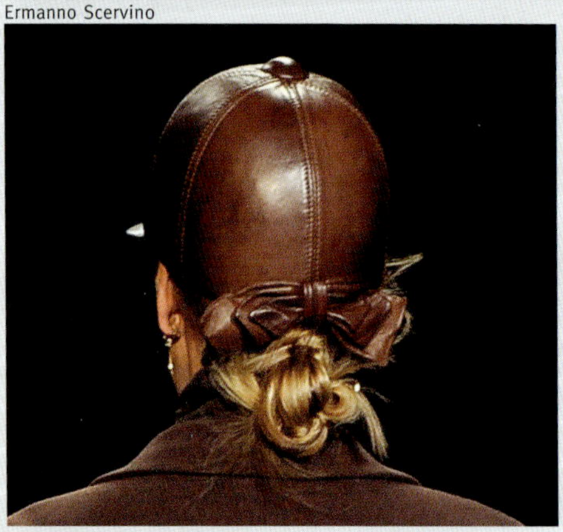

Nina Ricci

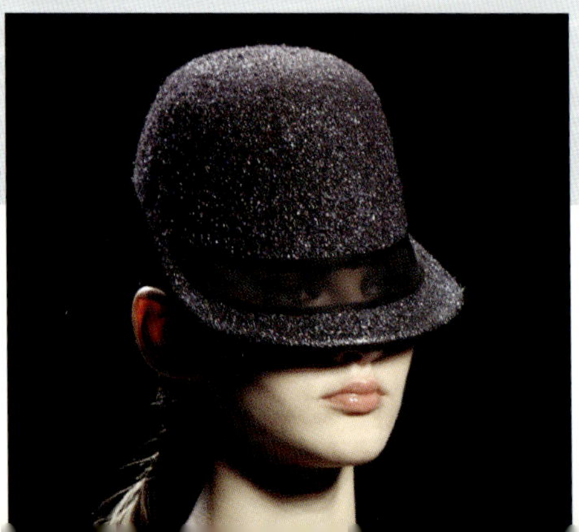

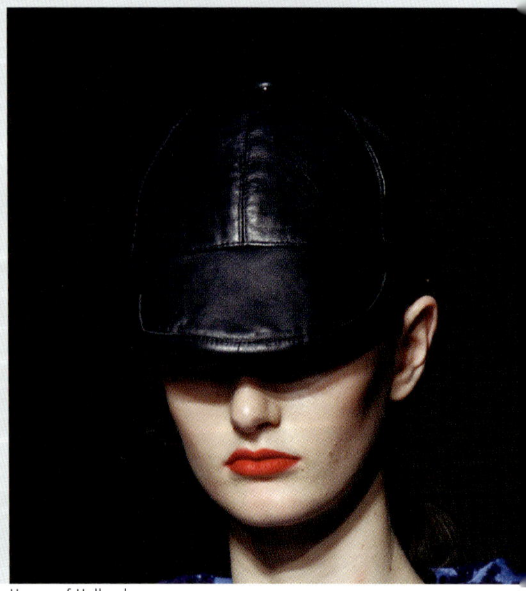

House of Holland

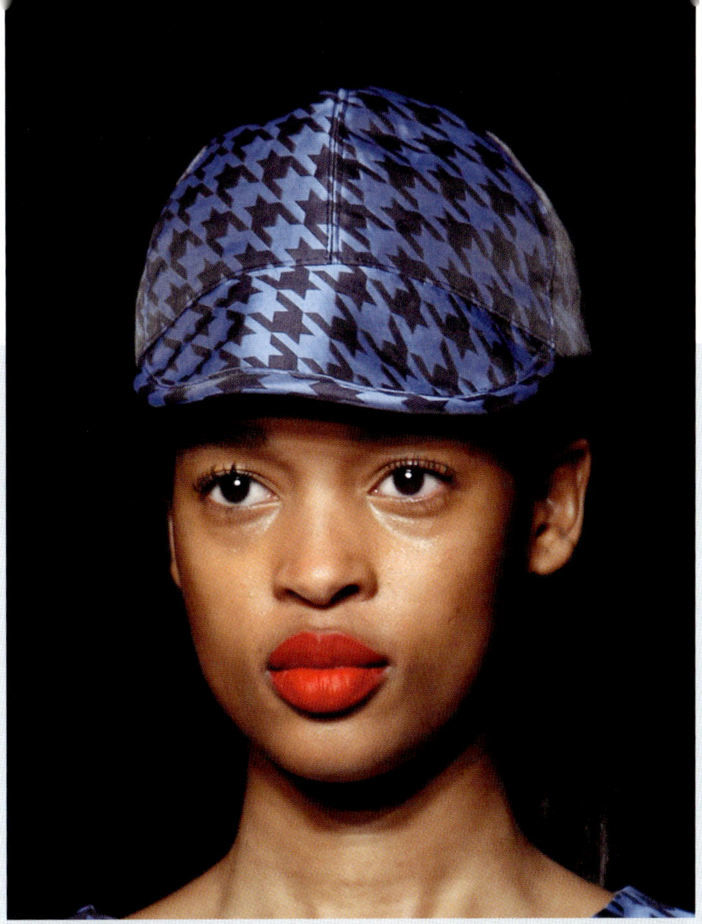
House of Holland

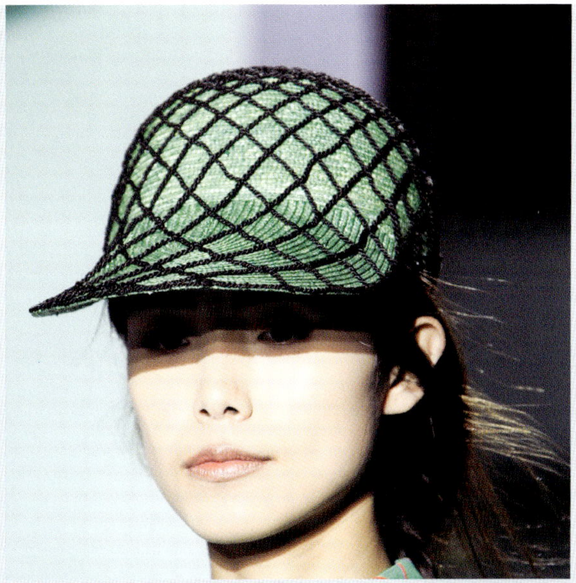
Kenzo

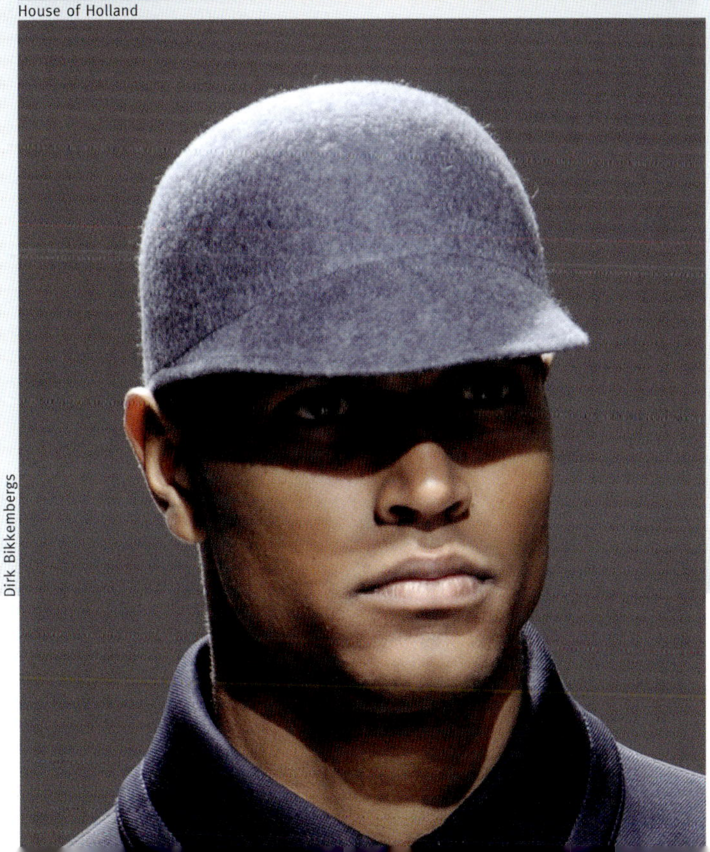
Dirk Bikkembergs

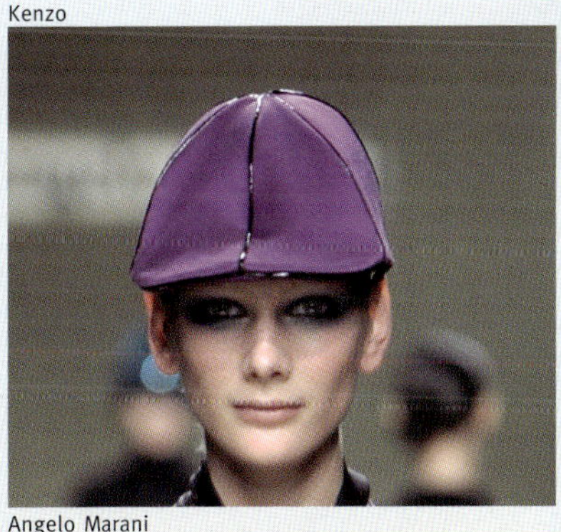
Angelo Marani

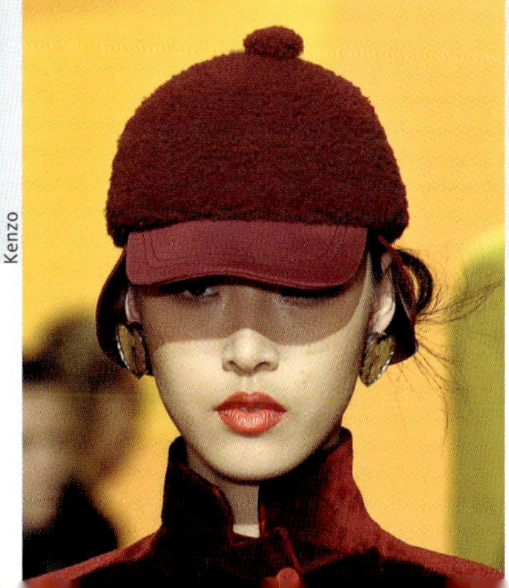
Kenzo

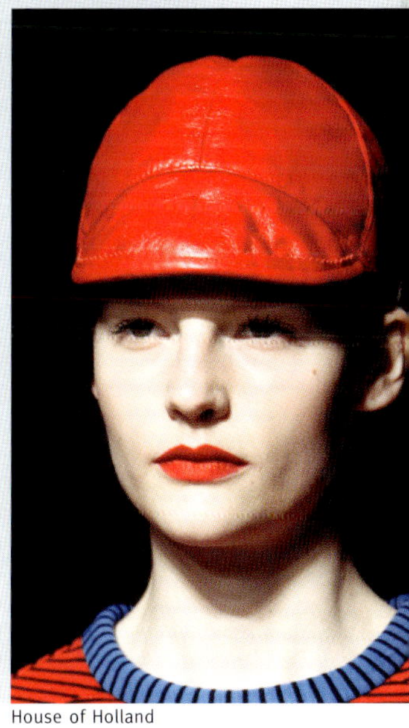
House of Holland

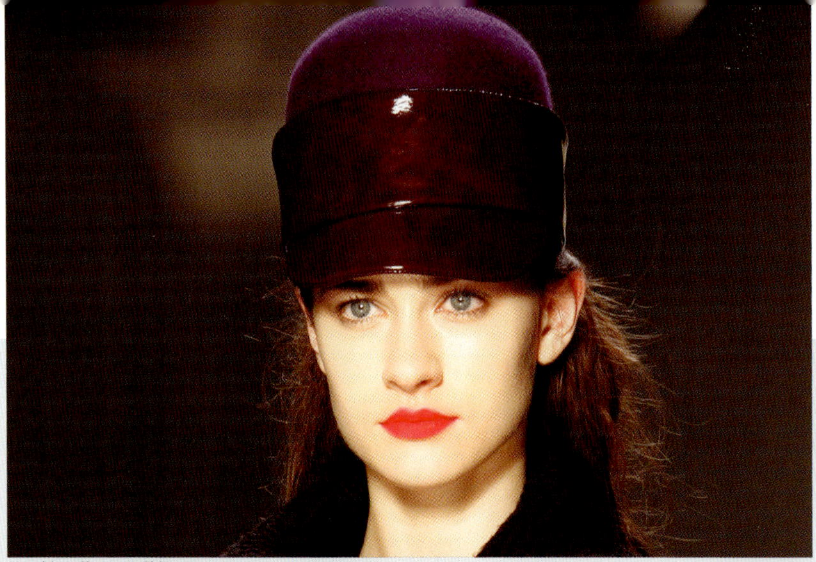

Moschino Cheap & Chic

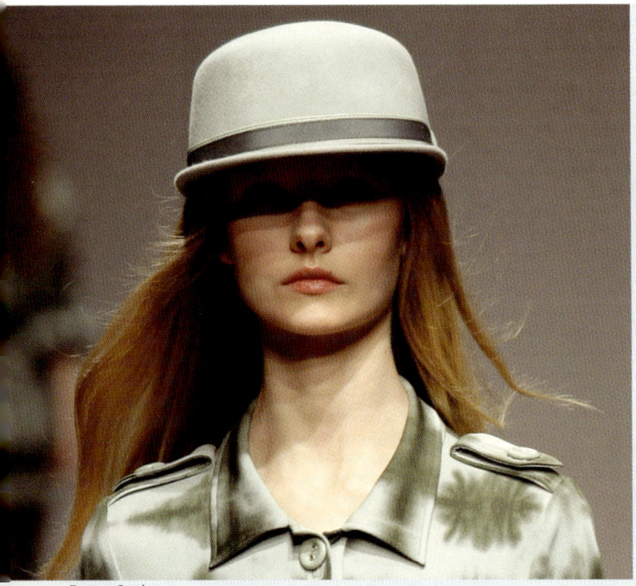

Emma Cook

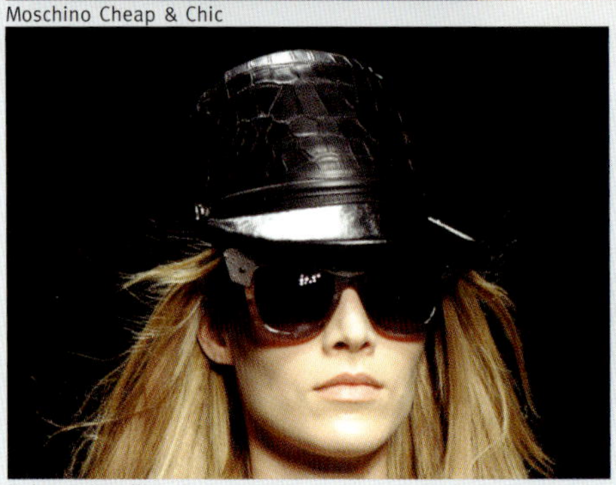

Roberto Cavalli

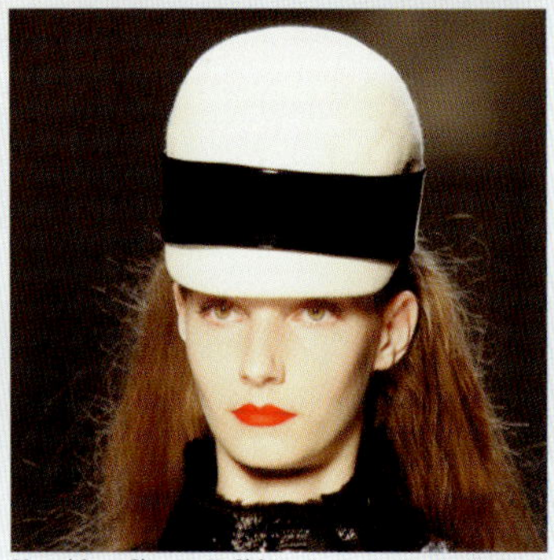

Moschino Cheap & Chic

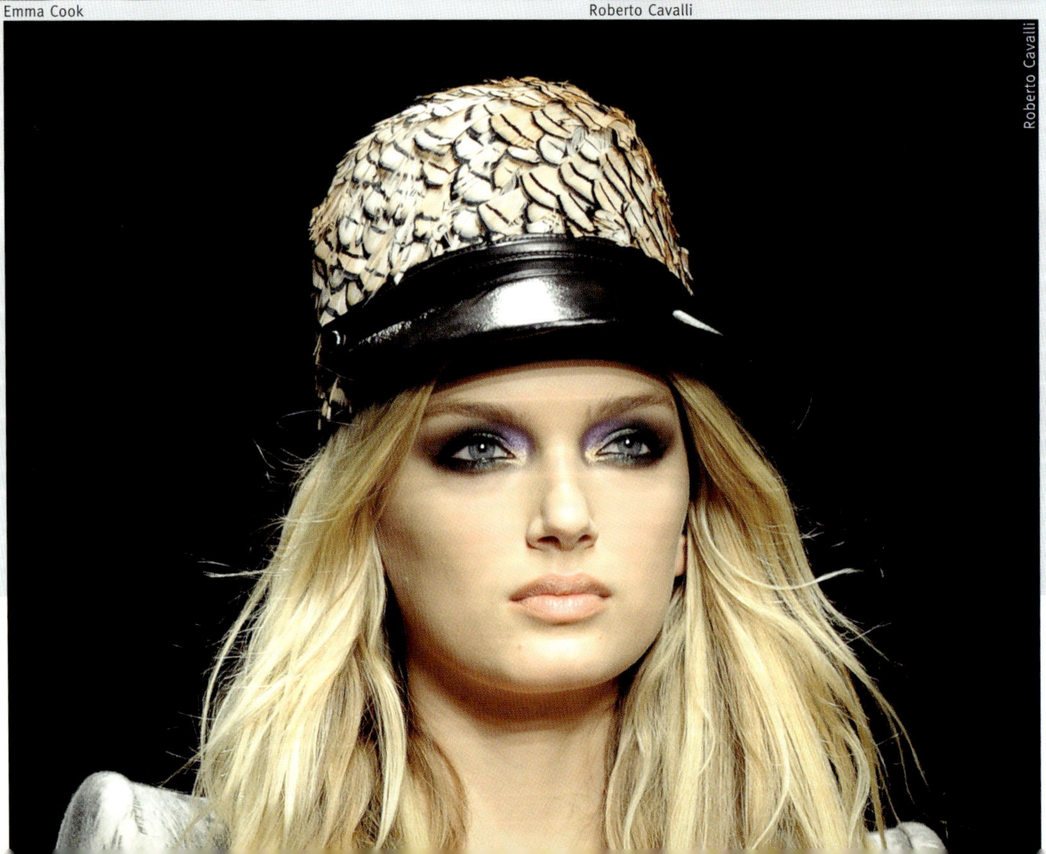

Roberto Cavalli

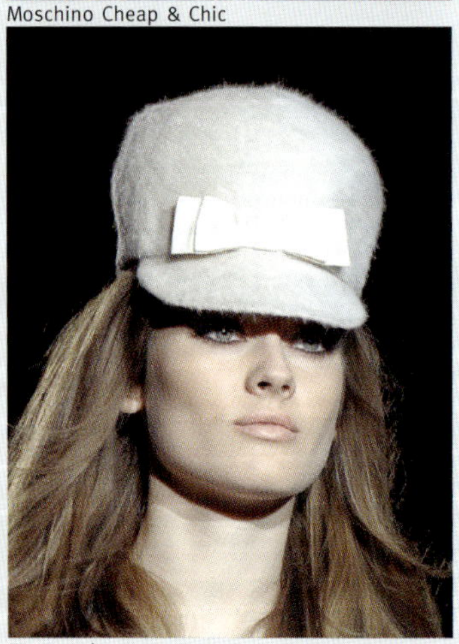

Dsquared2

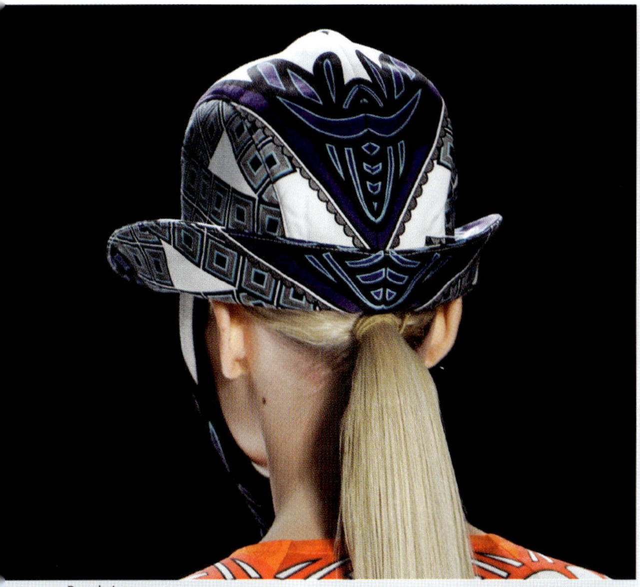

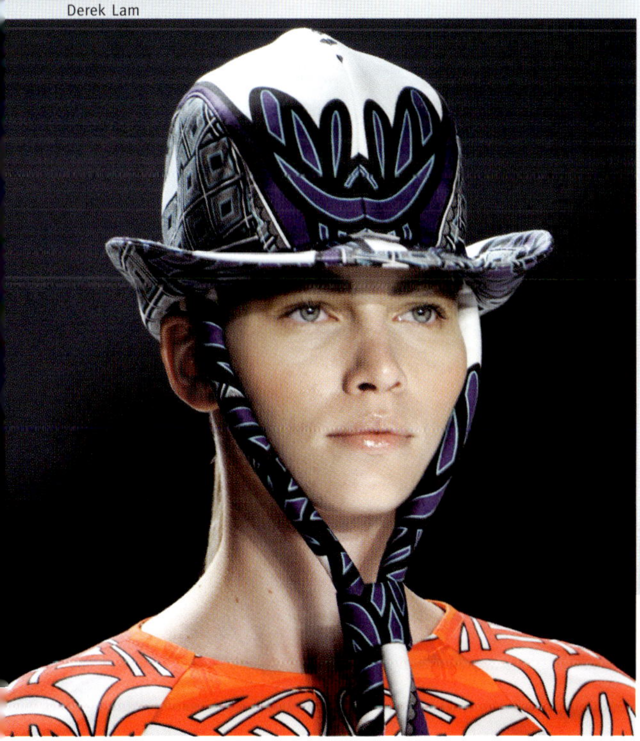

Derek Lam

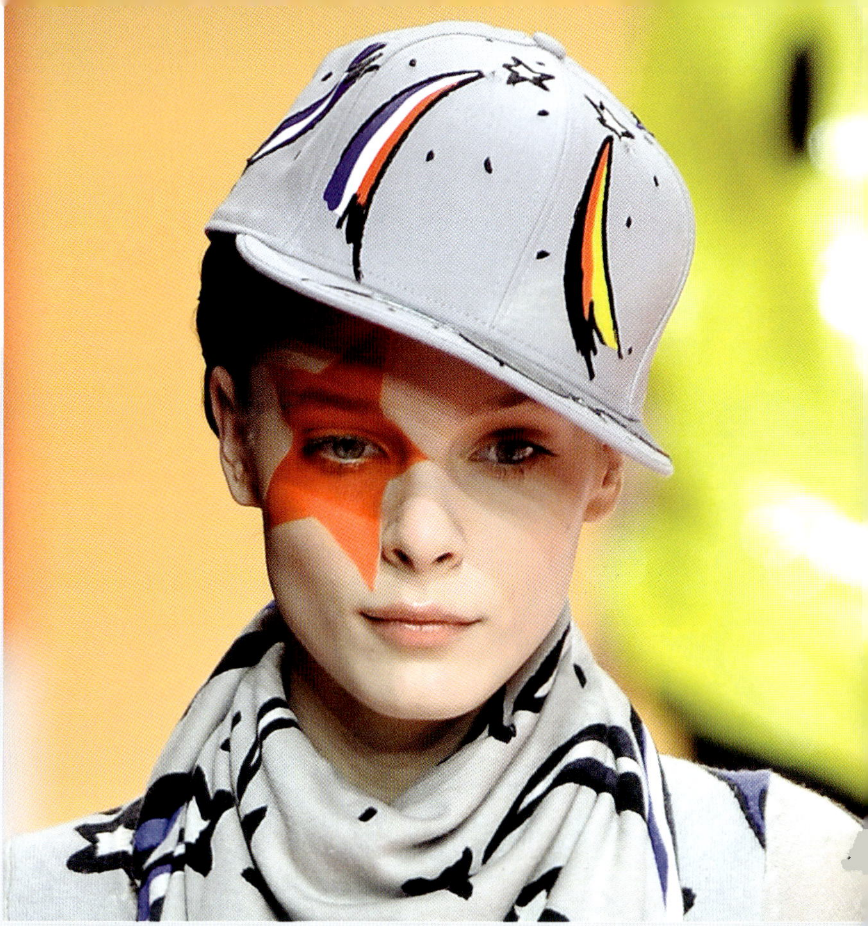

JC de Castelbajac

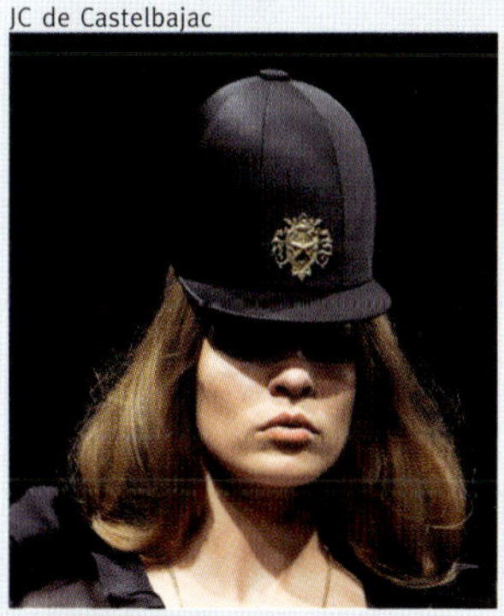

Francesco Scognamiglio

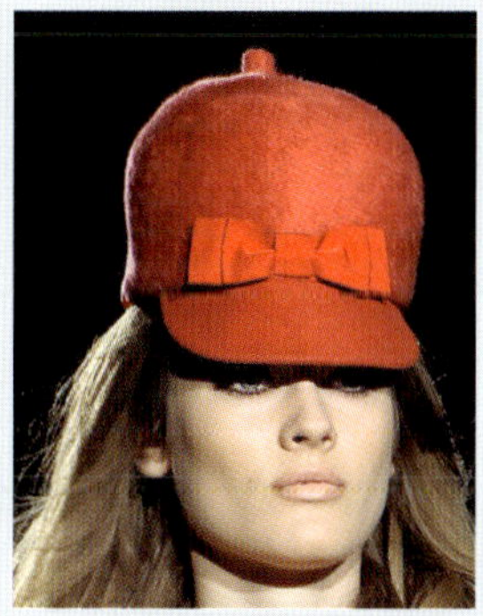

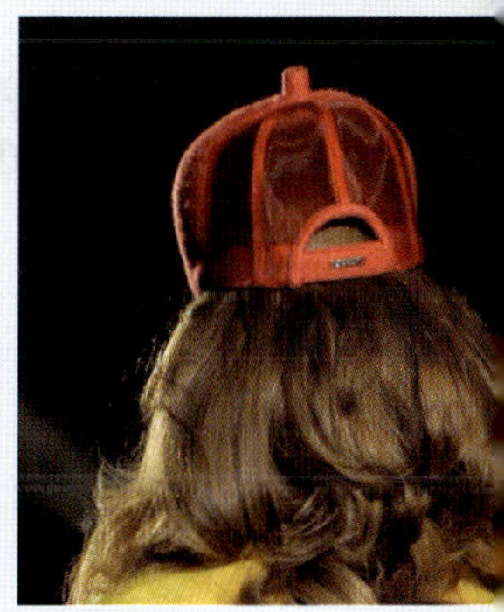

Dsquared2

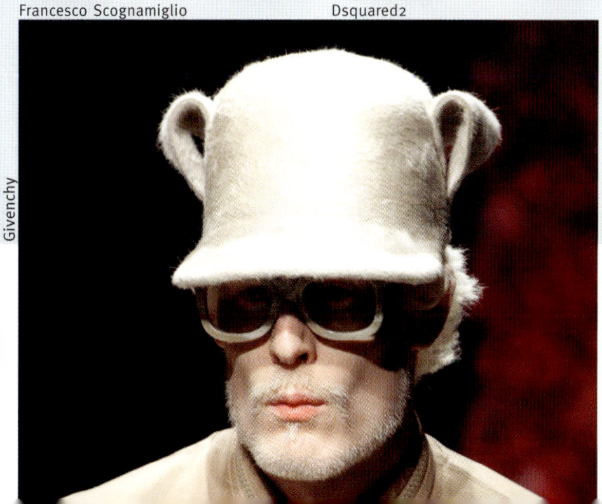

Givenchy

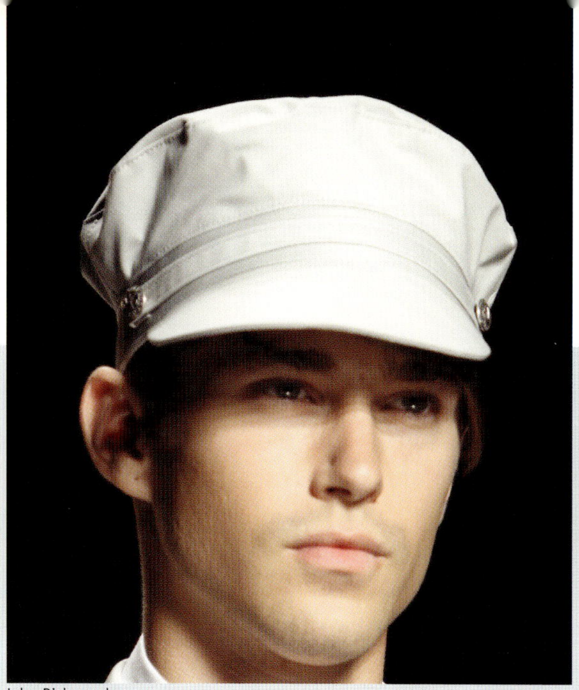
John Richmond

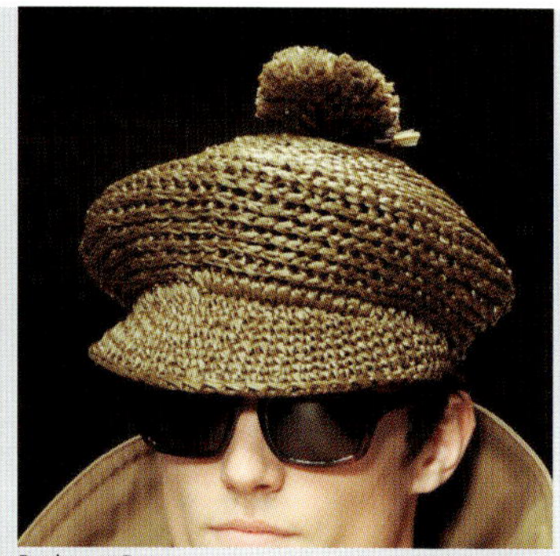
Burberry Prorsum

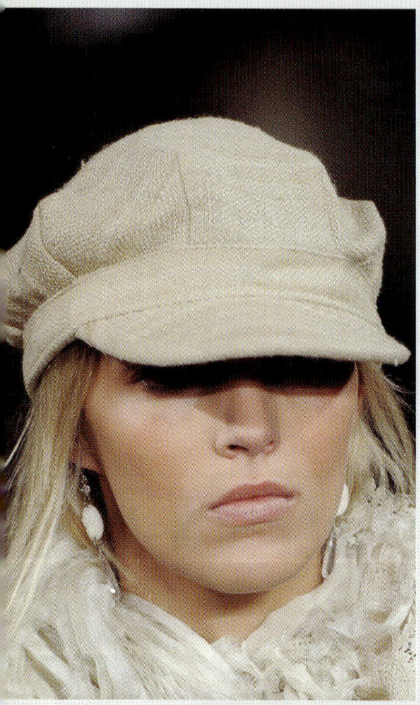
Ralph Lauren

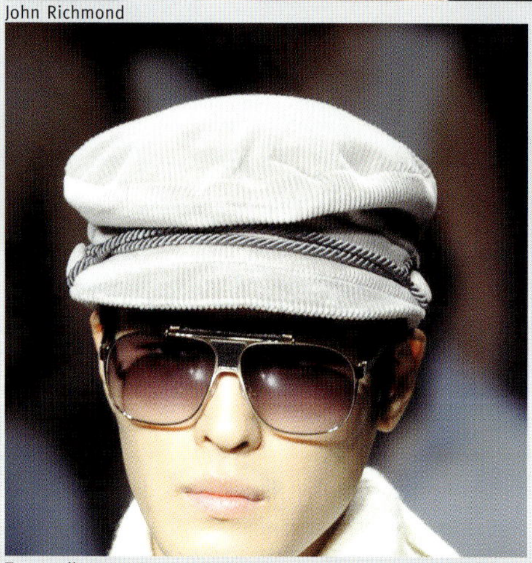
Trussardi

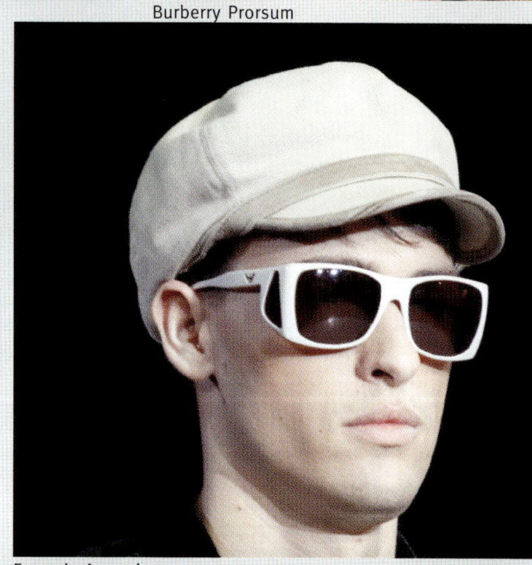
Emporio Armani

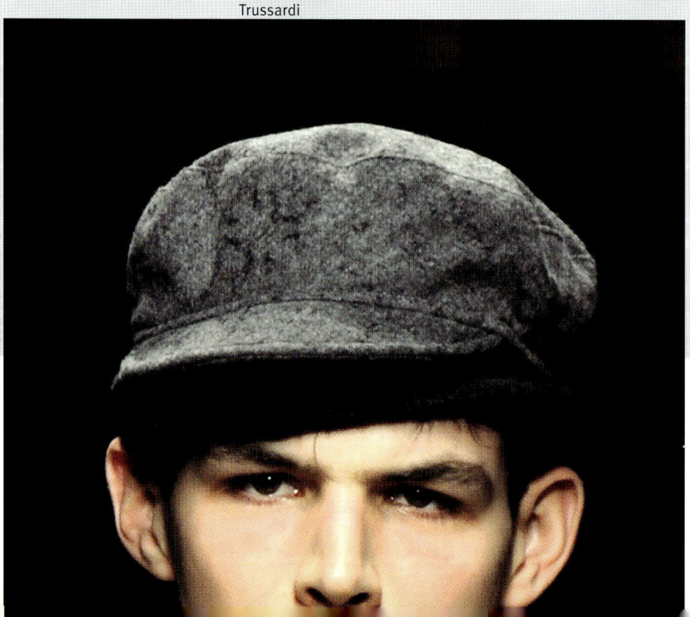
Costume National

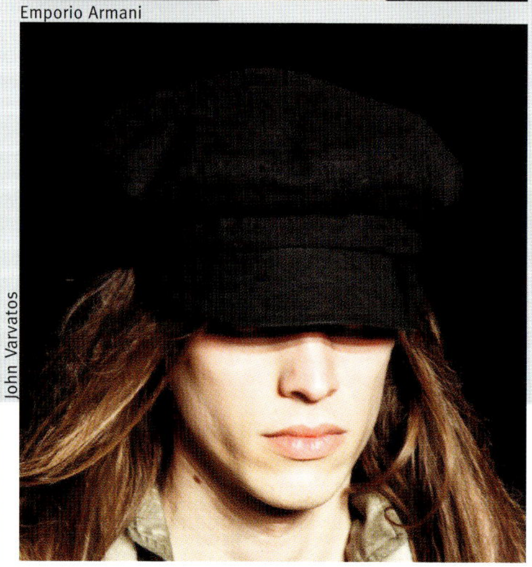
John Varvatos

Vivienne Westwood

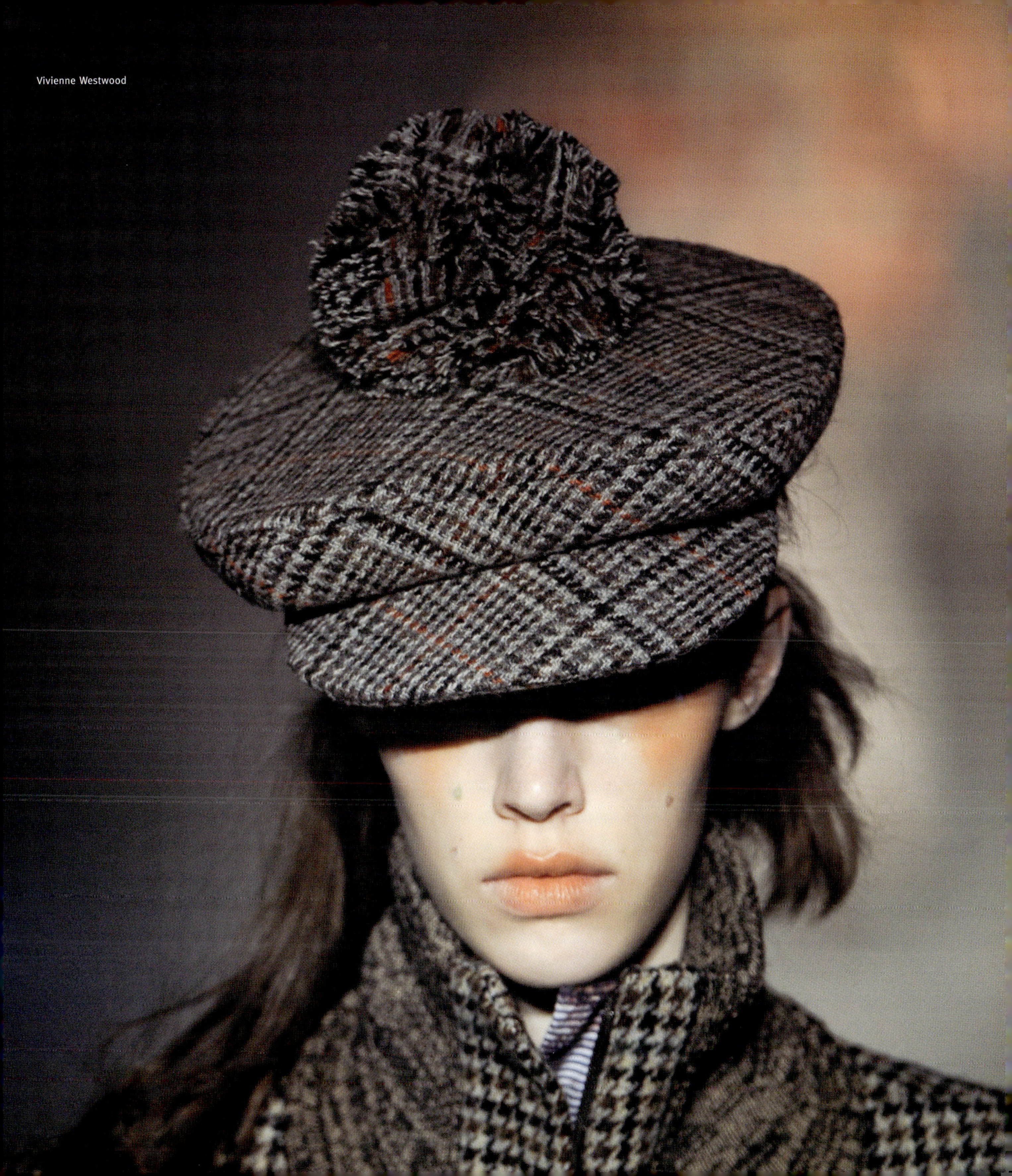

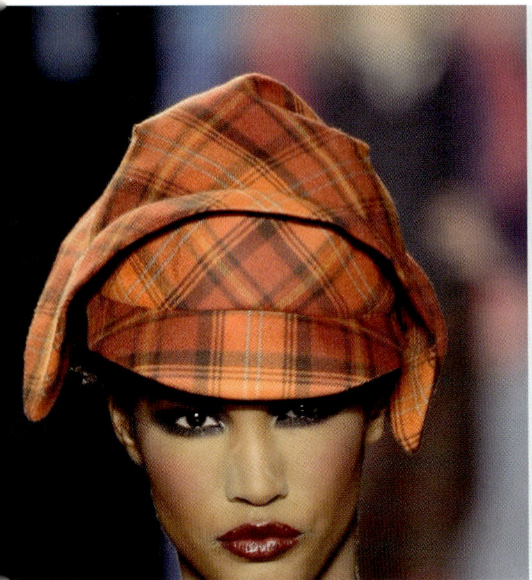

Vivienne Westwood Red Label

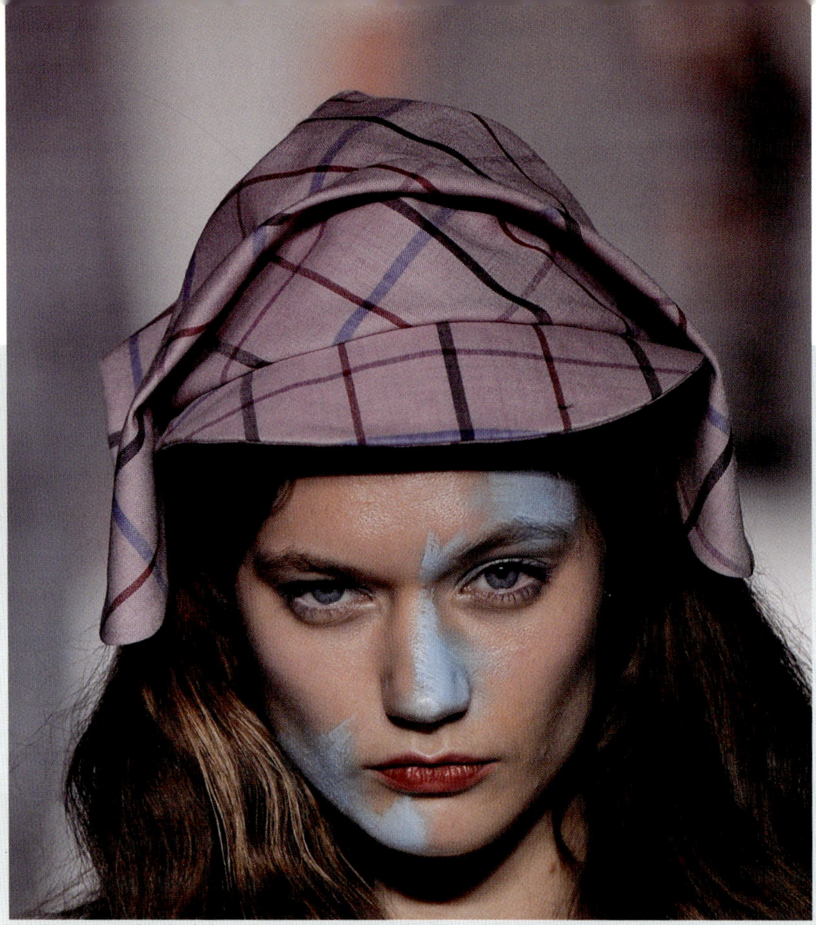

Vivienne Westwood Red Label

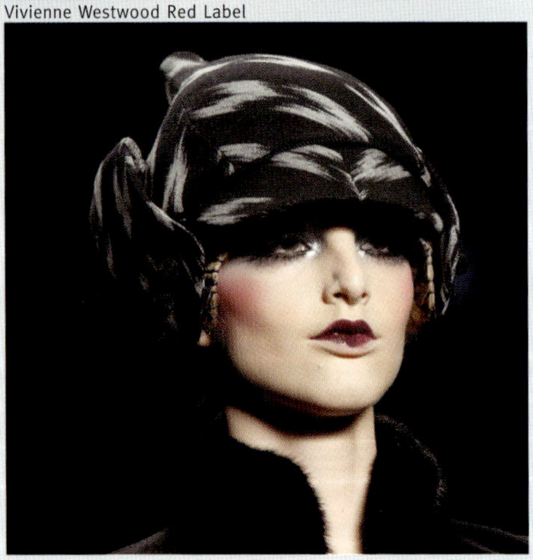

Dior

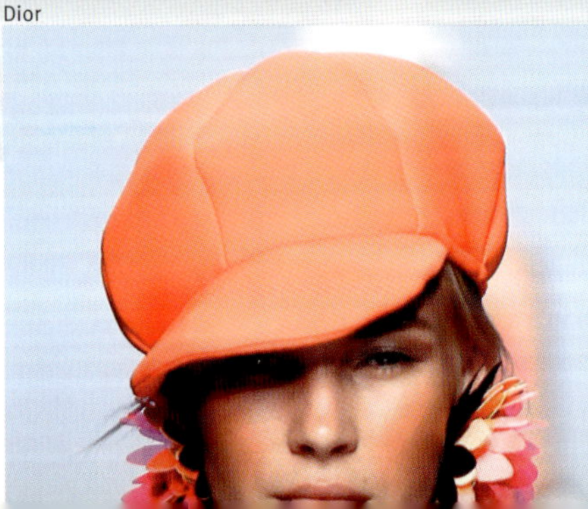

Blumarine

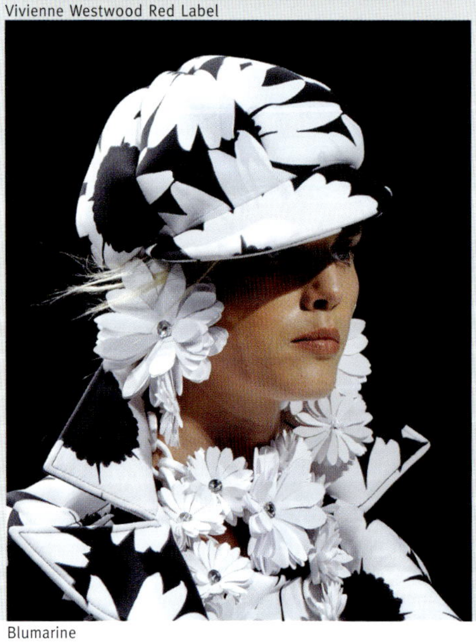

Blumarine

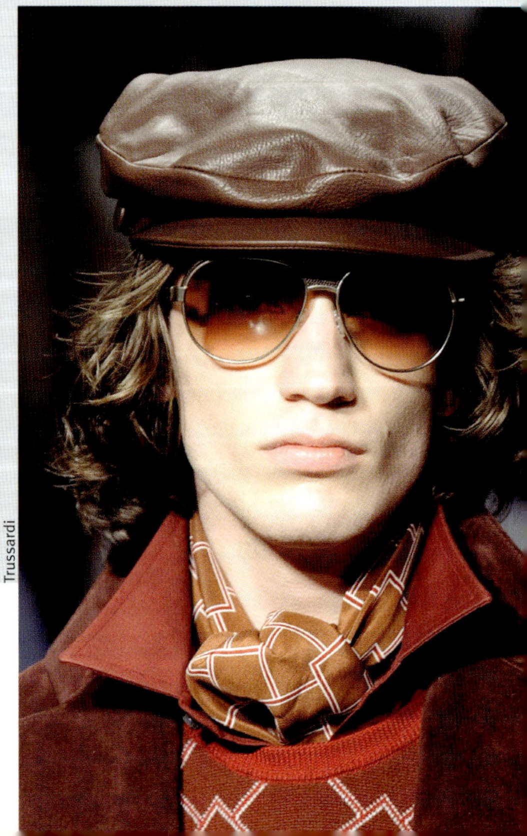

Trussardi

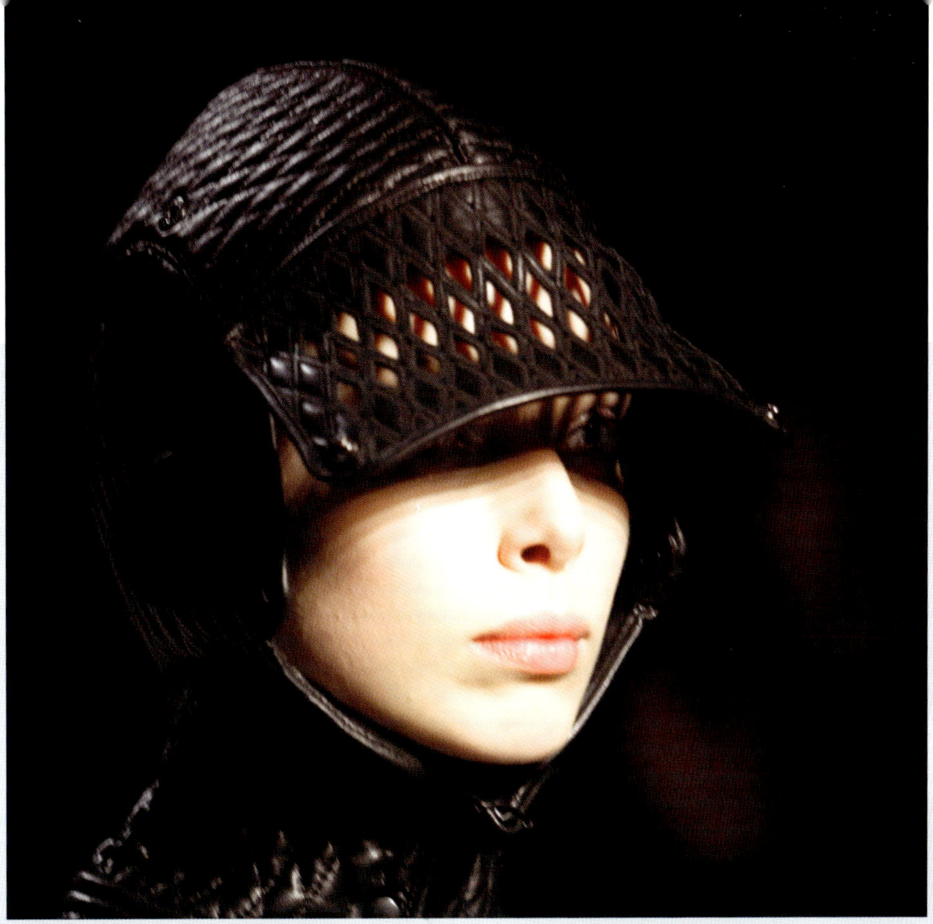

Jean Paul Gaultier

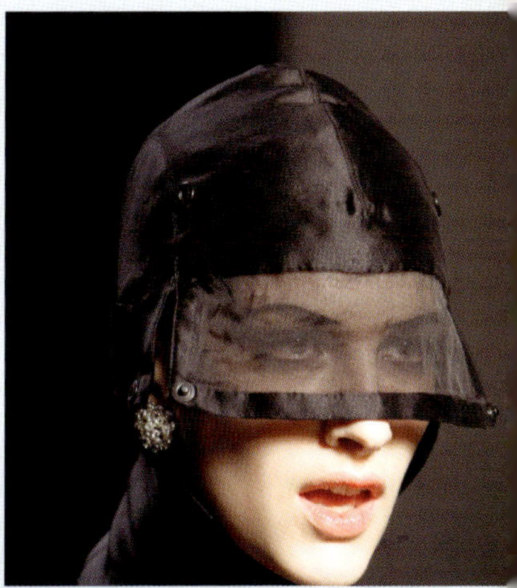

Jean Paul Gaultier

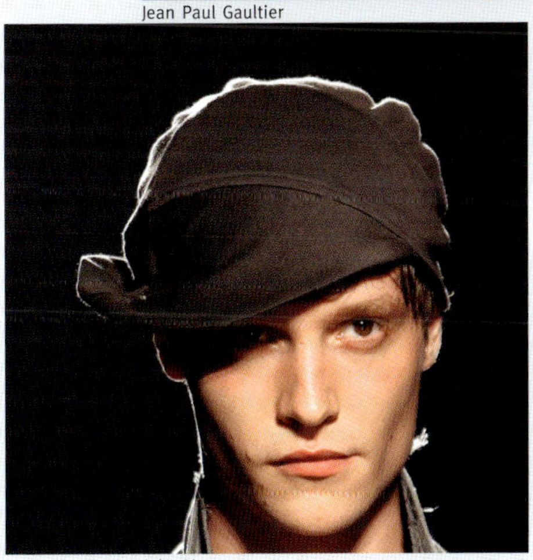

John Varvatos

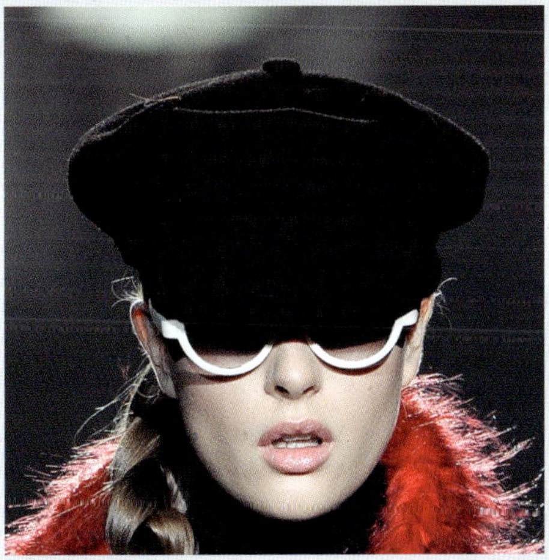

Betsey Johnson

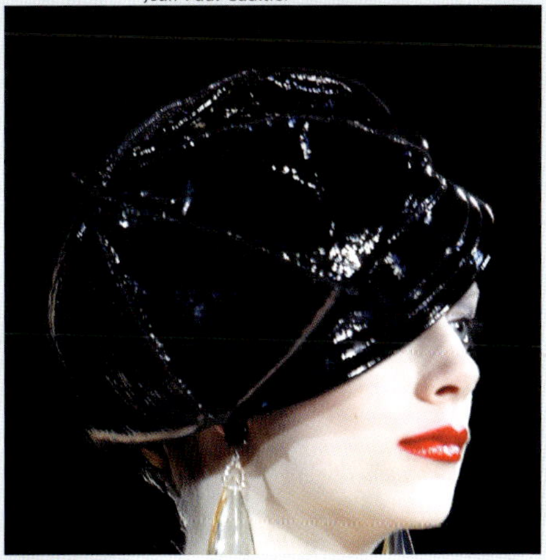

Giorgio Armani

Giorgio Armani

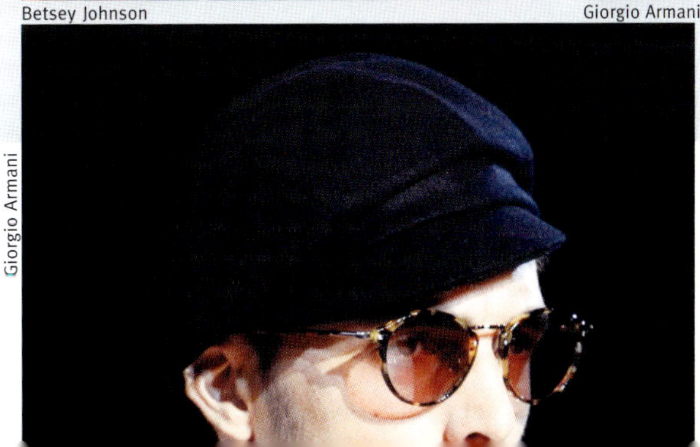

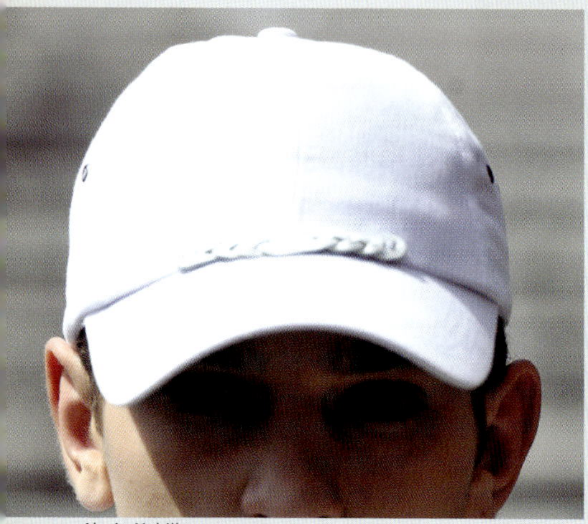

Alexis Mabille

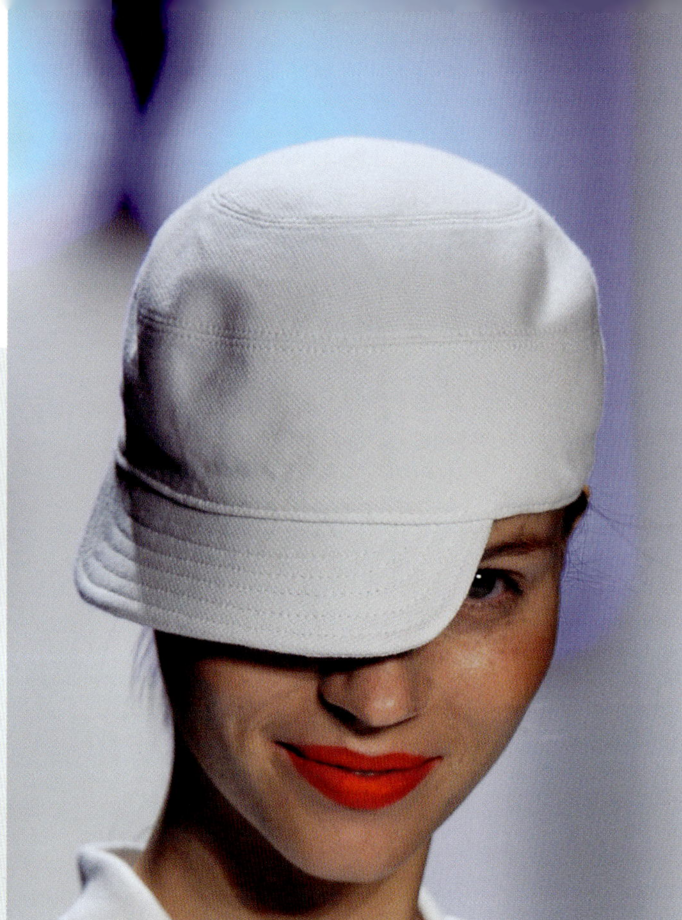

Lacoste

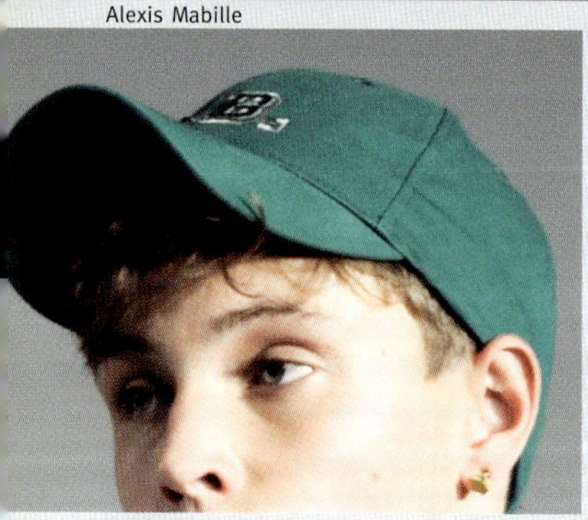

Agnès B.

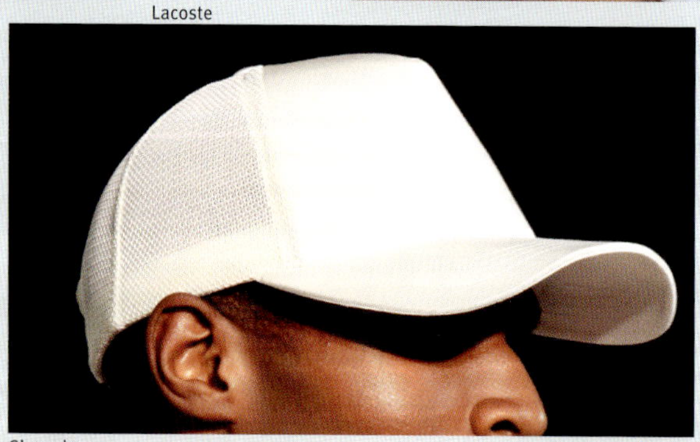

Givenchy

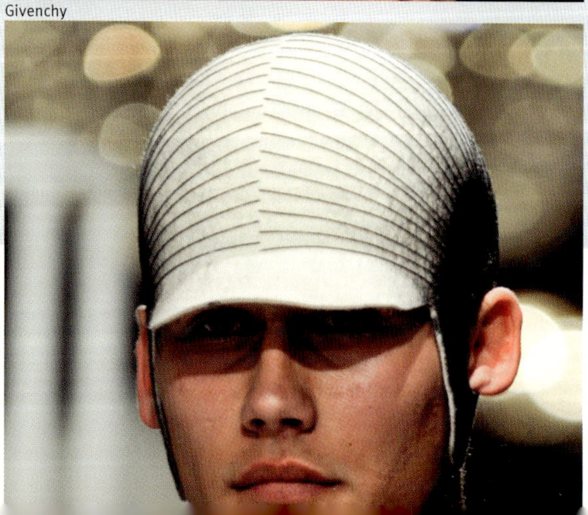

Henrik Vibskov

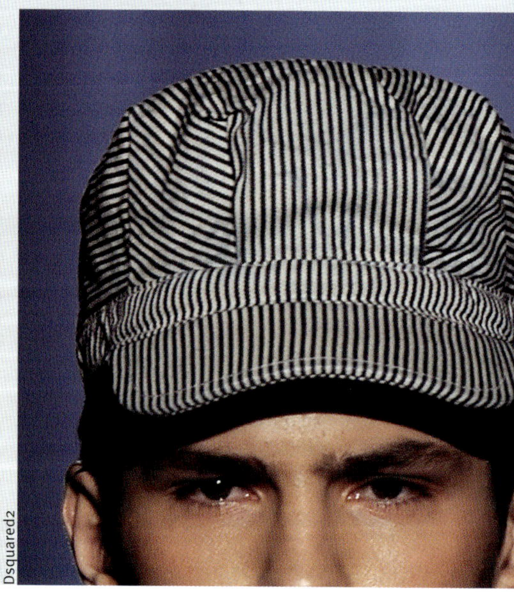

Dsquared2

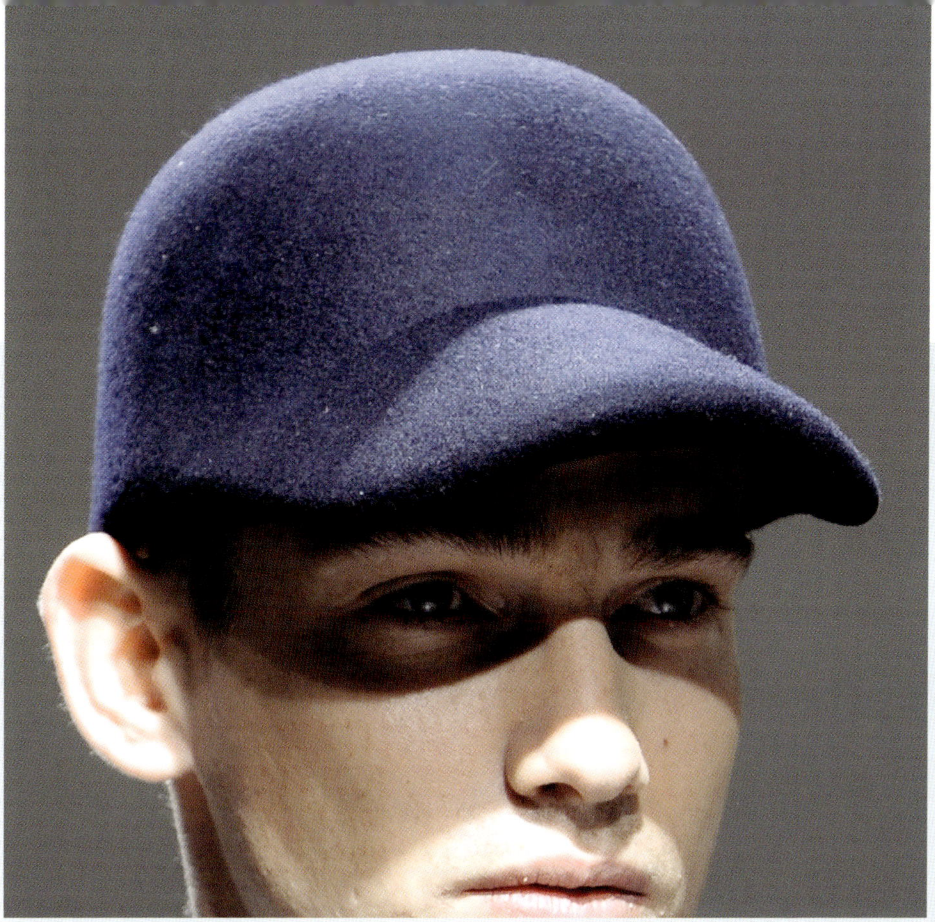
Dirk Bikkembergs

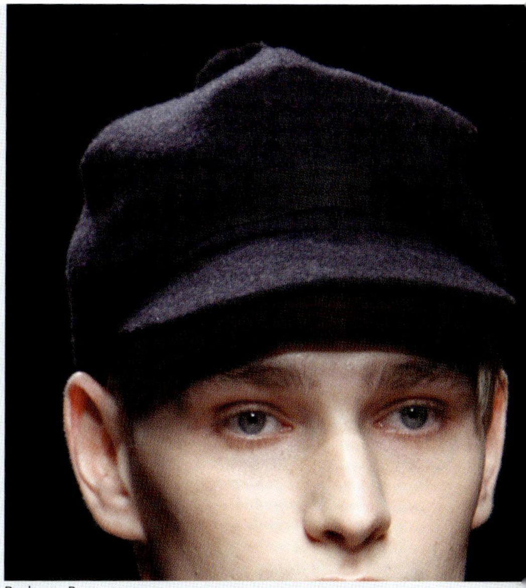
Burberry Prorsum

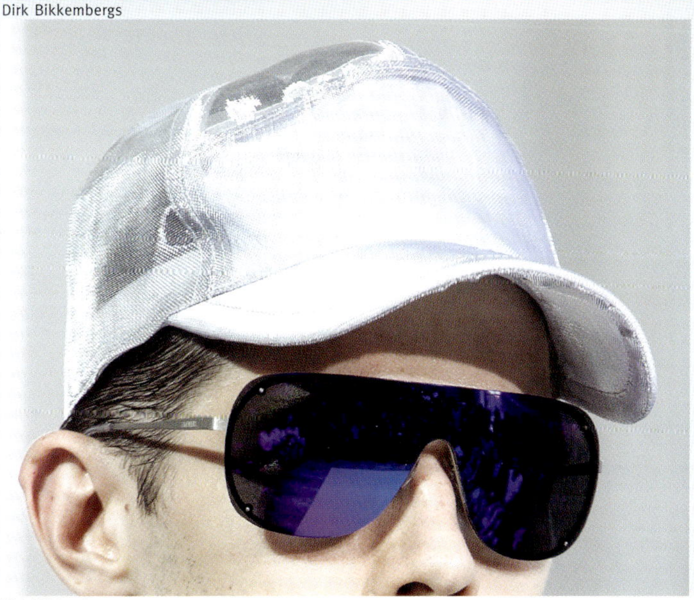
Dirk Bikkembergs

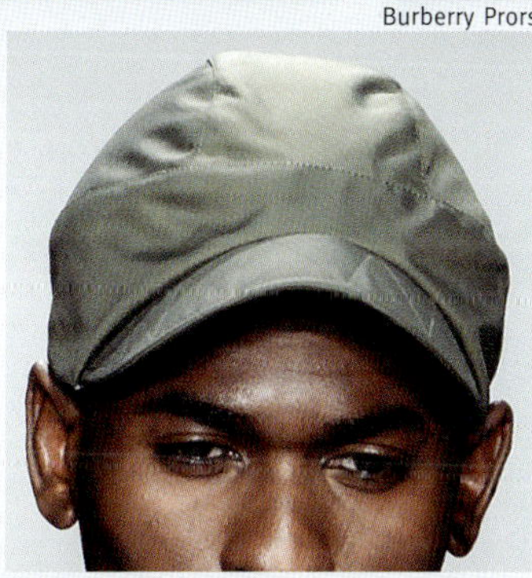
Christopher Raeburn

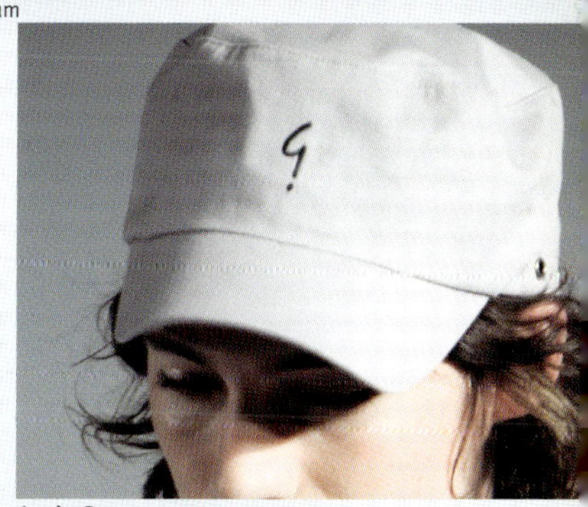
Agnès B.

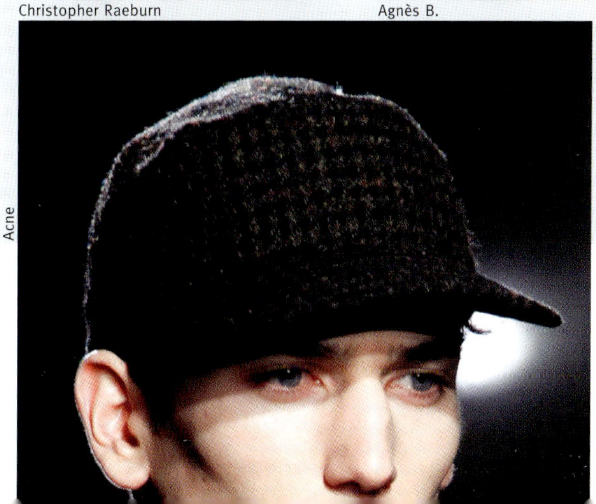
Acne

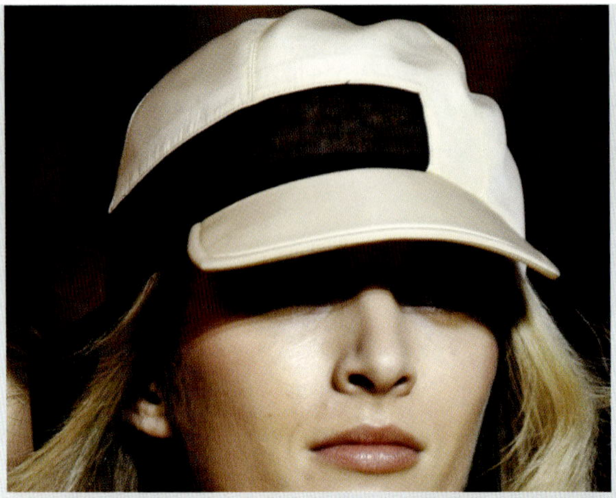

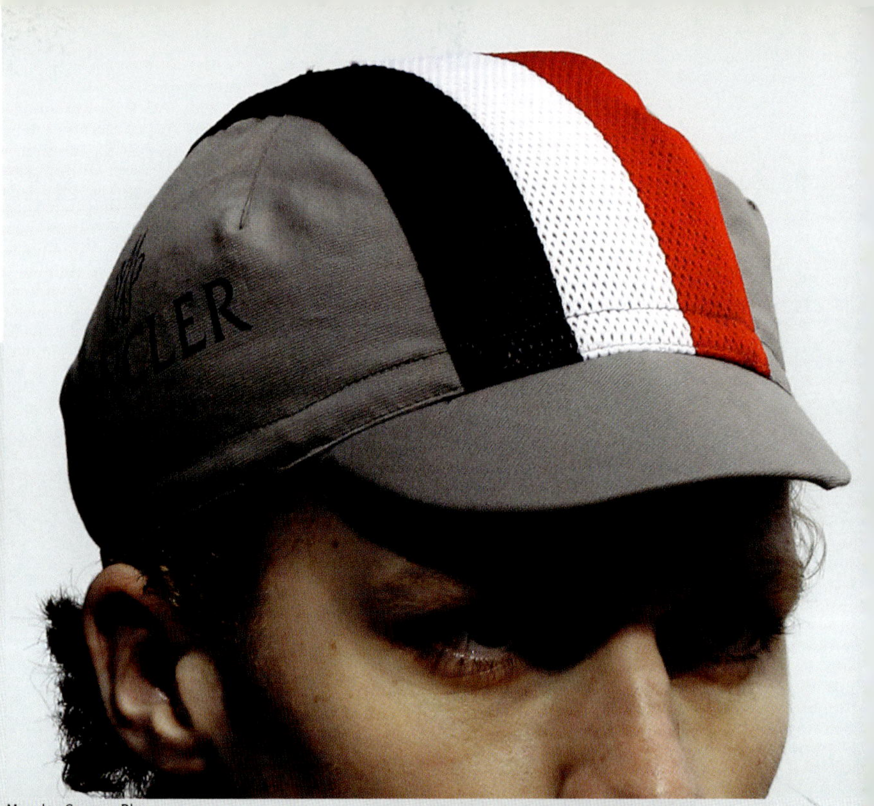

Moncler Gamme Bleu

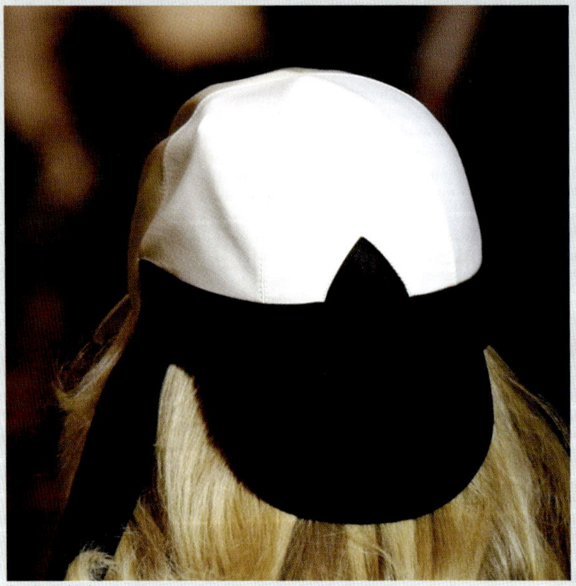

Sonia Rykiel

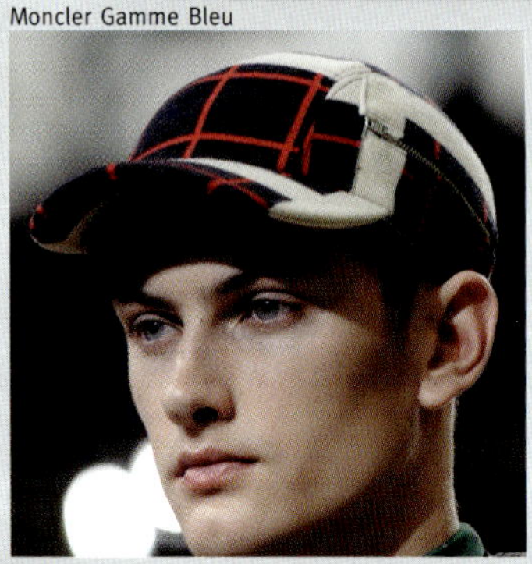

Kenzo

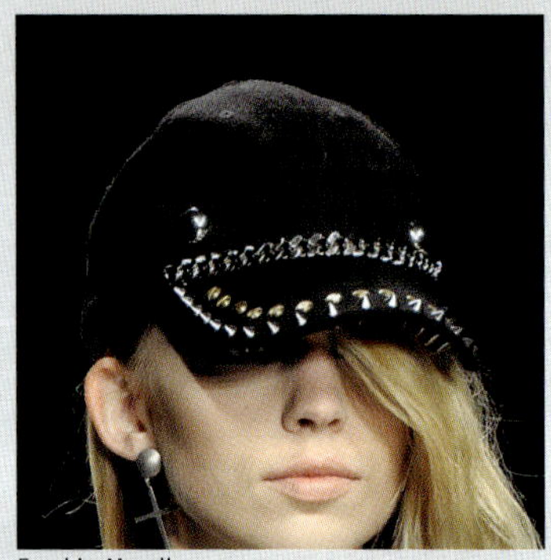

Frankie Morello

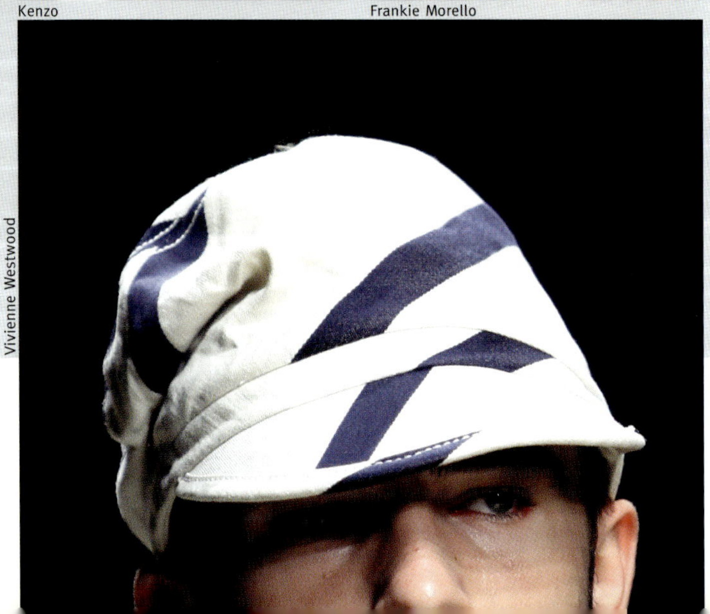

Vivienne Westwood

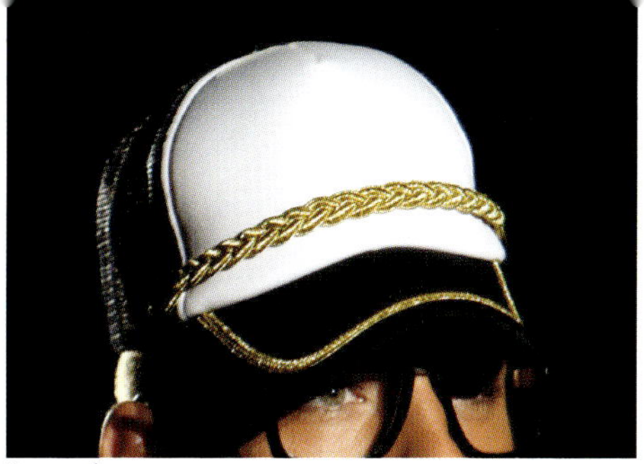

Dsquared2

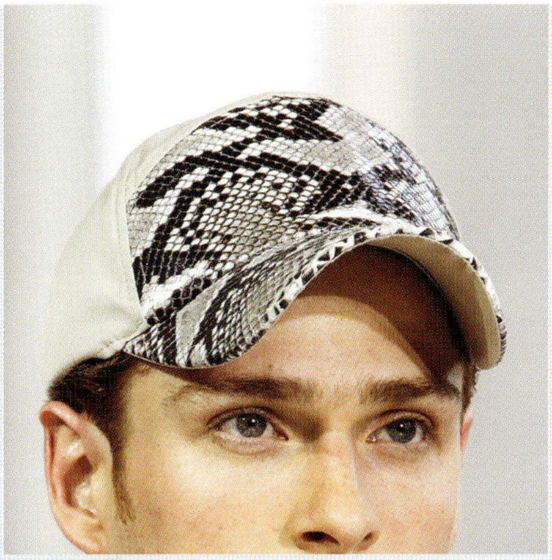

Dirk Bikkembergs

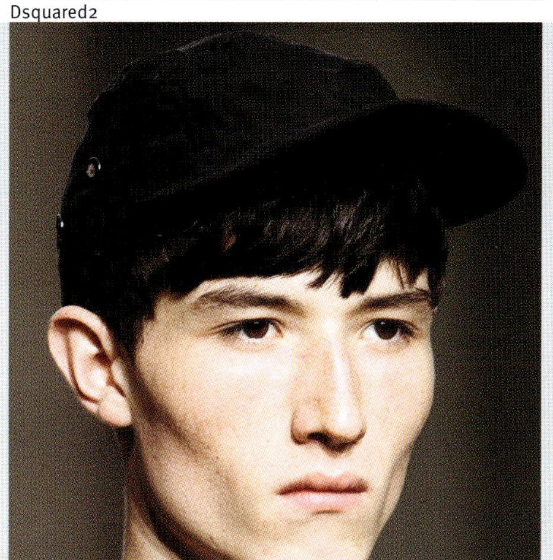

Neil Barrett

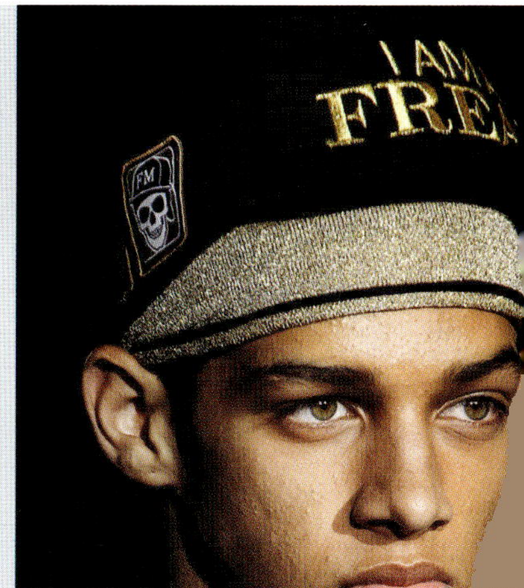

Frankie Morello

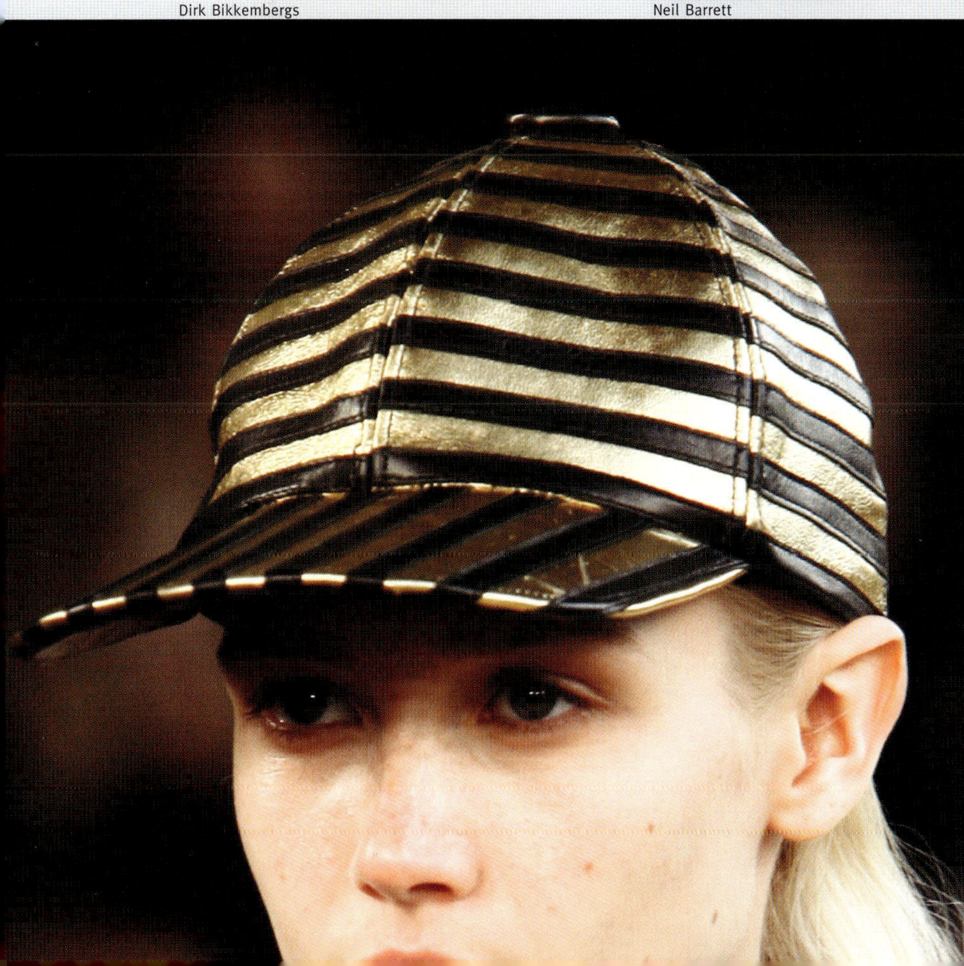

Unique

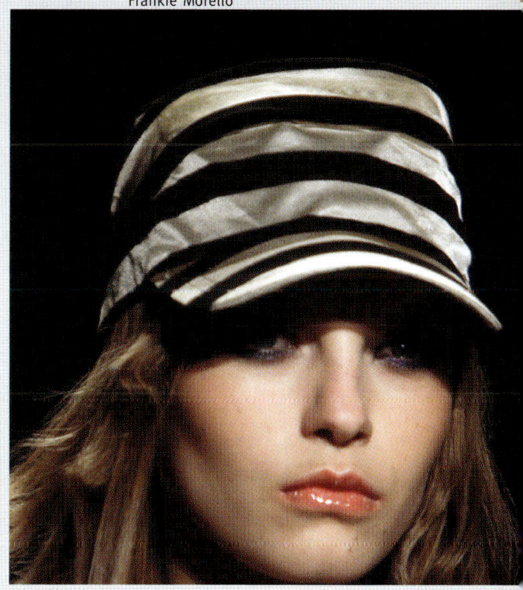

Miss Sixty

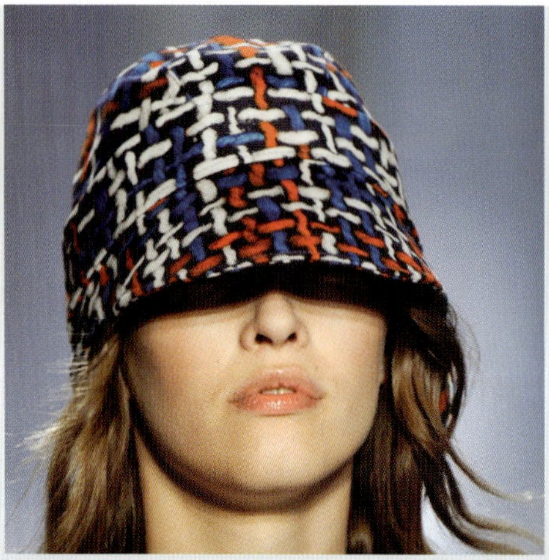
Lacoste

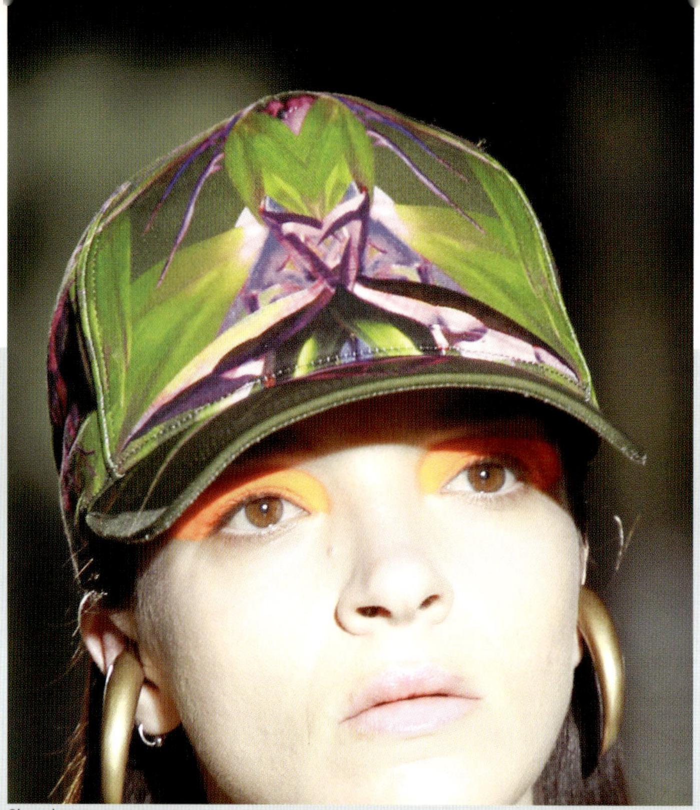
Givenchy

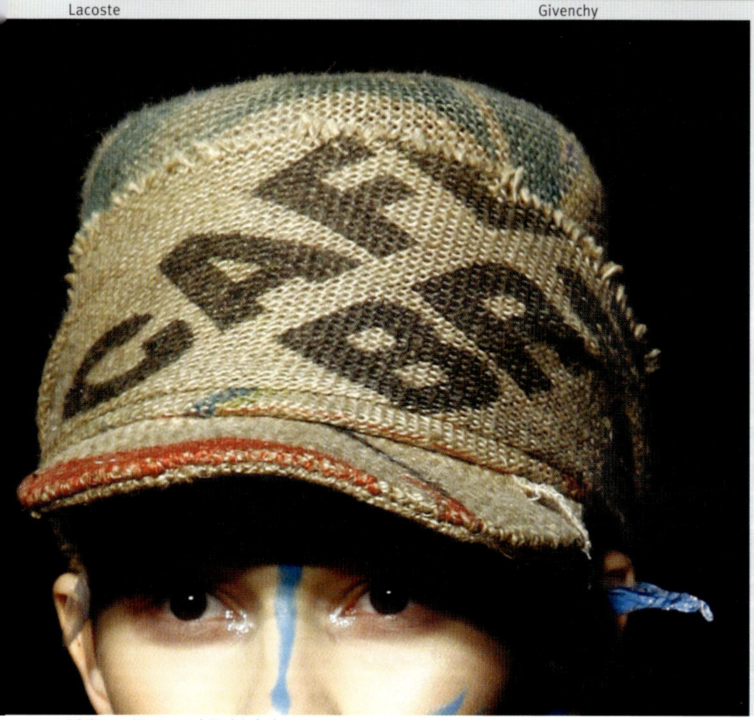
Vivienne Westwood Red Label

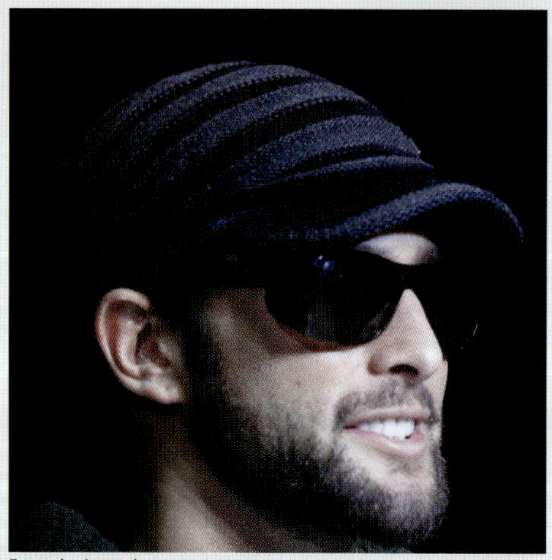
Emporio Armani

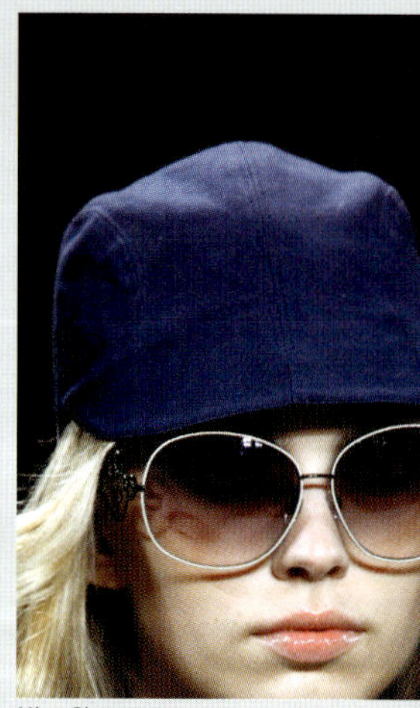
Miss Sixty

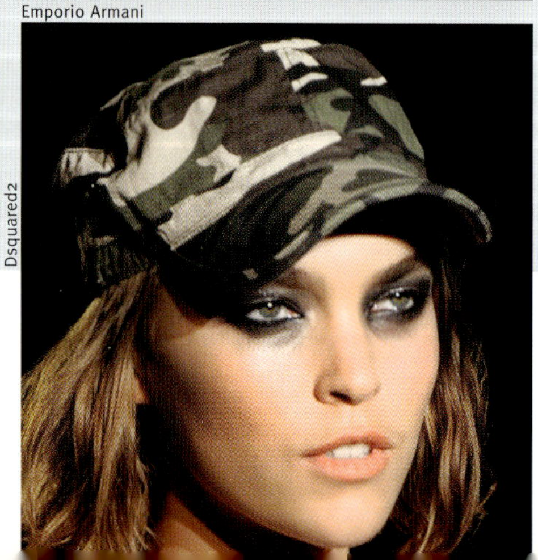
Dsquared2

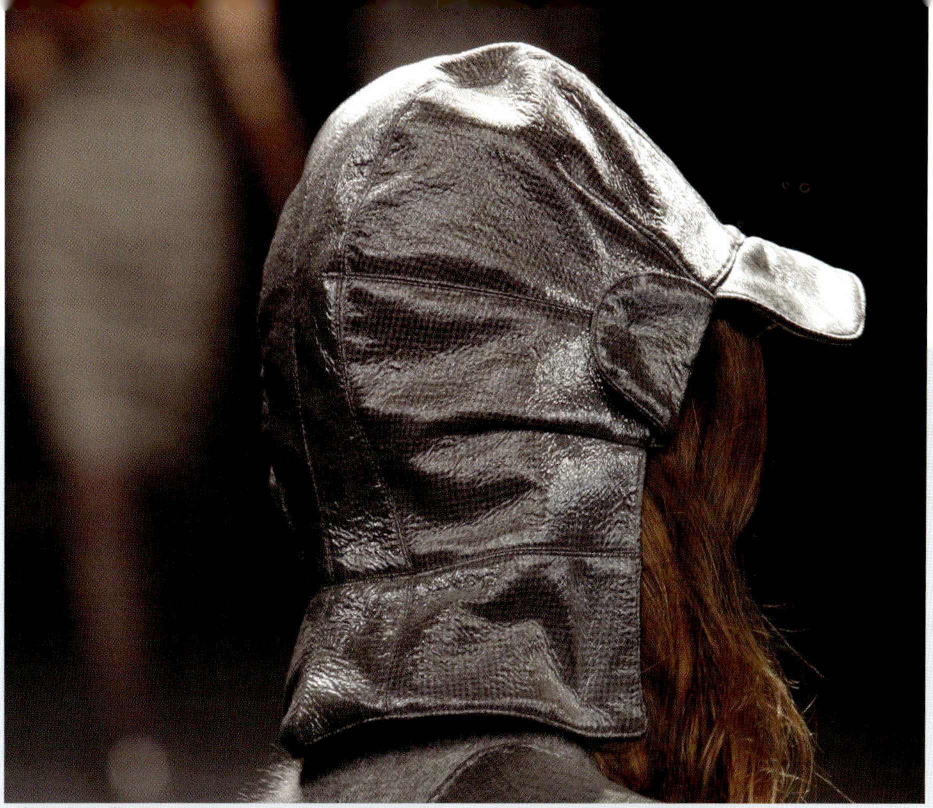

Federico Sangalli

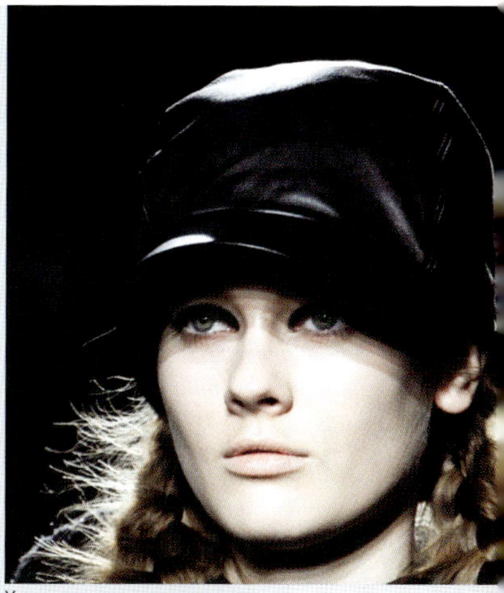

Y3

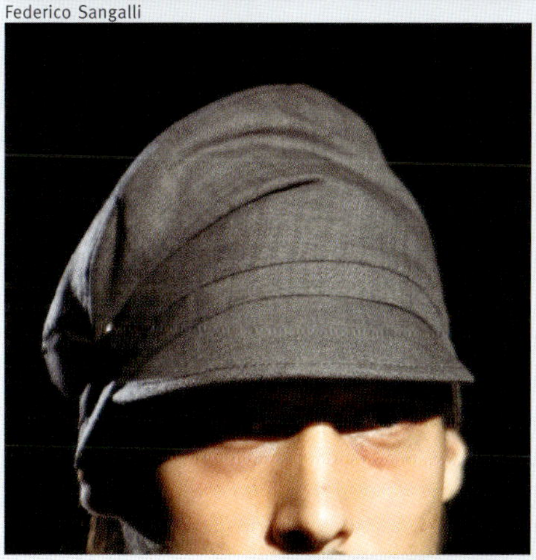

Vivienne Westwood

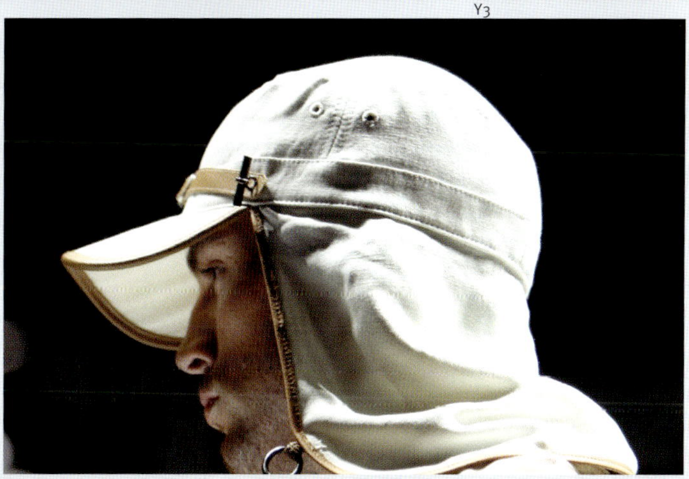

Versace

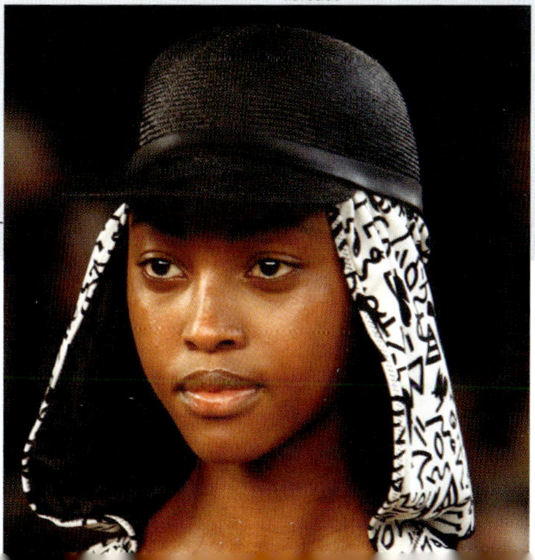

Unique

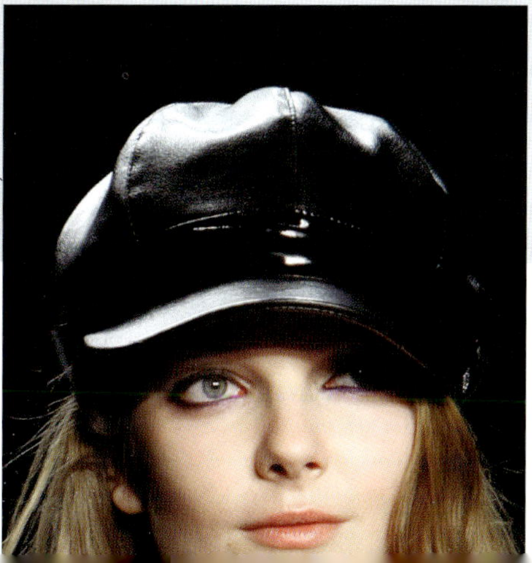

Miss Sixty

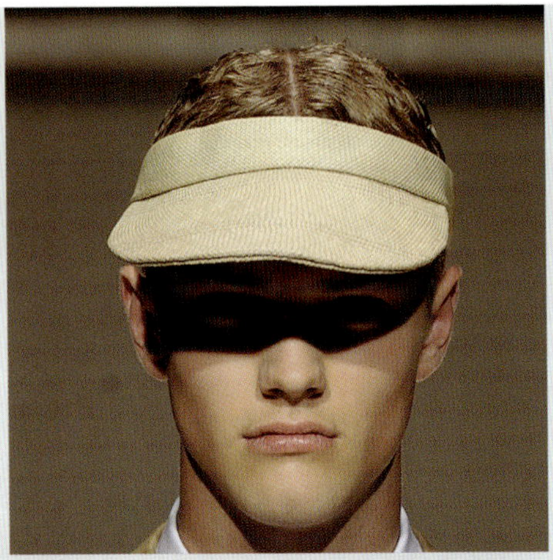
Les Hommes

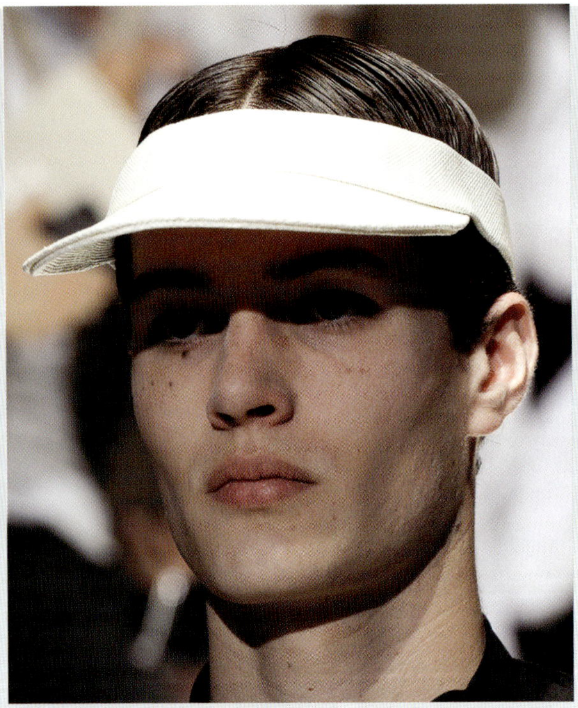
Les Hommes

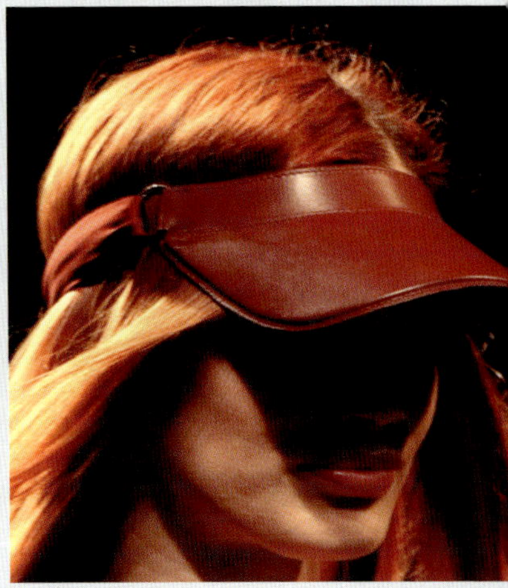
Hermès

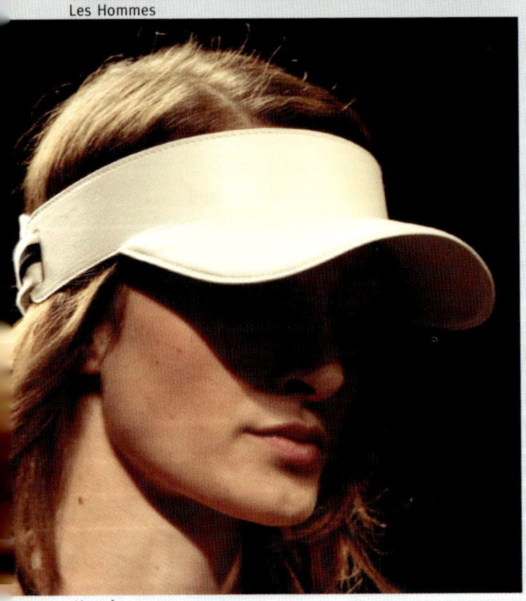
Hermès

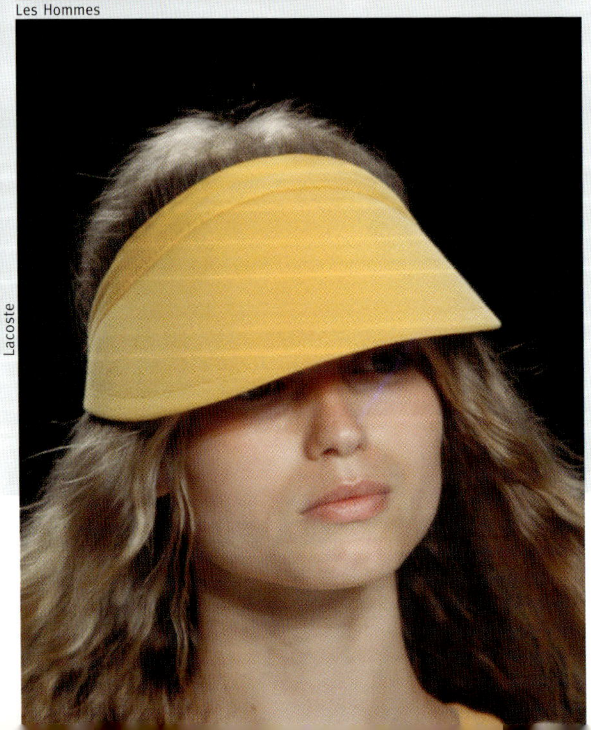
Lacoste

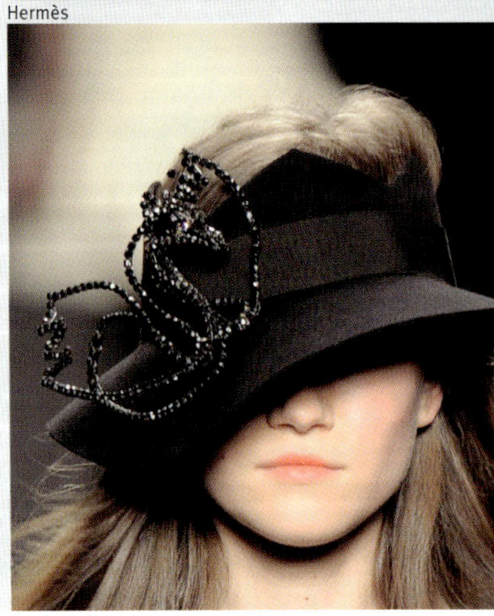
Sonia Rykiel

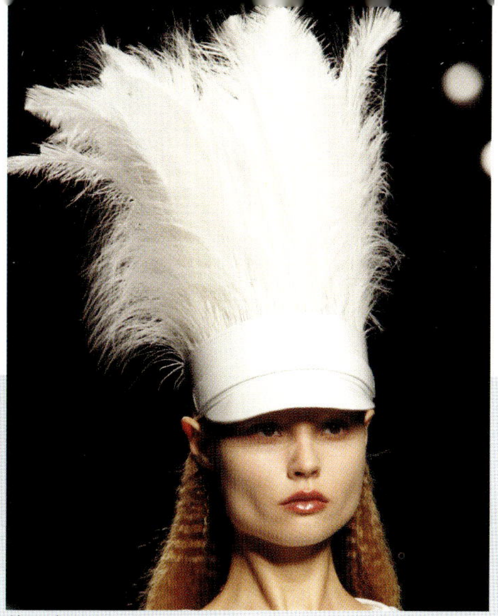

Givenchy

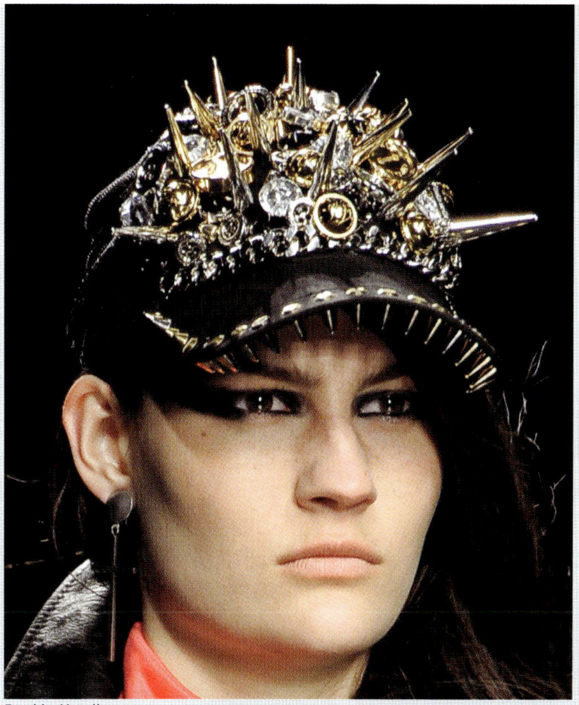

Frankie Morello

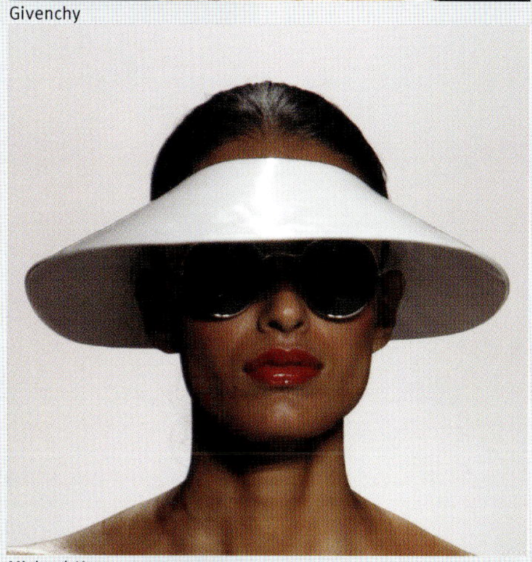

Michael Kors

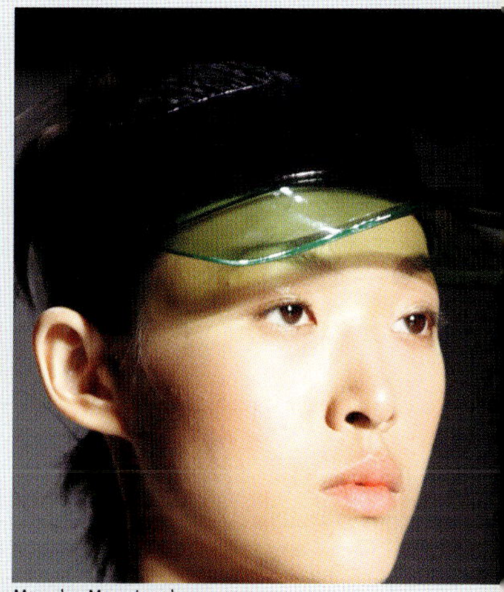

Marc by Marc Jacobs

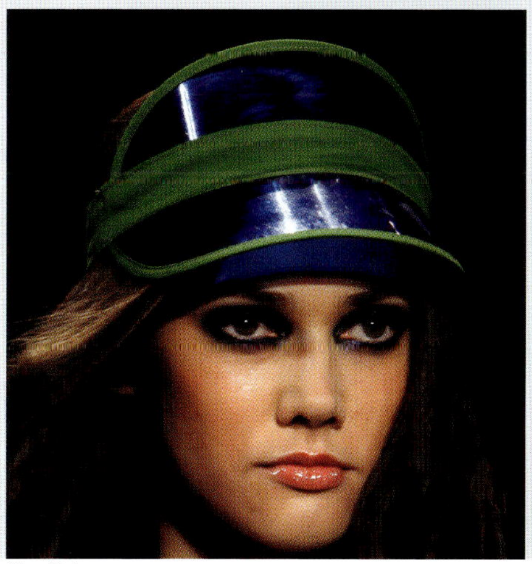

Miss Sixty

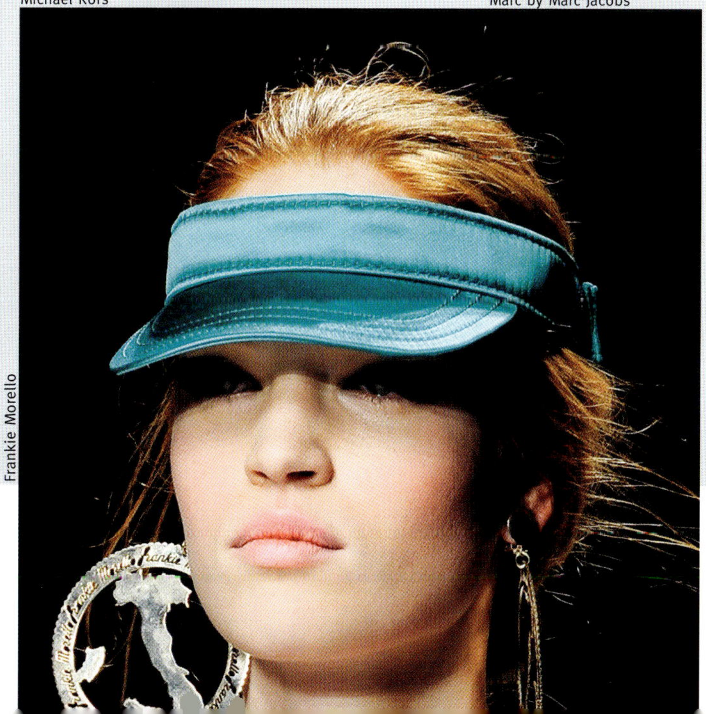

Frankie Morello

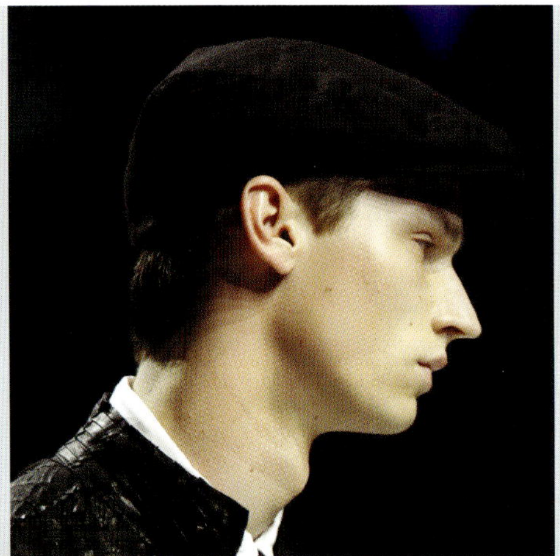

Dolce & Gabbana

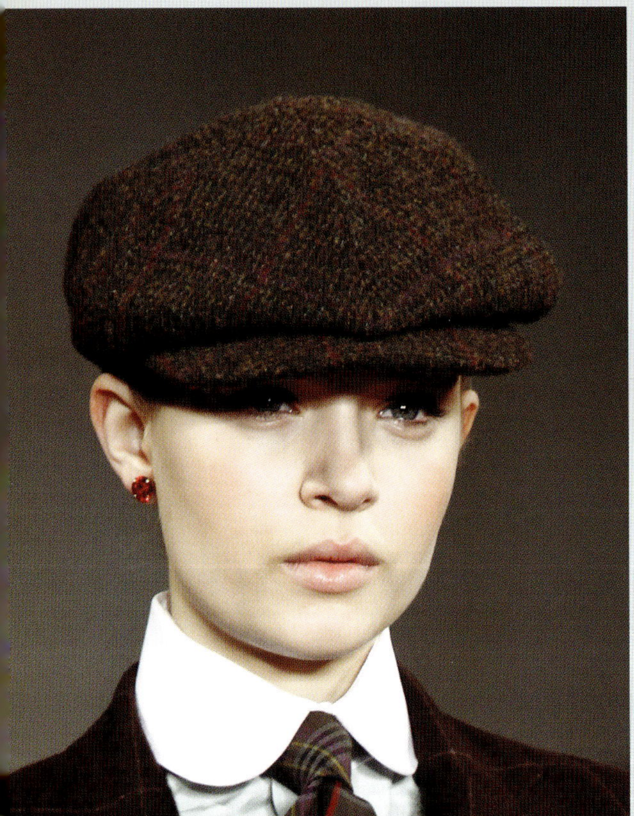

Ralph Lauren

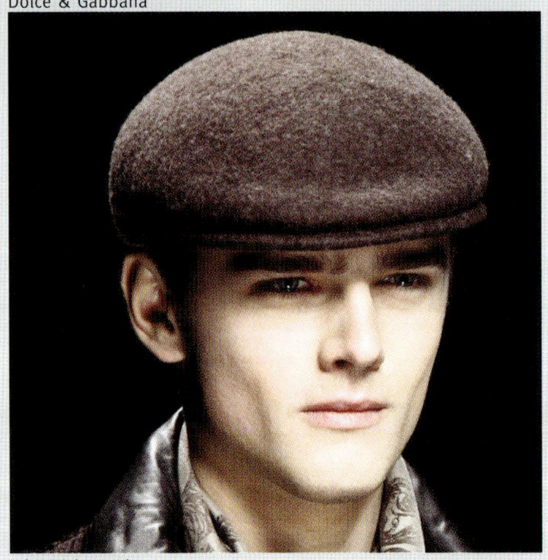

John Richmond

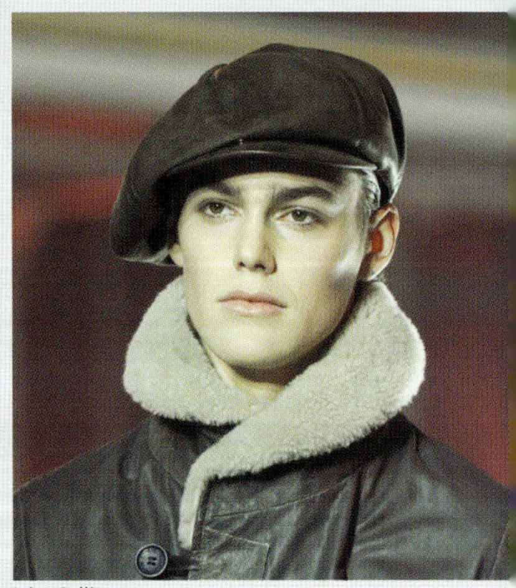

John Galliano

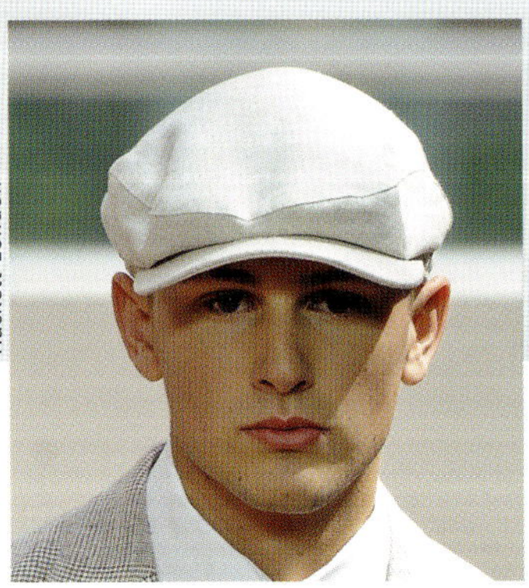

Hackett London

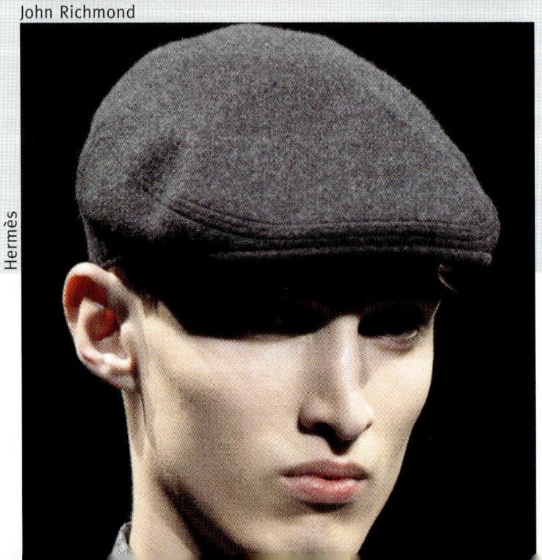

Hermès

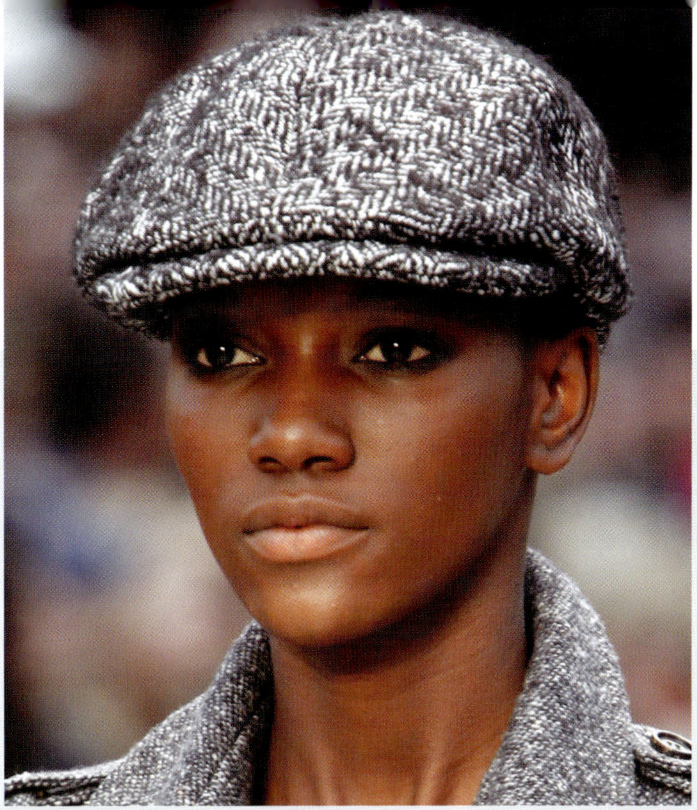
Burberry Prorsum

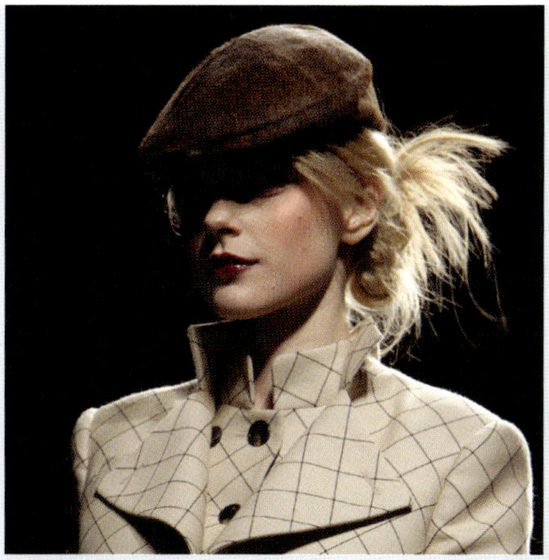
Dior

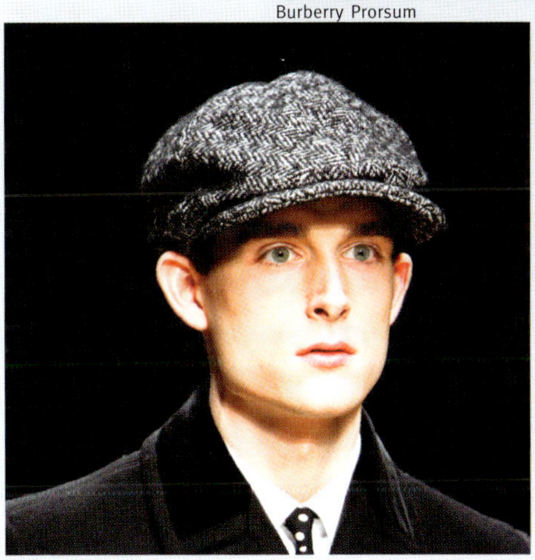
Burberry Prorsum

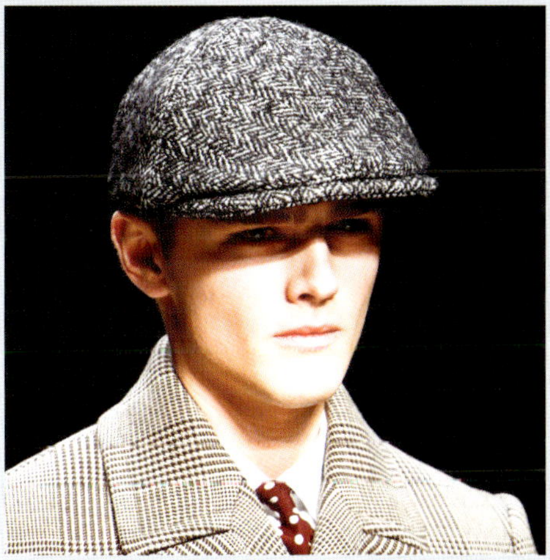
Burberry Prorsum

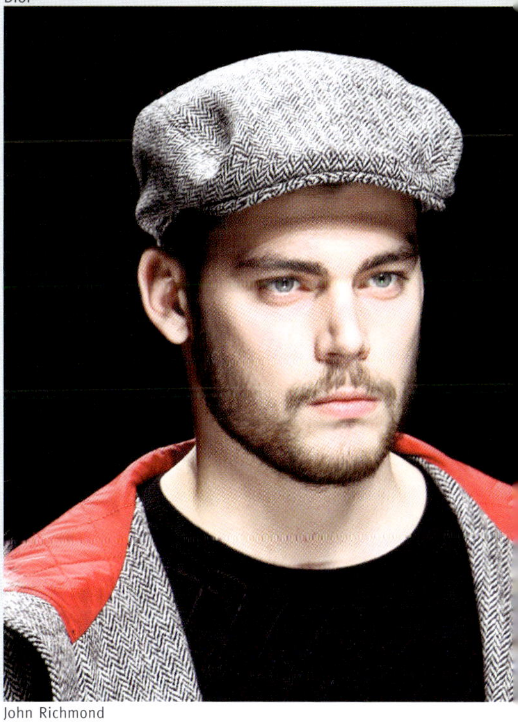
John Richmond

John Galliano
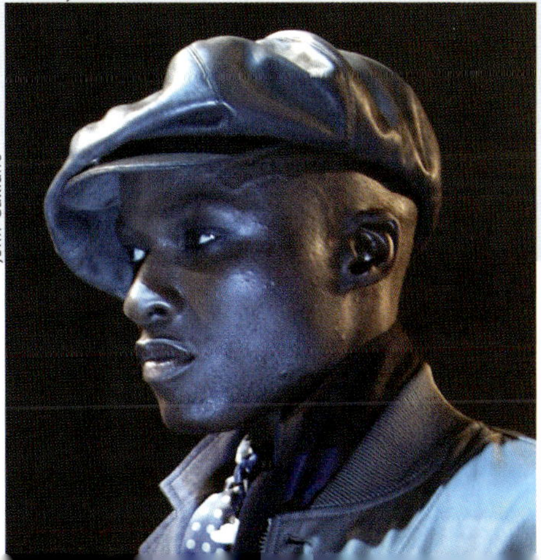

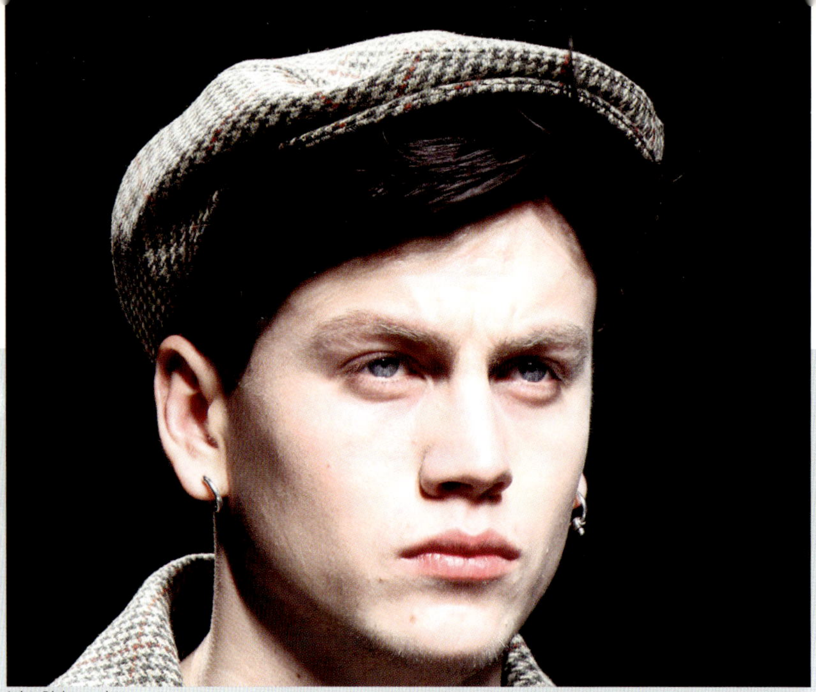

John Richmond

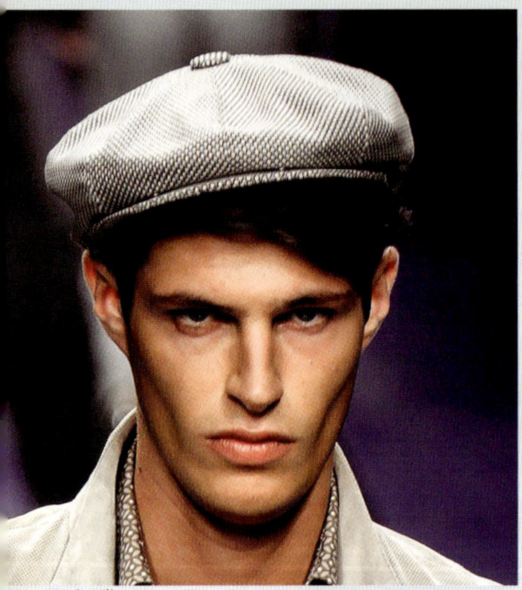

Canali

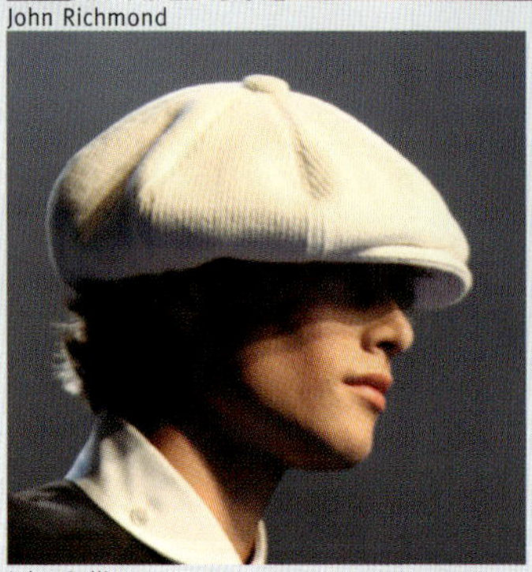

John Galliano

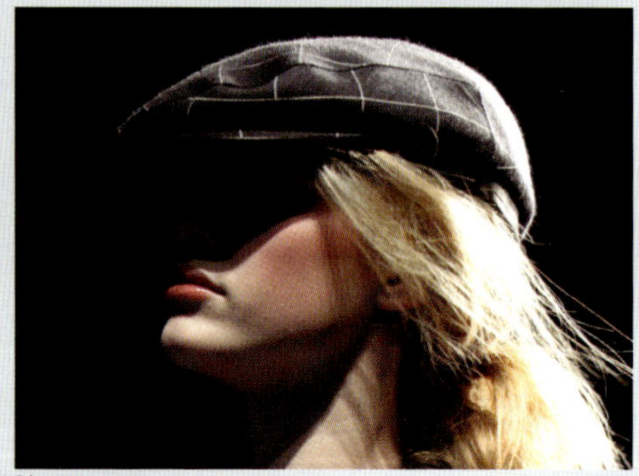

Dior

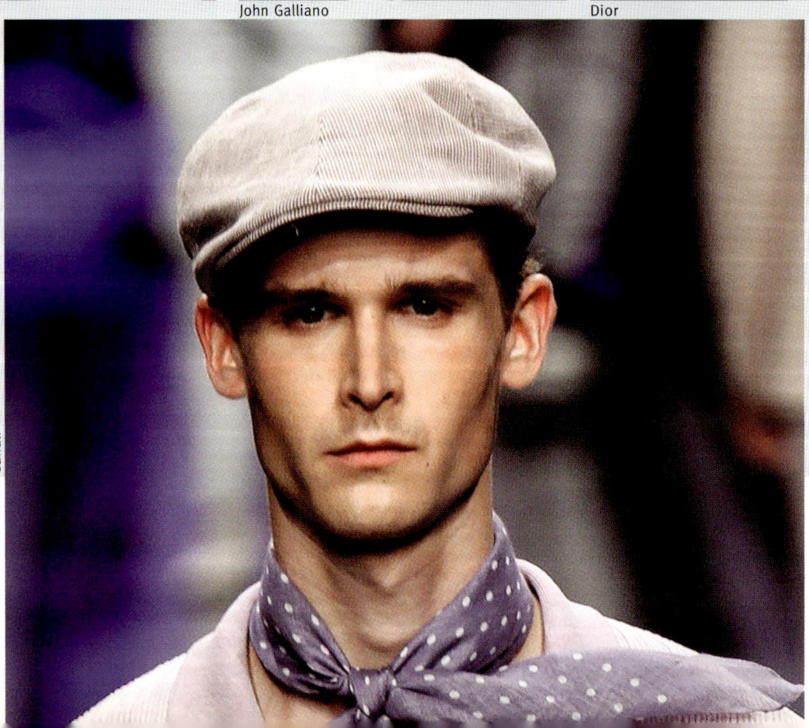

Canali

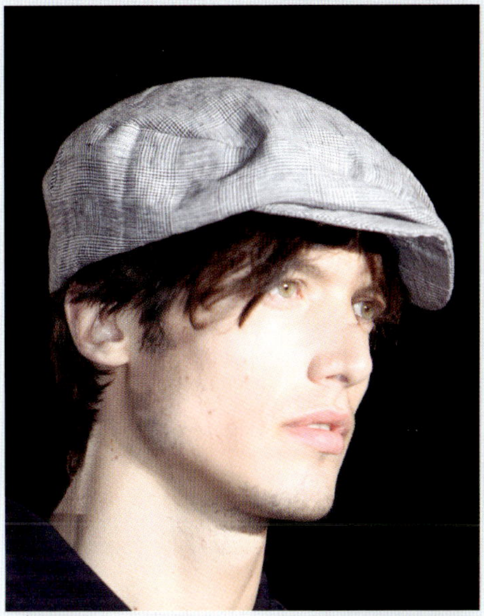
Iceberg

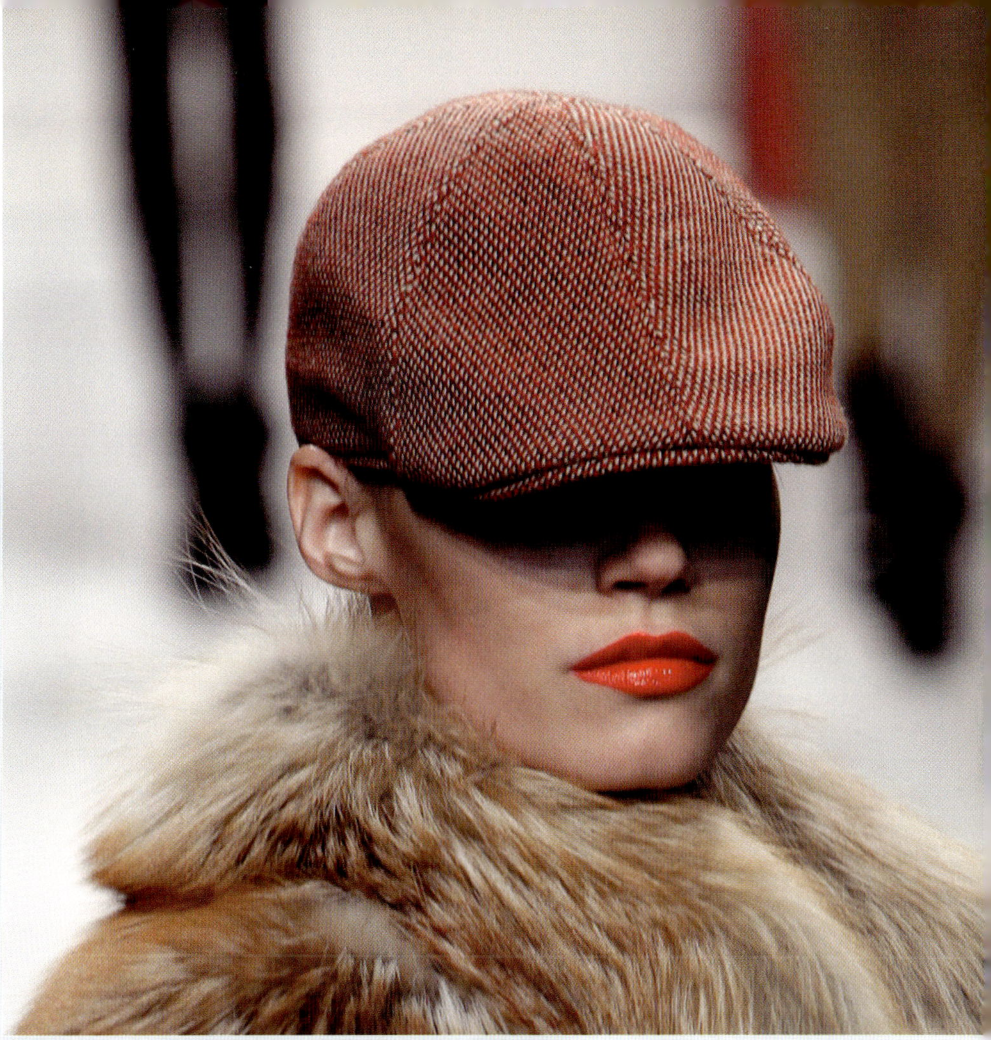
Aigner

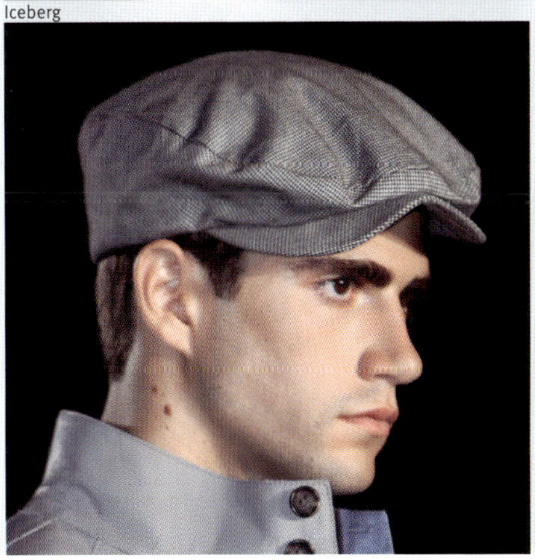
Iceberg

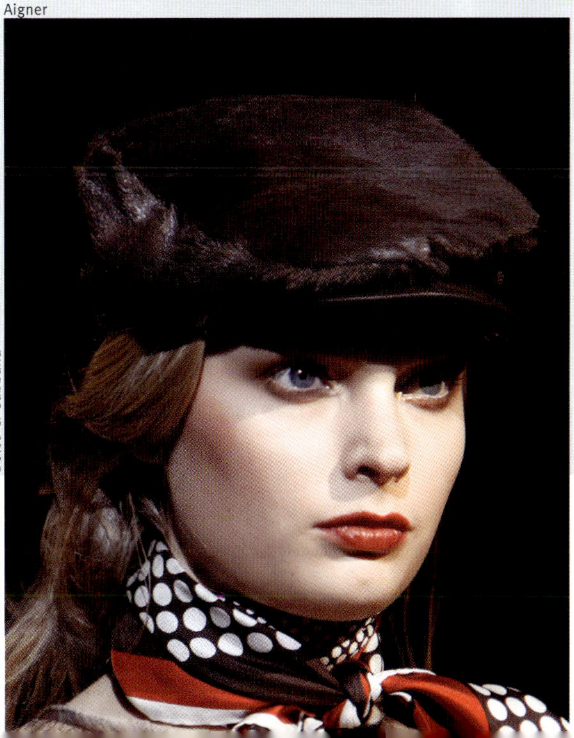
Dolce & Gabbana

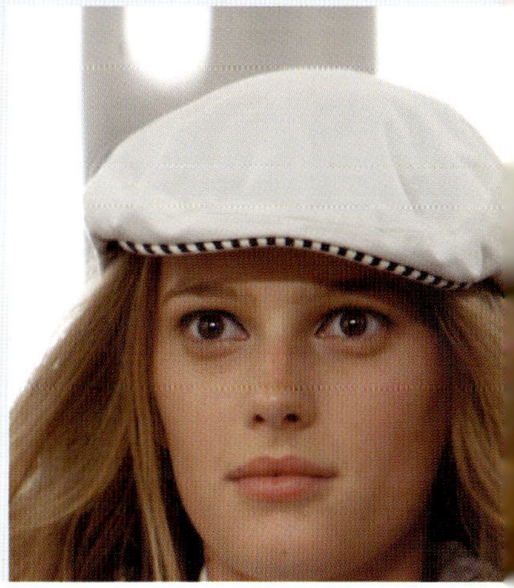
Y3

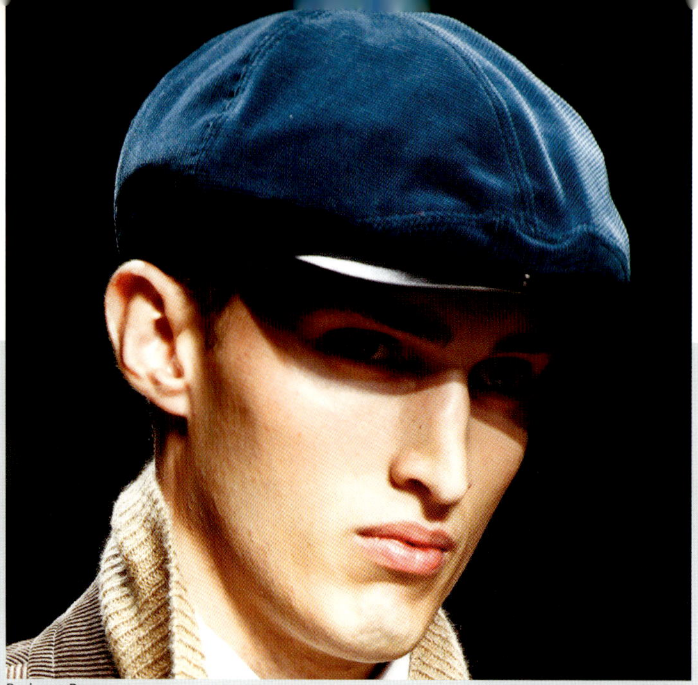

Burberry Prorsum

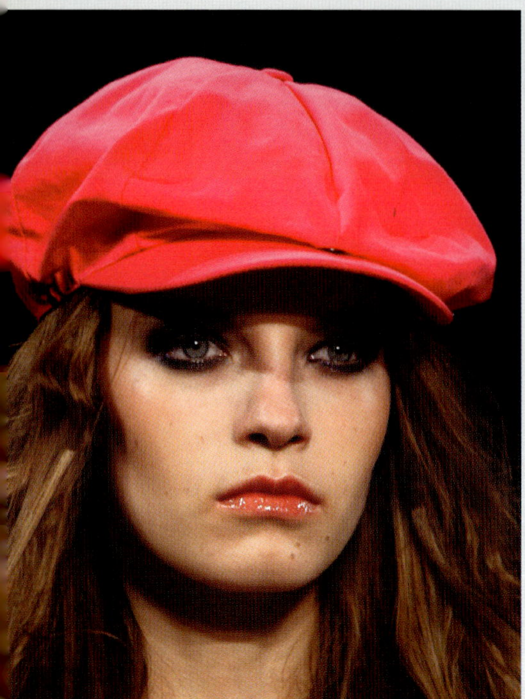

Miss Sixty

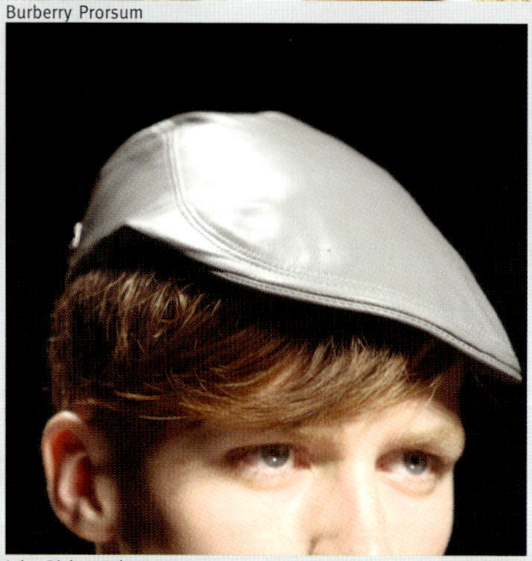

John Richmond

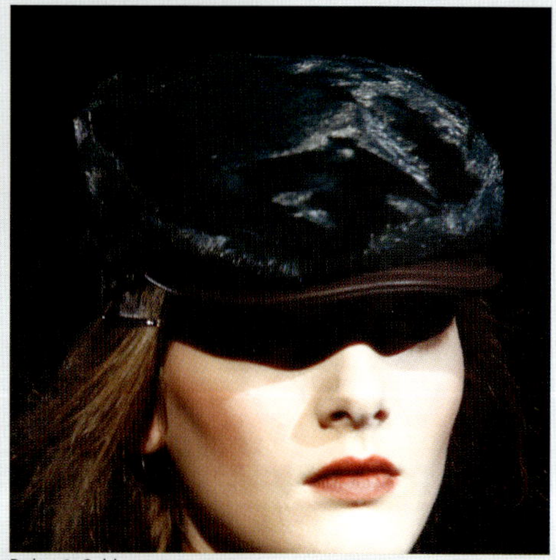

Dolce & Gabbana

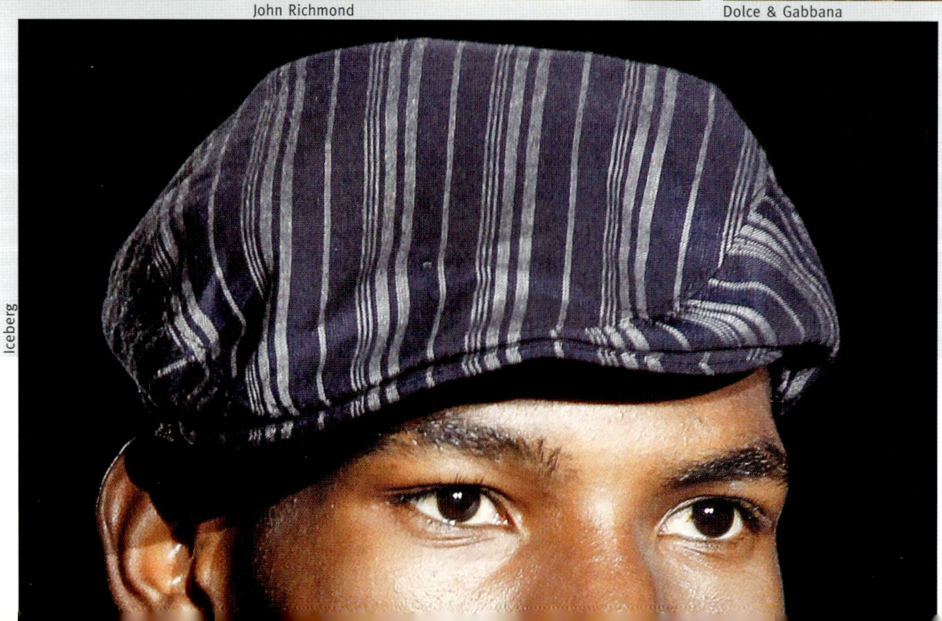

Iceberg

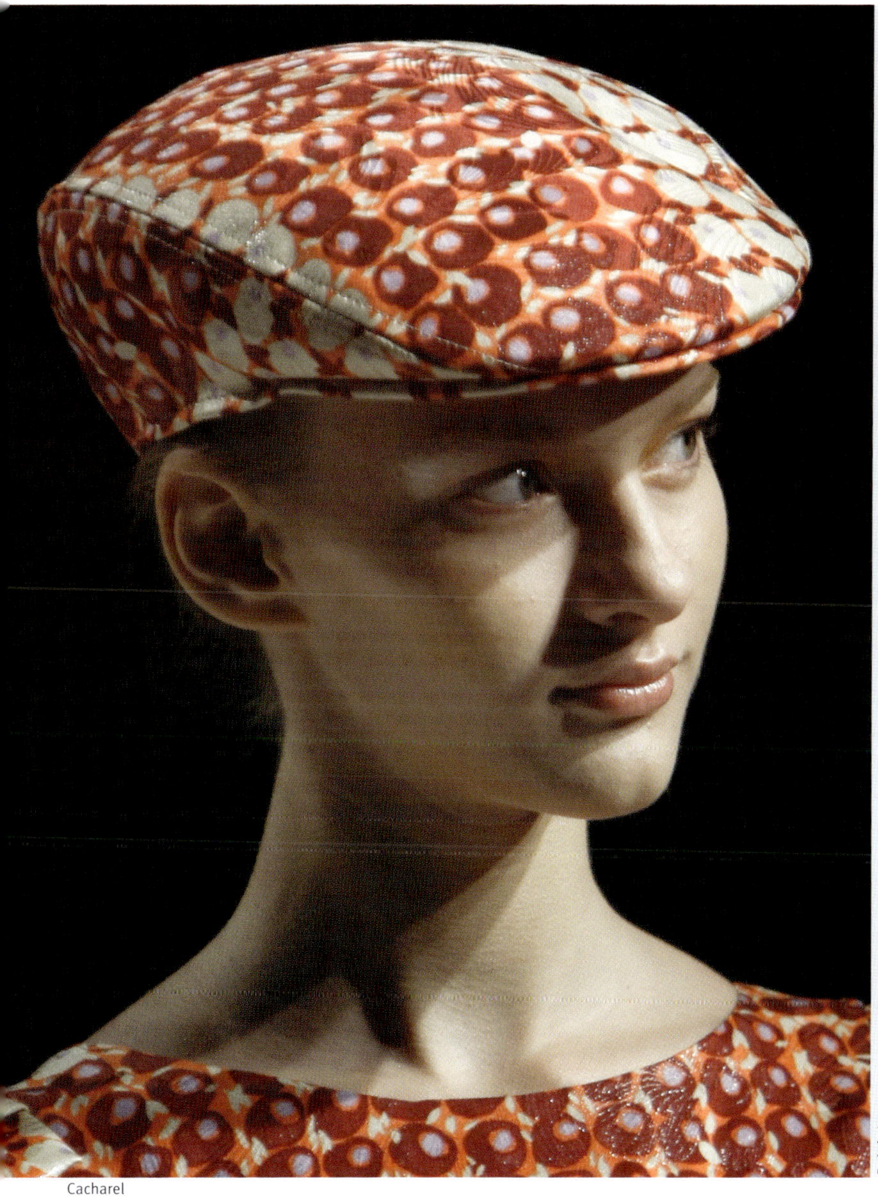

Cacharel

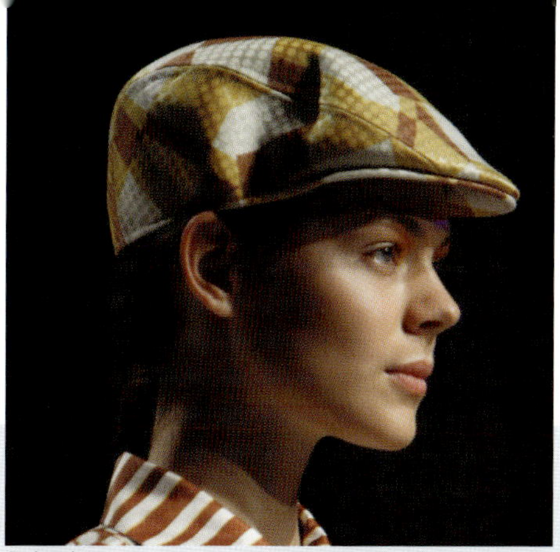

Cacharel

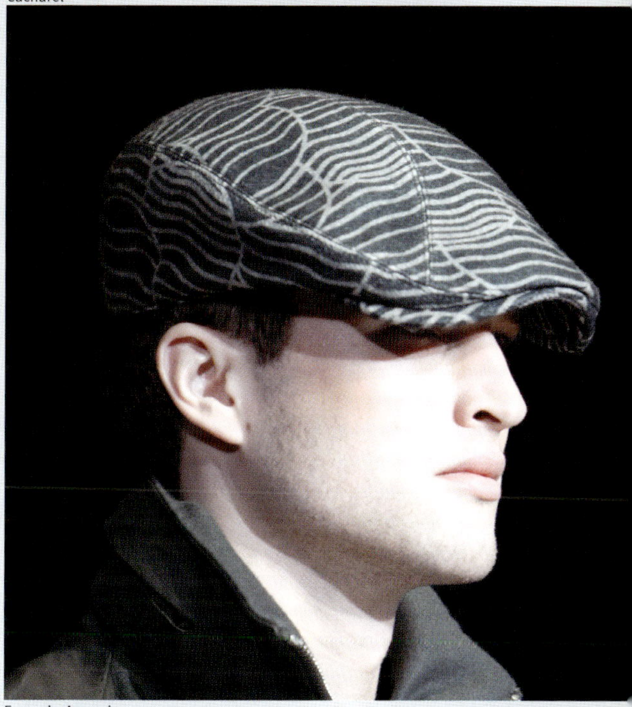

Emporio Armani

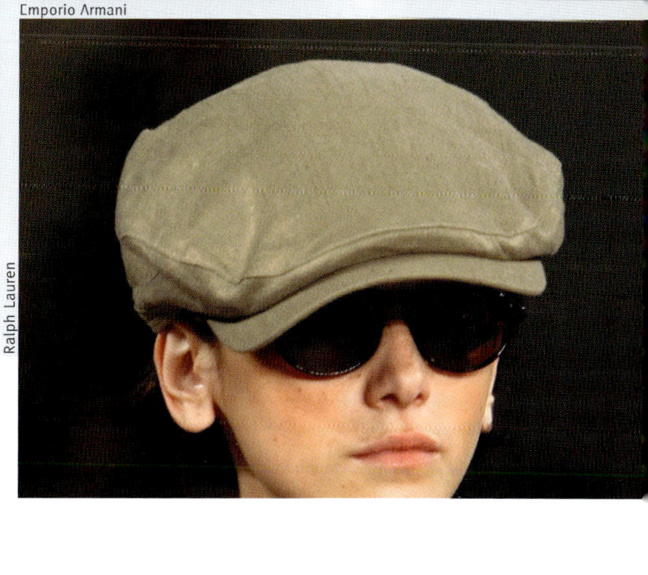

Ralph Lauren

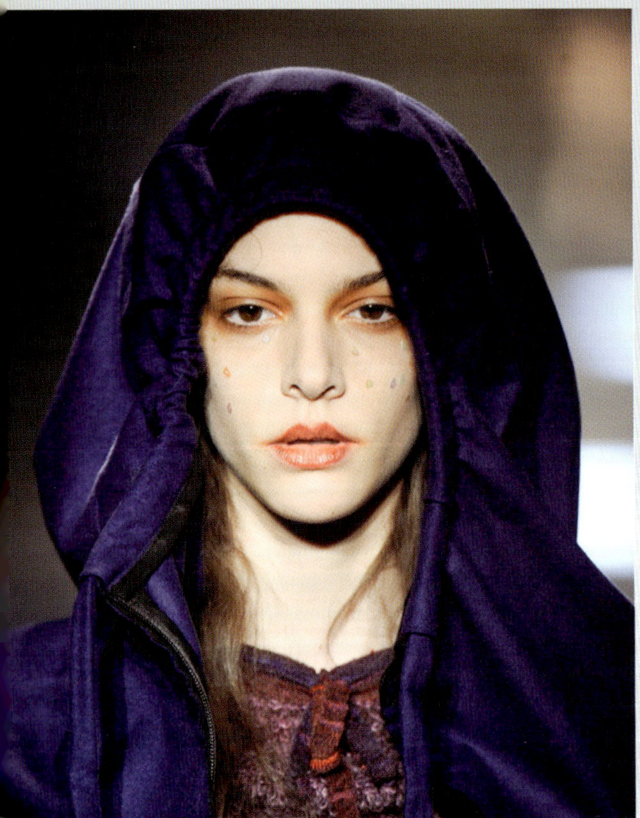

Vivienne Westwood

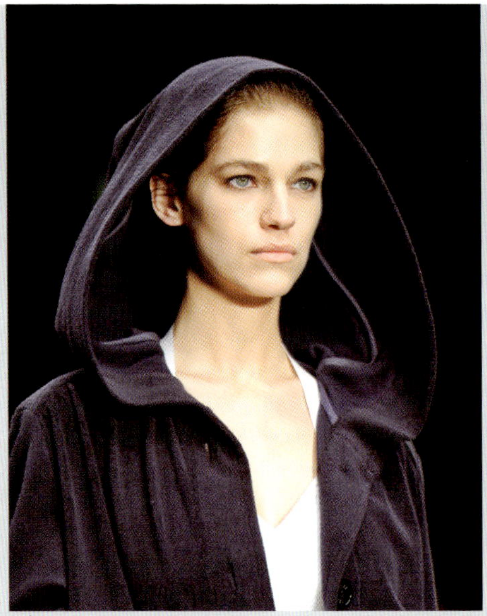

Daks

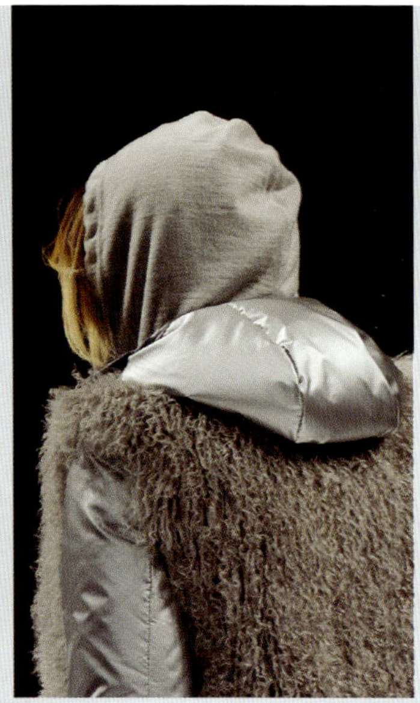

Blumarine

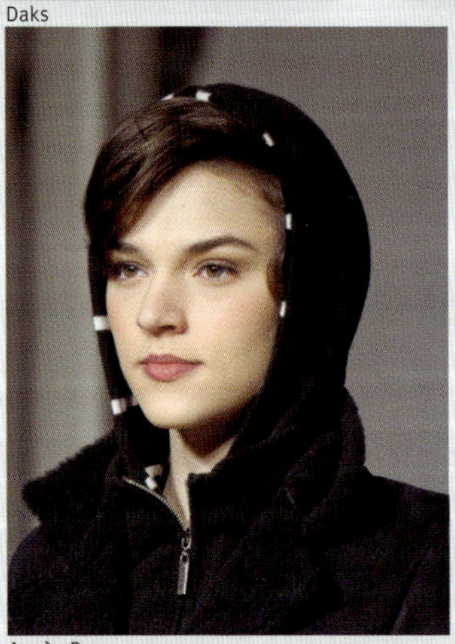

Agnès B.

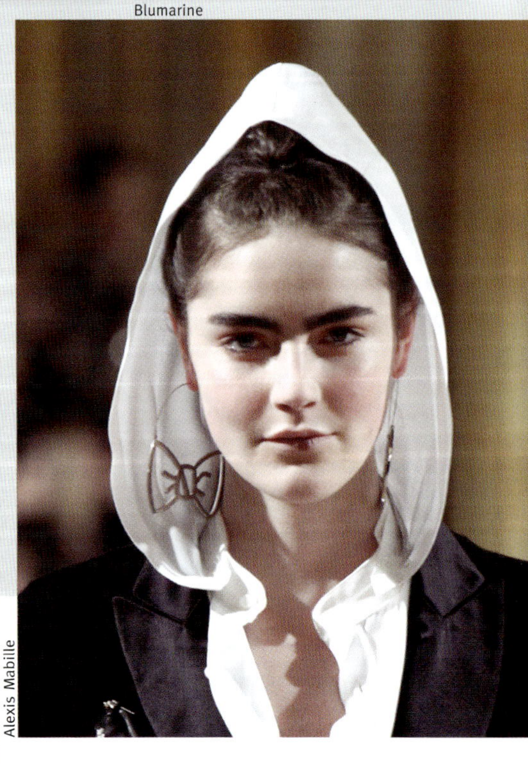

Alexis Mabille

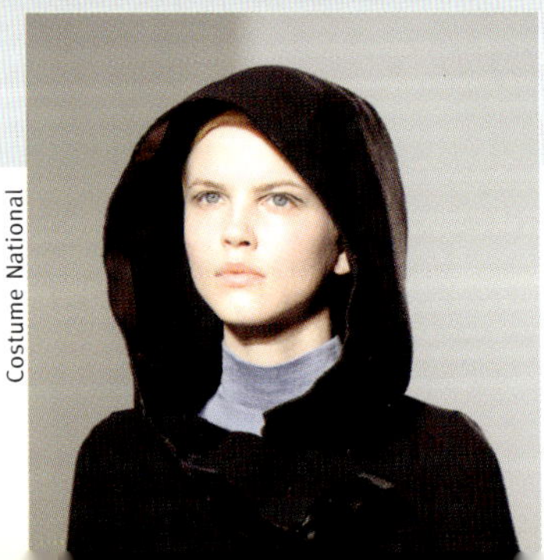

Costume National

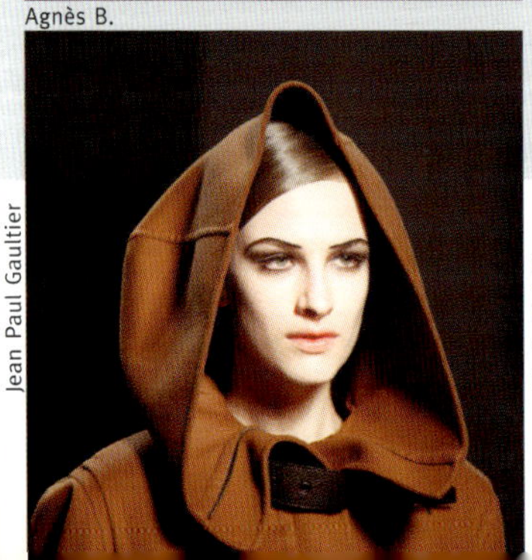

Jean Paul Gaultier

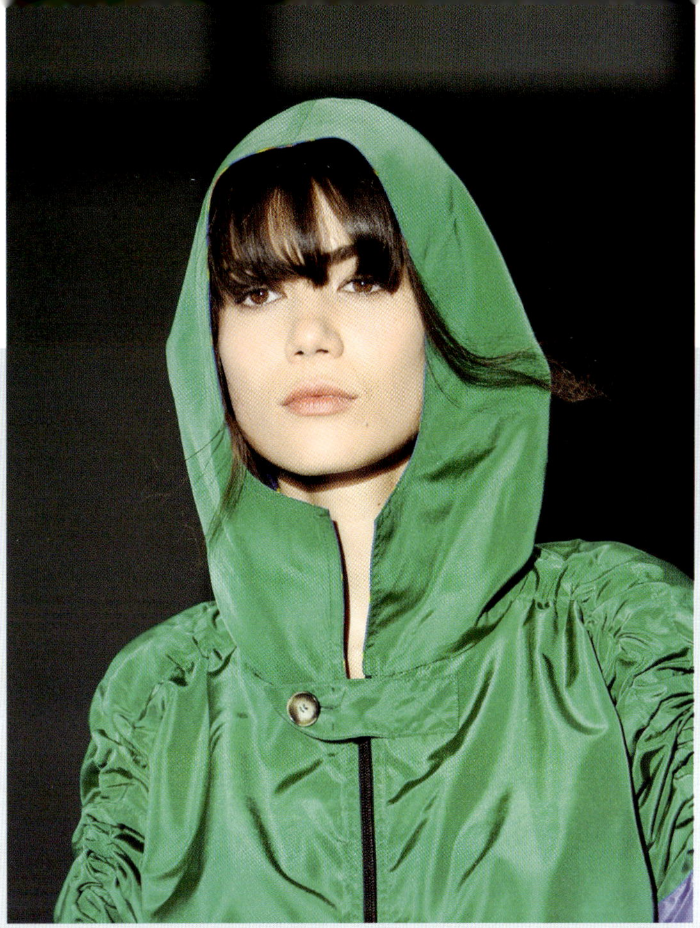

Kenzo

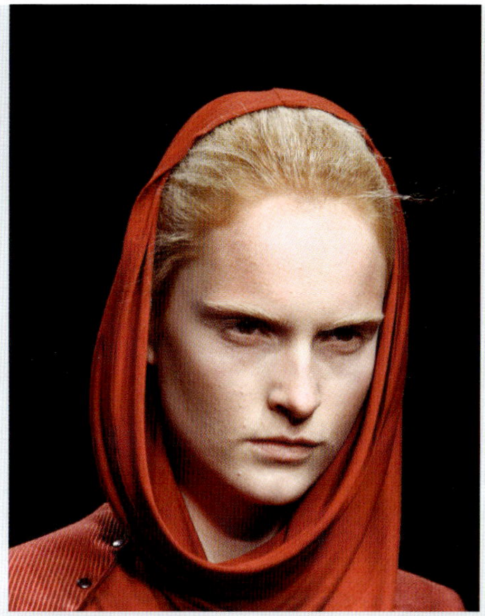

AF Vandevorst

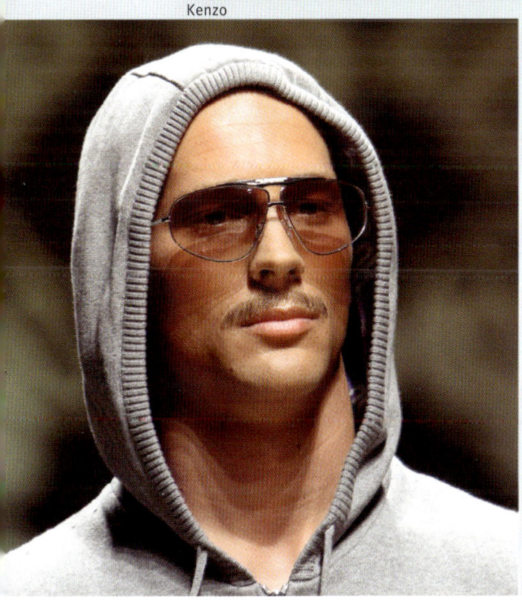

Dirk Bikkembergs

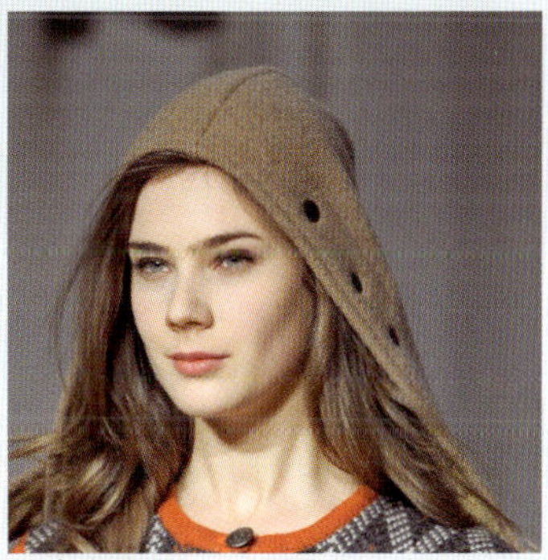

Agnès B.

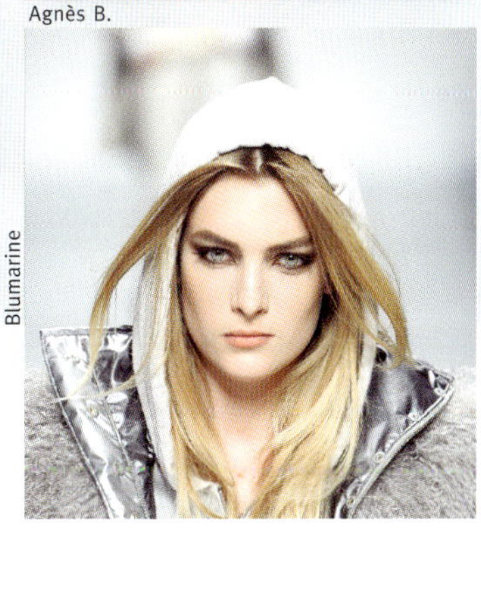

Blumarine

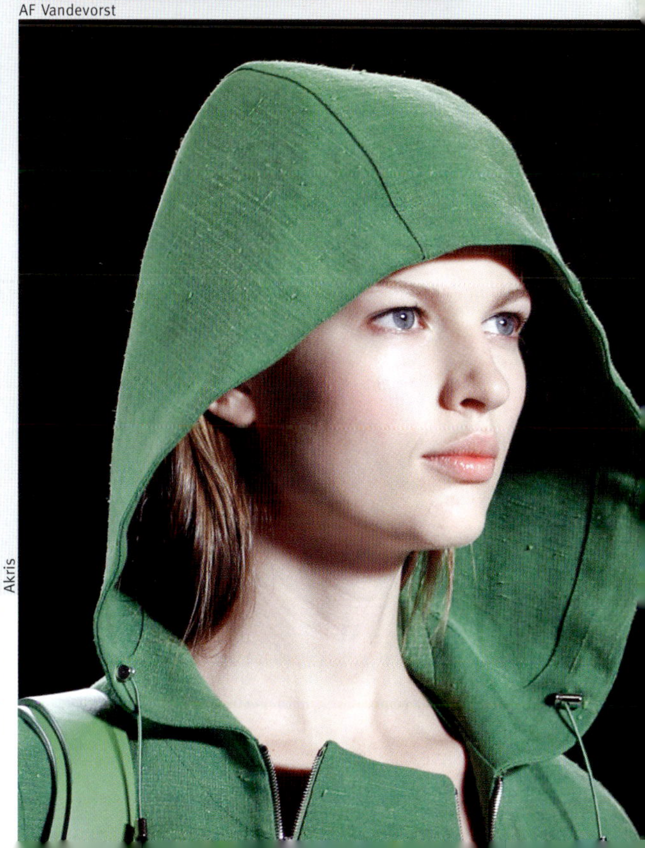

Akris

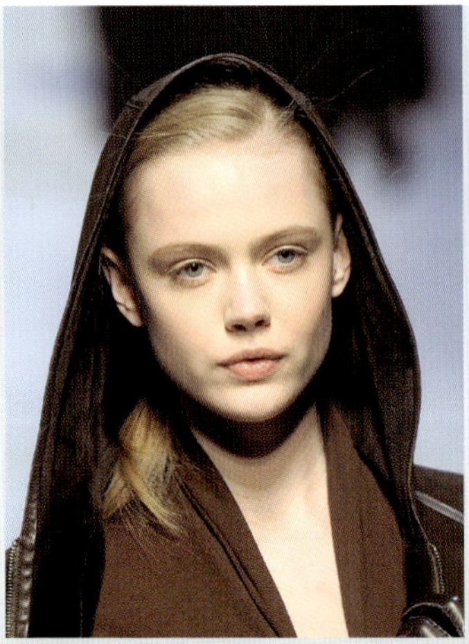
Hermès

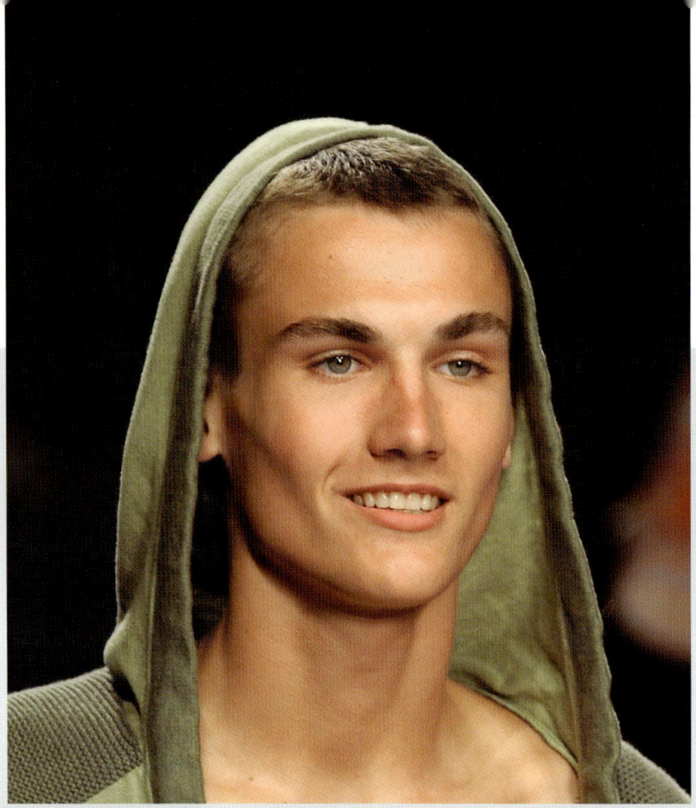
Frankie Morello

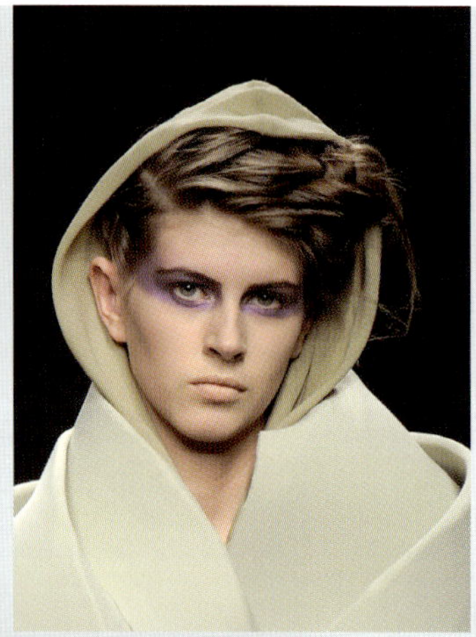
Malloni

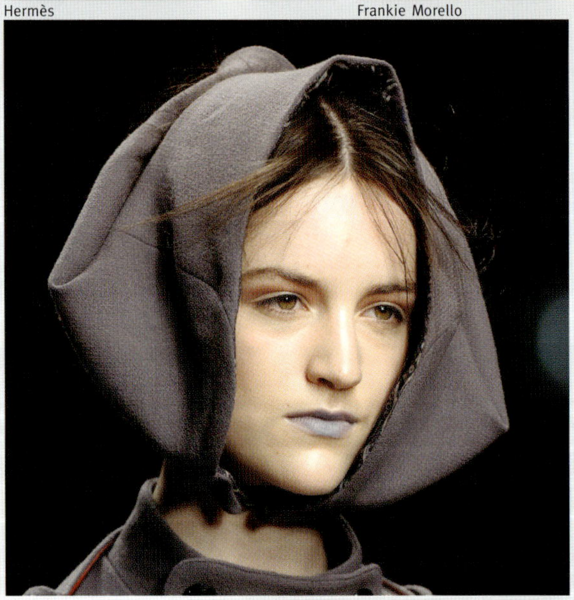
Bora Aksu

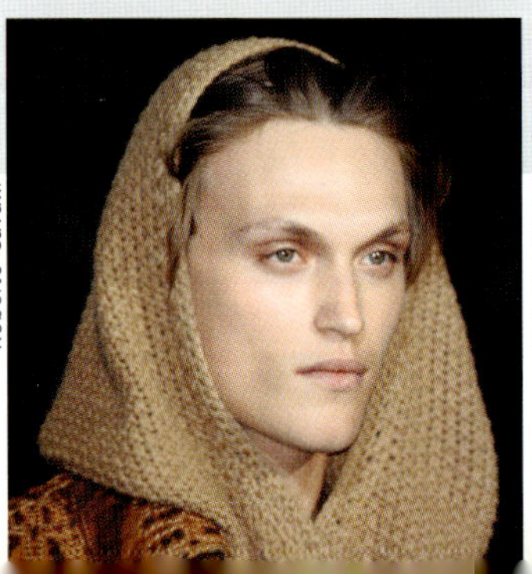
Roberto Cavalli

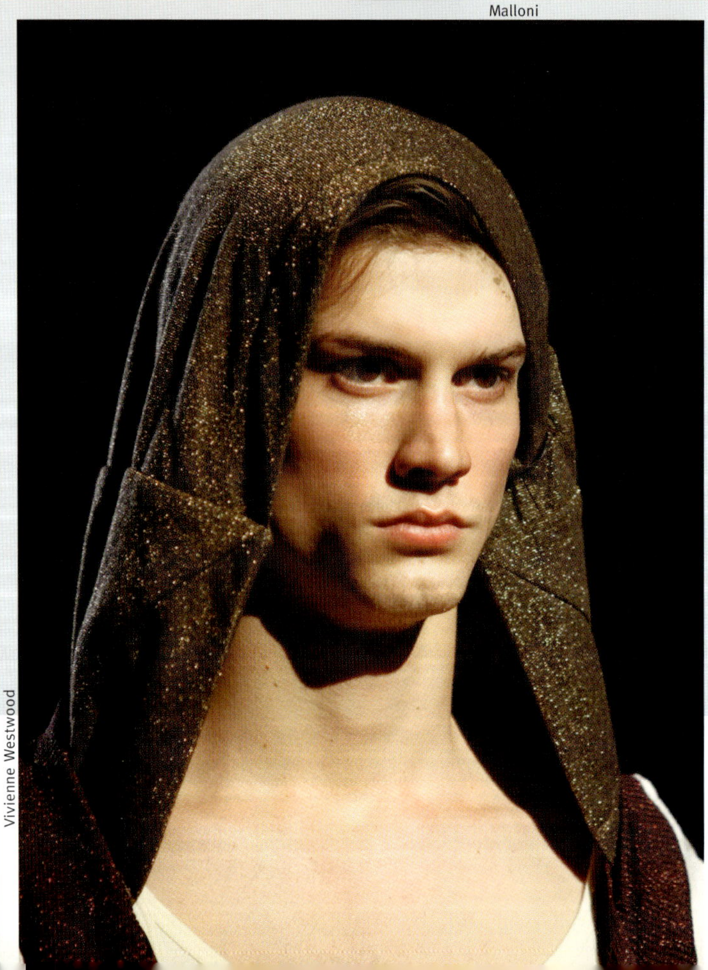
Vivienne Westwood

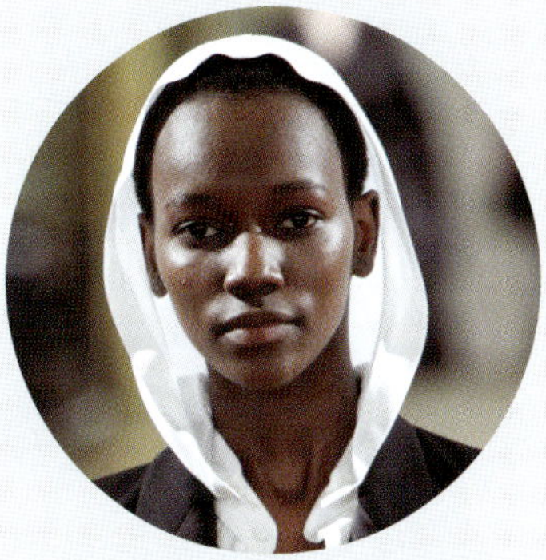

Alexis Mabille

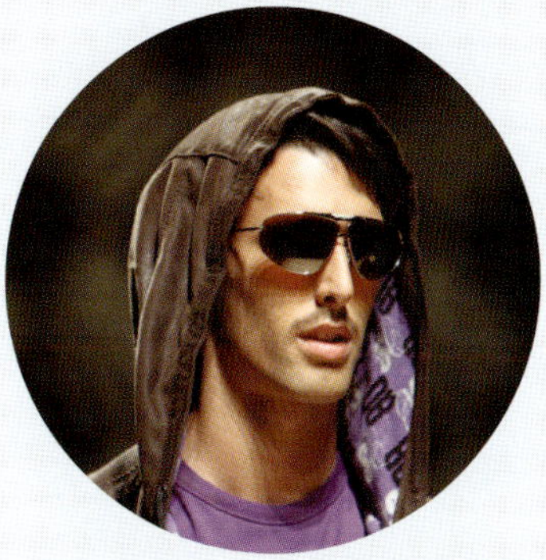

Dirk Bikkembergs

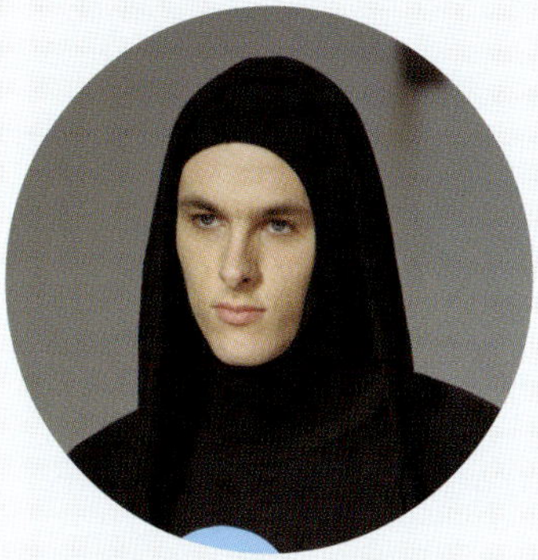

Agnès B.

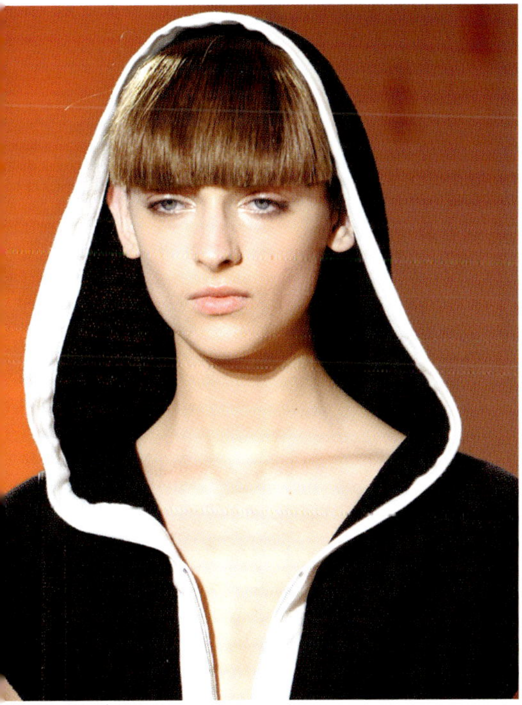

Hermès

Sportmax

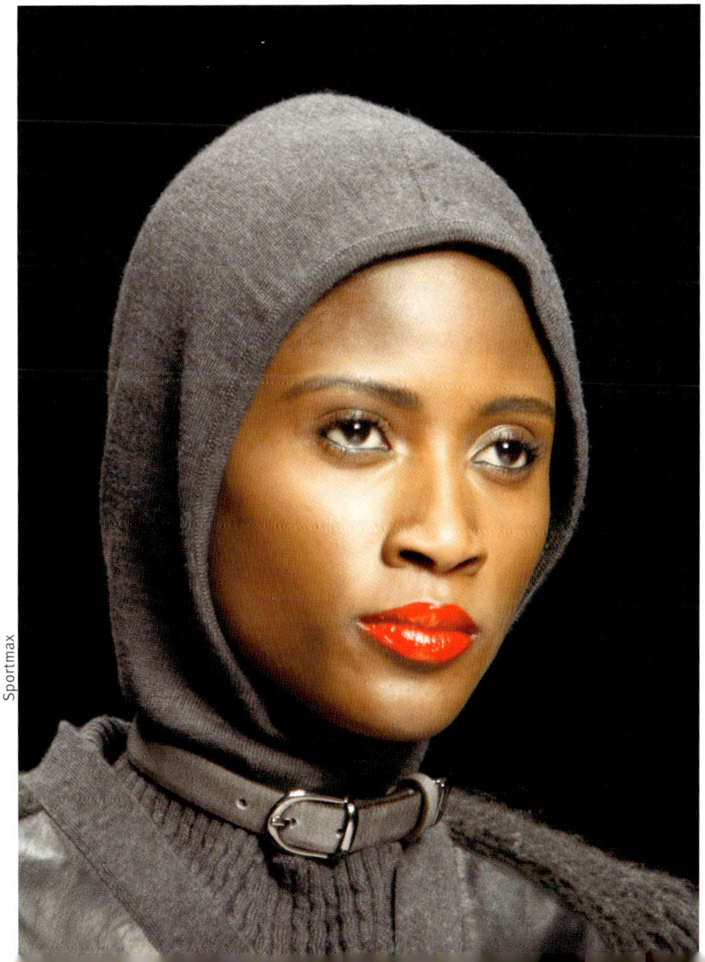

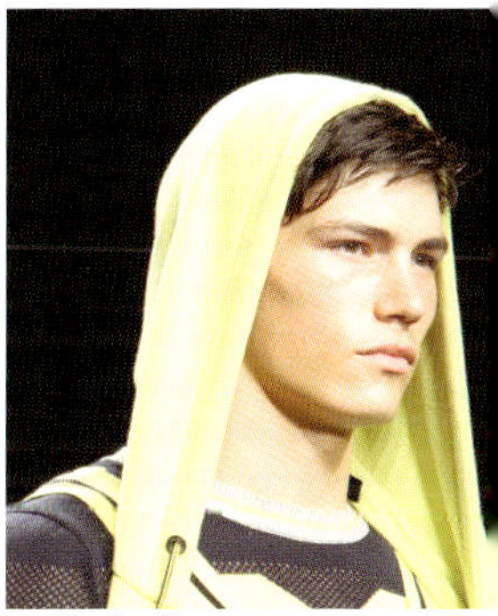

Frankie Morello

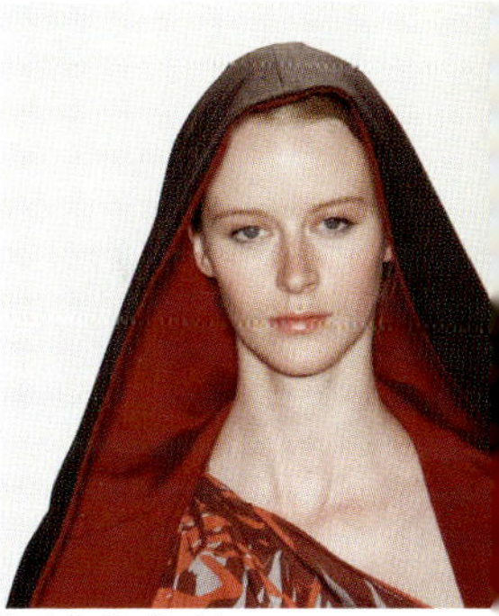

Costello Tagliapietra

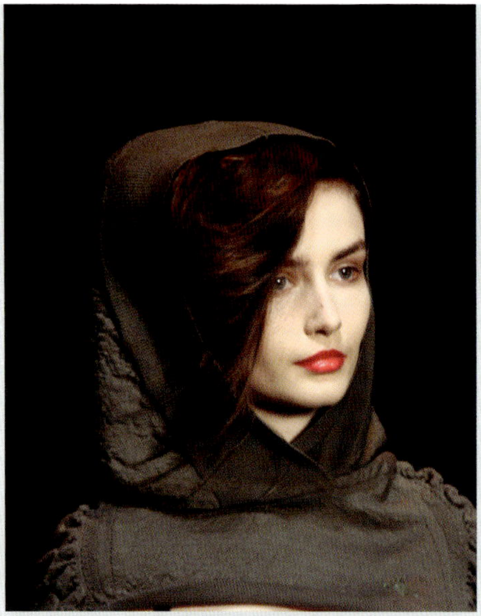
Vivienne Westwood Red Label

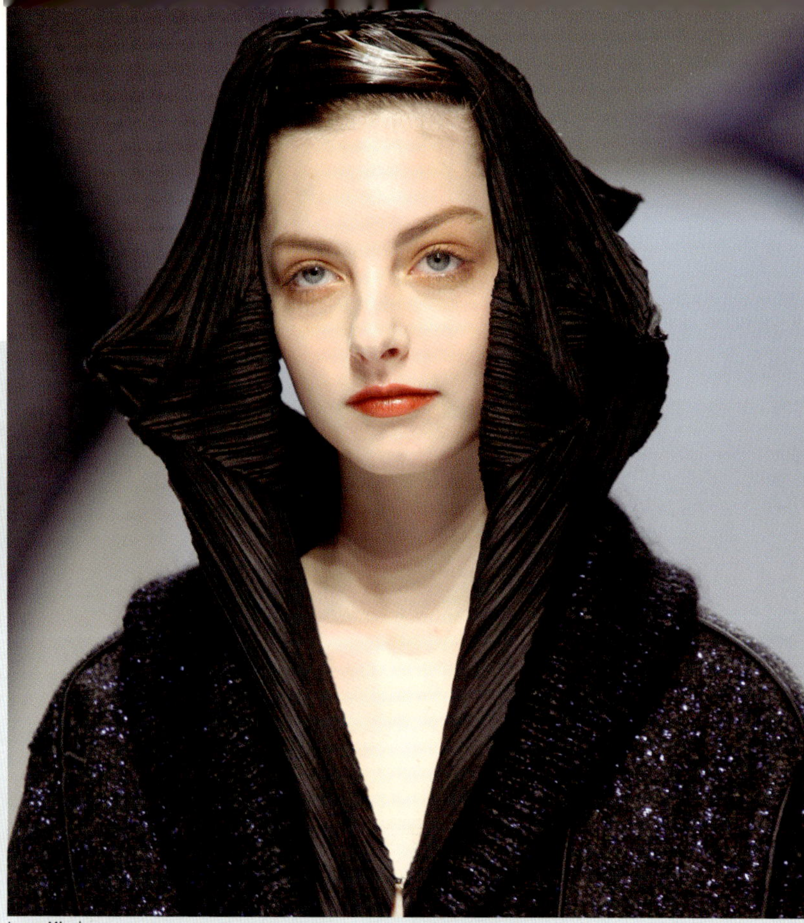
Issey Miyake

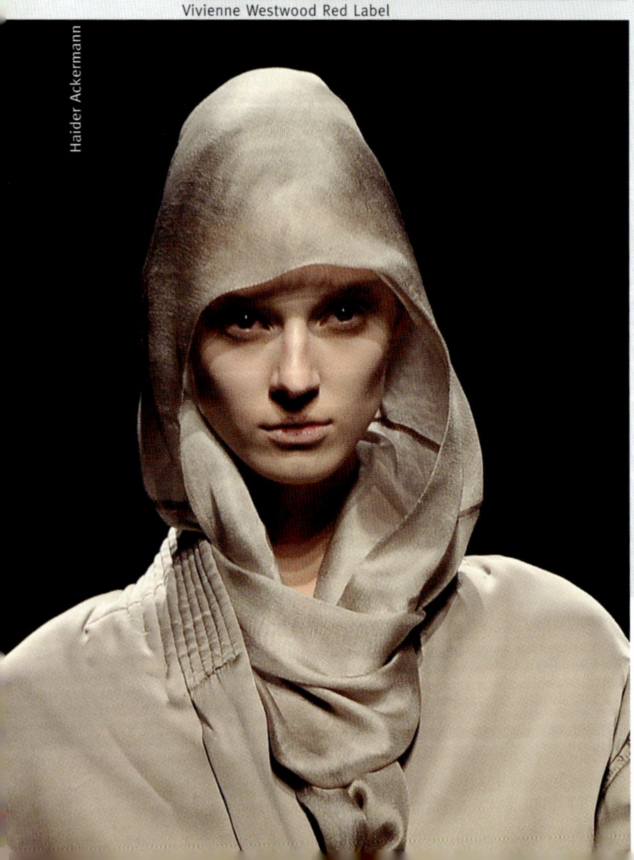
Haider Ackermann

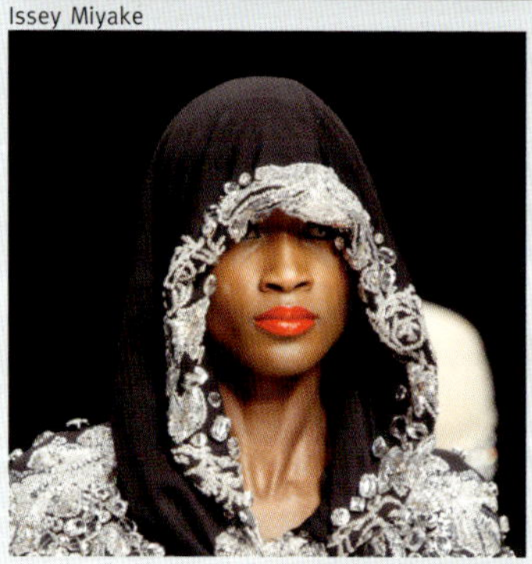
Sportmax

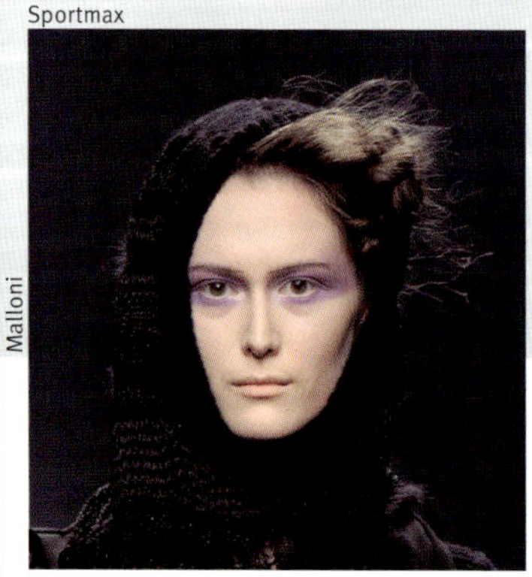
Malloni

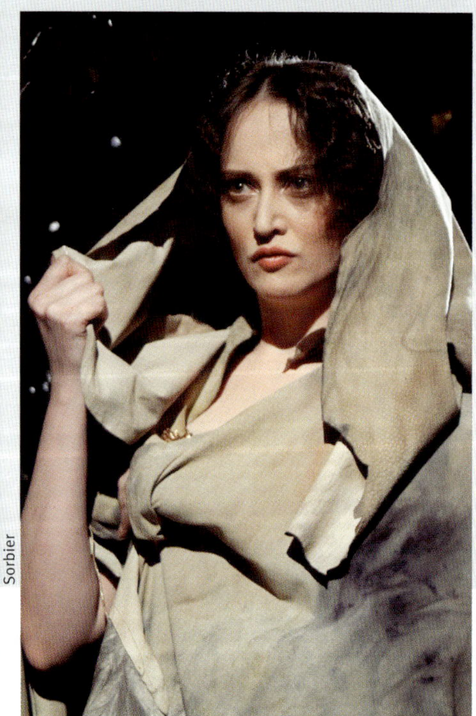
Sorbier

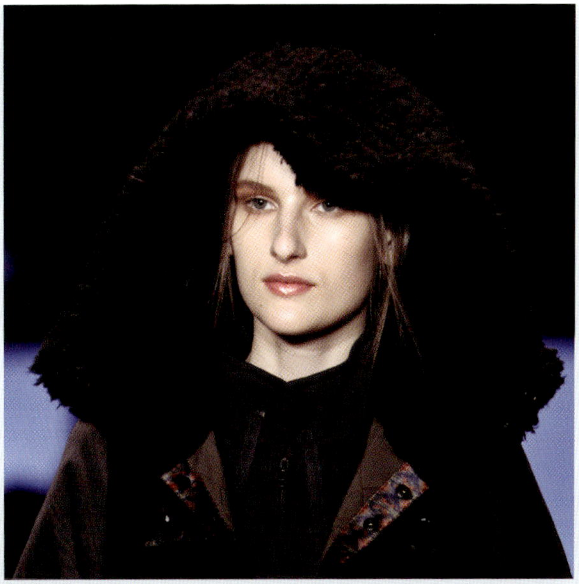
Y3

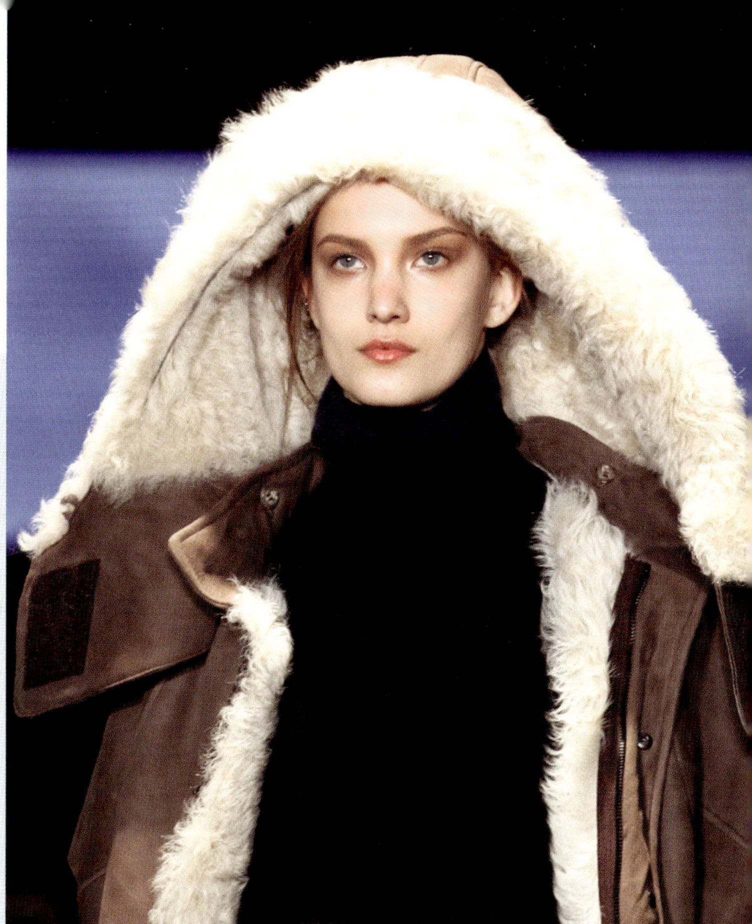
Y3

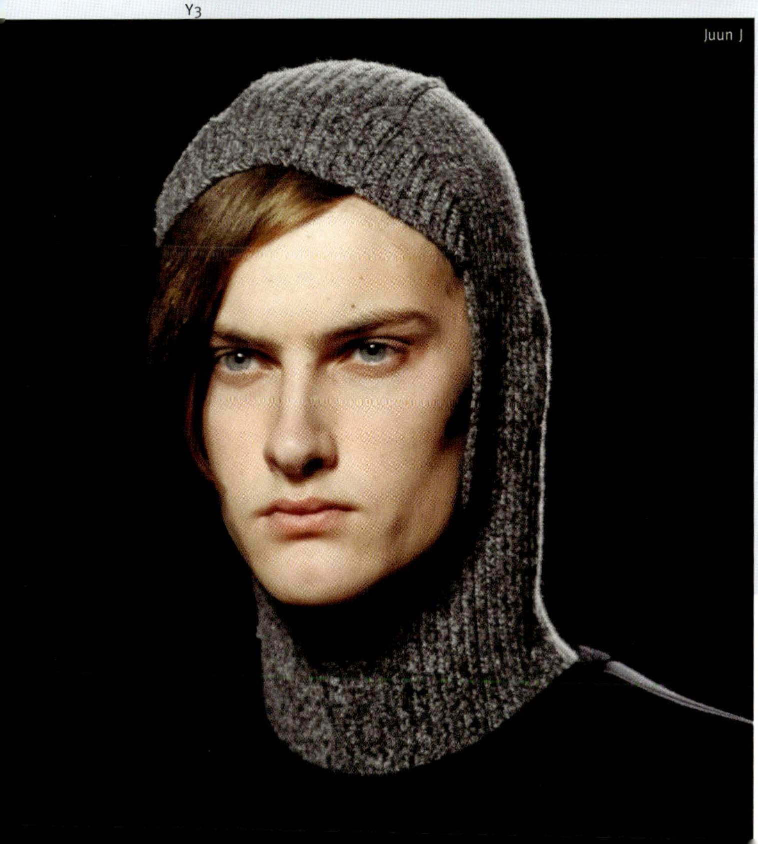
Juun J

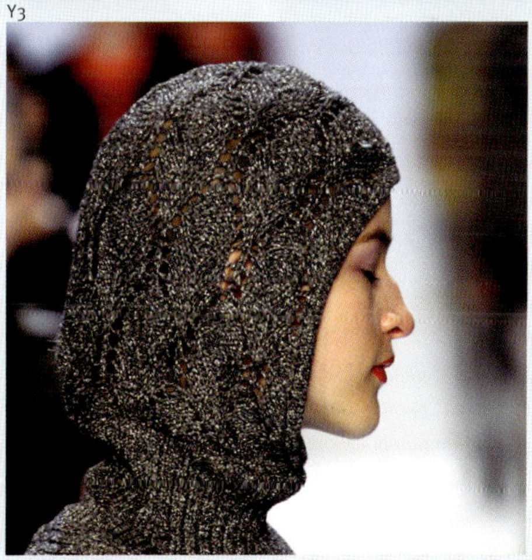
Charlotte Ronson

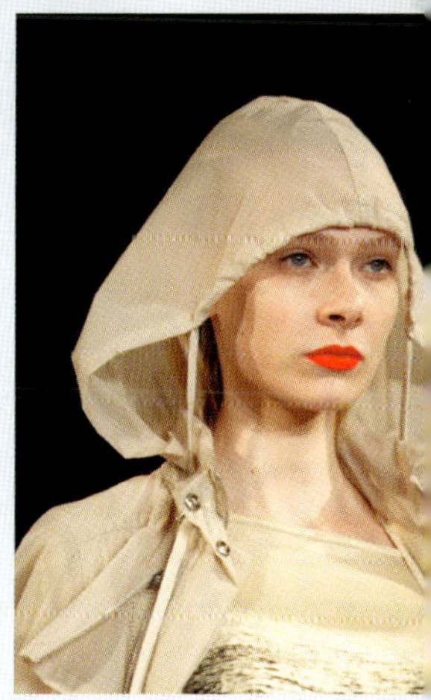
Véronique Branquinho

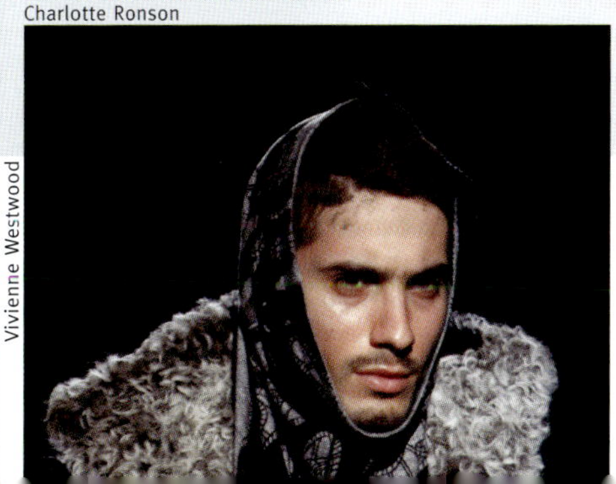
Vivienne Westwood

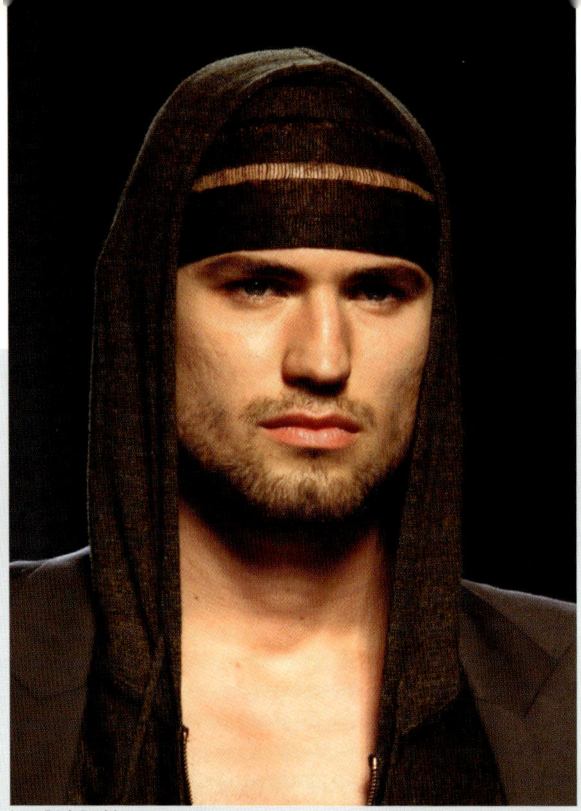

Jean Paul Gaultier

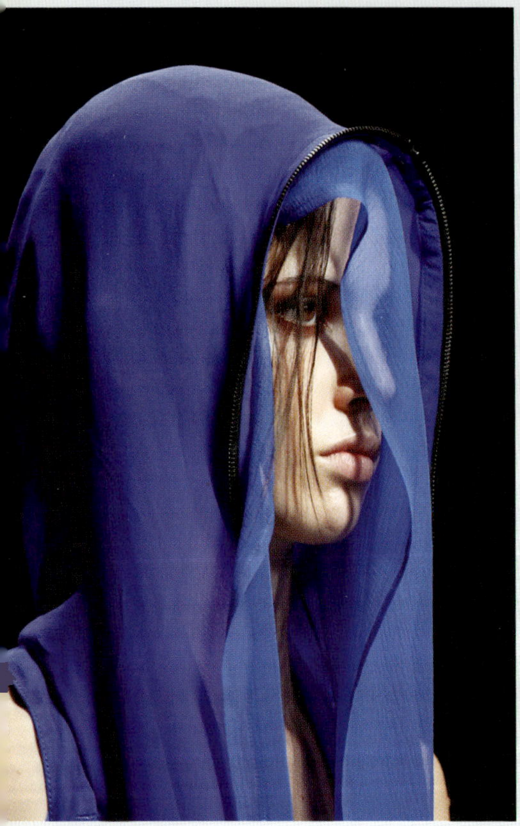

Haider Ackermann

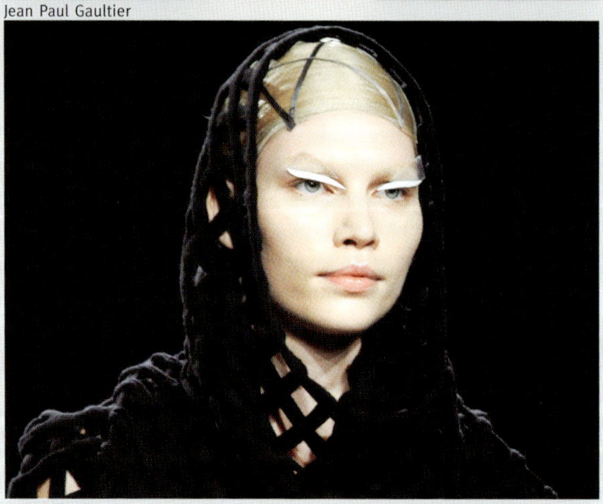

Gareth Pugh

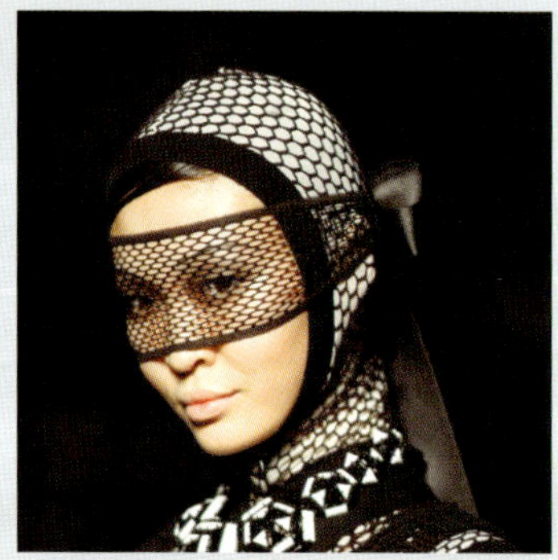

Jean Paul Gaultier

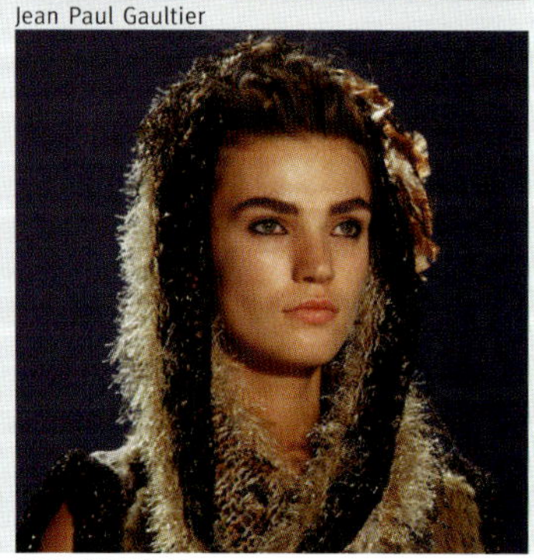

Custo Barcelona

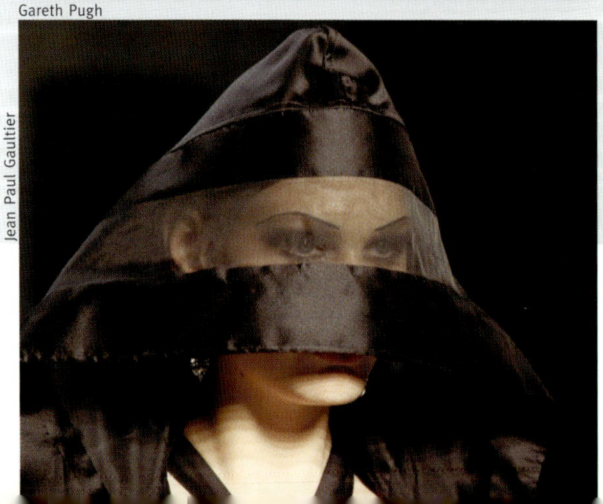

Jean Paul Gaultier

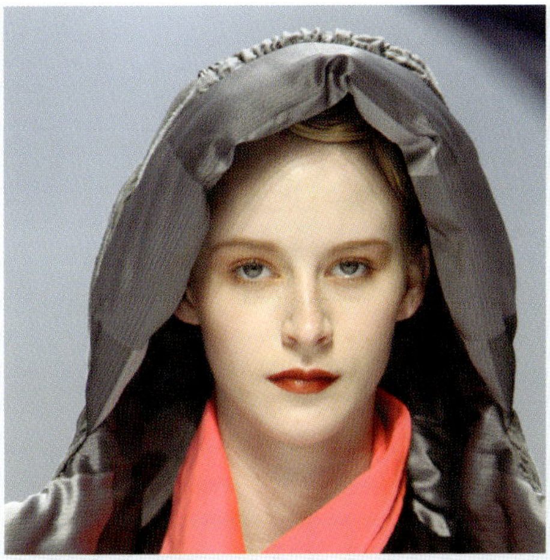

Issey Miyake

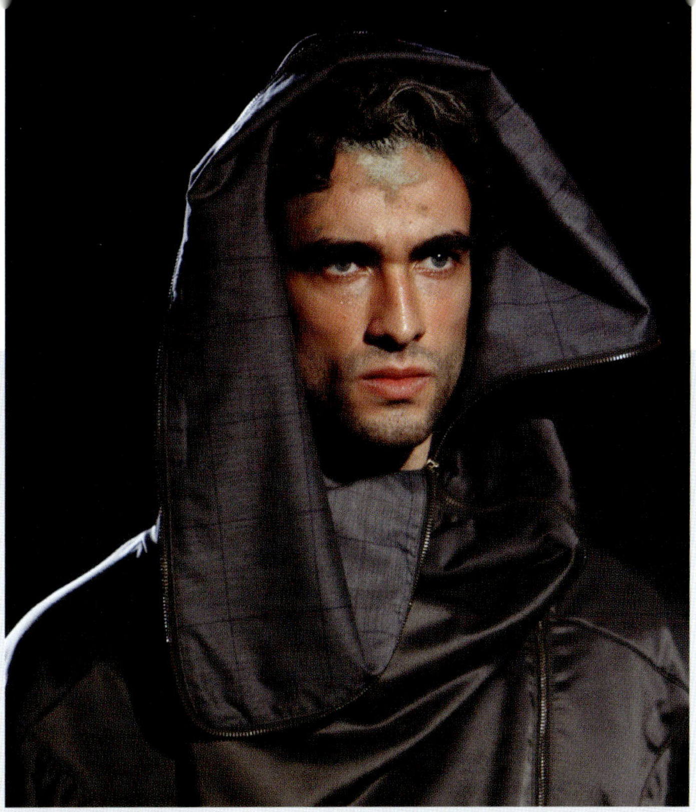

Vivienne Westwood

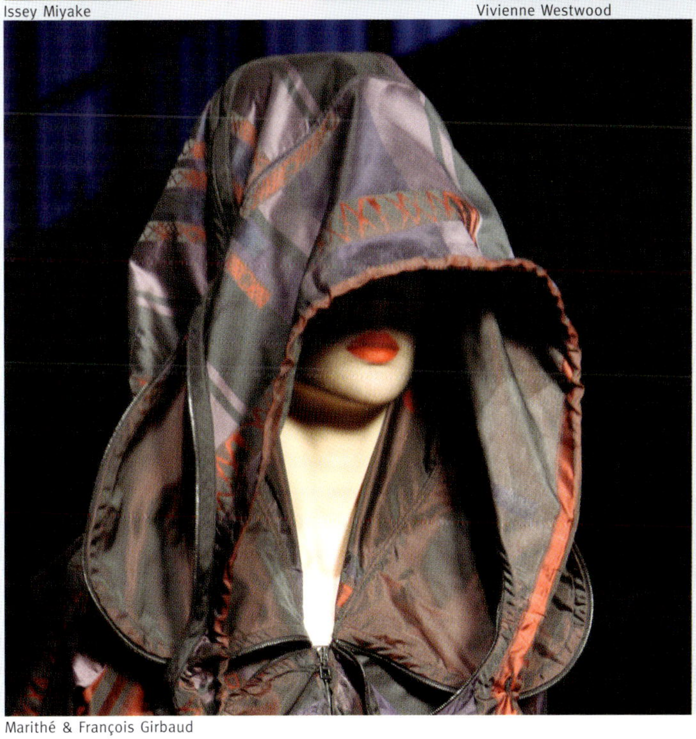

Marithé & François Girbaud

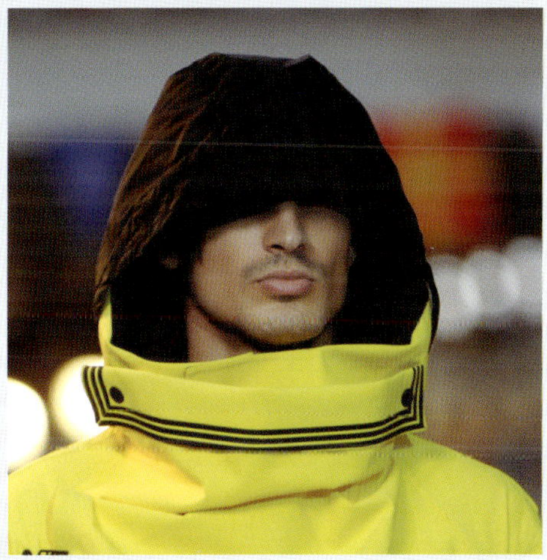

Moncler Grenoble

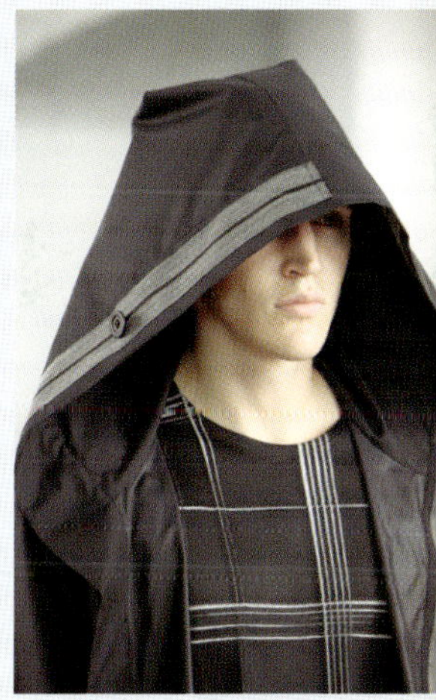

Issey Miyake

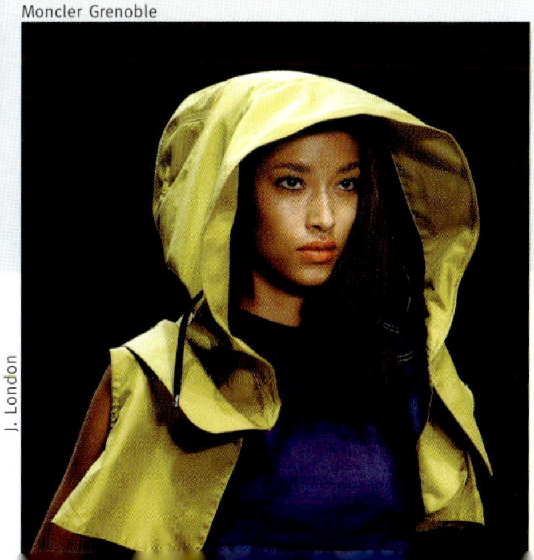

J. London

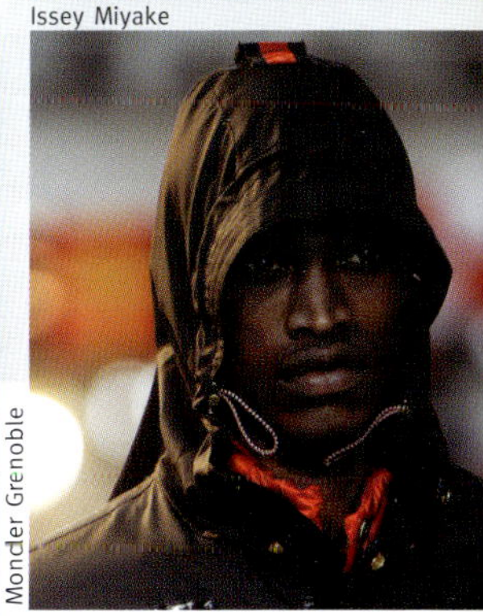

Moncler Grenoble

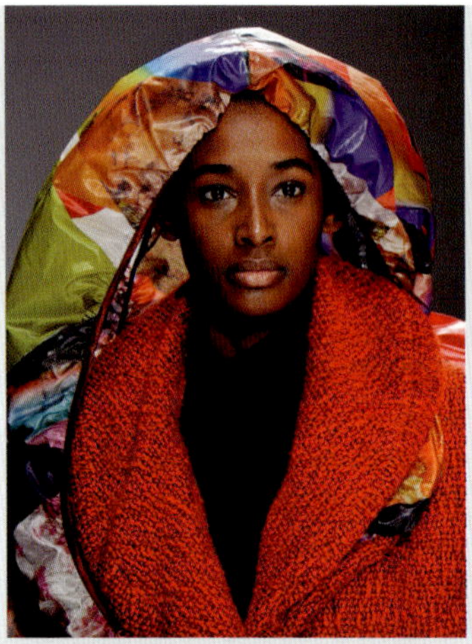

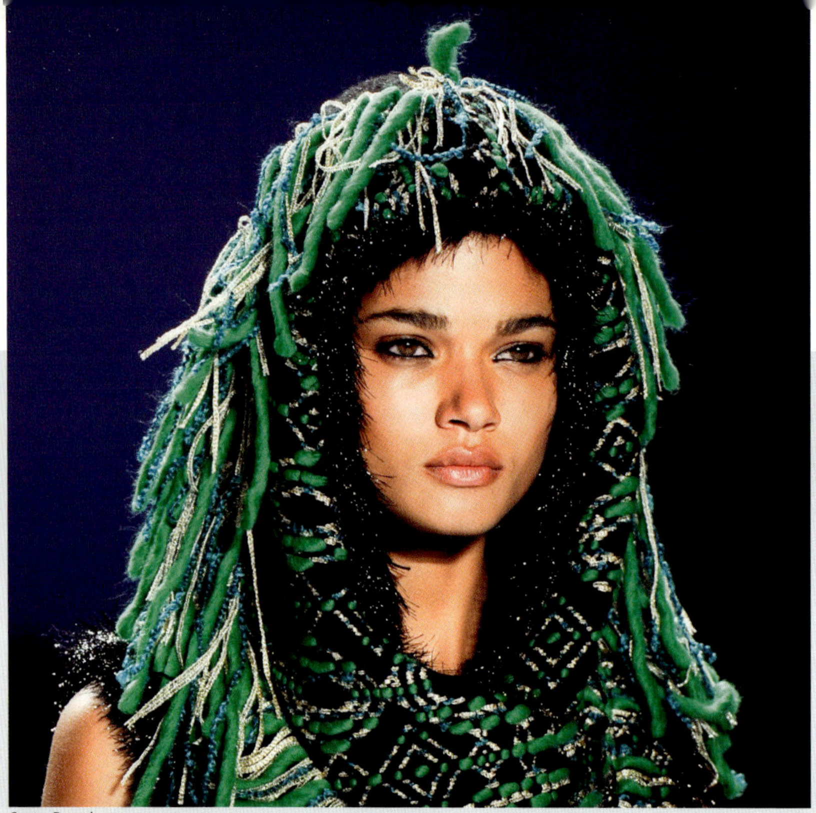

Custo Barcelona

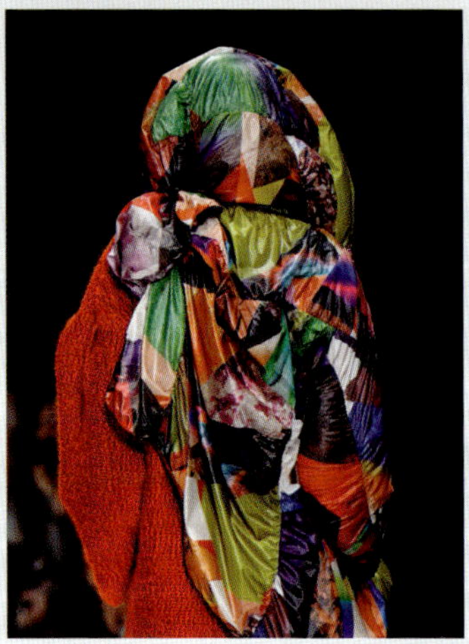

Issey Miyake

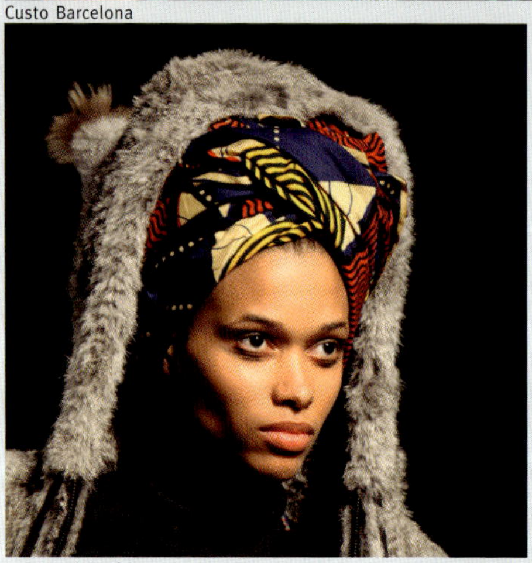

Jean Paul Gaultier

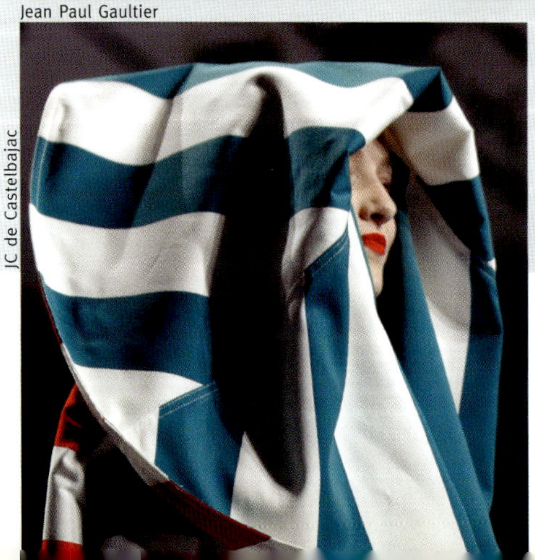

JC de Castelbajac

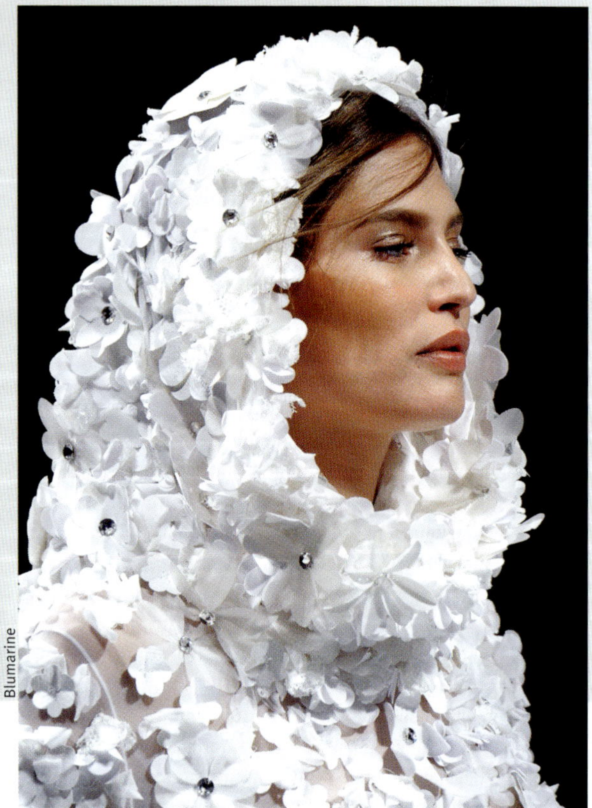

Blumarine

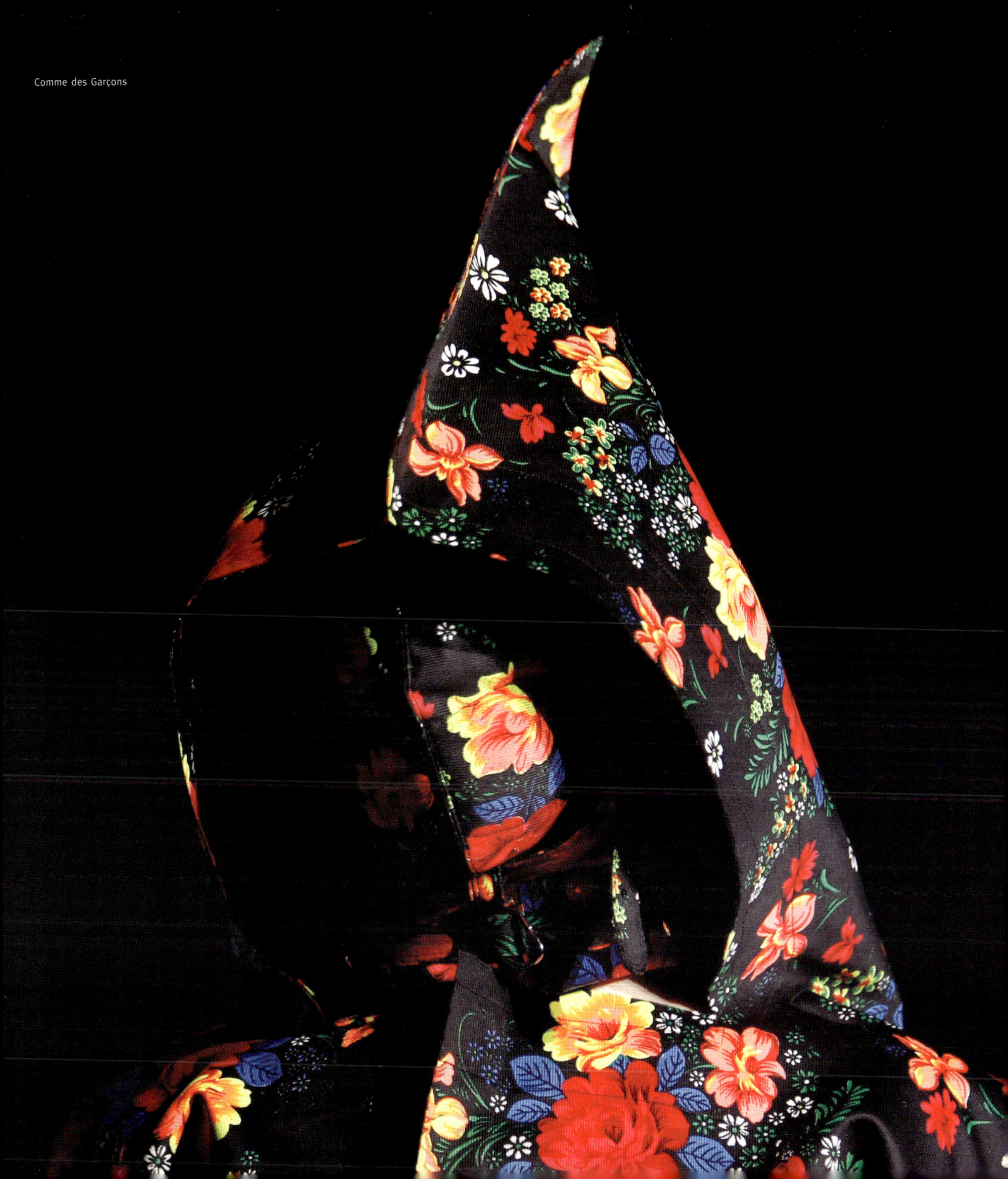

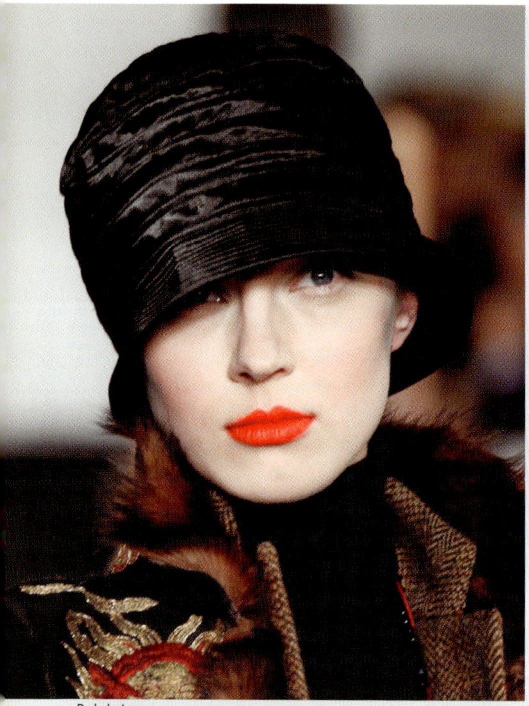

Ralph Lauren

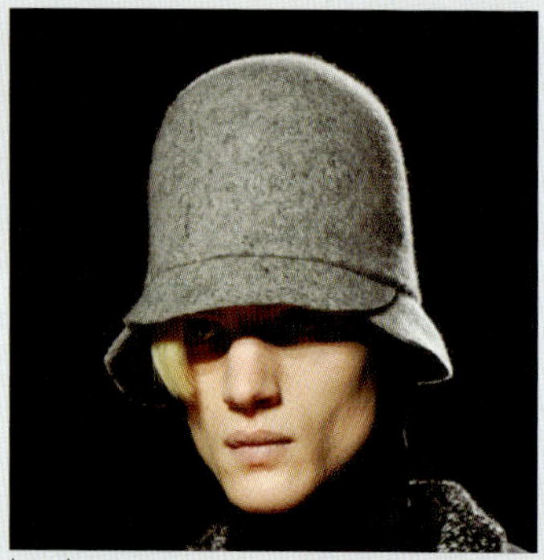

Juun J

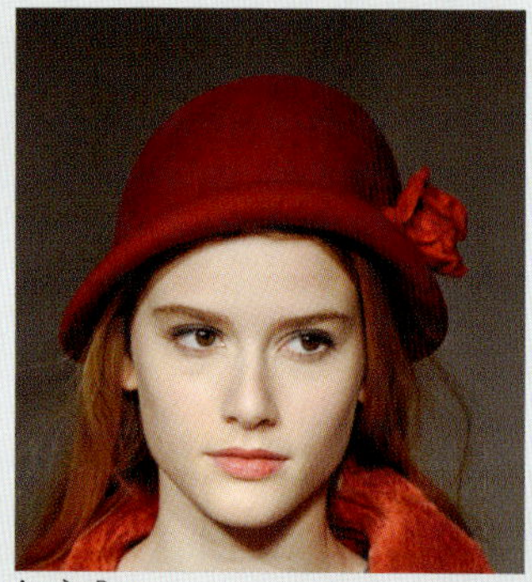

Agnès B.

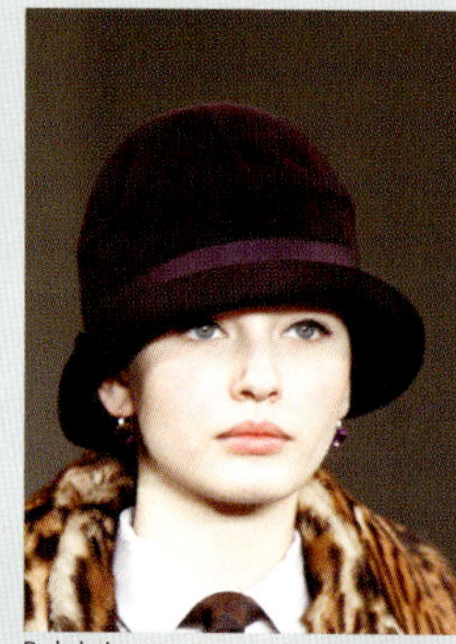

Ralph Lauren

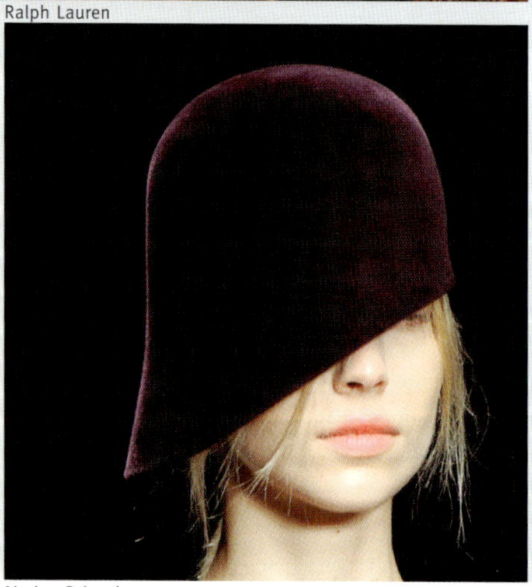

Marios Schwab

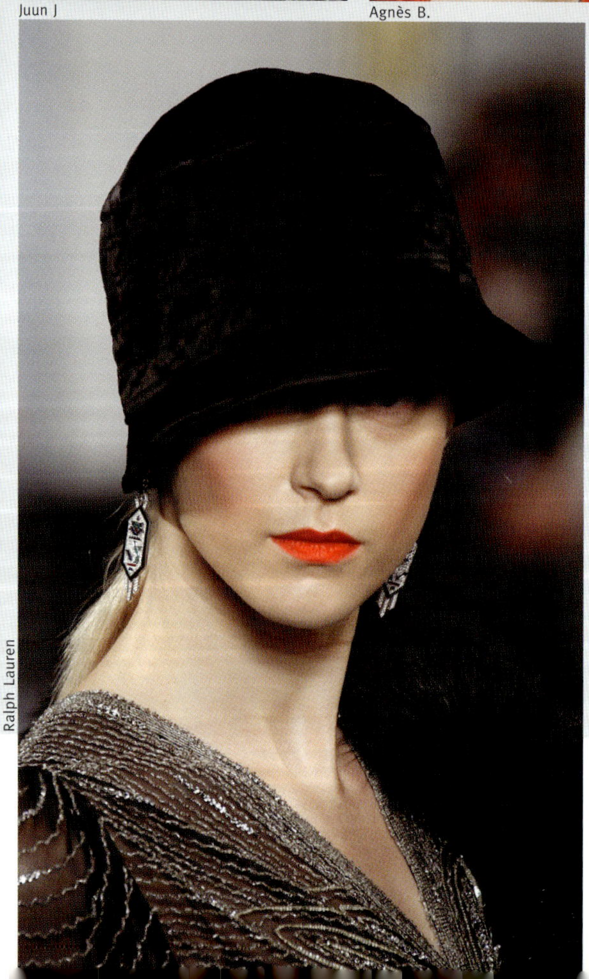

Ralph Lauren

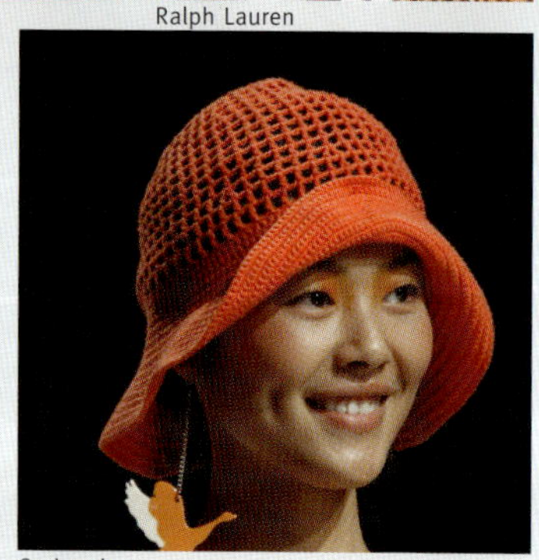

Cacharel

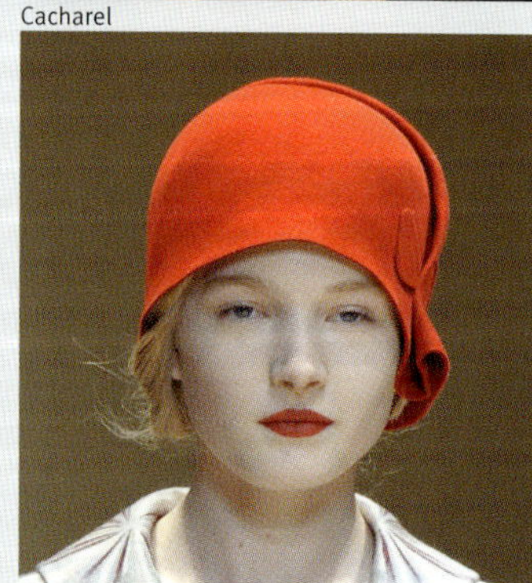

Cacharel

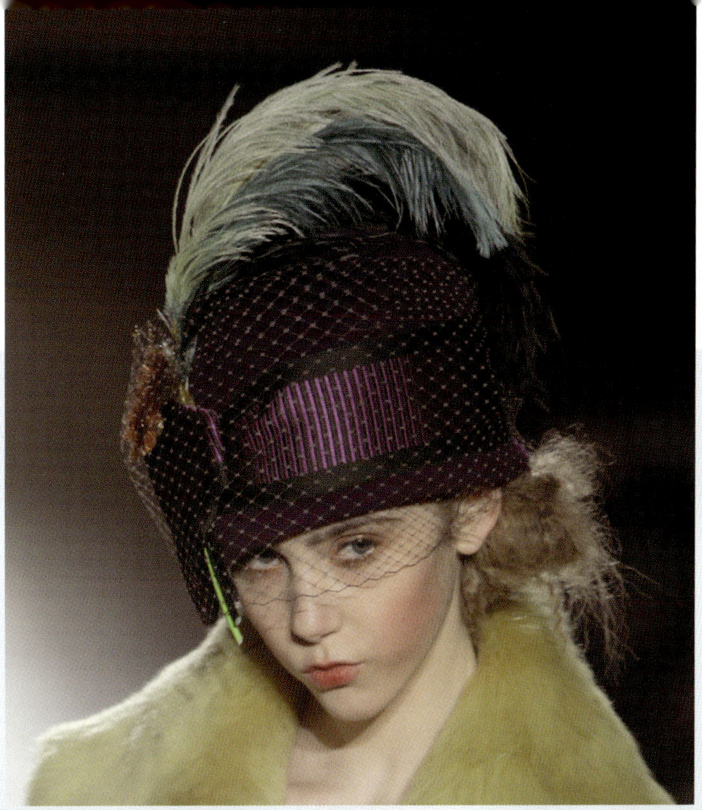

James Coviello

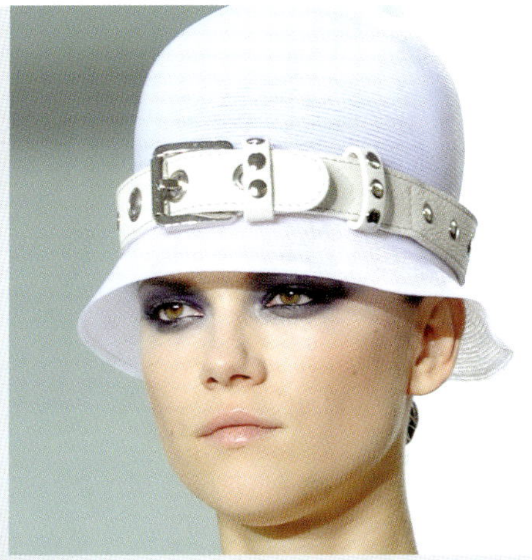

Temperley London

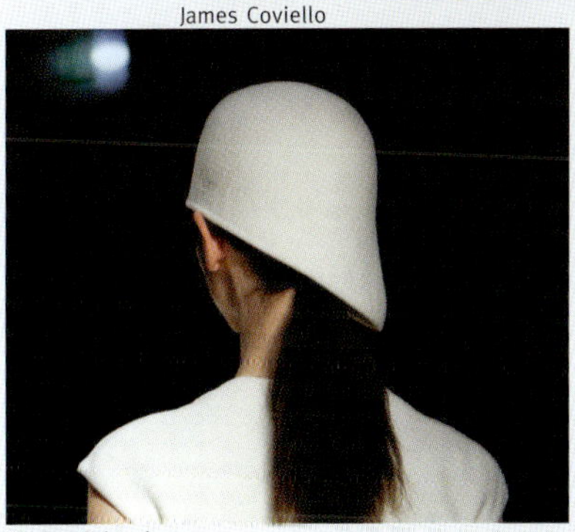

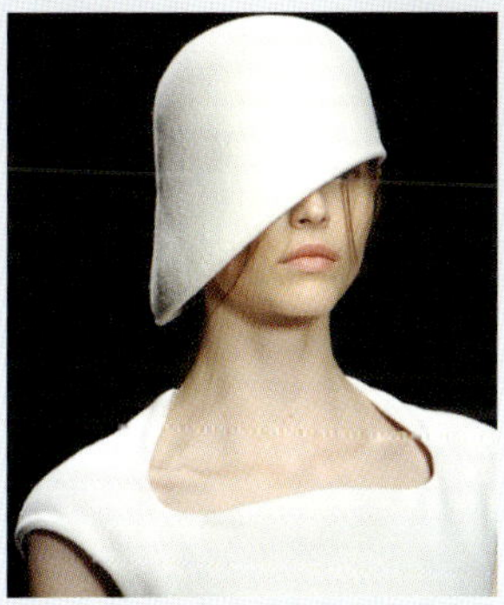

Marios Schwab

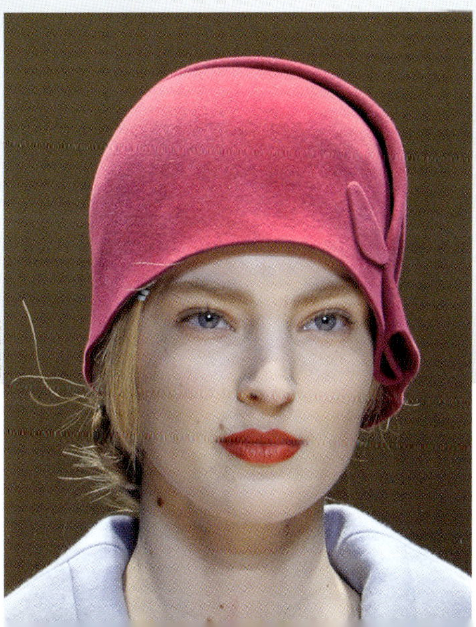

Cacharel

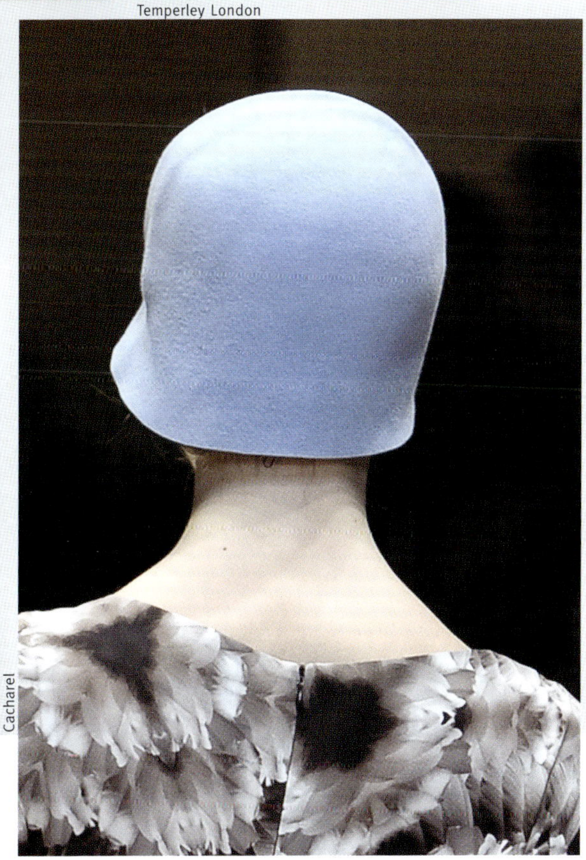

Cacharel

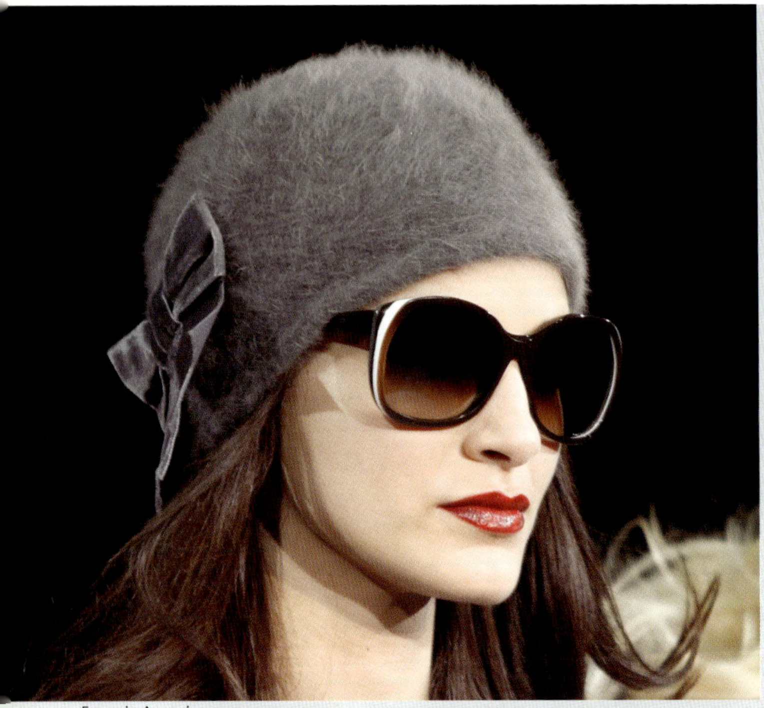
Emporio Armani

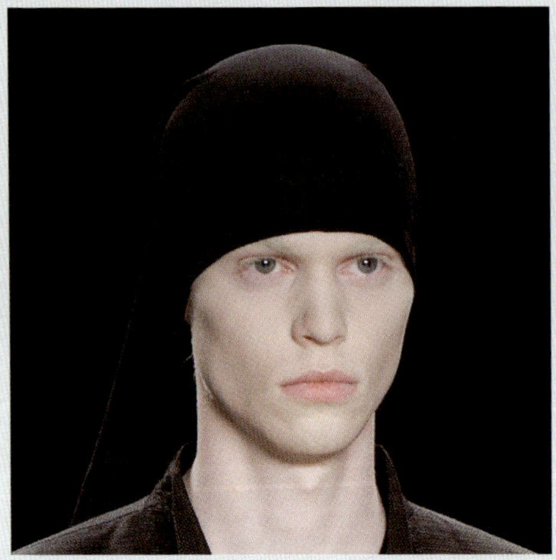
Rick Owens

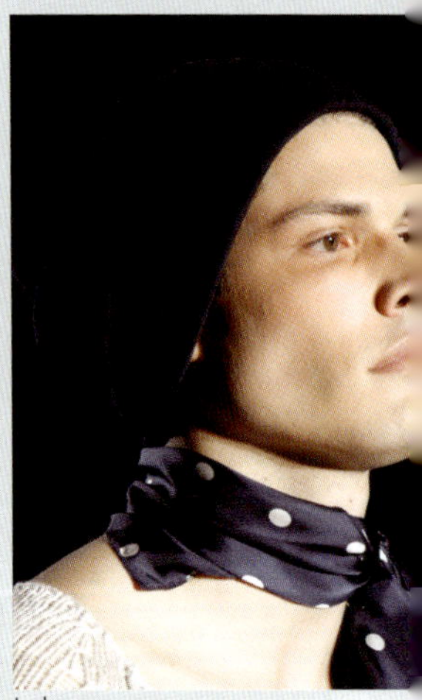
Iceberg

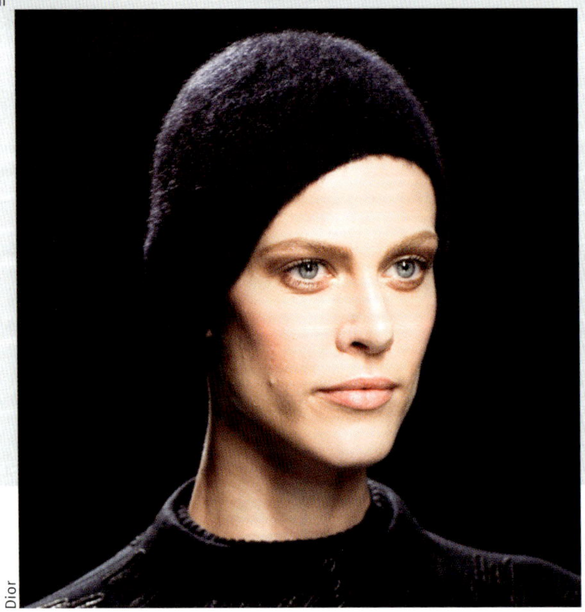
Dior

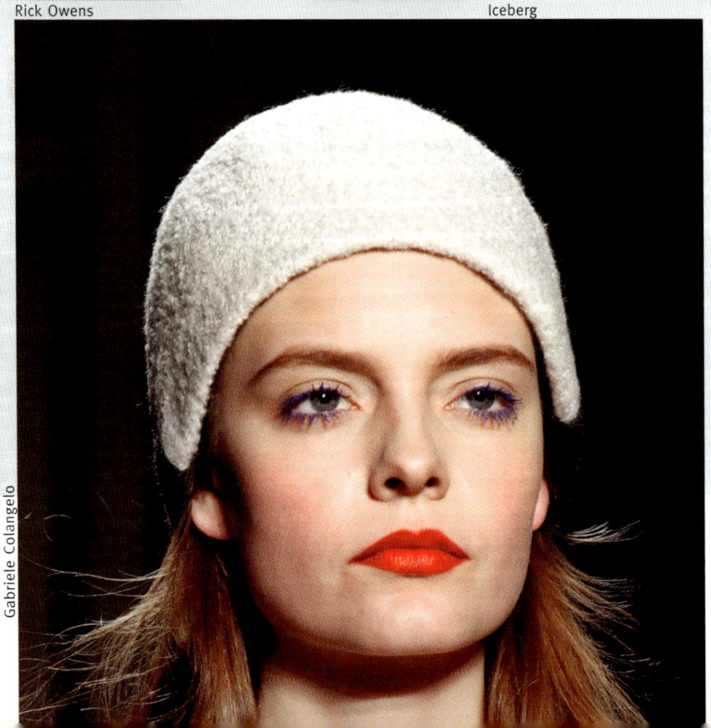
Gabriele Colangelo

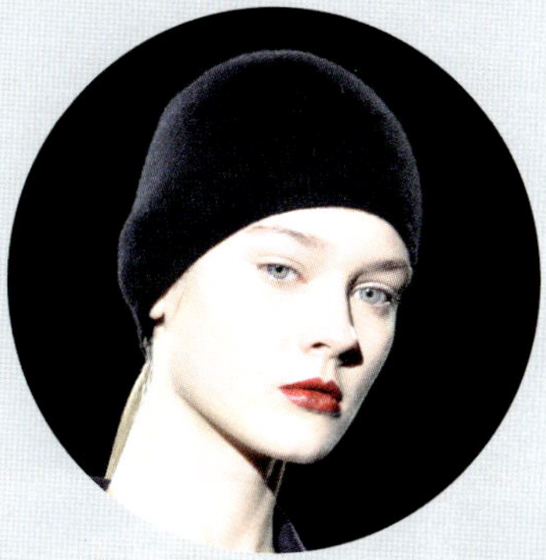
Hugo Boss

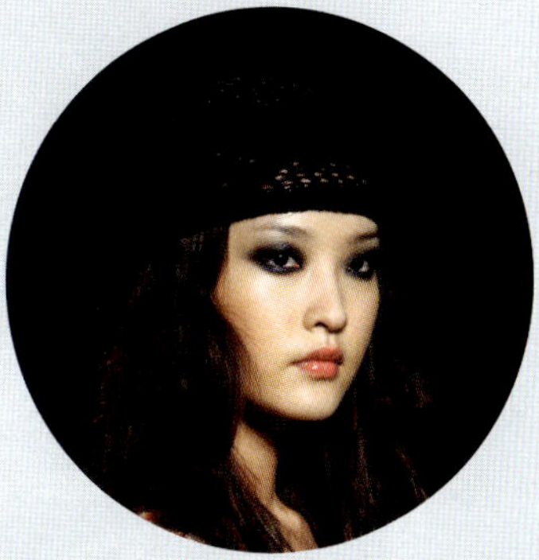
Miss Sixty

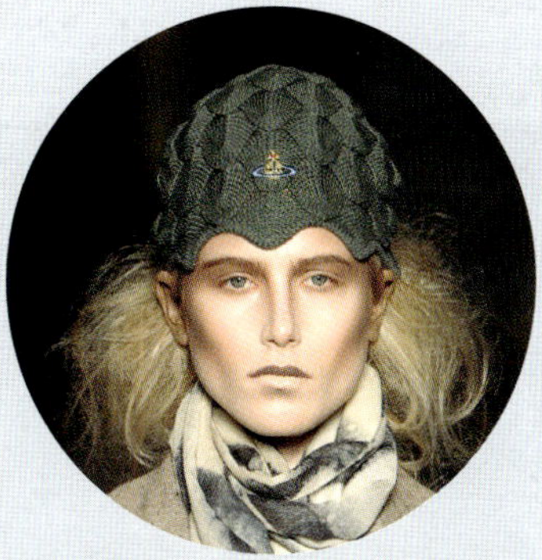
Vivienne Westwood Red Label

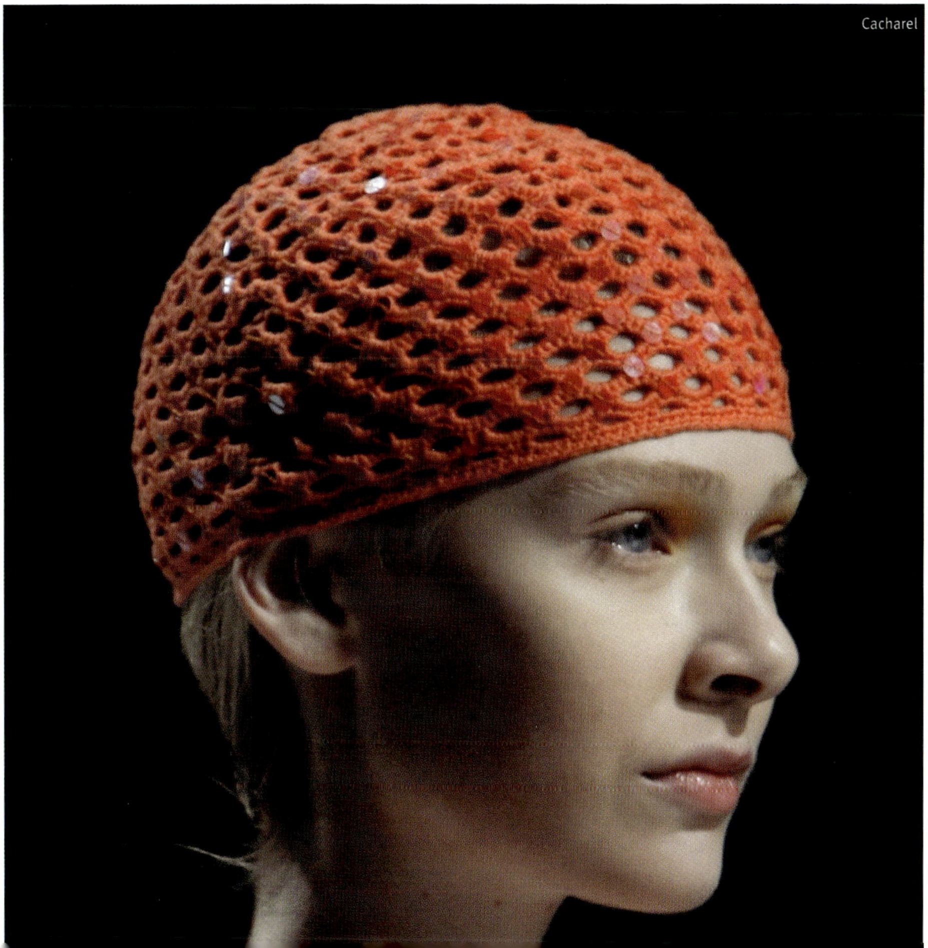
Cacharel

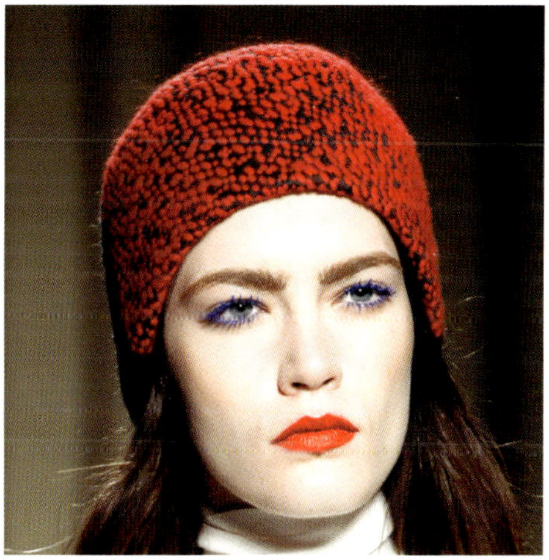
Gabriele Colangelo

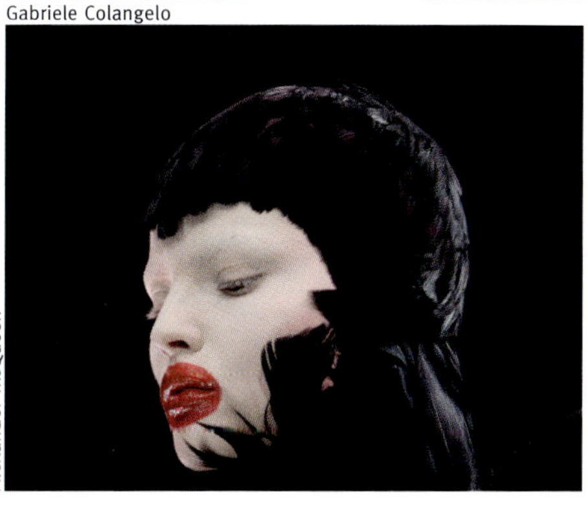
Alexander McQueen

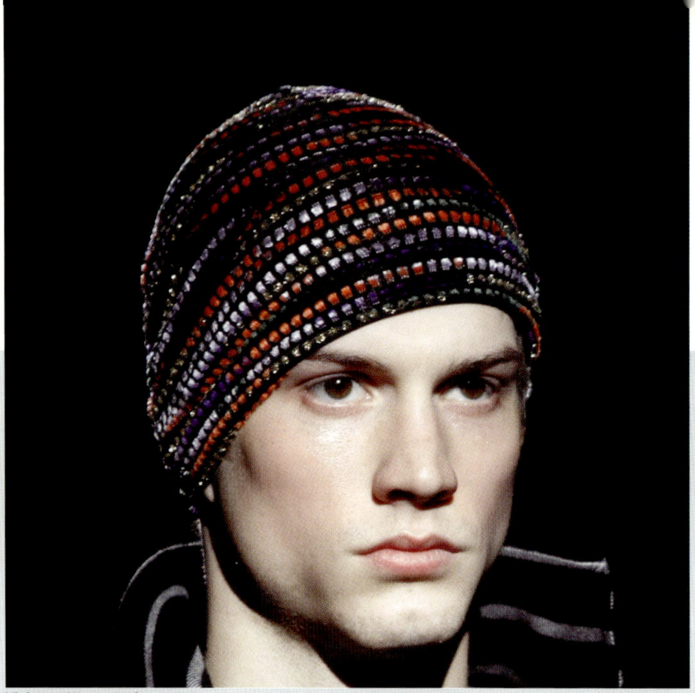

Vivienne Westwood

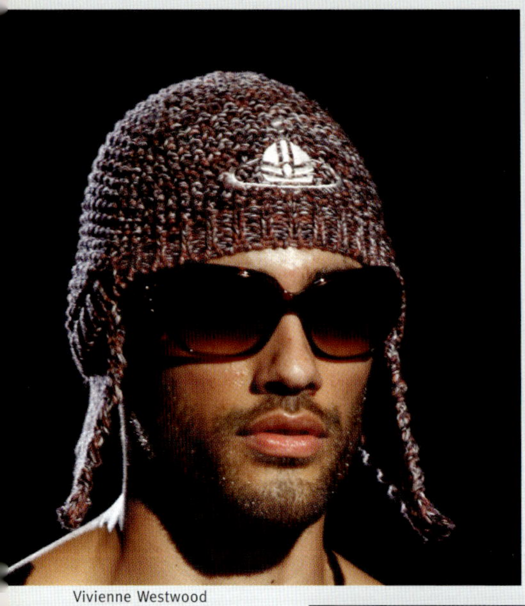

Vivienne Westwood

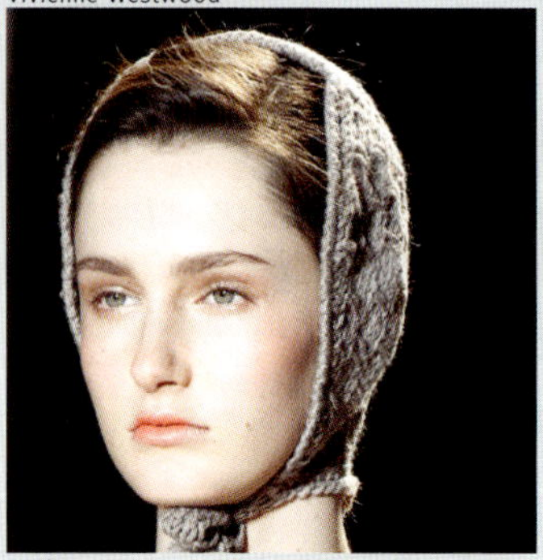

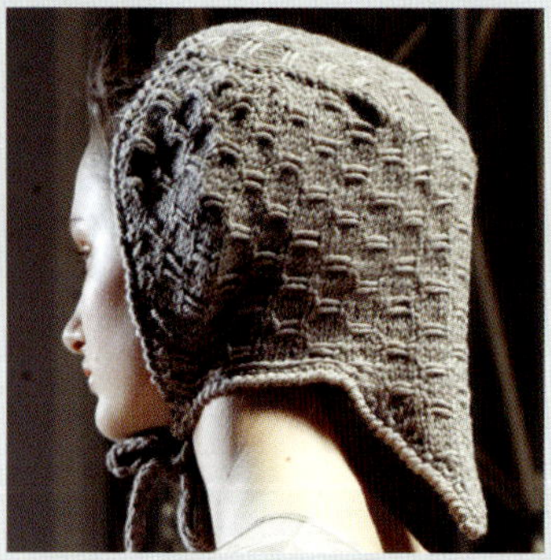

Rochas

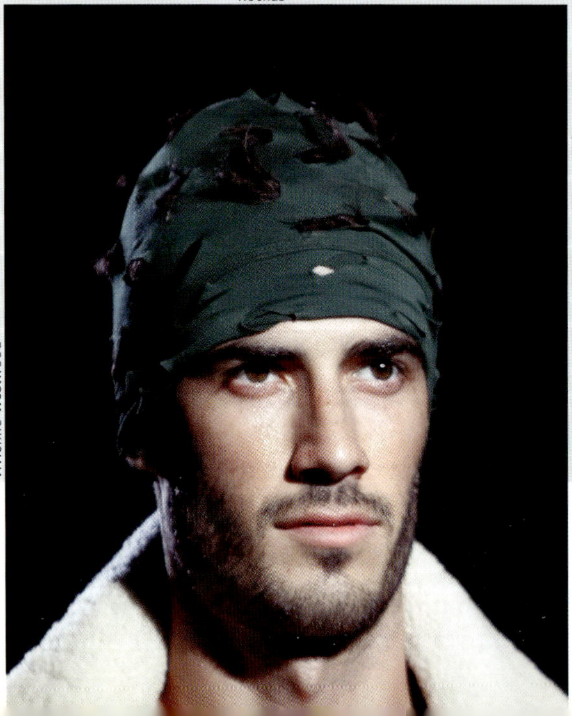

Vivienne Westwood

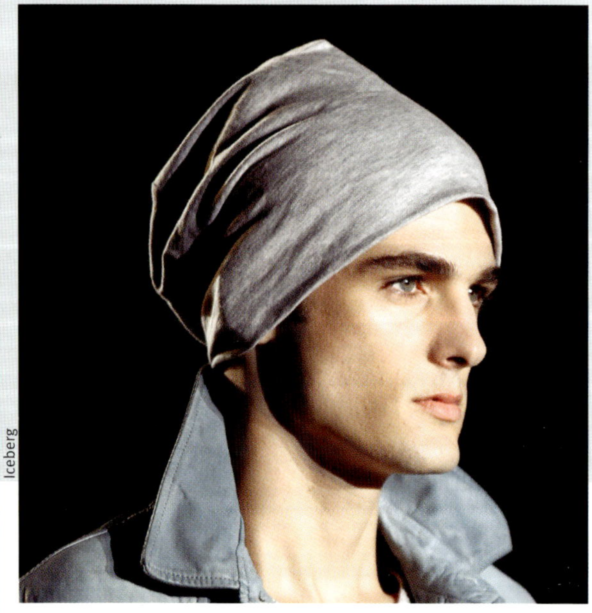

Iceberg

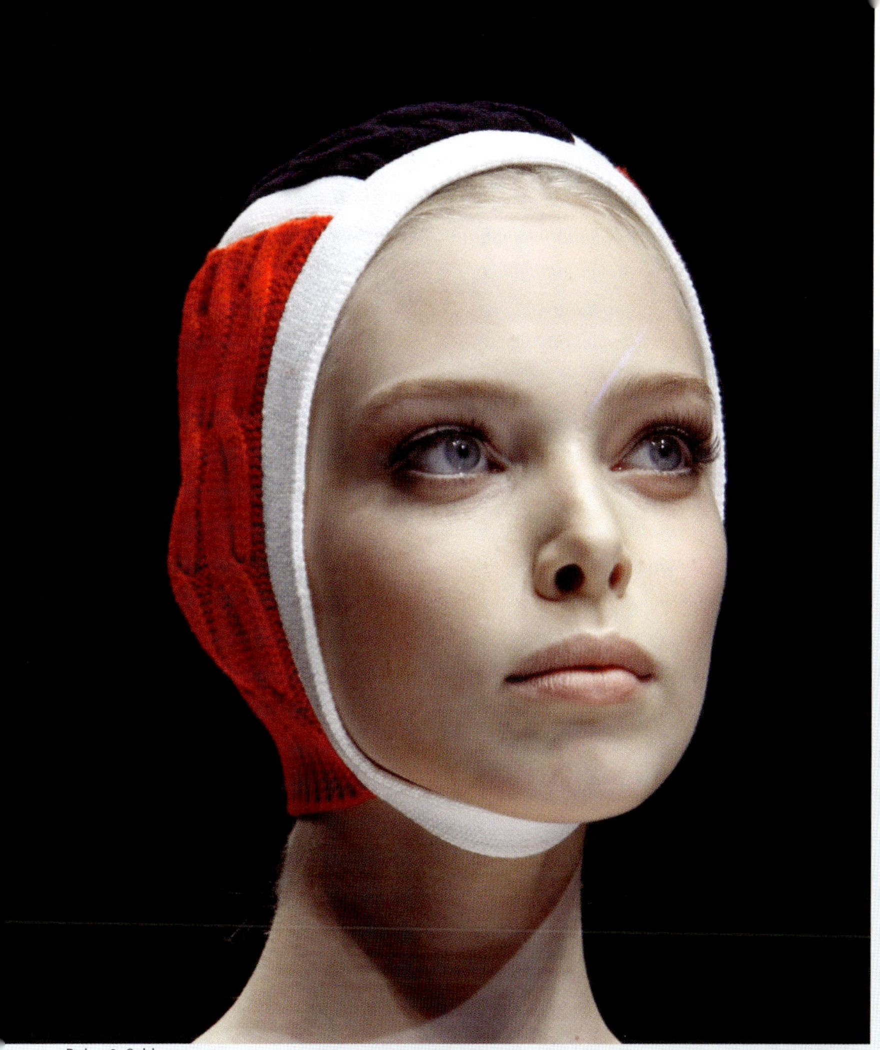

Dolce & Gabbana

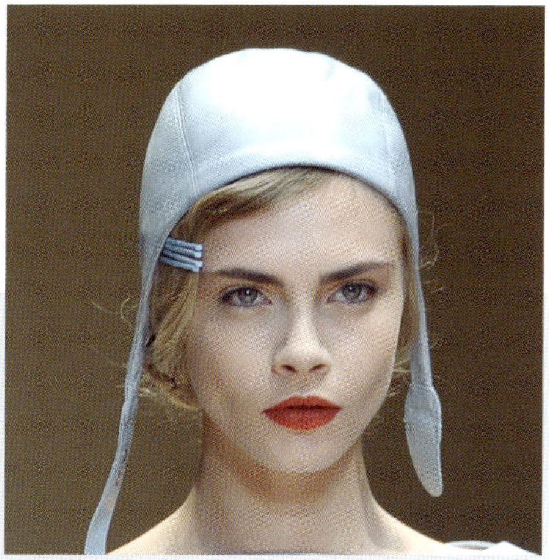

Cacharel

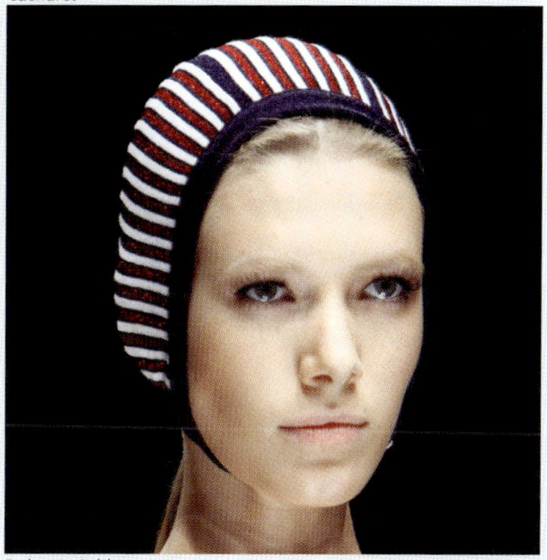

Dolce & Gabbana

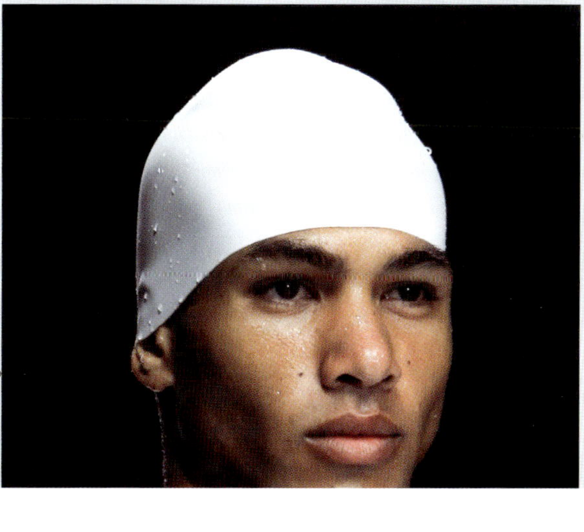

Dirk Bikkembergs

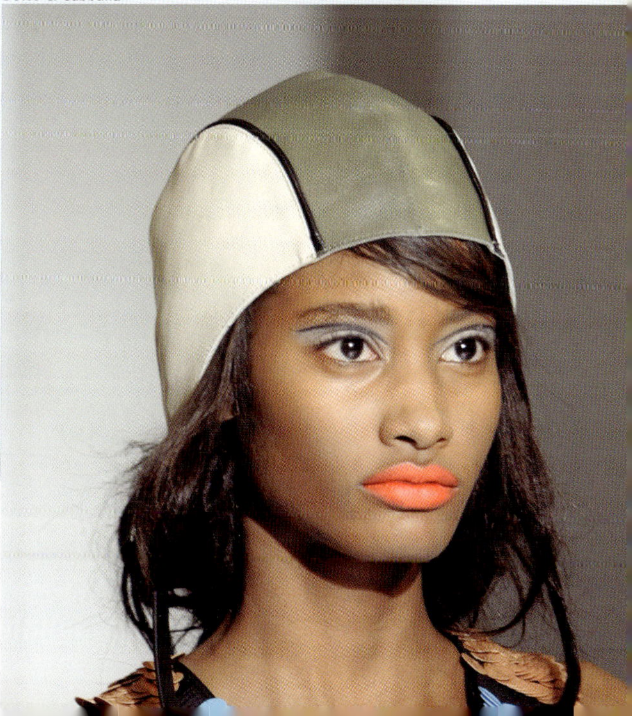

Marni

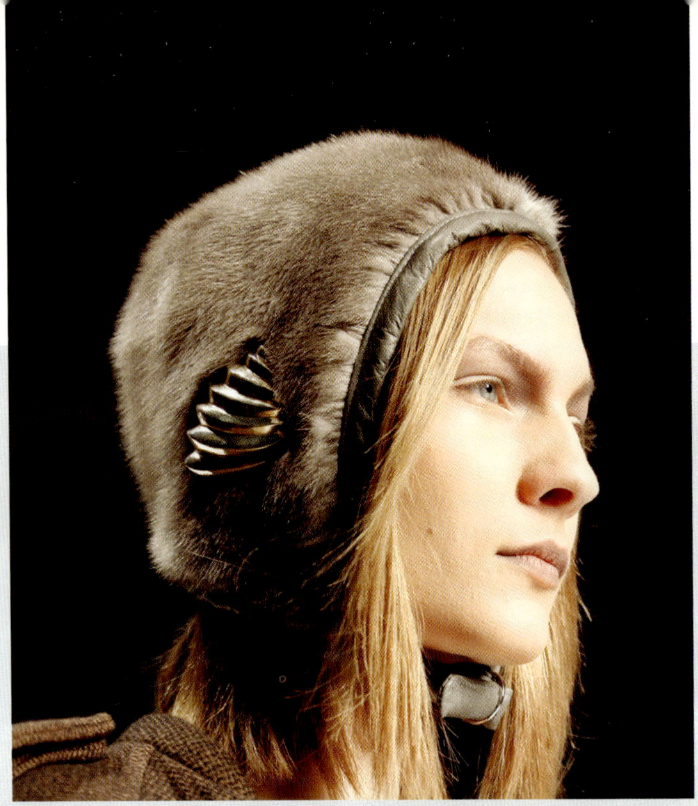

Max Mara

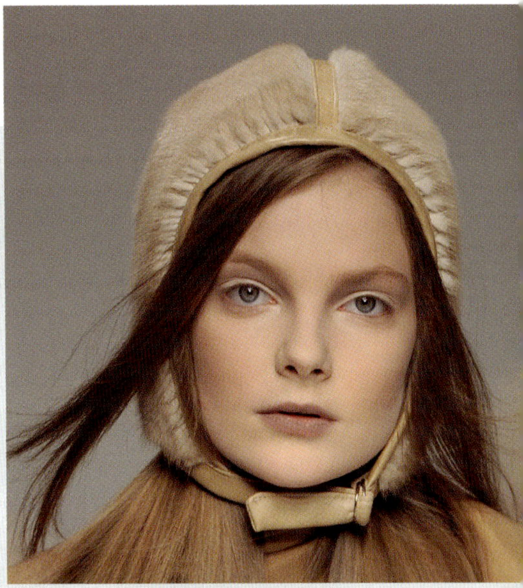

Max Mara

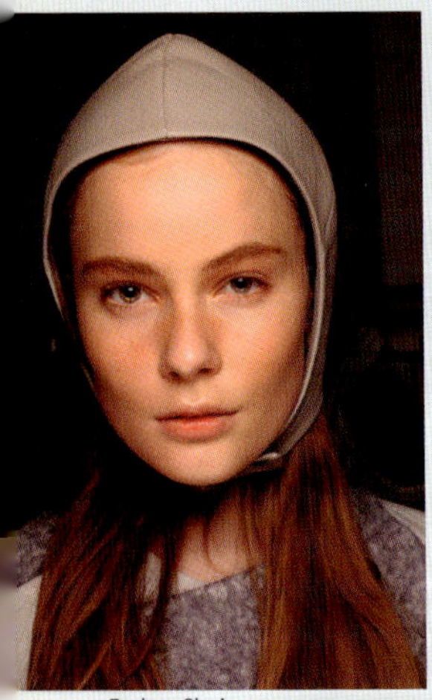

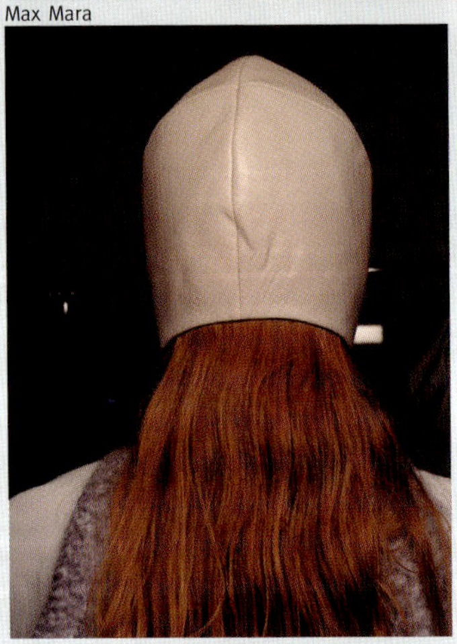

Eudon Choi

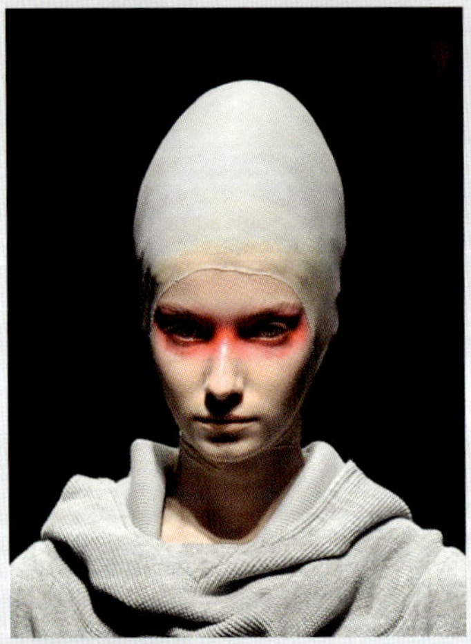

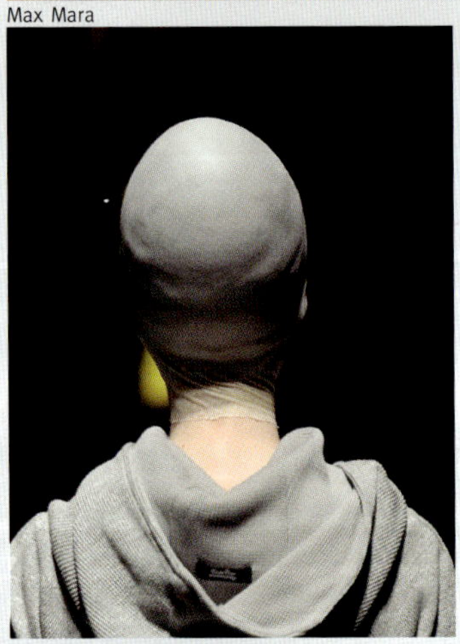

Undercover

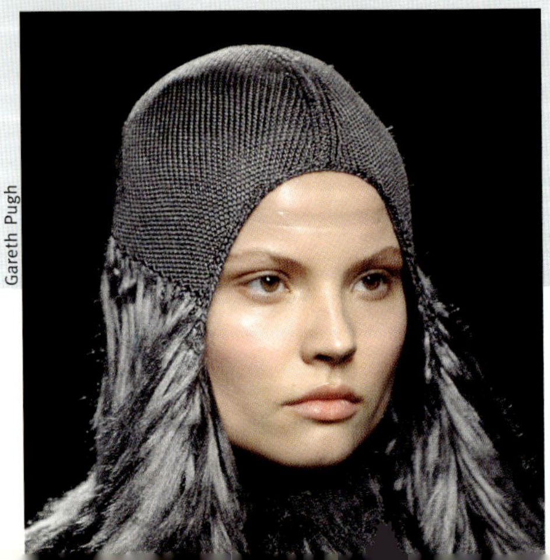

Gareth Pugh

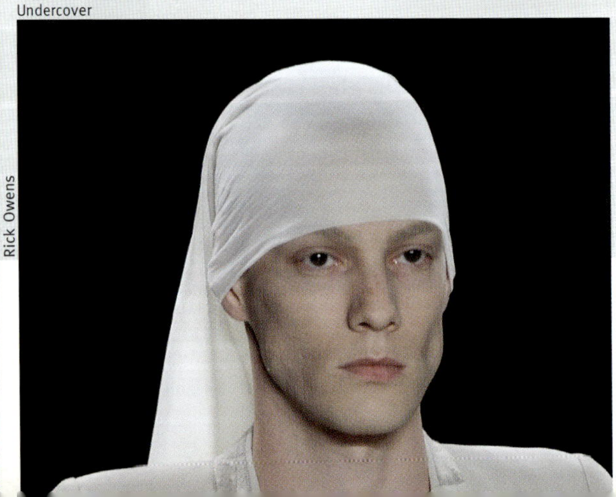

Rick Owens

Prada

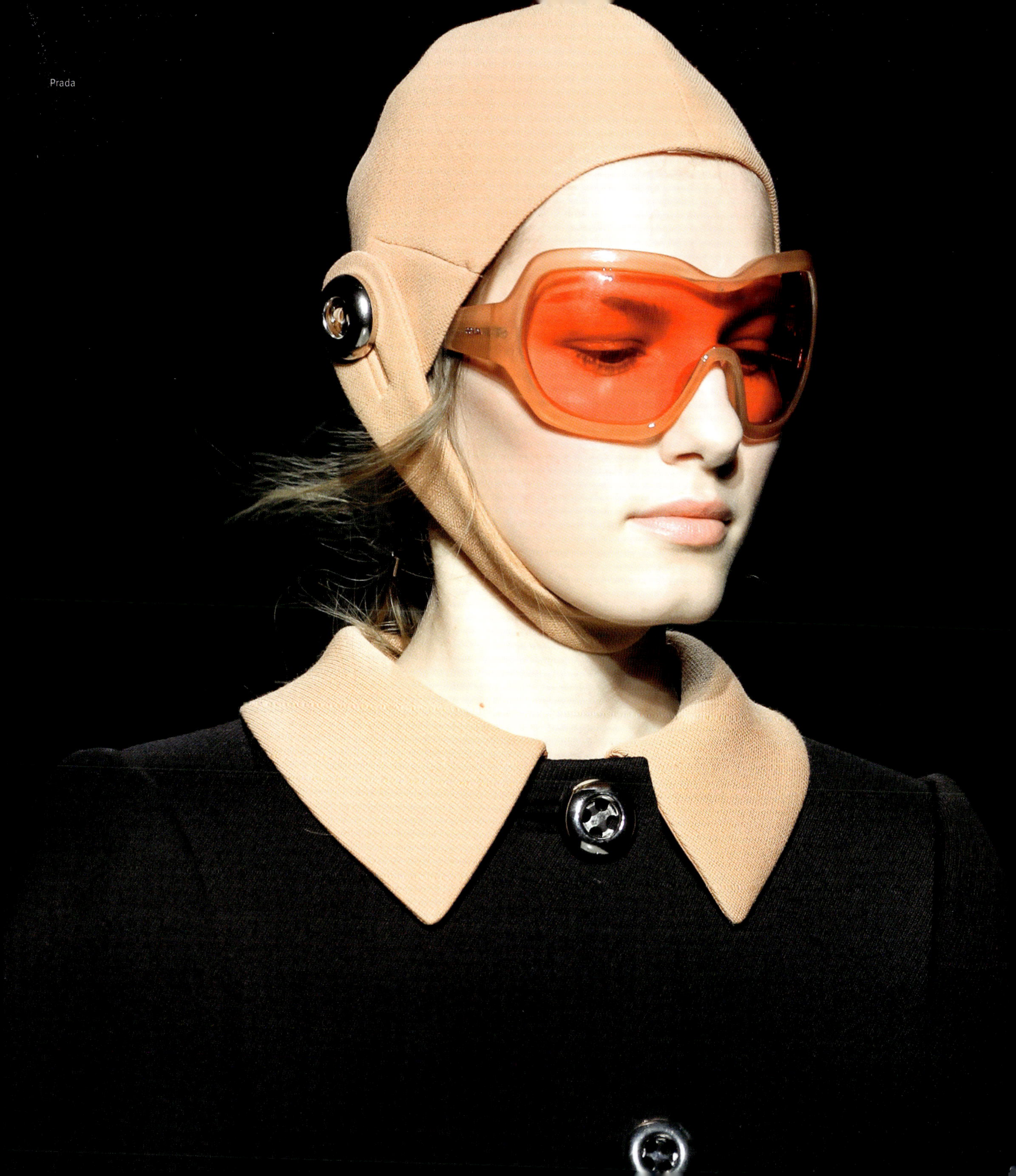

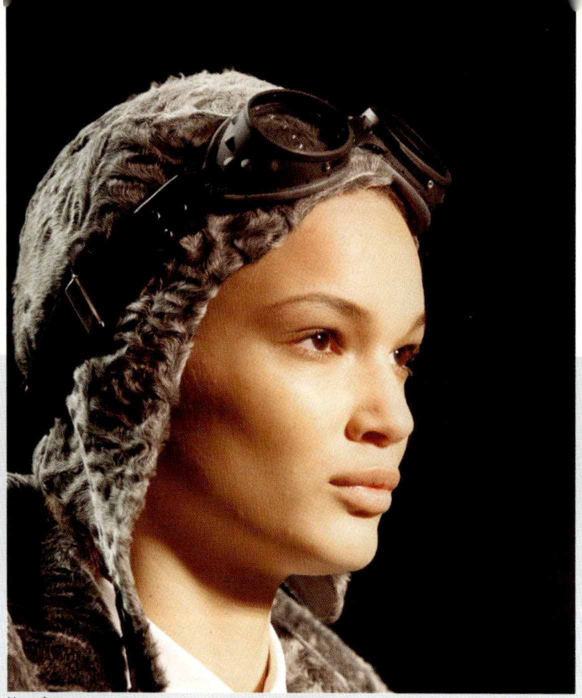

Hermès

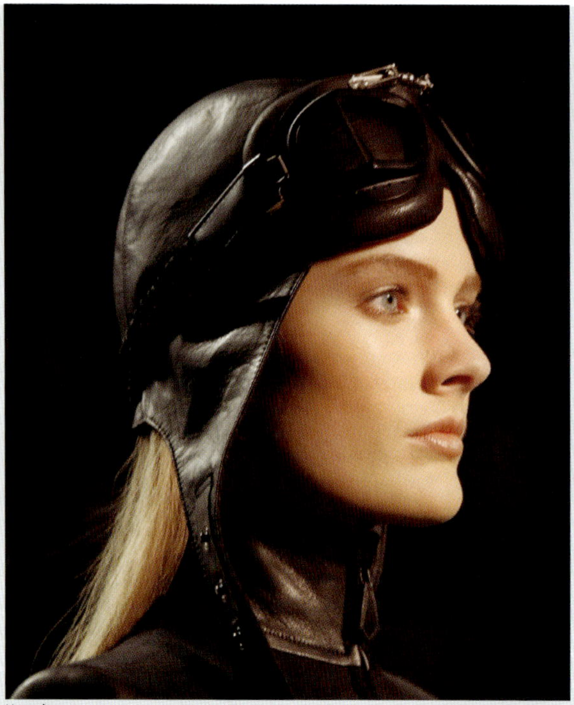

Hermès

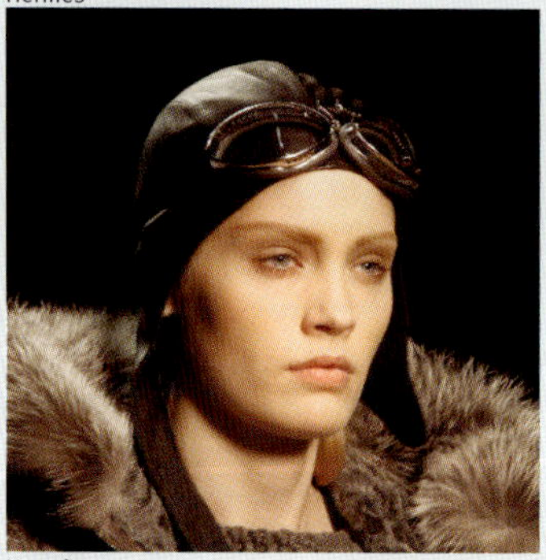

Hermès

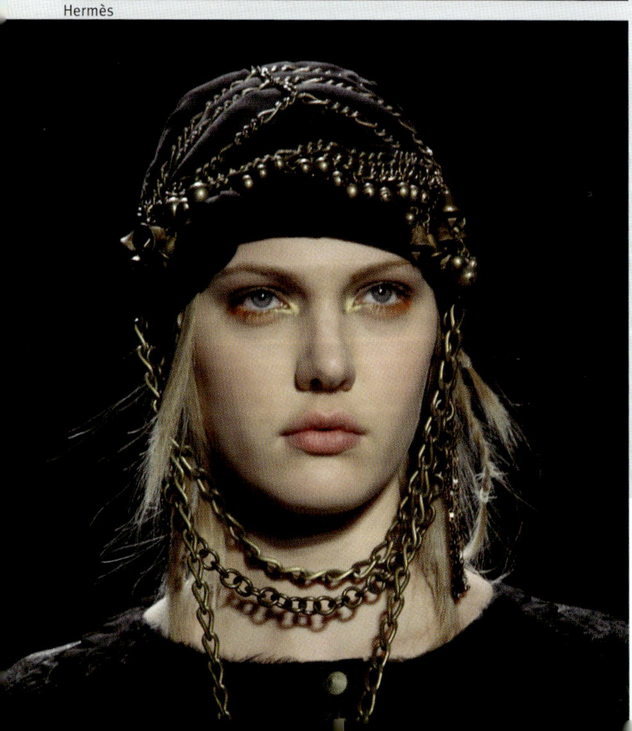

Alexandre Herchcovitch

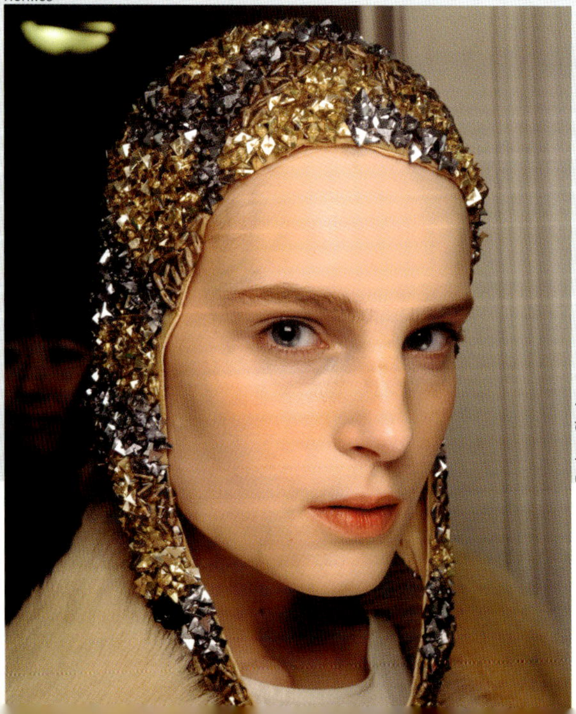

Eudon Choi

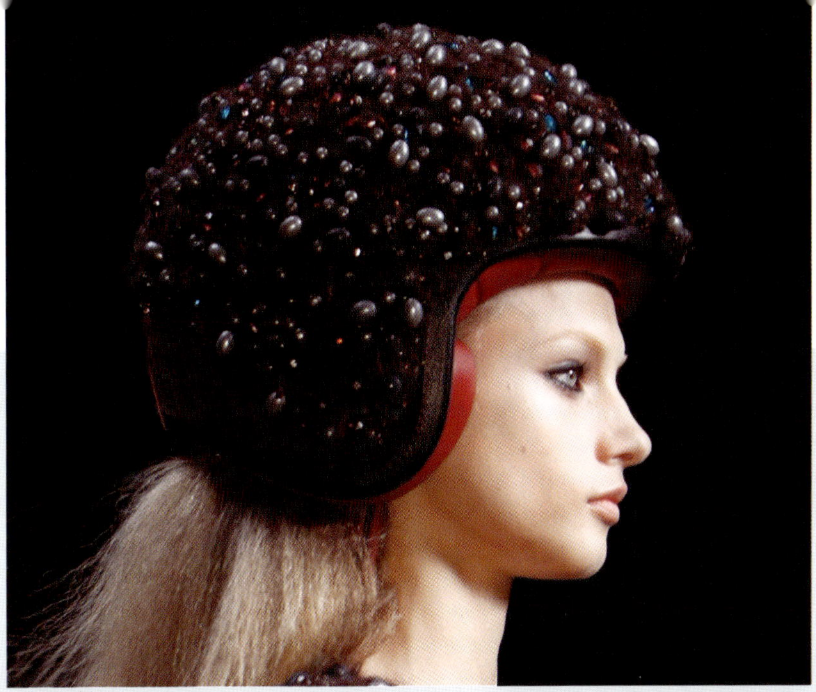
Karl Lagerfeld

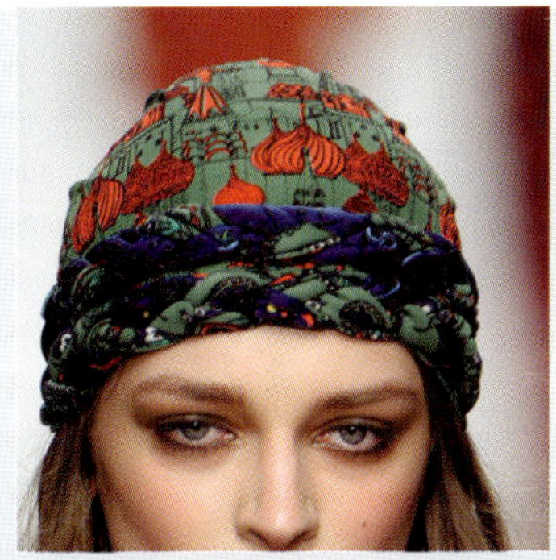
Issa

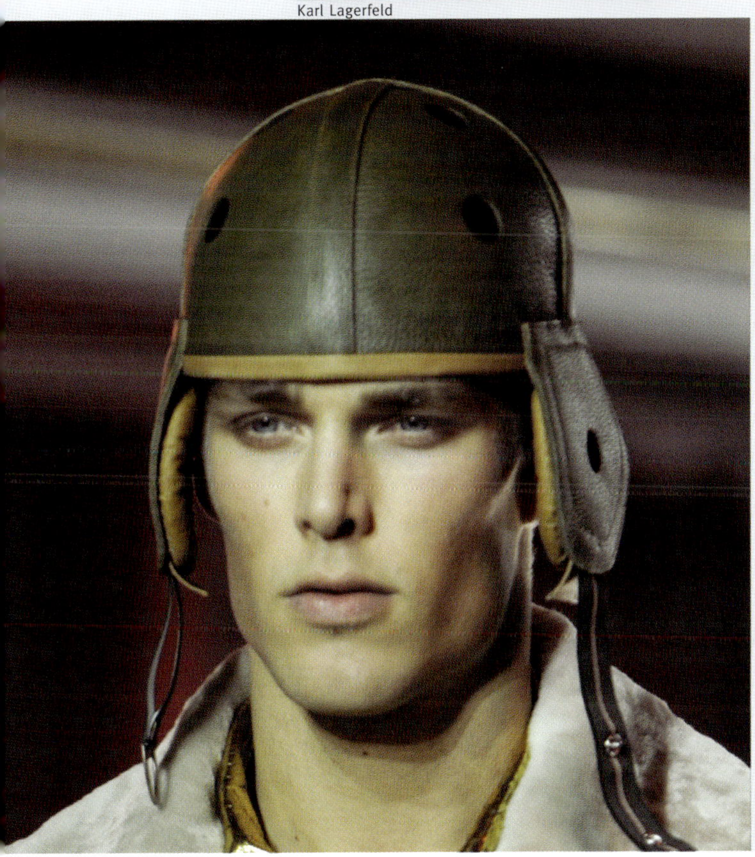
John Galliano

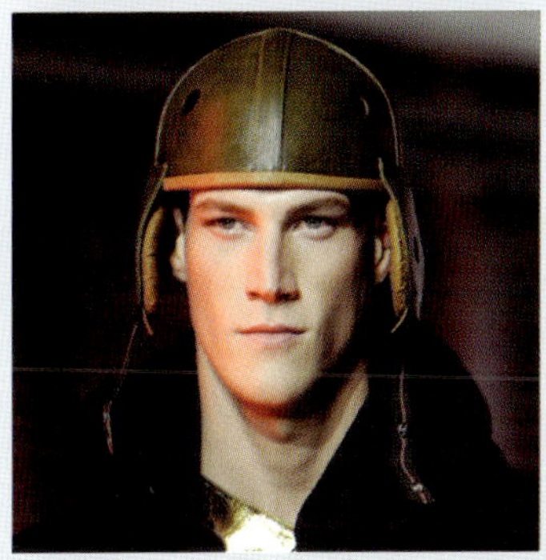
John Galliano

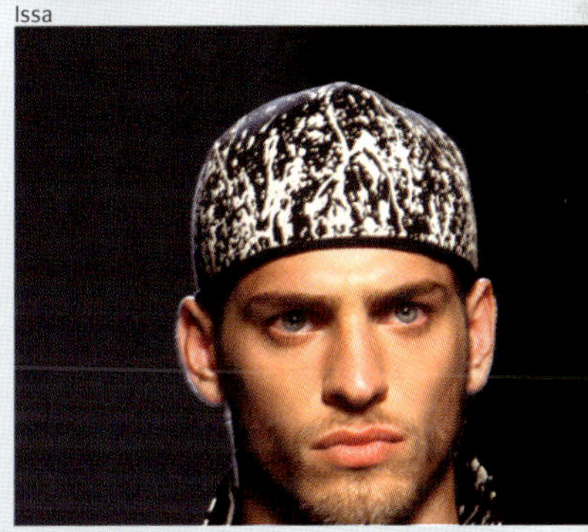
Jean Paul Gaultier

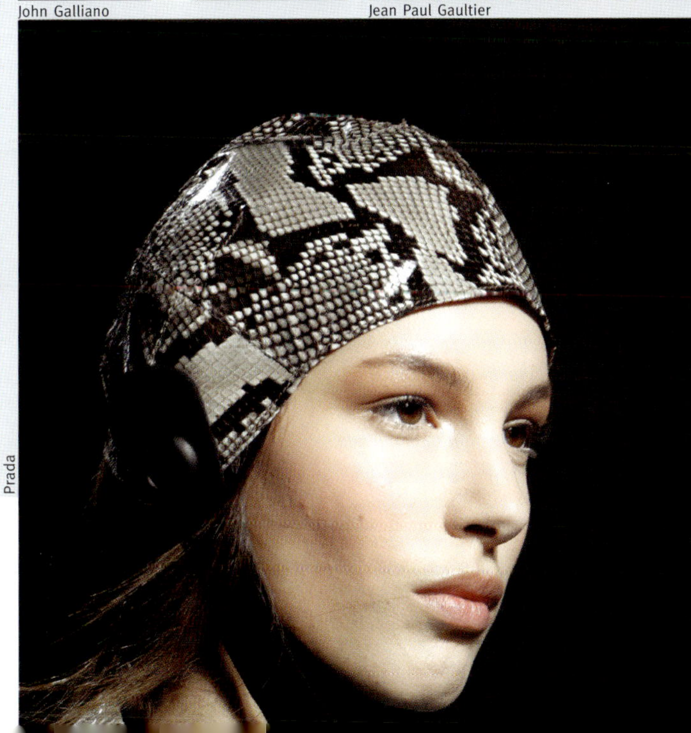
Prada

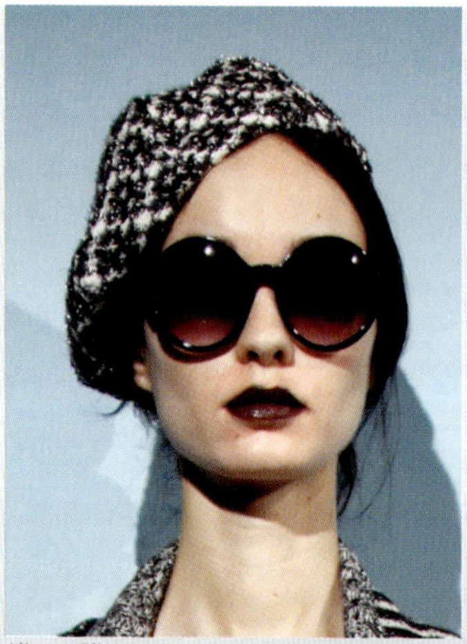
Alice + Olivia

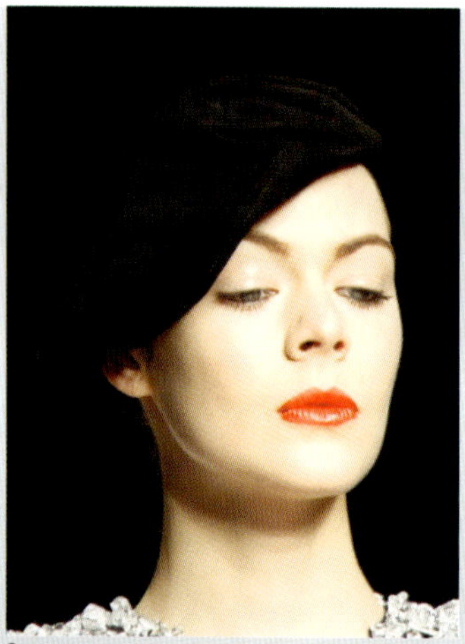
Sportmax

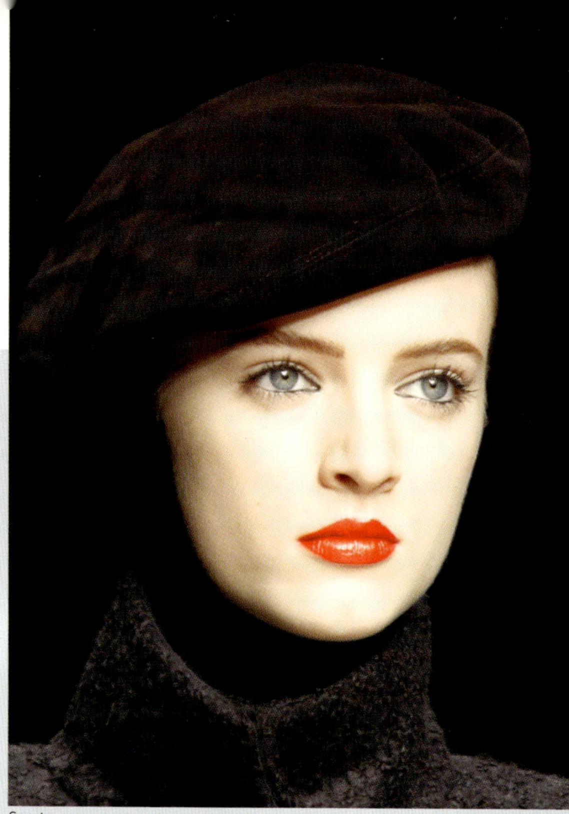
Sportmax

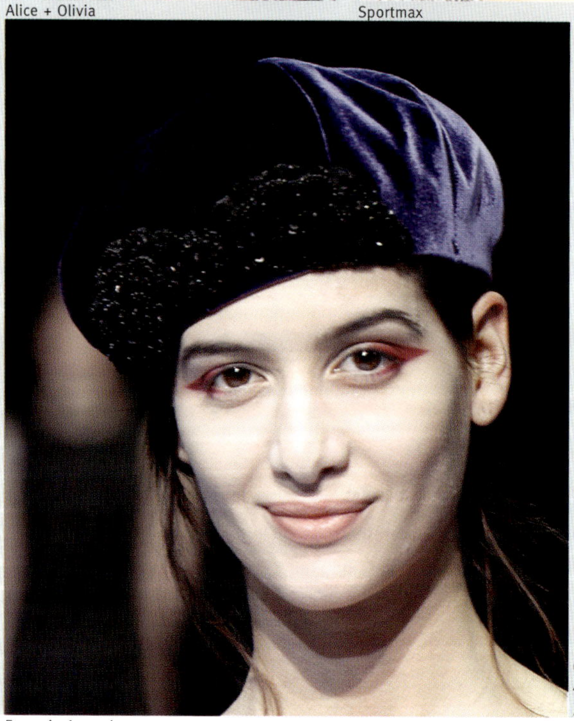
Emporio Armani

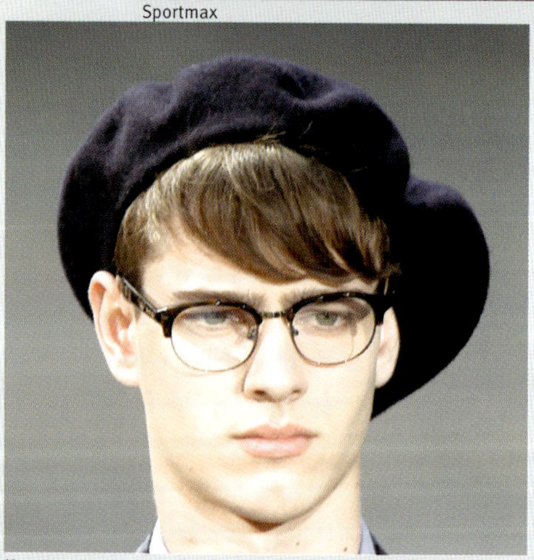
Kenzo

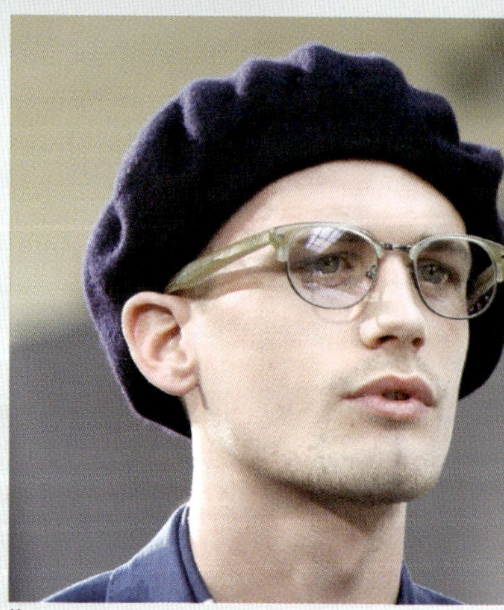
Kenzo

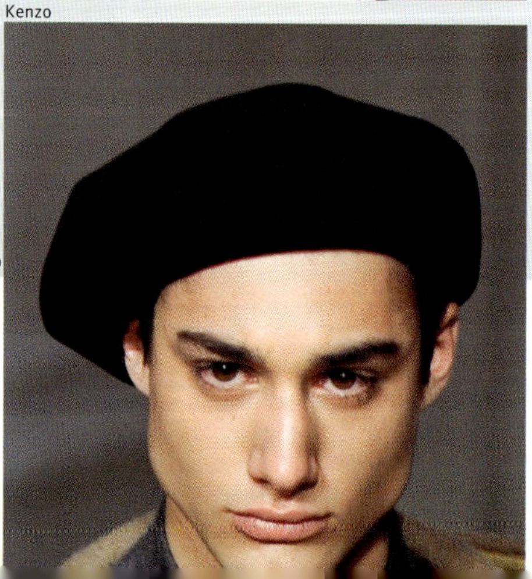
Agnès B.

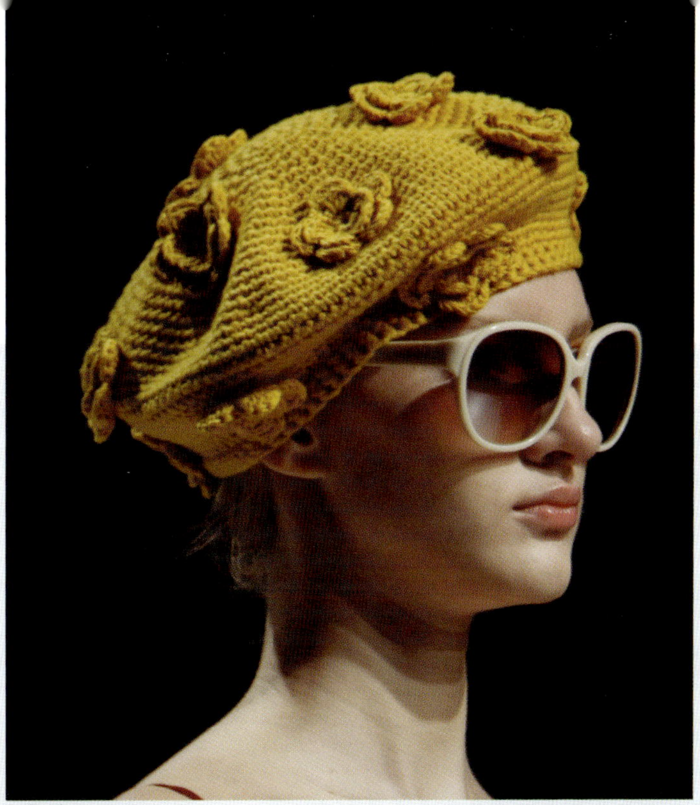

Cacharel

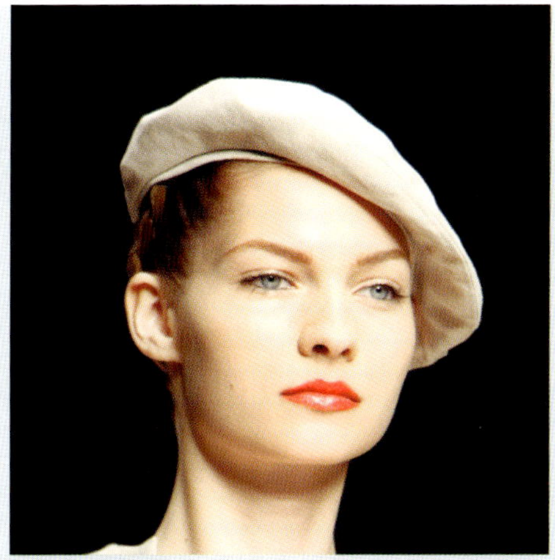

Sportmax

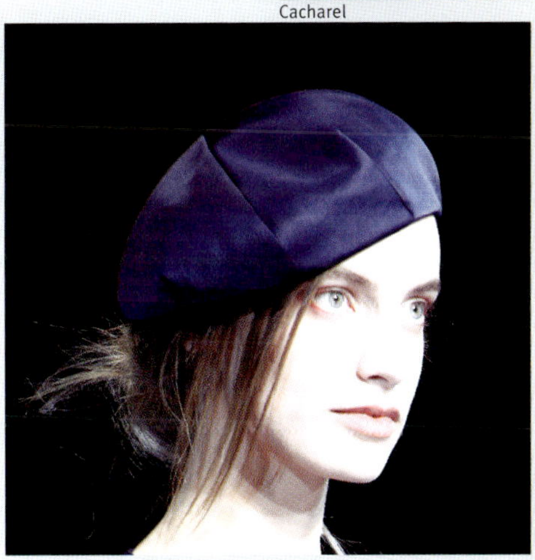

Emporio Armani

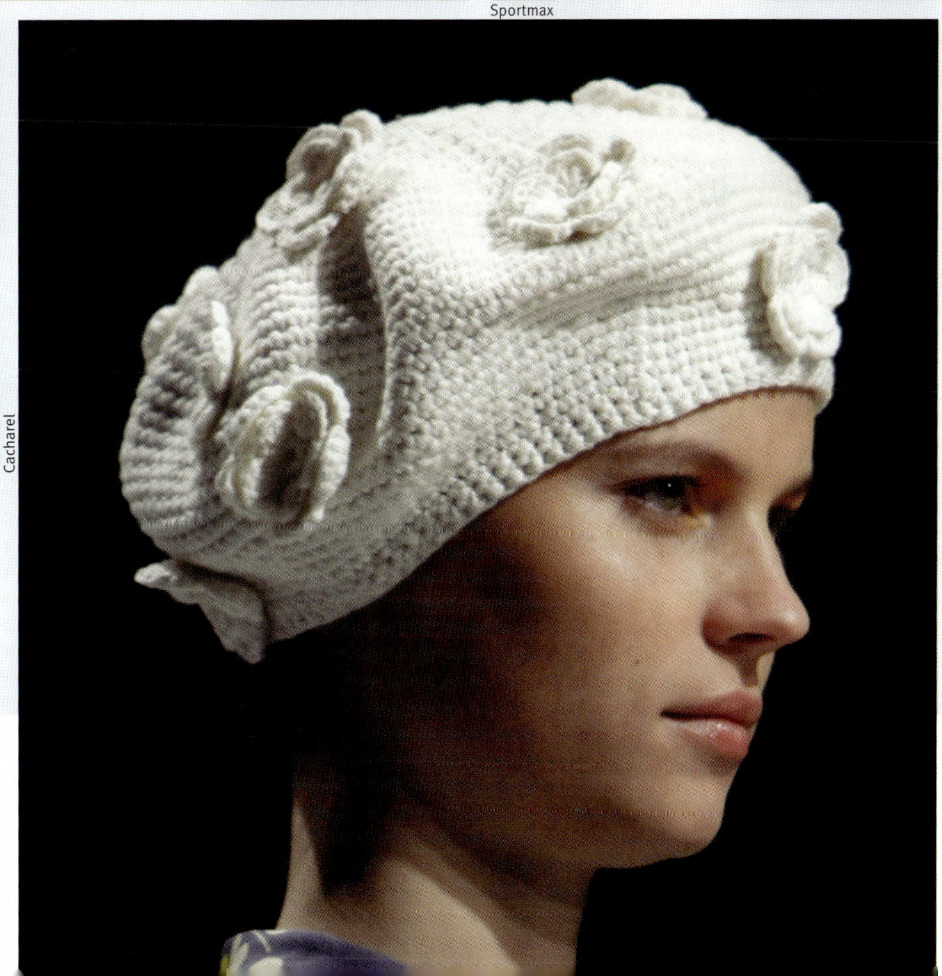

Cacharel

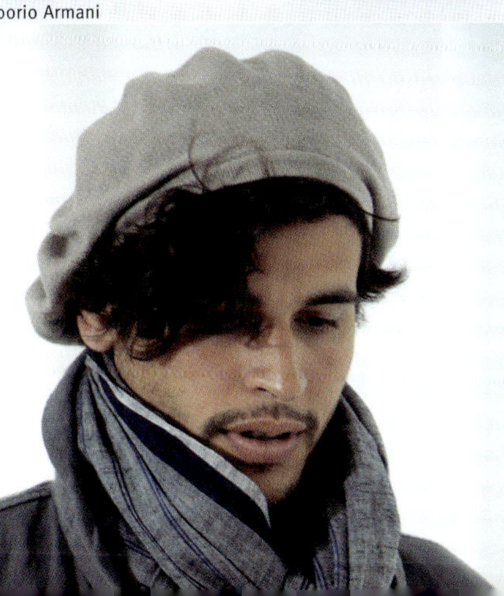

Agnès B.

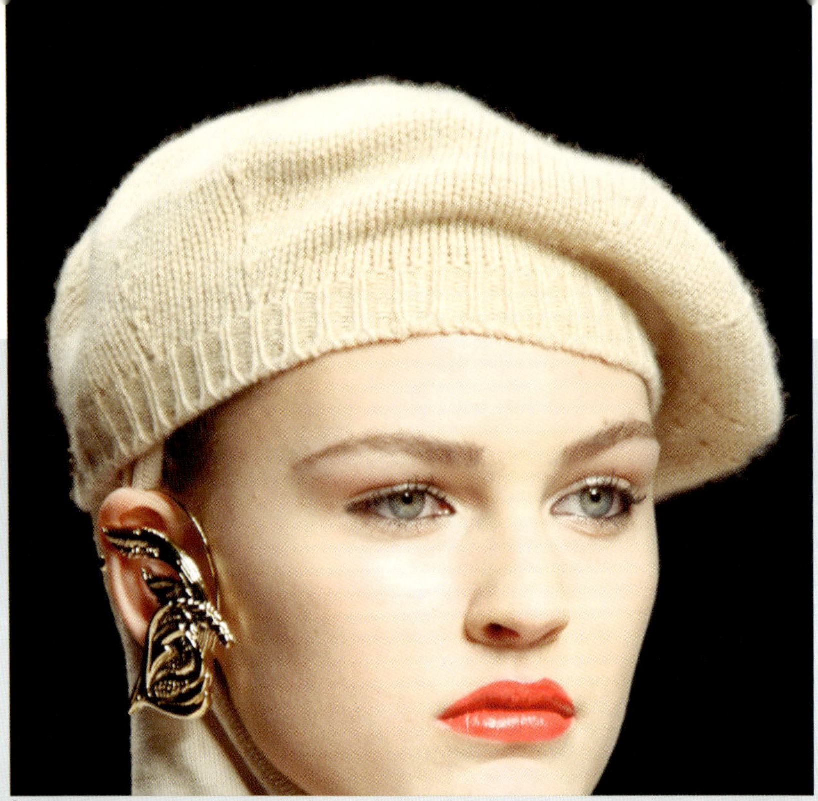

Sportmax

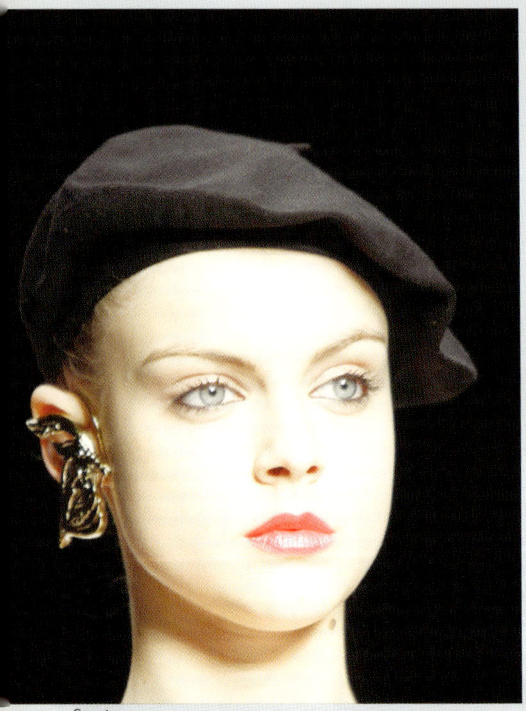

Sportmax

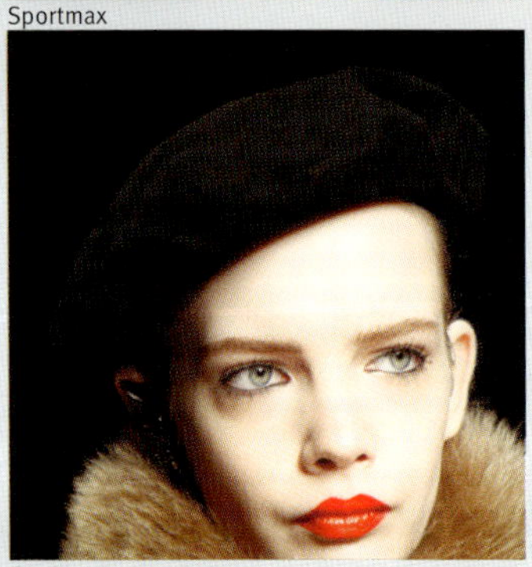

Sportmax

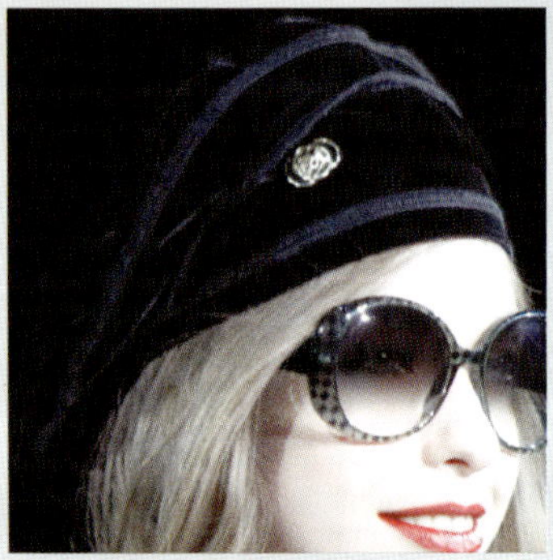

Emporio Armani

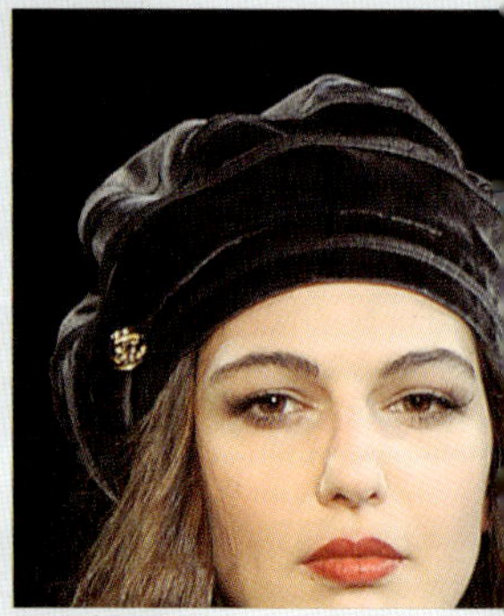

Emporio Armani

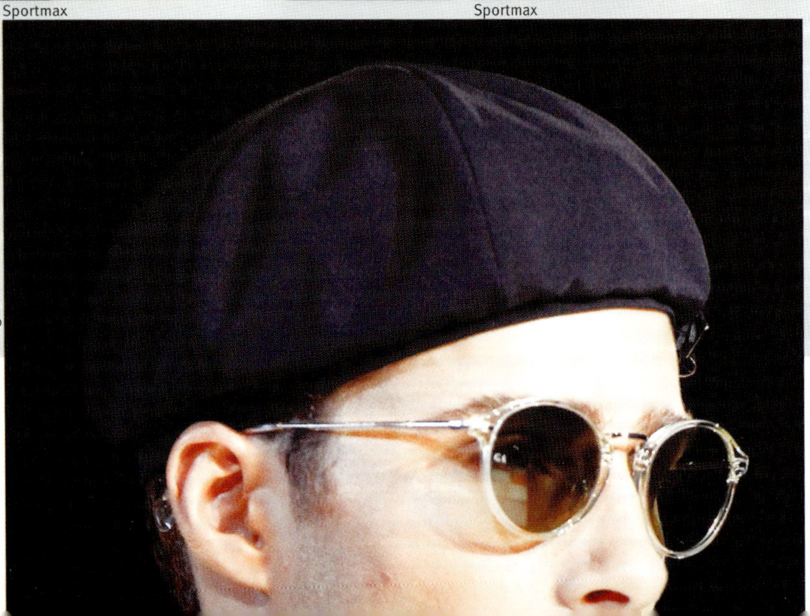

Giorgio Armani

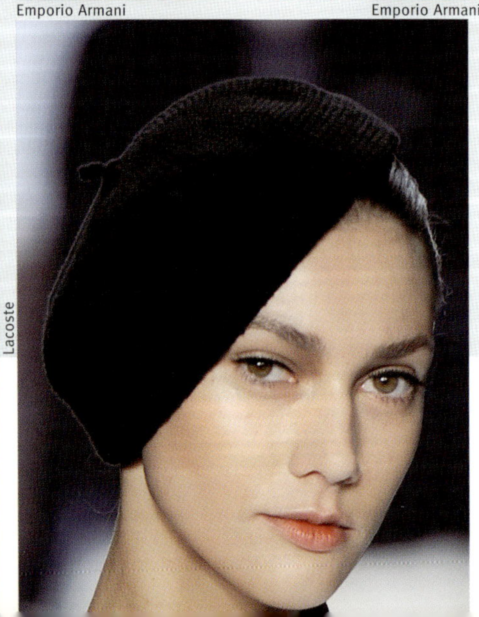

Lacoste

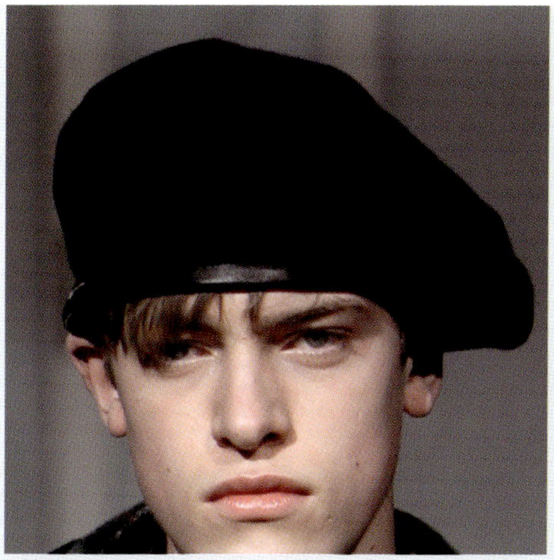
Yohji Yamamoto

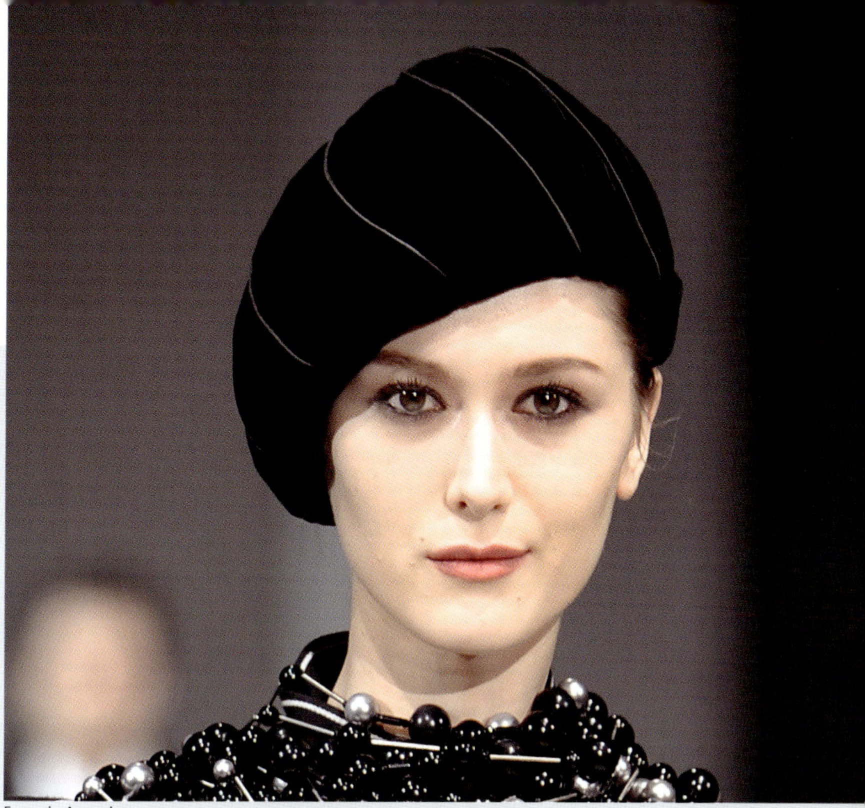
Emporio Armani

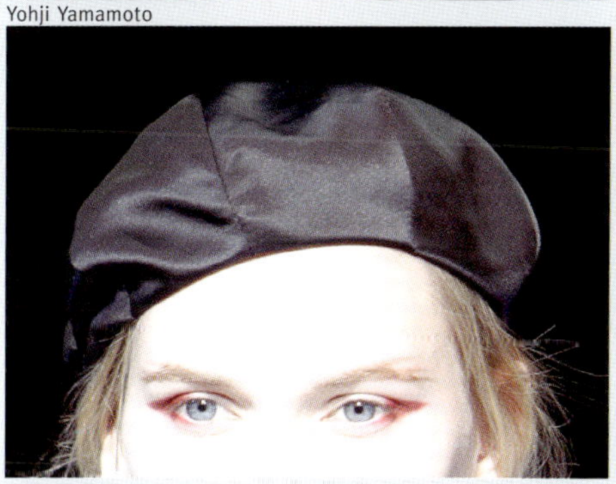
Emporio Armani

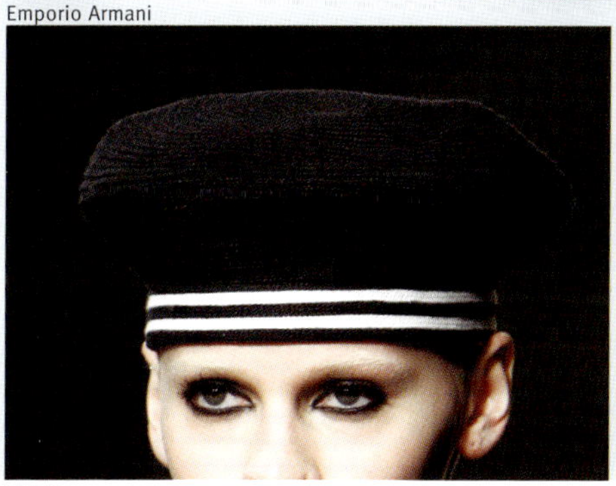
Unique

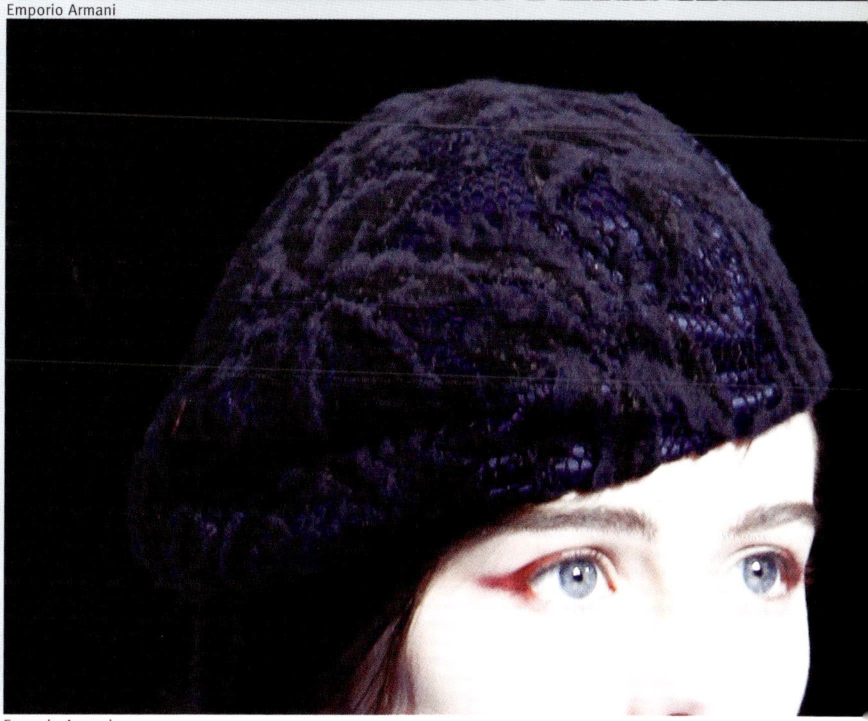
Emporio Armani

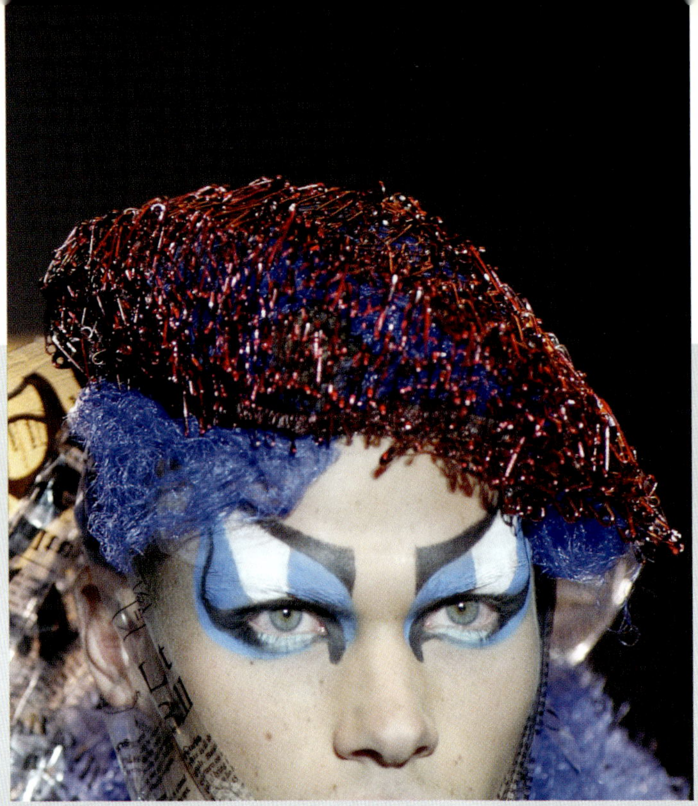

John Galliano

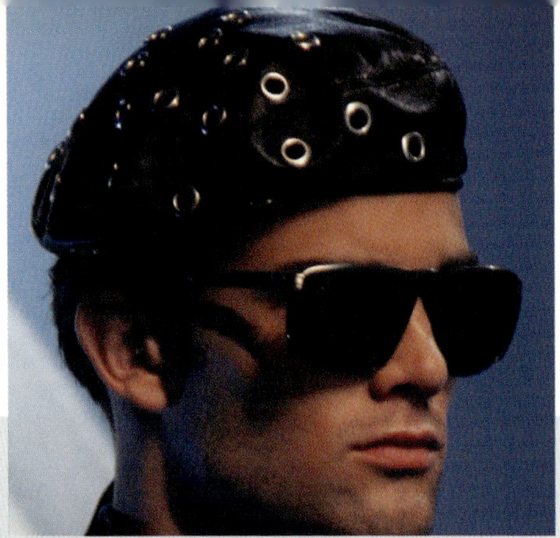

John Galliano

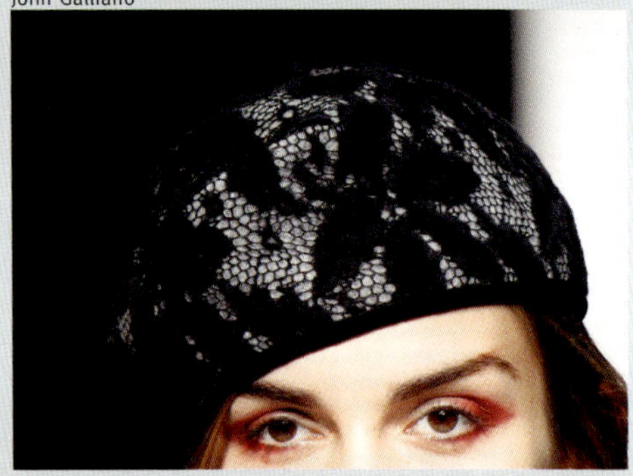

Emporio Armani

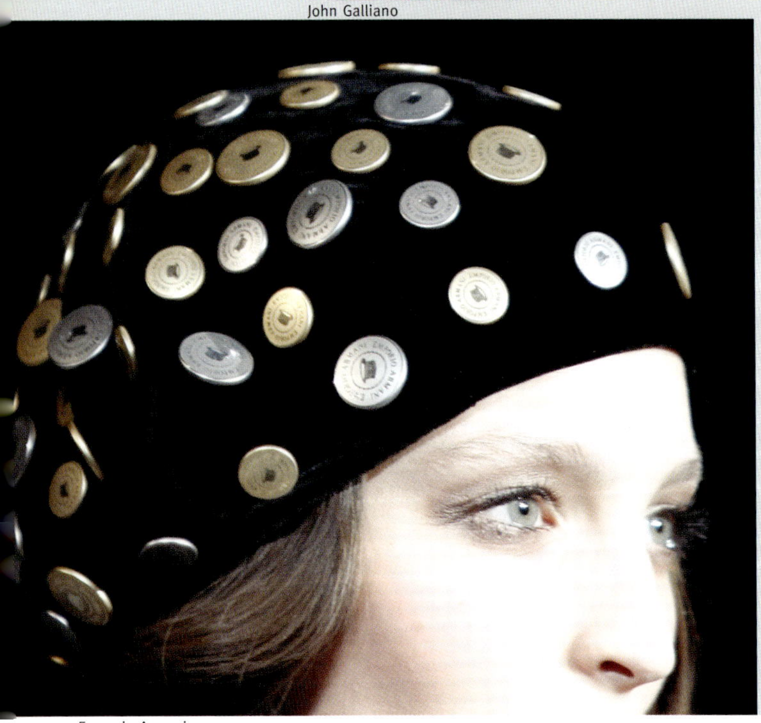

Emporio Armani

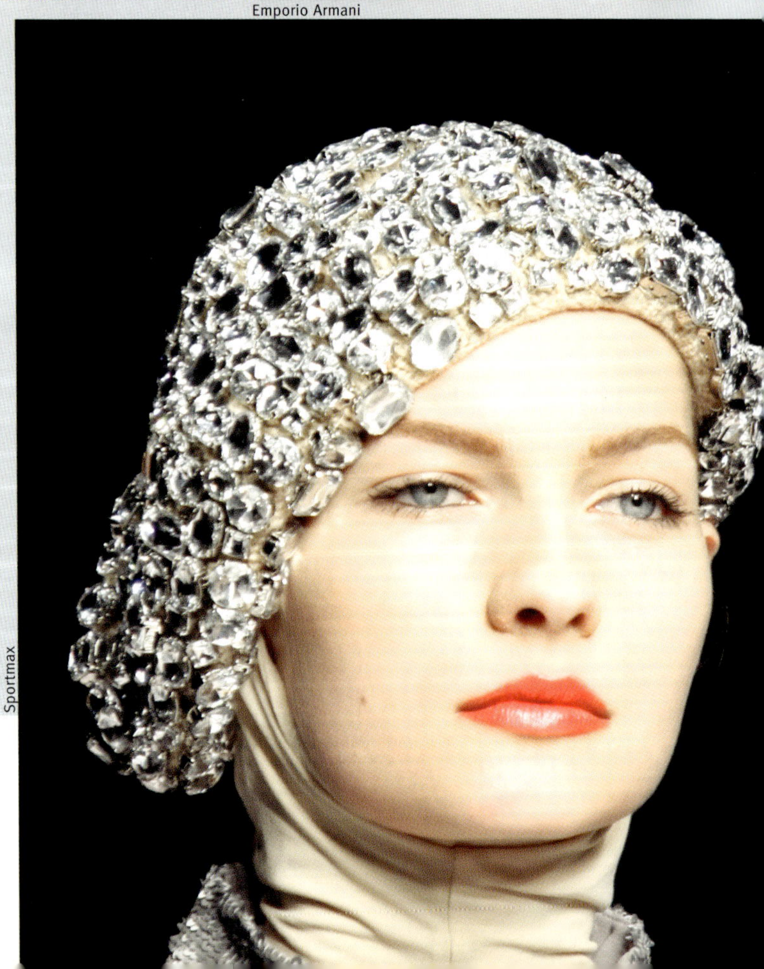

Sportmax

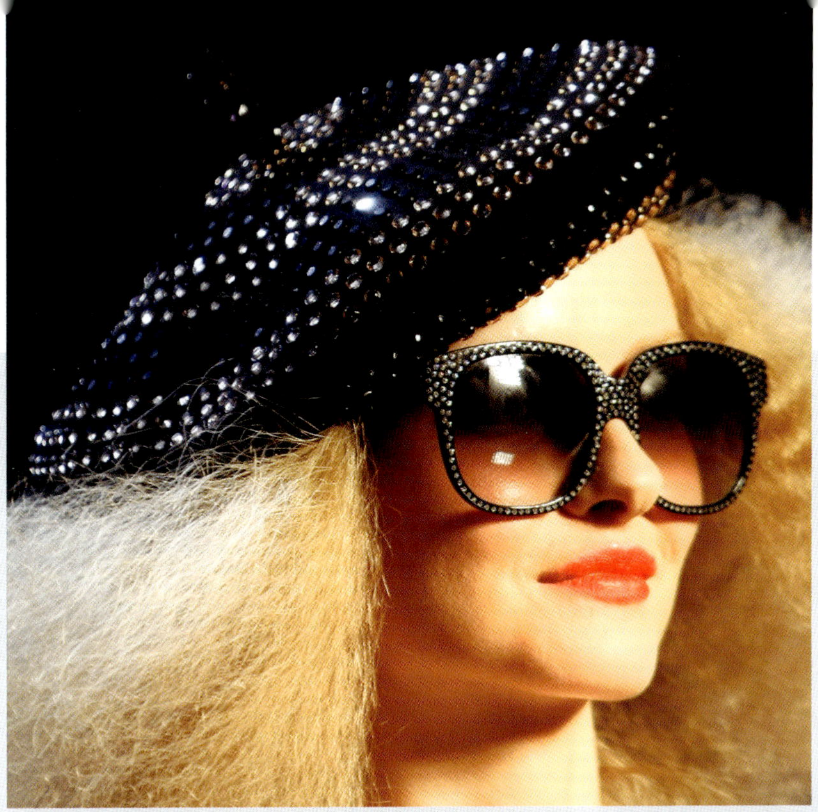

Sonia Rykiel

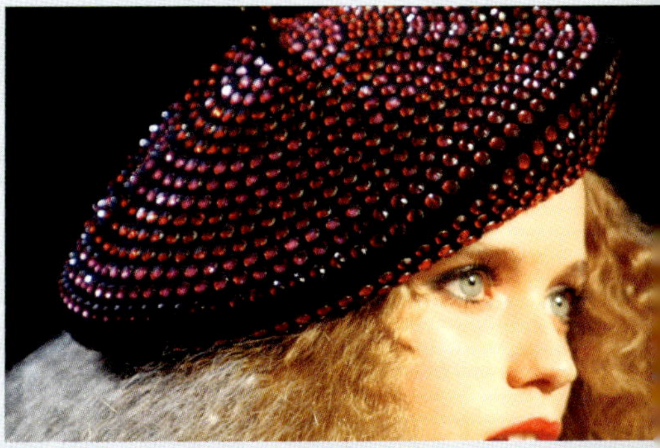

Sonia Rykiel

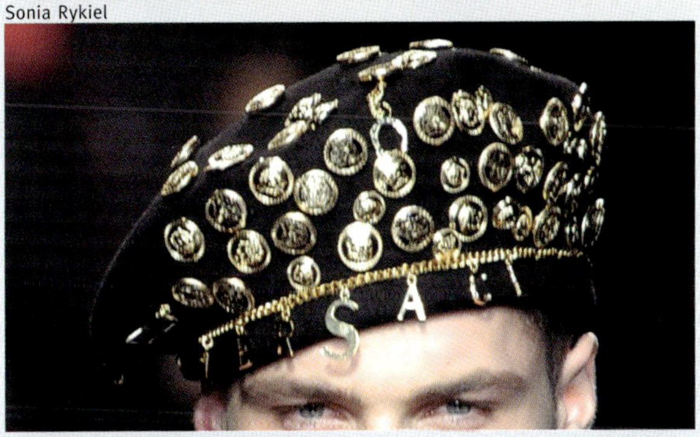

Versace

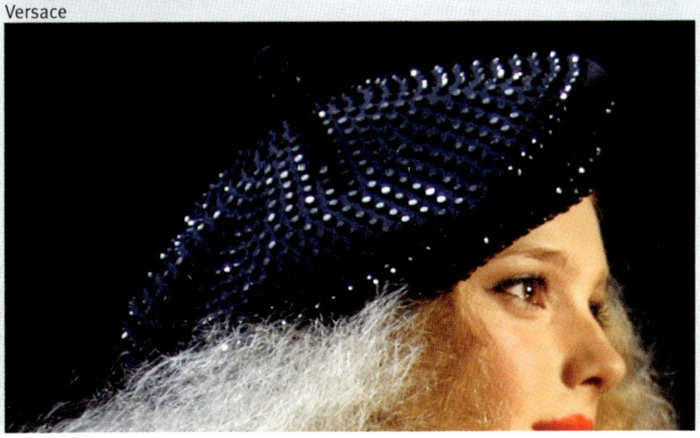

Sonia Rykiel

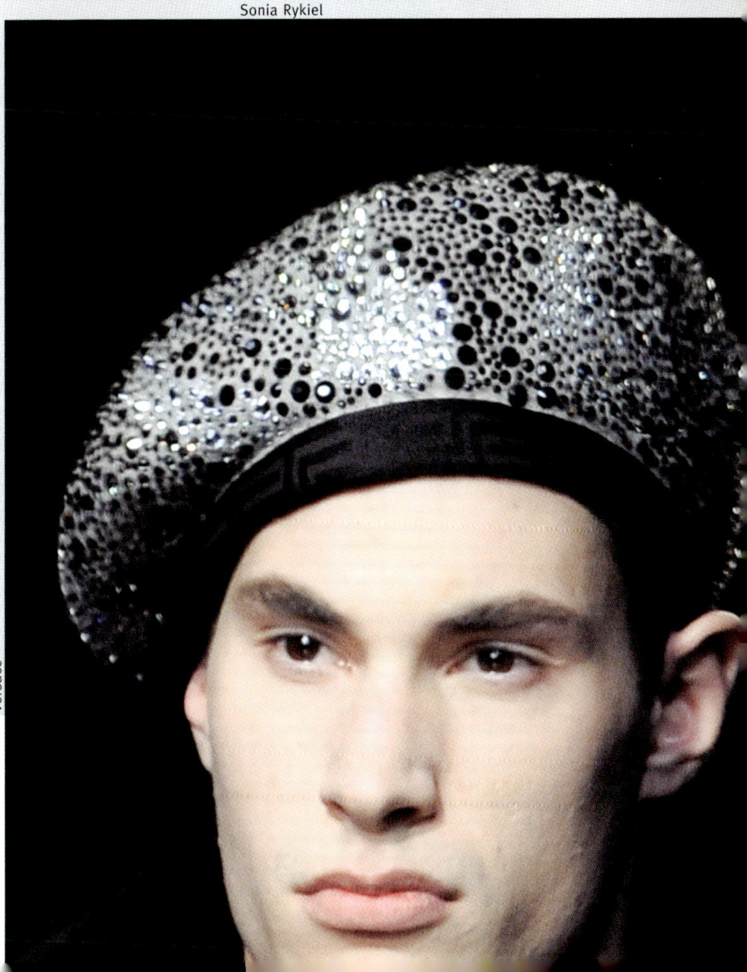

Versace

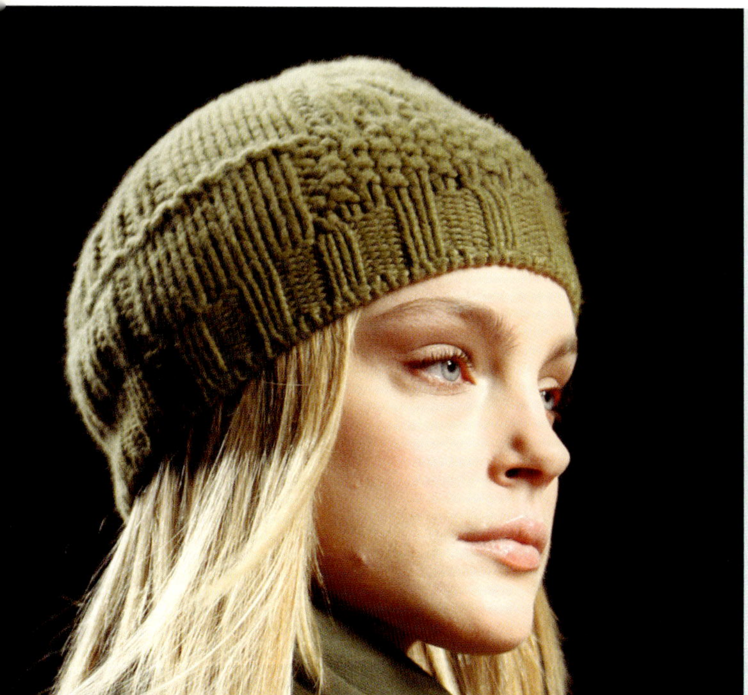

Hermès

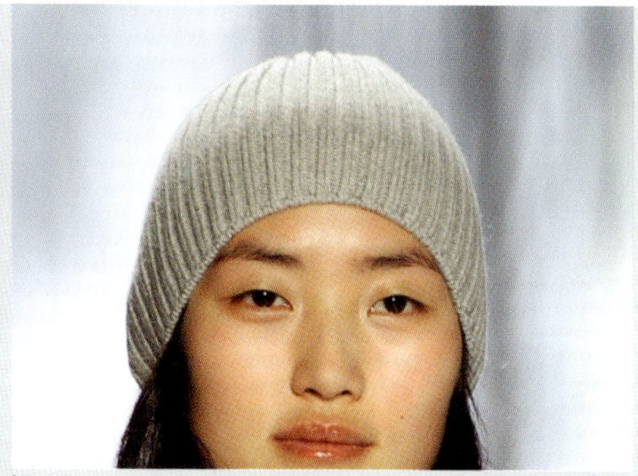

Lacoste

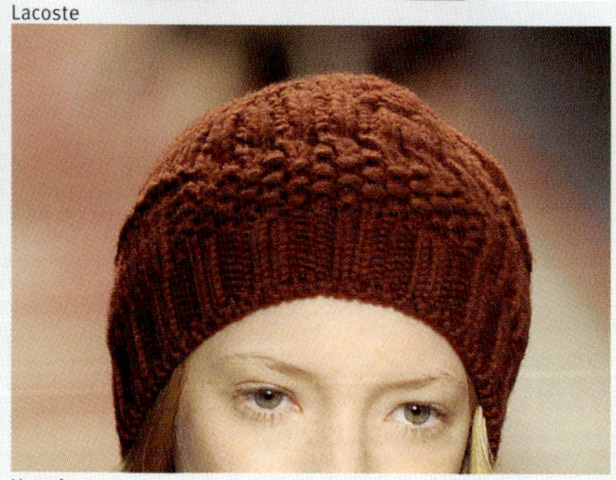

Hermès

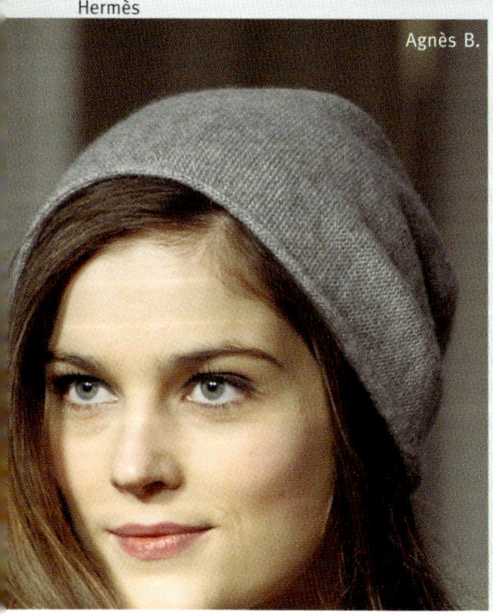

Agnès B.

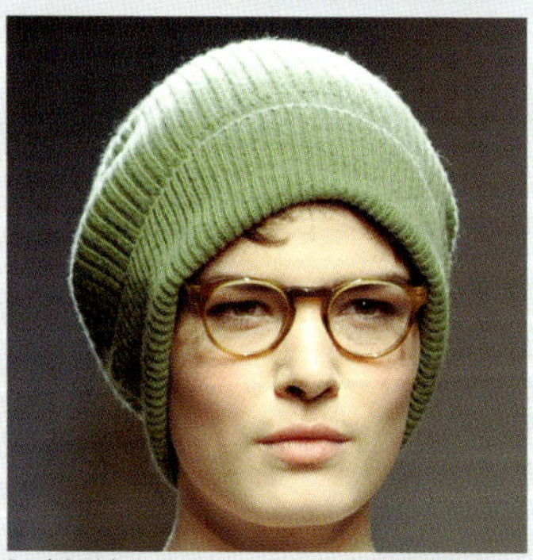

Paul Smith

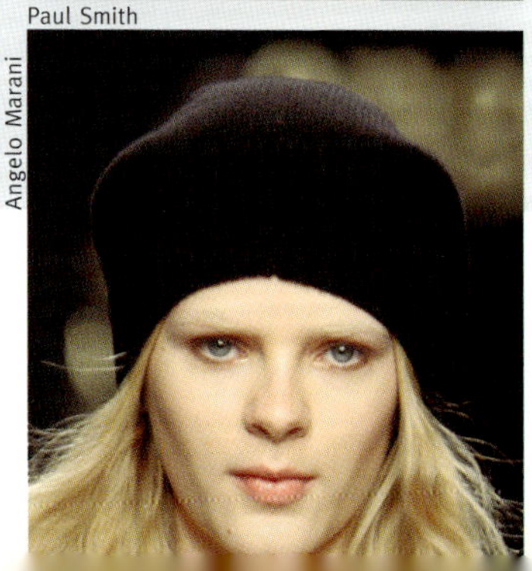

Angelo Marani

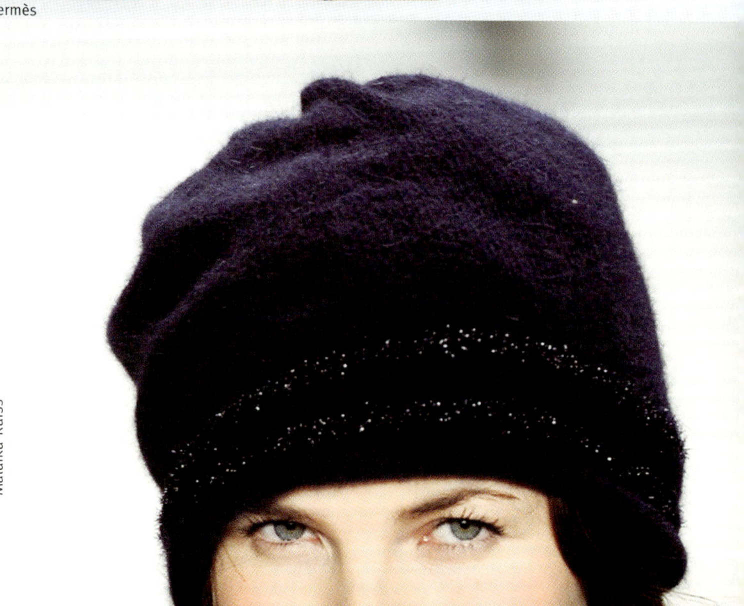

Malaika Raiss

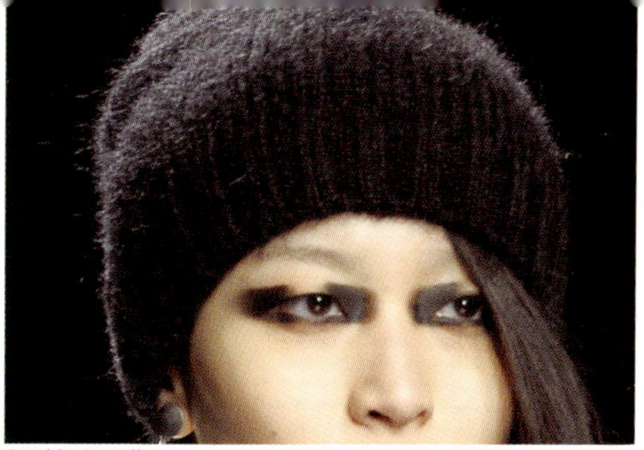

Frankie Morello

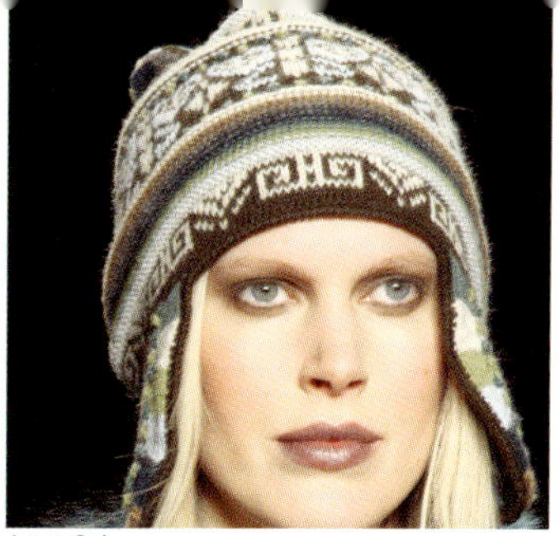

Anna Sui

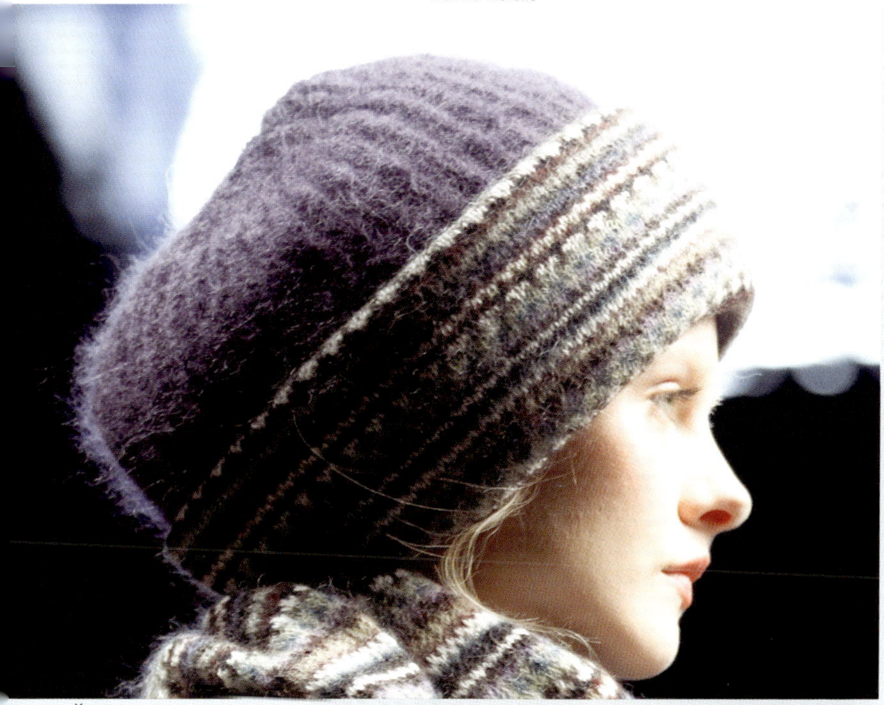

Kenzo

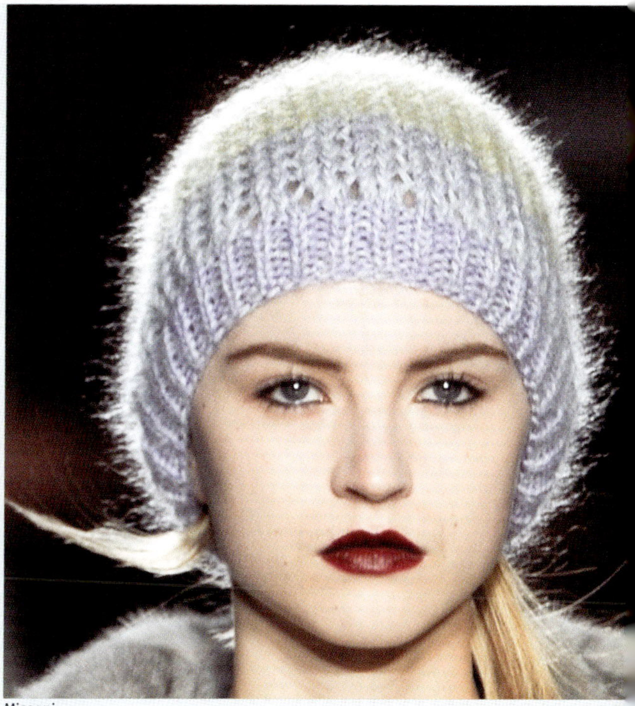

Missoni

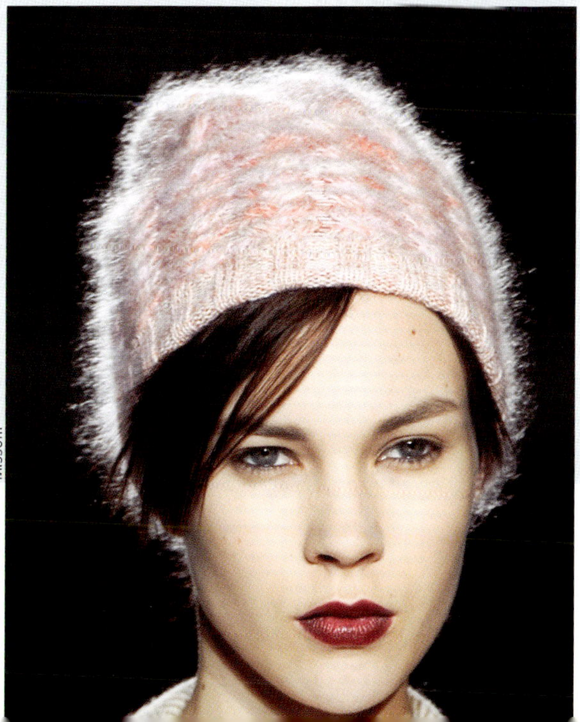

Missoni

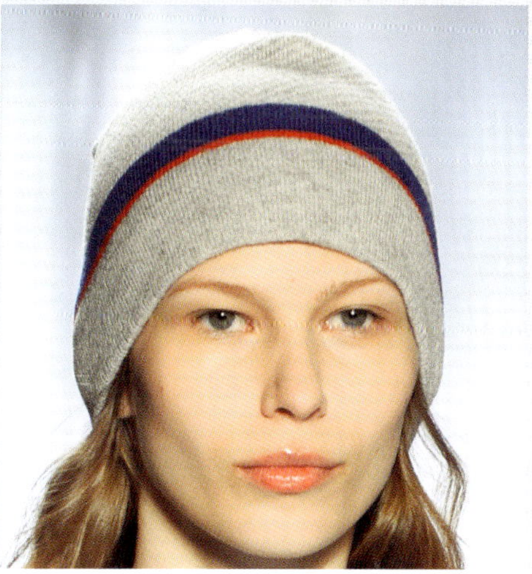

Lacoste

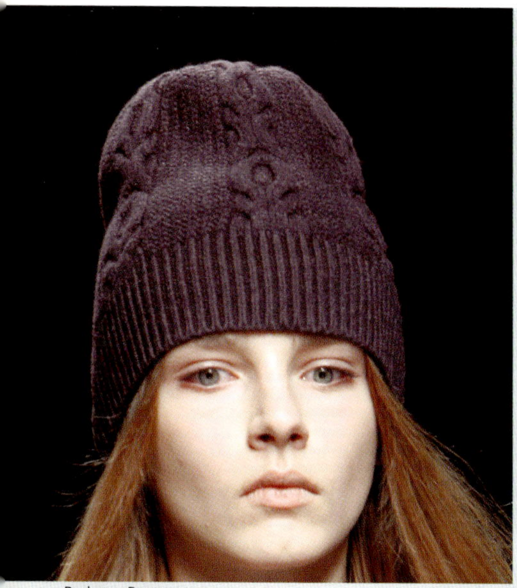

Burberry Prorsum

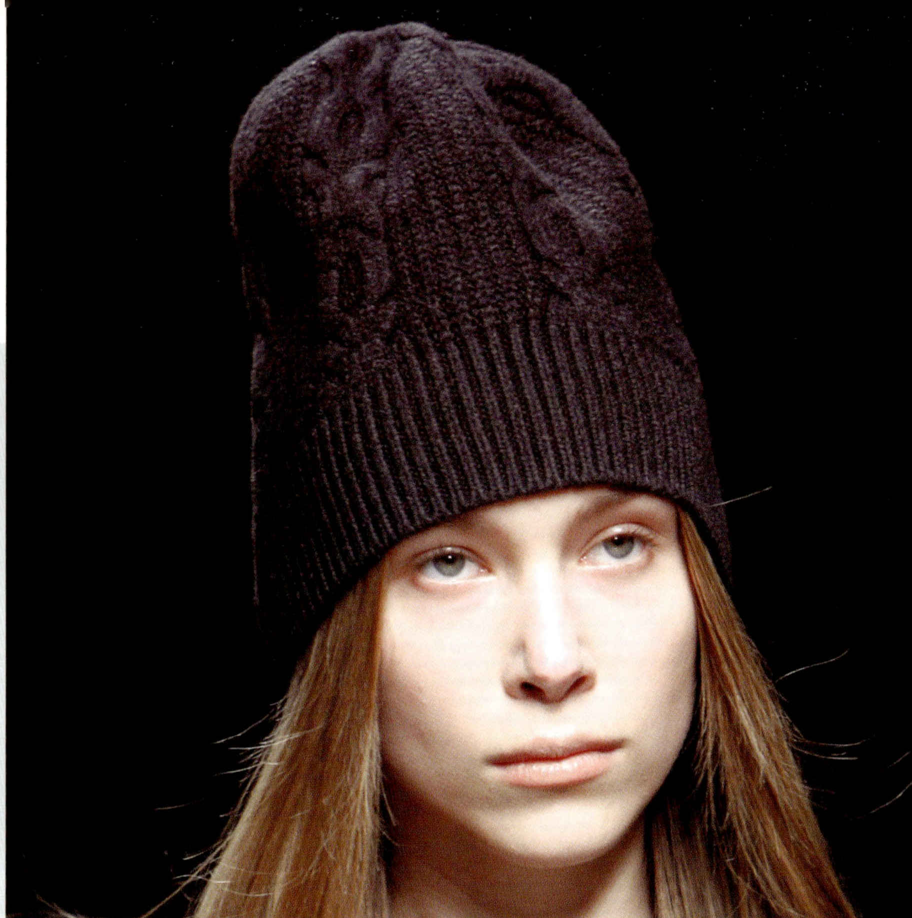

Burberry Prorsum

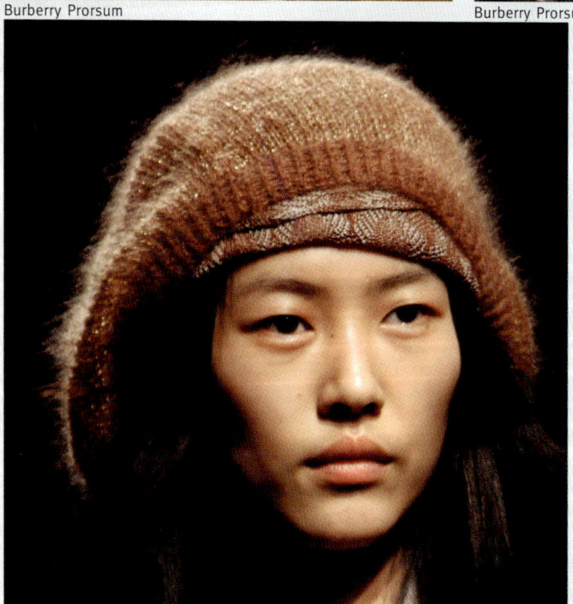

Missoni

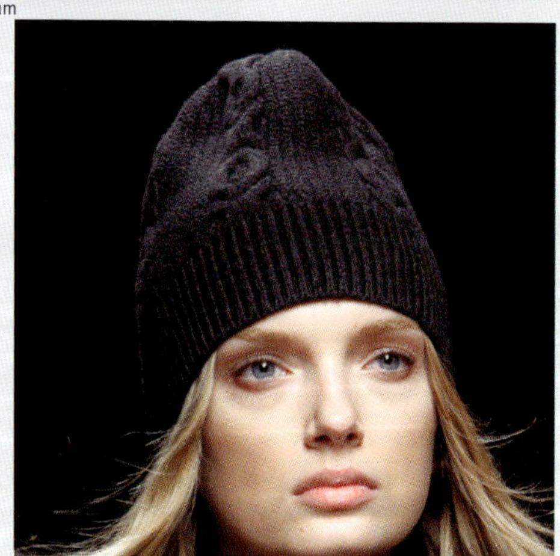

Burberry Prorsum

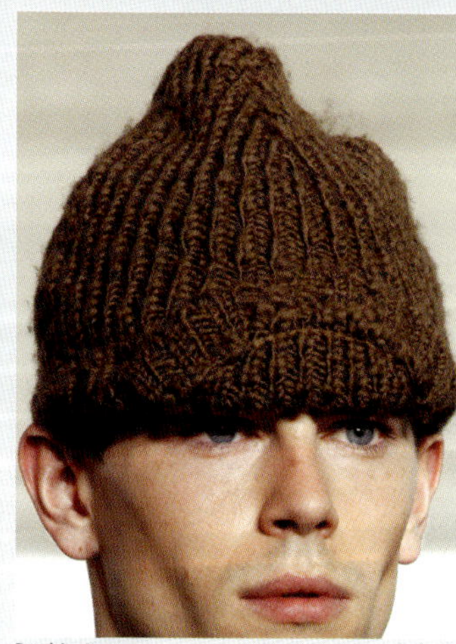

Duckie Brown

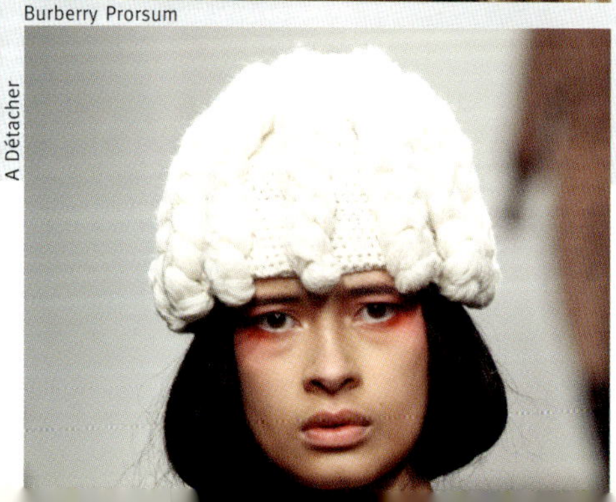

A Détacher

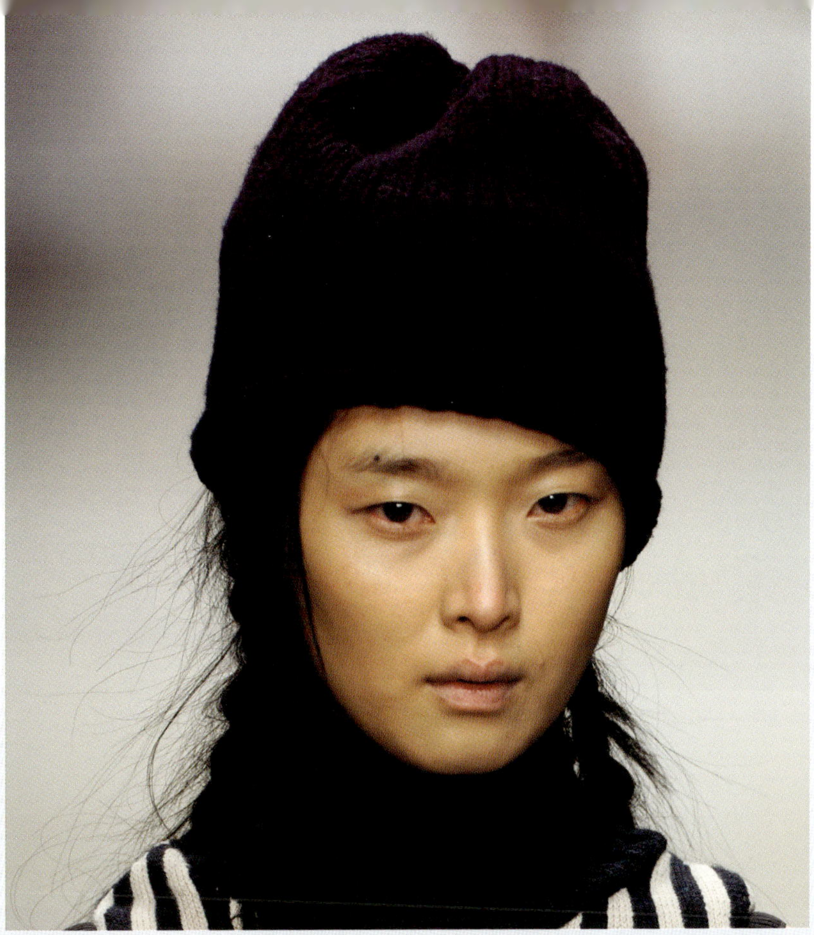
Mark Fast

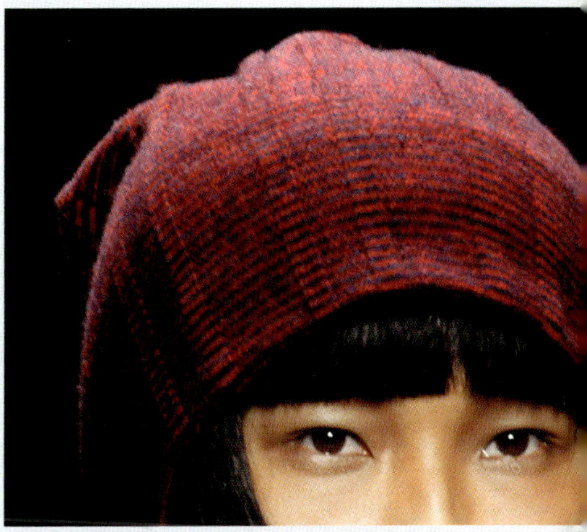
Band of Outsiders

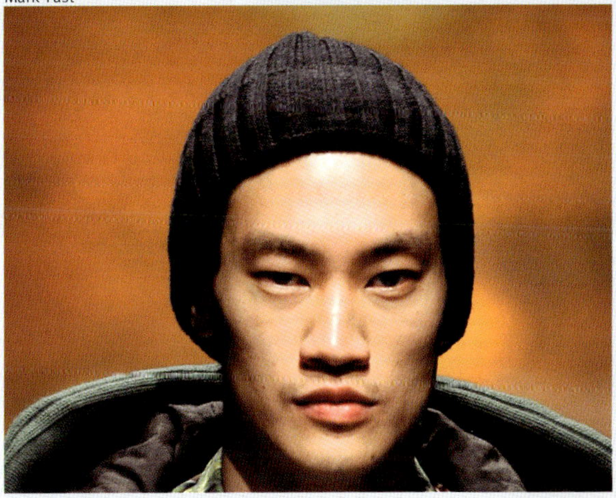
C .P. Company

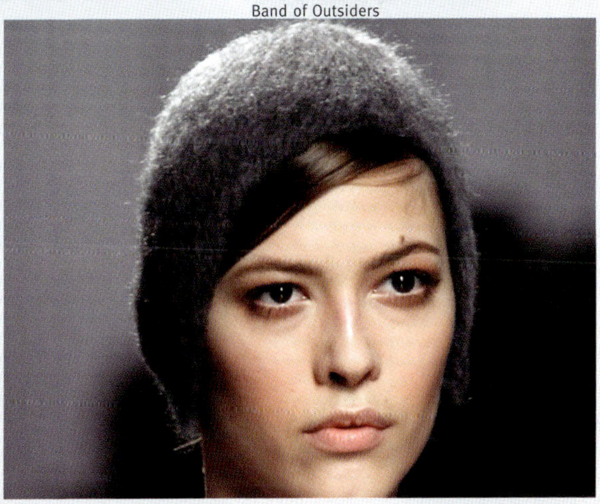
Dior

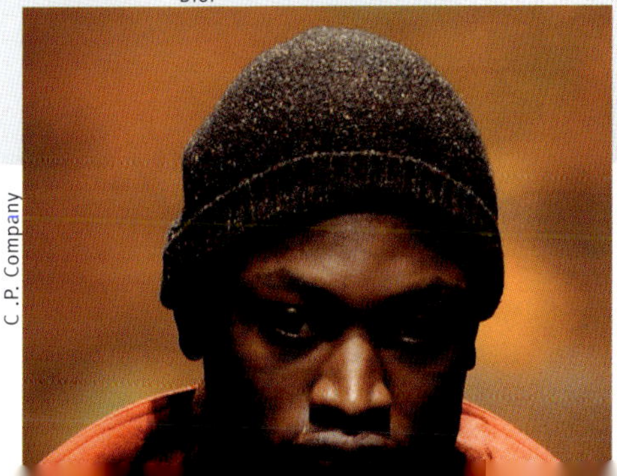
C .P. Company

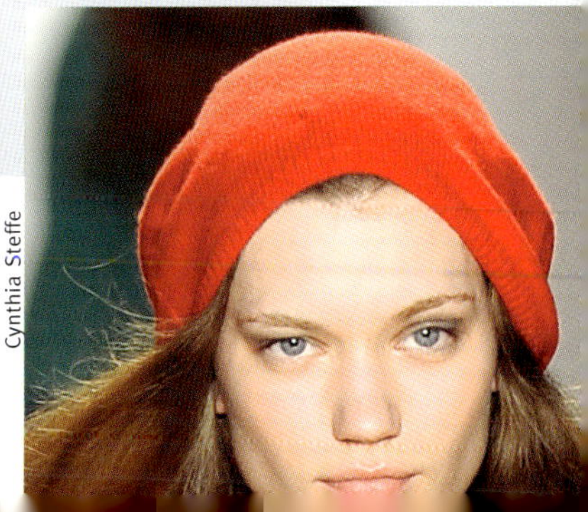
Cynthia Steffe

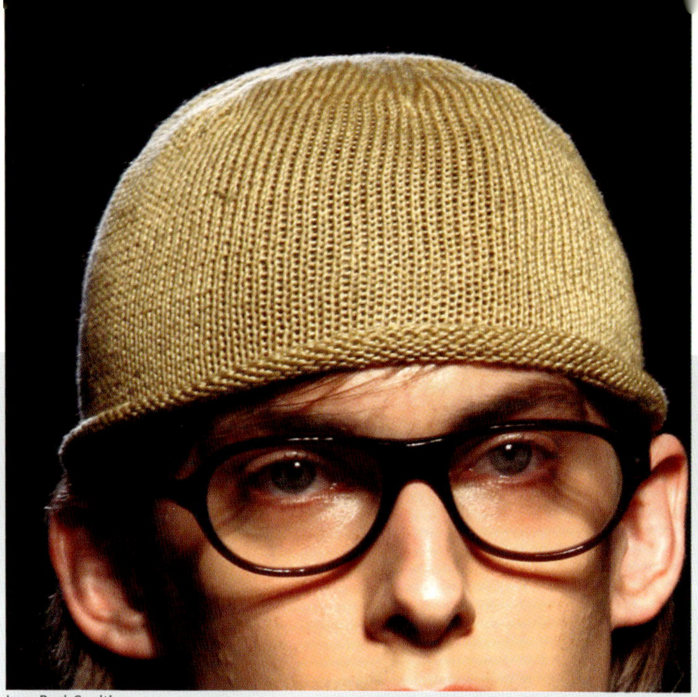

Jean Paul Gaultier

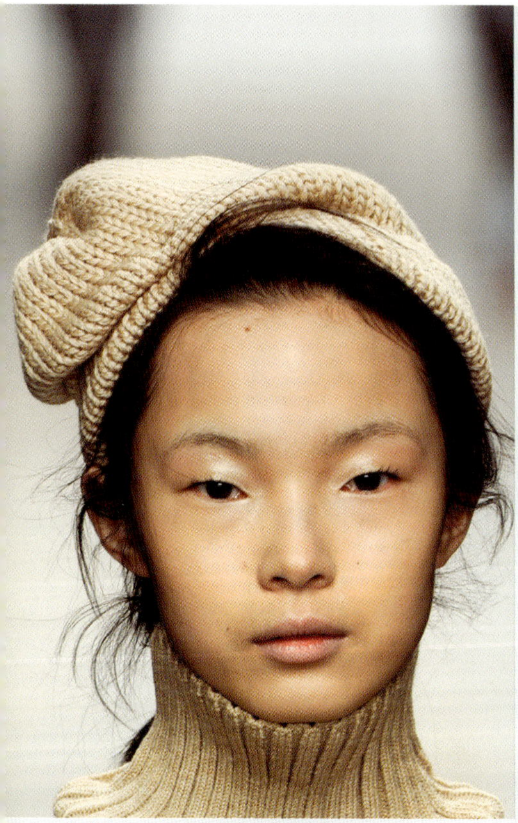

Mark Fast

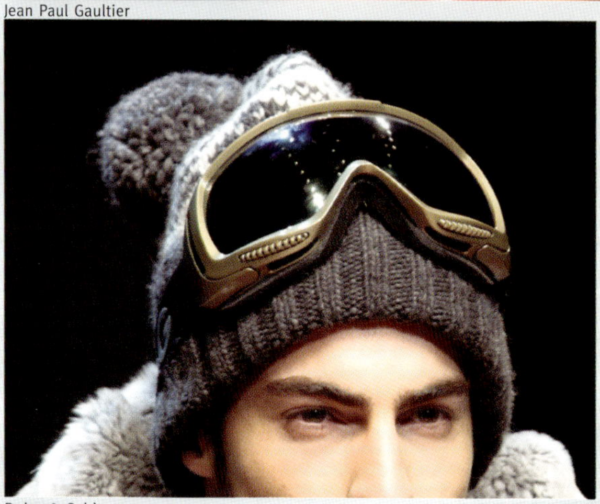

Dolce & Gabbana

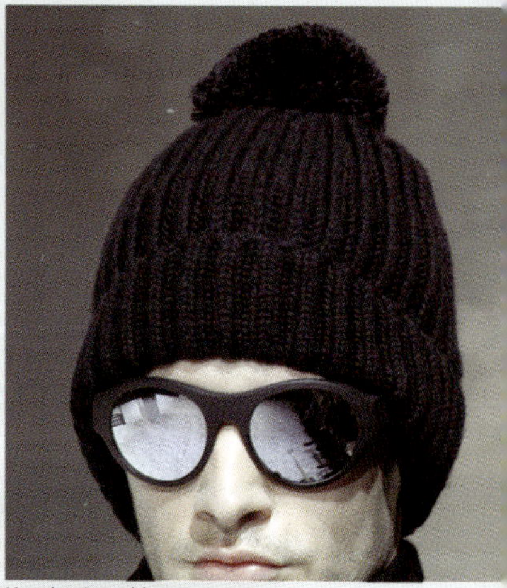

Moncler Grenoble

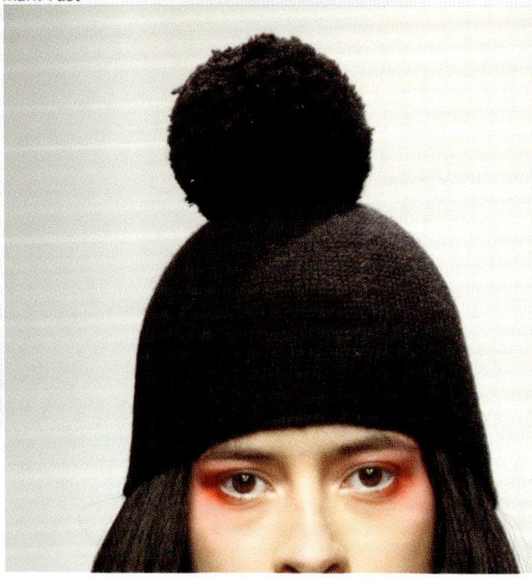

A Détacher

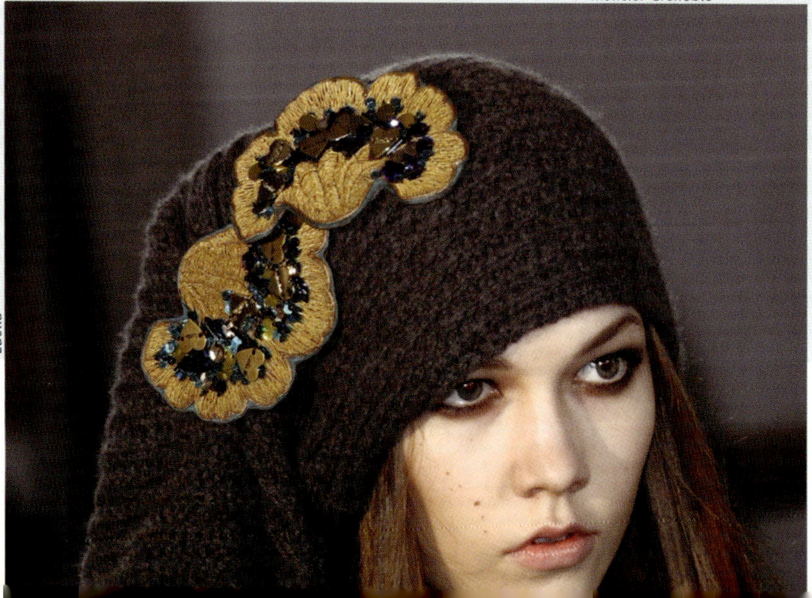

Luella

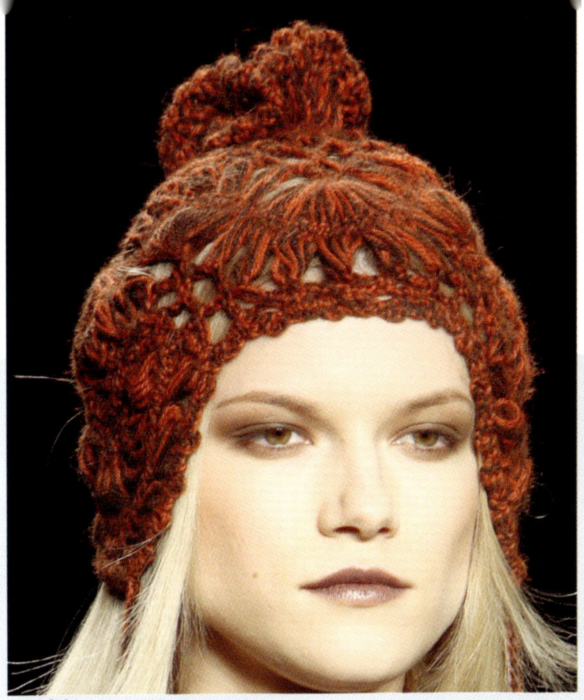

Anna Sui

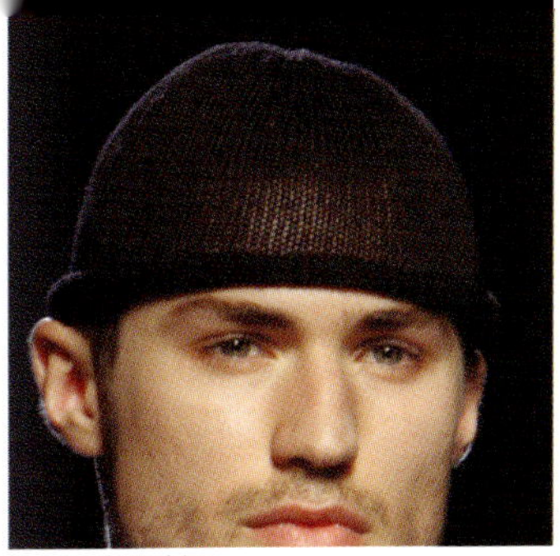

Jean Paul Gaultier

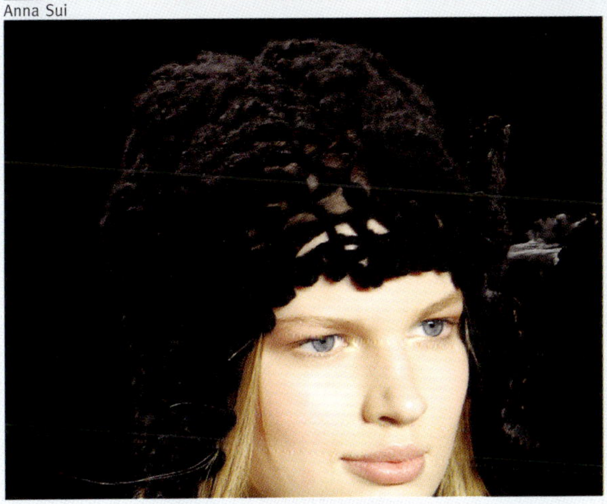

Anna Sui

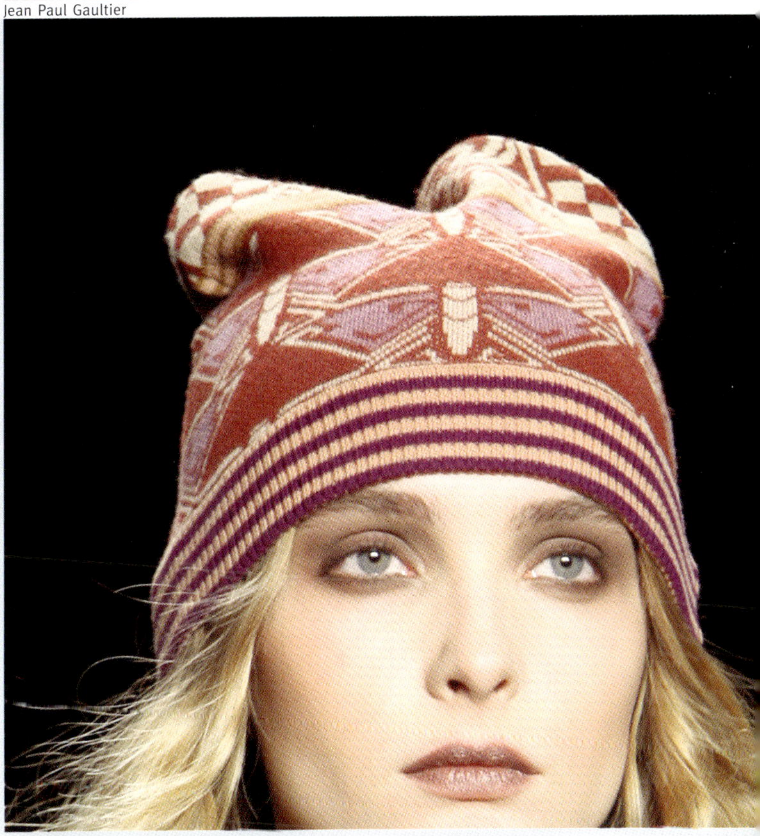

Anna Sui

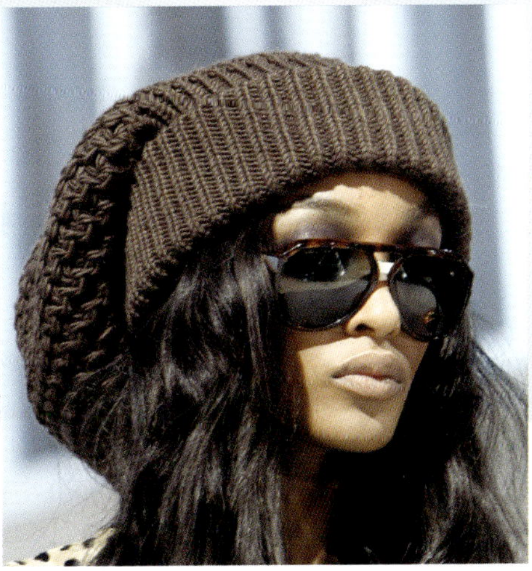

Dsquared2

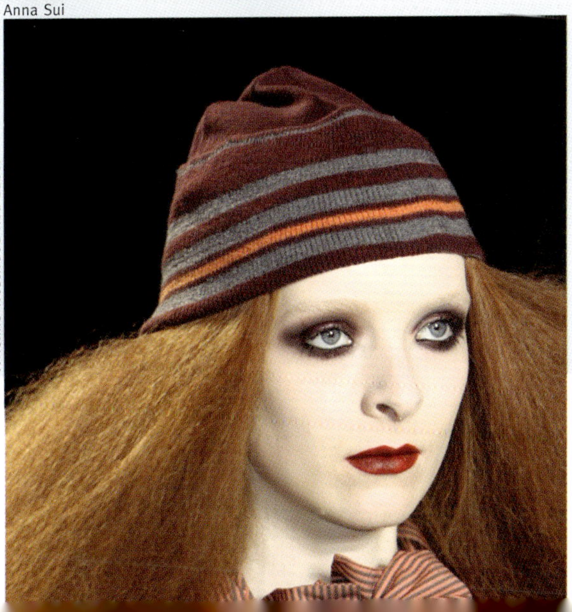

Vivienne Westwood Red Label

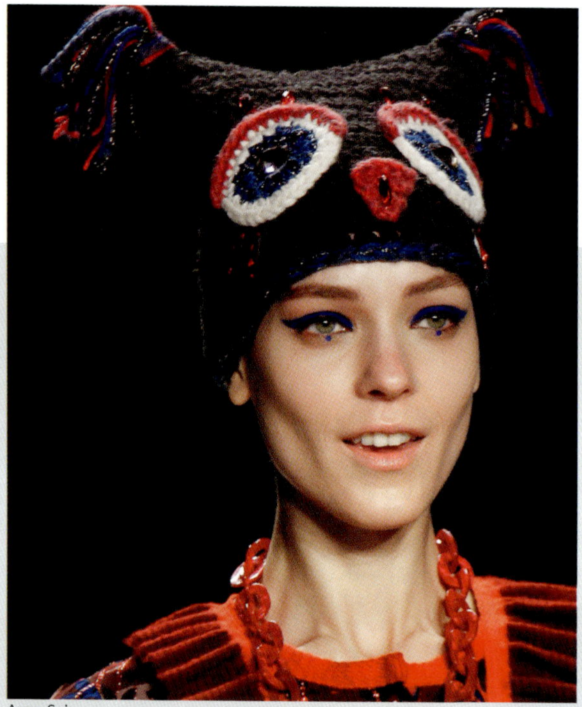

Anna Sui

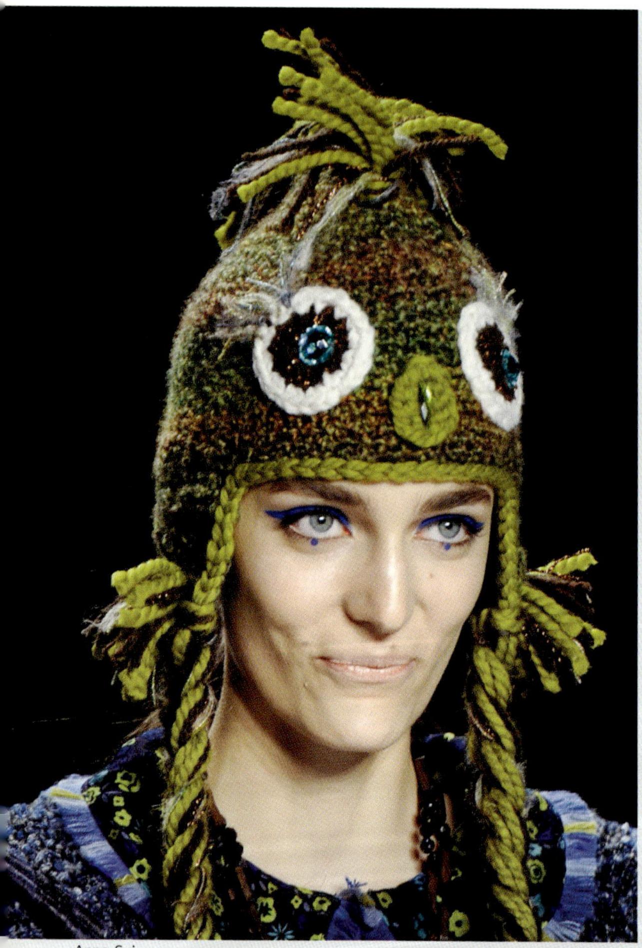

Anna Sui

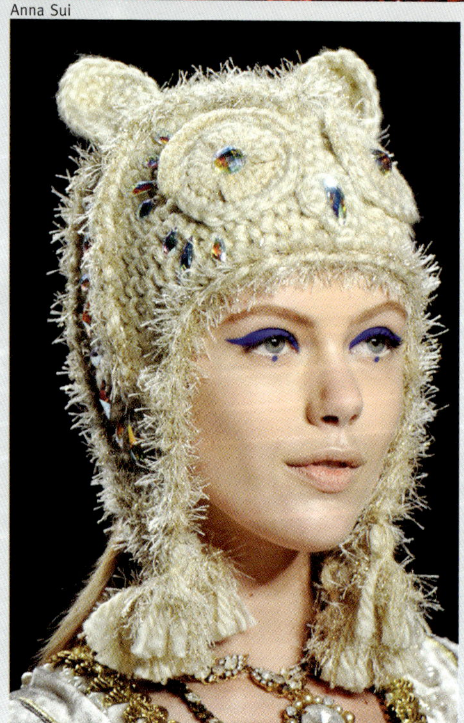

Anna Sui

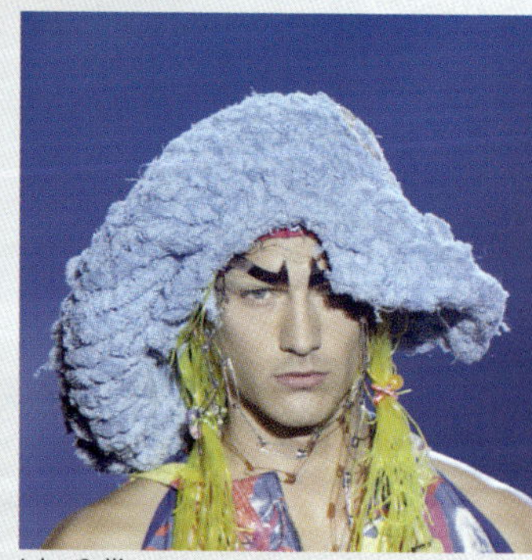

John Galliano

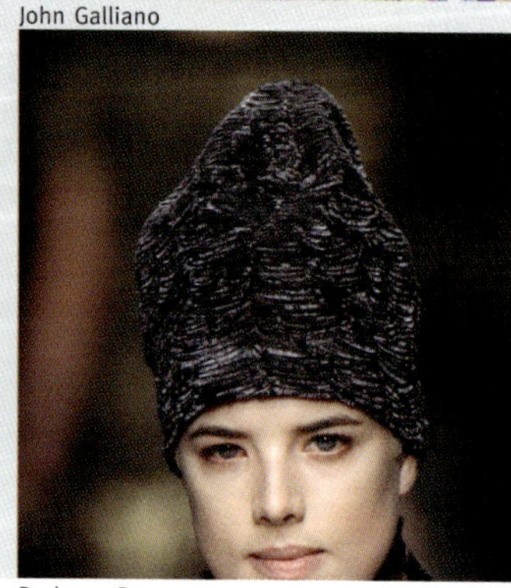

Burberry Prorsum

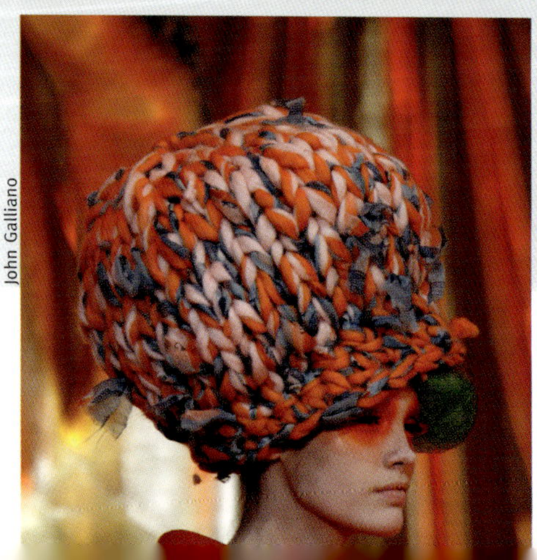

John Galliano

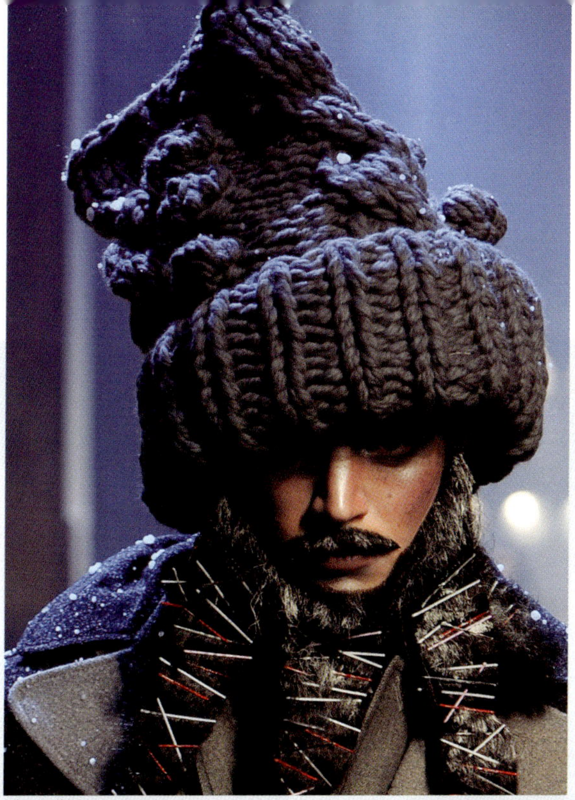
John Galliano

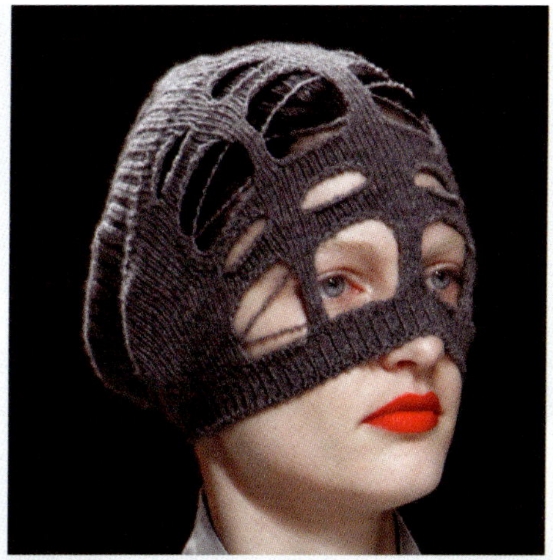
Rick Owens

Thakoon
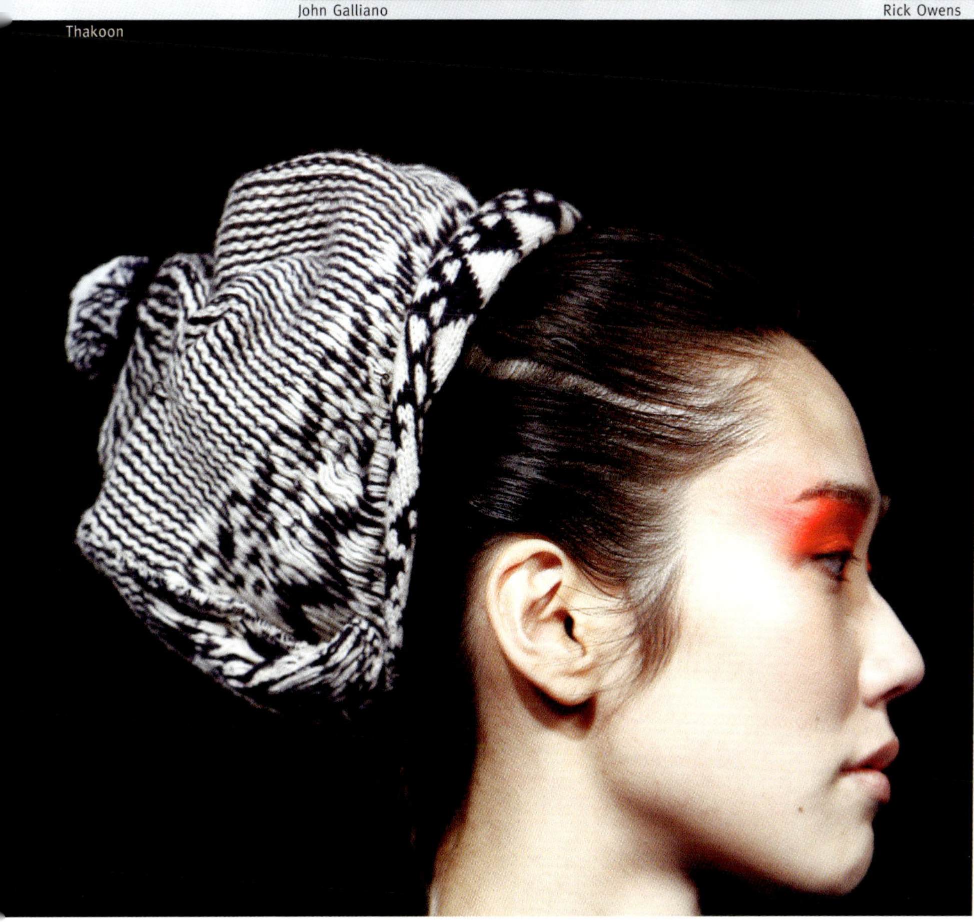

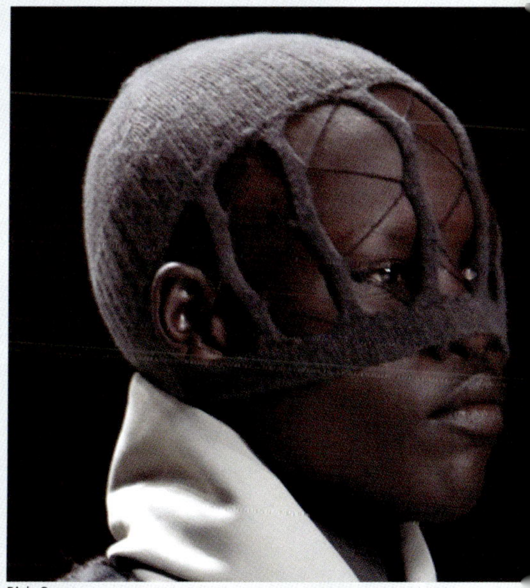
Rick Owens

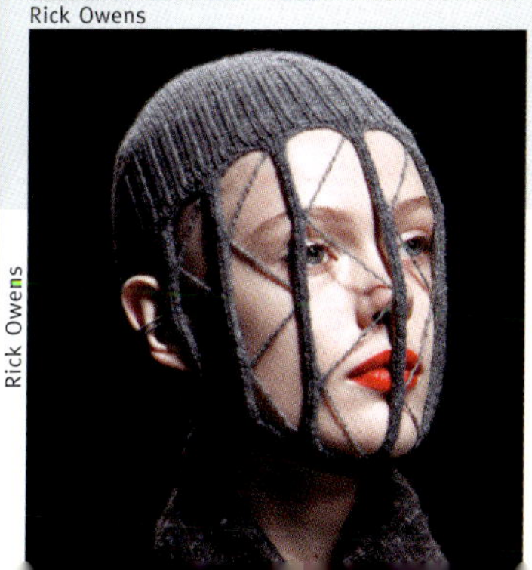
Rick Owens

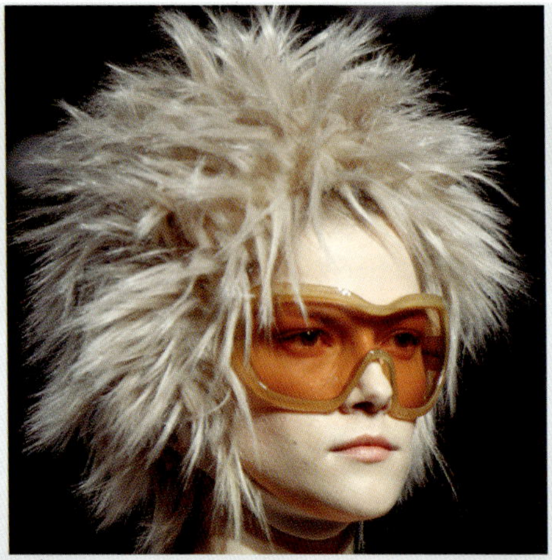
Prada

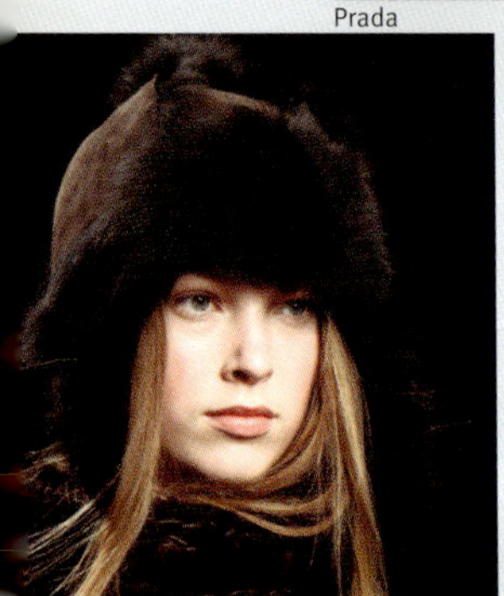
Trussardi

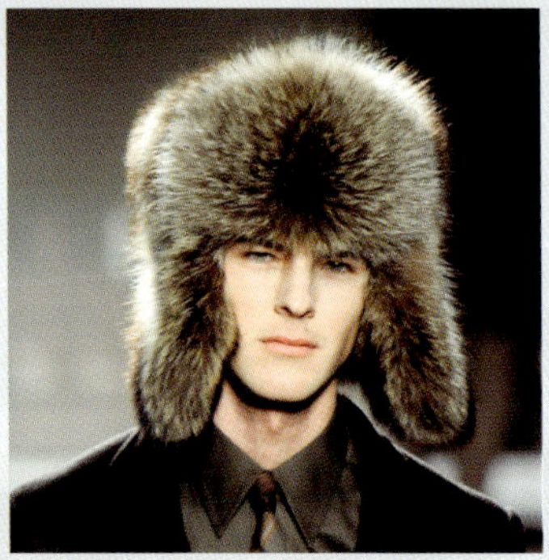
Ermenegildo Zegna

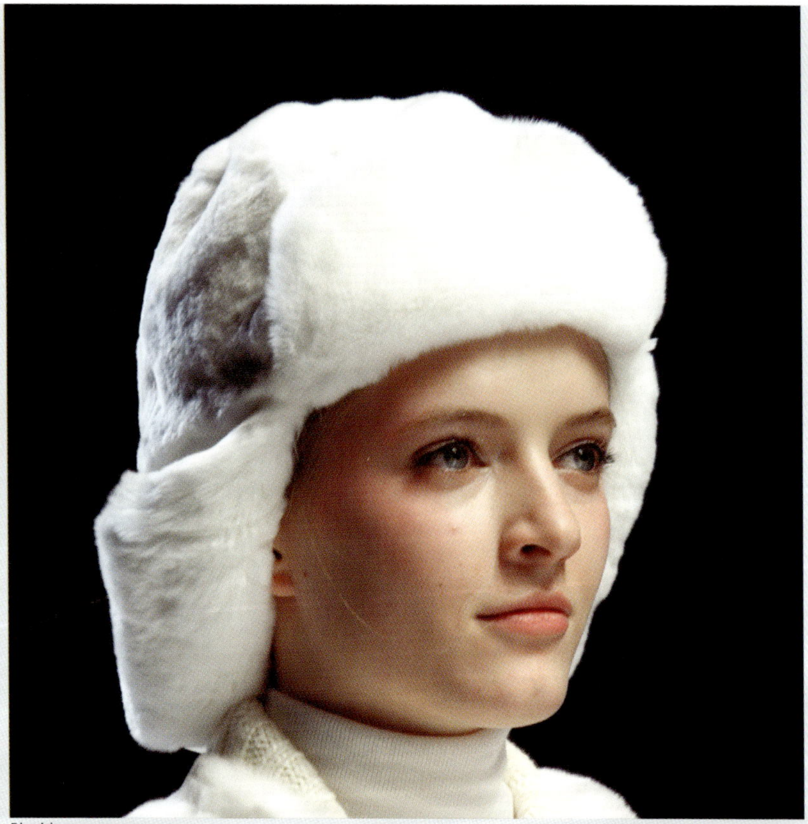
Blugirl

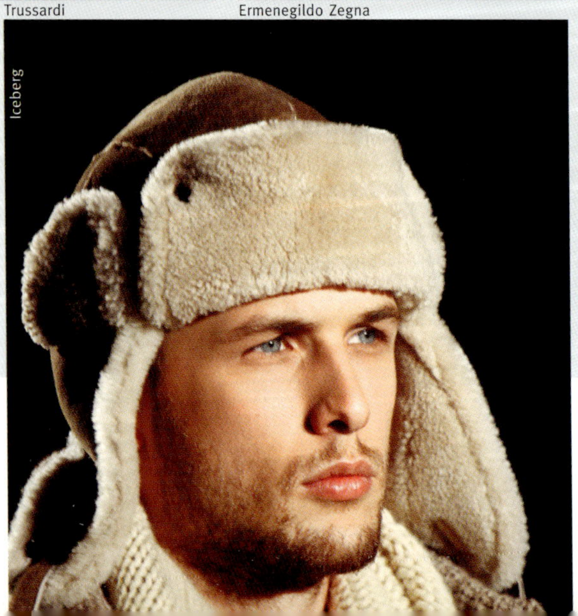
Iceberg

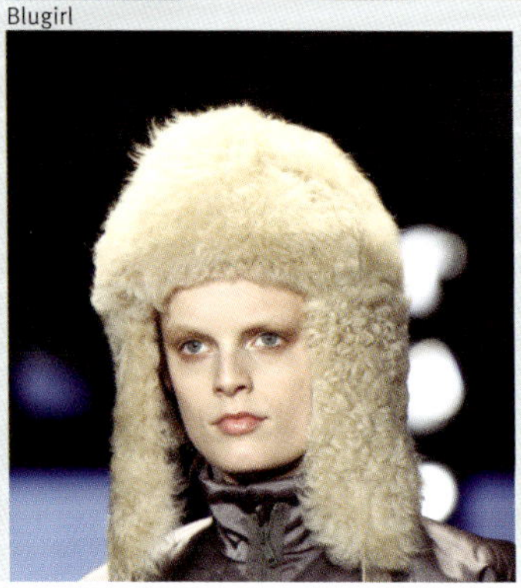
Y3

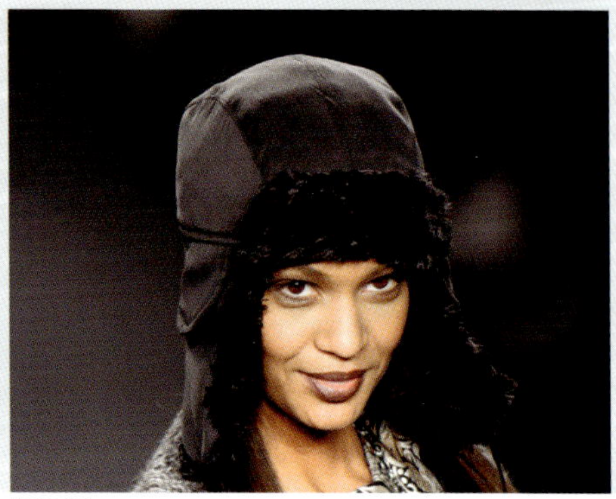
Anna Sui

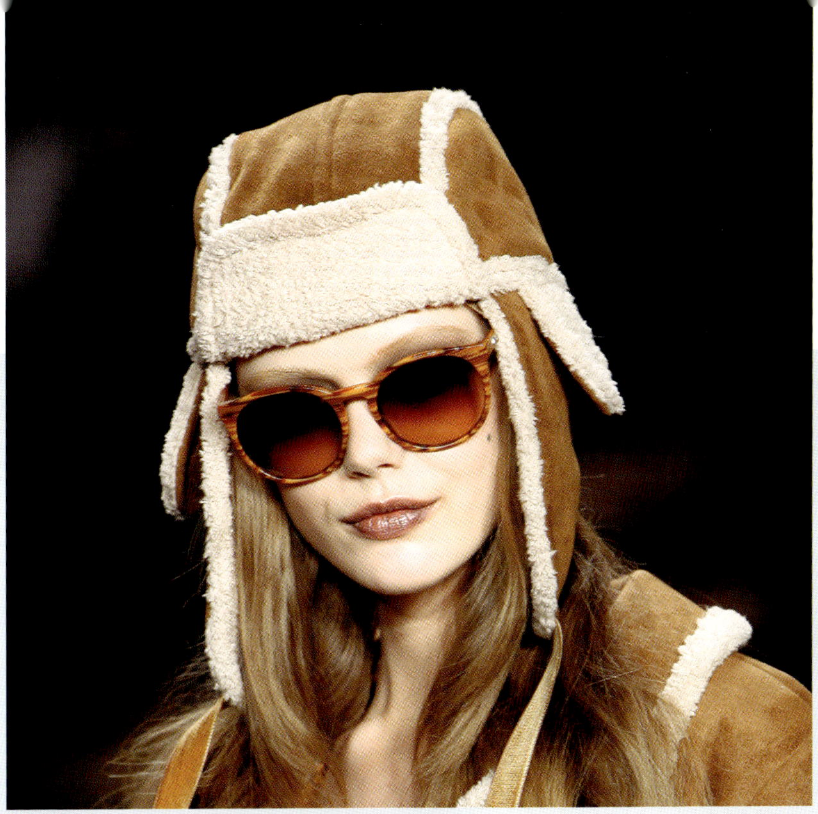

Anna Sui

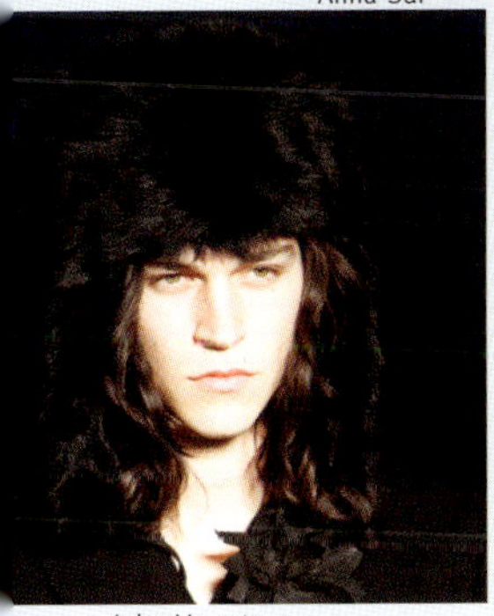

John Varvatos

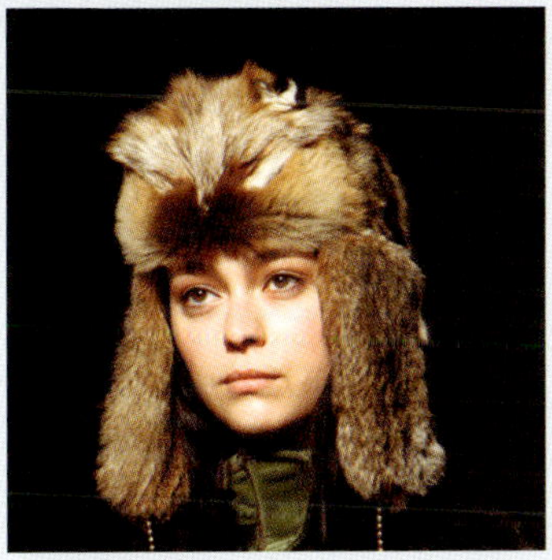

Jean Paul Gaultier

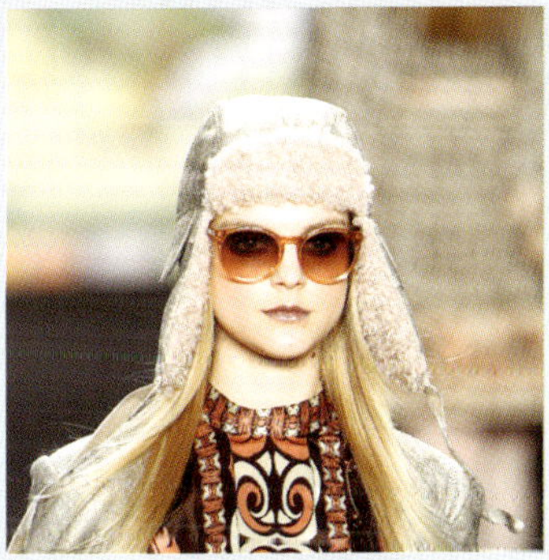

Anna Sui

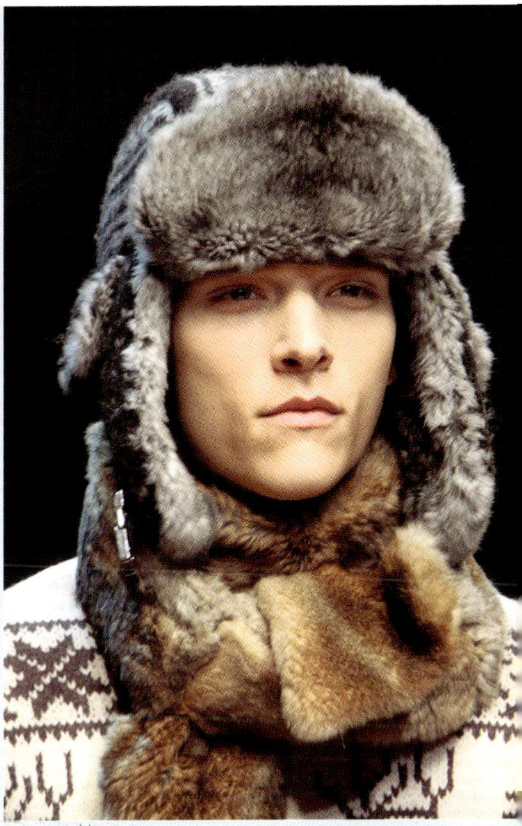

Dolce & Gabbana

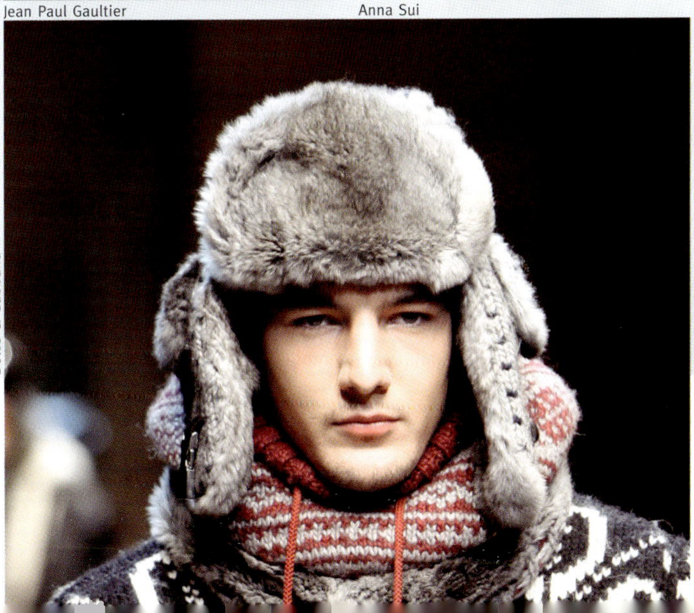

Dolce & Gabbana

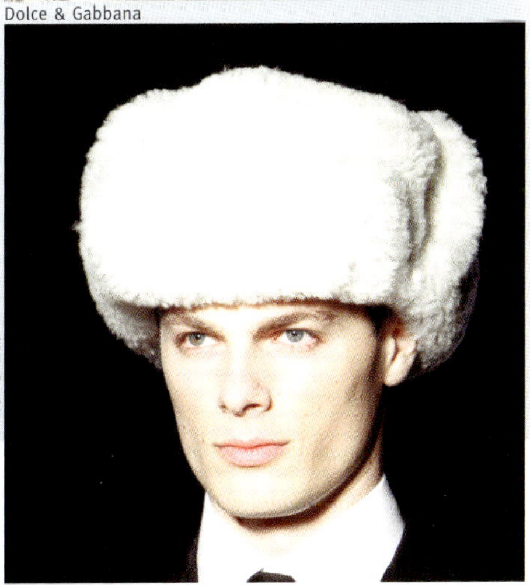

Viktor & Rolf

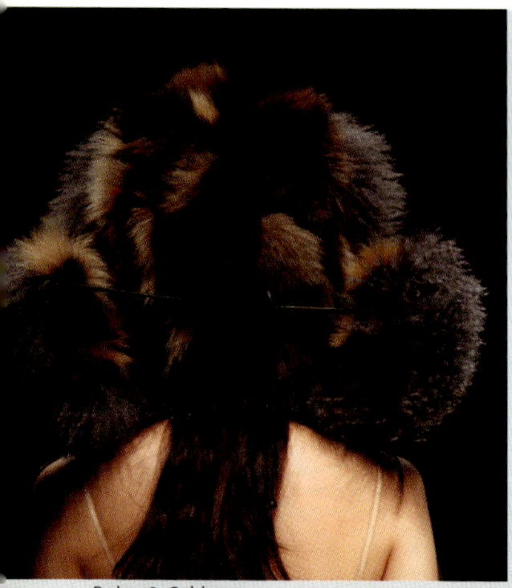
Dolce & Gabbana

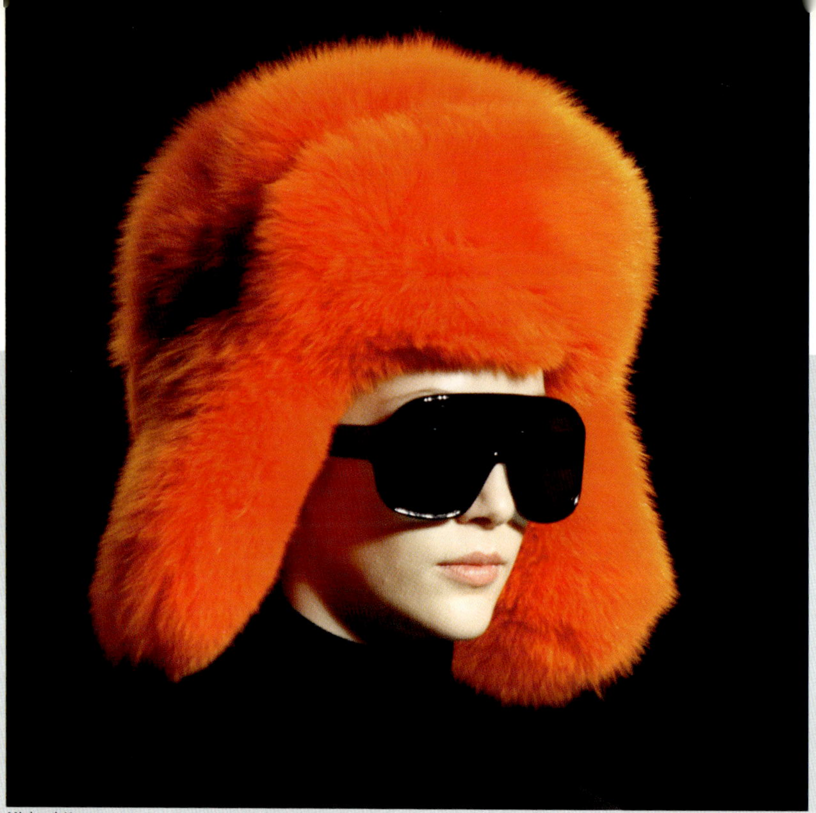
Michael Kors

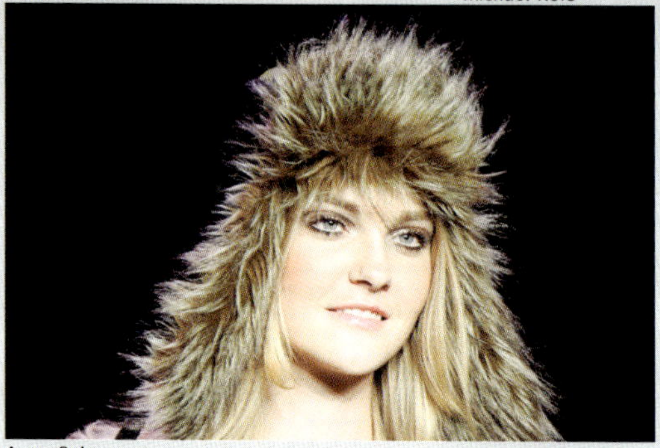
Anna Sui

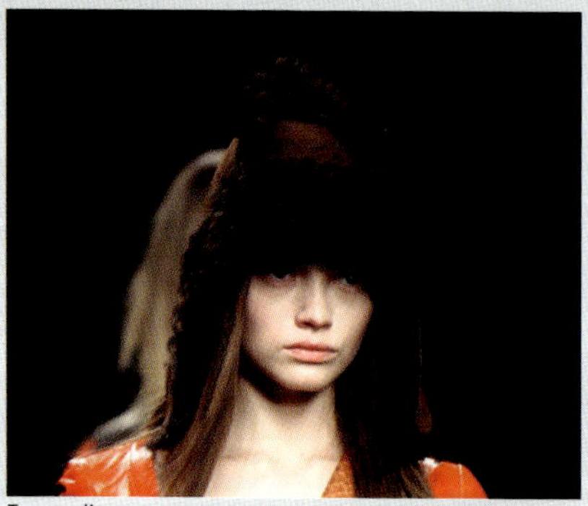
Trussardi

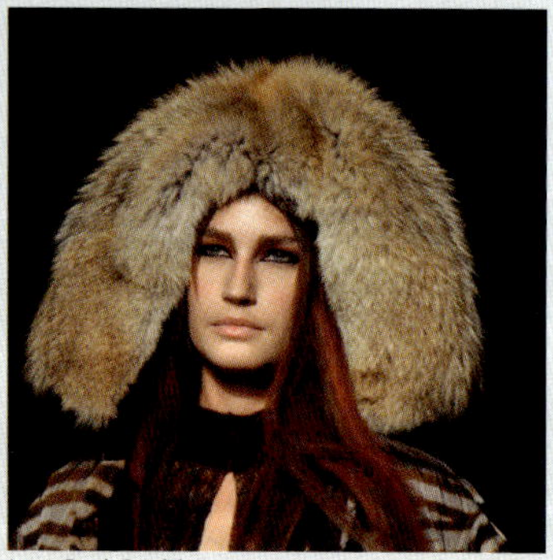
Jean Paul Gaultier

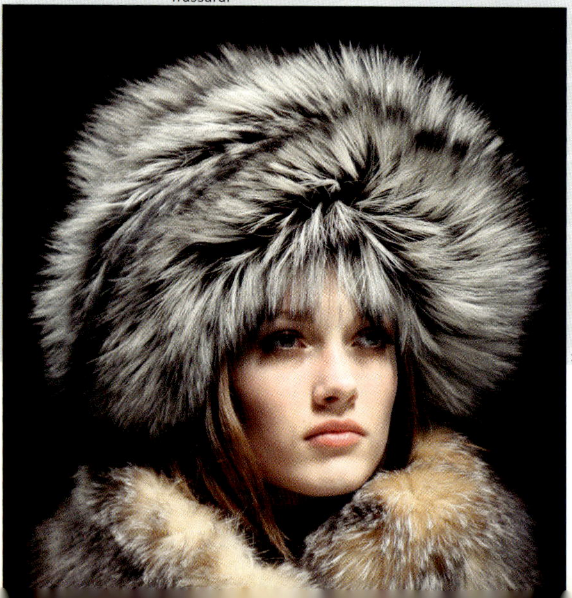
Blumarine

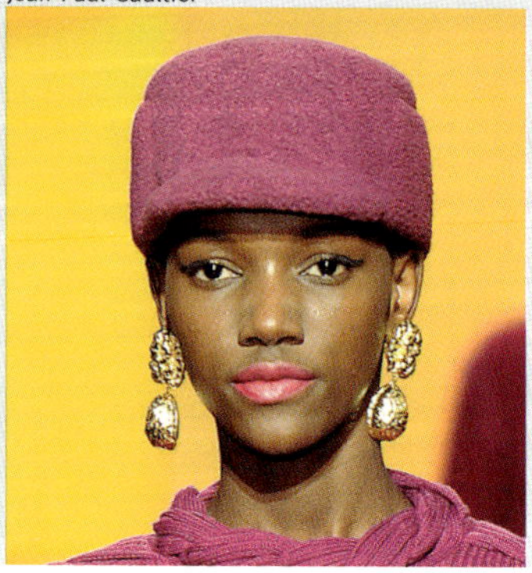
Kenzo

Michael Kors

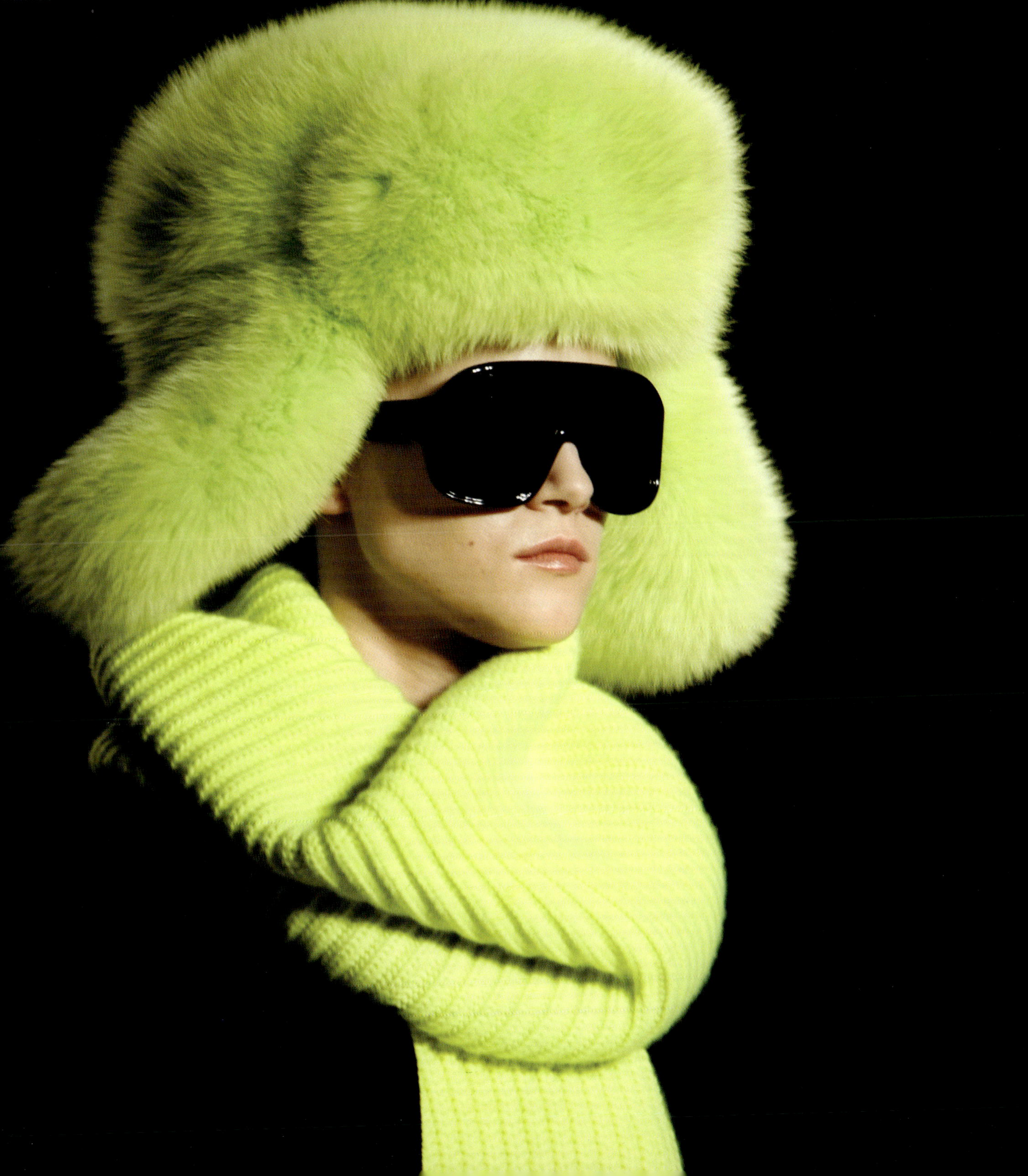

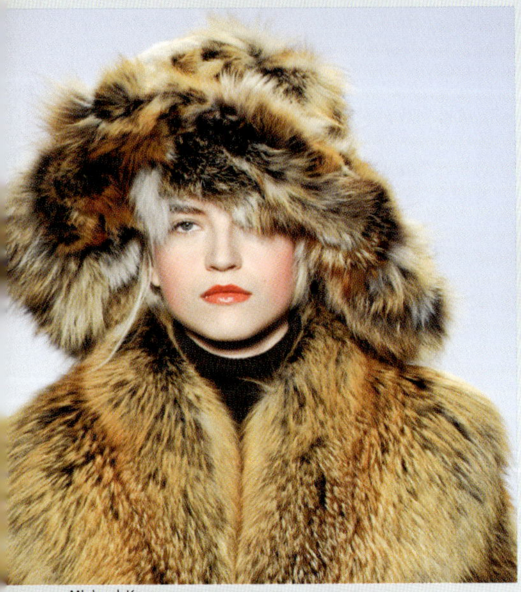
Michael Kors

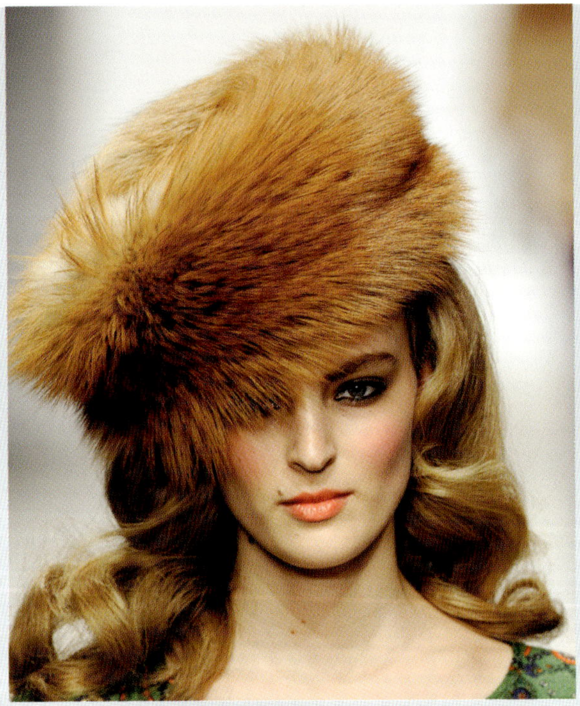
Issa

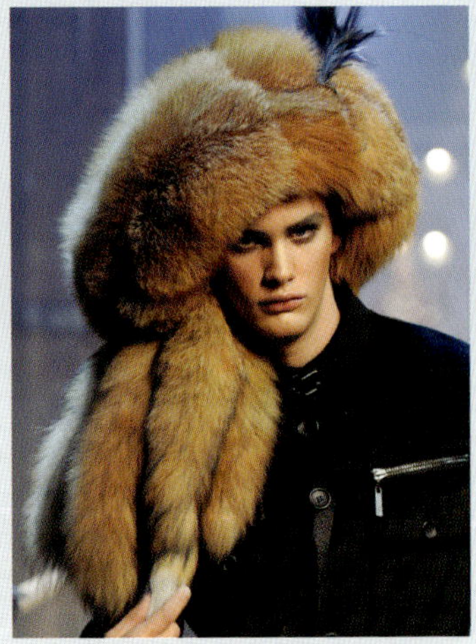
John Galliano

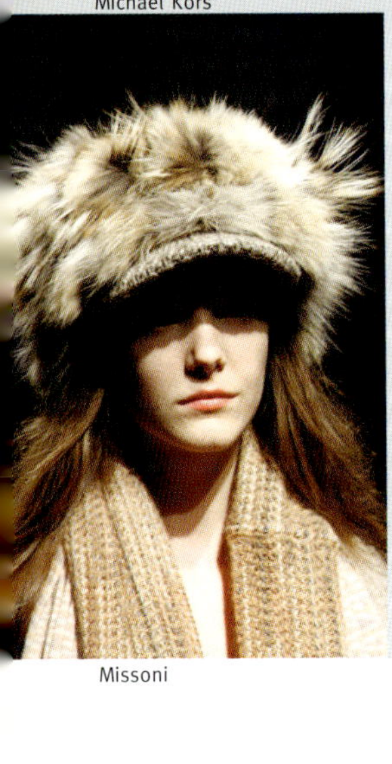
Missoni

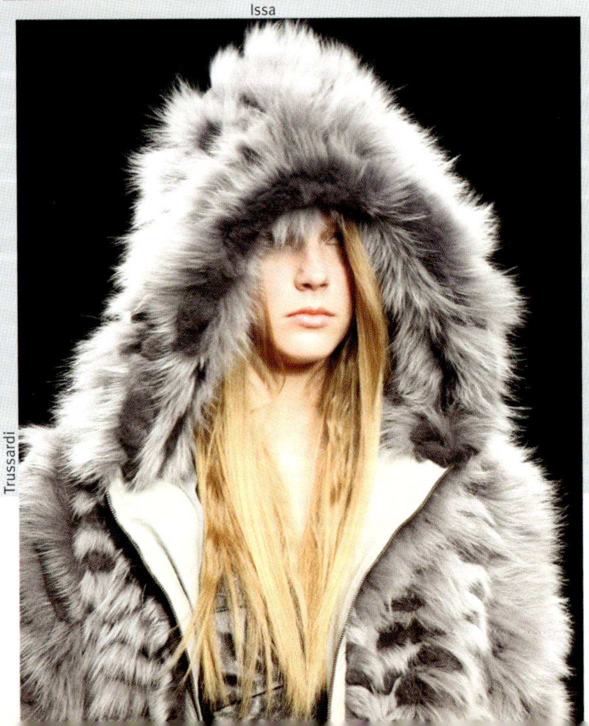
Trussardi

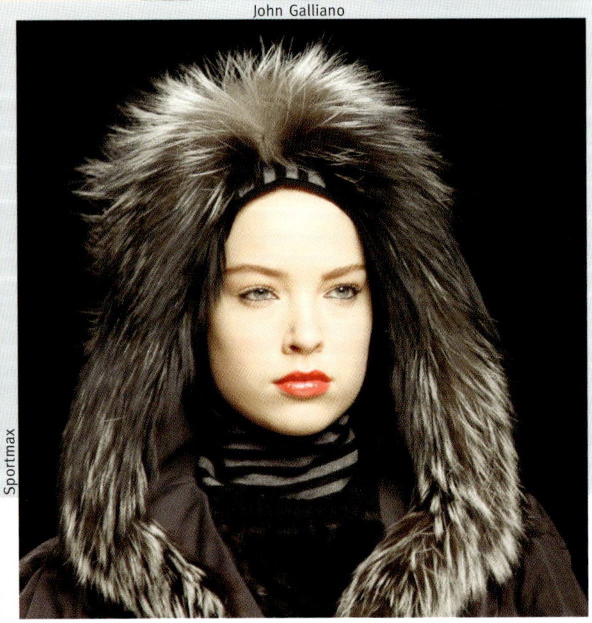
Sportmax

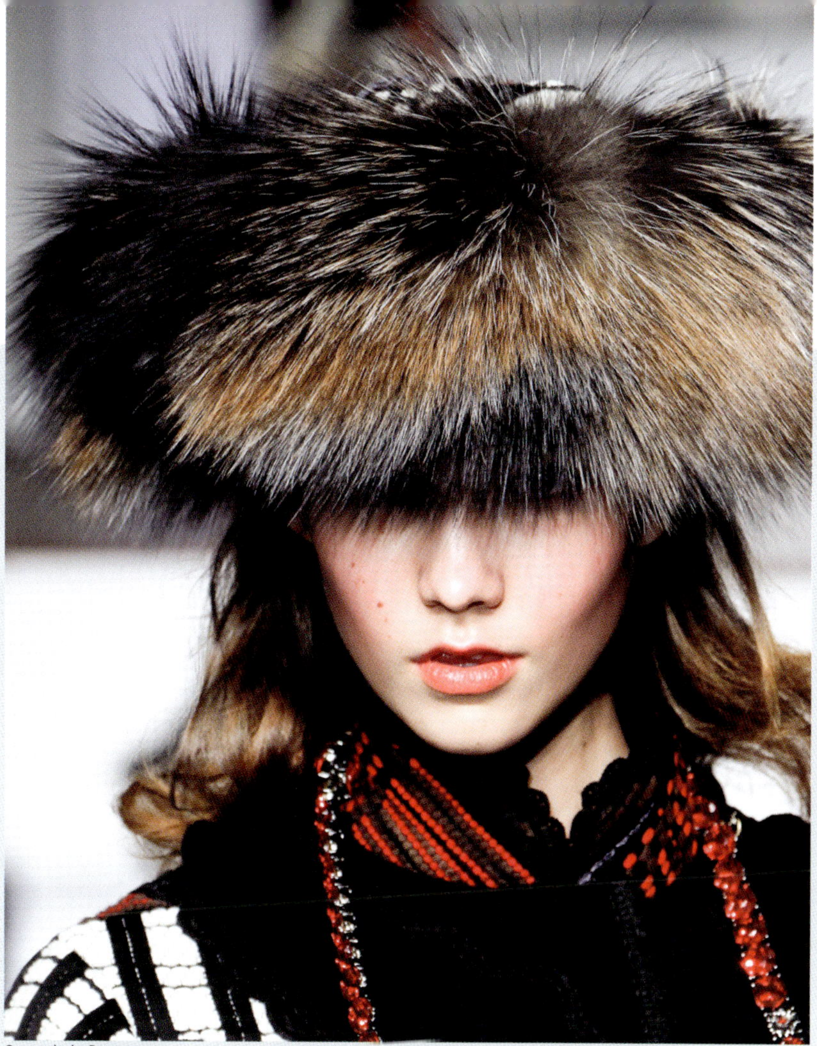
Oscar de la Renta

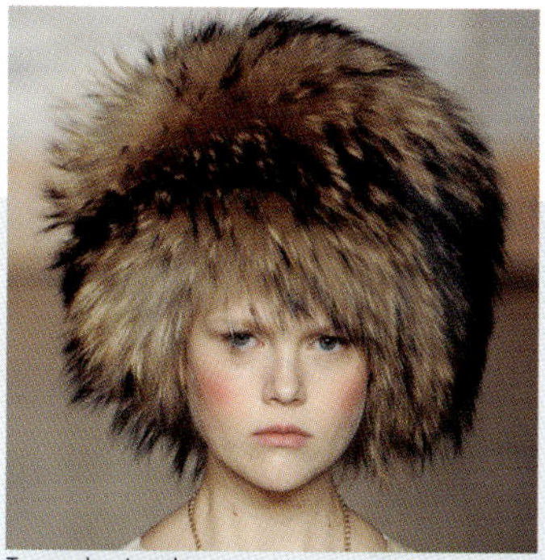
Temperley London

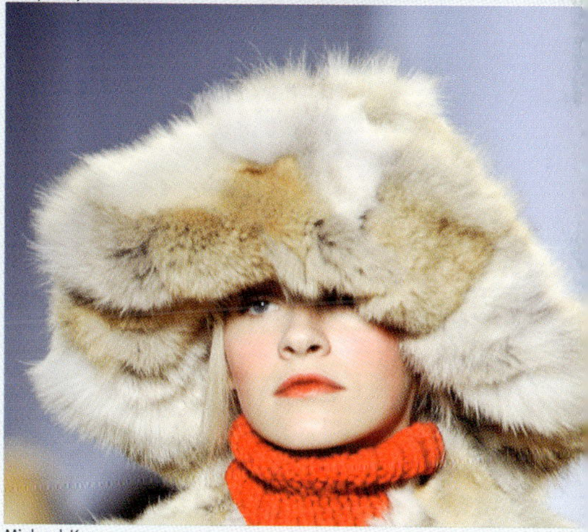
Michael Kors

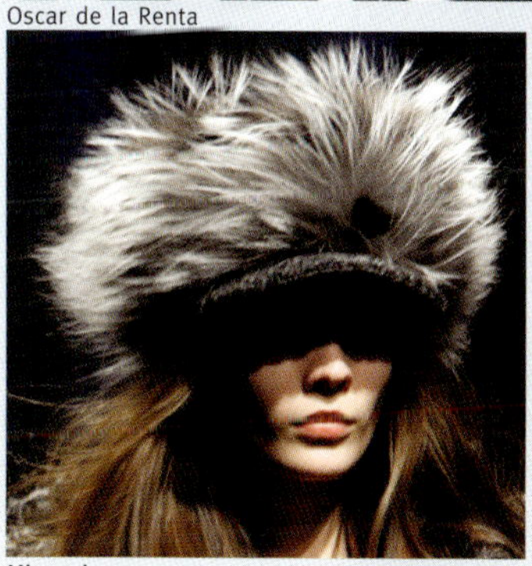
Missoni

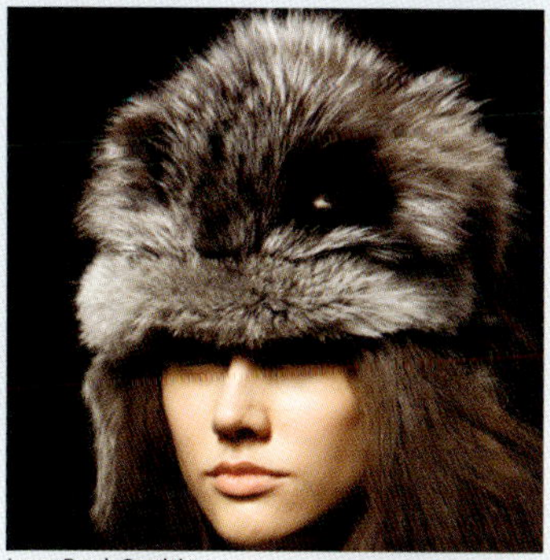
Jean Paul Gaultier

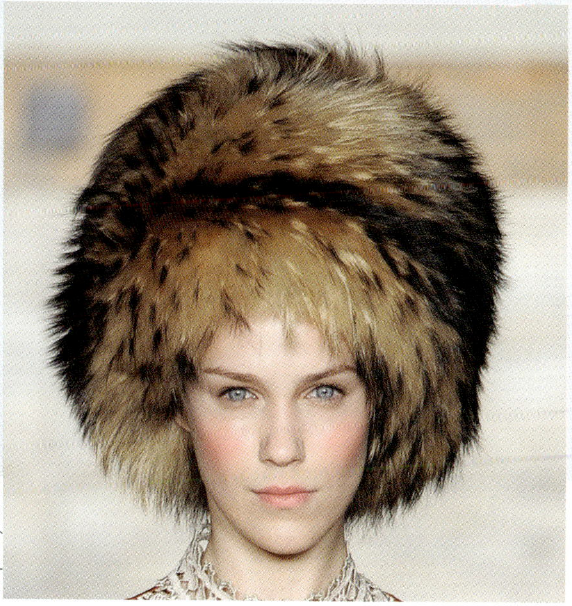
Temperley London

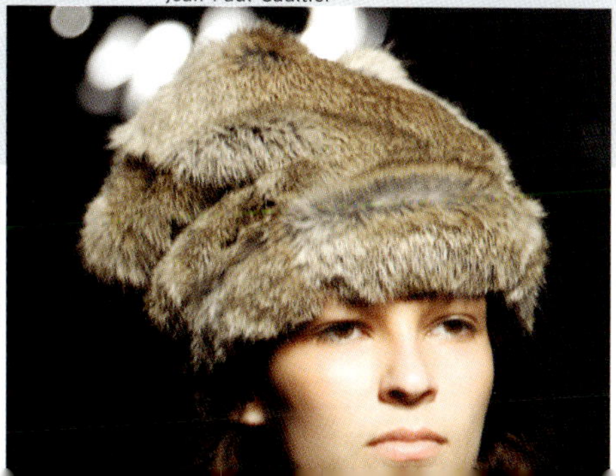
Band of Outsiders

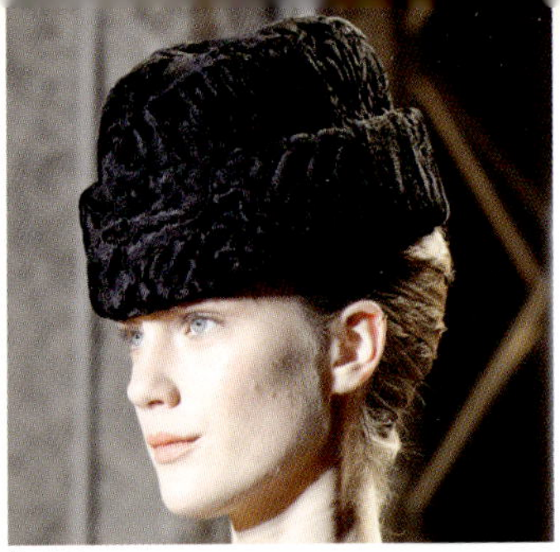
Rochas

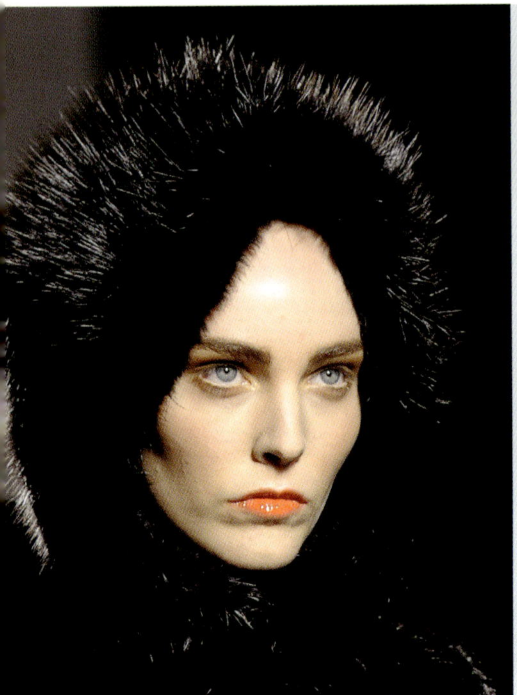
Sportmax

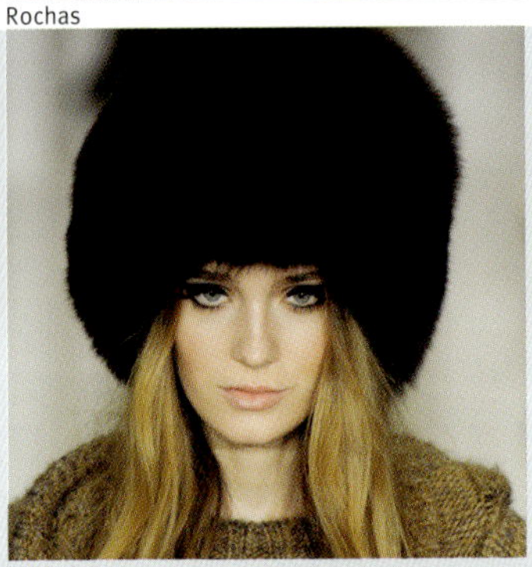
Rachel Zoe

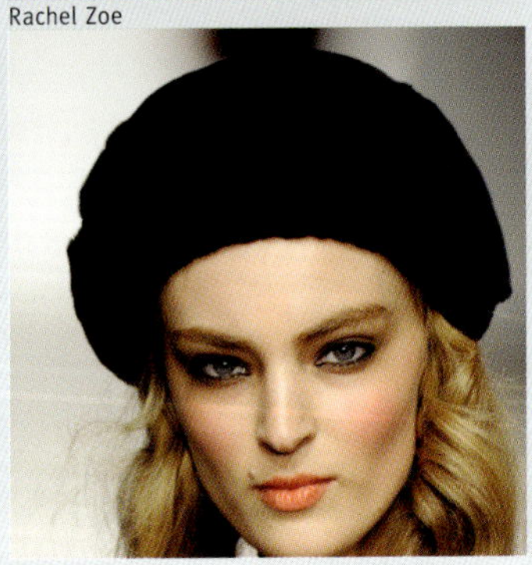
Issa

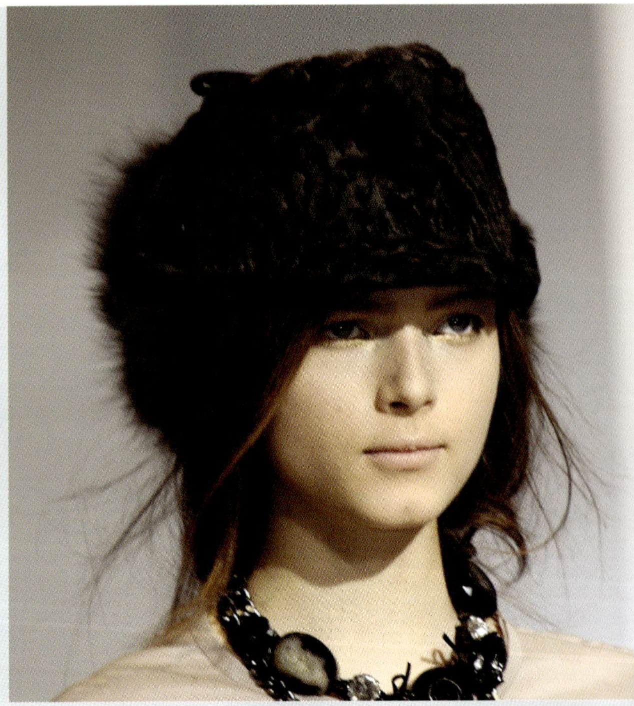
Marni

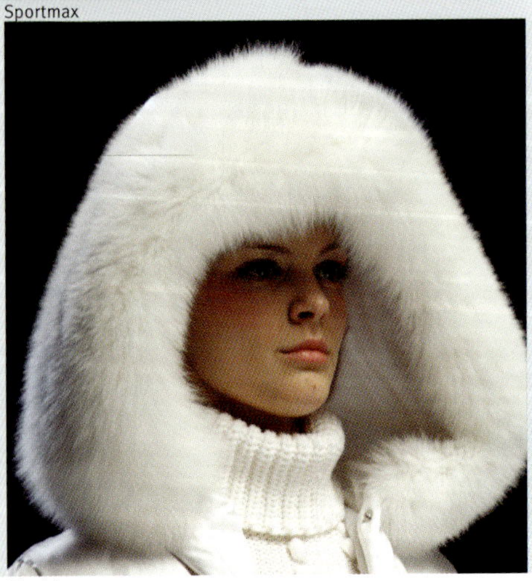
Blugirl

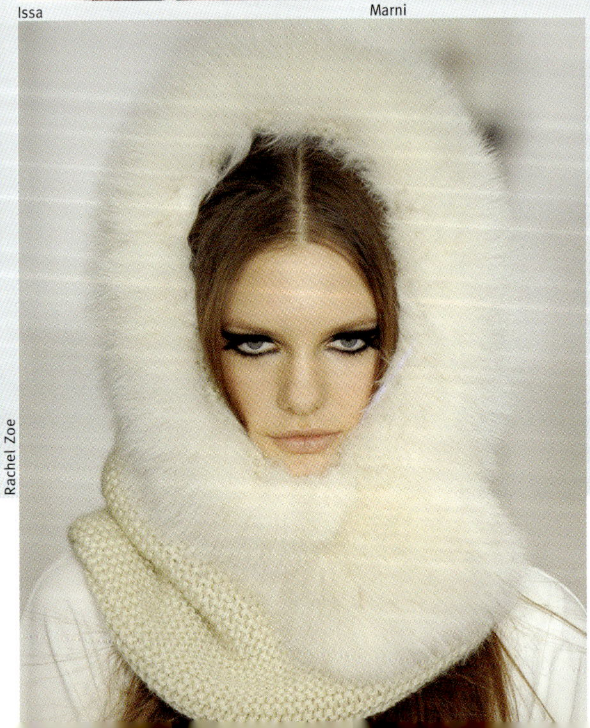
Rachel Zoe

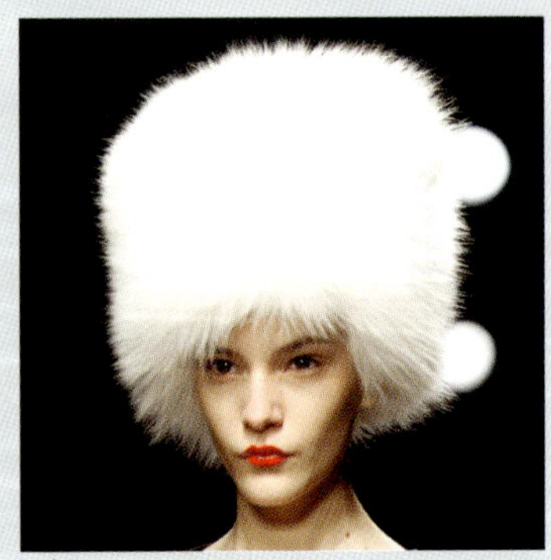
Iceberg

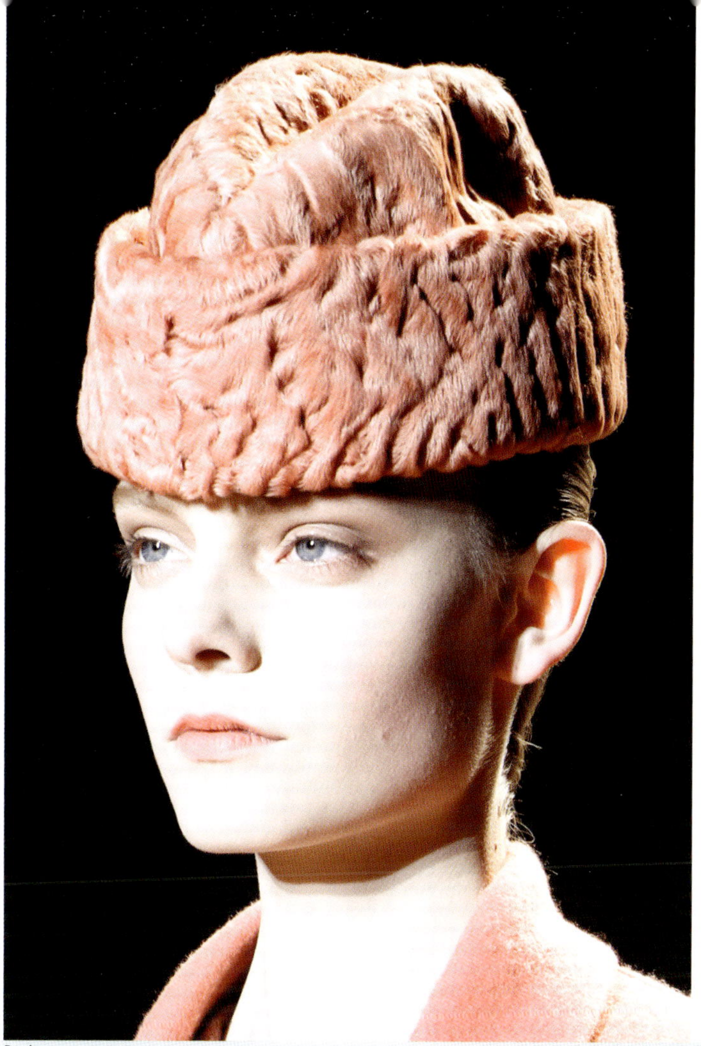

Rochas

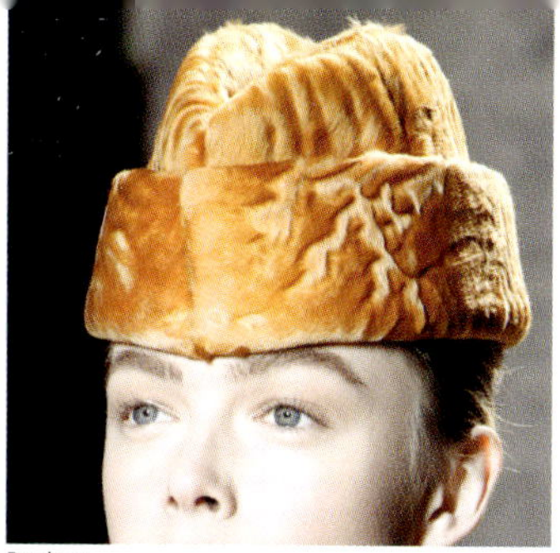

Rochas

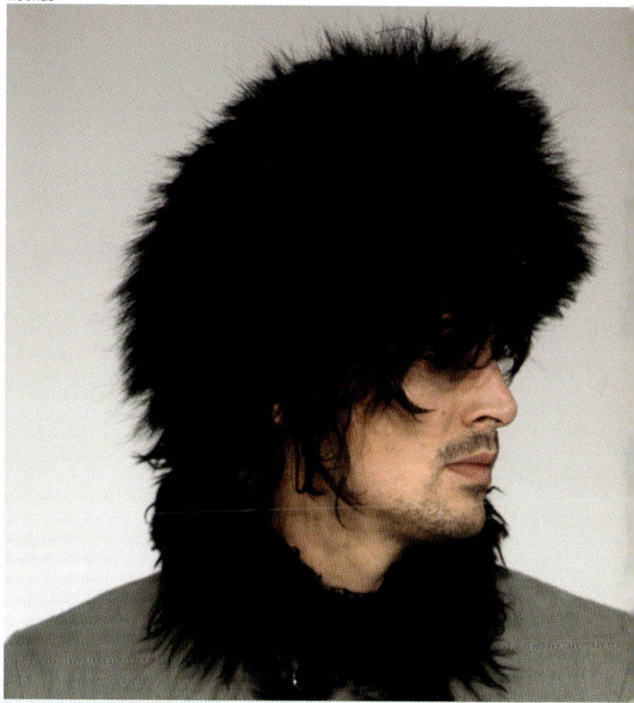

Agnès B.

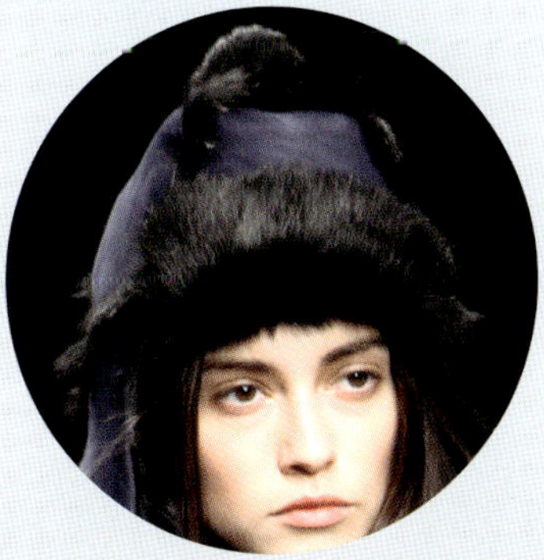

Trussardi

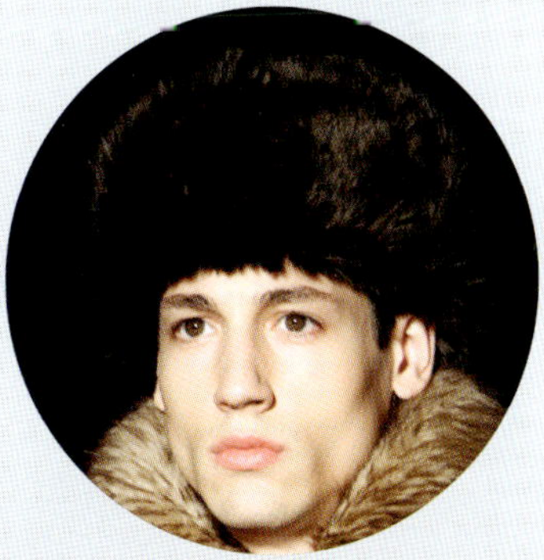

Viktor & Rolf

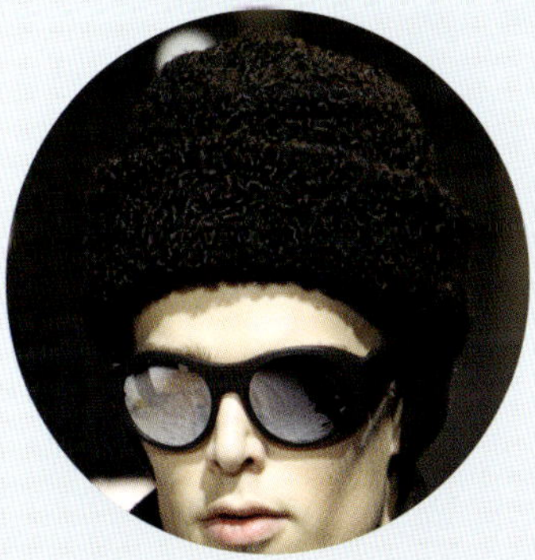

Moncler Grenoble

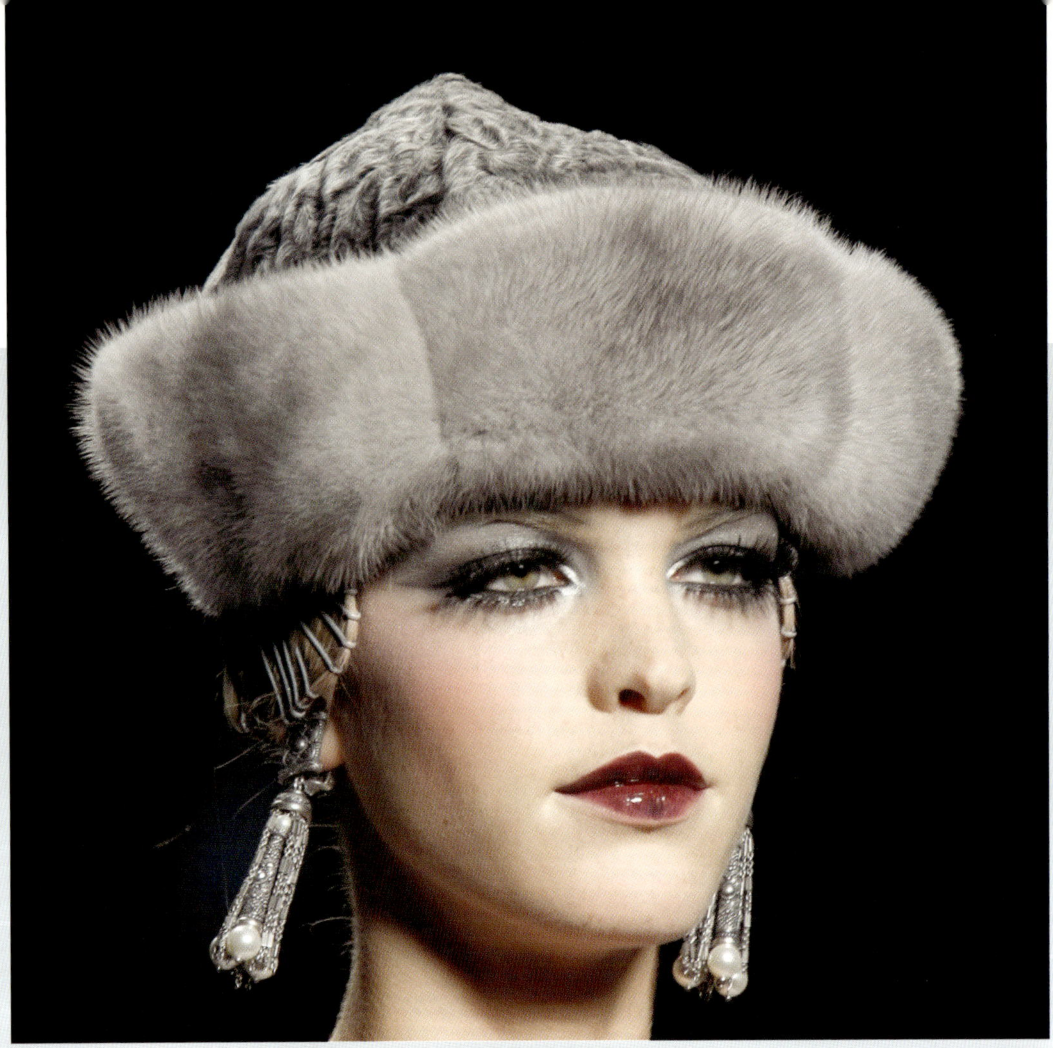

Dior

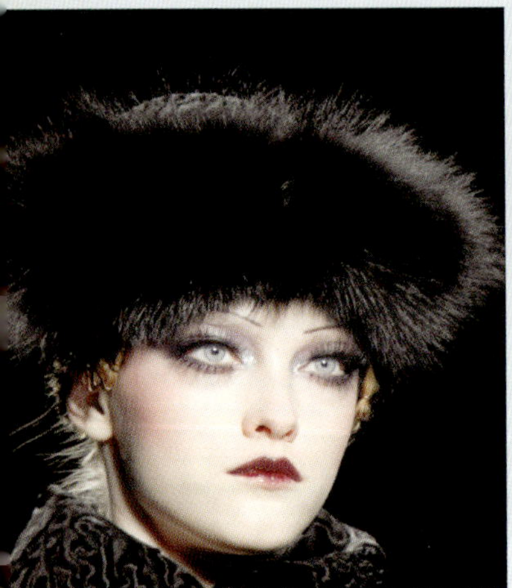

Dior

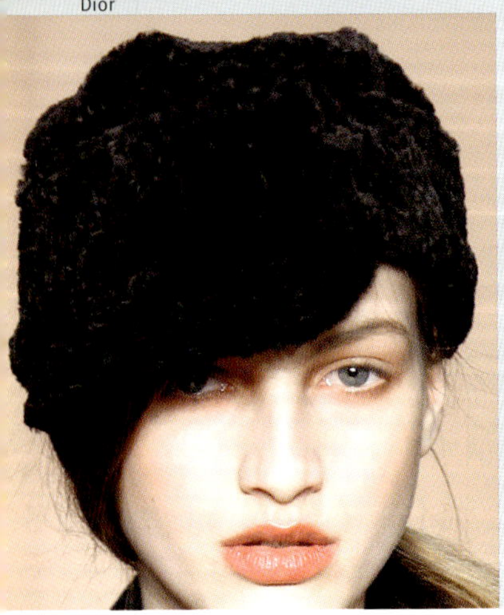

DKNY

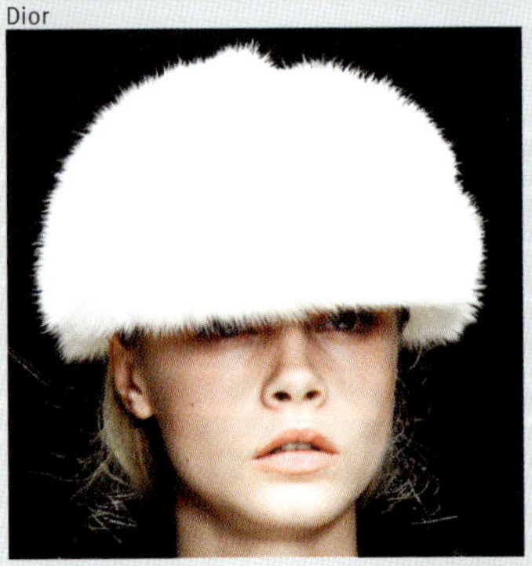

Burberry Prorsum

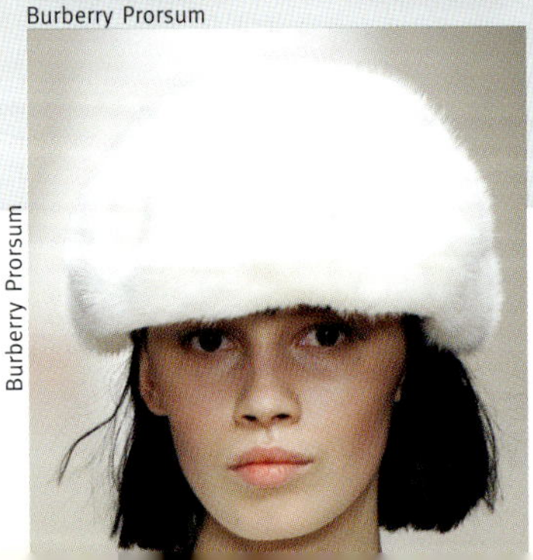

Burberry Prorsum

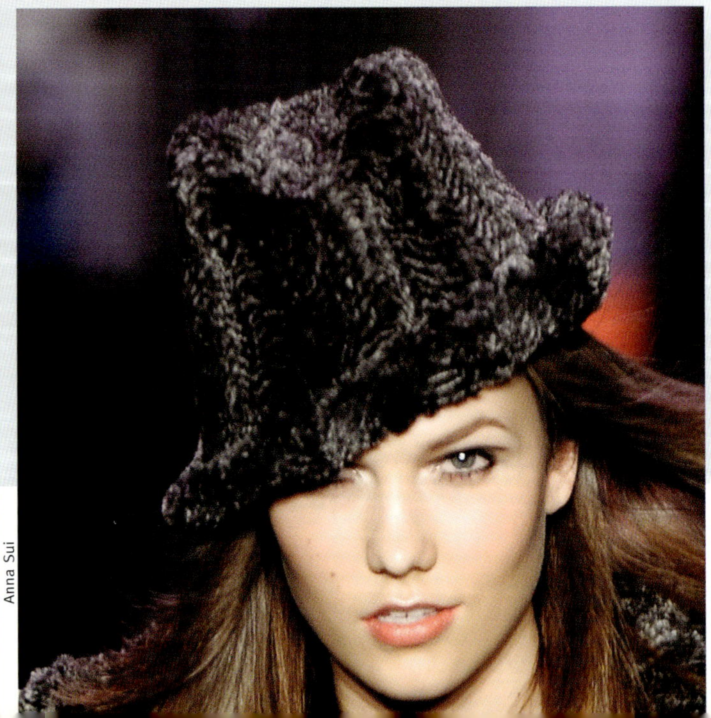

Anna Sui

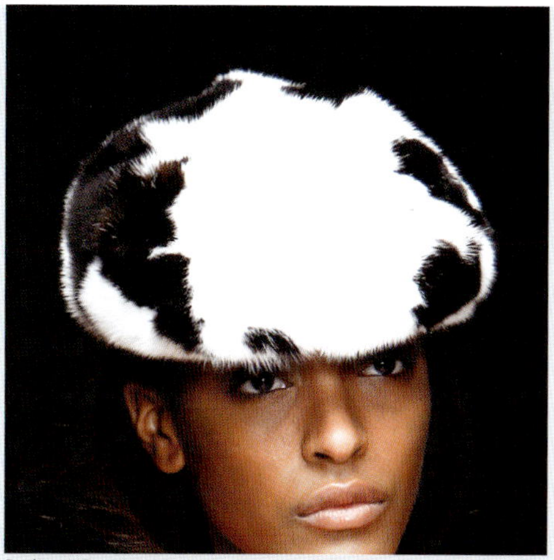

Burberry Prorsum

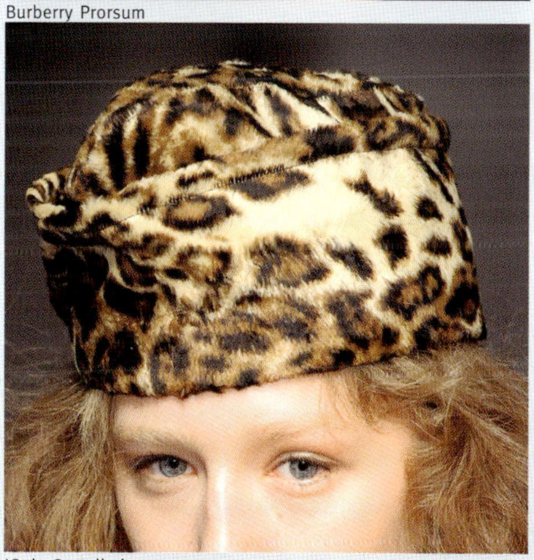

JC de Castelbajac

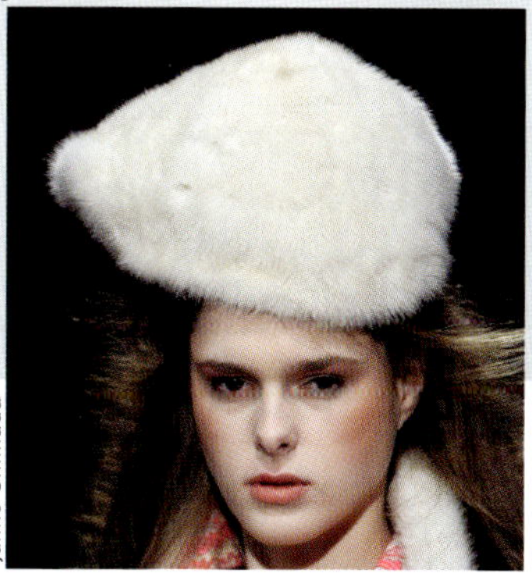

Junko Shimada

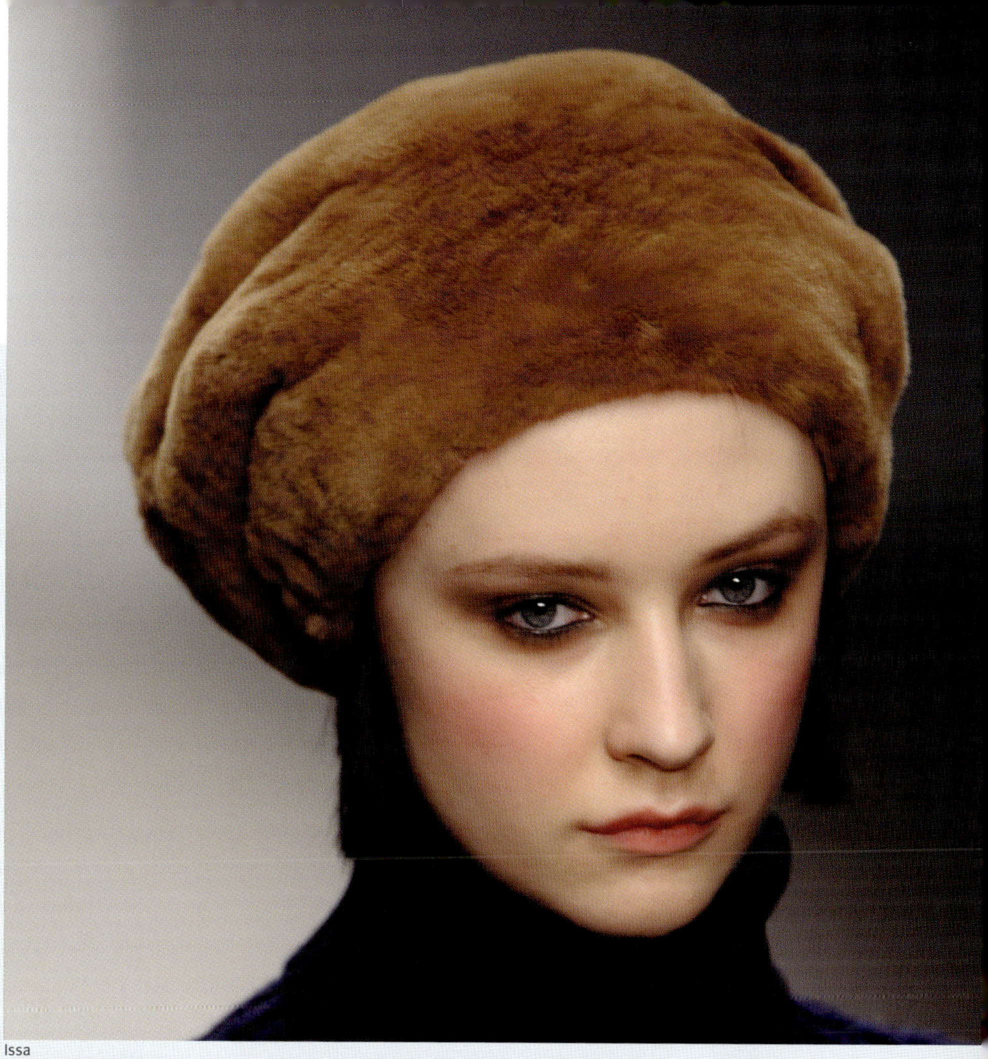

Issa

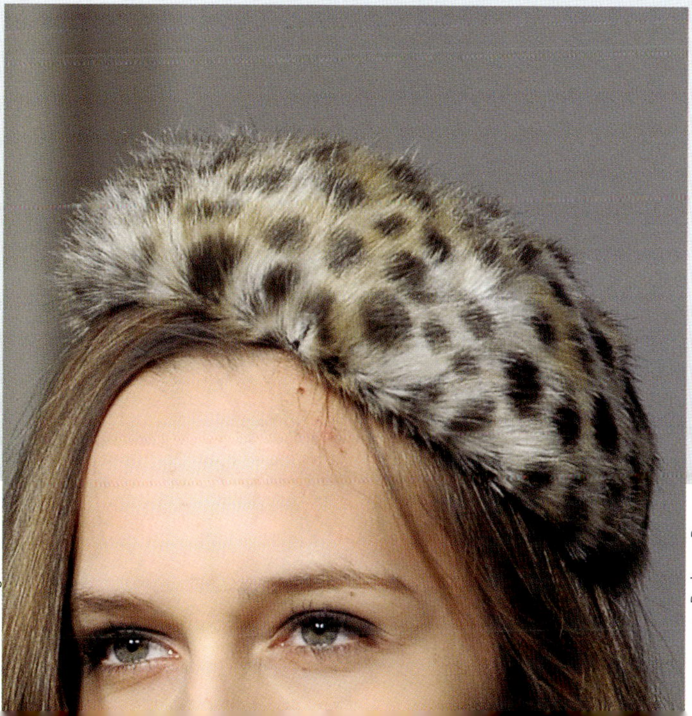

Agnès B.

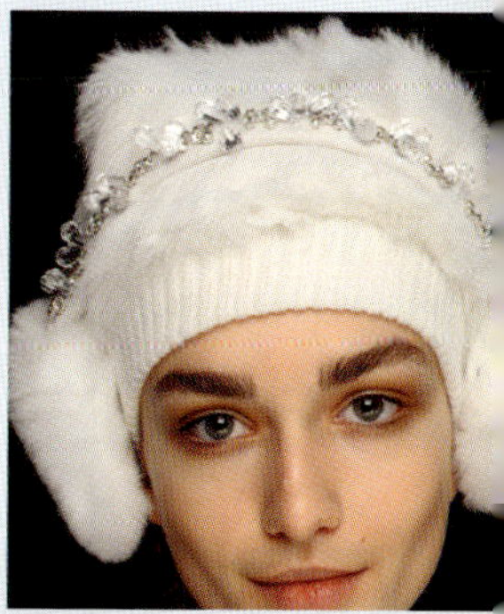

Blugirl

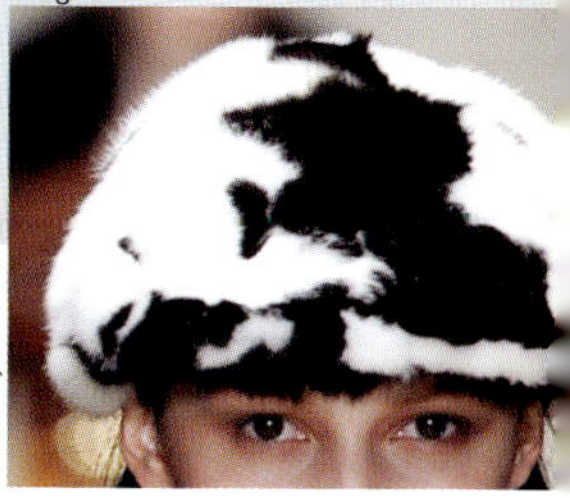

Burberry Prorsum

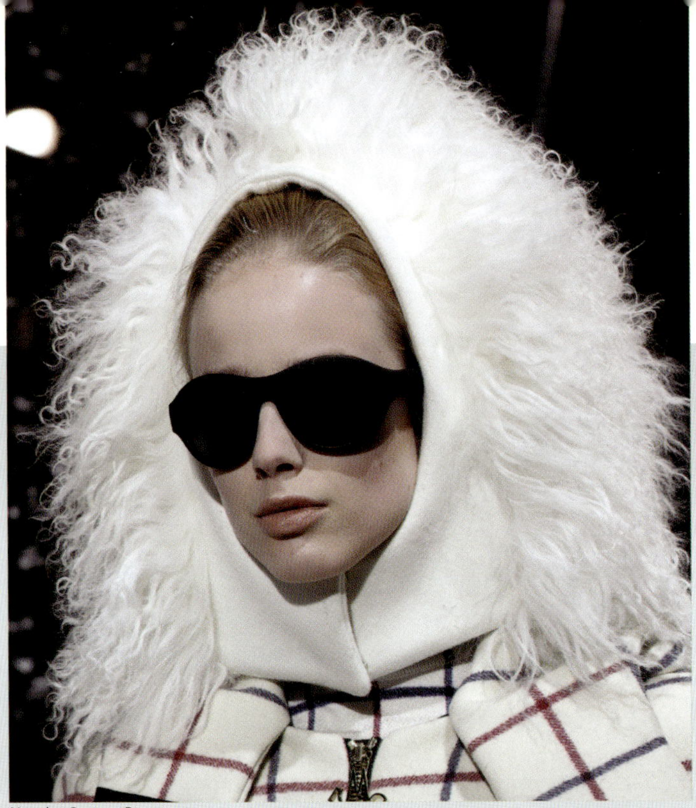

Moncler Gamme Rouge

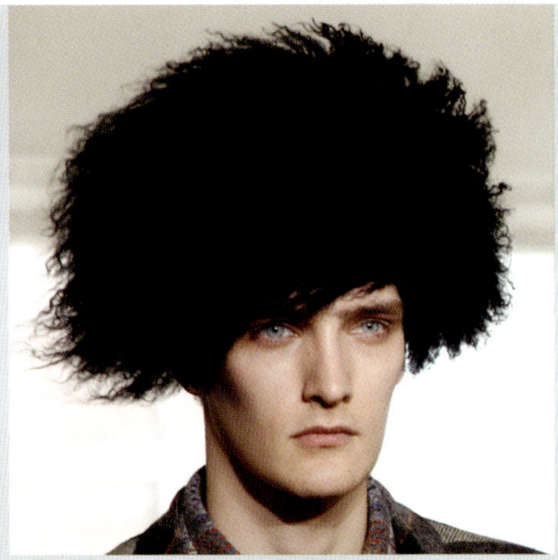

Duckie Brown

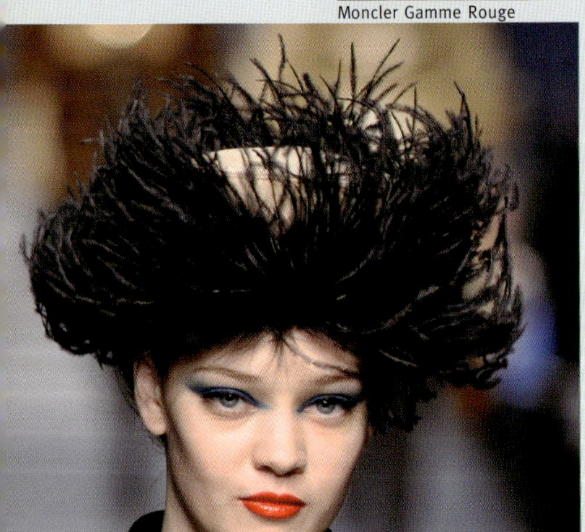

Frankie Morello

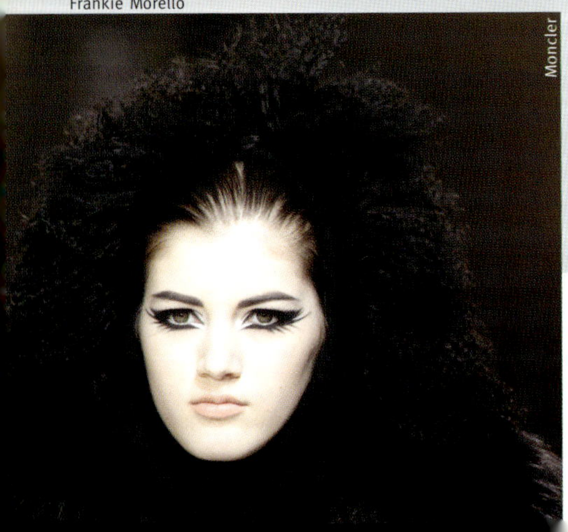

Moncler

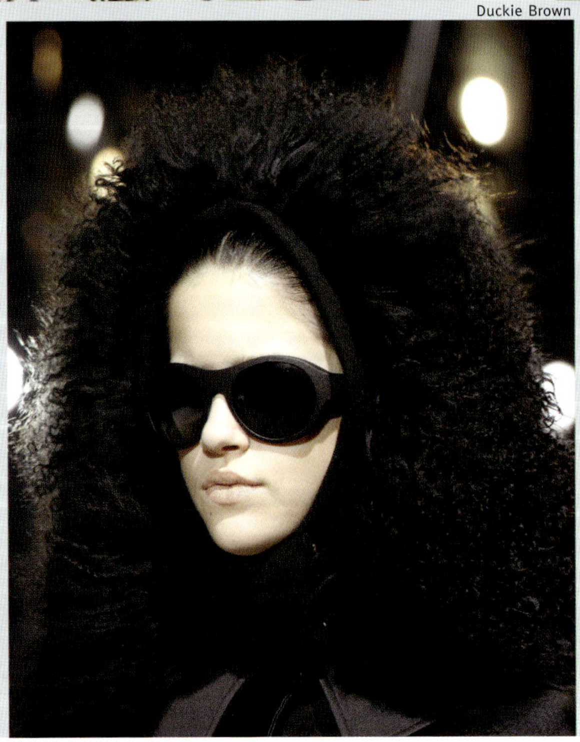

Moncler Gamme Rouge

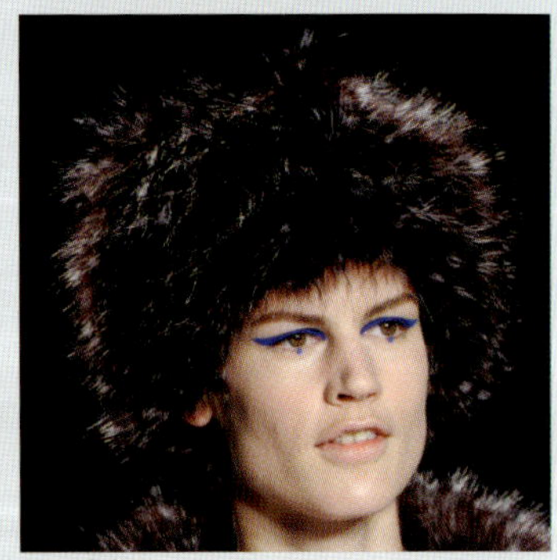

Anna Sui

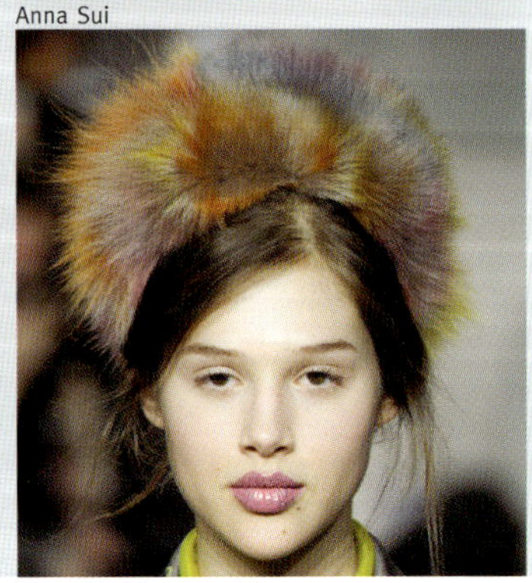

Moschino Cheap & Chic

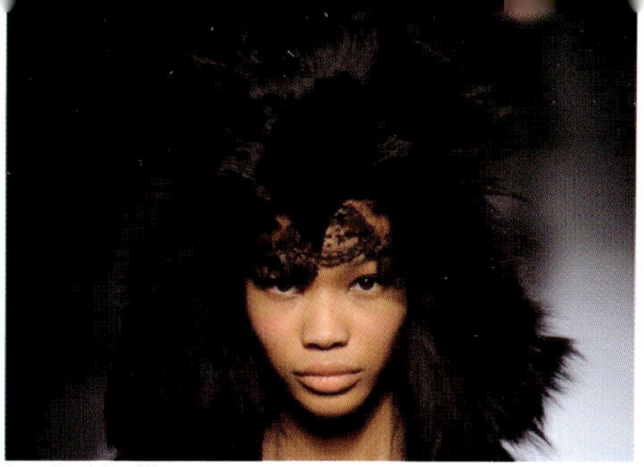
Jean Paul Gaultier

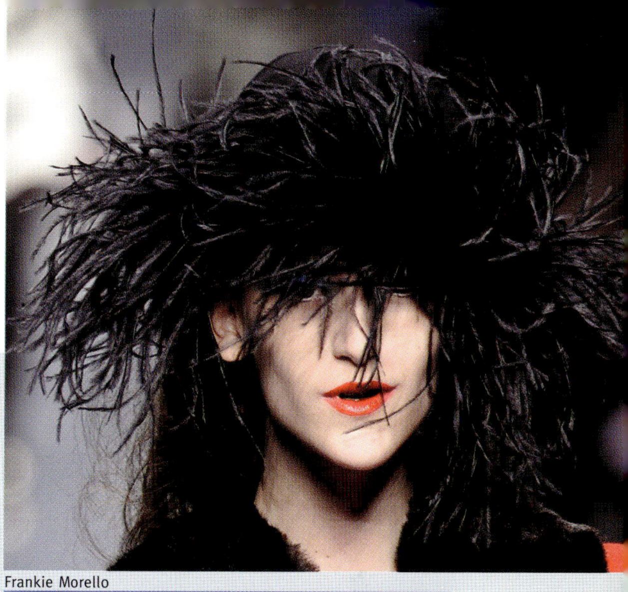
Frankie Morello

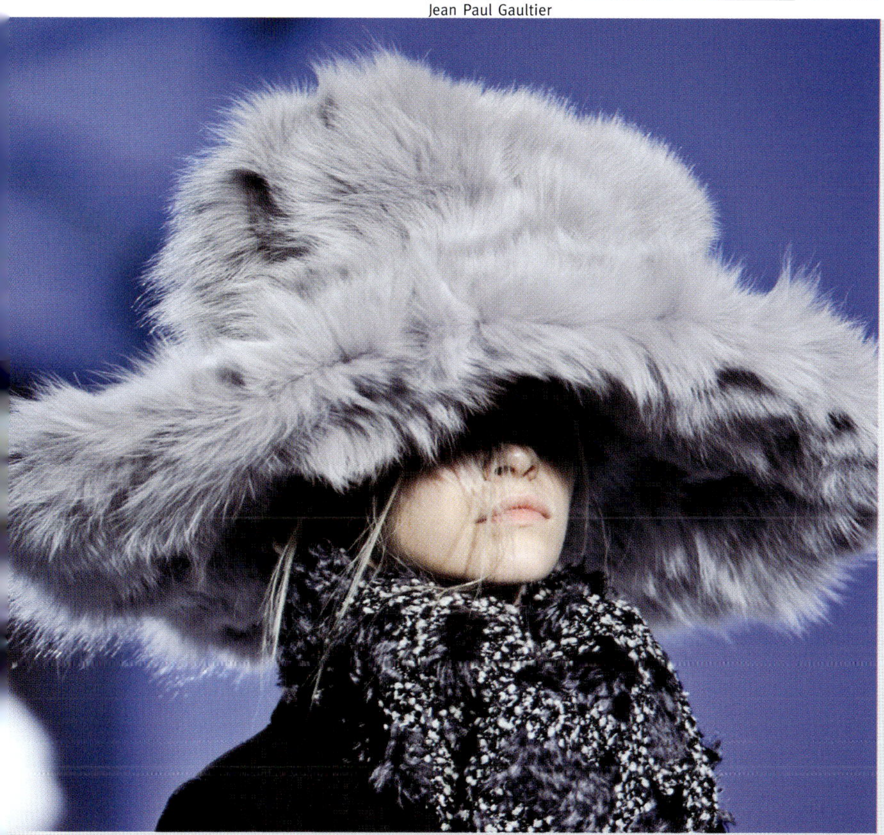
Marc Jacobs

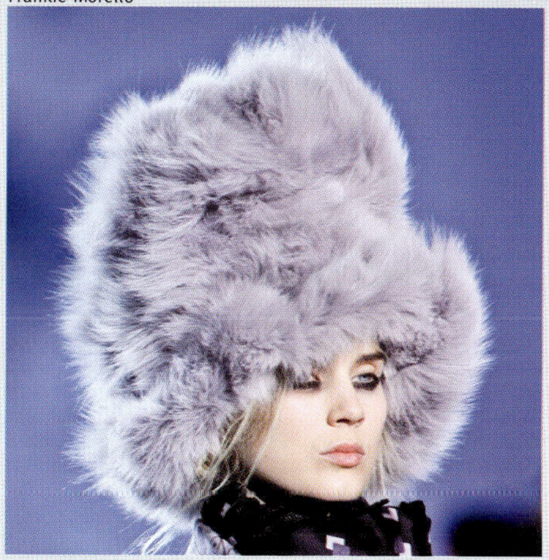
Marc Jacobs

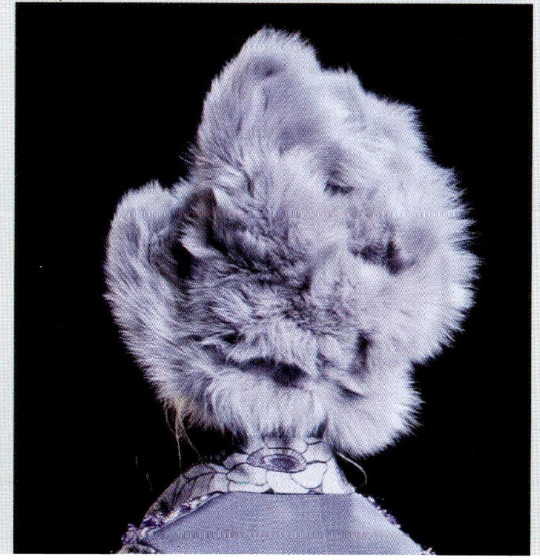

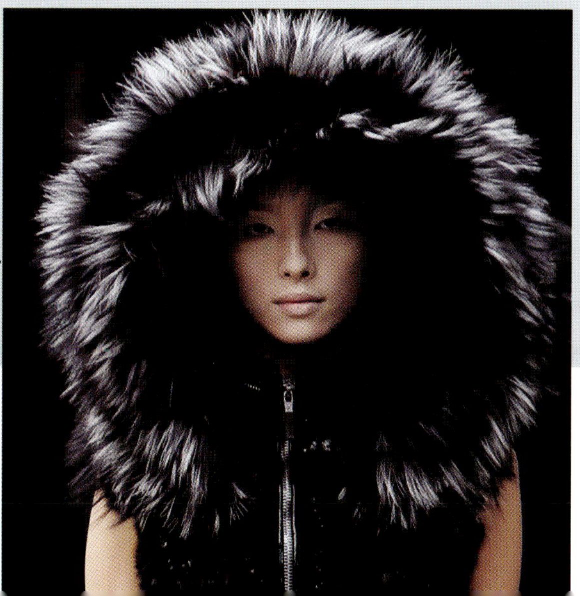
Alexander McQueen

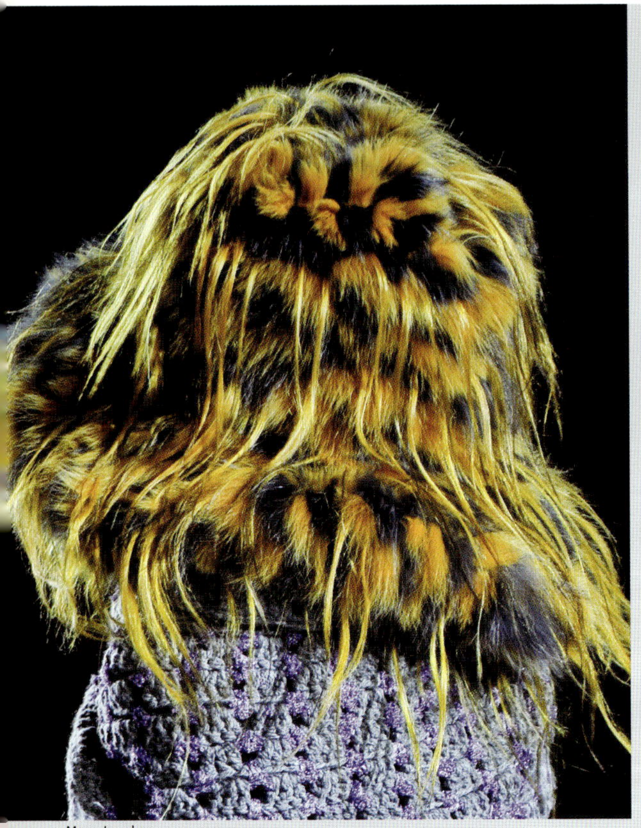

Marc Jacobs

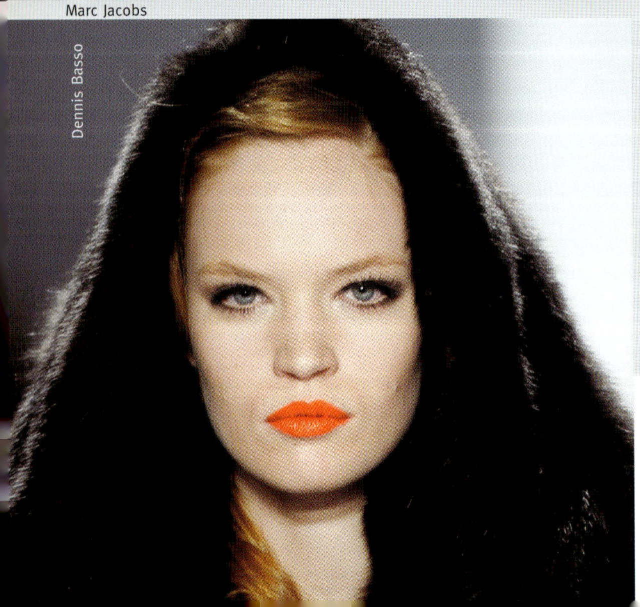

Dennis Basso

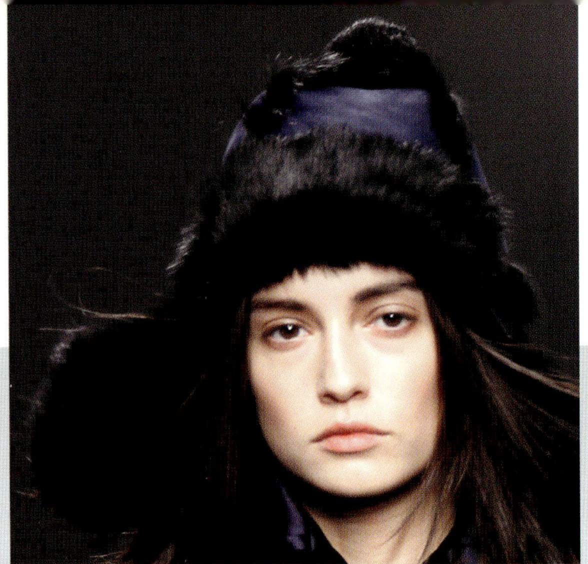

Trussardi

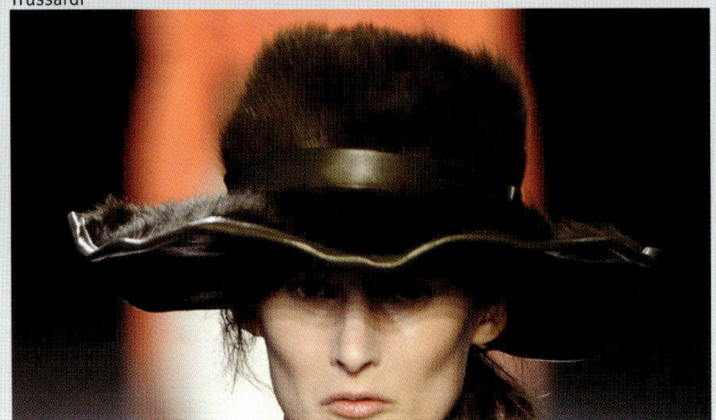

Acne

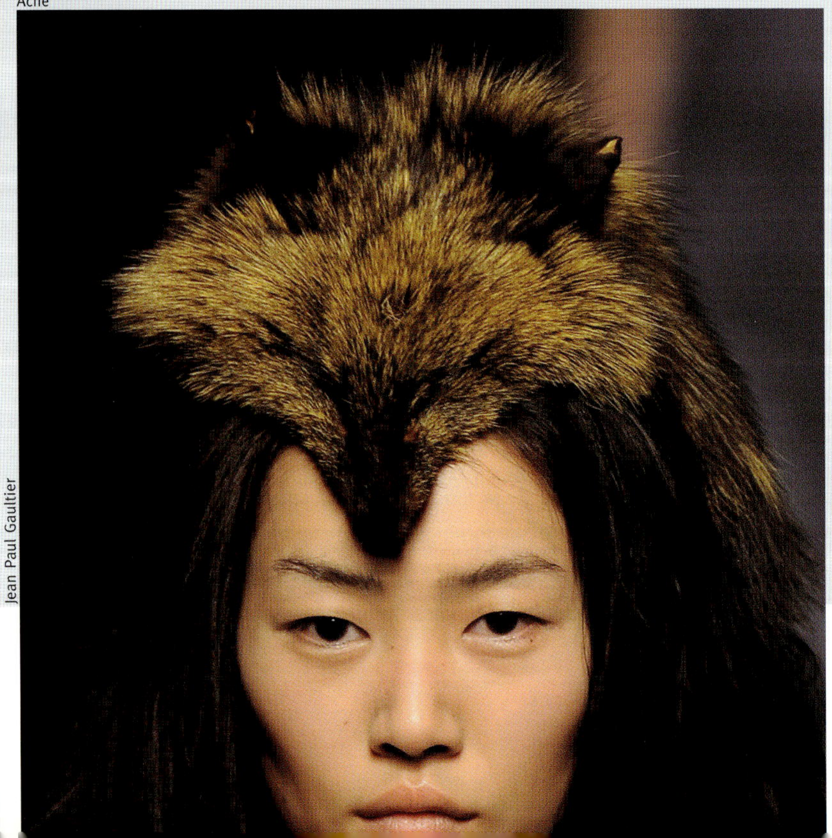

Jean Paul Gaultier

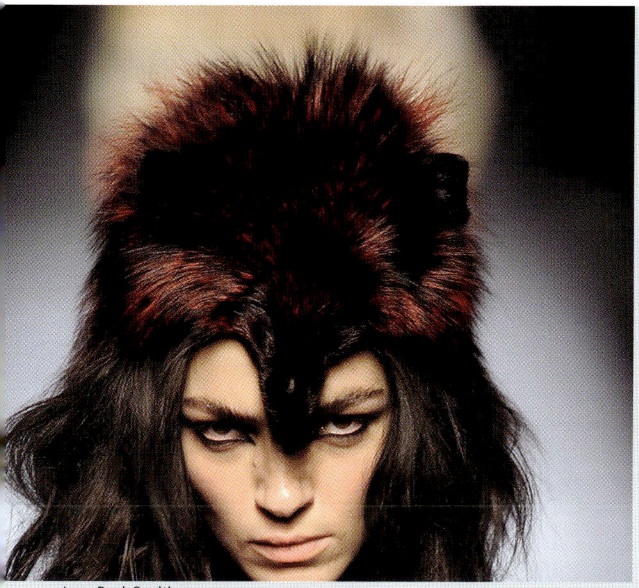
Jean Paul Gaultier

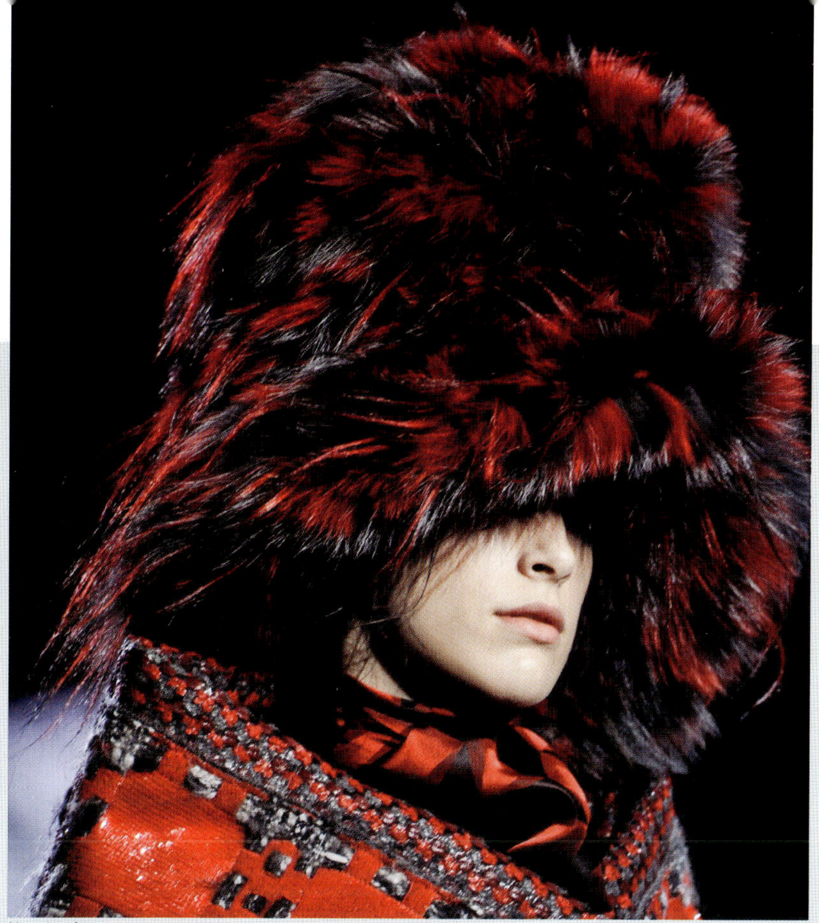
Marc Jacobs

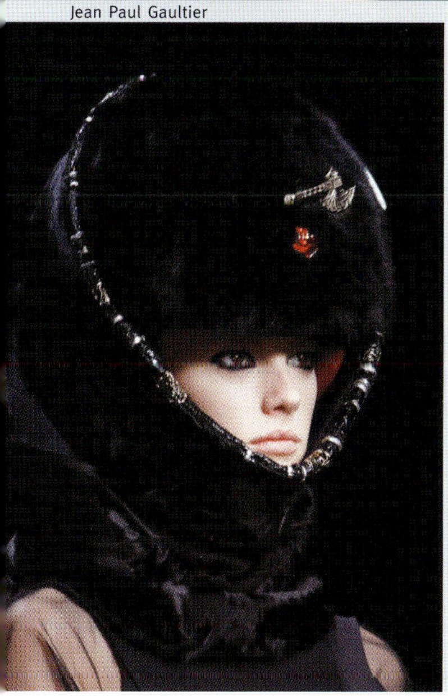
Karl Lagerfeld

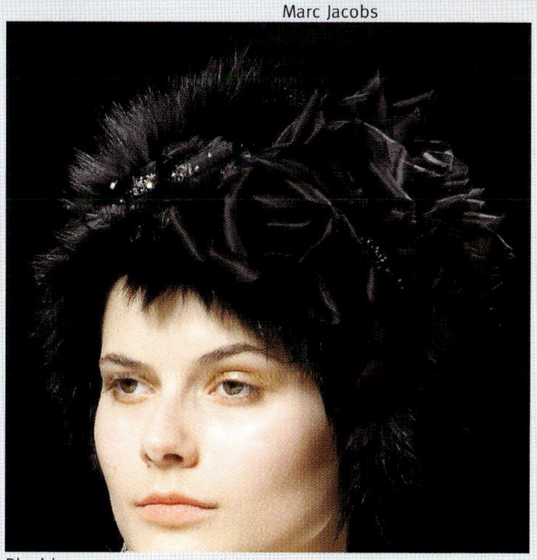
Blugirl

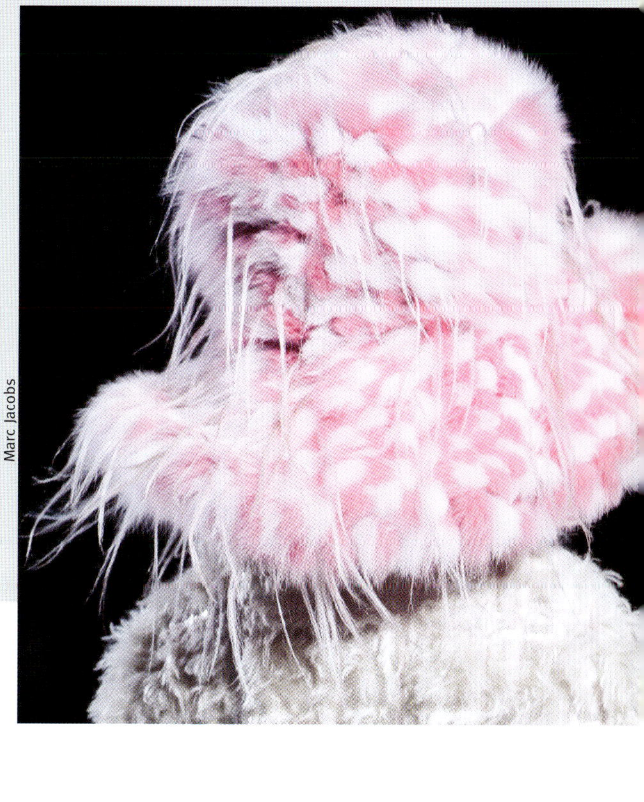
Marc Jacobs

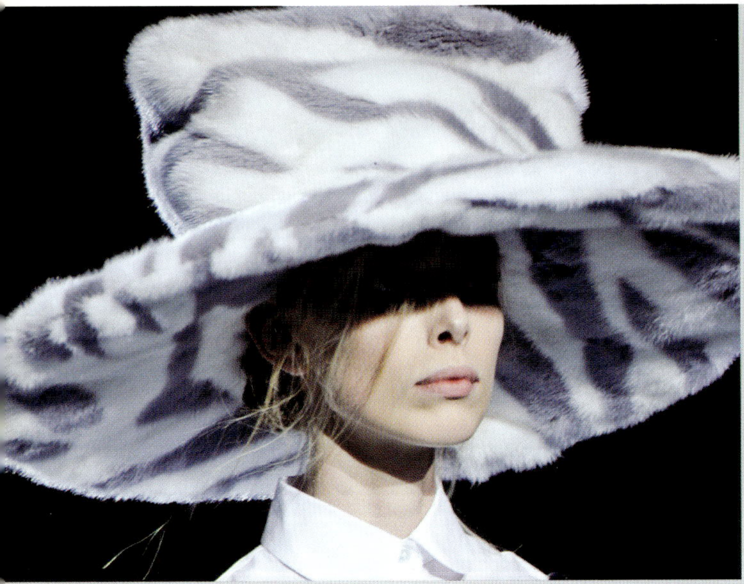

Marc Jacobs

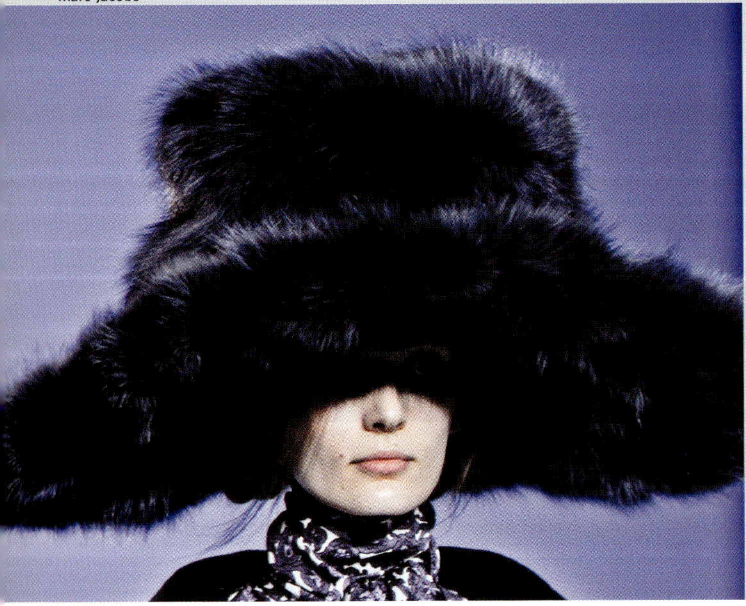

Marc Jacobs

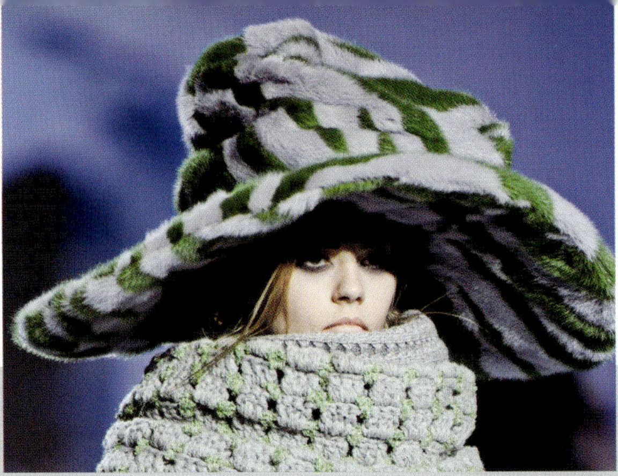

Marc Jacobs

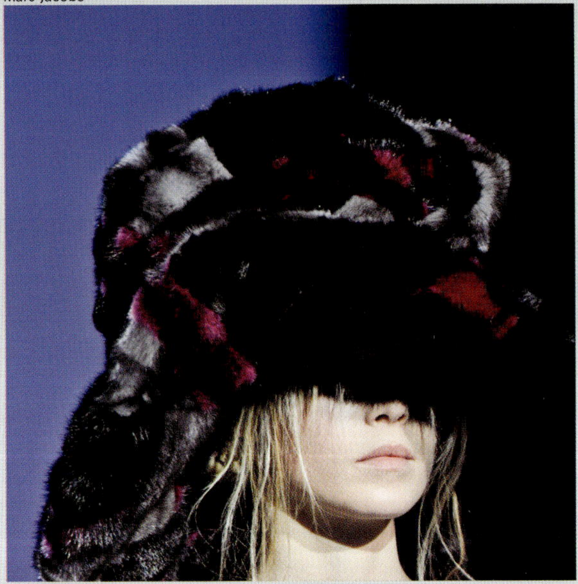

Marc Jacobs

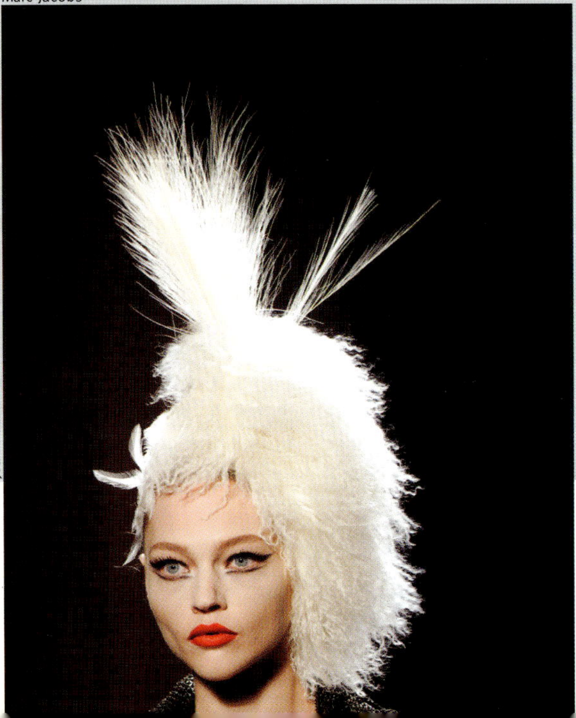

Jean Paul Gaultier

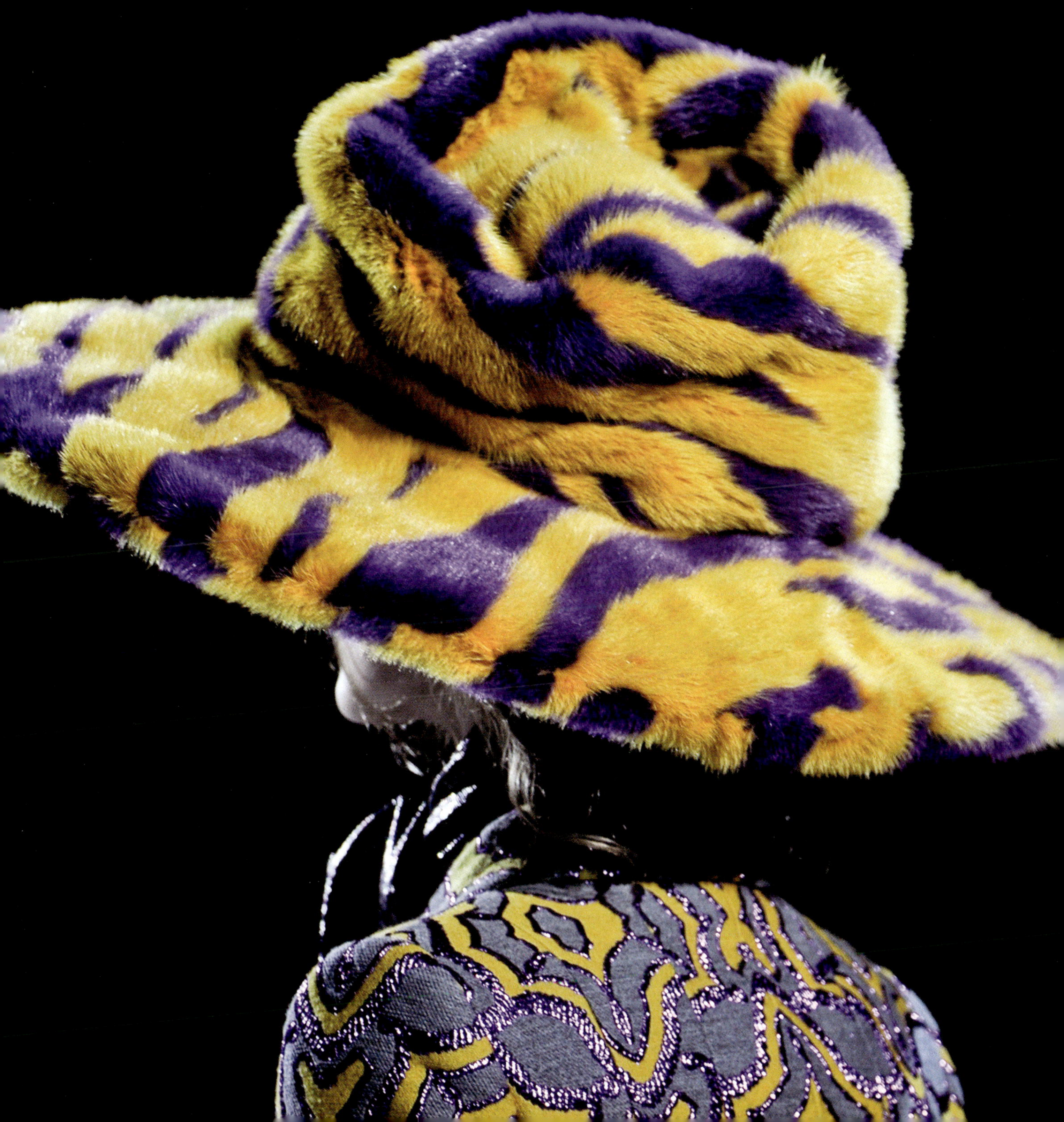

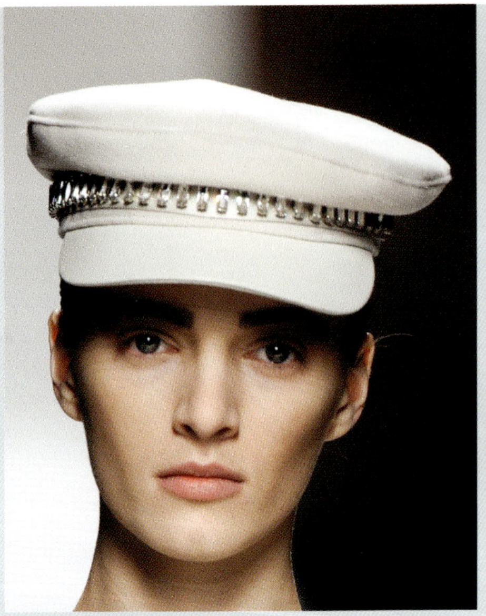
Max Mara

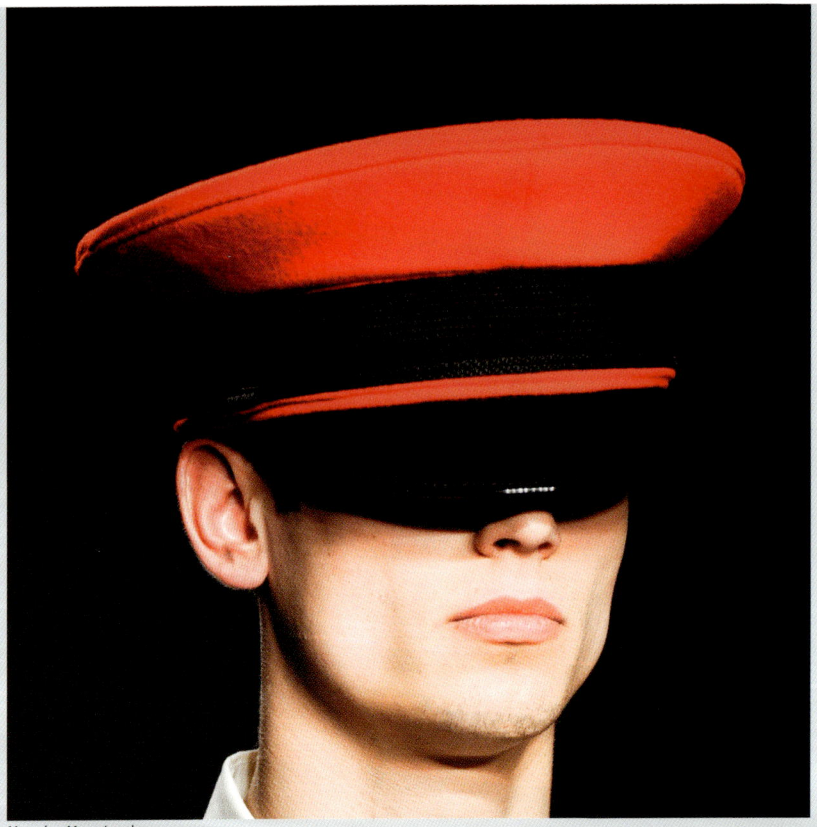
Marc by Marc Jacobs

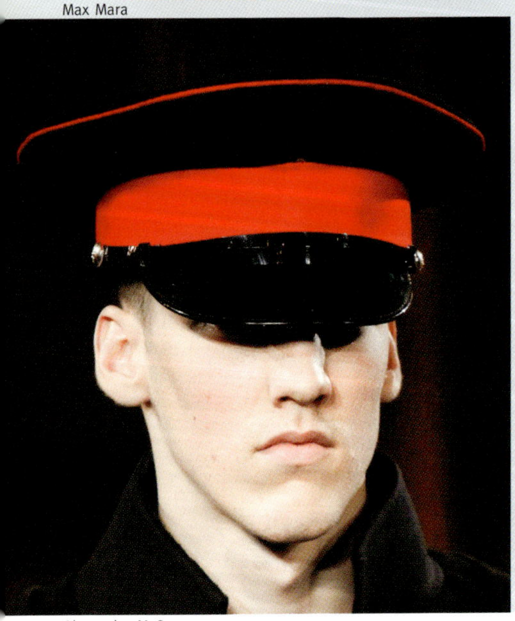
Alexander McQueen

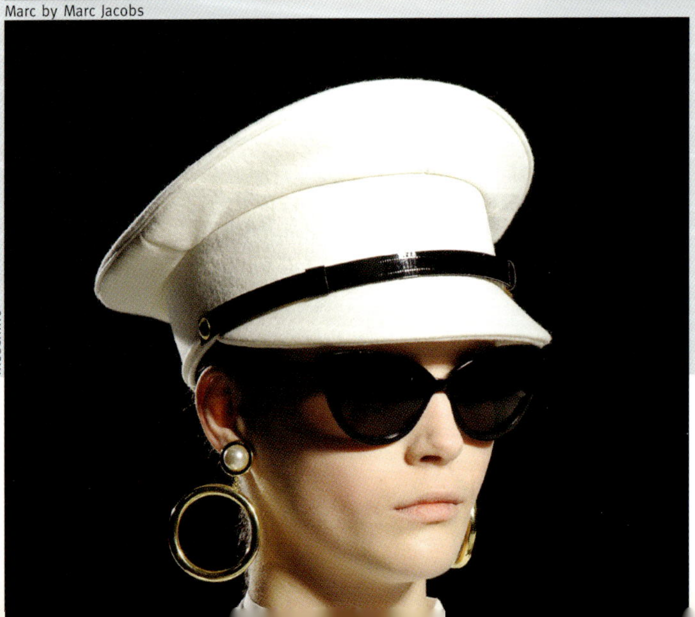
Moschino

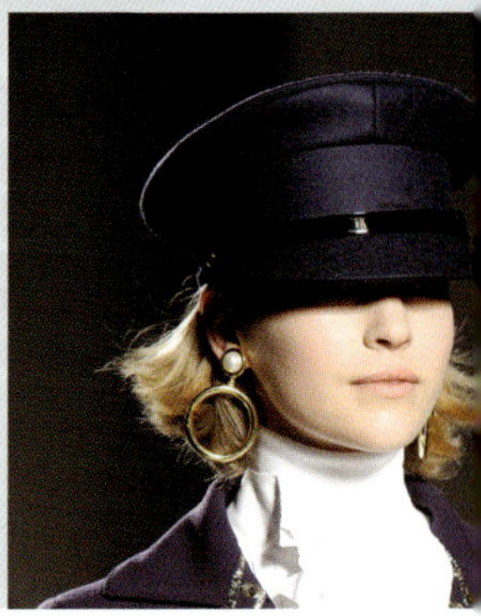
Moschino

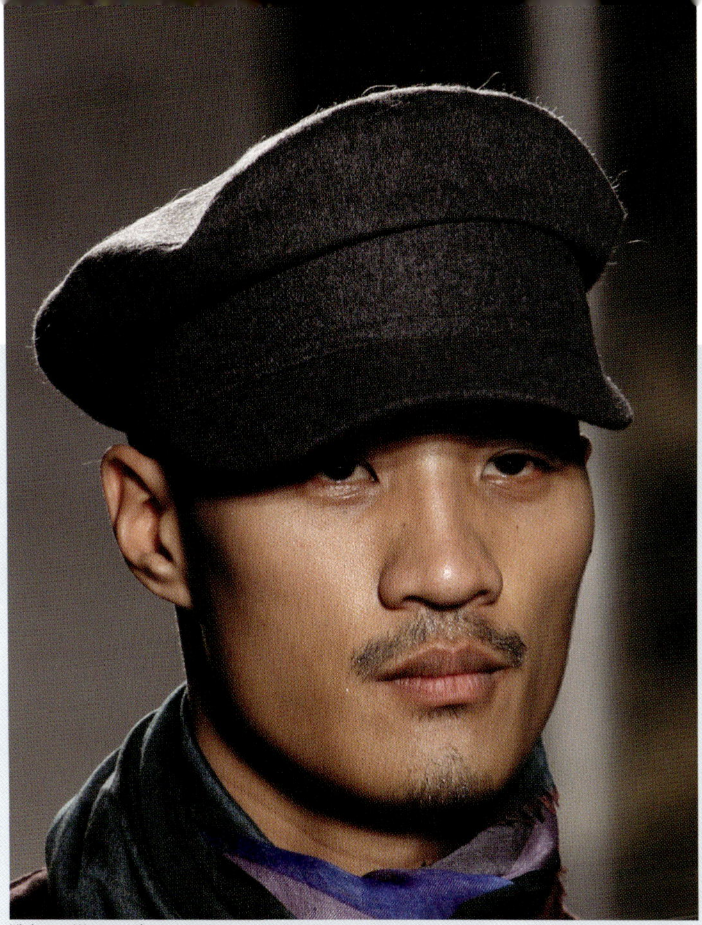

Vivienne Westwood

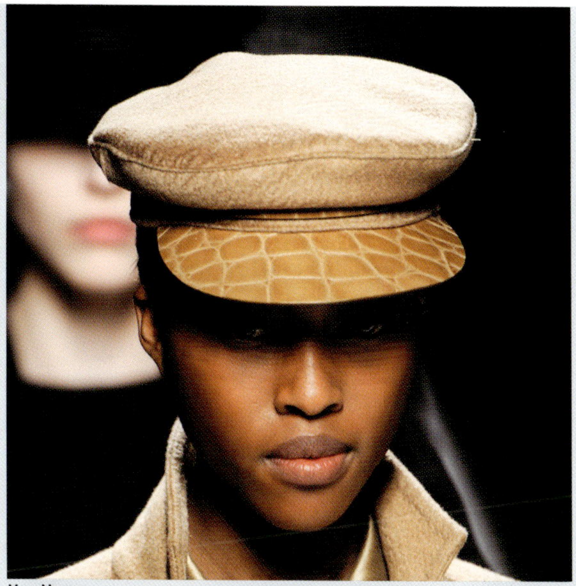

Max Mara

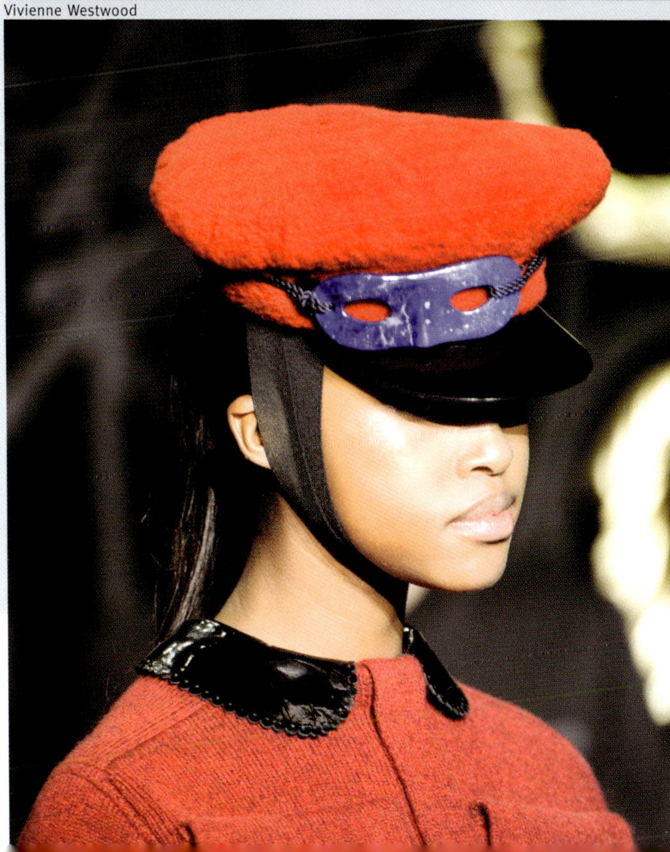

Louis Vuitton

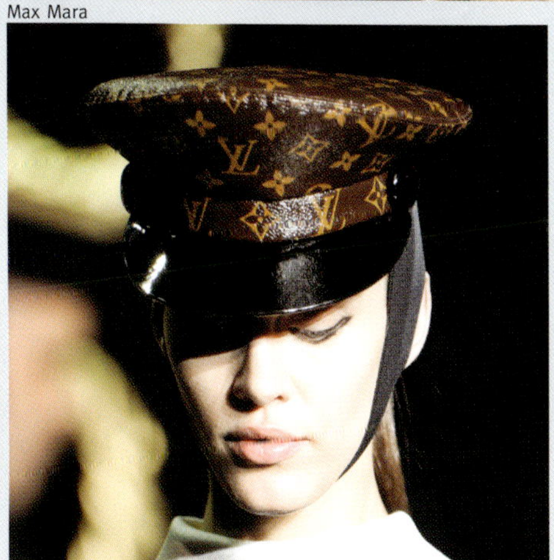

Louis Vuitton

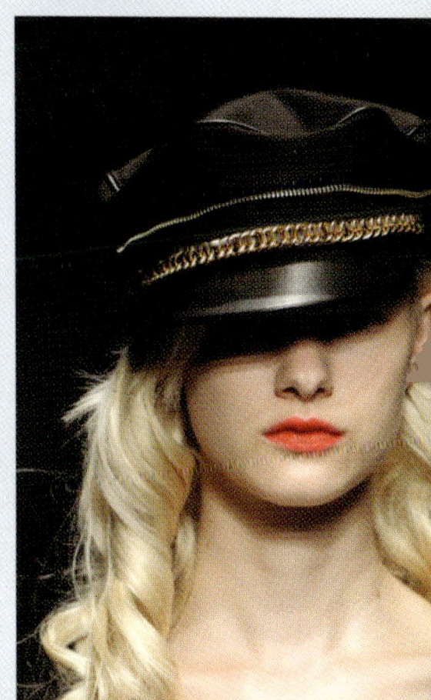

Jo No Fui

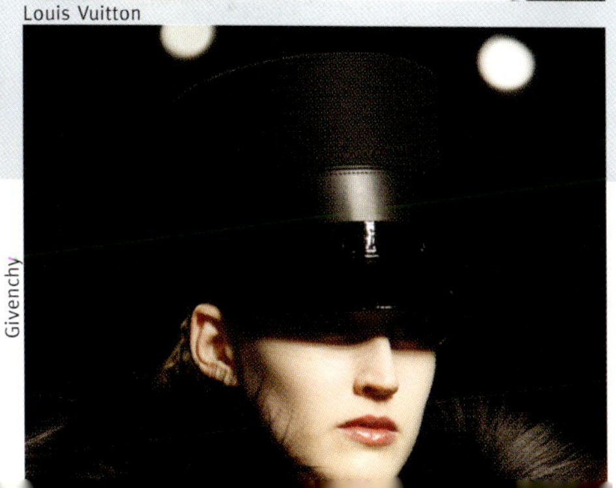

Givenchy

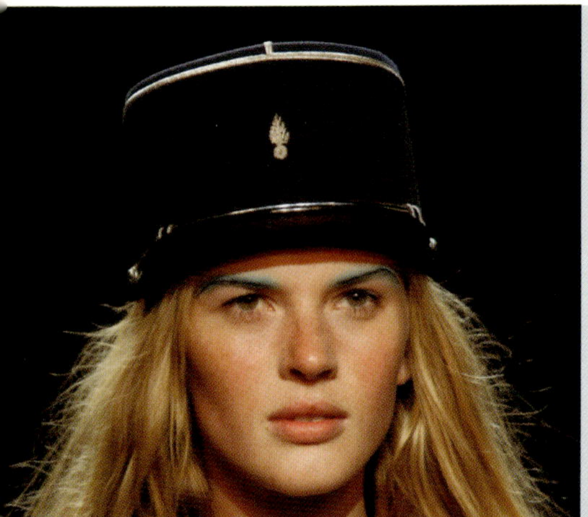
Diesel Black Gold

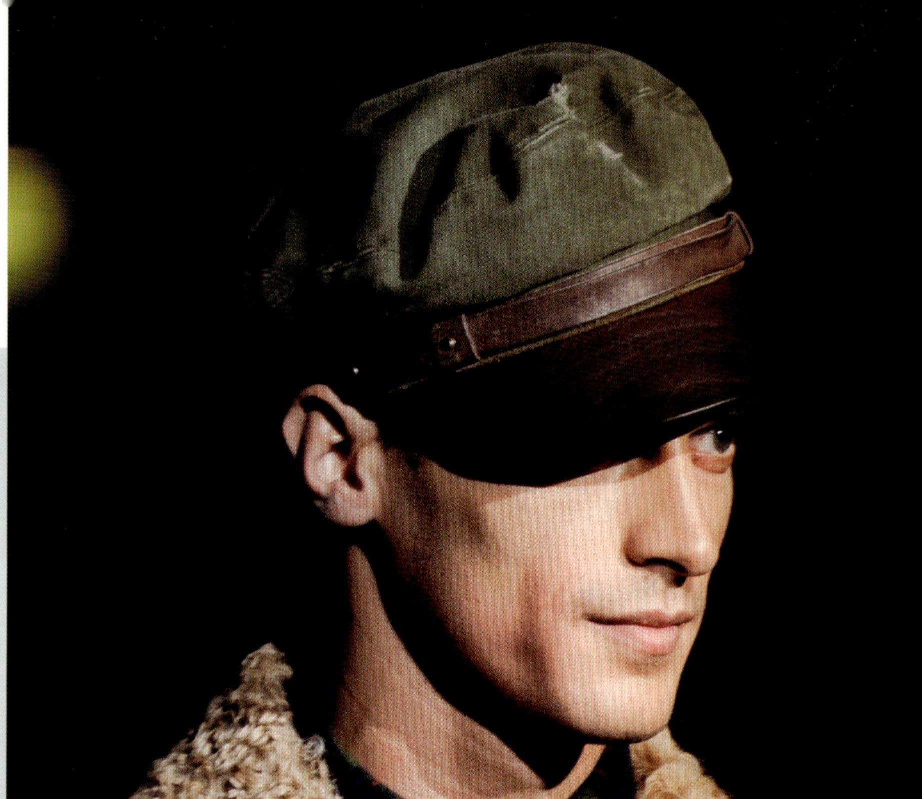
Dsquared2

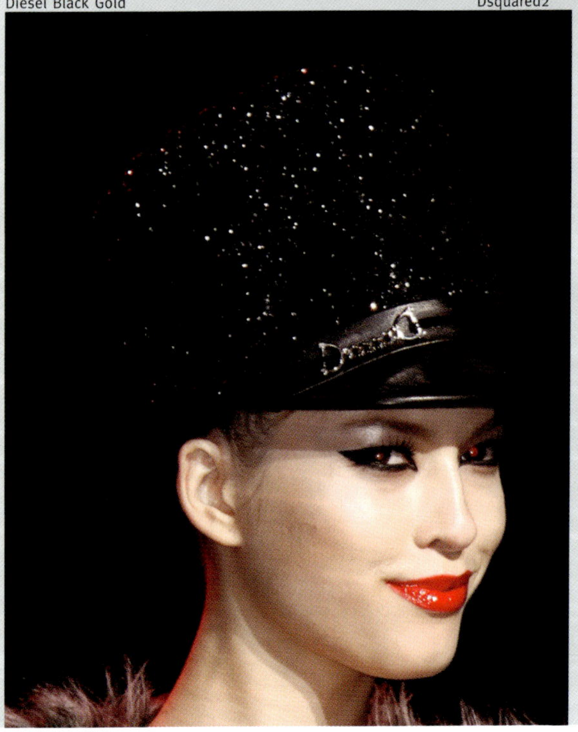
Barbie

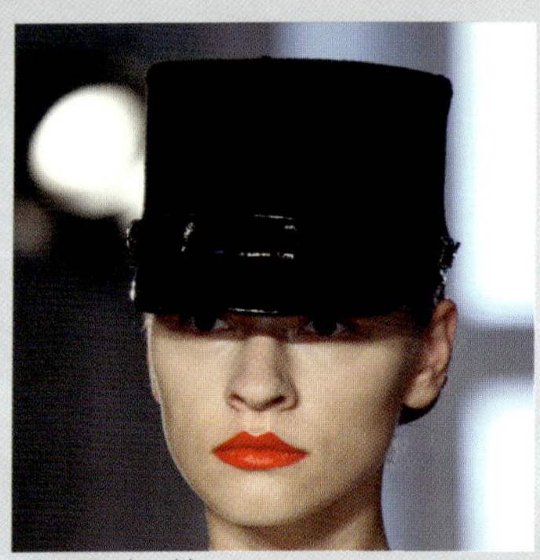
Julien Macdonald

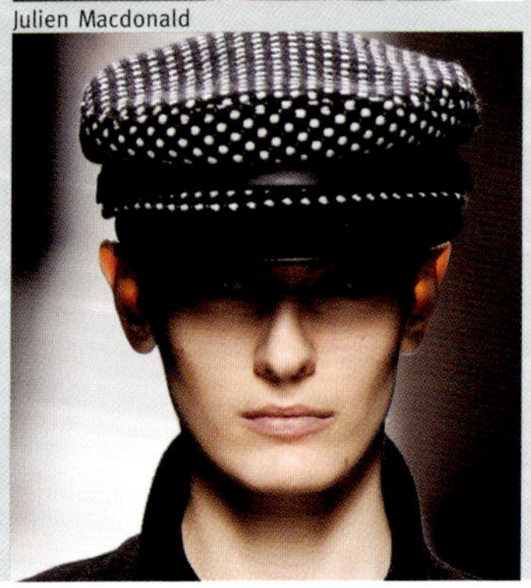
Max Mara

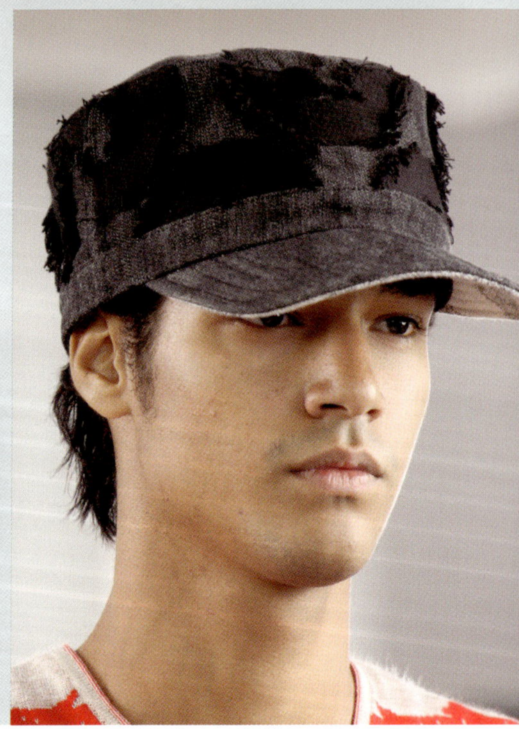
Issey Miyake

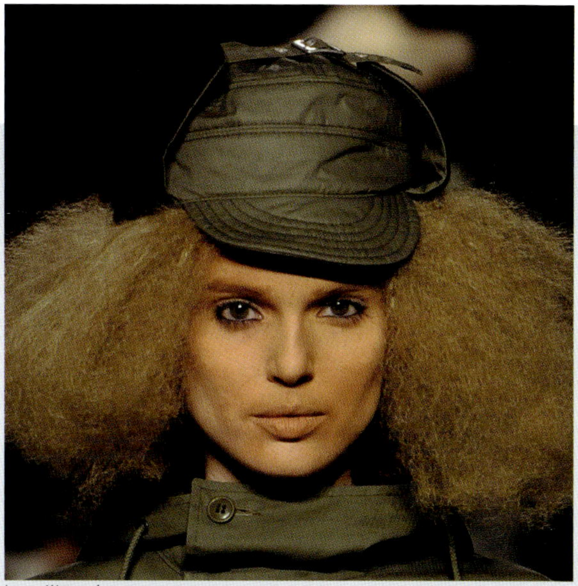

Junya Watanabe

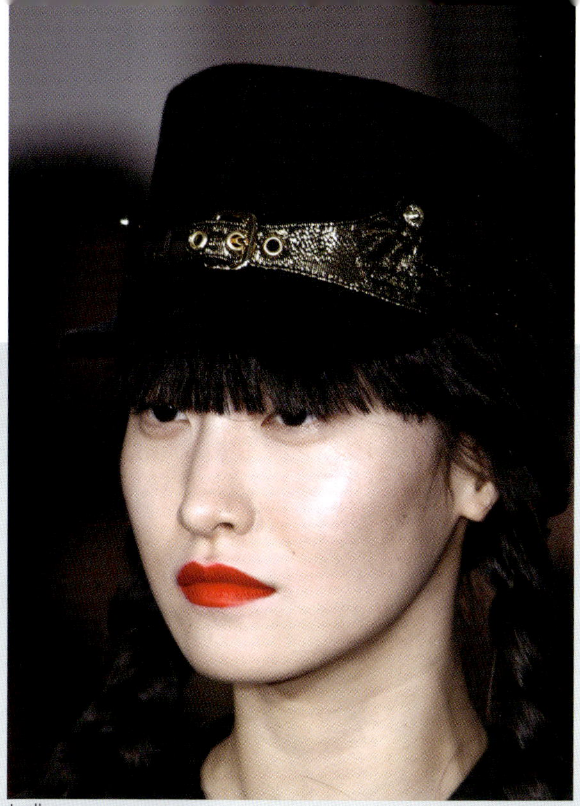

Luella

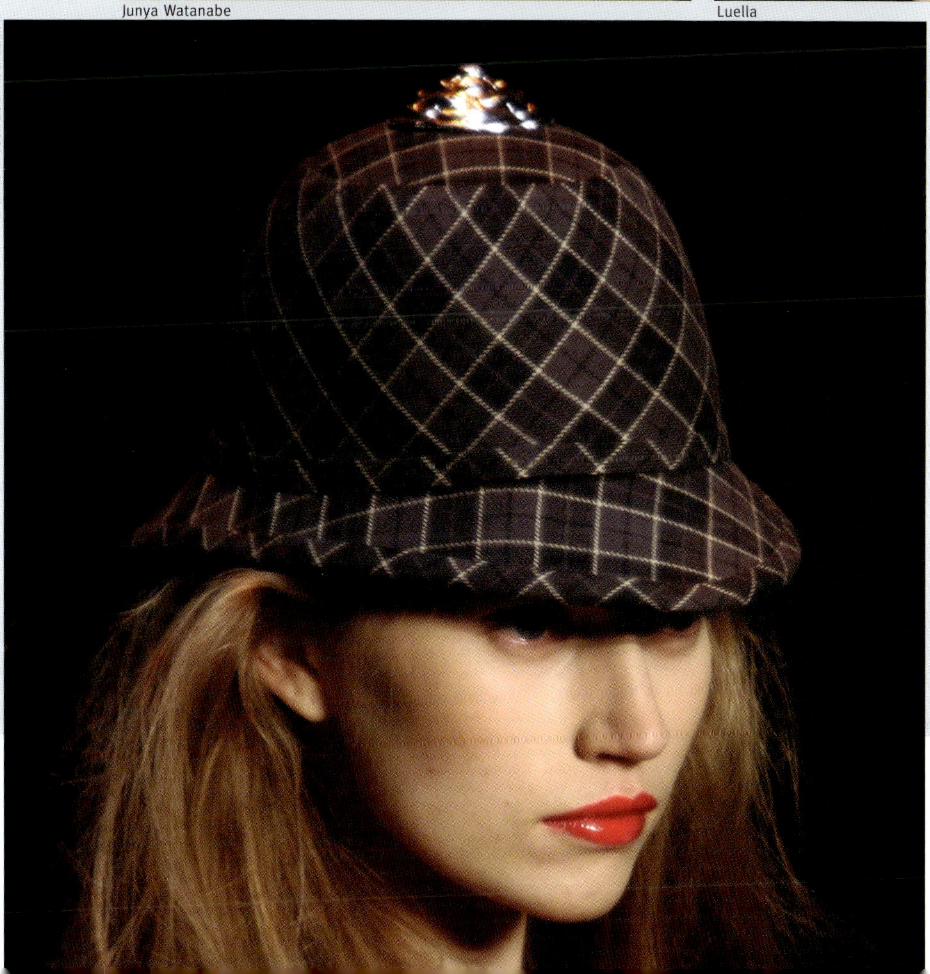

Vivienne Westwood Red Label

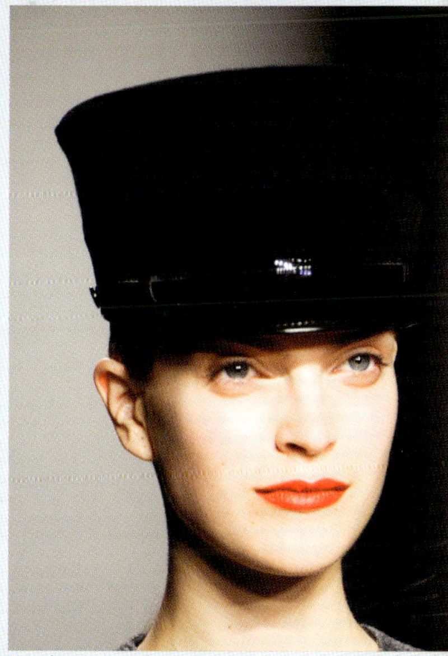

Marc by Marc Jacobs

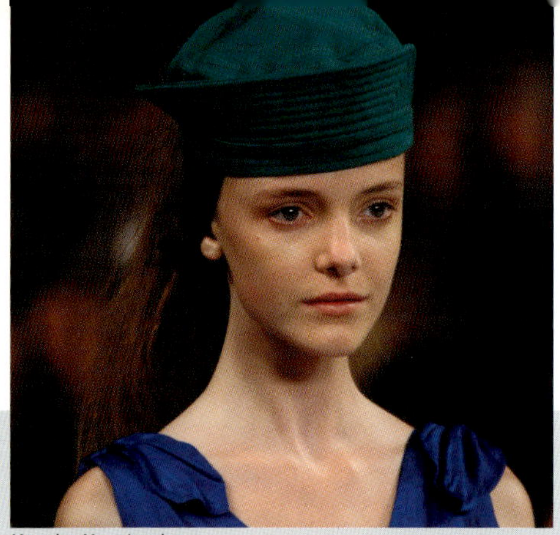

Marc by Marc Jacobs

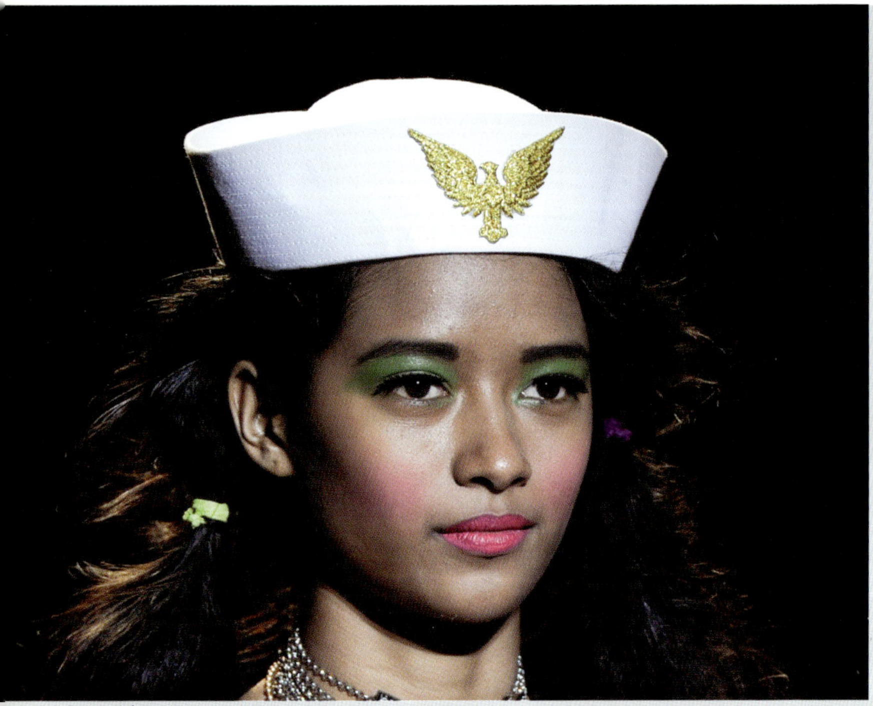

Betsey Johnson

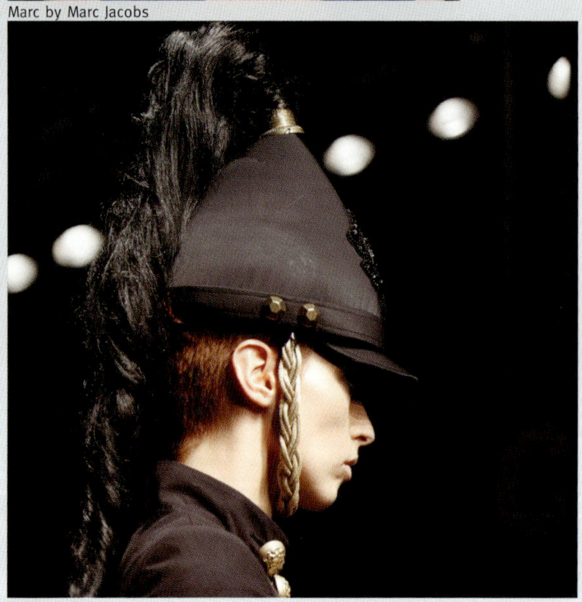

Gaetano Navarra

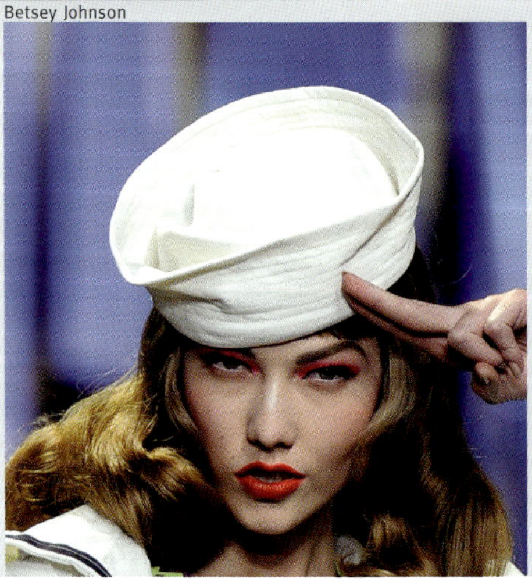

Dior

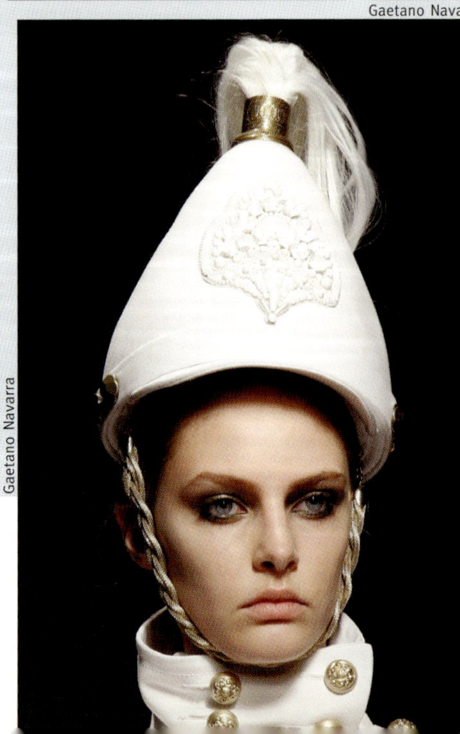

Gaetano Navarra

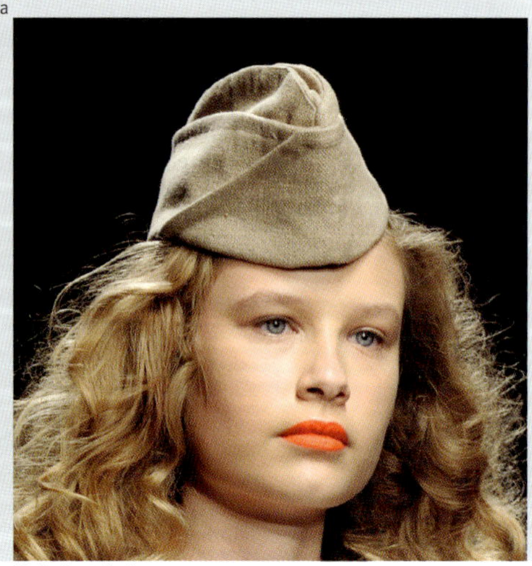

JC de Castelbajac

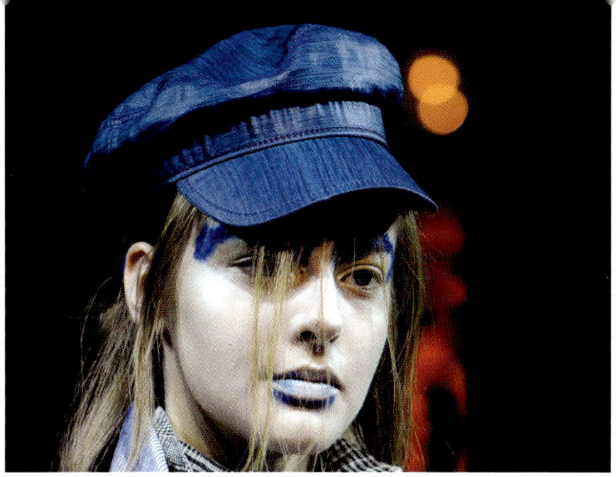

Vivienne Westwood

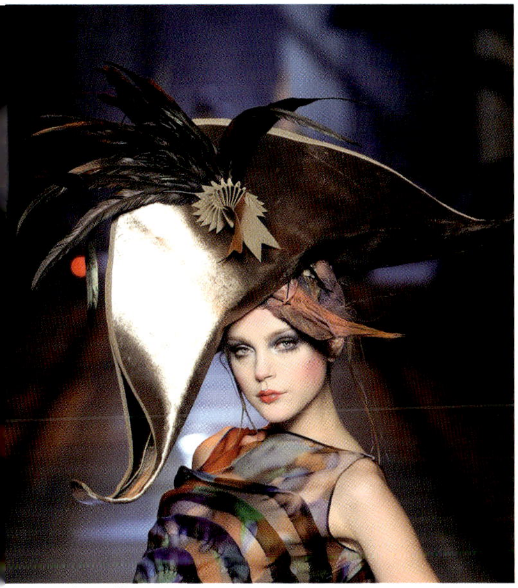

John Galliano

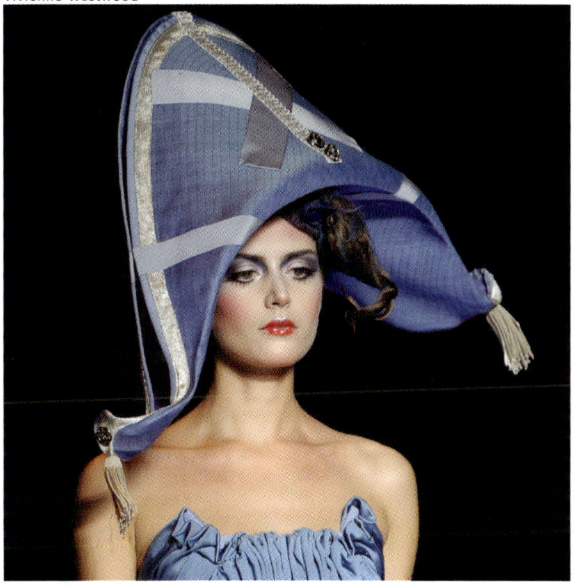

John Galliano

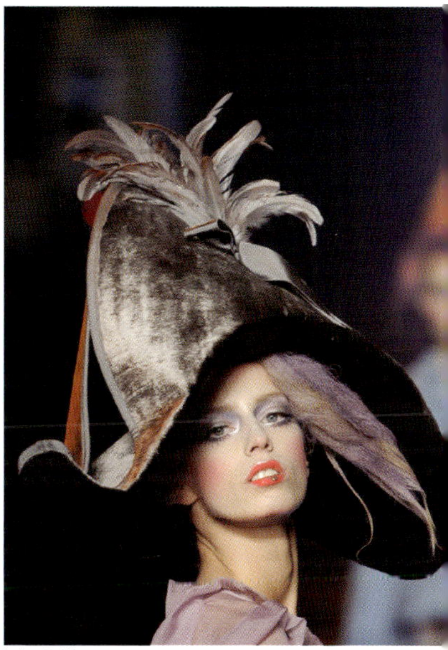

John Galliano

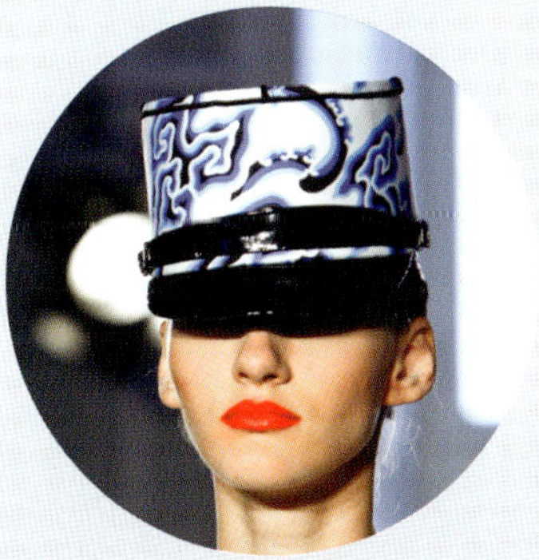

Julien Macdonald

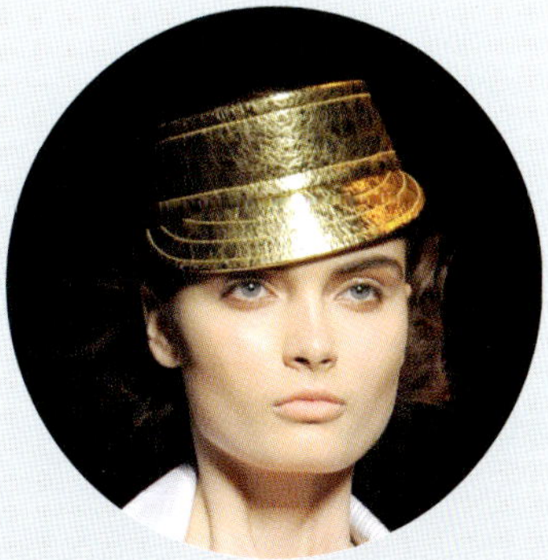

Vivienne Westwood Red Label

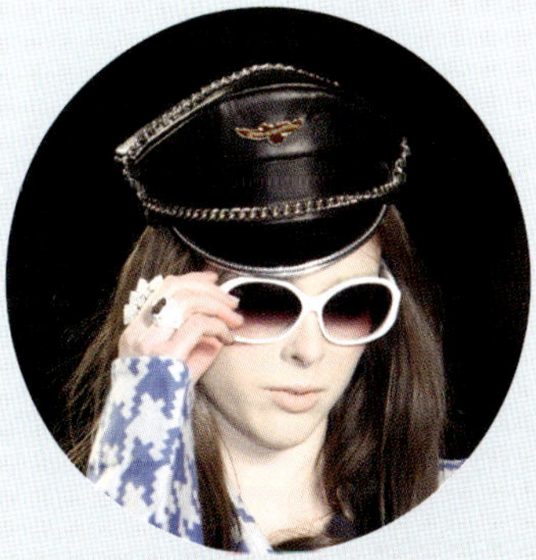

Vivienne Westwood Red Label

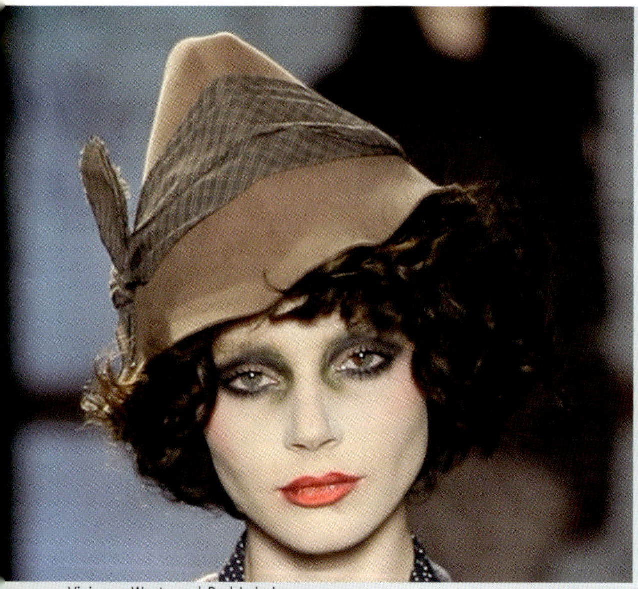

Vivienne Westwood Red Label

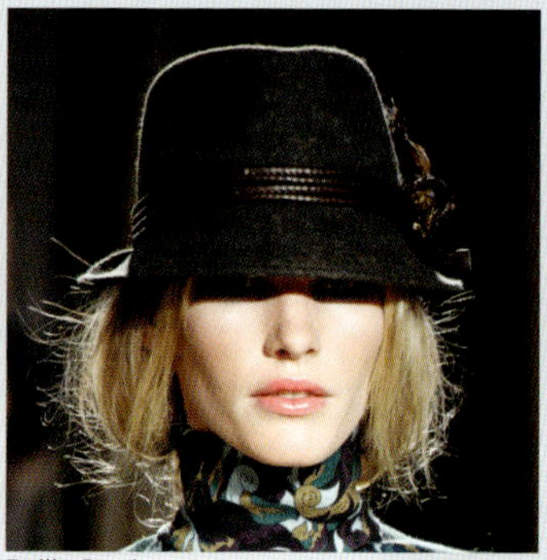

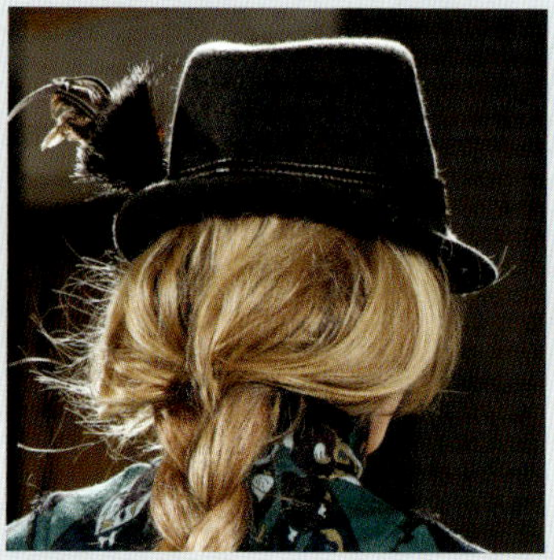

Emilio Pucci

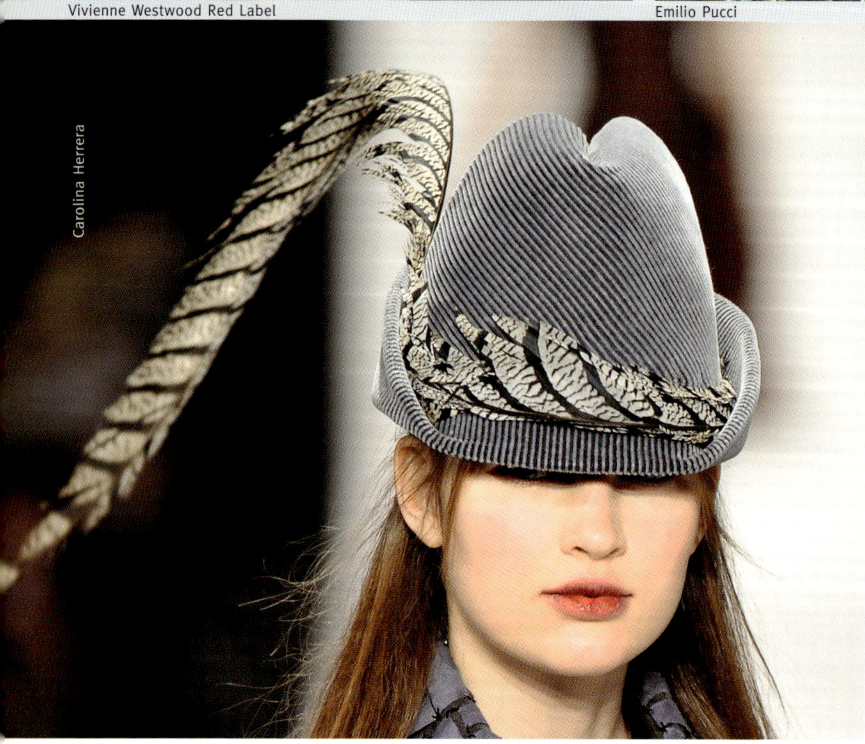

Carolina Herrera

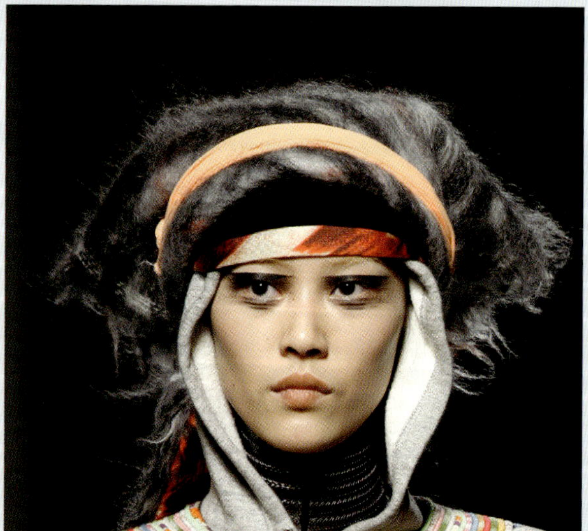

Jean Paul Gaultier

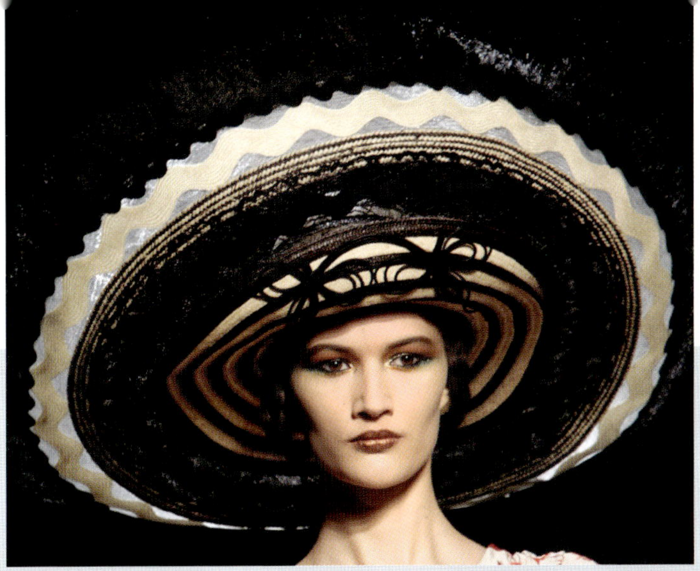
Jean Paul Gaultier

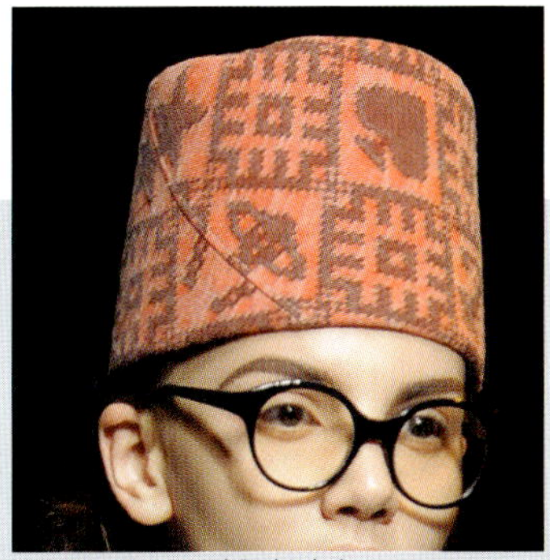
Vivienne Westwood Red Label

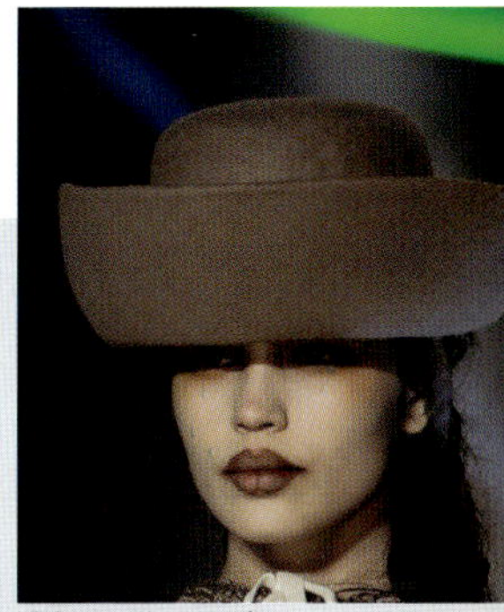
Vivienne Westwood

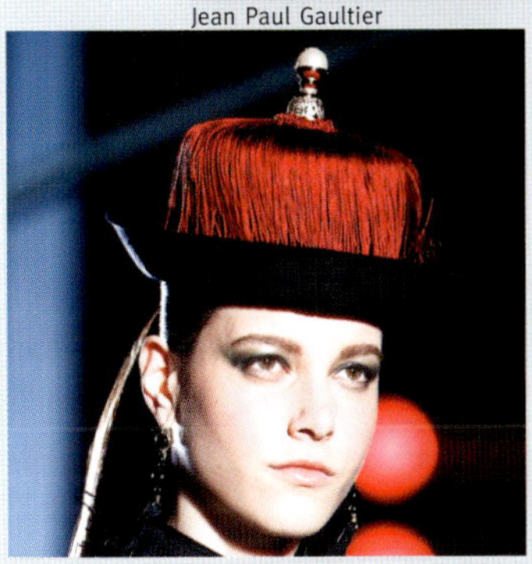
Jason Wu

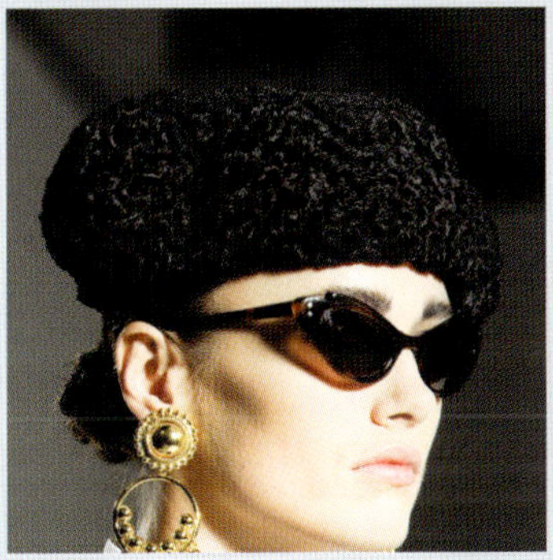
Moschino

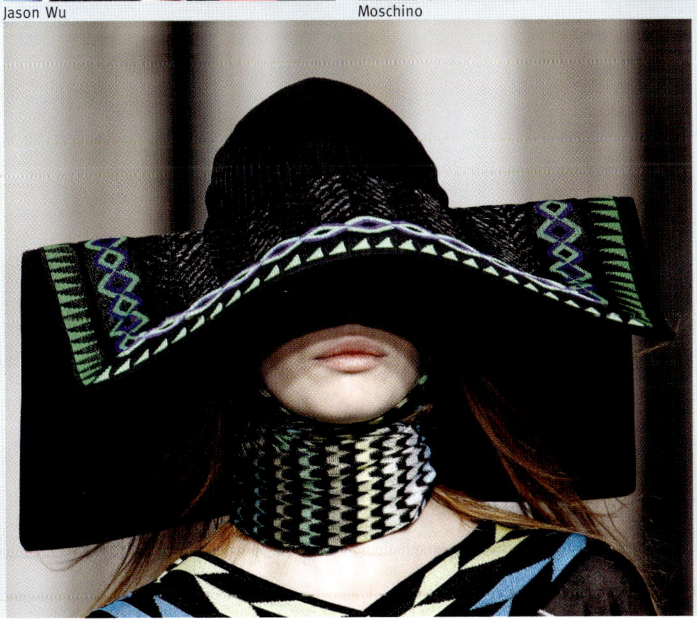
Missoni

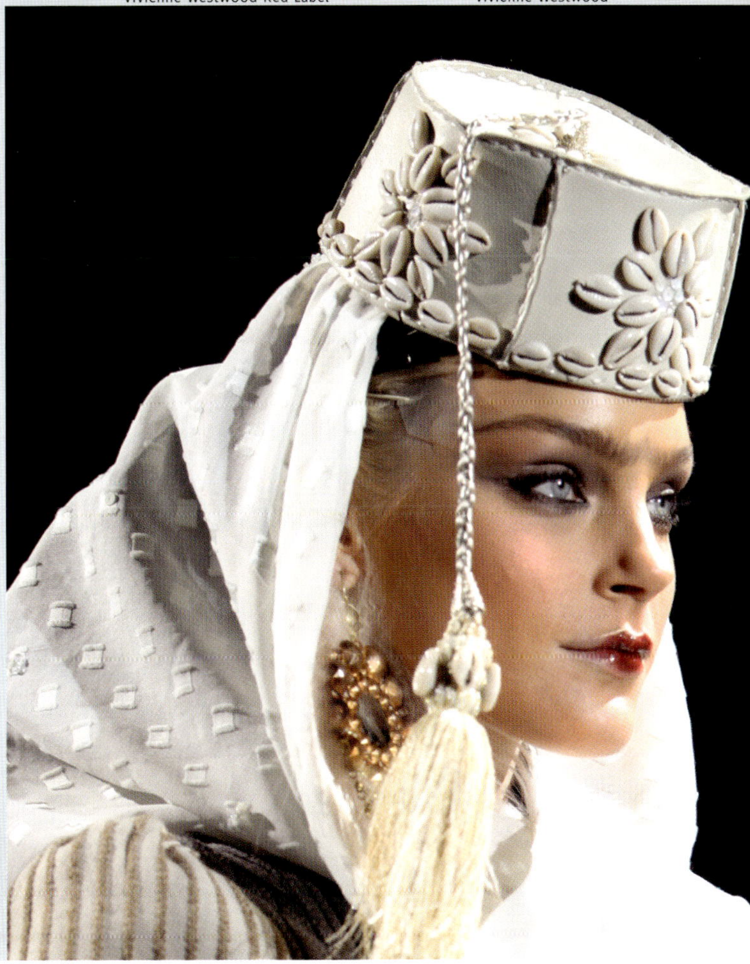
John Galliano

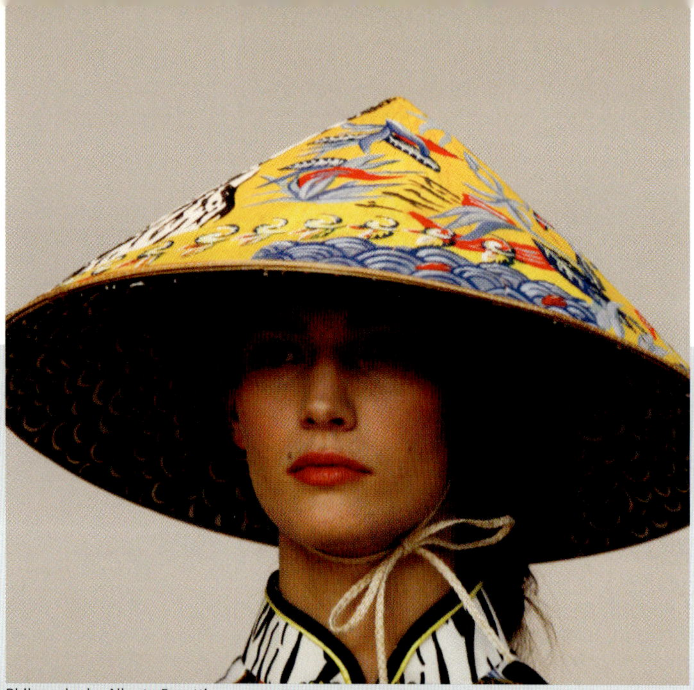

Philosophy by Alberta Ferretti

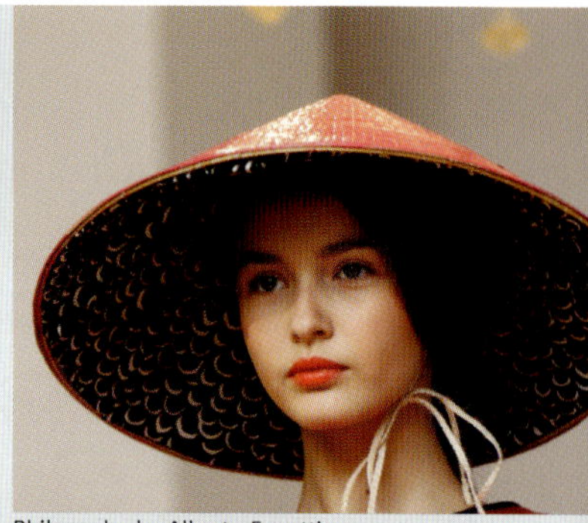

Philosophy by Alberta Ferretti

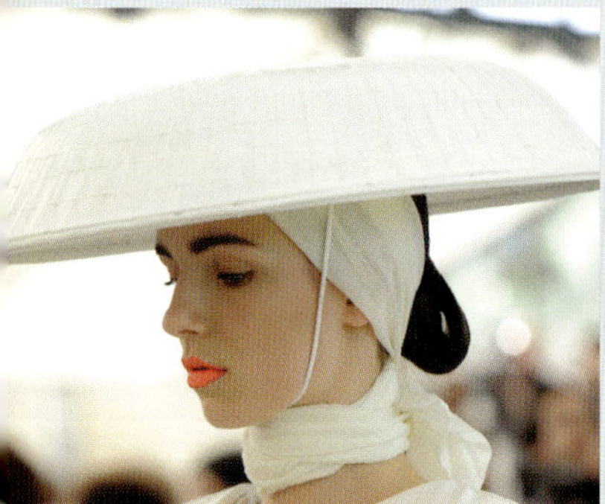

Osman Yousefzada

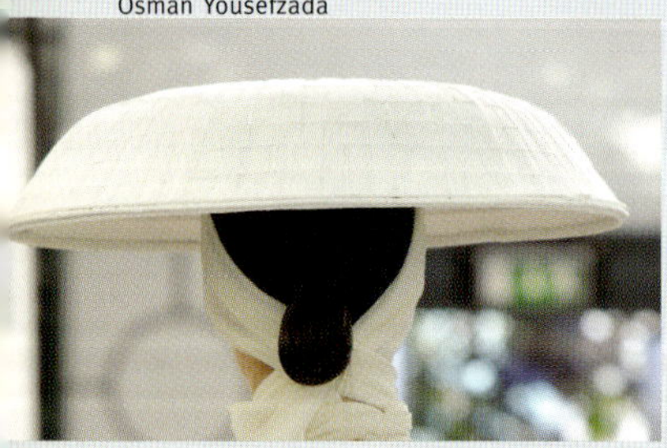

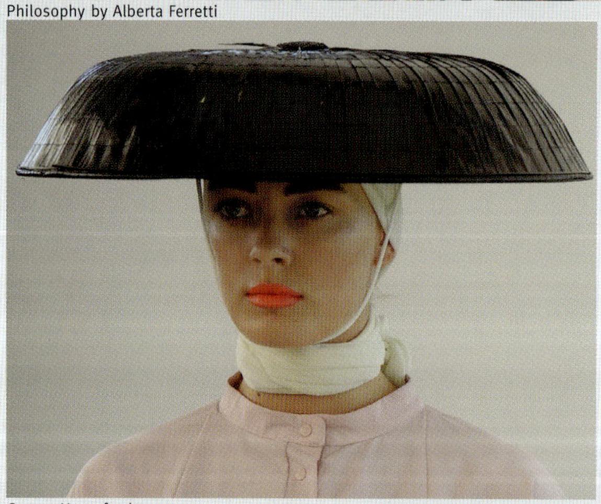

Osman Yousefzada

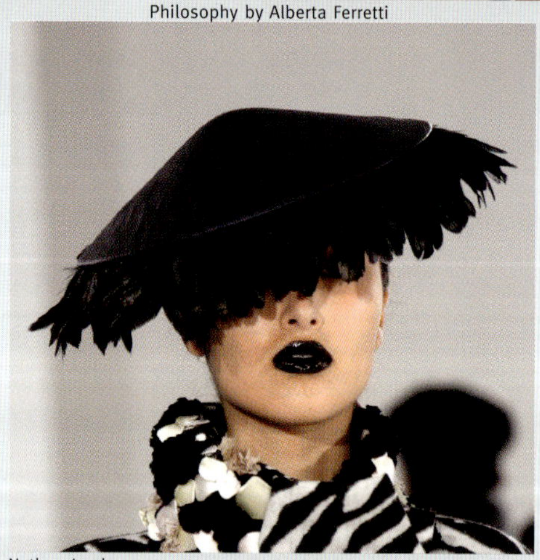

Nathan Jenden

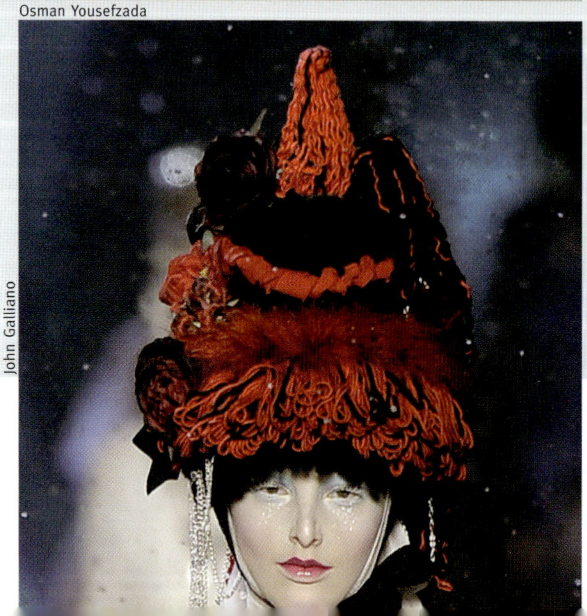

John Galliano

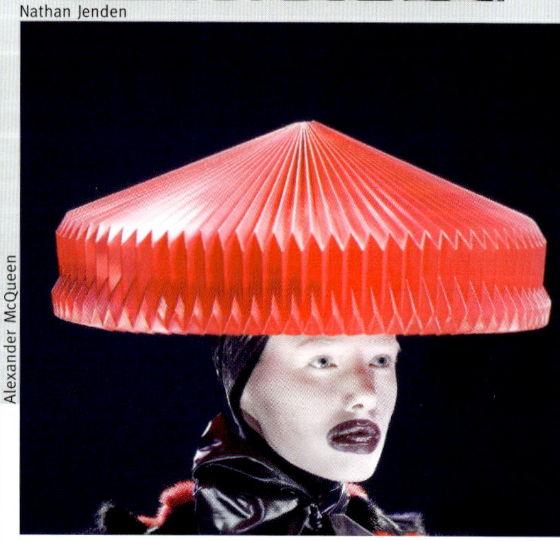

Alexander McQueen

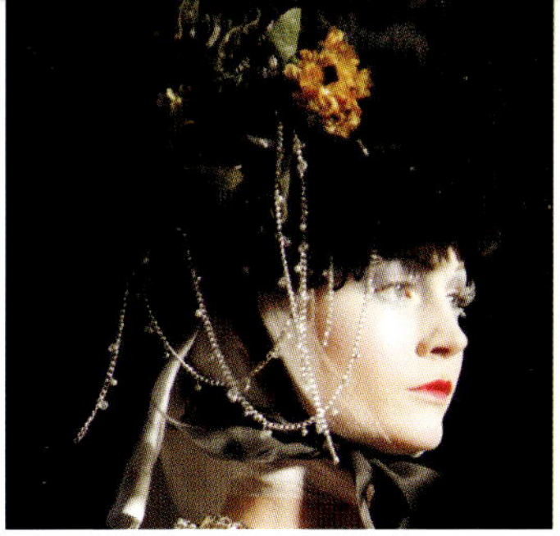
John Galliano

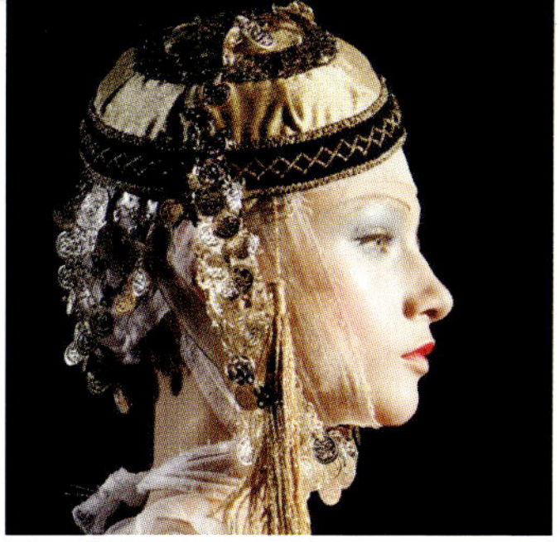
John Galliano

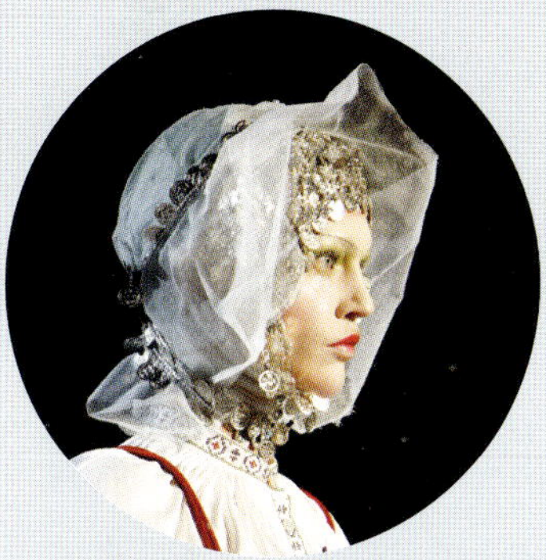
John Galliano

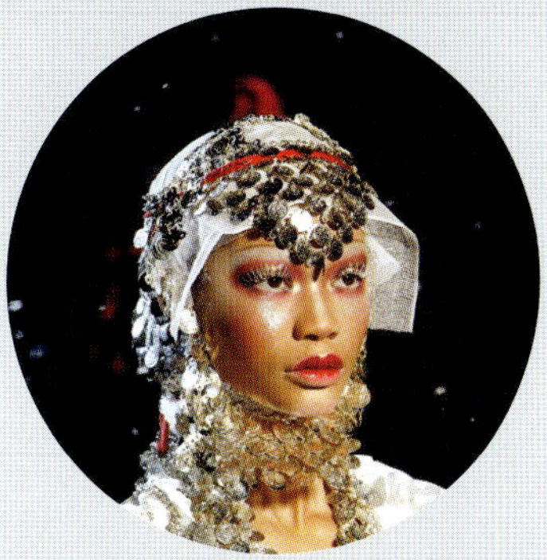
John Galliano

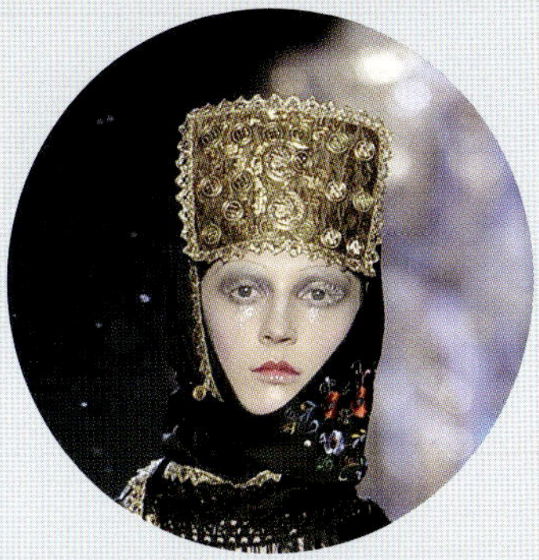
John Galliano

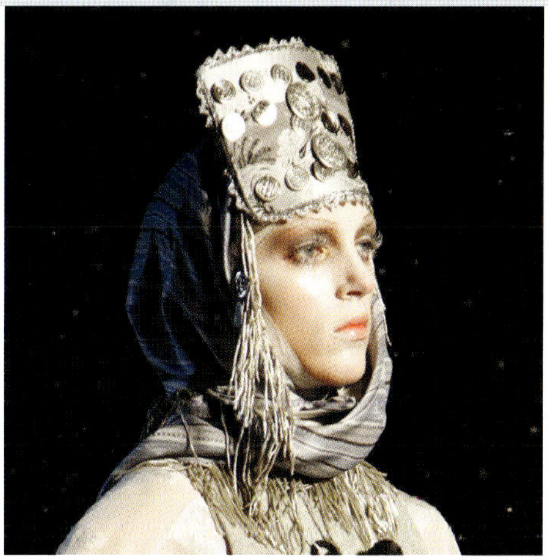
John Galliano

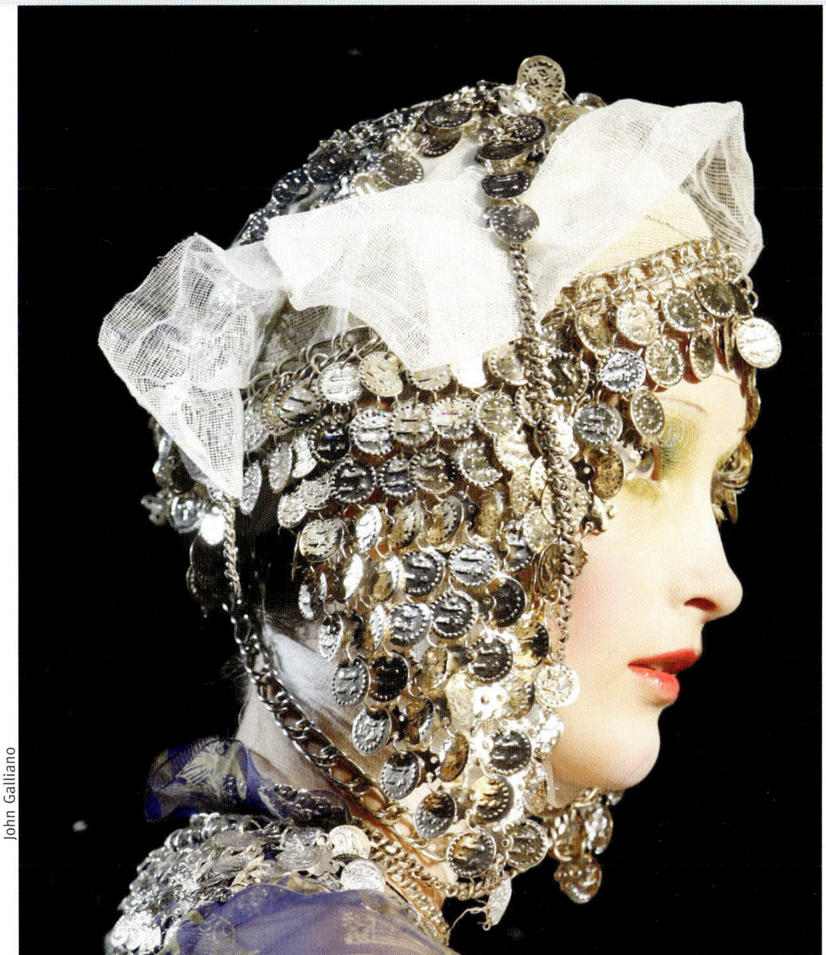
John Galliano